Almost A Born Loser!

Almost A Born Loser!

Annis Gregory Aleck

Library of Congress Control Number:		2011901845
ISBN:	Hardcover	978-1-4568-6510-8
	Softcover	978-1-4568-6509-2
	Ebook	978-1-4568-4403-5

This book was printed in the United States of America.

To order additional copies of this book, contact:
Xlibris Corporation
1-888-795-4274
www.Xlibris.com
Orders@Xlibris.com
88442

Introduction

I first learned to be optimistic about situations in life from watching the movie *The Miracle Worker* when I was sixteen. The teacher, Annie Sullivan, had a very difficult life and expected things to improve for her; but life got more and more difficult for her as time went on, but at the end of the movie, she had performed a miracle. Everything she went through had prepared her for the difficult task she was about to face, looking after Helen Keller. This was a true story, and I learned that when things beyond your control happen, it could look like something is going wrong; but it could be better that it happened that way, and at the same time, I learned that when people misbehave, something will happen back to them.

Looking back over the years, I realized that my life has followed much the same pattern. My parents, Art and Anna Aleck, had bitter memories of what they went through in the Indian residential schools; and I was their scapegoat. Although I was usually well behaved, they still lashed their anger out on me and didn't give me the same treatment my brothers got. I have two older brothers, Tony, the oldest, who's three years older than I, and Arthur (a.k.a. Isaac), who's two years older than I. I was born in 1955; and David, the youngest brother, is seven years younger than I. I often wished they would stop putting me down and not hold me back from doing things my brothers were allowed to do, but they didn't realize what they were doing. At home, everyone called me Baxter, so naturally that's what I thought my name was; then when I started school in grade 1, I walked into class and the teacher said, "Oh. You must be Annis." I was too shy to say anything, so at school and in my professional life, everyone knew me as Annis; and at home, everyone knew me as Baxter.

I did good in elementary school and sometimes got 100 percent or close to it on exams; but since I was naturally shy, continually teased, and often held back when I tried to do something for my own interests, I started withdrawing to cope with what I was going through. I was often put down just for being young and grew up so shy I got the reputation for being a loner and didn't make very good friends. As a teenager, on weekends everyone would be out having fun, and I was always forced to stay home and babysit David. I wasn't paid anything for babysitting, and life got incredibly boring for me as I got older. Then halfway through grade 10, I started joining sports, partly because I enjoyed it but also so I would have an excuse not to have to stay home and babysit David. When I wasn't available to babysit, my mother would hire a babysitter rather than get Tony or Isaac to stay home and babysit; but fortunately in grade 11, I chose bowling as one of my activities. One night as I was walking home from bowling, it was snowing and blowing; and I came across a fellow who lived a few houses down from us, lying there with a broken ankle. No one driving by could have seen him, so I helped him home; then a few years later, I realized that I saved his life. I don't know why some people laugh when I say "Just because he was gay and didn't like my dog was no reason to see him die."

Unfortunately, I got so bored with everything that by the time I reached senior high school, I barely made it through grade 11. Then when the summer came, I started drinking and having fun and exploded because so much tension had built up. I drank heavily during the summer then only on weekends when I got back to school and started studying hard again but wasn't doing very good and didn't know why. Then when the weather got too cold to drink, I had to quit drinking and my marks shot up. I realized I was allergic to alcohol and it was affecting my studying. I always was a deep thinker without realizing it because I learned not to say anything because it seemed like whenever I spoke up, everyone would laugh at me or my parents would get mad at me. I was never allowed to say no or express an opinion. My parents got mad at me for everything I did and even got mad at me when I didn't even do anything, so I was easily taken advantage of by unscrupulous, greedy people. As a result of being a deep thinker, I was able to see things other people couldn't see but couldn't communicate my ideas. I was so shy that if the feeling came over me not to say anything, I couldn't talk no matter what the situation; sometimes even in a dangerous situation or in a classroom,

I couldn't answer the teacher or warn anyone of danger if the feeling not to talk came over me.

In high school I was always very quiet, and whenever I would raise my hand to answer a question, the teachers would automatically choose me because they knew that if I spoke up, I would really come across with good answers. One day in my grade 12 English class, we read a poem about a doctor working in a third world country. The doctor was a heavy drinker, and the teacher asked why he drank, so I put up my hand and was automatically chosen. I said, "Because he didn't like working where he was. And to escape reality." The teacher heard my first answer and asked me to repeat me second answer, but the feeling came over me not to say anything, so I automatically clammed up. He said he didn't hear me, but luckily, another student heard me and she answered for me; then the teacher rambled on and on about why the doctor drank to escape the reality of where he was working.

As I reached senior high school, life got extremely boring for me because I was so much alone and realized it had been a mistake not to make friends when I was younger. High school education wasn't very difficult for me, and I graduated when I was 17. I didn't have any luck with finding girlfriends even though people said I was a very nice-looking boy, and my mother kept telling me to find one. I had tried to find one, but it interfered with my studying, so I felt better when I decided just to stay single; but I also instinctively knew I couldn't get anyone interested in me, so I preferred not to think about it.

As I was finishing high school, I told myself that I wanted to get a career right away so I could get away from my family then get on with my own life. I didn't know exactly what I wanted for a career but knew I wanted to do something with my life and what kind of working conditions I wanted but couldn't find a job anywhere, so I had no choice but to carry on with my education right away. It was 1973. I grew up in the middle of town in Merritt, British Columbia, and in school we were continually told everyone gets equal treatment in Canada; so naturally most of us believed it. I never really thought about the stories I heard and some of the things I saw happen as I was growing up, so I was still proud to be Canadian. My parents had decided to move back to the Indian reserve where we were registered. It was in Rosedale, ten miles east of Chilliwack, British Columbia, so my dad was in the process of having his house built during the summer.

Preface

Canadian Indian Residential Schools

Since approximately 1879 to 1986, Canadian Indian children were taken away from their parents when they were old enough to start school and placed in Indian residential schools. These schools were usually completely closed off from the outside world; they lived there at least ten months of the year and were very badly treated. They were beaten just for speaking their own language even though some of them couldn't speak a word of English, were kept from contacting their parents, often forced to work very hard, improperly clothed, and poorly fed. Indians still had to attend these schools even if they lived close to town, and some were sent to schools a long ways from home. These schools were operated by several Christian factions, and the Indian children were taught to be ashamed of being Indian and that their culture and religious beliefs were evil and of the devil. They were also stripped of their dignity, self-respect, and self-esteem.

These schools often did nothing to prepare the Indians for getting meaningful employment or a career when they left school, they weren't taught how to be responsible working people, and the quality of education was often substandard and far below the national standards of public schools. Many who survived often drank because of the pain and anger of what they went through, then fell victim to alcoholism. Many survivors didn't know how to parent; some didn't even know what was right or wrong, and this reflected on how they raised their own children. They often had to settle for Labourer's jobs, and even when they tried to do something for themselves, they were held back by the Department of Indian Affairs, DIA. DIA is a branch of the federal government who controlled everything the Indians did including education because they controlled the funding and could dictate what went on.

Most Canadian Indian reserves are nothing more than a tiny, useless, isolated swamp or rock pile where there's very little for the Indians to do for work, recreation, or even entertainment. The Canadian government tried to keep us on these reserves and on welfare, so life wasn't only difficult for those who survived the residential schools; it was hard on their families. They often wouldn't get hired when they applied for work and didn't get equal treatment even when they were lucky enough to get hired. Although life was difficult for the residential school survivors, it also made some of them stronger and more determined to do something for themselves and not let their children go through what they went through!

Some books have been written on what conditions were like in the residential schools and some try to hide, distort, or minimize the truth; but what some survivors had to say about it will be mentioned in this story. My life story will show what it was like to be the first generation after the residential schools and what it took for me to do something with my life. My father went to school with Jennifer's father and both of our mothers were residential school survivors, so our home life was difficult! I struggled against overwhelming odds to do something with my life then applied what I learned through the hard times to help Jennifer do something with her life. We didn't only have to struggle because of how our parents were affected by the residential schools and being held back by DIA but also because of how our siblings were affected and trying to get a meaningful job in the field I was educated in because of how Canadians treated aboriginal people!

In grade school we were continually told, "Everyone gets *equal treatment* in Canada!" so naturally, most Canadians believe it. My parents said very little about what they went through, so I knew very little about how Indians and other minorities were treated. Canada kept the truth very well hidden over the years; but I was able to gather much of the truth, put it in information packages, and exposed it to influential people. The events in this story are true and told exactly the way it happened. Some of the names of the people, the towns they lived in, and the names of the Indian reserves have been changed to protect their privacy. The names of the inmates when I worked for Corrections Canada taking them out on work release have been changed to protect their privacy; any resemblance to actual persons with the same names, living or dead, is purely coincidental. The towns are all in British Columbia, British Columbia unless mentioned as being in another Canadian province or Washington State, United States of America. We were called Indians, but eventually we were also called aboriginals and First Nations people.

Foreword

When this autobiography is read, several historical imperatives have to be well-known to the reader.

Canada is a settler state. Everything that is called Canada in real estate terms was the environment of several different language groups.

The settler state took drastic steps to take control of tribal groups; starvation, deprivation, and killing the languages using brute force and the rule of law became intertwined with the methods of colonization. There were antecedent actions. The Scot Highland story called Clearances is well documented for anyone who cares to read that hard history. The Acadian story of expulsion by the British of French and Micmac mixed blood who had intermarried with French who were simply put on boats and told to get out of what is now New Brunswick and Nova Scotia. The Acadians had thriving communities. They were able to feed themselves and live off the land and sea. While the Acadia story is famous in American literature, its story of gross human rights violation has been successfully ignored by the nation-settler state of Canada and the United States in their officially sanctioned histories.

At the same time, one has to take into account the human being in development, the necessity of nurturing, and a well-informed education to round out a healthy, well-developed person. Within the residential-school system, long-term child neglect, condoned or encouraged cruelty to children was bragged about in the Canadian parliamentary committee reports as successfully getting rid of the "Indian problem."

The role of Christian churches of European origin has to be understood not in any sentimental sense of what could have been transpired. For Native American children, residential schools were horror institutions without an ogre emerged in one form or another. Often, supervision was so lax that the children became sadistic to one another and a "Lord of the Flies" reigned to subvert normal emotion and understanding what it means to be a human being. *Lord of the Flies* is a fictional book about a group of children stranded on an island without any adults to supervise and guide them. It illustrates that children can be savages without any adult supervision and control to guide their actions and from harming one another.

The first generation of children free of residential schooling were still victimized by the machinations of introducing self-hatred, nondevelopment of a profound sense of thanksgiving for daily life and the absence of personal positive imaging of aboriginal peoples. If you are educated to believe only white Europeans had the keys to heaven, the means to become prosperous in the material sense, the seven pillars of self-esteem never were built into the child-wellness system. Any emergence of self-determination was pulverized by active oppressive means, and suppressive ways such as public hangings were part of that.

No one in the whole world has an excellent knowledge of child development. This is a very complex set and series of stages that are at once individual and universal. In this book, we see the emergence of the psychologist, the counsellor, and the social worker giving directions to the very troubled, the disturbed, and the violated. This is an arduous and often-hazardous journey into the past and fear of the future. This is too often a pain-filled journey that can only be made better by a stable reality of discernment.

Annis tells us his stages of trying to understand himself with his family and himself with Jennifer and her family. Jennifer seems childlike and appears locked into several ways of nonconnection to a present reality. Without any mental-health training, Annis knew instinctively how her childhood and parental attachments have been skewered and are impacting into twisted avenues of bizarre thinking and melodramatic acting out through post-traumatic stress syndrome. Annis held very little back, including his own way of problem solving.

The effects of grinding poverty are spelled out for us. No money, no food, no lodging, a seminomadic-existence basis of finding work seemed the only way these people made it through. It is difficult reading since Annis wrote it down; honor his struggles by reading the entire book.

There is relief in the book. Annis knows his work very well. We gain insight into how forest fires are fought and the training methods that have been developed. Forestry and harvest of the forest is well described by Annis.

Anne Acco
former editor for Pemmican Publications

Chapter 1

Getting a Career

I couldn't find a job when I finished high school, so my dad took me out to the woods and taught me how to use a power saw. He was a professional tree faller—in logging they're just called fallers—and had taught many men to be professional tree fallers. As we were walking in for lunch one day, a Cat, bulldozer, often just called a Cat and came in various sizes, was going in dragging a bundle of logs. There was a log in front of the blade of the Cat and I knew it would go rolling down toward us; but the feeling came over me not to say anything, so I couldn't say anything. I knew we would have time to get out of the way though because Dad was in good condition and I had been a distance runner; and when the log came rolling down toward us, we both ran in opposite directions, but the log was stopped by a snag. I only worked there for three and a half weeks, then we were shut down for fire season; but doing heavy work in the hot weather was a good experience for me because it motivated me to go back to school and get an education, but I still wanted more logging experience.

I was eligible for unemployment insurance (UIC) but didn't know it, and my father didn't know either because he had been in business for himself most of his life or was usually away working. My mother didn't know either, but I couldn't ask her because she was always moody and unpredictable; so after a long, boring summer with no money and nothing to do, I was happy to go to college because at least I would have something to do. I was prepared to settle down right away, get a career, then get on with my life because I almost didn't make it through high school because of drinking; and I wasn't going to do that again. I applied to go to college; and my dad went with me when I was interviewed by the counsellor, Gary (not his real name), from Department of Indian Affairs (DIA). Gary said, "We expect good attendance for classes. Many Native students have trouble adjusting to city life, so they drop out, but some also need a few years off to get partying and having fun out of their system."

All through grade school we were taught people are the same no matter what their race or nationality, so I was quite surprised that when I got to college, almost all Native first-year students were segregated and kept from taking regular college courses. Gary had forced most of the Native first-year students on to a special program called Native group studies and gave us the opinion that if we didn't take that program, we wouldn't get paid our college living allowance and have to go through on our own. For most of us, the program had nothing to do with what we were there for; and after classes, we had nothing to do but sit around all day. The only other person I knew at the college was Isaac, who hardly ever said anything to me so I started learning to open up and talk to people. After spending enough time in college and meeting people, I found out Gary was deliberately putting Native students on the wrong programs and giving them courses they didn't want or need, making them waste their time there. Consequently, many Native students would get frustrated, quit, then give up on their college education.

There were several Native first-year students who weren't segregated though and took regular college courses. I saw one Native student who wasn't on the program sitting back by himself; some friends said he looked like he was lost, so I went over and talked to him. I didn't ask what his name was, but he said he was from Whitehorse, a city in the Yukon Territory. I didn't know how long he attended, but it didn't seem like very long and he dropped out. There was also a rather nice-looking girl there, Maria (not her real name), who attended for a month or a month and a half then dropped out too. In high school, whenever I would get bored with school, my mother would tell me, "That's the happiest time of your life," to try and motivate me to stick it out; so when I got to college, I asked an Indian lady in her thirties, "Is school really the happiest time of your life?"

She said, "I went to the residential schools, so life in school was miserable."

Gary was also the instructor for one of our classes, and we all showed up for class one day, but he couldn't make it because he was in the drunk tank, so of course we all thought that was a big joke. On November 2, the front-page article on the college newspaper was titled "Native Students Angry at Segregation!" It stated how we were being treated, and in that article, Gary was quoted as saying, "There's a high dropout rate of Native students. Perhaps Natives can't handle postsecondary education." I couldn't believe it because right through grade school, we were told people are the same no matter what their race or nationality. The Native students called Gary to a meeting to discuss our discontent at how we were being treated, but he refused to show up; and in that article, he said, "The students just wanted to bitch at the program," so we called him to another meeting, but he didn't show up for that meeting either.

A week later, the front page of the college newspaper read, "Native Students Cite Segregation!" In that article, Gary tried to downplay the seriousness of the situation and how we felt about it and said those that didn't show up for the meeting didn't have a problem but the article said those who didn't show up were attending classes. Much political trouble was raised because of us being segregated, and when the chief of our reserve and the Union of British Columbia Indian Chiefs found out, more trouble was created. Another instructor for that program was extremely angry about all the trouble we created though, and when all the Native students were gathered for a meeting, he just yelled at us because that program may not be used again. We all just sat there and didn't say anything, but I thought, *That program should have been optional, not compulsory, then nothing would have been said about it.* But I was too withdrawn to speak up.

Being young and not sure of what I wanted for a career, I thought about accounting because I seemed to be good at math; but I also thought about joining the police force, so I started reading books and seeing movies about policemen. However, after being forced on to such a simple program for four months, my study habits were ruined because there was nothing to do on that program but sit around all day, so we started partying and having fun. The two-year technical programs started in the fall, and I didn't know the difference between a technical and a university-degree transfer program. I went to a regular college counsellor to get my courses for the second semester, and he thought I would be happy to learn how our ancestors lived, but I told him it would be interesting to learn in my spare time but that I wanted to get a career first. That program did nothing for my career goals.

"That's a very interesting answer," he said.

In my second semester, my study habits were ruined, and I soon found out accounting wasn't my line of work and should have gone on the university transfer program instead. Now there was nothing left for me to do but sit out the rest of the semester and work on the rest of my courses. I took a course in psychology, and in the textbook, I read a story about a priest trying to tell an Indian to go to town and get a job, and it went like this.

Priest:	Why don't you go to the city and get a job?
Indian:	What then?
Priest:	You'll work your way up to foreman!
Indian:	What then?
Priest:	You'll work your way up to supervisor.
Indian:	What then?
Priest:	You'll work your way up to manager.
Indian:	What then?
Priest:	Eventually you'll have so much money you won't have to work at all!
Indian:	That's what I'm doing now, so why should I go through that much trouble to get what I have now?

Since the other courses were easy and I had nothing to occupy my time, I started partying and having fun with my friends again. Sometimes we partied day and night for three days at a time and had a hard time staying awake in classes. I did so much dancing I wore a hole in the soles of my shoes. I missed one dance, and everyone wondered where I was. I was invited to a dance one night after a dance and thought I better not go because I was getting too drunk. I didn't want to get lost or stranded anywhere, then missed a strip-poker party. A number of us were partying one day; and after a few beers, everyone decided to go down the bars, so I said, "I can't. I'm only eighteen." The legal drinking age in British Columbia is nineteen.

Murray Hill said, "Here, use my ID," and passed me his birth certificate.

I put it in my shirt pocket but forgot where I put my own ID (identification card), and when we got to the bars, the bartender called me over and asked for my ID. I went to throw Murray's ID down on the counter and my own ID came out at the same time, so I pointed to Murray's ID and said, "That's my ID."

"No, I think that's your ID. You better get out of here!"

Instead of leaving, I went and sat down, and surprisingly, I still got served. I was supposed to go back to my parents' place in Rosedale that night but ended up partying for the next three days. Usually, when I say I'm going to be somewhere, I'm there; but no one knew where I was for three days. Later on I found out I almost gave my mother a nervous breakdown.

I always enjoyed cooking and sometimes thought about being a chef. After attending college for one year, I got a summer job as a dishwasher and busboy at the Hope Hotel, in Hope, British Columbia, twenty-five miles from where my parents live. Since I was young and energetic, I soon asked to work straight night shift so I wouldn't be tempted to run the streets drinking; but working in a restaurant made me realize I could never be a chef, and it motivated me to go back to college and try again. Physical education also appealed to me at that time because I had tried to be athletic in high school, so I thought I would make that my career choice. It was hard to find a place to stay that I could afford on my income that year, so I chose a small two-roomed housekeeping room because I thought I would be rooming with Isaac again. The landlady was a nasty old lady who knew she was overcharging everyone for rent, but there was nothing anyone could do about it because places were hard to find.

Isaac had gotten disillusioned with college after the first semester and couldn't settle down and study for the second semester, so he failed because of depression and was told to take a year off, and so he went logging. I started looking for someone to share my apartment with, and some friends at college suggested James (not his real name), and he agreed. Then I met his sister, Coleen (not her real name), who was outstandingly beautiful; so naturally I tried to get her interested in me. Later on I found out James was gay, and he told me about going to the Indian residential school in Port Alberni and seeing his father drown. He also hurt his back as a child, so he couldn't do heavy work, and told me a number of things, including an inferiority complex that made him turn gay. I suggested to him he try finding a girlfriend and try going out with a woman, so he agreed and started looking for someone.

I felt determined to do something with my life and took swimming as one of my electives. I wanted to get serious about my studies, so I took up a part-time job to pass time on weekends until basketball started. The manager of the restaurant knew I was a good worker, so she put me to work every chance she got; and the staff were lots of fun to work with, so I started partying and having fun again. I had so much fun in my first year of college that it was hard to settle down in my second year. It was lots of fun working there, but it was interfering with my studies, so I had to quit. It was almost too late to pass my courses by then, but I gave it my best effort to make it through. Since I changed programs, Gary made me sign an agreement stating that if I didn't pass everything, I would take a year off; and it looked like I wasn't going to make it, but I had a feeling something would come up for me. I was beginning to realize my psychic abilities but only followed my hunches once in a while. Sure enough, just before the semester ended, Gary got fired because of the program he put us on the year before; so I got to stay in college.

There was an Indian fellow from Ontario in his midthirties, Gilbert Oskaboose, who decided to go to college and get into journalism that year. He said, "I went to the residential schools back east. Those students who did well in school, they tried to convert them into priests and nuns."

When I started, my fourth-semester depression and loneliness started setting in because it looked like I would be spending more time in college than I wanted to. I was nineteen years old, old enough to go to the bars, and I wanted to have fun with my friends but couldn't because I was allergic to alcohol. Gary had tried screwing me around then started giving me a hard time, so I gave him a hard time right back; then he wouldn't go near me after that, but after he got fired, he went and talked to me in the cafeteria and he seemed all right. He even had a beer with me a couple times, so I thought maybe he was treating the Indian students that way because he was following orders. He was happy now because he got another job with twice the pay and half the work; usually, when people misbehave, things like that don't happen.

I couldn't study very well at home because the heat was always turned down too low, and to add insult to injury, the landlady raised the rent illegally and her son threatened me with violence. I knew something would happen back to them for misbehaving, but I didn't like the idea of being bullied. I knew I failed my fourth semester and got extremely depressed, so I started drinking heavily and couldn't wait to get out of Vancouver. When I first went to college, I was prepared to settle down and get a career; now two years later, I had the equivalent of one semester's credits. I had wasted my first two years at college because of partying and trying to find a girlfriend, so I decided I should give up on looking for one; but I also instinctively knew I wouldn't have any luck with them, and it was slowing me down with my career goals. I moved back home with my parents and continued to drink heavily because of depression. After wasting two years at college, the last thing I wanted to think about was finding a girlfriend, but my mother had been trying for years to get me to find one and wouldn't listen when I told her all she was doing was slowing me down and interfering with my career goals. She told me to find one every chance she got, and we started having heated arguments over it.

I felt very disillusioned about college and the world and wanted to give up; I wanted to do something with my life and nothing seemed to be working out, but my family got mad at me and told me not to give up. I also got a letter from DIA stating my application for funding my education was approved, so that made me feel a little bit better. I considered going to Vancouver to see about taking a trade, but on the day I decided to go, I got called for a job tree planting in Prince George, a town in Northern British Columbia. I was still recuperating from drinking when I got up there and didn't like the job very much, but this was my first time in a logging camp and the food was fantastic; not only that, it gave me a chance to stop drinking. Tree planting is very back-breaking work, and I wanted to quit but knew I wasn't a quitter. I was anxious for the job to end, but on the last day, we were asked to go further north to Mackenzie, British Columbia, for a week to ten days. I didn't want to go, but I knew there was nothing to go back to Rosedale for, so I went. And on our way to Mackenzie, we stopped in Prince George for a few hours, so we went to the bars and stocked up with liquor before leaving. Since the camp in Mackenzie was a dry camp, the boss took our liquor away from us while we were passed out.

Working in Mackenzie was miserable compared to Prince George, so half the crew quit. The ground was flat, so we were bent over continuously, making it very hard on our backs; we weren't earning as much money; the rooms were hot and we couldn't open the windows because the flies could crawl right through the screen; and the commissary ran out of insect repellent. I wanted to quit, but I knew there was nothing to go home for and I would just end up arguing with my mother over finding a girlfriend. On our last day of work, our boss drove us back to Prince George and gave us back our liquor, then I and another fellow, Dan, got a motel room for the night. It felt so good to sleep in an air-conditioned room on a double bed by ourselves that we decided to stay one more night. We went to the bars in the afternoon and ran into a fellow we had been tree planting with, and he said to Dan, "We need one more man for a crew on the CN [Canadian National Railroad]. Why don't you come and work with us?"

"No!" Dan replied. "I'm sick of the mountains. I want to go back to Saskatchewan."

"Why don't you apply then?" he said to me. "I'll go along and put in a good word for you."

We went to the CN station the next morning, and I got the job. After five weeks in camp, I had one day off and got a job with the railroad, so it appeared to me that when I stuck out a difficult situation, something would happen to make it worthwhile. When I got the job, I was told I may have to wait a month for my first paycheck, which was okay with me; but the fellow who got me the job was really lazy, and I almost got fired because I let him show me what to do. Not only that, the foreman liked to yell at the crew. I enjoyed working for the CN though, and when I started getting paid regularly, I was making money faster than I could spend it. I was tempted to make a career out of the CN, but I was drinking too much and I knew I couldn't go on like that.

I wrote to James and told him I was thinking of making a career of the railroad, and he wrote back a nasty letter telling me to go back to college because everyone believed I could make it. I also realized I had to go back to college because I was drinking too much and didn't want to be traveling like that all my life. We worked nine hours a day for twelve days, which I enjoyed; but I noticed that the foreman would often only see his family for two days in twelve, if he saw them at all. The highways were narrow and winding back then, so if he saw his family, sometimes he would drive all night to see them for two days then drive all night again to go back to work. I didn't want to be travelling like that for the rest of my life and also would have preferred a job with more responsibility and opportunities for promotion, so I decided to go back to college and give it one more try; if I had any more setbacks, then I would quit!

My father had found a place for Isaac and me to stay, so everything was set up for me to go back; not only that, I thought I could get killed from drinking too much and wanted to get into unarmed-combat training and settle the issue with my ex-landlady's son. After registering in college, I knew I couldn't drink very much and decided to go to a movie one night but had a little over an hour to wait, so I thought I would go for a couple of beers while I was waiting. I told people I got to the street corner and turned around and walked the other way, and one fellow said he wished he had done that; so later on, I told people an old man tried to pick me up, so I turned around and went the other way. When I got back to Vancouver, my cousin Eddie Dale tried to tell me I had to find a place of my own because he was there first; he didn't care that I was up north working and he had all summer long to find a place of his own, so his mother obviously didn't tell him he was supposed to find a place of his own. Billy Jack movies were popular at that time, and after registering in college, I noticed posters advertising a Korean style of karate, hapkido, that Billy Jack took. I also had a feeling I should play soccer, so I signed up for hapkido and found an Indian soccer team looking for players. Eddie Dale owned a car and ended up staying with Isaac and me, which I knew would happen. He's two years younger than I and for a little while as a child was nicknamed Days and Days. All three of us grew up together and got along well, so it was all right. He helped coach me on how to play soccer, but his car gave him and Isaac a chance to run around and have fun. I tried telling Isaac to settle down and study to secure his future, but he just laughed and said, "What for?" After taking a year off and making good money logging, he couldn't see any point in studying.

Eddie Dale, Isaac, a friend from college, and I went walking around town drinking one night. And when we walked by a clothing store, there was the bottom half of a mannequin set up outside the store, displaying a pair of pants; so Eddie Dale yelled out, "Grab that ass!" I could only drink once a month or have the occasional beer for burnout; any more than that and it would affect my studying.

I wasn't sure what I wanted for a career yet, but I refused to give up trying; and in the fall semester, I took the second half of courses I had already taken so I could get university credits. I enjoyed playing soccer because I liked running and was training hard in hapkido because I had an issue to settle. I noticed again I was rather good at math but had to wait until the spring semester to take a Math 12 and thought if I had started a university transfer program in the spring of 1974, I may have completed my math by now. The Christmas break was also fantastic that year. I played soccer for the team in Rosedale and didn't seem to have any luck with finding girlfriends, so I usually tried to keep myself too busy to feel lonely. This was also my last chance at postsecondary education, so I had to settle down to my studies and close myself off from the rest of the world. When we got back to college, Isaac was told on his transcripts to take time off; he did too much running around and failed at college again. Everyone knew he was depressed, so some friends suggested we get some liquor and go to our place to let him know everyone cares about him. We were quietly sitting around having a few drinks, then Isaac finally said, "When I was logging, a log flew over me. Instead of running, I just walked." Everyone was upset that he felt that way, and I knew he was depressed because of the way things had gone in college.

After registering for the spring semester, I went home for the first weekend to play soccer, and my mother had kept telling me to find a girlfriend, and it was getting extremely annoying. After the game, I went back to the parents' place and Auntie Irene and Uncle Joe were there and they tried stepping in to force me to find someone and kept saying, "Who is your date for tonight?" They could see I didn't appreciate what they were doing, but they did it anyway. I decided that was too much for me. I had my career goals to think about and didn't want anything interfering with them, so I stopped going home altogether. I was also tired of people trying to run my life without listening to my opinion and continued to train hard in hapkido and play soccer; and as I was training, I noticed how much strenuous exercise took my mind off my studies, so that was great! Not only did the exercise take my mind off my studies, I was also still thinking of joining the police force if getting a degree didn't get me anything.

In the 1970s there was much racial tension against the East Indians, even in Merritt before I moved out. Often there was writing on the washroom walls against them, and one comment written was "Kill the Punjabs! I'm up to 2 Paks a day!" A comment beside it wrote, "Down to 2 Paks a day!" but we became very close friends with two of them,

Rick Klare and Paul Mahal. Rick had a girlfriend who was a blond girl and she said, "When we went down the bars one fellow was looking at me wondering why I was going out with an East Indian."

John Delorme was an Indian, but he looked more like an East Indian, so we nicknamed him Abdule and I went up to him one day and said, "Hey, Abdule!"

He got really mad and said, "What was that you called me?"

I was surprised he got that mad, so I said, "I said John!"

"That's better!" Later on I found out he went to a college dance and got punched out because people thought John was an East Indian, and Rick saved himself by grabbing a tire iron to defend himself. Sitting in the cafeteria, I sometimes heard East Indians talking about being harassed at college dances but saying there was enough of them to prevent trouble.

Rick said to me one day, "I don't know why people give us a hard time."

"Some of you make a bad name for the others," I said but didn't tell him it's the same way with Indians.

When we lived in Merritt, I had a foster brother named Wesley Pierre, and he mentioned attending the Indian residential school in Lytton. A friend from Merritt stopped by to visit one day and said Wesley cut himself with a knife again, but I didn't hear about the first time he did it. Mother couldn't get him to study no matter how hard she tried, and I couldn't understand why he was like that; then when he moved out, all he ever did was drink.

Tony, some friends, and relatives dropped over to visit one night before going to a rock concert; and I said, "I think it would be fun trying to catch a greased pig."

One cousin said, "Those pigs were hard to catch. That time we had to castrate them."

So I said, "Wouldn't you run too if someone was going to castrate you?" and everyone burst out laughing.

In high school, people kept saying how hard Math 12 was, so I only took math as far as grade 11; but when I did my Math 12, I wasn't studying very hard and was still passing the course. I had tried dating a few girls in the fall, but they treated me like poison ivy; and I went home so bored I couldn't do any studying, so I gave up looking completely to devote my time and energy to studying, soccer, and hapkido. Isaac wasn't working or attending college in the spring, and his interests and activities were slowing me down. I tried to tell him, but he wouldn't listen; so I decided I wouldn't room with him anymore if I had to study, but he seemed to do that deliberately!

Just before the spring semester ended, I got an interview for a job with DIA timber cruising on Indian reserves up north; and at the interview, I was asked if I didn't mind working with an East Indian. Often, when I walked by them on the street, they would glare with extreme anger; so I tried to just ignore them unless they were friendly with me first. I was glad I got the job though because I didn't want to go home and put up with my family trying to run my life. I only went back home for one night to pack my things then went back to Vancouver to catch the plane to Terrace the next day, Dad was surprised that I had stopped going home altogether and knew something was wrong!

The other people hired were Charles (not his real name), an Indian student I went to college with, and Herman Hans, a forestry student from the University of British Columbia (UBC). Charles left his wife at home, who was pregnant and needed a gall-stone operation, which made her cranky, but couldn't get the operation until after she had the baby; so he was glad to get away. The East Indian said he was very prejudiced against the white race because of the way they were treated by the British; then I realized that's probably why many immigrant East Indians have a chip on their shoulder and some of them make a bad name for the others. We don't hear about it because the British wrote their own history books that we read in school.

In junior high school, my science teacher was from England and he got very angry at us because we didn't read any books on the Indian revolution. At our age, he read nothing but books about the Indian revolution and told us about the Black Hole of Calcutta and a false religious rumor that started the whole revolution. At that time, I was really into books on nature, trappers, and explorers and didn't know if there were any books on the Indian revolution in the library; but I wondered if that was really the cause of the revolution or a story made up to hide the truth. It's hard to believe people would do something like that, put them in the Black Hole without good reason and read the book *Bury My Heart at Wounded Knee* that summer and learned the truth about the American Indian wars.

While working up north, the East Indian said, "If you want to go into forestry, take economics." I couldn't see the connection, but I told myself I'll take economics when I get back to college. I still had to finish my Math 12, and I wanted to set myself up for a number of career options because everything I tried so far didn't work out. I still wasn't sure of exactly what I wanted, just that I wanted to do something with my life. Then the East Indian got me fired because I didn't follow the customs he was used to, and I couldn't understand why I got fired because I tried to be a good worker. For some reason, immigrant East Indians found it offensive when people laugh or smile because they think you're laughing at them; I smile a lot because I try to be happy and optimistic, but that got me fired. The day I got fired, Charles and I went to the bars, and he tried to pick up some girls. We stayed in the bar until closing time then went to a bootlegger; at that time, beer only cost $3.50 a case in the liquor store, and he charged $7.00. It was two o'clock in the morning, and I yelled out, "Seven dollars for a case of beer!"

Everyone went "Shhh . . . !"

Charles and I stayed up all night drinking and I caught the bus to Chilliwack the next morning; it was a long ride, so I was happy I would be sleeping most of the way. When I got back to Chilliwack, I moved home with my parents, but right away I told my mother I would move out and not go back if she tried to run my life again. Our family got invited to a barbecue in North Vancouver one weekend at my aunt's place, and there was a very nice-looking Indian girl there, but I didn't try to go out with her because I had my career goals to think about. Later on she went to a dance and got raped, so I felt guilty about it because it may not have happened if I tried to go out with her. About two months after I got fired from DIA, I ran into Charles in Chilliwack. He said the East Indian got fired about a month ago and he quit because I was getting beat up too many times. Later on he told me each time he ran around on his wife, he got beat up but didn't notice that each time he did something wrong, something would happen back to him for doing it. I also had a hunch the East Indian got fired before he told me about it.

I met Charles's sister-in-law that night and asked her out to dinner and a movie and didn't want to drink. We went out for dinner, but I had to bring the car back to Rosedale right away for my dad. She stayed in Chilliwack, so Tony gave me a ride back to Chilliwack. She treated me like poison ivy and only wanted to drink, so I ended up going home so bored I didn't know what to do with myself. Then I realized it was too much trouble getting around without a car where my parents lived, and when I was in college, I didn't have time to go out with anyone. I got lonely, but there was nothing I could do about it except block it out of my mind and try to keep myself too busy to feel lonely.

I got a job logging for two weeks with our neighbour, Sam Douglas, who was the chief of our reserve and a logging contractor. I only drank one bottle of beer a day and it slowed me down at work, so I was realizing how sensitive my body was to alcohol. On the job, I noticed a situation for a possible accident; when the logging-truck drivers tightened up the hinges of the cinch straps around a load of logs, they put a pipe on the handle for more leverage, producing a force like a catapult. I thought they should stand to the side in case it slipped because it could give a powerful blow; but unfortunately, I was too shy to speak up because my family was always putting down my opinion, and a truck driver got hit that way.

I was off work for two weeks, then Tony got me a job high-lead logging where he was working for two weeks before college started. High-lead logging is where a steel pipe is up in the air, supported by cables strapped to stumps in the ground for support and cables going out to yard logs toward the tower in an area widened for piling the logs called a landing to be loaded on to a logging truck. A fellow I was logging with mentioned Ron Gabriel being a very good logger. Companies have to pay him an extra $20 a day to get him to work for them; at that time, that was about two and a half hours pay above the union wage rate. Everyone I talked to advised me not to make a career of logging, so I thought I better listen to them because they know more than I do; and while I was there, a forestry student in camp told me that if I wanted to go into forestry, I should take some physics courses. When I got back to college, all my friends were going out to logging camps, working, making good money; and I felt like going with them, but I chose to stick it out with college. Then a month later, they were all coming out and had quit their jobs; but eventually they went back logging, so it looked to me like I made the right decision.

In my fourth year at college, I tried to give up my athletic activities so I would have time for a girlfriend and romantic adventures, but it didn't work. I never had any luck finding girlfriends, and I didn't have anything to take my mind off my studies; and by the time I realized I needed the exercise to get my mind off my studies, my grades were dropping, so it looked like my seventh semester was going to be a waste of time. I passed physics without too much trouble, but I had to drop my math class and one of my economics classes. I could have done better in physics, but I needed my time to catch up in my other economics class and got very depressed about the way things were going and wished people would just leave me alone to live my own life or at least listen to my opinion. My dad still kept putting my down for being young and calling me a scrooge, a name synonymous with an old miser, and other people tried forcing me to find a girlfriend and wouldn't listen when I told them all they were doing was slowing me down with my career goals.

I continued training in hapkido and didn't play soccer because I hurt my ankle from not kicking the ball right and didn't want to get into too many activities like I did the year before because I knew I had to save more time for studying. As I was hitting the bags one night, I started thinking about what I wanted to do to my ex-landlady's son and started hitting the bag as hard as I could with my feelings showing on my face. Then the instructor started giving me angry looks because he knew what I was using the training for, so I settled down and tried not to think about it. Since I didn't do very good in the fall semester, I couldn't get the courses or the teachers I wanted in the spring semester and got very depressed and felt like drinking, but I knew my limits, and that would only make the situation worse. I thought about taking forestry at the British Columbia Institute of Technology (BCIT), but some students told me they have a long waiting list to get in. Some people I graduated high school with had applied there and were turned down, so I wasn't sure if I would get accepted or not. One day, my speed-reading teacher, who also taught one of the courses during my first semester, saw me standing in the hall; and she said, "Annis! You're beginning to be a permanent fixture around here!"

"I wasted my first two years because of the program DIA put us on."

"I was against that program right from the start. So were a number of other instructors, but there was nothing we could do about it."

"I was thinking of taking forestry at BCIT, but maybe I should go to the college in Prince George instead."

"Maybe you should go to Prince George. BCIT has a long waiting list to get in."

I ended up dropping my English and physics classes because of the way things were going and got extremely depressed. I went to one of the Pink Panther movies—which were usually incredibly funny movies starring Peter Sellers—in the evening to try and cheer myself up, but I was so depressed I couldn't laugh until near the end of the movie. Then I got really uptight and phoned my mother to tell her the problems she was causing me and that she should see what I'm going through before she tells me what to do, but I couldn't get through. I called again the next night and really yelled at her and told her she was lucky I couldn't get through the night before! Since she never listens to anything, I sent her a long letter explaining my setbacks, the reasons for them, and how much trouble she was causing me.

One day, I was sitting in the cafeteria, talking to a white student about how dominating mothers can be; and he said, "Whenever I went anywhere, she always said, 'Where you going?' I got tired of it, so one time I just said, '*Whoring!*'" Then he said, "You know how White Spot advertises 'service with a smile'? I went to the White Spot one day, and the waitress was real grumpy, so I said, 'What's the matter? Haven't you been getting yours lately?"

It appeared to me like I wasn't going to make it through the semester, but just before the final exams, my economics instructor gave us a makeup exam and said she was going to take our marks from the best four out of five exams. It was an easy exam, and the final exam was easy so I knew I would pass the course, but I didn't think it was necessary for forestry. While attending college, I met many Indians who went to the Indian residential schools, and most of them told the same story: they were treated very badly and life was miserable. I didn't hear very much about Merritt after I left, but whenever I did, it seemed like an Indian I went to school with died or committed suicide. I talked to a lady there from Merritt, Vivian Ignace, about it; and she said, "There's a lot of apathy there."

Isaac and Murray were staying in an apartment just around the corner from where I was staying, so I went over to visit them one day. Abdule was there, and I said, "What happened to Rick?"

Abdule said, "He's working in the sawmill like all good East Indians!"

So I said, "Well, how come you're not out there with them?" and everyone burst out laughing.

Although I met the minimum requirements to be sponsored for education by DIA, I wasn't very happy with the way things were going, and the Native students' advisor asked me what I was doing and called me a professional student. I also knew my record could affect my ability to transfer to other institutions; but a few days later, he suggested I apply for a scholarship from Parks Canada that were available to Native students going into natural resource management, so I applied. I also talked to another student, a white fellow with a black belt in karate who was trying to get into the police force and told him, "I might take forestry in Prince George so I can keep up with hapkido."

"Go to BCIT. It's a better school. Hapkido can wait."

Abdule went back east to the girl who was to become his wife, and I narrowly made it through my fourth year at college. When I moved back home, my parents had taken in a foster child, Jimmy Stewart; so my youngest brother, David, would have a playmate his own age since they lived in a rather isolated area. When I moved home, my mother was still trying to tell me to find a girlfriend and I told her it's more trouble than it's worth and it's too much trouble getting around where we live. We had a very heated argument about it in front of many friends and relatives, and my dad saw the arguments we were having because all I wanted was to stay single. My mother still wouldn't listen and threatened to embarrass me about being a virgin until I found one, so I told her all she was going to do was start another big fight.

I settled right down and hardly ever drank, and not drinking at that age cut out much of my social life since very few people in my age group didn't drink, and those who didn't were usually busy raising a family. It was a bad year for finding jobs, and I hadn't worked long enough the year before to draw UIC. I was left alone quite a bit and got extremely bored; so I started taking David and Jimmy out to movies, the drive-in theater, hunting, etc. People said I looked older than I was, and some people thought Jimmy was my son. I went to the Seabird Island Indian Festival and canoe races and ran into some of the Indians I went to college with who had quit, and they called me a professional student, and one of them laughed when I said, "It wasn't my fault."

Since it was a bad year for finding work, I went to Merritt to look for work and couldn't find anything there either, and some friends wanted me to stay there longer; but my horoscope book said I would get a job on a certain day, so I made sure I was home that day. Luckily I did that because I got a job logging, setting chokers on a high-lead tower in Hope. It was incredibly hard work because I was a green logger, we were working in a brushy setting, the weather was hot, and the boss didn't have very much experience handling a crew. Quite often after work, I would take Jimmy swimming because it was hot and he was such a bundle of energy. One time he swallowed some water and panicked, but I knew what to do to save him because I had done a year of physical education and took swimming as one of my electives. Then I went home from work one day and got a letter from BCIT saying I was accepted in the forestry program, so that was one of the happiest days of my life since finishing high school because I knew if I could handle the course load, my future would be secure.

My logging job only lasted two and a half weeks, and I got laid off because I was replacing an injured worker who went back to work. I didn't tell my dad what my mother and I were arguing about, until after I got accepted at BCIT, but he was still angry enough about it. Then Isaac went around telling everyone I would have flunked out at college anyway but didn't say anything to me though because he knew I would get mad about it. Dad still continued to put me down for being young even though he knew I usually just stayed home and spent most of my time studying, so if I had a choice, I would have gone back up north to get away from my family. Another one of my uncles, Percy Roberts, who worked as a counsellor for Indians told me, "You're told BCIT graduates have a high employment rate, but you're not told half of them drop out before they make it." That made me wonder if I could handle the course load, and at that time, the Chilliwack RCMP was looking for an Indian constable. There were also jobs available for Indians in salmon-enhancement programs, but I decided to try and get a forestry diploma before making any other decisions.

It was a bad year for finding work, but I got the $1,000 scholarship from Parks Canada; that and knowing I would have a good chance of getting a job if I graduated motivated me to continue with my education. I made many friends at college and talked to many people, but I instinctively knew that the students at BCIT were going to close me off, but I was determined to get a career and nothing was going to stop me. I didn't have much money when I started there, so I rented a cheap one-roomed housekeeping room. It wasn't much, but it was all I needed: a fridge, stove, sink, bed, table, and chairs, all in one room. When I attended classes, the students closed me off and wouldn't associate with me like I knew they would, and the students who would associate with me were few and far between. One very religious fellow, Roland Syens, was friends with me though; and whenever he forgot his lunch or bus fare, he would go to me for help. I didn't mind though because I could live quite comfortably on the money I got from DIA because I hardly ever drank or went out, so money was never a problem. As I was standing outside a classroom one day, a lady going out said "Hi!" to me.

I was surprised and said, "I thought you were talking to me."

"I was. I'm Cindy Werebowsky, from Merritt." Eventually she noticed I was closed off by the other students and felt bad that no one wanted me in their group.

Before I got accepted at BCIT, I felt like Charlie Brown, a cartoon character who could never do anything right no matter how hard he tried, a total failure at everything after trying my best. When I got accepted in the forestry program, there were many job openings for graduates, and this was where my natural talents and interests were; so I started getting the opinion that nature has compensations, for people who aren't very good in one field are better in others. Everyone has the potential to do something with their life if they have the determination to find and use their natural talents. Previously I had changed career choices, so often people started asking me if I was going to change my mind again, and some were still calling me a professional student.

The first month at BCIT was difficult because I needed strenuous exercise to get my mind off my studies and couldn't find anything. I also wanted to be a boxer in case the course load was too hard then I would try and join the RCMP, but the nearest boxing club was closed down for a month, and it would have been too inconvenient to go to any other club because of the bus routes I would have to take. Having nothing to take a break from my studying made the work difficult for me because I couldn't drink liquor unless I had three days to recuperate. My mother still kept trying to get me married off and insisted that I had time for sports then I also had time for a girlfriend and always insisted that would take my mind off my studies.

I couldn't understand why I couldn't get any ladies interested in me because people sometimes said that I'm a very nice-looking boy. I got lucky on a few one-night stands but never anything more than that. I started getting tired of going to the bars, dances, and cabarets and started going out less and less. Abdule had moved back to BC with his wife Silvey, and I sometimes went out to the cabarets with them. They couldn't understand why I was always getting turned down either, and I was reaching the point where I would just sit back and listen to music if I went out to the cabarets. When I was over visiting them one day, I asked John, "Does anyone ever call you by your second name, Ramon?"

"That's my first name."

"Are you sure you weren't East Indian originally?"

He just laughed and said, "Yes, I'm sure I wasn't East Indian originally!"

After the boxing club finally opened, I had something to take my mind off my studies, but I was falling behind on my studies and didn't know if I would pass all my courses. I also couldn't find anything to do on weekends to get away from studying, and that slowed me down even more. I always dropped everything at midnight and went to bed but sometimes got up at four or five in the morning to complete my assignments; a couple of times I even got up at three in the morning to study. The first semester was an extremely busy one for me partly because of the course content but mainly because of things slowing me down, but I still stuck it out and gave it everything I had; I passed everything in the end, but my marks weren't very good. I went downtown for breakfast one day and ran into a friend from Merritt, Roger Swakum, and he told me Wesley Pierre committed suicide about four months ago. Wesley didn't only drink continuously; when he moved out, he cut himself with a knife two times, lost his front teeth in a car accident, and now he committed suicide! I didn't hear about it because one of the other tenants was stealing my newspapers from Merritt.

It was okay for me to drink during the holidays, so I tried to live it up as much as I could in my two weeks off. Then just before Christmas, Abdule decided he wanted to buy his wife a watch for Christmas, and Isaac wanted to look for a stereo system, so we took a trip to Seattle to look around. When we got to Seattle, Isaac and Abdule went looking in the jewelry stores and I went for a drink. At first the barmaid didn't think I was old enough to drink, so she just ignored me. Then another customer came in; she served him then asked me for my ID. When she saw I was twenty-two, one year over the legal drinking age, I ordered a Singapore Sling. It didn't taste very good, so I drank it fast then left because I knew Isaac gets very impatient at times. Abdule bought his wife a watch, then we went down the street to another jewelry store and told the owner we were just down from Vancouver, Canada. He was really serious and said, "Is there snow and dogsleds up there?"

I started laughing and said, "Oh yes! Yes! I forgot my six gun and Stetson at home! We chase wild horses during the summer!"

He cut me off and said, "Hey, I was just kidding!" before I had a chance to say, "We just took a week off our trap line to come down here!"

They were trying hard to sell Isaac a watch, so he asked me to finance him if he didn't have enough money. I agreed, but I only brought enough money to have a good time for the day and that was before bank machines came out and all banking was done in person at the bank or by personal check. The store owner kept lowering his price until he offered it for $80, then his partner said, "Give it to him for half price. Otherwise, we'll be eating them after Christmas!"

I wanted to save my money for having fun, so I started saying, "Give him sixty! Give him sixty!" The owners were ready to tell me to get out, but Isaac walked out when they offered him 16 percent exchange on Canadian currency. Later on, everyone was laughing at me because it was a $150 watch and I was saying, "Give him sixty!" Lots of money back then!

Although the other students wouldn't associate with me, they didn't want me to drop out either; and when I went back for my second semester, I did everything I could to have some activity to take my mind off my studies on weekends. I joined the boxing club again and signed up for racquetball lessons and cross-country ski lessons. I had the urge to see Whitehorse and go up north for a long time, and a job opening came up with the British Columbia Forest Service (BCFS) in Lower Post, British Columbia's most northern town; so I thought if I get the job, I may have a chance to see Whitehorse. The second semester wasn't as difficult as the first, but I still had things slowing me down; the schedule for cross-country skiing changed, so I had to get Abdule to drive me to Manning Park; and I wasn't able to get much studying done because of the time involved. The racquetball course was just a little bit of an introduction and didn't do anything at all to take my mind off my studies; then the transit buses went on strike for a week, so I wasn't able to go boxing.

One night, the boxing coach told us we could never do enough running for that sport; so I started running during my lunch hour, which helped me take a break from studying and escape feeling lonely.

In one hour, I did a two-and-a-half-mile run, had a shower, ate my lunch, then made it back to my next class. I'm not a natural athlete, so it took me a long time just to start sparring, but I noticed right away that the beatings I was giving out were the beatings I was getting back. Then whenever I wished too strongly that the students would accept me rather than close me off, James would call when I had lots of work to do, so I thought, "Perhaps it's better that it's happening this way."

As I was learning more at BCIT, I realized the East Indian I worked with for DIA didn't know anything at all. It surprised me that he didn't even know the basics about timber cruising that a first-year forest technician would know, yet he said he cruised timber for sixteen years in the jungles of Malaysia, and was also incredibly lazy. At the job interview, I was told I may have trouble keeping up with him because he hasn't gained any weight since he was fifteen, but I wondered how they could believe that because people are still growing at fifteen, and he was also a chubby little fellow. I was very angry about that, but I noticed what would happen whenever I would think about it. When we were on field trips walking through the woods and I would start thinking about him or my ex-landlady's son, a branch would slap me in the face or I would slip and fall. How much it hurt would depend on how angry I was thinking about it; it was almost like something was saying "Don't think about it! They've suffered enough!" so I learned how to tell when people were thinking evil thoughts.

Abdule started working out with the boxers too and was my sparring partner. He was bigger and stronger than I and almost knocked me out with a good blow to the chin one night, so I was rather hesitant about sparring after that. One day as I was getting changed to go jogging, a fellow kept saying hi to me. I didn't recognize him, but he knew me. He was Dave Maratina, from Merritt, and was one of the few people who would associate with me; but he was in a different technology.

I kept applying for jobs, going for interviews and getting turned down, and was getting so discouraged I was ready to stop applying, but kept trying anyway. When we wrote out our résumé in our communications class, some students said I've had lots of jobs; but in spite of my work record, no one would hire me. I kept trying for the job in Lower Post, and each potential applicant was given a second interview. I made it to the second interview, but there was still nothing definite, so I asked my father and brothers to help me get a job logging. As the end of the semester drew near, I didn't know what I was going to do, my marks weren't very good because of outside influences slowing me down, and one instructor gave us a major assignment just before our final exams. I didn't want to go home, so a week before the semester was over, I phoned home and told my mother I wasn't going home because all she was going to do was tell me to find a girlfriend. Then just before the semester ended, I found out I needed more high-lead logging experience to do logging layout, in forestry called engineering. Now it was a toss-up: should I go up north to get away from my family or try and go logging? I didn't know what to do.

Then three days before the semester ended, I was offered a job in Lower Post, so I was really happy I could go away for the next four months where no one could bother me! The next day, Roland told me he was offered the job; but he had already committed himself to another job, so he suggested the Forest Service hire me. That meant I would have one day off after my final exams, fly up north to Smithers, then drive to Lower Post. Now I was glad I only had a cheap one-roomed housekeeping room because I could keep it over the summer without packing up and looking for another place when I got back. I was learning more and more to be optimistic and that perseverance pays off. I got a job where I wanted one the most but kept wishing there would be some way I could get more high-lead logging experience before I graduated. Then I heard a number of students laughing and yelling out, "Up in Lower Post, the Forest Service puts up eight-foot fences to keep the Indians out!" I never saw any eight-foot fences when I was there; there wasn't even a fence around the compound. I wasn't going to add this in, but people told me to do it because that is what happened. The truth is the truth.

I wrote the last of my final exams, took a night out to the bars, then went home to get packed; and the next day, my mother and one of my aunts drove me to the airport in Vancouver. I met some people I went to BCIT with, then we flew to Smithers to meet Jim Dunlop, the district manager. We met the rest of the crew in Smithers and went for the two-day drive to Lower Post; spent one night in Stewart, British Columbia, a town near the Alaska Panhandle; then drove to Lower Post. I enjoyed the trip along the Stewart-Cassiar Highway even though it was mostly gravel road and there was much highway construction going on.

When we got to Lower Post, I was told I was going to be the lookout assistant and the rest of the crew was the rappel or rap-attack crew. Rap attack consists of sliding down a rope from a helicopter to access and fight fires, and this was the second year it was tried because there were very few roads to get to fires that far up north. There were many applicants for the job, and the competition was stiff. We were known as the IA (initial attack) crew, the first people on a fire and the first ones off. The object was to try and get a fire under control right away before it can spread and become a major forest fire. Our first two weeks was job training, which consisted of safety, fire control, helicopter safety, first aid, and radio communication. Helicopter safety was most important because we would be around helicopters much of the time. Then after initial training, I had to fly back to Smithers in a single-engine plane to pick up a one-ton truck to be used for deliveries. I would then be going around to the lookout towers to prepare them for accommodation while the rest of the crew got their firefighting and rap-attack training. I enjoyed flying around to the lookout towers on helicopters. The head lookout man was fun to work with, and when it was over, I had to bring the one-ton truck from Dease Lake to Lower Post.

I always knew I was withdrawn and couldn't understand why then I must have gotten scabies soon after I got to Lower Post because I seemed to be rather short minded and unable to think clearly. About a month after arriving, I got my marks for the second semester and thought my marks would go up, but they went down. I passed everything but was still depressed because I had tried so hard and nothing ever seemed to work out the way I wanted it to.

I did some of the training with people who were going to be operating the lookout towers, then got sent back to Smithers to trade a truck in. The crew was then divided and three were sent to Dease Lake, three stayed in Lower Post, and two were sent to Atlin, an old gold-mining town in Northern British Columbia. The weather started getting warmer, and the crew had to be available and on call, called standby, in case there was a fire; and the crew got one-third of their wages for each hour they were on standby. As I was burning some garbage one day, a fire started in the yard, so I ran to get the garden hose to put it out; but the garden hose was too short, so I grabbed two washbasins and dumped water with one while the other was filling up. I tried to get the fire out before Jim Dunlop got back, but he went driving in just before the fire was out. He just laughed, and a fellow with him said, "Put the fire-hazard rating up another notch!"

I wasn't put on standby because I was the lookout assistant. It was hot, and I started getting bored, so I went to the bar one Friday night. The next day, Jim went to Watson Lake, a town just inside the Yukon Territory, to pick up the cook; and some people at the nearby Indian reserve were burning garbage and a fire broke out. The reserve was right beside the forestry station, so we were on the fire right away. I didn't have any firefighting training, but the rest of the crew was trained, so I did what they did. As we were setting up the pumps and laying out the hoses, children were pushing and pulling buttons on the pumps, wondering what they were there for; so I got really mad and yelled at the people to keep their kids out of the way.

The grass was dry and the trees were very pitchy, so the trees would smolder for a few seconds, then you would hear a swish; the whole tree would go up in flames. It was the cook's first day on the job and there was a big fire right beside the station when she and Jim went driving in. Jim was well experienced at fighting fires and immediately called the bombers in because we had to get the fire under control before any houses were burnt down and lives lost. Bombers are airplanes that drop fire retardant, a chemical compound that helps put fires out, keeps them from spreading, then breaks down into fertilizer for the forests. After we got the hoses laid out, the pumps operating, and some of the Indians working with us, the subforeman told me to take the truck and get some more hose. Someone had already taken the truck away, so I ran back to the station to get the one-ton truck. Jim told me to take some hose and equipment to another part of the fire, but when I got there, I was told to take it back to where we first started trying to control the fire. The RCMP had stopped traffic and I pulled out in front of everyone and people were glaring at me, wondering what gave me the right to pull out right in front of them, yet they could see the fire. I had my hard hat on and the equipment in the back. After I dropped the equipment off, I was told to get a group of workers and go to another part of the fire. When I got there, I was sent back to where I came from and kept driving back and forth until finally someone said, "Send them out the bush!"

"What about the bombers?" I said.

"They'll hear the sirens before the retardant is dropped!"

Right after I sent the crew in, the bombers went and dropped their retardant right where I sent the crew without sounding their sirens, so I got someone to call them back. After the bombers got the fire under control, we got the hotel to make sandwiches for the workers; and the assistant ranger, Ron Last, said we're going to take a Cat to build a fireguard. We worked steadily until dark then went in for supper, so it must have been an exciting day for the cook because it was her first day on the job. The next day, Ron and I went to work on the fire again, and the rest of the crew had to stay at the base in case they were called to another fire. I worked ten and a half hours before I finally got a chance to take a break, but I had a tendency to get overexcited in emergency situations and not think too clearly. After the emergency was over and everything calmed down, the area of the fire was traversed. It was only twenty-one acres but cost $18,000 to put out, a large sum of money in 1978 because firefighters were only paid $4 an hour; but thankfully, none of the houses were burnt down and no one was hurt.

Then things started going smoothly, and I was busy making deliveries to Dease Lake, finally, a trip to Whitehorse, then to Atlin. To get to Atlin, a person has to go up the Yukon on the Alaska Highway then go back down into British Columbia. It was raining hard when I got back to Lower Post, so the crew was off standby and Jim let us use a Forest Service vehicle to go for a drive to Whitehorse and Atlin for the weekend, so I was in Whitehorse two times in one week. We went to a dance in Atlin and had a good time, but my luck with finding girlfriends was the same: they treated me like poison ivy.

When we drove back to Lower Post, my wrist was aching, an indication that more rain was coming because of arthritis. It rained again in Lower Post, and there had been a lightning strike in Atlin, causing a fire; so all the crew were sent to the fire but me, so I had nothing to do but sit around the office. The crew were getting much overtime and I wasn't getting any, but I knew things seemed to work out right for me. A week later, the crew were sent back to their units and I had to deliver some equipment to Atlin. There weren't any roads into the fire, so everything had to go in by plane or helicopter to a camp setup for the firefighters. The Atlin crew and I ended up getting more overtime than the other crew, and all we were doing was working on a dock, loading food, helicopter fuel, equipment, and fire retardant onto planes. Since the days were long, we worked seven days a week from seven o'clock in the morning until ten o'clock at night.

Working up north was quite isolated, so the crew thought up all kinds of jokes. If we were in a hurry, Carl Schultz, the clown, would say, "And we're off like a whore's drawers!" If it got too hot, he would say, "It's hotter than a whore's drawers on payday!" The airplane pilot serviced his plane one day and left a can of grease on the dock, and a young kid working with us picked it up and said, "I guess I'll grease my joints!"

When the fire was under control, our work was cut down to eight hours a day; then a back fire was lit to control the fire, but it jumped the guard, so we were back working long hours again. I was happy to be working the long hours because I wouldn't have time to get bored or lonely and was having the time of my life but kept wishing I could get more logging experience before I graduated. Toward the end of the summer, the fire was under control and firefighters started getting laid off. There was very little for us to do, so I asked to be sent back to Lower Post to work on my summer technical report. I noticed I was getting short minded and not able to remember very much, but I thought I was just tired from the long hours I had been working. I flew back to Lower Post on a patrol plane while the pilot was watching for fires. I only had one day off in the five or six weeks I was in Atlin and enjoyed the trip back. Every summer the IA crew does a run from Lower Post to Watson Lake, a distance of fifteen miles. I wanted to do it, but missed it. Some of the crew were getting ready to leave since the summer was almost over, so we all went out for a steak-and-crab dinner; then the next day, half the crew was sick from food poisoning.

I gathered information from Jim Dunlop about setting up a camp in a remote area for my report, and he asked me to send it to Hank Doerkson (BCFS) in Victoria, so in my report, I stressed the importance of physical fitness as a safety factor for the IA crew. The crew often have to work long hours, often in steep terrain; and since most accidents happen when people are tired, it would reduce the chance of an accident if they're in good physical condition. Not only that, it reduces mental tension; and if a fire gets away and they have to run, it would increase their chance of survival.

I had some time off coming to me, so I left a week and a half before the summer was over and asked if I could go back next year, but it looked like I wouldn't get out of BCIT on time. I flew back to Vancouver feeling proud of myself because I made really good money and had a great time. Most of the other students only made $5,000 or $6,000; and it had to pay for their second year at BCIT. I made over $8,000 and it was all spending money because DIA paid for my education. That was lots of money back in 1978; and as usual, whenever I went up north, my mother would ask if I had any girlfriends up there when I got back.

As I was walking around Vancouver one day, I ran into James; so we walked around and talked for a while, then I asked him, "Where's your sister, Coleen?"

"Working by the Hotel Vancouver."

"As a chambermaid?"

"No. As a prostitute."

Even though she was outstandingly beautiful, I knew she wouldn't go out with me if she never had anyone, so I guess I didn't miss anything. After I got back to BCIT, I couldn't understand why I still had trouble remembering and learning things. When I went to bed at night, I had a hard time sleeping because I was so itchy and almost scratched myself right through the skin on some parts of my body. There was another Indian student there in first-year forestry, and he told me he attended previously to be an X-ray technician. Then he asked me, "What do you think of the T'shamas? These white students?"

He didn't know I knew what he meant, but I said, "How do they treat you?"

"They're just acquaintances."

"How did they treat you when you came here before?"

"It was the same way." A white girl listening felt bad that we were treated that way though, and I noticed he was being closed off the same way I was.

I thought this was going to be my last year in Vancouver, so I was determined to become a boxer and thought I may have some fights this year, so I tried to spar with someone every time I went to the club. I still subscribed to the *Merritt Herald*, and the other tenant was still taking them, which wouldn't have bothered me; but he wouldn't give them back so I would have a chance to read them. Then there was a mail strike, and when mail started flowing again, I checked the date on my paper and thought he was stealing them again, so I went upstairs and threatened to beat the shit out of him. The next day, my papers came in the mail.

The itching went on for a long time and was affecting my studies considerably. I thought it may be nerves, so I went out to the bars for a night out, but it didn't do any good. Later on I phoned my mother and she told me to go home and see the doctor, so I took the bus to

Rosedale and got off at the pub and got good and drunk. I was hoping the incredible itching was just nervous tension that could be let out by having fun, but it wasn't. The next day the doctor told me it was scabies and gave me some lotion to keep applying until it went away. It was late in the semester by now and I was way behind in my studies, but I wasn't about to give up. I thought if I made a supreme effort, I might be able to pass this semester; but unfortunately, I didn't pass and had to wait until next fall to try again. I didn't find out I failed until after Christmas, and got very depressed but tried to be optimistic about it. Dad also told me not to give up; otherwise, I would be throwing away five and a half years of my life, so I moved home again because my parents always let me move home when I was down on my luck.

I had nothing to do, so I started taking David and Jimmy out to movies, dinner, breakfast, etc., again. It was rather cold that winter, and Jimmy wanted to go for a bike ride and said his tires were low, and the air compressor wasn't working as he was standing by the patio door. Then he said, "There's a dead bird there."

I said, "Well, put it inside until Dad gets home." So he put the dead bird in the house.

"What did you do that for?"

"You said put it inside until Dad gets home."

It was very boring living with my parents, so I kept going to Vancouver to try and get a job logging out the coast and asked my brothers and friends to put my name in where they were working. Being unemployed was extremely boring and lonely, but I instinctively knew I couldn't get anyone interested in me no matter how hard I tried, yet my mother still kept telling me to find someone. She was making life miserable for me, so I had to put it to an end. I was twenty-three now, and my father was getting concerned about me because I never had a girlfriend yet. On one of my trips to Vancouver, I met a girl and took her out for the weekend. She was twenty-nine but only looked twenty-two, but after I found out she was an alcoholic, I stopped trying to go out with her.

Then just when the boredom was getting unbearable, I got a job working on the reserve. I was making more on UIC, but at least I had something to do; and when I had two days of work left on the reserve, I got called out logging. Eddie Dale, the last person I ever expected to get me a job, got me a job. Where I went logging, the crew went in to the logging camp Sunday nights or Monday mornings and we went out Friday nights. I really enjoyed the work, but fortunately, I knew well enough to listen to people who knew more than I did and didn't intend to make a career of it. I also worked for the government first and wasn't making much more than I was with the Forest Service and couldn't stand the thought of seasonal work, only working six or eight months of the year, so I knew education was the way to go.

When I went to town Friday nights, I usually went to the bar at the Empress Hotel in Chilliwack because there wasn't much else to do; and at that time, the Empress had a beer parlor, lounge, and restaurant. One night I was having supper there with Margo Coutlee, an Indian girl from Merritt, and three times, a group of Indians walked in; and as soon as they walked in, the waitress sharply said, "Sit in the corner if you're only going to have soup!"

Margo called her prejudiced, and most of the customers just turned a blind eye; but one lady said, "She has a lot of nerve saying 'Sit in the corner if you're only going to have soup!'" I was too withdrawn to think anything of it until years later though.

The company was happy with my work at first; then I drank a little bit and it slowed me down, almost cost me my job, and I lost a promotion. So after that I only drank Friday nights so I would have two days to recuperate. One night I went to a cabaret and was just going to call a taxi home when a taxi driver went in and said, "Taxi for Peter!"

So I said, "Yeah, right here!"

When I was logging, I worked with a Canadian fellow close to my age and had lived in Australia for a number of years and spoke with an Australian accent. I asked him what the Aboriginals in Australia were like, and he said they live in reserves, where there is a high rate of unemployment and alcoholism. I was also working with a WWII veteran, and he proudly said, "The Allies never took second place to anyone in how we treated our prisoners of war!" The movies and history books talked about how the enemy treated their prisoners of war, but I sometimes wondered how the Allies treated their prisoners of war.

I was still tempted to make a career of logging because I enjoyed it so much, but I had met many loggers who enjoyed it at the start but got tired of it ten years later. I also wanted to finish my education so I would have more than one career choice; the idea of finishing something I stated also appealed to me because I thought something good could happen if I persevered. When we got shut down for fire season, I had time to find a place to stay when I went back to BCIT. It was hard trying to find a place to stay that year, and all I could find was a rather large one-bedroom apartment, which I thought was great! I wouldn't get cabin fever if I stayed home too much because I didn't think the students were going to associate with me again.

My third year at BCIT was great though; it seemed like everything was working out for me except for finding a girlfriend. The students accepted me and associated with me like a normal person; and I found a boxing club where I could work out Monday, Wednesday, Friday nights, and Sunday afternoons, which worked out perfectly for my studies because I could work out one night then stay home and study the next night. One of my sparring partners was stronger and faster than I and gave me a black eye. Then a few days later, I was in a bad mood from writing exams. He had a hard day at flying school, so we got in the ring and just flew at it. I hit him and knocked him back and thought, *If you want to come back swinging go right ahead!* I thought we were sparring normally, then the coach said, "Hey! If you're going to fight like that, go to the bars and do it! And use broken bottles! You don't need me here to teach you that!" He said to him, "I saw you taking some good blows!" Then he said a little more softly to me, "I saw you taking some good blows too. Settle down and spar normally! I don't like to see my friends get beat up!"

The next day I found out the exam wasn't worth very much and my sparring partner had a black eye. I had punched him out for no reason, so I thought I better not get mad anymore; I better wait and see what happens. A Native fellow went in one night to join the club and didn't want to talk to me because he wanted to associate with non-Natives and break the color barrier. He was obviously an experienced boxer, yet he was still ignored. He noticed I was treated the same way, so he got frustrated and walked out, but I tried to be optimistic about it. Everything was going good, and I wished things would happen like that all the time. However, I instinctively knew that if I were to find a girlfriend, she would run around on me. It seemed like no matter how hard I tried, I couldn't get them interested in me, so I tried to block it out of my mind. After I completed my third semester, I went home for Christmas. Sometimes when I went home during my holidays, it was incredibly boring; but this time, the holidays were great and had a great time partying and having fun.

Chapter 2

When I went back for my fourth and final semester, I thought I would finally graduate and have a career; but if I drank, I had to be extra careful and make sure I could spare three days to recuperate. The second weekend after starting the semester, I thought I could spare the time for a night of partying and had a hunch telling me to do so. I went to Chilliwack and asked Tony to go to the bars with me; but he had invited some people over, and Isaac and his girlfriend at the time, Tracey, were also going over. It was a nice, quiet social gathering and I enjoyed it; then when the party was over, Tracey said to me, "Baxter. You should come over to our place and meet this girl. She's sixteen and has a crush on Isaac."

"I'm twenty-four. Am I too old for her?"

"No. Age doesn't matter."

"Okay, I'll be over next weekend."

I took the bus to Abbostford the next weekend and Isaac picked me up in and we went out for coffee then to Laughing Raven, an Indian reserve just outside of town. We sat around most of the day then went to the bars in the evening, but I didn't drink. The next day, Tracey made a pot of coffee; and a little while later, Jennifer went over for a visit. When I spoke to Tracey alone, I said, "Is that the girl?"

Tracey laughed and said, "Yes." Tracey and Jennifer had coffee then made a pot of duck soup, and after lunch, Jennifer and I were sitting across from each other at the table, both nervous and wondering what to say. I was used to getting turned down, so I hardly ever got excited anymore and asked Jennifer where she was from. She said Agassiz, so I asked if we were related, and she said no. She was a very homely girl, but I was lonely and knew things seemed to work out right for me. She was seventeen, not sixteen. A little while later, Eddie Dale called and asked Isaac to go to town to play pool and go bowling, so Jennifer and I went with him and took an interest in each other. It was Sunday afternoon, so I couldn't stay long because I had to go back to Vancouver to get my homework done; and Jennifer said, "Is it that important to you?" I was surprised she didn't seem to think career goals were important.

Jennifer was staying with her sister Geraldine and her husband, Ben, so I called her on Thursday to tell her I was going back on the weekend to visit her. She was out on the road, playing street hockey, and I was surprised she was seventeen and playing street hockey. Geraldine answered the phone, and Jennifer thought it was her ex-boyfriend calling and got depressed. I was sure happy she was excited to hear from me and told me she missed me, then I said, "I'll meet you at the bus depot Saturday morning. Isaac can give you a ride to town."

As the bus pulled into Abbotsford, I didn't see Isaac's car there, so I thought I had been stood up again. It wouldn't have bothered me because I was used to getting turned down, but when the bus pulled into the depot, I was really happy to see Jennifer sitting there waiting for me. She said, "Isaac went to Kamloops to visit his friend, so I took a taxi to town." Then we went out for breakfast, walked around town for a little while, then took a taxi to Laughing Raven. I visited Jennifer and her sister's family for the weekend, then I told her I couldn't see her for two weeks because next weekend I had to go back to Rosedale to prepare for my spring field trip to the interior of BC, but I would be back the weekend after.

I was going to pay for the field trip myself, but one of my cousins told me to get DIA to pay for it because that's what they're there for, so I agreed and was given two weeks' living allowance. I didn't sign up for where I wanted to go and was sent to Williams Lake. One instructor said half the people will be staying in town and the other half will be going to Chezacut, then asked who wanted to go to Chezacut. I volunteered because I consider myself adventurous and game for anything, and on our way to Williams Lake, I realized I had the flu; but I still had a good time there. We stayed in Chezacut for three days and got free room and board, steaks, pork chops, and chicken, then spent the last night in town. Things seemed to be working out right for me, and I enjoyed being accepted by most people and not closed off like I was previously.

I got back from my field trip earlier than I expected and rushed back to see Jennifer, so I went to Isaac's place and he sent someone over to get her. As I got to know Jennifer, I found out she wasn't on the pill; but I was used to getting treated like poison ivy whenever I dated any girls, so I never made any sexual advances on her other than hugging and kissing. Then Jennifer slowly started telling me about herself, but it took a while before I found out about the child abuse because that was something totally unheard of to me. Geraldine, the kids, Jennifer, and I went to a house outside of town; and I met Jennifer's half sister, Veronica, who grew up with their mother's aunt and uncle in Laughing Raven. When I phoned Jennifer a few days later, she said Veronica wondered if I was twenty-seven or twenty-eight because people sometimes said I looked older than I was.

I went home to visit my parents the next weekend, and I still had the flu. I wished I could get over it so I could study, but my father's friend said it was the Bangkok flu brought over from the boat people from Vietnam and lasts six weeks; but I just thought, *No problem. I can pull up my marks in the final exams.*

I spent the next weekend with Jennifer then went back to Vancouver, and several days later, she phoned me up and said she was at Sears, right behind where I lived. I was surprised she was able to find her way around Vancouver to where I lived and was happy to see her and glad she seemed interested in me. She said she had done some skiing before, so I took her skiing up Grouse Mountain; and the next day, we went for a walk down Stanley Park. And as we were walking around near the end of the day, she started crying. When we got back to the apartment, it took her a long time to tell me what was wrong; she said the day before, I got impatient and said, "Come on! Hurry up!"

I didn't think I said it harshly, but it still upset her; and earlier that week, she was riding a bicycle with her niece, Amanda, and had an accident. Amanda cut her foot and Jennifer was scared Ben was going to beat her up. I thought she was just doing that for attention. I still couldn't study or keep up with boxing because of the flu but thought I could pull up my marks in the final exams, and Jennifer and I continued to see each other quite regularly even though Geraldine didn't want us together. I thought her family would be happy to have her going out with an ambitious, successful fellow like myself, but Geraldine said I was too old and serious for her.

One day in Vancouver, Jennifer said, "I cried really hard last night."

"Why?"

"I didn't think I was good enough for you!"

We were seeing each other just about every weekend, the flu lasted five weeks, and Jennifer's depression was slowly coming out. When we were walking around Central Park in Burnaby, she told me about edible wild plants, and I thought she knew about them because our parents knew about them; then she told me she used to eat them because she was hungry, and I didn't think I heard her right. I did a word jumble in the *Province* newspaper one day and couldn't get the last word, but Jennifer did it fast but didn't believe it was right; so I wondered, "How could she do it so fast if she's not very smart?"

Jennifer told me about some of her experiences with other men and running away to Vancouver. I asked her why she didn't just say "No!" but she said she didn't know how. I tried to get her to go on the pill, but she kept saying she didn't know how and wouldn't remember to take it and mentioned running away to Vancouver one time and a bus driver offered her a place to stay then tried to take advantage of her. She dropped her cassette recorder and the sudden noise scared him and she ran away.

Several years later, I asked her, "How did you get home?"

"I don't know!"

"Where did you spend the night?"

"I don't know that either!"

Another time she ran away to Vancouver because she was worried about being pregnant and went down to the water in North Vancouver to get a drink but didn't know it was salt water. She was lucky because a couple from Burrard Indian reserve picked her up as she was walking down the street and let her stay with them for a week. I also had a feeling Jennifer had a baby previously before she told me about it and was lucky she only got pregnant once after all the times she was taken advantage of, and Geraldine advised her to give it up for adoption. Jennifer said when the baby was born, she knew it was coming but she was too scared to wake Geraldine up to take her to the hospital. Geraldine was always putting her down, and I didn't realize the effect it was having on her. Then she went to the Sto:lo ("people of the river") Eagle reserve to visit her family for a few days then went back to visit me, and when I went home from classes, she said, "I scratched myself all up when you were gone!"

"Why did you do that?"

"I thought you would be mad at me for going to Sto:lo Eagle!"

I couldn't understand why she thought I would be mad at her for going to Sto:lo Eagle, and as we were seeing each other more, more of what she went through was coming out. She told me about going to school in Agassiz, and people didn't want to associate with her, not even her sister Elizabeth (called Liz). She told me about stealing from the store because she was hungry and one time she put some oranges in her toque and got caught and was told not to go into the store anymore. The next year, some of her cousins started going to school in Agassiz so she had friends who associated with her. Her father had taken her out of the school on the Sto:lo Eagle reserve and put her to school in Agassiz because he thought she would do better there, but she did worse. In her second year in Agassiz, she was taken away from home because Liz had reported the sexual abuse to the police, but Liz would later become her closest sister.

Jennifer told me about the beatings she got from her father and being picked on by the other children. She said one time her father called her and she was scared to go, so she pretended to be asleep; then he punched her in the stomach so hard she peed in her pants. After being taken away from home, she was put in St. Mary's Indian residential school in Mission; and when she first got there, she couldn't believe all the new clothes the staff were buying for her and wondered, how could people be so nice to her? Then she told me about looking down at the Fraser River and wanting to run down the hill and drown herself. She walked a long ways to phone her Dad one day, but they weren't allowed to talk very long, so she couldn't say very much. Although the students picked on her there, she was lucky one of her cousins there protected her and Uncle Joe was the administrator there at the time.

Jennifer was a very homely girl, and people said I was a very nice-looking boy; so sometimes, in restaurants the waitresses would wonder why we were together, but she seemed to be the only girl interested in me. I met some ladies who were outstandingly beautiful, but most of them wouldn't go out with me if they were single, so I never got excited by them. I also saw some ladies who were very homely when they were young who grew up to be very nice looking, so I thought this could happen to Jennifer. Jennifer and I got along quite well, but her depression was coming between us. She mentioned contemplating suicide and how easy it would be and eventually told me about some of her attempts to commit suicide. She tried to overdose with aspirins and hoped she would die in her sleep but woke up. Then she tried to slash her wrist one time when Geraldine put her down, but didn't succeed, then Tracey went over, so she didn't try to do it again that day.

The forest economy was good at that time, and jobs in forestry were plentiful. I didn't want to take her with me, but I didn't want to leave her behind either; so when some job openings came up in Lillooet, I decided to try and get a job there because it wasn't too close to my family or too far away from her and I wouldn't be living in a logging camp. Another reason for getting a career was so I wouldn't have to spend the rest of my life in logging camps; then right after I committed myself to a job in Lillooet, some really good job openings came up in Terrace, Northern British Columbia. I told myself, "That's where I should have applied."

Jennifer had a sister, Brenda, living in Lethbridge, Alberta, who had a baby girl named Cheryl; and I was told Brenda had her father's baby, but incest was something I had never heard anything about. Because of the religious upbringing my parents had in the residential schools, I was actually taught sex is bad; and whenever I tried to go out with anyone, they just treated me like poison ivy. Brenda hurt her back and wanted Jennifer to go over there and help look after her baby, but Jennifer was mixed up about going. She didn't want to go because of me and didn't know if she should move back to Sto:lo Eagle or not. She knew her father wouldn't want us together, and after talking to her when she thought about moving back, I realized why. I had been trying to teach her to be optimistic and said maybe it's better that it's happening this way. Her depression was starting to interfere with my studying, and I was still behind because of the Bangkok flu. I didn't mean to make it sound like I wanted to break up; I just needed time to catch up on my studying.

Liz went back to Laughing Raven for two weeks after going to upgrading classes in Lethbridge, and now she was going to London, Ontario, for a course in journalism. Jennifer and I had been going out together for four months before my family knew about it, and my father was surprised because several other people on our reserve also found girlfriends from Sto:lo Eagle. I borrowed my mother's car to go to Sto:lo Eagle to visit her family that weekend, and her father wasn't home. We didn't stay long. I met her mother, Emily, and I knew just before we left that Jennifer was going to start crying as she hugged her mother good-bye.

After Jennifer went to Lethbridge, I thought I could catch up on my studies and perhaps go in at least one boxing tournament; but right after she left, I got the Bangkok flu again and couldn't write my final exams. I didn't go to the doctor the first time I got sick and was told I would just be given my marks to date, so I didn't know if I was going to pass or not. During my last month at BCIT, my check was late, so I phoned DIA. And they said it would be put in the mail. Two weeks later I phoned them again and they said they would send it; then a week later, it was still on someone's desk, so I said I would just go down and pick it up. They wouldn't tell me whose desk it was on, and later on I thought it could have been another try to get me to give up on my postsecondary education.

I wasn't able to continue with my studies and had two weeks off before I started my job in Lillooet, and I wanted to do some sport fishing and take some time off. I needed a vehicle right away, so I bought a Datsun King Cab 4×4. Datsun, now Nissan, was the only dealer with this type of vehicle at that time; and it suited my needs perfectly. My father cosigned for the loan; and I put $3,500 down on a $9,000 truck. I was still sick though couldn't function properly. Dad went back to camp working, and my parents had a little boy from the reserve staying with them. Everyone else was busy, and my mother wanted to go to Merritt for a few days, so she made me give up what little free time I had so she could go to Merritt. David also took advantage of how caring I was and did a lot of driving around on my truck. Things like that would eventually build up a great deal of tension between me and my family.

I enjoyed the work I was doing in Lillooet, and my logging experience was helping me do my job better. Logging was in a recession, but there were still jobs in forestry. I enjoyed laying out roads and cutting boundaries for logging settings but still missed logging. I sometimes wished I were several years younger and knew what I know now and thought I would have been working my way up in some large company and not have wasted so much time in college. I couldn't drink more than once a month because I knew it would affect my work, and this cut out much of my social life, so I wished I could work seven days a week so I wouldn't have time to feel lonely. Jennifer and I continued to write to each other, and before she left, I tried to teach her that when people do something wrong it will happen back to them. I worked in Lillooet for about month then phoned home, and Dad told me I didn't graduate and would have to go back. That was a big disappointment, but I thought, *Maybe it's better that it happened that way. I only need one semester, five months to finish my education, and I'm too close to finishing now. Giving up would throw away seven years of my life.*

On our way to work one day, I had a feeling I should look under the hood while we were gassing up. I didn't always follow my hunches because I didn't trust my own judgment. I had the drive to succeed but lacked confidence because my family was always putting my opinion down. When we got out of the woods, the truck had no brakes; so the fellow I was working with, Paul Bernier, checked around to see why. He couldn't find anything, but my instincts kept telling me to look under the hood. Finally, Paul looked under the hood and someone had taken the cap off the brake fluid and it drained out.

I went for a beer one afternoon and started drinking with a Native from Lillooet, Willard Ned. I had gone to college with his son Dave. I told Willard I was doing logging engineering, but I missed logging, and he told me I was far better off engineering than logging. He was a carpenter, had gone to the Kamloops Indian Residential School, and said the Indian children were beaten until they were old enough to fight back then they were kicked out of school. Then he showed me some of the scars he got from the beatings. As old as he was, he still had physical scars from the beatings he received as a child in the residential schools. Dave was four years older than I, so Willard was old enough to be my father. When I first met Dave, he said he went to church to get his kids baptized, so naturally I thought he was a responsible family man. Then later on, Dave said whenever he and his old lady go to a party, if she wants to get drunk, he has to tell her not to get mad at him, because he gave her VD twice.

I went back to Rosedale on some weekends because there wasn't very much to do in Lillooet. I couldn't play soccer anymore because of my ankle, and baseball wasn't as popular with the Indians as it used to be. I went to Laughing Raven to visit Isaac and Tracey one weekend and saw someone riding down the road on a bicycle; it was Jennifer. She had gone back from Lethbridge and didn't phone to tell me. Jennifer told me about the good times she had in Lethbridge with Brenda and Alvin. They went on a two-week camping trip, went fishing, and did other activities; but after she told me about the good times, I was surprised she still talked about committing suicide. She said they went to Kamloops for a week to visit one of Alvin's uncles and she walked out on a bridge one night and was contemplating suicide but the police arrived and drove her home.

I started going back to the coast every weekend to see her because I was lonely, and she asked if she could spend a week up there with me, so I rented a kitchen unit at a motel for a week. It's hot in Lillooet, so the first night we were there, we went out to a lake to go swimming. Jennifer talked about being a good swimmer and how far she could swim out, then said she would like to swim out until she drowned. She started swimming out a ways, then I realized she was serious about what she was saying, so I swam out to stop her and pulled her back to shore. I was in good physical condition and knew lifesaving techniques from having done a year of physical education in college.

Living in Lillooet was very boring for her because she didn't know anyone there and I was away working during the day. Her depression was coming out more and more, and she wanted to stop in Lytton to see her brother, Ryan, on our way back to the coast because she wanted to ask him if their father molested the girls because she didn't want to believe it happened. In the morning, Ryan told Jennifer their dad did molest the girls and he was really mad at him for doing that, especially after what he did to Brenda. The hardest thing he ever did was to lie in court because he didn't want to see their mother get hurt, yet Jennifer still didn't want to believe he was like that. We went back to the coast the next day, and Jennifer went back to spend a week with Ryan and Desiree. She started getting interested in Desiree's brother, Don, but nothing came of it; and I thought she would be more interested in a successful man like me.

One weekend when I went to visit Jennifer, Geraldine took us and her kids to Sto:lo Eagle to visit their parents. It was the first time I met Henry, and they still had two brothers living at home, Andrew and Henry Jr. While we were walking around the backyard, Jennifer showed me a stump that was still a tree before she was taken away from home, and said, "That's where I hid from my dad one time when he came home drunk. Another time he came home drunk, I hid in the closet. Grandpa told Dad his daughters are going to scatter far and wide and was right. Geraldine's in Laughing Raven and Ben doesn't like to see her go home. Brenda is in Lethbridge and Liz is in London, Ontario."

Liz wrote back and asked Jennifer to go out and stay with her for a month because she was lonely, and would pay her way there and back. Jennifer was going to go, but Liz sent her belongings back and said she was going back to British Columbia. When Liz got back, Jennifer told her about her desires to commit suicide. I didn't know what to do, but Liz suggested she see a psychiatrist; so I checked the Yellow Pages in the Chilliwack and Abbotsford phone books but couldn't find any, so I still didn't know what to do. Sometimes when I went to visit her and we would be lying in bed, I would try to be affectionate; she would get really scared and suddenly jump up, holding her arm by her ribs and her hand by her mouth and start crying. I would ask her what's the matter, and she would say, "All I saw was a shadow by the door!" Previously, Jennifer told me about trying to go to jail so she wouldn't have to worry about being pregnant. I was very lonely and still trying to get her interested in me, so I was very protective of her and enjoyed how she stuck to me like glue. Jennifer was ashamed of her sexuality because of the abuse but I didn't know it at the time and it was very easy for me to suppress my sexual desires because I was so used to being treated like poison ivy whenever I tried to go out with anyone.

Jennifer continued to drink rather heavily and her depression was coming out more and more and I was transferred to Gold Bridge, an old gold-mining town that is a two-hour drive from Lillooet. I could feel Jennifer was losing interest in me, so I kept trying harder to keep her interested in me. One weekend when I went down to visit her, she was drinking again and we ended up going back to Rosedale. She was undecided about whether or not we should stay together. Then she went to sleep for several hours. When she woke up, she was feeling better and decided she wanted to go to Gold Bridge with me. I told her it's a very isolated community and there would be nothing for her to do, but she went along anyway.

The house I was staying in was isolated and there was nothing in town but a hotel, grocery store, and hardware store. I was working with two other fellows, UBC students; and we forgot to empty the garbage, so it attracted a bear. Being forestry workers, we weren't too worried, but found Jennifer hiding up in the attic. She was sleeping on the way up, and when I went to work one day, I left instructions for her to bake some chicken for supper. She wasn't sure how to cook it, so she phoned Geraldine, and she wasn't sure what to do either. Then she got scared and wanted to run away but didn't know which direction to go. I still wondered why she was so scared of making a mistake. She lived in Laughing Raven for two years before I met her, and Geraldine was always criticizing her if she did things wrong and putting her down if she did things right, but I still didn't realize the impact it was having on her. I continued to go down on weekends to see her, and we sometimes went to Sto:lo Eagle to visit her family; but whenever we went there, she wanted me to keep my distance in front of her family. On one visit, she thought I was sleeping, and she asked her dad about beating them. Henry denied beating them, but Jennifer told me later she'll never forget the time he punched her in the stomach so hard she peed in her pants.

I was used to working and making good money, so I bought Jennifer clothes when I thought she needed them. She was losing interest in me, and I was starting to miss being single. I was still lonely, but more concerned about her depression. I continued working in Gold Bridge, and one weekend, she decided she wanted to go up with me again, and the two other fellows had gone back to UBC. She brought along my tape deck so she could listen to music and try to keep herself occupied during the day, and after work, I tried teaching her how to drive to give her something to do and make her feel better about herself. There were some wooden stakes in the ground with ribbons tied to them, but she couldn't see them and didn't know those stakes meant there was a hole in the road and almost drove into the river, so I didn't do that anymore. One night we decided to go out for supper, and I was surprised to run into Linda, a lady I worked on the dock with in Atlin. Jennifer got bored, so on the last day of the week, she wanted to go to town; and she ran into Linda, so they spent part of the afternoon watching television in her hotel room. And by the end of the week, Jennifer decided she wanted to break up.

I only worked four days that week because I had to go to the dentist, and when we got back to the coast, she changed her mind again and decided she didn't want to leave me. We went to a dance that weekend and she got interested in another fellow there, but he didn't go out with her because he already had a girlfriend. Most people would have given up by then, but I was concerned about her depression. I started driving back to Gold Bridge the next day, but when I got as far as Lytton, I realized I had the flu, so I turned around and headed back. The next day, I phoned the company and told them I couldn't make it to work then told my mother that if Jennifer called, she tell her I was not home, and my mother had already decided she didn't want us together. When I went to the doctor for a note explaining my absence, I saw some pamphlets on depression, so I asked the doctor about them. He said, "That's just a come-on. They offer help for depression then ask for money. That's why I don't advertise them."

"My girlfriend has trouble with depression and I don't know what to do about it."

"You're helping her just by being there."

I went to visit Tony and his girlfriend, Terri Dargatz, but they were separated at the time; and I told her Jennifer and I had separated and I didn't know if I should go back to her or not. Then Terri told me I should go back to her, and if she hadn't said that, perhaps I might not have gone back to her. During my time off, I applied for more funding to go back to BCIT; getting a career made me feel good about myself, so I thought that might make Jennifer feel better about herself. So I asked a counsellor, Theresa Neel, if Jennifer could get into upgrading. There was one seat left, but it didn't start until October.

Being single again should have felt better, but I was extremely bored and only slightly lonely. I still wished I could work seven days a week so I wouldn't have time to feel lonely. I couldn't drink because I knew it would affect my work, I didn't have any luck finding girlfriends, and most people I knew were either raising a family or partying on weekends. I was often left by myself with nowhere to go and nothing to do, and my mother wanted me to leave Jennifer because she was so possessive. Toward the end of the week, I phoned Jennifer to see how she was doing, and she was really happy to hear from me and said she was tempted to hitchhike up to Gold Bridge to see me. Geraldine wanted her to go to their aunt's place to help can fruit, but she was too excited about me going, so she didn't go and Geraldine got mad at her.

Jennifer insisted on going back to Gold Bridge with me that week and said she could go to work with me. I was glad she did that because she's very observant and pointed out to me I wasn't holding my compass right when I was taking compass bearings. It was also very convenient for the company because I used my own vehicle to go to work and took Jennifer and the compass man with me while Grant Hadwin, the engineer, went to work somewhere else.

Jennifer was very observant but also seemed to be good at figuring things out, giving me the opinion that she's very intelligent but just never had a chance in life, so I was determined to give her one. Sometimes her immaturity and irresponsibility would bother me, but whenever I got angry at her, I noticed things seemed to work out in her favour; good luck seemed to be following her. When we were working, Jennifer was very scared of bears and kept looking around for a tree to climb in case a bear went along, but most of the branches were high up on the trees, so they were impossible to climb. When Grant Hadwin heard about it, he asked her, "Well, Jennifer! Have you seen any bears?"

We worked until Friday then went back to the coast, and when we got back to Rosedale, my mother said, "Bad news! Your sister Geraldine slashed her wrist and tried to commit suicide!" Geraldine survived the suicide attempt, and I was surprised she did that because she always seemed so happy. When we went to see her, she said she lied to the doctors and nurses about how many times she tried to commit suicide so she could stay out of the psychiatric ward.

I got Jennifer registered in upgrading classes in Sardis, a suburb of Chilliwack; and a lady from Laughing Raven was working there, so Jennifer caught a ride with her. Jennifer got $100 a month for going to upgrading, but Geraldine acted like putting her back in school wasn't any big deal. I was still working in Gold Bridge, and when I went down to see her, Liz said Jennifer wasn't taking her studies seriously; when she got home, she just went off and visited her friends. Liz found a job in the newspaper up in Destruction Bay, Yukon Territory, and asked Henry if she could borrow $100 to go up north for the job. I was in Laughing Raven when their parents came and Henry said, "Next year's humpback year. Many couples are going to separate. That's what the old Indians tell me." The odd-numbered years are when humpback salmon go up the river to spawn, but I didn't think Jennifer and I were going to separate, because I thought we were getting along quite well. Humpback salmon are sold as Fancy Pink Salmon in the store.

Jennifer was drinking heavily and was losing interest in me now, and I tried to get her to slow down on her drinking, but Geraldine kept giving her more beer. I instinctively knew she was going to run around on me, so I kept trying to get her interested in me. Jennifer and her family just didn't understand the importance of getting an education; she had attended her upgrading classes for about five or six weeks by now and wasn't doing very well. She continued drinking heavily and was crying and depressed all the time; she actually cried so much her eyelids swelled up. Eventually she got her braces removed, and I didn't know what to do except keep trying to help her, and Ben was also getting tired of her being depressed all the time. I often asked Jennifer to do things for me, but it was hard to get her to do anything. I finally talked her into cooking pancakes for my breakfast one day, and when she started cooking, I told her to match the size of the burner with the size of the frying pan. Then she started crying, so I hugged her and tried to reassure her; and Geraldine sarcastically said, "You don't have to suck up to her!"

I went down the next weekend, and she had an appointment to see the doctor the next day. Geraldine mentioned how hungry the kids were when she was living in Sto:lo Eagle, but they weren't allowed to eat the sandwich meats because it had to be saved for their dad, and he even made the kids put his socks and shoes on for him. I was tired from working all week and the long drive, so I went to bed. Jennifer and Geraldine sat up talking, and Jennifer was wondering if I was too old for her. Geraldine said, "A psychiatrist can't tell you if he's too old for you or not." Jennifer came to bed a little while later and almost cried because she didn't know I was awake and heard her.

We took Jennifer to the doctor the next day, and she was in the doctor's office for a long time and seemed to be taking forever. Finally she went out, even more depressed than when she went in; was crying; and said, "He wants me to see a psychiatrist!" This was the first time she went to the psychiatric ward for depression and sometimes said, "I think Daddy's the best father anyone can have! I don't care what anyone says!"

Her depression, immaturity, and irresponsibility were taking its toll on me, and I was also too shy and withdrawn to express my opinions or assert myself with the other workers; so some mistakes were made. I knew I had to work on my own emotional problems, but getting a career was my main concern at the time. Winter was coming, and I knew I could get laid off at any time, and there was still much work to be done before we got snowed out, and it also was time to burn slash on areas after logging to prepare the ground for planting a new crop of trees. We put in some long hours burning slash and putting out fires if they went over the logging boundary, but weren't paid any overtime for it. Some people took time off, but I worked as long as I could because I knew I had to go back to BCIT.

Then my mother and I started having arguments over staying with Jennifer, and I kept telling her I wanted to stay single, but no one would hear of it. I kept reminding her of when I almost flunked out at college and Isaac was still telling everyone I would have flunked out anyway even though I had kept telling him to stay home and study. Mother said I should leave her because she had a nervous breakdown at that age so there's no hope for her and she's too set in her ways. Uncle Joe told her he had to bring in a special counsellor just for her when she was taken away from home and put in St. Mary's residential school. I was rather happy Jennifer was in the psychiatric ward, so I could leave early enough for work to get a good night's sleep though.

One time when I was visiting Jennifer in the hospital, she was talking to Dr. Nichols, her psychiatrist, a trained professional close to retirement. In spite of everything that happened, she didn't want to believe her father had molested the girls, her sisters all tried to convince her that he did and one of them even had his baby, but she still didn't want to believe it. This was weighing heavily on her mind, and it looked like it was going to take Dr. Nichols a lot of work to get her over it. Then I took Jennifer out on a pass that night and told her, "You don't have to worry about it. If you sit back and watch, you'll see that when people misbehave, something will happen back to them. When I was working up north, that East Indian who got me fired for no reason got fired later on. The other worker who was always running around on his wife. Each time he did that, he got beat up, so he quit his job because he was getting beat up too many times. He didn't realize that each time he did something wrong, he suffered for it.

"People who hold grudges should learn to watch what happens when they think evil thoughts towards someone. I trained hard for years in unarmed combat to punch out my ex-landlady's son, then I noticed what would happen whenever I would think about it. A branch would slap me in the face, I would bump my head, slip and fall, or something like that would happen. It was almost like something was saying, '*Don't do it! They've suffered enough!*' If your dad didn't do anything, he has nothing to worry about. If he did something wrong, he has probably already suffered for it." Jennifer felt incredibly relieved after that. It took me about twenty minutes to get a major problem off her mind that would have taken Dr. Nichols lots of work.

I got laid off in Lillooet on the fifteenth on November, and I spent a week in Lillooet before coming home then went to Vancouver to find a place to stay so I wouldn't have to rush around when I got back to BCIT. After that I went to Laughing Raven to visit Isaac and visit

Jennifer in the hospital. It really snowed hard one night when I was visiting her, and on my way back to Laughing Raven, it was snowing and blowing so hard I could barely see the highway. Isaac was going back from Chilliwack and missed the turnoff, so he and one of my cousins had to walk one-fourth mile through the snow and wind. It was still snowing hard the next day, but Isaac was able to get his car pulled out of the snow and back home. After it stopped snowing, Isaac, Tracey, and I went to Abbotsford to do some Christmas shopping. Jennifer said she wanted radio earphones, so that's what I bought her. I also bought her a dress because I thought it was a nice one.

When Jennifer was in the hospital, she got her eyes tested and realized she needed glasses; but when she went out on a pass, Geraldine said she was just using them for a decoration. After Jennifer got out of the hospital and the swelling on her eyelids had gone down, she was a very nice-looking girl, but she was still mixed up and had many problems to get over. She was still on medication for depression and got really cranky and we broke up again and I couldn't understand why! I had tried really hard to get her interested in me, but I just couldn't do it. We got back together again just before Christmas, but I couldn't understand why she was treating me so badly; and when she opened her presents, she got mad at me and said I had poor tastes in clothes.

One night when we were visiting her parents in Sto:lo Eagle, Andrew was serving himself some soup and the pot slipped out of his hand and broke the bowl. I could see how scared Andrew was, but Henry didn't do anything because I was there. Now I finally realized Jennifer wasn't only criticized for making a mistake; she was also used to being beaten for making a mistake. My mother went with Jennifer and me to visit Isaac and Tracey one night, and Jennifer mentioned how ugly Geraldine would get when she was drinking and she was scared of her, so my mother said she would ask Dad if she could move to Rosedale with them. I knew Dad would say it was all right, and she moved to Rosedale to my parents' place.

Chapter 3

1981

I went back to BCIT for my last semester, and Jennifer asked if she could go to Vancouver with me. I was still lonely, so I was happy to have her go with me, but problems arose because I was in classes all day and she was home with nothing to do. Then when I got home, I had my studying to do and she wanted my attention; and when she stayed in Rosedale with my parents, it was rather isolated and there was nothing for her to do. I tried to get Jennifer back into upgrading when she got out of the hospital, but all the seats were taken and there was a long waiting list to get in, but Theresa Neel said she could get into a course called Skills for Occupational Survival (SOS) though. The course wouldn't start for another month; it didn't cost anything, but she wouldn't get paid for it either. Dad mentioned having gone to school with Henry in the Indian residential school in Mission, and when Jennifer was staying in Rosedale, he noticed she was afraid of her own shadow.

I had applied for funding again from DIA to go on the field trip to the interior of British Columbia, and the day after my funding was approved, I was told I couldn't go on the trip because I had already been on it. They had to balance their budget, so I had a week off but had to read a book and write a report on it, so I just took the money and made another truck payment. I had no conscience about taking money from DIA after seeing how much they held the Indians back from doing something for themselves.

Jennifer was losing interest in me, and her depression was starting to interfere with my studies; and the boxing club only worked out

Monday to Friday evenings now, so I couldn't work out as much as I wanted to because of her. The students also closed me off again and I let it bother me more than I knew I should have because I learned to be optimistic before I finished high school. Jennifer had been having an affair with her brother-in-law before I met her, and she said it was because she was lonely; she wanted someone to love her and he was there. She started talking about wanting to go out with him one more time because he looked after her when she was young, and I tried telling her that was his responsibility as her guardian and he didn't make her go to school, but she wouldn't listen. I was doing everything I could to try and keep her interested in me, but it wasn't doing any good and I also knew it wasn't worth trying to go out with anyone else because they would just treat me like poison ivy. So I kept telling Jennifer that when people misbehave, something will happen back to them, but she still wouldn't listen. I was in Rosedale one day and Jennifer was out somewhere, and my mother and I got into a big argument. I said, "I wish I was free!"

"You only have a few more months of school left!"

"I mean I wish I didn't have a girlfriend!"

"Well, why don't you just leave her!"

"Yeah, and all I'll hear from you is 'Find yourself a girlfriend! Find yourself a girlfriend!'"

"I never ever told you to find a girlfriend!"

"Bullshit! I had to go way up north so I wouldn't have to listen to you tell me to find a girlfriend!"

"Well, I didn't tell you to find that one!"

"But you called me a virgin when I told you I never had any luck with finding girlfriends!" Then she went storming off to work, and both of us were incredibly mad!

When I got my extra week off, I was still trying hard to get Jennifer interested in me; so whenever she asked me for something, I would get it for her. She said she never had a dresser for her clothes, so I bought her one; it didn't hold all her clothes and she didn't show very much appreciation. She went to Vancouver to visit and we left to visit Ben and Geraldine in Laughing Raven. We were going to spend the night there then go visit her parents in Sto:lo Eagle. We spent the night there, then the next day, Geraldine asked Jennifer to go to town with her. I said no, so she sent her son Riley in to get her. Jennifer got up and went running out before I could stop her, and I got really mad about that because I knew something was going to go wrong. I got tired of waiting for them to go back, so I went to Chilliwack to watch a soccer game then went to Rosedale. Jennifer was still taking medication for depression and phoned me at five in the morning because she wanted her medication. I got mad about it but brought it to her anyway, and when I got there, she was wearing a turtleneck and was rather cranky. I was tired, so I just went to sleep; and when I woke up, Jennifer said nothing happened. So I asked her four-year-old niece Amanda what happened, and she just said they made several trips back and forth to town.

Jennifer and I went back to Rosedale, and eventually we went into the bedroom, and she lowered her turtleneck. There were hickey marks all around her neck, and she told me what happened. I was totally devastated because I tried so hard to get her interested in me and just couldn't do it! Not only that, everyone kept telling me to find a girlfriend and no one would listen to what I had to say about it, so I was really hurt and cried hard! She tried to cheer me up, but that didn't do any good. Then the next day, she told me I could go out with someone else if I wanted; but I knew I couldn't get anyone interested in me no matter how hard I tried, but I was more concerned about her depression. I kept getting mad at Jennifer and being spiteful and told her I wanted to go out to a logging camp and not go out. She cried and asked me to stop picking on her, but I told her she shouldn't have done that in the first place. Then a couple of days later, Liz called and said she was in Sto:lo Eagle. I didn't want to go over there, but I didn't want her to hitchhike over there either, so we went to visit her. Whenever we went to Sto:lo Eagle, Jennifer didn't want me to sit too close to her in front of her family because she knew her father didn't want us together. This time she wanted to sit close to me, but I wanted her to keep her distance. Before she went out with Ben, she was getting interested in my father. He didn't appreciate it, and my mother was getting mad.

We stayed in Sto:lo Eagle for a couple of days then went back to Rosedale. Geraldine called and asked Jennifer to go back to Laughing Raven to help her with the housework because she was having trouble with her hand after she slashed her wrist, but I wouldn't let her go. I told her Ben has two good arms and two good legs, so there's no reason he can't help her. I also didn't want her going out with him again and never went back to Laughing Raven again for a long time, not even to visit Isaac and Tracey. Jennifer's depression was interfering with my studies, and I didn't know what to do about it; it seemed like I wasn't going to make it through BCIT because I wasn't doing as good as I could be doing, and was getting worried. I told a fellow at the boxing club about Jennifer's depression, and he said he had a girlfriend like that once and she committed suicide.

I got Jennifer into the SOS classes, but one day during the spring break when we were in Rosedale, Henry stopped by with a fellow named Mark to take Jennifer to an Indian spiritual doctor named Isadore Tom, in Lummi Indian reserve, near Bellingham, Washington. I didn't know anything about such things but just thought, *If it works, it works.* I hoped Isadore could cure Jennifer or at least help her feel better, but when she got back, he didn't seem to help her very much. Jennifer told me, "He was crying when he was working on me. He said I should have come to see him much earlier. He saw an eagle in a tree. Someone has a hold on me. Dad said it's Geraldine. Isadore said I'm going to have to get stronger or become an Indian Dancer. He also told me I can't be left alone."

I didn't know very much about the Indian Dancers and the smokehouse used by coastal Indians, but it seemed to be like other religions; people turn to it because they have problems, and most people who go into the smokehouse to become Indian Dancers have problems. Some went in because they have alcohol or drug problems or were put in there by their parents for disciplinary reasons. The initiation rituals are rather harsh and can change people, sometimes for the better, sometimes for the worse, and sometimes not at all. I was worried about my studies and Jennifer's depression and didn't know what to do, but luckily, Henry stopped by and took her back to Sto:lo Eagle; and neither of our fathers wanted us together.

I was happy to be free again so I could concentrate on my studies now, but the frustrations of studying and my family always trying to run my life were getting to me. I knew I couldn't get anyone interested in me no matter how hard I tried, so I preferred not to think about it; then finally, out of anger and rebellion to get my mother off my back, I started thinking about calling James. For most of my life, I never was much for sweets and didn't use very much sugar; then all of a sudden, I started craving sugar and couldn't get enough of it. The only other times I craved sugar was when I quit drinking altogether, but I still didn't crave it the way I did now, so I phoned my aunt in

North Vancouver and asked her what I should do. She described my symptoms and told me I better go to the doctor right away, and I realized my instincts were telling me not to think about James, but I also got the flu at the same time and ended up missing two days of classes. It was raining hard and blowing at the same time the class was scaling logs on the Fraser River delta, so I was lucky I got sick then.

Darlene Rivers, a young lady boarding with my aunt in North Vancouver, asked me to help her move her things from Port Alberni. She had just recently met her brother, Wayne Rivers, who grew up on the same Indian reserve in Merritt as Wesley Pierre did. Wayne said he knew Wesley before he committed suicide, and when Wesley quit drinking, he changed so much he didn't even recognize him.

I didn't try very hard to get a job because I wanted to move to Terrace, way up Northern British Columbia, away from my family! I also thought about working with Indian bands to help them manage their resources, and one of the instructors said he had some contracts with some Indian bands and could use someone with my experience, so I kept checking up with him to see if the job would come through or not. I also called DIA about work, but they didn't even ask my name, where they could contact me, or say where I could apply. I continued studying, attending classes, and trying to find time to work out with the boxers. I had a little over a month of classes left then started to feel sick half the time then felt sick more and more, so I finally went to the doctor. This time I would have a note from the doctor so if I couldn't carry on, I would have a chance to write my final exams. I thought I had the Bangkok flu again, so I went to the doctor right away. I kept checking with the instructor about the job and it looked like a sure thing the job would come, but just before I went to the doctor, he said the job didn't come through and there weren't many other jobs to apply for. I wasn't too disappointed though because there were usually lots of jobs to apply for in the fall.

Right after I got a note from the doctor saying I couldn't go on, I phoned BCIT to tell them my situation. They said I didn't have to attend classes anymore and I would be given an average of my marks to date, so as soon as I heard that, I made a beeline for the bars to celebrate. I didn't know if I made it through or not, and the next thing I knew, the bartender was waking me up, telling me to take a walk around the block. I was still feeling sick and tired all the time, so I couldn't go back to work right away. Then I went to the doctor again, and both of us thought it was just a flu, so I was given some antibiotics.

After Jennifer moved home with her parents, she kept attending her SOS classes because her father made arrangements for her to catch a ride from Sto:lo Eagle to Chilliwack. Henry told her we should break up because I was too old and serious, we weren't going to have any friends, we would get tired of each other's company, and she would be pushing me around in a wheelchair because I was so much older than her. Jennifer was going to wear to class one day a dress she got from Geraldine. The dress could have been worn to church or to a formal banquet, but Henry made her change into her blue jeans and said, "You don't want to go there looking like a slut!" One time when someone called, Henry answered the phone and said, "Jennifer doesn't want to see you anymore because your shoulders are too fat, your ears hang down, and your teeth stick out!" Jennifer asked who that was, but Henry wouldn't tell her, and it wasn't me.

During the years I was attending college and BCIT, I sometimes visited fortune-tellers who did tarot-card readings as a source of entertainment when I was bored. An elderly man was doing tarot-card readings in a restaurant in Vancouver, and I thought he was good; so I went to see him, but he moved to Harrison Hot Springs, not far from Rosedale. I noticed an ad in the Agassiz newspaper about a tarot-card reader in Harrison Hot Springs, so I booked an appointment and went there expecting to see the old man but met a lady in her forties who was confined to a wheelchair. Her name was Wylma. Wylma said she tried to commit suicide four times before she was fifteen years old and was in a wheelchair for four years but it felt more like four days. She was as happy as could be and I thought maybe she could help Jennifer feel better about herself.

I still felt weak and tired all the time and thought it was a flu because I had the same symptoms. I didn't know whether I passed or not; then one day, I got a letter from BCIT stamped Graduated. I was so happy I finally made it, and thought, *I've got it made now! I'm twenty-five, have my career, and still young enough to do more logging if I choose to!* One fellow from the reserve who said I was going to spend the rest of my life in school said he wished he were twenty-five had a career and his whole life ahead of him. I thought my hard times in life were finally over and thought I knew much about life. I was too sick to celebrate but glad I finally made it! I called Sto:lo Eagle one night to talk to Jennifer, but Henry told his son to say she wasn't home, but I knew he was lying because Henry never let his kids go anywhere.

While Jennifer was living in Sto:lo Eagle, she was training for canoe racing. She missed me and often thought about hiding notes by the trees at the Agassiz Secondary School. While she was training, she tore a ligament in her knee, so her father had to take her to the hospital in Chilliwack for an operation. It was a very painful accident, so she stayed in the hospital for a few days; and while she was there, she asked me to visit her secretly. I went to visit her, and she was happy to see me and told me how her father was treating her. He was ready to hit her for forgetting to put the soy sauce on the table, got mad and said, "Oh, you're useless! You're nothing but a burden! You'll never amount to anything!

"Then he said I was a mistake and I make his life miserable!"

I had been trying to help Jennifer get a job, and she was offered a job in Harrison Hot Springs as a kitchen helper; but he wouldn't let her go because it was too far, so I told her and later told her father I could have driven her. When she got out of the hospital, she moved home with her parents and needed crutches to walk around, so I sometimes went over to visit her and take her to physiotherapy. Jennifer sometimes stayed in Rosedale with me, and one time she grabbed my UIC cards and was going to tear them in half, acting like a really bratty child, and wouldn't listen when I tried to tell her how important they were. She went home again, and the next time I saw her, she said her dad was ready to beat them all up because he couldn't find his UIC cards. Then she realized how important they were.

Before Jennifer got out of the hospital, people in Laughing Raven noticed I never went around anymore and only went to visit Isaac and Tracey once after leaving BCIT. She knew why I stopped coming around and tried to get me to go back again but I was sick all the time and didn't know what was wrong with me. Jennifer wanted to go to the Seabird Island canoe races, but I didn't want to go because I knew Ben would be there and I didn't like the way she was more interested in him than in me. After much talking, I finally agreed to go for a little while, but going there built up so much tension that most people avoided me. I spoke to Ben a little bit and told him I never went around because I had too much studying to do and was sick again. Jennifer saw how uptight I felt, so she never said a word about going back the next day.

Jennifer moved home with her parents again, and I met her at the Cultus Lake canoe races a week later. She was really cranky because she was more interested in someone else even though I was always trying to be nice to her. I stayed home on the second day of the races, and late that afternoon, Ryan dropped her off in Rosedale. She was very shaken up and said her dad made a pass at her as she was getting into the truck. She got mad at him and said she would catch a ride home with Ryan, but instead of going home, she got Ryan to drop her off in Rosedale. Jennifer said, "Dad was getting mad and yelling at me again. He said, I'm not hurt. I'm just psychosomatic! Ryan came in and saw him yelling at me, but he didn't do anything."

Ryan couldn't really do anything against his father anyway. Jennifer wasn't only scared for herself; she was also scared for me because she thought her father would beat me up. She said Mark started going over to visit and they seemed to be getting interested in each other, but nothing came of it. Mark was older than I, but Henry didn't seem to mind them getting interested in each other. The next weekend, she said, "Daddy's going to the canoe races in Lummi Island, so we can go to Sto:lo Eagle and get my clothes when they're gone. There's a trapdoor you can crawl through under the house." After we got her clothes, she continued to live with me in Rosedale and I continued taking her to physiotherapy, but she was really cranky because of her nervous condition. She wanted to go to Laughing Raven, but I wouldn't go, not even when I went back to BCIT to look for work.

She continued going for physiotherapy, and her physiotherapist was happy with her progress, but I still felt weak and sick all the time. The International Woodworkers of America, IWA, on the coast went on strike that summer; so there weren't any jobs available in forestry or logging. Liz called Jennifer from Spences Bridge to offer her a job at Smitty's Pancake House, where she was working; but I didn't know if she could take it because of her knee, and Liz said the job would be there if she chose to take it though. Jennifer's leg healed to the point where she almost didn't need crutches anymore; and Tony's first wife, Sue, and my nephew Eric went down to visit. My mother asked me to drive them back to Merritt, and Jimmy would meet us there on the bus; then I would take Jimmy to Kamloops to meet his mother. I was excited about going back to Merritt and drove around to all the sawmills and tried to get a job there, but none of them were doing any hiring. The recession, which started last year, was getting worse;

and although I couldn't find a job and didn't see many people, I knew I still enjoyed the trip. One night, Jennifer got really ugly and went running down the road on her crutches; and even though I didn't do anything, she sometimes got like that, so I let her go down the street a ways before I went and picked her up. She cooled off by then, but I couldn't understand why she did that.

We picked Jimmy up at the bus depot the next day then went to Kamloops, parked at one of the hotels, and walked around town for a while. Later on we drove around town, and Jimmy said his mother parked just opposite us at the hotel parking lot when we first got there, so I wondered why he never said anything to her there. Jimmy phoned his mother eventually and we went over to visit her, left Jimmy with his mother then got a motel room for the night. When we headed back to the coast Jennifer got really cranky and almost got us into an accident by telling me how to drive.

We went back through the Fraser Canyon and stopped off at Spences Bridge to visit Liz, and she suggested Jennifer get a job there because they needed workers. I thought Jennifer would need her physiotherapy more, but Liz said she could transfer it to Ashcroft. The manager thought it was a good idea and gave Jennifer a uniform, so I took her back to Chilliwack the next day to get it dry-cleaned and buy her some shoes for work; but when we got to Chilliwack, Jennifer somehow lost the pants to the uniform. We went to one-hour martinizing and were lucky to get it done the same day. Then it took her all day to decide which shoes to buy, and I tried to get her to move faster and make up her mind, but she wouldn't listen. And after it was over, my mother got mad at her because of her indecisiveness.

We went back to Spences Bridge the next day, and Jennifer started working as a waitress. I just lived there, and Liz and I tried to encourage her as much as we could. There was an ex-trucker, Bill, who lost his driver's license due to impaired driving working at the fruit stand next door to the restaurant. Although he had a drinking problem, he claimed to be near genius; everything came too easy for him, so he created his own excitement. I could see Jennifer was interested in him, but I was still determined to try and look after her. Living in Spences Bridge was fun even though it's rather isolated; the people there were fun, and we had parties almost every night after the restaurant closed. We became friends with Bill, and he seemed very knowledgeable. And he thought I was lazy because I wasn't working, but I told him I was sick and the doctor couldn't find what was wrong with me. On Jennifer's days off, I took her back to the coast to visit Wylma because I thought she could make Jennifer feel better about herself and give her some idea of what was coming in the future. Wylma told Jennifer not to feel bad about being a waitress because it's an honourable profession, and she answered most of the questions that were on her mind.

Then the people at Smitty's suggested I go to work there too, so I bought some extra clothes for becoming a waiter. It was fun working there, and I caught on to the job right away. And a friend from Merritt stopped there for lunch on his way back, and I told him, "Just for the fun of it, I smile at the ladies to get more tips."

A white fellow sitting with him said, "Put a banana down your pants!"

I enjoyed working there and the parties after work, but I had an ulcer and didn't know it. I just knew something seemed to be wrong with my stomach. We continued working but were growing apart because she was losing interest in me. Sometimes Jennifer would show up at the hour she was scheduled to start work, have something to eat, then she would start working. She didn't even know she was supposed to start work on time until I told her. Last year when I was taking her to the doctor, Geraldine said to me, "You mean when you're supposed to be somewhere, you're used to being there right on time?"

Jennifer got more interested in Bill and we separated again; he told her I was doing too much for her and she didn't need it. I asked the manager, Dennis, two times about her work; and he said she was doing fine, but finally he told me she was slow. Sometimes at night even though I was tired, I had to sit up and talk to her because her nervous condition was slowing her down. I had to encourage her to keep trying because she was really depressed and talked of suicide. Most of the time I was able to calm her down, but one time my stomach acted up and I got annoyed, so she ran off and everyone went looking for her. When Dennis realized her condition, he suggested she join the army and said when he was in the Canadian Armed Forces, there was a fellow just like her. The training snapped him out of it, and you never would have known it was the same person.

I still felt sick all the time and finally tried going on a special diet to avoid fried foods. Bill had his twelve-year-old daughter stay with him for a week and said Jennifer had the mind of a twelve-year-old because he saw the two of them play together all day and get along well. I knew it could be true, but I didn't want to believe it because it made me feel even more depressed. Then when it was time for Bill to take his daughter back to his ex-wife, I offered to drive them to Kamloops. The cook caught a ride with us to Cache Creek and said he was going to visit his brother but caught a bus in the opposite direction he said he was going and never went back, so no one knew where he disappeared to.

Bill left a few days later, so it wasn't as much fun working there anymore. Jennifer and I separated, but I still continued to do what I could to try and make her feel better about herself and thought, *If I don't look after her no one will be willing to do it!* Bill wasn't really interested in Jennifer, but we still didn't get back together. Since it wasn't as much fun working there and my stomach couldn't take it, I had to quit but thought I better wait for Jennifer to go back so she doesn't commit suicide. I went to the doctor again, and he told me to get my stomach X-rayed and finally found out I had an ulcer, so I had to go on a special diet. I also bought a 30-30 rifle because I thought I would finally have time to go hunting and do some of the things I always wanted to do.

My parents gave David a car, and for several years, I had been doing many things for him and Jimmy. When I bought my truck, he drove around in it like it was his own; but after all the things I did for him, he said I couldn't touch his car, and claimed to be a good mechanic. But if he did any repair work on my truck, I would have to pay him for it. If I treated someone that way, I would have been surprised if they didn't get violent. I couldn't though because I was too weak because of my ulcer and knew something would happen back to him for doing it. Sure enough, about three weeks later, some woman hit him and totalled his car; so he was without a vehicle for a while and tried to use mine again. After all the things I did for him, I couldn't believe he was treating me like that!

Jennifer stayed and worked at Smitty's with Liz for about three weeks after I left. I went on a fishing trip with my dad and a few of his friends where we had to fly in by helicopter, and when I got back, Sue was visiting again and said Jennifer called for me. I didn't know where she was, but I was home the second time she called, so I secretly met her in Abbotsford. We both knew no one wanted us together, so we lived in my truck for about two weeks. It was fairly warm yet, so it wasn't too bad, but I had an ulcer and hemorrhoids at the same time. Jennifer and Liz were staying in a sleeping room in a house in Abbotsford and weren't allowed overnight visitors.

I only went home to pick up my UIC cards so no one would know Jennifer and I were back together. Geraldine didn't want us together, so we also had to stay away from Laughing Raven. I couldn't understand why her criticism bothered her so much, but I was glad I waited for her to go back because of her depression. Dennis had talked Jennifer into joining the armed forces because he believed it would help her come out of her nervous condition, so she applied for an interview. Her rent at her room was almost due, she didn't have a job or very much money, and her depression was getting worse. Then when my mother found out we were back together, she got really mad and went for a long drive somewhere in the middle of the night. I asked her friend what was wrong, and she said my mother was mad because Jennifer and I were back together. I also heard Geraldine did the same thing when she found out we were back together.

I suggested Jennifer try and get a job as a dishwasher, and I had a feeling she should try at a restaurant in the middle of town. Sure enough, she got a job there working Monday to Friday, eight thirty to four thirty. She also needed a place to stay, but all we could afford was a sleeping room. The landlady wanted two months' rent in advance, Jennifer had to supply her own meals, and all her groceries had to be kept in her room so the children wouldn't have to ask which groceries they were allowed to eat. I paid her rent and bought her some groceries, but it ruined my plans for doing anything I wanted to do.

Looking after Jennifer was getting expensive and hard on me because of my ulcer, so I decided to take a chance and work on a farm. We were paid cash, so I thought I could get away with, it but this would be the last time I would ever do anything dishonest. Jennifer's nerves made it difficult for her to work, and I didn't know what to do except be there to look after her. I took her out for supper one night and she got really ugly, and one customer thought I looked like I was ready to start wailing on her. I enjoyed working on the farm, but I should have known better than to get greedy. Sure enough, when I started up my truck then left it out of gear and went back into the house, my truck rolled and hit a post, causing my insurance rates to go up.

Jennifer didn't work at the restaurant very long because of her nervous condition and thought she was going to join the army. While she was working, her sister Brenda and her husband, Alvin, went over from Lethbridge, Alberta, to visit. Brenda was an outstandingly beautiful woman, but I was used to getting turned down, so I usually gave up without trying and didn't get excited. Not only that, most ladies like that wouldn't go out with me if they never had anyone, so I was going more and more into a shell. Jennifer talked about quitting her job, and I tried to talk her into staying with it. I said, "Often when you stick out a difficult situation, something happens to make it worthwhile."

"Like what?"

"I don't know. It's something that makes life interesting."

Jennifer quit her job anyway because her interview to join the army was coming up, but before the interview, she phoned the recruiting center and found out even if she got accepted, she would be lucky if she could join in six months. I continued trying to help her as much as I could though; then when she got her paycheck and saw how much it was, she wished she hadn't quit, but it was too late. The Canada Employment and Immigration Centre (CEIC) at BCIT phoned two times to offer me a job. One job was with the British Columbia Forest Service in Port McNeill, and the other job was juvenile spacing out at the Queen Charlotte Islands, but I had to turn both jobs down because I was still too weak from my ulcer and had to help Jennifer out. Juvenile spacing is when there's too many trees on an area, some of them are thinned out so the remaining trees will grow better and faster.

I continued working on the farm and gave Jennifer enough money to go to Vancouver and back when she went for her interview and told her I would be there for her when she got back. In college, an East Indian friend, Rick, said when he was undecided about something, he would flip a coin; so I started doing the same thing. Heads was always yes and tails was always no, and I was surprised at how accurate it was, so Jennifer started doing the same thing. Jennifer and Liz both went to Vancouver to get interviewed, and both of them failed to meet the entrance requirements, but Jennifer was told she could try again in two years. Jennifer was totally devastated by that and felt like nobody wanted her, nobody needed her, and that she was a total waste and a burden to everyone. She knew I would be there to look after her, yet she still flipped a coin to see if she should commit suicide. Luckily it said no.

When she got back to Abbotsford, she called me and said she was turned down because of her knee; but eventually she opened up and told the truth: her test results didn't meet their qualifications. She was really depressed, so we went to a drive-in movie that night. It was a horror movie she wanted to watch to take her mind off her depression. I had always been laughed at and put down for being young, so I tried to act older and serious most of the time; therefore, I preferred watching true stories. I started getting bored and stamped my foot, not realizing what it would do to Jennifer, so she started crying and getting depressed. I said I was sorry, but it was too late. She got really depressed and started crying "Mommy! Mommy! I don't want to go! I don't want to go!" like she was being taken away from home. Then she started crying "Stop it! Stop it! Stop it!" like she was being beaten by her father. She wasn't crying very loudly, so we stayed until the movie was over and she calmed down; then we went to Laughing Raven and she asked me to call her father, but no one would get up and answer the phone. Now all I could do was stay beside her as much as possible.

I was still working on the farm, and my ulcer was slowly getting better, but I didn't know what to do for Jennifer! I considered taking her to see Isadore Tom, but one of my aunts suggested I take her to see an old man in Sardis; so I called the old man, but he refused to do anything. I tried to explain the situation to him, but he still said no. One night we were checking mail in the post office, and she went down on the floor curled in a ball on her hands and knees and started crying "Mommy! Mommy! I don't want to go! I don't want to go!" Then she started crying "Stop it! Stop it!"

I thought, *Oh my god! Is there nothing I can do for her!* If I tried to slap her out of it, she wouldn't have felt it, and that would only make the situation worse. All I could do was be there when she came out of it, but two times when she told me she could feel it coming, I was able to talk her out of it. One time, I told her, "Your parents are going to get old and they'll need someone to look after them! If you get stronger and get a career of your own, you'll be able to look after them!" Another time when she felt the depression coming, I said, "Jennifer! Your family is a really hardworking family! Try and get stronger and live up to your name!" Those were the only two times I was able to calm her down; the other times all I could do was be there when she came out of it.

I continued working on the farm and spending as much time with Jennifer as possible. We had a week's work left when I had a feeling, saying, "Go to Vancouver and apply for a logging job," and usually took the bus to Vancouver since I didn't like driving or looking for a parking spot in the city. I was in a bad mood from my ulcer and the stress of looking after Jennifer, so I went for a beer before going to the logger's agency. The fellow applying in front of me looked and dressed like a seasoned logger and was turned down flat, but I applied anyway and was told the same thing. Since I was in a bad mood, I stood there wishing I had stayed for one more beer when Nick, the hiring agent, looked at me and said to the clerk, "Get his name! Quick!" My older brothers had made a name for themselves as good loggers, so he was anxious to hire me.

Two days later, Nick called me and said I had a job in Security Bay, I had to be in Vancouver in two hours to get my plane ticket or I would lose the job, and I would be flying out the next day. I took Jennifer with me to get the ticket, but I wouldn't be flying out for two days. Then we went back to Laughing Raven, then to Rosedale to get packed, but I didn't know what I was going to do about Jennifer's depression. The next day, we were looking around in a shopping mall in Chilliwack and ran into Henry and her uncle Junior, so we talked to them a bit then went back to my truck, and Jennifer told me to go get her father. I went back and told him Jennifer wanted to see him, and as we were walking to my truck, I told him I wanted to help her; but he just waved his hand as if to say, "You're doing absolutely nothing for her!"

When we got back to my truck, Jennifer was just screaming! Henry tried to talk to her, telling her to only think happy thoughts, but she couldn't hear him. She just sat there and kept on screaming! Then he said, "Her nerves must be shot!"

"Probably from beating her up!" I said. I knew he hated me and thought, *If you want to beat the shit out of me, go ahead!*

Henry just stood there and thought, *I try to like him, but he's so outspoken!* He knew Jennifer was a nervous wreck and actually believed it was Geraldine who was doing it to her and he had nothing to do with it; actually, it was both of them, but he couldn't see it.

Henry left, and Jennifer and I drove back to her sleeping room in Abbotsford. She calmed down quite a bit, but when we got there, she ran off when I was in the house. The landlady's children were bratty like normal children were, but they stopped soon enough and told me which direction she ran off in; and she was still crying hysterically when I picked her up, but she calmed down eventually. I knew the worst of her depression was over, but it would still take an awful lot to get her stronger, if ever, but at least now I knew she would be safe when I went out to camp. We spent the night at Isaac's place in Laughing Raven, and he drove me to the bus depot the next day. I caught the bus to Vancouver then to the airport, the plane dropped us off in Port Hardy, and we had to wait an hour before flying out to camp when I realized I still had some of Jennifer's money and forgot to give it back to her. I went out to camp leaving her in town with no job, no income, and very little money. I felt bad about leaving, but there was nothing I could do; she would have to ask Geraldine for help.

Going out to camp was very relaxing for me, almost like a holiday, and it cured my ulcer. However, I soon realized I couldn't make a career of logging because it was seasonal work, the opportunities for promotion weren't very good, and I didn't want to spend the rest of my life in logging camps. Veronica just had a baby and wanted Jennifer to spend a few days with her to help look after the baby and her house while I was in camp. After that, Jennifer applied for work in every restaurant in Abbotsford and Clearbrook but couldn't find work anywhere. She got a job removing tape from refrigerators where apartments were being built, but only worked one day because of her knee. She had some groceries that I bought her, but there wasn't very much there.

While I was logging, I noticed what may seem like trivial errors were very costly to the logging company. I was used to everyone trying to convince me I was wrong or getting mad at me when I used my own judgment, so I didn't say anything. I wished I had sent the following note, but I didn't:

To whom it may concern,

Re: Costly breakdowns that can be avoided

I would like you to have a look at your fixed costs then consider the following:

Item	Cost per Hour
Hook Tender	$14.14
Yarding Engineer	13.57
Chaser	12.10
Rigging Slinger	12.88
3 Chokerman	$11.97 × 3 = 35.91
Loader Operator	14.44
Total Wages	$103.34
WCB = 4% × 103.34	4.13
Holiday Pay = 4% × $103.34	4.13
Union Benefits = 15% × 103.34	15.50
Camp Costs = (8 × 132)/8 hrs	32.00
Vehicle Costs = $40/8 hrs	5.00
Travel Time = $103.34/8hrs	12.92
Yarder (includes sales tax, insurance, transport, etc.)	150.00
Loader (includes sales tax, insurance, transport, etc.)	150.00
Subtotal	$515.17
Book Keeping and Administration = 12% × $515.17	61.89
Total hourly fixed costs	$577.66

Although these costs are rough estimates and don't include a logging truck and driver sitting in the landing, waiting for a load, it should bring to your attention the money lost due to seemingly trivial errors.

Each time the lines break, an hour is spent getting a hold of the camp handyman, and another hour is spent waiting for him to bring splicing equipment from one tower to another. That costs close to $1,200 a breakdown. This loss can be avoided simply by having splicing equipment at each tower, which would pay for itself in one breakdown.

> Also, on one setting, the ground was flat as a golf course and the faller didn't buck the roots off a windfall at the back end. The crew was yarding a long way out; the hook tender had to buck the roots off, so consequently, it took several hours to yard one log. How much money was lost there?

I often got the flu for three weeks every fall (and I couldn't understand why I was like that) then drank coffee at night, so I wasn't getting a good night's sleep, which was affecting my work. One day, the rigging slinger was walking toward the lines and it looked perfectly safe, but luckily, he wasn't walking very fast when a voice said to me, "*Tell him to stop!*" I didn't say anything, and the line shot up incredibly fast right at his neck level; if he had been any closer, it would have sliced his head off. I didn't tell him but knew I had to follow my hunches all the time from now on and also had to quit drinking coffee at night! There was a French Canadian on the crew who was very close to my age and said he was very bitter about how the French were treated in Quebec. I said, "All we hear about out here is how the government seems to favor the East."

While I was in camp, Jennifer didn't have very much money or groceries and nearly starved for two weeks but got some lucky breaks when Isaac dropped by and took her out to a Laundromat and for dinner. One afternoon, the hostess at a restaurant gave her a sandwich; and another time, Geraldine gave her some groceries. Jennifer also sent me a letter begging me strongly to go back to her, so I just couldn't say no. She also said she was getting stronger than ever. On one occasion, Jennifer went for a job interview and her feet got sore and started to bleed, so she called Geraldine to go give her a ride back to her place. Geraldine got mad, but she did it anyway. Jennifer applied for welfare when Isaac took her out to dinner, but was turned down and was told they couldn't give it to Indians off the reserve, so Jennifer had no choice but to move back to Laughing Raven with Geraldine and her family.

I didn't work very much that year because I had to finish my education then developed an ulcer and couldn't work, but thought there would be job openings in the fall for forestry graduates. I also thought I could go back to work as a waiter or dishwasher if I had to. By the middle of November, I was starting to feel burnt out and wished for a rest, but the camp was going to stay open for four more weeks then shut down for five weeks. I was going to stay in camp for ten weeks; then the yarding engineer said we were shutting down that day. I went back to Rosedale and didn't phone Jennifer right away, but I guess I should have. I told Dad I had no regrets about what happened even though it took me eight years of studying just to get a two-year diploma, and he said I was being religious. I tried to tell him I was only being optimistic, but he wouldn't listen; then my mother started trying to run my life again, so I thought I better phone Jennifer right away. She was visiting her parents in Sto:lo Eagle and was happy to hear from me, so I went to visit her, but when I saw her, I knew she still had a severe problem with depression.

We went back to Rosedale, and I said we should go to BCIT and see if there are any jobs available. She wanted to have a few drinks the day before, so that's what we did, but when we got to BCIT, there were only two jobs on the board and people had already applied for them. After all those years of studying, there weren't any jobs available and I couldn't work long enough to draw UIC. On our way back, Jennifer wanted to look around in one of the shopping malls for something to do; but when an old man was turning off, I misjudged how fast he was turning and stepped on the brake. But my foot slipped and I rear-ended the corner of his truck. He pulled into the service station, and I pulled in behind him and offered to call the police; but he said, "No, don't call the police." We got each other's phone number and license number, and I reported it to the Insurance Corporation of British Columbia (ICBC) right away. I phoned him later that night to see if he was all right, but he was sleeping and his wife wouldn't wake him.

I thought I was still eligible for three weeks of UIC from before I went to camp, so I sent in my cards, but they were sent back to me because I sent them in too late. I inquired why and was told I should have let them know in writing that my cards would be sent in late, so I realized I was still suffering from what I did wrong and thought, *I'll never do that again! I'll try to be totally honest from now on!*

Henry went on his annual moose-hunting trip up north that fall, never got anything, and ended up with an $800 repair bill on his truck. I brought my truck to a service station in Agassiz for a tune-up, and when I thought it was ready, I asked David to drive me over to pick it up; but he just said, "Get someone else to do it!" After all the things I did for him, he was treating me like that! When I was in camp, not only did he use my firearms, which I told him not to do, he also shot off my shells. After I got a ride over to Agassiz, the mechanic said a cylinder head was gone on my truck and it would be expensive to repair; it had to be fixed, so I told him to do it. When I got home and asked my dad if he could help me out, he just said, "No! I've helped you out enough already! I have to draw the line somewhere!"

I tried to tell him it wasn't my fault I couldn't work, but he refused to listen. Christmas was also coming, and I didn't know what to do! Luckily, I paid my truck off until the end of April; so I was safe there and told myself, "I'll never do anything dishonest again!" While we were shopping in Sears, Jennifer showed me a housecoat she wanted for Christmas, but it cost $35 and I couldn't afford it. Her depression was dragging me down; and when Uncle Joe was visiting, he wondered, "Why does he stay with her when she's just making life miserable for him! I had to bring in a special counsellor just for her!"

I was talking to Tracey one night and Dad happened to be listening, I told her I wanted to try and help Jennifer get a career so she can do something with her life. I had tried to encourage Jennifer to do things previously, but he did what he could to stop me. Jennifer and I looked around Chilliwack and Hope for work but couldn't find anything, many places weren't even taking applications, so my mother suggested I try a cafe at the Seabird Island Indian Reserve because it's a twenty-four-hour truck stop. She took us there and I got a part-time job as a waiter and could learn short-order cooking on my own time.

On my way to work, I started to feel nauseous, and Dad thought I shouldn't help Jennifer out at my own expense, not if she's dragging me down that much. My mother said, "I noticed that as soon as you get a job, you get sick. It happens every time." When I worked for the Forest Service in Lower Post, I was told I lacked confidence, and didn't know this nauseous feeling was because I was unsure of myself. My family always treated me like they were always right and I was always wrong and got mad at me for everything I did. Nothing was ever enough.

Jennifer and I continued to do our Christmas shopping and bought many things on sale because we didn't have very much money. We were both in Sears when I noticed the housecoat she wanted was on sale for $20. I could afford it now but had to hide so she wouldn't see it, so the clerk told me to go to the cashier at the back of the store. When I went to pay for the coat, I saw Theresa Neel sitting by the door, so I paid for the coat then asked if Jennifer could get back into upgrading.

"No!" she said. "Our classes are filled right up and we have a long waiting list to get in."

"I just graduated from BCIT in forestry and I'm looking for a job."

Just then an accountant, a Filipino fellow, went along and we stood around talking for a few minutes, then I left. After I walked off, he said to Theresa, "I need someone to fill this position."

"That guy right there! I think he just graduated from BCIT in forestry."

As Jennifer and I were walking away, I could sense someone following me, and it was the accountant. He told me to go to Lytton, look up Nathan Spinks, and apply for a job; so we went to Lytton the next day and tried to find Nathan Spinks. We drove around Lytton and asked where he lived; and when we found his place, he wasn't home, but his wife took a copy of my résumé. Several days later, Nathan called and asked me to go to Lytton for an interview. I went to the interview, and when I met him, the first thing I thought was he and Jennifer's father looked like twins. As I was going to BCIT, I thought I would like to work with the Indians and help them manage their resources. I got the job with the tribal council in Lytton and was really happy and surprised. By trying to help Jennifer, I ended up in the right place at the right time to find work when jobs were extremely hard to get. I also thought, *Of all the towns I worked in, I never thought I would end up living in Lytton.*

Jennifer was still such a nervous wreck it looked like she was beyond recovery; sometimes in her sleep she would cry "Mommy, Mommy! I don't want to go! I don't want to go!" followed by "Stop it! Stop it!" like she was being taken away from home and being beaten by her father. Ryan and Desiree stopped over one day to take Jennifer to see Isadore Tom. Ryan was taking Desiree to see him because of her nerves and wanted Jennifer to see him too. The session with him helped her for a little while but didn't last very long, and I still didn't know what to do except keep trying to help her.

I was still into Christianity at that time because I was taught to be a Christian as a child, so I kept praying that Jennifer could do something with her life; and as I prayed, a voice seemed to say, "Come on now! You know she can do it!" I ignored the voice and kept praying for her every night, but the more I prayed, the stronger the voice got. The voice got stronger, and I knew it would soon force me to stop praying because I knew she could do something with her life. Then I stopped attending church regularly because if I tried to say anything, they would say I was being religious merely because I went to church regularly on Sunday. As I was growing up, I always heard my dad firmly say, "When someone tells me something can't be done, I try harder to prove it can be done!" I bought Jennifer the book *You Can If You Think You Can* by Norman Vincent Peale to try and motivate her to try and do something for herself, but when my dad saw the book, he said I was being religious. I tried to tell him it's the same thing he does, but he refused to listen; if he said I was being religious, then I was being religious and that's all there was to it!

Chapter 4

1982

Jennifer and I moved to Lytton on New Year's Day, were a little late leaving, and got there about seven o'clock at night because she took her time getting ready. The clerks at the Totem Motel didn't know if we were going or not, so our apartment was given to someone else. The owners were on holiday and the clerks didn't know if the other unit was saved for us or would be rented out by the month, so we just got a room for the night. The unit we stayed in was small, dingy, drab green, and had no heat and hot water. Jennifer walked in, walked out, and started crying; so I stopped her and told her, "Don't worry about it! Maybe it's better that it happened that way! Something better could come up!"

"Like what?"

"I don't know! Let's stay the night and see what happens."

We went to bed that night, and I got up early so we could pack up and have coffee before going to work. It was cold out; and when I got outside, the truck had a flat tire, so I told Jennifer what happened and to stay inside. But she still went out while I fixed the tire. We got the tire changed and got packed just in time to get to work; and I met the band manager, Fred Henry, so I told him about the apartment and the flat tire, and he just laughed. When I went to the office, the receptionist, Nathan's daughter, Alice, bought us coffee; and I told Nathan what happened, and he just told me I could take some time off to find a place to stay and get settled.

Lytton is a very small town, and it can be hard to find a place to stay. But we got an apartment in another motel, but when we moved in, it had no heat and no cold water. Living in Lytton was good except there wasn't very much to do after work and Jennifer was too nervous to meet people. It was cold and the snow was one and a half feet deep, so I couldn't do any fieldwork. Before we left Chilliwack, Jennifer saw a coat at Sears that she wanted, but we couldn't afford it and we got our social assistance check just before we left; but when she went to buy the coat, it was gone. During my second week in Lytton, I got sent to Kamloops for a meeting and Jennifer went with me. Instead of going to the meeting, she shopped around in one of the malls and found a coat similar to the one she wanted; but it was a nicer one and on sale for half price, so she was slowly learning to be optimistic.

Ryan and Desiree were planning on getting married that year; and her sister, Gladys, was the secretary where I was working. Gladys said, "I met Jennifer in the summer of 1980 when she stayed in Lytton for a week. I wondered why Jennifer kept to herself the way she did. I thought she was stuck-up. Then I remembered I was withdrawn like that when I was young."

"How did you come out of it?"

"I just made up my mind I was going to come out of it, and if I fell on my face in the process, that was too bad." Gladys seemed to come out of it quite well, and I wished Jennifer could do the same thing.

Since there was too much snow to do any fieldwork, I had to read material available in the office and ordered forest cover maps of the Indian reserves I would be working on and noticed the reserves were incredibly small, even on a 1:20,000 scale map. What little the Indians were cut off with, some of it was taken back by the BC Hydro lines, and on the maps it looked like BC Hydro made sure their lines went through the Indian reserves. I also came across a booklet on the Indians in Boston Bar. The Indians were given land and started growing orchards; when the Indians could have become self-supporting, the land was taken away from them, but it didn't say what year it happened.

I inquired about trying to get Jennifer into upgrading and didn't think it would be possible in a small town like Lytton; but fortunately, Jack Ned, the outreach worker, had applied to Cariboo College, now Thompson Rivers University in Kamloops to sponsor adult basic education (ABE) in Lytton. His application was approved, so I immediately asked if Jennifer could get in. At first it looked like she wouldn't get accepted because Lytton Band members got first priority, but she got one of the last seats available. Jennifer would get $50 every two weeks for upgrading, but it would take six weeks for her money to start coming in, and I told her she could spend it on herself because I wanted her to feel she was trying to do something for herself and getting something for her efforts.

We went to Chilliwack one weekend and went to a movie. I was always taught to save money and often tried to teach her to do the same thing, and when we got to the theater I said, "I thought you were going to pay your own way in."

"I thought you were going to pay for it."

"Well, you have money of your own, don't you?"

"I'm trying to *saa-ve* it though!"

Jennifer always managed to outwit me or find a way to get her own way. She got a T4 slip from when she was working at Smitty's in Spences Bridge and paid a little over $29 in income tax and was going to throw it away because she didn't know it was worth anything. I tried to tell her to keep it, and her father said she could give it to him if she didn't want it; and after I did her income tax return, she got back just over $169. She asked me to buy her the book *Sybil*, about a girl with sixteen different personalities, so I bought it for her; and once she started reading it, she hardly put it down until she finished it. It was one of the few books she ever read because Henry always wanted the kids to pay attention to him. After two months we got a notice from the motel that our rent would go up to $40 a day at the end of June, so I thought we better find another place to stay soon. One of the students at Jennifer's upgrading classes said she and her husband were going to move out of the Totem Motel and she would inquire about us renting their unit, so we asked the owners, and they said we could rent it out. I sometimes had to go to Vancouver or Kamloops for meetings, so I was happy to get a place to stay in town. I didn't like leaving Jennifer home by herself, but at least she could still attend her upgrading classes.

Liz went back to work in Spences Bridge, and we sometimes went to visit her, and she went to Sto:lo Eagle with us one weekend to visit their parents. We went to visit Wylma for a tarot-card reading because I thought she could help Jennifer out, but she helped me more. Wylma told me, "You're not having enough fun in life and burning yourself out. You're too obsessed with the future and financial security. Read the book *Think and Grow Rich* by Napoleon Hill and apply what it says."

My dad always wanted scientific proof for everything and always tried to force his opinion on me. My attitude was "If something works, it works! Why wait for scientists to prove something works?" So I followed her advice.

When Jennifer was going to upgrading, I sometimes almost had to force her to go and she wanted to give up, but I wouldn't let her. She said she didn't know what she wanted, but I told her I went through the same thing and eventually found what I wanted. I told her I bought her lots of nice clothes; she got free room and board and $50 every two weeks to spend on herself. She wanted to give up anyway because she was too nervous to carry on, so we went to the doctor to see what we could do about it. We explained the problems of her depression to him and he made arrangements for her to see Dr. Nichols, a psychiatrist in Abbotsford who also treated her when she had a nervous breakdown in 1980, so I was glad she was seeing her.

When Jennifer went to see Dr. Nichols, she left at eight thirty in the morning and didn't get back until ten o'clock at night and I thought, *That's a long day with nothing to do.* At that time, we could go out for a hamburger, french fries, and something to drink for $9; and arcade games first became popular in British Columbia. It cost $21 return for bus fare, so I gave her that and $9 for meals and entertainment because I wanted her to feel secure and looked after when she went away; then I always went out to meet her when the bus went in. There was very little for us to do in Lytton, and Jennifer was too nervous to meet people or do anything, so we usually went back to the coast or to Kamloops on weekends. I couldn't get out and meet people either because she always wanted me to stay beside her.

Henry was a strong believer in spiritual doctors like Isadore Tom and said he had a really bad temper before Isadore calmed him down, and I thought to myself, *If he treats his kids like that now, what was he like before Isadore Tom calmed him down? He makes his kids put his socks and shoes on for him and he beats them if they make a mistake! He actually believed he had a happy home, and it was his stepdaughter, Geraldine, who broke it up. Sometimes when I look at him, he looks like he's going insane!* I didn't think it was a very good idea to tell Jennifer that though, but even Liz, she said, "I think Dad is going insane! He won't let Andrew and little Henry grow up!"

One time when we were visiting him, Henry was snacking as he was watching TV and Andrew and Henry Jr. were waiting on him hand and foot. The next morning, I heard him yelling at them, "How come the kitchen's a mess?" Henry knew one of the main reasons I was staying with Jennifer was to protect her from him and Geraldine because both of them were always putting her down and she couldn't take it. I was outspoken with Henry at times, but I only spoke the truth. I believed in being totally honest, whether the truth hurt or not.

Looking after Jennifer was getting increasingly difficult and I could feel my parents pressuring me to leave her, so I started drinking more coffee at work and more liquor after work to cope with the stress. Previously I used to only drink once a month and two cups of coffee a day, but now I was drinking more to relieve tensions since I didn't have anything else, and one time, Jennifer and I were arguing so much we didn't eat for three days. We went to visit Liz, and the lady there took her time serving us because she knew us and thought we were just visiting. I started getting concerned about the stress of looking after her and how it could be affecting me; so I asked the alcohol-and-drug counsellor, Gary Abbot, for help. But he just said, "No. She's just doing that for attention." I couldn't understand why he did that but didn't let it bother me.

Jennifer was slowly getting stronger, so I was able to teach her some of the things I learned over the years. Previously when I tried to encourage her to do things, she usually just automatically said "I can't," but I taught her how to control anger because you can tell when people are thinking evil thoughts. One time I bent over and bumped my head as I was getting up, and she said, "You're mad at me because you don't think I've been doing enough housework." My instincts told me not to feel that way, but I still didn't follow my hunches as often as I should have. One time when we were visiting Liz, she said, "Jennifer must be psychic because she knows what happens when you think evil thoughts."

"I taught her how to do that."

"My boyfriend burnt himself with a match on time and I said, 'Oh! You must have been thinking evil thoughts!' He just looked at me as if to say, 'What does she know?'"

Henry told me about some of the things that happened in his life and that he was a heavy drinker until his daughters were taken away from home, and when he stopped drinking, he noticed his kids weren't as scared of him. He also talked about being beaten as a child and how he worked and travelled around Kamloops; that's how Jennifer got a half sister, Rhonda, and half brother, Timothy, in Kamloops. If what Henry said was true, then I guess he would be naturally bad tempered and hold grudges; so I told him, "If you sit back and watch, you'll see that when people misbehave, something will happen back to them. If you want to hold grudges, watch what happens when you think evil thoughts towards that person. It's almost like something is saying 'Don't do it! They've suffered enough!'" Then I told him I learned to do that when I was training to take a round out of my ex-landlady's son; that's why I didn't do anything after all the training I did. I also told him a number of stories about what happened to me when I was thinking evil thoughts.

One weekend when we went to Rosedale, my mother had bandages on two of her fingers; so I said, "Don't think evil thoughts, Mother!" but she just laughed because she thought I was joking. Then she started telling me about her job, so I said, "That's what you were thinking about when you cut yourself!" She gave me a really surprised look, and I realized not everyone can see these things, but I could never get anything through to my parents because they never ever listened to anything I had to say.

Gladys came from a rather large family, and Ryan and Desiree were planning on getting married in Lytton; and although they went to Lytton quite often, I wondered why they never visited us. One night, Jennifer and I went to an auction that was raising money for a treatment center for people with alcohol and drug problems. I saw Johnny Jackson there, a logger who used to work with my father in Merritt. I asked him where his brother-in-law Barney was; Barney and I had gone to school together for several years in Merritt. Johnny said, "He's dead. No one knows if it was murder or suicide. I can't see him doing it to himself though. He was found dead on a fish boat and a .22-caliber rifle was found on the boat."

I thought, *Another Indian I went to school with is dead!*

I sometimes had to go to Vancouver to attend meetings about forestry or fisheries, and one fisheries meeting resembled a courtroom with a top executive from the Department of Fisheries and Oceans sat up like a judge and a number of people took the stand and said whatever they had to say. One commercial fisherman old enough to be my father stood up on the stand and said, "I wish my son was an Indian because of all the grants available to them!" Then at lunchtime, he and a few other fellows were standing around talking and laughing about how some Indians are too lazy to do anything for themselves. I knew there was a high rate of unemployment and alcoholism on Indian reserves and I sometimes heard people talking about how DIA would try to hold back Indians who tried to do something for themselves. Now I was seeing it more and more for myself, and people would often look at us as if we're too lazy to do anything for ourselves.

Looking after Jennifer was hard, but I knew that if I didn't do it, no one else was going to do it. I kept her in school and sent her to see Dr. Nichols regularly; and her teacher, Chuck McCann, got a note from her, saying Jennifer had a problem with depression. Sending Jennifer to see Dr. Nichols also gave me a welcome break from looking after her, but whenever we went to Rosedale, my parents would pressure me to leave her and I couldn't get a word in edgewise to explain anything to them. I tried to tell Dad that Henry is a child beater and molester. I'm protecting her but also trying to push her to do something for herself, but he refused to listen. I knew Henry hated me and was often looking at me like he was waiting for an excuse to take a round out of me even though he knew I was only protecting her and trying to give her a chance to do something with her life, so I outright told him she wasn't moving home to do her upgrading.

One time, Henry was bragging about what a man he was and said, "My daughters tried to put me in jail and they couldn't do it!"

I didn't say anything but thought, *That's only because Ryan lied in court to save his mother.*

"I used to go to the Log House Café after work then go to the bars."

"Nothing for the kids?" I asked. "When your kids went picking berries, you shouldn't have taken every cent they made!"

"Yes. They have to get used to paying room and board."

"So you can drink!"

Ryan and Desiree got married along with her oldest brother, Don, and Darlene in a hall just across the street from where we lived. Jennifer and I were arguing that day, so I ended up getting quite drunk that night and into a drunken brawl because of it; a lady tried to go out with me and her boyfriend got jealous. Ryan said it was more of a drunken pushing match than a drunken brawl, so I was glad Henry refused to attend the wedding because he would have helped me out, but nothing would have happened if Jennifer and I weren't arguing that day.

Another time I was at a meeting in Vancouver, Jennifer heard on the radio that Vancouver was going to fall into the ocean because of the Jupiter effect, so she tried to get me to go back to Lytton that night. Liz and a friend, Franklin Brown, were over visiting her and they seriously talked about taking my truck to Lethbridge to Brenda and Alvin's. They phoned, and Alvin said, "Go ahead, come over. Stay as long as you want." They were sipping a bottle of wine and thought the end of the world was coming.

When I got home, I met Jennifer at the hotel for lunch and she said, "I phoned about twenty hotels, looking for you last night."

I got mad and she went running out the door toward home; so I got her, apologized, and told her, "You shouldn't have told me when I was tired! You should have waited until I had a chance to rest!"

"I want to go see Isadore Tom again!"

When our phone bill came in, it wasn't too high. And I used to get mad at her but was surprised at how often she made the right decision, so although I don't like to be told what to do, I learned to go along with her decisions. But it was like the whole world was against her. Her father and sister were always putting her down, my family was against me for trying to help her, and I usually had to stay right beside her or people would start harassing her. Sometimes when Jennifer would get really depressed, she would start crying, "Nobody wants me! Nobody needs me!" and I would have to talk her out of it. I told her she's important and she can do something with her life and we're going to prove it. Sometimes she would tell me she didn't think she would live past twenty-five because she saw it a couple of times in her dreams.

One weekend, we were visiting my parents and I got into an argument with my mother and was ready to throw my coffee on her, then Dad got mad at me because it's hot and thought I should leave Jennifer. I tried to make her realize how lucky she is to have someone supportive of her who's trying to help her, but her family knew I was getting her jobs and putting her back in school yet they acted like it was nothing. Geraldine even wondered why I spent so many years studying to get a career, because Ben didn't; she didn't realize that if the plant went bankrupt, he would have nothing. I never got any support from anyone, so I tried to get Liz to tell Jennifer how lucky she was; but Liz just said, "I've always been able to look after myself."

Sometimes people would look at me and wonder, "How can people be so miserable?" At a tire shop, an attendant thought I looked really cranky, but he soon realized I wasn't; and if I said it was because of my parents, I would have been stereotyped as a "spoiled kid." Sometimes I hated being young because I was blamed for everything. I went home from work one day to get some lineament for my wrist and ankle because my joints were aching, and when I got home, Jennifer there doing her schoolwork and seemed to be working quite well when she was alone. She laughed and said she was too scared to go to school so she went home and did her work. I continued keeping her in upgrading and sending her to see Dr. Nichols. She started getting happy the way I looked after her like a father, so she bought me a cup that said "I Luv My Dad!"

I went to a forestry meeting in Vancouver and met an Indian forester named Dave Walkem. He didn't look Indian, but he was an Indian from Spences Bridge. On that trip, I bought Jennifer a pair of jade earrings shaped like totem poles, and everyone in her upgrading class liked them. Then a month later, I went home from work and she was scared. It took her a long time to tell me she dropped one of her jade earrings down the sink, so I told her it was all right because it was just an accident.

Dave called me one day at work and suggested I go to a Junior Forest Wardens meeting in Surrey. I heard about them on TV but didn't know they actually existed in British Columbia. The meeting was on a weekend and across the Surrey Place Mall, so I was able to take Jennifer with me and gave her some money and told her to buy me some clothes. She enjoyed shopping because it was a way of taking her mind off her problems; then at supper time, a lady there said she knew Jennifer from when she was a nurse in the psychiatric ward in 1980. She said Jennifer looked a lot happier now. After dinner, we watched films and slides, had a talk session, then went back to our room. The shirts she bought were nice, but one of them was too small and it was too late to bring it back so I said, "Don't worry about it. Maybe it's better that it happened that way." Instead of listening to me, she got really mad and started a big argument until eventually I said, "Why did you run around on me when I tried so hard to get you interested in me?"

"I thought you were trying to buy me."

"Well, if you didn't love me, why didn't you just leave?"

She got really hurt by that, started crying, and said, "But I do love you!" Then she grabbed my coat and threw it behind her. The coat hit the lamp. It fell over and broke. Then she went running and slouched against the wall, crying, and said, "I'm gonna go throw myself off a bridge!"

"No, Jennifer, don't do that!" I said and put her on the bed and held her down for a while.

I thought she calmed down, but she didn't; about fifteen minutes later, she jumped up crying and went running and slouched against the wall again and said, "I'm gonna throw myself off a bridge!" I had to take her back to bed and hold her down again so she wouldn't do anything to herself, but the next day, she calmed down and was feeling better. She was used to being beaten and criticized for making a mistake, and that's what she expected to happen, but I still had to pay for the lamp.

I helped get a Junior Forest Wardens club organized in Lytton but couldn't get involved with it because looking after Jennifer was more than I could handle. When we went to Sto:lo Eagle one weekend, Henry mentioned Rhonda having children live at their place for some time then they were given up for adoption; then he said, "Brenda done the same damn thing!"

"Wasn't that your kid?" I said. Then I thought, *It's a good thing they didn't have that kind of upbringing.*

Henry just glared at me; but that night, he said rather proudly, "I don't care if they hate me or not!" So I told Henry how David was trying to treat me after all the things I did for him. Most people would have gotten violent in a situation like that, but I was too weak with an ulcer at the time. Then I told him all the bad luck David was having for what he did.

Jennifer went to Vancouver for a field trip with her upgrading class, but I couldn't go because I had to work and was scared for her because she could get lost if her nerves acted up again. She almost got lost, and the rest of the class got mad at her then when her upgrading classes ended and she didn't have to write any exams but she passed her grade 10 level but just said, "It was probably just given to me!" But I thought at least it's one step in the right direction.

There wasn't very much to keep me busy at my job, and I'm not the entrepreneurial type because I'm too used to being told what to do most of the time, so a job like this was better for people who enjoy promoting projects. Lytton Band got a tree-planting contract to promote employment, and I gave some advice, but not enough. One day I decided to go to work with them and met them at the Forest Service office. I picked up some of the tree planters, and the foreman left before me and someone said he went to the post office, so I went there and picked up some more planters. The planter who took the crew to work had his vehicle impounded the day before; and Buck Thomas, the foreman didn't know about it until I got out to the woods. The first thing Buck asked me was if I had any ribbon, and luckily, I had a feeling telling me to bring some and brought four boxes of ribbon. We worked long hours and didn't get home until seven o'clock, so Jennifer got angry and scared and looked all over town for me. Liz was there and said, "Don't you trust him?" but she still searched all over town for me.

Wood tick season was on, and one night on my way home, I felt something in my hair. So I pulled it out, and it was a wood tick. When I got home, I found another one on me and flicked it on to the table. Jennifer almost panicked and sprayed it with Raid for ten to fifteen seconds. The next day when I got home, she said she stayed in bed all day because she thought the wood ticks might get her. The tree-planting contract wasn't going very good because many of the planters were first-time planters and it looked like the contract was going to be a failure, but we kept trying; and luckily, the Forest Service ran out of trees and cancelled the rest of the contract.

There was an outstandingly beautiful Indian girl there, Lisa Dunstan, who became friends with Jennifer and I and sometimes went over to visit. Lisa started getting interested in me, and most people would get excited if someone that nice looking got interested in them; but I just thought, "What's she doing that for? She's going to change her mind." I was also used to ladies like that not being interested in me, so I usually gave up without trying.

Liz got fired from her job in Spences Bridge, so she asked me to help her move; and Jennifer had to see Dr. Nichols that day, so I told her we'll be in the bar when she gets back because I thought Liz would be depressed after getting fired, so I would buy her a few beers. Lisa was working at a restaurant between Lytton and Spences Bridge, and Liz asked me to stop there and pick up her sleeping bag. Sure enough, Lisa changed her mind about me, but it didn't really bother me; I just couldn't understand why I never had any luck with finding girlfriends.

Jennifer joined us for a couple of beers then said, "I'm hungry!"

Liz stayed with us for a little while, went back to Laughing Raven then went back to stay with us then started going out with an irresponsible alcoholic named Frank. Usually when Ryan and Desiree went to Lytton they never came over to visit us, but when Liz was going out with Frank, he started going over to visit and I couldn't understand why he was like that.

One time when Jennifer went back from seeing Dr. Nichols, she said, "It made me feel good to press the button to cross the street and traffic would stop just for me!" Then she said, "I'm hungry!" Another time she went in and she said she bought a shirt from a secondhand store for Liz then said, "I'm hungry!" Other times she went in and just said, "I'm hungry!" One time she had to see a regular doctor in Clearbrook, and said it costs $3.95 to take a taxi, so I gave her $5 extra; but instead of taking a taxi, she walked and went home hungry. I noticed every time she came in from seeing Dr. Nichols, she was hungry, so I wondered what she was doing because I gave her enough money for two meals. Then I thought maybe she just missed supper, so I didn't bother asking; and in May, Dr. Nichols finally made her realize how lucky she was to have me there to look after her.

Lytton Band got more tree-planting contracts, and I was able to get Isaac a job and let him stay at my place. The band was also relying on my services because that's what I was there for. The contracts didn't start out very good because of delays by the Forest Service, and it was frustrating for the crew, so some of them quit; but I managed to talk two of them into sticking it out and seeing what happens even though I didn't say something good could happen by doing so. Sure enough, a contractor backed out of a contract and we were asked to do it. The Forest Service asked us how we wanted to get paid, so we said hourly. So for seven days, the crew was making good money working only eight hours a day. Buck Thomas and I were getting paid by our regular job, which was tax free because of our Indian status and by the Forest Service at the same time, so we were paid twice for the same job. When that contract was over, we went back to our original contract and ended up working nineteen days straight.

One day when we were working, a small cat was brought in on the back of a dump truck to clear the snow off the road so we could get in. On his way out, he took a turn too sharp and tipped the truck on its side on a blind corner. When we came across it, the first thing I said was "We should put a ribbon up so no one will come around the corner and hit it!" Then I said, "No, I don't think so."

Luckily, Isaac heard me and said, "No, Baxter, go do it!" I almost shied away from doing it.

I couldn't make many friends or meet many people because Jennifer was too nervous to meet people, and even when we did our laundry, we had to go out of town. Closing myself off didn't bother me too much because I was used to being closed off and not drinking very much had cut out much of my social life. Sometimes when I went home from work, Jennifer would be slouched down in the closet, crying with her face against the wall. One time she had my shotgun against herself, wishing to shoot herself, but it wasn't loaded! I wondered why Gary Abbot wouldn't help me counsel her and said she was just doing that for attention; other times she would start crying and say, "I can't go on, Baxter! It hurts too much!" and I would have to talk to her and try and calm her down.

People in Lytton noticed Jennifer really hung on to me and we were hardly ever apart. One night she was playing around and wrapped the telephone cord around my neck and started pulling it, and I felt really happy because if she kept pulling it, I wouldn't have to put up with my family anymore. I saved my days off from tree planting until there was a statutory holiday and took a whole week off, and we went to Laughing Raven. We told Geraldine we were hesitant about going to Rosedale because my parents keep pressuring me, so she said we could stay at their place if we wanted to, so we stayed there for a few days then went to Sto:lo Eagle. Jennifer's uncle Vern and one of his sons were visiting, and Vern's son mentioned how Mark was strung out on drugs and about to give himself up to the Indian Dancers, so I wondered why Henry didn't mind Jennifer getting interested in someone older than I and a drug addict.

Jennifer worked for several days as a chambermaid at the Lytton Hotel but couldn't take it. I tried to get her to keep working because I thought she might feel better about herself, but her nerves were too bad. Since Jennifer was nervous of meeting people and held me back, I thought exposing her to nice people would help her come out of it. We went to Merritt one weekend and decided to go to a movie; we had some time to spare, so I thought we could go visit my cousin Meredith and her husband, Kirby. They're a nice, fun-loving couple and I thought she would enjoy meeting them. We visited them for about fifteen minutes, then Jennifer said, "Come on, let's go!" I hesitated, then she said, "Baxter, you said we were going to a movie!" and suddenly she got up and went running outside to the truck.

I said, "I guess she's too nervous to meet people!" then left.

I went out to the truck and we drove off, parked behind the bowling alley, where there wasn't any houses or people; and she got out and walked away. I ran after her and stopped her and she was crying and said, "You know I'm nervous of meeting people! Why did you do that to me?"

I didn't answer her and she kept on crying; then suddenly she peed in her pants. I realized that wasn't the solution and I would have to keep closing myself off until she got stronger. Now we had to go to the store and buy her a new pair of pants. Jennifer was also getting scared of insects and her fear was getting worse and worse. I took her to the woods one day to check some reserve boundaries, and she got panicky because of the bees and grabbed on to me. I told her she might cause an accident and we might fall on the rocks, but she still hung on to me. One weekend, Liz went with us to Merritt and a grasshopper jumped in the truck when we were at a stoplight in town. Jennifer panicked and started screaming, so I had to get it out as fast as possible so she wouldn't cause a commotion. Jennifer told Dr. Nichols about it, but she couldn't figure out why she was like that.

Sometimes when I went back to Merritt, former classmates, neighbours, and friends would see me and wonder what I was up to. I usually said hi to my friends but didn't say very much or talk to them and they were surprised, but I had to close myself off because Jennifer was too nervous to meet people. We went to a store one day and the clerk thought I was a cranky customer and would give him a hard time, but I slightly smiled and lifted one eye to assure him I wouldn't give him a hard time.

We didn't stay home very much on weekends, and on one trip to Rosedale, Dad finally realized he had always been putting me down just for being young. I was twenty-six, hardly ever went to parties, dances, or even to the bars; but he still refused to listen to anything I had to say and still got mad at me whenever I tried to use my own initiative. One weekend during the summer, Jennifer, Liz, and I went to Rosedale and everyone there was cranky toward us. We were going to go riding horses, but it was too hot, so we went swimming in Harrison Lake; and by the time we got there, all three of us were in a bad mood. One day, Jennifer and I brought our truck to a service station in Agassiz for servicing and I saw my dad's truck at the doctor's office, so we caught a ride to his house with him. He was logging in Boston Bar and had cut his arm when his power saw kicked back, so he needed a number of stitches because of the accident.

Jennifer thought about going to Lethbridge and spending two weeks with Brenda and Alvin, which would have given me a break from looking after her, but I don't think she would have enjoyed herself very much. I also would have had to worry about her being taken advantage of because I couldn't get her to go on the pill, but luckily, Brenda and Alvin were going on a two-week camping trip and they weren't sure when they were going. After living in Lytton for six to eight months, Jennifer said she didn't use a towel when she had a bath because when she lived at home, the towels had to be saved for their father. I didn't know about it then tried telling her to try and develop her psychic abilities, but she automatically said "I can't," so I told her to just follow her inner feelings when they go then sit back and watch what happens; eventually she'll be able to tune her mind to it. I got interested in developing my psychic abilities and read several books on the subject. I had more books to read but didn't get a chance to read them because sometimes when Jennifer's nerves would act up, she would start destroying my things.

Toward the end of the summer, Liz, Frank, Jennifer, and I went out to the woods to pick soapberries. When the berries are canned, they're beaten with an egg beater until they form foam we call Indian ice cream. We picked and canned the berries for Henry and he didn't even thank us. Often when we would visit him, I could see him grinding his teeth with anger; and I knew he hated me, but I had to protect Jennifer from him. One weekend when we were walking around a mall in Chilliwack, Jennifer told me she had $80. I asked her where she got that from and she just laughed and said, "All that money you were giving me to see Dr. Nichols. I wasn't spending it." Then she spent it all on her parents like she was taught to do.

Nathan Spinks, the administrator, told me I was going to be transferred to an Employment Bridging Assistance Program (EBAP) and my position would be filled by someone else. This was the first year these programs were started. People on UIC would work and get their income topped to a higher level. I felt happy about it because it was more my line of work; working with the Tribal Council was better suited for someone who could promote projects, but I was always told I was wrong, and it was hard for me to break out of it. I gathered a list of people eligible for the job and Isaac was one of them, so I told him he could stay at my place while he was working there and the job was supposed to start in July but didn't start until September.

After the job started, Isaac talked about getting a place of his own. There was much tension between me and David and my family wanted to put it to an end and treated me like I was the guilty party. I wouldn't put up with how he was treating me from anyone, not even my own brother! Isaac mentioned Dad helping him out, but he admitted he would do it for my brothers but not for me because of Jennifer. Dad looked at my bank statement one month and I didn't like him doing that, so I had them sent to Sto:lo Eagle. He was mad at me for the way things were going but wouldn't listen to anything I had to say.

I enjoyed hunting but never had time for it since high school, so now I had time and asked Jennifer to go with me; she didn't want to go because she was scared of bears and insects, but I took her along anyway. We got a little ways out of town and ran into Ryan and two of Desiree's brothers. They were on their way back from hunting and we had to turn back because my truck needed a new fuel filter. I knew some of the symptoms to watch for and what to fix from working in Lillooet and from driving my dad's car. Dad knew much about mechanics and what to fix when something went wrong; luckily, I knew some of the theory of auto mechanics because my truck only needed a $5 part that could be replaced in two minutes. Frank said another fellow spent $300 on repairs for his truck and all it needed was a new fuel filter.

When I got back to Lytton, the service station didn't have any fuel filters for Datsuns, so I would have to go all the way to Chilliwack to get one. I had to park my truck for three weeks before I could get a ride with Isaac back to Rosedale, and when I got to Rosedale, David wouldn't even let me borrow his car, which was given to him by our parents, just to go to Chilliwack to get a fuel filter. In spite of all the things I did for him, he was treating me like that and my family treated me like I was the guilty party doing something wrong. The tension between us built up so much I outright disowned him; I didn't want him to go visit me and didn't even want to know him. If I treated

David that way, I'm sure my family would still lay all the blame on me; even my dad would have said something.

After I got my truck operating again, we went to Sto:lo Eagle to visit Jennifer's family. Jennifer promised to get Henry some blueberries, and he said, "I thought you were going to get me some blueberries!"

"My truck wasn't running for three weeks because it needed a new fuel filter." He was still angry at me but didn't say anything.

Not long after the job started, Jennifer went back to upgrading to work on her grades 11 and 12. The job started out pretty good and I enjoyed working with the people in Lytton. I continued to let Jennifer keep her $50 every two weeks and $9 spending money each time she went to see Dr. Nichols. It still looked like she was beyond recovery, but I didn't hear her crying in her sleep anymore, but she was still scared of insects. Isaac saw how she was acting and said, "The way I see it is Jennifer wants everyone to cater to her just because she has bad nerves." Isaac was sometimes as dense as our father: the answers could be laid out right in front of them and they would just ignore it because they knew everything.

One weekend when we went to Sto:lo Eagle, we gathered up all the laundry at their place and took it and their mother to Chilliwack to the Laundromat. It cost us almost $50 to do that much laundry, and when we got back, Henry was glaring at me for taking his wife out of the house. I told him what we did; then he stopped glaring at me. He didn't even thank me, but the boys did.

Most EBAP programs seemed like a farce, and I read in the paper that people had to wait five or six weeks for their first paycheck, one of my cousins in Merritt said they were given a loan but had to pay it back with interest, even if they paid it back right away. The work was going well, but the crew was working without pay and getting discouraged; and when their pay came in, they were even more discouraged because they were making very little above their regular UIC. Some of them were only making $3 or $5 a day and their pay was very irregular in coming in, so I couldn't ask them to work hard.

Liz eventually broke up with Frank because he was just an irresponsible drunk and started going out with Jeremy, Gladys and Desiree's brother. Liz moved up to Jeremy's house in an area of Lytton known as Snake Flat, two and a half miles out of town, and we often went up to visit them because Jennifer; and Liz were always close to each other. Liz got a job at the hotel, and one day, she and Jennifer were walking toward the hall and Liz was on her way to work. Jennifer saw a very large caterpillar and got scared and went running home and didn't go to classes that day. One weekend, Ryan and Desiree took us up to Snake Flat to visit Liz and Jeremy, and we all sat around drinking and stayed the night. The next day as we were sitting around eating breakfast and drinking coffee, Jennifer got really cranky; she started crying and slapping me, so Liz got mad and told her I wasn't doing anything. Jennifer went out crying and started walking back to town, so I followed her. It was only her family there and she still got extremely nervous. When we got back home, she went into the bedroom and went to sleep; she was even nervous around her own family.

I really felt down and a friend, Casey, stopped in; so I asked him to go to the store and get some pop so we could have a few drinks. I was glad he went over, so I could talk about something rather than think about what I was going through. Sometimes after Jennifer went to sleep, I would sit up and have a few drinks and think about how peaceful life was when I was single. Casey said he knew Wesley Pierre at the residential school in Lytton and stopped over a couple more times for a drink on Sundays because the bars weren't open, and since he didn't want to appear like a free loader, he dropped off a couple of packages of deer meat on top of my truck. I was playing cards with Jeremy and his youngest brother, Gordon, one night and said, "I found two packages of deer meat on my truck one day! I thought I had a secret admirer!" Then I put my hand on my crotch and said, "Before I found out who put it there, it sure felt like I was coming down with romantic fever!"

Henry and his nephew, Freddie, stopped off in Lytton on their way back from their hunting trip. They went to Quesnel and never saw a thing. I thought it was too warm to go hunting that early in the year.

Jennifer went to upgrading for two months in town; then the class got moved to a house at Two Mile, just down the road from Snake Flat, because the hall was being renovated. Liz quit her job and went to upgrading with Jennifer, and I was happy because she always made Jennifer feel better. One day while checking the mail, I saw an ad for an industrial first aid course and thought I should take it because if someone on my crew got hurt, it would help if someone on the crew knew first aid. I applied to take the course and got accepted, but it didn't start until October. It was hard to work full-time with a crew, take the course, and look after Jennifer at the same time because it was like doing three full-time jobs at once with no breaks. One day after work, Jennifer and I were looking around in the hardware store and she asked me to buy her something and I said no.

She immediately said, "But I studied hard today, so you should buy it for me!" so I had to give in to her. Whenever she wanted something, she always managed to find a way to get her own way.

Jennifer was never taught to be responsible for anything but her father's demands and always wanted my attention. She didn't care if I made it to my first aid classes on time or not, but I thought to myself, *If a man gets hurt, it's better to know what to do whether I pass the exam or not.* She went into a fit of anger and depression one night as we were standing outside on the street, and she started hitting me, so I slapped her solidly on the shoulder and she snapped out of it and didn't even remember me doing it.

One day, Isaac and I had the day off, so we left early and told Jennifer we were going to work, but we went hunting instead. All we got was a couple of grouse, but I still enjoyed myself. Isaac knew his UIC was going to run out soon, so I let him and one of my crew use my truck to go hunting. They were willing to shoot any kind of big game because of the hard economic times, and many people were unemployed because of the recession. Jeremy had an accident while riding a horse and sometimes had to go to a doctor in Kamloops, so Jennifer always promised I would take them then go home and tell me about it; but luckily, Buck Thomas always let me have a day off to take them to Kamloops.

Since many people were having a hard time financially, our family decided to draw names for Christmas presents and I kept hoping I would get Isaac's name because I knew he needed a new pair of work boots badly and couldn't afford them. I got his name, so that's what I bought him. Later on, he talked to my mother about the job and thought he would have been better off not to take it; even though I paid all the room and board and he got a six-week extension on his UIC, he still almost went deeper in debt.

Christmas was coming, and Jennifer and I went to Chilliwack to do our Christmas shopping. I was making good money because my work was on Indian reserve, so I didn't have to pay any income tax. I gave Jennifer some money and told her to do some shopping. She wanted me to stay with her, but I wanted some time alone; and when

I got back, she was upset and crying because people were harassing her. I didn't get a chance to see who it was, so I couldn't do anything about it. People were always harassing her when I wasn't around, so I had to stay right beside her all the time whether I wanted to or not. We were going to spend Christmas Eve in Sto:lo Eagle then go to Rosedale and Laughing Raven the next day, and when we got to Sto:lo Eagle, I heard Henry in the back room, yelling at someone. He was drunk and yelling, "You know how to fight! I can fight better!"

I wondered whom he was yelling at, but he calmed down when he saw Jennifer and me there, and Andrew went out like nothing happened. I wondered, *Was he yelling at Andrew? Henry is big and strong and an ex-boxer. Andrew is smaller than me! Why does he treat his kids like that?*

After opening presents and having turkey dinner, the next day I told Jennifer we should get going because we agreed to go to Rosedale and Laughing Raven. I kept telling her we should get going, but she wouldn't move. We ended up arguing in the back room and she started slapping me and everyone could hear it. I don't believe in hitting a woman, and Andrew went back to protect his sister even though he is much smaller than I, but he realized I wouldn't do that to her.

My horoscope said this was going to be a very good Christmas for me, but I thought it was quite the opposite. Jennifer's cousin Cyril went over, and as I was talking to him, I told him I was thinking of going back logging. Henry heard us and knew the reason Jennifer and I were together was to protect her from him; then he got up and started walking toward his gun rack and I wondered, *What's he doing that for? Usually when he wants something, he gets his kids to get it for him.* He picked up one of his .22 rifles and gave it to me for a Christmas present, and I couldn't believe it! I tried not to take it, but he insisted. He knew I enjoyed hunting, but it was hard to find time for it, so it turned out to be a very good Christmas after all. After Boxing Day I went back to Lytton to write my first aid exam, and Jennifer stayed in Laughing Raven. I passed the written exam but failed the practical exam because I was just too burnt out from working and looking after Jennifer at the same time.

Chapter 5

1983

Jennifer and I went to Laughing Raven for a New Year's Eve party, and that night, Henry set off a dynamite blast right behind his house. He claimed to have been a blaster at one time, got drunk, set off some dynamite; and someone said he set it off then calmly walked away, taking his time. The blast cracked or broke some windows on his house, Ryan's house, and his brother Sunny Boy's house. Henry didn't associate with or talk to his sister-in-law and she got really mad and said white carpenters from Chilliwack were going to go over and fix their windows and he was going to have to pay for it. Henry wouldn't be allowed to fix them himself.

Jennifer and I went back to Lytton for my job and her upgrading classes and Isaac went back because he had two more weeks of work left, and just before he left, the brick building that was St. George's Indian Residential School burned down. Lytton Indian band had wanted to do something with the building previously through Cariboo College, but it had to be approved through DIA first, but DIA was so slow to respond that Cariboo College gave up waiting. Finally when DIA gave their approval and Cariboo College was ready to begin renovating the building, it burned down and was a very expensive building to lose.

Isaac worked until his UIC ran out, Jennifer continued to go to upgrading, and Jeremy sometimes had to go to Kamloops to see a specialist because of his accident. Jennifer always promised to take them then went home and told me about it, but the other supervisor always let me take the day off. Looking after Jennifer was incredibly hard and I sometimes wondered what I did to deserve something like this because I always thought I was a nice guy. I told a crew member, and he jokingly said, "Maybe your personality!"

Jennifer continued to get $50 every two weeks for upgrading and $9 for meals and entertainment when she went to see Dr. Nichols. I wasn't worried about the money, but I wondered if I was doing too much for her and what I could do about it; so I thought, *Perhaps I'll start cutting her down on the money I give her to see Dr. Nichols. I'll cut her down to $7, get her used to that then cut her down to $5.* So the next time she went to see Dr. Nichols, I said, "Here, I'll give you $28 this time."

I didn't expect her to say anything, but she squealed, "Awe! *Do I have to!! Do I have to!!*" and kept repeating it even as I was getting my wallet out until I gave her the extra $2.

I thought, *So much for that idea! It didn't work.*

In 1982, the federal government set up a fisheries sting operation to catch illegal sales of salmon. Status Indians were allowed to catch salmon by gill net for food and ceremonial purposes in the Fraser River, but it was illegal to sell it or even give it away. The penalties could be severe if caught and people could end up losing their nets, boat, motor, vehicle and receive a stiff fine. One day on the news, a large number of Indians got their vehicle towed away early in the morning for selling salmon to people involved in the sting operation, so Jennifer and I phoned her father to see if he was one of them; sure enough, he was. When the weekend came, we went to Sto:lo Eagle to see him because we knew he would be upset and angry, and decided to take him to see Wylma and try and find out what's going to happen, whether he would lose his truck or not. We took Henry to Wylma, and she said Henry would probably get his truck back; and after the reading, she said she knew a clairvoyant in Abbotsford who may be able to help him out. We phoned her up, and her name was Phaye Sutton. She charged $40 and could give Henry a reading then gave us her address, so we went to see her the next day. Phaye turned out to be a very interesting person, and we would end up visiting her many times in the future. She said Henry was going to get his truck back and told him many things about his past and future.

We went back to Lytton that night and Jennifer was happy that she helped her father. She went back to upgrading classes and my hours at work were getting shorter because the crew's pay was so slow and erratic in coming in, and one time, either the UIC or the band office lost their cards, so their pay was even slower than usual. I finally found time to read the book *Think and Grow Rich* and thought to myself, *If it works, that's great! If it doesn't, there's no harm in trying!* I had read a few pages previously but gave up right away because I thought, *Sometimes when I wanted something, it seemed to come to me. The most dramatic case was when I wanted more logging experience before I finished BCIT, got scabies, didn't go to the doctor soon enough, and flunked out. That's when I got my logging experience.*

I read the book right to the end and enjoyed hearing success stories about people who succeed with perseverance and determination against overwhelming odds. It mentioned people making major decisions even though other people may not agree with it and some people put their lives and careers on the line. Some such as Abraham Lincoln became famous, while others went down and were forgotten about. My decision was to help Jennifer out; my life and career weren't on the line, but my family was continually pressuring me to leave her. They were treating me like a black sheep and were ready to disown me. Even Terri Dargatz could see quite clearly that I was being treated like a black sheep. When I got near the end of the book, it mentioned reasons why people fail, and one reason was fear of criticism. When I read that, I could see it was word for word how Jennifer acted. I knew what the problem was, but I didn't know what to do about it except keep trying to help her the way I succeeded.

One weekend when visiting my parents, I said that I had a good year in 1982, but Dad got mad at me because much of my money was spent because of Jennifer. It was my first full year that I worked without attending college or BCIT. My older brothers had worked for years, had nothing to show for it, and nothing was said to them. I got mad about that, so as we were walking around in a mall in Chilliwack, I saw Uncle Joe and I walked by him with clenched fists and an angry look on my face, but he just walked by like I wasn't there. I was glad he did that because he was just a scapegoat for the way everyone was treating me.

One weekend I finally convinced Jennifer not to go anywhere because I was tired of driving around all the time on weekends. I thought I finally got a break from all that running around, but on Sunday the phone rang and Jennifer answered it. Henry was calling and asked for me, so I knew right away something was wrong. He asked if I could go to Chilliwack and pick him up because he thought the Indian Dancers were after him and wanted to initiate him. He told me where I could meet him, so I said I would be there in two hours, so I still had to drive around that weekend. When we got to Chilliwack, Liz and Jeremy were there with him and we stood around talking for a few minutes; then someone waved as he went driving by. Henry got scared and said, "That guy's an Indian Dancer! He might tell them where I'm at!" On our way back to Lytton, Henry said, "I don't know why they want to initiate me! I did everything for them! I bought them groceries, drove them to powwows, and cut firewood for them!"

We stopped at a restaurant on the way back and I bought everyone a hamburger and a coffee, and as we were eating, Henry said, "One thing you never talk about is the girlfriend you had before Jennifer."

I didn't want to tell him I never really had one, so I just said, "I didn't have a girlfriend for seven years." Henry didn't believe anyone could go that long without a girlfriend because of the pleasures of a woman and pretended he was flat broke as usual.

We all went up to Snake Flat for supper that night, and Henry didn't give me any thanks at all. He went back to town with us and spent the night at our place, so I cooked breakfast the next morning and served him coffee in the cup that read "I Luv My Dad." When Henry saw it, he thought, *She calls him Dad instead of me. He taught her it's all right to make a mistake as long as you keep trying. I used to beat them for making a mistake.*

One Friday night, Liz and Jeremy asked us to take them to Lillooet to do their grocery shopping; it was raining hard and rocks were rolling down on the road and I was still very mad at David for how he was treating me. I felt like knocking his teeth out but should have known better than to think evil thoughts because I knew something bad was going to happen. Sure enough, I hit a rock that I should have missed, but thinking that way took away my concentration from driving. I stopped and Jeremy got out and told me I had a flat tire and I looked up to the hillside and thought, *We better keep driving because some rocks could come rolling down on us.*

We drove ahead and changed our tire and another car passing by offered to help us, but we were okay. He drove a little ways farther and got a flat tire too, so we stopped and helped him with our flashlight so he could see what he was doing. When we got to Lillooet, my tire was beyond repair and it cost me $155 for a new one. We did our grocery shopping and started driving back but turned around because there were too many rocks on the road, so we got a motel room in Lillooet. We cooked breakfast in our room the next day then went out for coffee and met some people from Lytton who said the road was clear, so we went back and my anger toward David cooled off a lot after that.

One day when I was at work, Jennifer was at home and moved a couch; she hurt her wrist in the process, and I told her she should have waited until I got home. I started getting more interested in developing my psychic abilities and tried tuning my mind in. Looking after Jennifer was extremely hard, and everyone was pressuring me to leave her, so I tried tuning my mind in after going to bed and wondered what I could do about the situation. I couldn't believe the answer I got and didn't want to believe it! Why was this happening to me? My intuition seemed to be telling me to stay with her longer, but this was very difficult for me to accept!

Since I didn't have a very big crew and some of them didn't like operating a power saw, I used a saw and worked with them. As I was working, I started thinking against my intuition, and suddenly the gas cap came off my saw and spilled gas down my leg, then a trickle of smoke started coming off my saw. I saw a power saw start on fire before while operating it and hoped it wouldn't happen here because I had nothing to put it out with and it could severely burn my leg, so I just put it down for a little while then went back to work. Jennifer's wrist was sore, so I had to do the dishes and as I was washing them I started thinking against my intuition again then my hands started to shake back and forth as I was washing the silverware and kitchen knife and knew that if I didn't stop thinking that way, my hands were going to get cut up.

Normally I only make a mistake twice, but looking after Jennifer with my parents continually pressuring me to leave her was more than anyone would want to go through. She was a nervous wreck and seemed to be getting better, but I went to bed thinking against my intuition again. Sometimes when clothes are hung on a hook, they cast a shadow that resembles a hooded monk. I woke up in the middle of the night and saw two spirits looking at me that resembled hooded monks. Both spirits looked incredibly evil, and I could just see the evil radiating out of their heads; but when I started following my intuition, they faded away and the clothes just hung straight down. Now I knew for sure I had to look after Jennifer and the feeling wasn't just my imagination.

When my job ended, Jennifer still had a month of classes left and I didn't have another job to go to. I had applied for other jobs and got turned down everywhere I applied, but Wylma told me I would get something that was more than I ever had before. I didn't know what she meant, but I was depressed about not having another job to go to. Jennifer's classes were still two miles out of town, and I went there with her even though I wanted some free time. We usually went home for lunch, and one day, some students asked for a ride to town. I was still mad at David and knew something was going to happen for thinking that way; and sure enough, as they were getting out of the back of my truck, the canopy window broke. A student, Ted Raphael, went to close the canopy door; and an arm of the door got stuck and went through the window. Ted asked me what he owed me for the window, but I told him not to bother. I didn't want to tell Jennifer what I was doing, so I said, "I wonder why that happened to me."

"Probably because you think down on people," she said.

I wasn't like that, but Jennifer tended to be critical of just about everything. We went back to Rosedale on the weekend, and Dad got mad at me for not charging Ted for breaking my canopy window; he knew I would say "I was thinking evil thoughts!" but didn't realize that's what saved David from doing what I wanted to do to him.

I phoned Henry from a pay phone in Agassiz, and he was cranky as usual; he still insisted I was doing absolutely nothing for Jennifer, I didn't appreciate him giving me that .22 rifle, and that he would protect me if I was ever harassed. I held back when I could have said, "You saw what you were doing to her! At least I don't drill into her head she'll never amount to anything then hold her back when she tries to do something for herself! You didn't even thank me for saving you from the Indian Dancers!

Just before Jennifer finished her upgrading, the class went to Kamloops for an education fair and toured Cariboo College. I went along, and when we got to the cafeteria where students were taking chef training, Jennifer saw a student decorating cakes and decided that's what she wanted for a career. We checked into it, and students had to take a cooking or baking course before taking cake decorating. Then just before her classes ended, I could hear Jennifer talking in her sleep, saying, "Come on, Baxter! Maybe it's better that it happened that way!" Then she went, "Hmmm, hmmm, hmmm, hmmm!" like I always do. I was so happy to hear that because now I knew she wasn't beyond recovery; fifteen months earlier I still wondered if she was beyond recovery.

Her upgrading classes lasted until the end of April, and I was offered a course in outdoor education on Vancouver Island, in British Columbia, often just called the island. Henry helped us move our things back to Rosedale, and after we got everything moved, I found out Jennifer gave him our love seat; and I didn't know she was going to do that. David was at home when we moved, and he finally realized I had good reason to be mad at him; he took advantage of me and used my things when I told him not to. Then he wouldn't help us unload our things and said he wouldn't even help me if I wasn't feeling well.

I wanted to take Jennifer to Strathcona Park Lodge on Vancouver Island with me, but I couldn't; so she had to stay behind in Rosedale, and it gave me a welcome break from looking after her. I went to Campbell River and was told the lodge was halfway between Campbell River and Gold River, and when I got there, I told the desk clerk I was there to take a course in outdoor education, so she showed me where I would be staying and offered me supper. On my first night there, a trapper from Northern Alberta, Helgi Martin, went in; and he was my roommate. The first few days was a hunter-safety course and I already had my ticket, so I put a roof on another tent cabin. I was given first option to move in, so I took it with Helgi and another trapper from Northern Alberta, Archie Marcel; and the three of us hung out together for most of the course. The course was the happiest time of my life, and other people said the same thing. The people there were lots of fun, and Helgi and Archie were also fun to hang around with.

Helgi was twenty-eight and I was twenty-seven and he told me he went to the residential schools for the Indians run by the church. He said the nuns were supposed to get "none" but that wasn't the way it was because he had fun with the nuns. Years later, I told a barber about that, and he said, "You missed out on that one!" and we both laughed.

There was a very nice-looking girl there, Val Hayden, who was either Native or part Native, who kept wondering why she didn't excite me, but I wanted to be sure she would go out with me if she never had anyone first. She said she would then also found out I never had a girlfriend yet, so I just told her I was looking after and supporting a girl at home. She found out the truth.

We did lots of camping and did a backpacking trip out to a lake where there were no roads in. We followed an elk trail in and practiced survival techniques. One exercise was to spend the night sheltered under a log to stay warm and dry as if we had been lost, and did a seven-day ocean-canoeing trip, which was lots of fun; and everyone enjoyed themselves. Sometimes in the evening we had parties or just a few drinks in our cabins. I drank a few beers one night and went to a first aid course the next day; so during a break, I told the trappers, "You have to let loose once in a while. Otherwise, too much tension will build up. Then you'll end up losing your hair, losing your teeth, losing your sex drive!" I said it as a joke; but several months later, a lady on a TV talk show said the same thing, and she was quite serious.

We went to the lounge at the lodge one night for a beer and I sang a song:

Tra-la-la-la boom dee yay,
Did you get yours today?
I did not get mine today!
Tra-la-la-la boom dee yay!

A white fellow sitting next to me always had a sense of humor and replied:

Well that is too bad for you!
You did not get a screw!
Perhaps some other day,
Good Luck will come your way!
Tra-la-la-la boom dee yay!

The canoeing and camping trips were what I enjoyed the most; the ocean-canoeing trip was fun, but I enjoyed taking kids out even more. We took a group of twelve-year-olds out on a canoe camping trip and they were lots of fun. I liked it when they started telling jokes and wished I had listened to them more. They said, "What's an orgy? Peeling oranges! Everyone's going to go upstairs and peel oranges!" It reminded me of when I was twelve years old and the jokes we used to tell. "What happened to the spider who crawled up the elephant's leg? It got pissed off. Jack and Jill went riding up the hill on an elephant and Jill helped Jack off the elephant!" I went to army cadet camp for six weeks during the summer when I was fourteen. When we first got there, we were checked for VD then got checked again just before we left; and as we were standing in line, people were saying, "Well, it's time to go to the pecker checker!"

The course was so much fun I wished it wouldn't end; the only thing that held me back from total happiness was knowing I would have to go back to looking after Jennifer and my parents would be pressuring me to leave her. Now I started drinking more because of knowing how my parents were going to treat me. While I was at the lodge, my family treated Jennifer rather badly; they went places and never let her go along or took her anywhere. She wrote to me and told me how lonely she was and she used to hug my shirts and wish I were there with her. One day she was home alone and everyone else was gone. It was hot and she locked herself in her bedroom because there was a large fly flying around in the living room. Then she told herself, "I'm not going to let that fly hold me a prisoner!" so she went out and killed it.

One day while I was working in the kitchen, I stuck my hand in some hot water and jumped then said to myself, "Don't think evil thoughts, Baxter!" A fellow behind me heard me and started laughing because he thought I was joking. I guess it sounded funny, but I was serious. I started wondering what would happen if I took two boxes of matches because I knew something would happen back to me, so I did it; and a few days later I lost my pen, worth three times as much as the matches. I realized even trivial things people do wrong will happen back to them.

Near the end of the course, we took a canoe instructor's course. I wasn't a very good canoer but took the course anyway. People didn't think I would pass the course but encouraged me to keep trying, so I did my best and kept thinking to myself, *I'm going to pass the course!* I didn't start off very good, but I kept getting better and better. When I did the test, I did quite well and got reasonably good marks and I was discovering the power of the human mind. When the course was over, I had lost a lot of weight and felt and acted ten years younger. When I first got there, people thought I was over thirty. Now, two months later, they didn't believe I was twenty-seven. Since the course was over, we all went to Gold River for a party and dance and I started drinking more because of the stress of knowing what I would be putting up with soon. I got very drunk that night and dreaded the thought of going home.

Just before I left, Jim Bolding, the owner, asked me and another Native fellow to be liaison workers with Indian bands and offer to advertise the course to Indian bands in Chilliwack and Agassiz. When I got back to Rosedale, Jennifer almost didn't recognize me; not only did I get darker, I also looked and acted many years younger. She was sure surprised and happy to see me and I told her I had a week off and she could go back with me.

During my week off, I told my parents, "I was happy when I was alone! No one would hear of it!" Those were the only words I could get in edgewise to explain myself, but they still refused to listen. Dad usually just laughed things off, and my mother got really mad because I didn't even want to find a girlfriend. Dad wondered why I stayed with someone who ran around on me, so I told him that's what usually happens when I take an interest in someone. I hardly ever try to change their minds if they say no because they would just run off with someone else. He realized why I hardly ever looked for anyone, yet he still pressured me to leave her. I found out my cousin Chester and his girlfriend were going to get married at the end of the summer and was happy about that because now my mother couldn't try and force me on her. Mother got mad at me because I wasn't interested in a very nice-looking girl like that, but it was more like she wasn't interested in me; I just didn't have the energy to flog a dead horse.

Just before we left, my mother and one of my aunts offered to take Jennifer for a drive, so I thought I better go along to protect her because I knew they were going to put her down. We went to Harrison Hot Springs, and my aunt asked Jennifer, "Jennifer? How come you're so fat? When I was that age, I wasn't that big." My family was always trying to break us up, and none of them would listen to what I had to say about it. Jennifer and I went to see Wylma for a tarot-card reading the next day, and she told me there was going to be a generation gap and I had one more hill in life to climb and I thought it was to become a registered professional forester (RPF) or do a year of business administration. We stopped off in Laughing Raven before going to the island and took Geraldine and the kids to play in the park. I was eating an apple, and the core was rotten and bit right into it and told Geraldine, "I was thinking evil thoughts. The core is rotten and I bit right into it."

"Coincidence?"

"No, it happens every time."

We went to the hospital in Abbotsford to visit Veronica because she was having another baby, and while visiting her, she thought, *It was like the whole world was against Jennifer! I wouldn't let her come and visit me.*

Then I thought, *Geraldine was always putting her down!* It didn't matter though because Jennifer was too nervous to meet people and was sometimes even too nervous to talk to Veronica when we saw her in a store. She didn't know I was from Rosedale and thought I was from somewhere else. When we got back to Strathcona Park Lodge, I was sick for a few days; when we first got there, it wasn't nearly as much fun as the outdoor-education program and people wouldn't associate with us. It didn't really matter though because Jennifer was still too nervous to meet people and our whole world revolved around each other.

I told Jim Bolding I could go on the EBAP job and went to Campbell River to apply, and the clerk at CEIC said the person in charge of those programs was away that day, so I just sat around the office, reading various pamphlets. Then someone else went in and inquired about EBAP jobs and was sent to a certain person upstairs, so I followed him and asked to see the same person. I wasn't questioned about what I was doing and was allowed to work but had to get my UIC claim transferred to Campbell River. I worked a little bit in the kitchen because I told the cook I enjoyed cooking and almost made it my profession. Most of the time I was beachcombing for logs because I logged before and was reasonably good at using a power saw, and Jennifer did volunteer work as a chambermaid and cook's helper. One day, she was working in the kitchen and saw a worm in the lettuce, panicked, then ran back to our tent cabin. She was scared to go back because she thought the cook would be mad at her, and it took a lot of convincing to get her to go back to work. Sometimes at dinnertime she got so nervous she wouldn't even go for supper; some people could see how much Jennifer held me back from meeting people and wondered how I could live like that because she had been the only woman in my life. I didn't know why things were happening this way either, but I tried to be optimistic about it.

Time was coming up for my ten-year high school reunion, but I was too busy working and couldn't make it because UIC had put a stop payment on my claim, so I didn't have very much money. I wrote to them, explaining what I was doing in Campbell River, but they just sent the same letter back asking what I was doing there. They had been paying $60 a day for my fees and still asked why I was there, but I finally got it straightened out, but I still l had to wait for my checks.

Moving back to the lodge seemed a little difficult at first because not too many people associated with us; however, I knew many situations may start out difficult but usually improve with time and perseverance. Sure enough, more people went and didn't mind associating with us. Working at the lodge also seemed to do Jennifer a lot of good; she was slowly becoming more relaxed and opening up. The owner's wife, Myrna, said the lodge does that to people; so I hoped we could stay there long enough for her to become more sure of herself. While we were there, Jennifer's wrist was still bothering her, so a doctor in Campbell River put a cast on her arm. The cast was removed two weeks later, but her wrist was still weak and I was told there was a job in a remote area in Northern Alberta managing a tourist resort. I was interested in the job but never heard any more about it; then my UIC checks finally went in and I was able to pay my room and board.

I phoned my parents one night, and they told me Dave Walkem called and gave me his number. He was living in Vancouver for the summer and had one more year left to work on his master's degree in business administration. I started getting mad at my mother because she was always telling me to find someone and thought, *I'm going to hit you yet!*

She got mad and answered, "I'll get you to find one yet!"

I got offered a job in Mission, British Columbia, and thought about taking it even though it didn't pay as much as my regular UIC, because I could start another claim when it was over and jobs were very hard to find. One of the workers didn't think it was a very good idea because it could screw up my UIC, but I thought I better take it anyway, and I also had a feeling I should take it. I gave my notice that I was leaving, and Jim Bolding said the Mission Friendship Centre had reserved an opening for me; and his nephew, Dave, said it's all right because they have another applicant who's not making very much on UIC, has a family to support, and needs the job badly.

We left the lodge and caught the ferry back to Vancouver. We stopped in North Vancouver to visit my aunt and uncle, but they weren't home, so I decided to go to the Tomahawk for a cup of coffee. When we got to the Tomahawk, I decided to phone Dave Walkem and see what he was up to; so I called the number he left at my parents' place, and he said I was lucky to catch him at the office that late in the day. He said he put my name in for a forest technician's job with Western Indian Agriculture Corporation, WIAC.

We went to Laughing Raven and asked Ben and Geraldine if we could stay at their place since the job I had didn't pay very much. They said it was all right, and Geraldine was pregnant with her fourth child. Jennifer was always spending our money on her family and wouldn't listen when I tried to tell her not to spend so much. Geraldine was still very critical of everything and was always putting Jennifer down, then Jennifer would get cranky at me because of it. As I was working in Mission and Jennifer sometimes went with me and spent the day in Mission to get away from Geraldine's constant criticism. The first thing we did at work was an orientation and explained what our job would be. We would be working with problem children and delinquents, taking them out camping, canoeing, and teaching them wilderness survival.

When Geraldine's fourth child was born, it was a girl she named Isabella. Jennifer was always taught to be responsible for everyone else, so she spent most of our money on them. We helped look after Ben and Geraldine's other children, and when she got out of the hospital, she was back criticizing her again; so Jennifer went to Mission with me one day. And at the end of the day, she was severely depressed again. Her depression was bad and she asked if we could get a place of our own, but I told her it would be hard because the job didn't pay very much and she was spending too much money. One evening, we had a meeting to discuss an upcoming camping trip, and she went with me to get away from Geraldine's criticism.

The friendship center had a direct line to Vancouver, so I called WIAC about the job. The general manager, Gordon Antoine, was from Merritt and knew me and my family and asked me to go for an interview. Jennifer and I caught the bus to Vancouver, and when we got to Vancouver and started walking toward the office, she completely and unexpectedly kicked me hard in the calf muscle when she was behind me. It came as a complete surprise to me. People who saw it were also surprised, and one fellow walking by thought he wouldn't put up with that. I went for the interview and told Jennifer she could look around Pacific Centre Mall and I would meet her later. The other applicant was Harry Spahan, a forest technician and the general manager's foster brother, who had gone to school with my oldest brother. There were two job openings for forest technicians and one agrologist.

I was told I would be called later about the job, so Jennifer and I went back to Laughing Raven to prepare for a camping trip. The trip would have been fun, but for many years I seemed to get the flu for three weeks in the fall, and I got it just before we went camping. We took a number of young people out camping at a lake just outside of Mission. Some of them were problem children living in foster or group homes, and one young girl about fifteen years old tried to commit suicide the day before we left, so she didn't go. I was a qualified canoe instructor and was also there to teach woods survival, but the lake didn't have proper facilities to teach them how to paddle a canoe, and they felt embarrassed with people commenting on where they were learning. I tried to teach them strokes of the paddle on dry land because they would drift too much in the water. It wouldn't have been a problem if they knew the strokes as I called out to them. The teenagers weren't interested in canoeing with other people watching, so we taught them woods survival, then we had supper, and toward the evening, we started playing games; but I wasn't able to play very long because I was getting sick.

Jennifer was scared of slugs, but I told her where I set up the tent, there shouldn't be any slugs. Then it rained the next day, so we didn't do very much and Jennifer stayed in the tent for a while. She was either nervous or tired, and when she woke up, a number of slugs had crawled up the walls of our tent; so she called me over to get rid of them. It only rained one day and night, and the next day, we all packed up to leave; and as we were packing, some of the young girls talked about not wanting to live past their teen years. They were from troubled homes and felt better off if they didn't live much longer. I felt bad that they felt that way, but there was nothing I could do about it because I had enough trouble looking after Jennifer.

We went back to Mission, and a lady in the office said we could take the rest of the day off, so Jennifer and I went to visit Phaye. She also told me I had one more hill in life to climb, looking after Jennifer; she was the last test of my patience and then there would be a whole new beginning. I asked her when it would be over, and she said, "In May. But you're going to go through some very difficult times until then!" But I thought it couldn't be any worse than what we've already been through; sometimes Jennifer still said she didn't think she would live past twenty-five.

I continued to read books on the subconscious mind and how it worked and books on psychics and their life story. The book on Peter Hurkos, a psychic, used to help find the Boston Strangler, was a very interesting book. The books I read said if you keep wishing and visualizing something in your mind, somehow it may come to you. Some religious people call it praying and I sometimes did that in the past and got what I wanted without realizing what I was doing. I often wished I could break Jennifer's depression and help her do something with her life and kept thinking to myself, *I want to help her do something with her life!*

We went to visit Henry and things I had been telling him were beginning to sink in and I told him about blowing a tire, how much it cost me to replace it, and getting a room for the night. Then I told him about the guy breaking my canopy window and eating the apple, and Henry looked away and started laughing because he knew I was thinking of taking a round out of David when all that happened. If I said no, he would have said I was thinking of taking a round out of my ex-landlady's son.

I made several trips to Vancouver to WIAC's office when I was told I got the job. Harry Spahan and Ross Douglas, the agrologist, were also hired. All three of us were given our own area to monitor forest-improvement projects on Indian reserves and send in reports to the main office. Ross and I were based out of Kamloops and Harry was based out of Merritt. I was to cover projects in Barriere, Kamloops, the Okanagan, and the Kootenays, southeastern British Columbia; so the job involved much travelling. Ross asked me if I needed an advance to move to Kamloops, but I told him I had enough money to move and Jennifer and I were both really happy to move away. Before we moved, my mother went to Reno, Nevada, for a holiday and brought me back a shirt that read "Everyone Is Entitled to My Opinion!" But even after that, no one would listen to anything I had to say.

We didn't own any furniture; so we just moved our clothes, blankets, and dishes and stayed in a motel for the first month. I worked out of an office at the Indian residential school in Kamloops; and a lady I went to college with, Vivian Ignace, was also working there. So I usually went and had coffee with her and her friend, Chris, in the morning. Right after we moved to Kamloops, WIAC put on a fall fair and Jennifer was too nervous to go, so she stayed in the motel room. I felt extremely depressed and uptight there and I thought it was because of how my parents were treating me. Gordon Antoine couldn't understand it because he thought I had the nicest parents and wondered why I preferred to stay single. I was getting more withdrawn, and if I got excited at all, I would have given up for the slightest excuse; and when I got home from the fair, Jennifer was extremely depressed again.

We were supposed to get new trucks leased from a car dealer in Vernon for work, but they were late arriving, so I had to use my own truck temporarily. I wasn't really sure what my responsibilities were at first, but I found out soon enough. I was to travel around to various Indian reserves and give reports on the work progress and safety procedures followed by the crew. I took Jennifer with me whenever I could and tried to contact Dr. Nichols to see if Jennifer could somehow see her again, but she had retired. Then I finally took her to the doctor for depression because she wouldn't even go to the doctor by herself.

The doctor asked, "Did she ever have periods of extreme happiness as well?"

"No," I told him and knew he thought Jennifer may have manic depression and was surprised I knew that, so the doctor gave Jennifer a prescription for antidepressants and asked if I could stay home with her for a day. He offered to write a note if I needed one, but I told him I probably wouldn't need it and he sensed I was into mind control and didn't believe it worked.

We got the prescription filled and I stayed home with her the next day, but Jennifer only took one pill because she hated taking pills, and I was able to help her because she was slowly getting stronger. We stayed in the motel for a month, then we found a furnished two-bedroom apartment on top of the hill near Cariboo College. I thought we were lucky to get a furnished apartment because we didn't own any furniture. Jennifer and I didn't drink very much and we couldn't join any clubs or activities because she was too nervous to meet people and her wrist was still too sore from when she hurt it in Lytton; therefore, our only activity to pass time was shopping, garage sales, and flea markets. Jennifer was a compulsive shopper and I tried to get her not to spend so much, but it didn't do any good because she usually found a way to get her own way, but I thought the money I lost would be worth it if I could save her from suicide.

We moved into our apartment and realized we didn't own a TV. Sitting at home can get awfully boring if you just sit and look at the walls, and I thought it could be like going to jail and looking at the walls. Right after we moved into our apartment, the vehicles were ready to be picked up in Vernon; and when we got to Vernon, the lease manager took us to an insurance agent to get insurance for the truck. But instead of getting a new four-wheel drive, I got an old, run-down two-wheel drive. When I went to start the truck, nothing happened, so I told the lease manager it had a dead battery and he sent a mechanic out to fix it. I told the mechanic it had a dead battery, but he just said, "I make a living at this!"

I didn't say anything, but thought, *That's fine. I'm not paying for it.*

Jennifer and I walked around for a little while, and when we went back, the lease manager said I was right—it had a dead battery and it would take a couple hours to recharge. I asked him where a good place to buy a TV was, and he said, "Down at the end of the street."

We went over there and Jennifer wanted a TV with remote control, but I said, "Is it too much trouble to just walk across the room to change the channel?" So I bought a manual TV.

I learned more about what I was expected to do and travelled to various Indian reserves and didn't trust that truck to go very far, so I didn't travel to the more distant reserves. I got called back to Vancouver for a meeting with WIAC, but we didn't stop at Laughing Raven anymore because Geraldine was always putting Jennifer down. At the meeting, we met some staff from DIA and discussed the job, how it was going, and what was expected of us. I had made some mistakes and spoke up on why it happened. Ross asked DIA a number of questions, but all they did was sit there and say no. Harry and I were more withdrawn and didn't say very much, but I couldn't understand why we weren't expected to spend more time on each project to give technical advice and record the species and stem count after working the area. This should have been recorded and put on file, but I didn't say anything though because I was just happy to have a job.

Some of the staff at WIAC were unhappy with the car dealer because of the vehicles we ended up driving: Ross had a rundown club cab pickup, I had a rundown two-wheel drive, and Harry had a small diesel pickup nicknamed the Bush Buggy. After the meeting, we went back to Kamloops, and I was supposed to make a trip to the Kootenays, but I didn't trust the truck to go that far. I continued working with the two-wheel drive, and one day, the lease manager called and said I was accidentally given car plates instead of truck plates. He also asked how I did on buying a TV, and I told him I saved $100, and he noticed I wasn't too worried about it even though that was quite a lot of money. When I went to trade in the license plates, the truck broke down because the right rear wheel wouldn't turn forward; it would turn backward, but it wouldn't turn forward. I was glad it broke down where it did because it was in a parking lot in the middle of town, so I just had to walk across the street to a bus stop to catch a ride home; and the fellow who was riding with me, his girlfriend was just passing by, so he caught a ride back to work with her.

I called the lease manager in Vernon, and he arranged for the Dodge dealer in Kamloops to have the truck towed there for repairs, so I got my own truck and drove out to the Dodge dealer to see about the two-wheel drive and was surprised the tow truck driver was Bill Peerenboom, a white fellow I went to school with in Merritt. The truck ended up with an $800 repair bill, paid for by the dealer in Vernon. I was supposed to make some trips to the Kootenays, but I still didn't trust the truck to go that far; and luckily enough, the British Columbia government employees went on strike and the Department of Highways was among those on strike. The roads were covered with snow and therefore impassable high in the mountains, so I could have ended up stranded in the Kootenays.

Dad had cut his arm at work a year earlier, and when I found out he was mad at me for staying with Jennifer, I should have known right away; but I didn't figure it out until now that he was thinking about me when he cut his arm at work. I phoned home to ask, but he wasn't home and my mother answered the phone, so I told her to ask him if he was thinking about me when he cut his arm at work; he didn't deny it, but he still wouldn't listen to anything I had to say.

The new trucks finally arrived, and I was given a brand-new four-wheel drive pickup; but for some reason, the lease manager kept trading me back with the two-wheel drive. Some of the other workers weren't trading for the other vehicles because we were supposed to be leasing the new trucks, and one day when I went to start the two-wheel drive, I had a hard time getting it started. I called the lease manager and told him the starter was going on the truck, so he started giving me a hard time and said, "You claim to be a mechanic! What else is wrong with it!"

I didn't answer but thought some of the other staff must have been giving him a hard time. I used the two-wheel drive for a little while longer; then it was time to trade it for the new truck again, and when I left Kamloops, I didn't dare stop the truck because I knew it may not start again. When I got to Vernon, I parked the truck in the car lot; and when they tried to move, it wouldn't start because the starter had gone on it. I told the lease manager that it was better that the new trucks didn't go in right away and that I was accidentally given car plates instead of truck plates. If I went to the Kootenays, I could have gotten stranded there because of the British Columbia government employees' strike; the two-wheel drive broke down when I went to trade in the license plates, but it was no problem getting back home because I was in a parking lot in town. It was better to break down there than in the woods, where it could have been a long walk home, or break down while driving down the highway and get into an accident.

Just before I left, I saw a fellow with his back turned to me and I knew right away it was Patrick Hill, another white fellow I knew from Merritt. His mother went to school with my mother in Abbotsford because my mother didn't always go to the residential school. Pat told me he was a truck driver; his oldest brother, Robert, was living in Enderby; and his youngest sister was living in Kelowna. But I couldn't ask him to go over and visit because Jennifer was too nervous to meet people. I continued working with the two-wheel drive and went to Rosedale one weekend to pick up my freezer and rifles because it was hunting season. It was raining when we got there, and my mother rushed us off because she was worried about road conditions, so we left in such a hurry I forgot my rifles.

The lease manager called and arranged to meet me at a restaurant in Chase; he said it would be the last time we trade trucks and I could now keep the four-wheel drive for work. When I met him, he was happier than the last time I saw him because he learned that when things beyond your control happen, it could look like things are going wrong but it could be better that it happened that way.

Since I had a reliable truck, I finally made a trip to Penticton and Oliver. When I got to Penticton, Jennifer said she would wait for me in town and I would meet her about one o'clock, but I was late getting out of the woods and she was really mad at me. I wished she would be more understanding and realize it couldn't be helped, and a lady listening to us argue thought she wouldn't get mad if I was late getting out of the woods. The next band I went to was called Osoyoos, but when I phoned them, they were in Oliver. I went to the band office and the receptionist said the crew was in another building doing a workshop and I was surprised when I walked in because an Indian fellow I went to high school with in Merritt, Wayne Bent, was there.

I continued taking Jennifer to work with me if I had to stay overnight somewhere or if she just wanted to go with me. She started reading the book *Hope and Help for Your Nerves* by Dr. Claire Weekes, and it seemed to be helping her with her nerves. Usually in the morning I went to the library to have coffee with Vivian and Christine and told Vivian what a nervous wreck Jennifer is and my parents keep pressuring me to leave her. Vivian said, "You should tell them you're not mad at them for their past mistakes. They shouldn't be mad at you for what you're doing."

Vivian told me she had a very difficult life too; her parents broke up and her mother got pregnant during the breakup and she was the result. She was rejected by her parents because she had a different father from the rest of the children; her parents put her down so naturally that the other children did the same thing. She said even when children are still in the womb, they know if they're wanted or not. We sometimes went back to Sto:lo Eagle, and on one visit, Henry finally realized he was the one who made Jennifer a nervous wreck and caused her to go into those fits of depression.

Since I had to make some trips to the Kootenays, I went after the British Columbia government employees' strike was over; and whenever I did, I tried to rush with my work so we could go to Lethbridge, Alberta, to visit Brenda and Alvin. I enjoyed the trip, and it only cost us $50 for gas. They were going through some rather difficult times, so I usually just bought some beer and we drank at home. On our first trip, I took what looked like the shortest route on the map; and when I got there, I found out it was also the most difficult. On our way back, we stopped at the bands in Oliver and the Okanagan so we could spend an extra day in Lethbridge.

One day when I went to Enderby, Jennifer decided to stay home, so I phoned Robert Hill and had a cup of coffee with him but couldn't do that if Jennifer was with me though. Jennifer's wrist still didn't heal from when she hurt it in Lytton, and when we went out for dinner, I often had to cut up her meat for her because her wrist was too weak.

She continued to spend and give our things to her family because she felt guilty that we had things and they didn't, but I couldn't get through to her that I worked hard for everything we have. I spent many evenings and weekends staying home studying while everyone else was out partying and having fun, and lived on a low income for many years while everyone else was out working.

Jennifer had a half brother she never met in Kamloops, Timothy, nicknamed Calf-eye. We were visiting Allan Casimer at the Kamloops band office and a fellow walked in, talked to Allan, then left. Jennifer asked about Timothy, and Allan said he just left. Calf-eye was injured in a barroom brawl, went to work later, and he and I eventually became good friends.

I ordered some films on forestry practices in British Columbia so I could put on some workshops at various bands. One place we did a workshop in was Enderby, and just before we did the workshop, I tried to join a kickboxing club. I attended for one practice and Jennifer went with me; she said the ladies there were getting interested in me, but I didn't believe her. When it became time for the next session, I had to spend the night in Vernon to put the workshop in Enderby; and my instincts also told me something would keep interfering if I tried to join the kickboxing club, so I had to quit. I knew I had to stay with Jennifer and the ladies there were getting interested in me. Sometimes when we walked around the malls in Kamloops, we would run into Garry Lafferty, another Indian I went to school with. He used to stop and talk to everyone, and he said to me, "Every time I see you, you look worse. What's the matter?"

"I miss being single. It's not so much that I miss being single. My parents keep pressuring me to leave Jennifer. I enjoy being single, but I want to help Jennifer do something with her life."

"Then you would rather put up with loneliness than find someone?"

Christmas was coming, and Jennifer and I went out to one of the shopping malls. I was getting tired of her possessiveness, so I made up the excuse that she should look around on her own; but when I left her, I began to feel extremely depressed. And sometimes at work I would feel the same way. When I went back to find her, I asked her if she felt the same way when I left and she said she did; then I realized I was feeling her moods. I continued working and looking after Jennifer, and she sometimes got really ugly, but I knew I had to put up with it. Sometimes at work I would start feeling depressed and knew something was wrong, so I would call her and ask what was wrong. She wondered how I knew, so I told her I can feel her moods. I considered giving up on developing my psychic abilities because I didn't like feeling her moods when she was depressed, but when I told Wylma about it, she didn't think it was that bad.

When I studied anthropology in college, I learned that people can't say one religion is right and all the others are wrong, because there's no way to prove it; and if people want to follow a religion, it's their option to live the way they want to live. In Canada, Christianity or some form of it is the most commonly accepted religion, and many Canadians have been taught Christianity of some type at one time in our lives. I was taught to be a Roman Catholic as a child and I was taught to consider people who weren't Christians as pagans and pray for them. Movies also portrayed other religions, especially Native Indian, South Sea Island natives, and black Africans as foolish superstition, something to be laughed at. I started getting interested in Indian spiritualism and what their beliefs were like, but all I knew was that they sometimes went to the mountains to fast and see visions. I asked a Native fellow named Pat about it, but he refused to tell me, but I thought, *That's fine. I learned much about life over the years.*

Just before Christmas, I got called to Vancouver for a staff meeting; and on our way, it snowed heavily, so we thought it would be safer to get a motel room in Hope. Jennifer didn't want to go to Rosedale because she was too nervous around my family. WIAC booked a room for us at the Blue Horizon, a hotel on Robson Street. I went to the meeting and Jennifer looked around a shopping mall. I was under so much stress I couldn't function very well and couldn't comprehend very much of what they were talking about at the meeting. We went back to Kamloops for another week's work then back to the coast on my own truck because the office was shut down for a week between Christmas and New Year's Day.

Jennifer and I agreed that we would spend Christmas in Sto:lo Eagle that year and next year in Rosedale. We were going to spend a day or two in Rosedale then go to Sto:lo Eagle, and when we got to Rosedale, David and Isaac were getting the turkey ready for the Christmas dinner. David asked me to help him with the cooking even though he knew full well he would just have given me some sarcastic remark if I asked him to do that for me. I asked him if he could tell

Dad about the time that guy almost got his head sliced off that's why I have to follow my hunches now, but he refused to do it. After all the things I did for him, he refused to do even a trivial thing like that for me and I felt like kicking him in the head, but I knew better. Then Jennifer started feeling nervous and depressed, so we left. Both David and Isaac thought David was starting to get on my nerves after talking to him for less than two minutes, so now I was glad I could feel her moods. Henry knew we were going and had a platter of sandwiches ready when we got there; he was happy to see us because I had calmed him down without realizing what I was doing.

Christmas wasn't too bad that year, but looking after Jennifer was getting hard on me; we were having more arguments and it was beginning to look like we may end up separating. Jennifer's mother saw us arguing and hoped I would stay with her until she got a career, so I told her Jennifer ran around on me in the past, so she offered to go out with me if I stayed with Jennifer until she got a career. Although her mother was very homely and they were a poor family, I appreciated what she was willing to do for her daughter. I didn't know she could see what was happening all the time I kept putting Jennifer back in school and wouldn't let her give up, because she usually just sat back and didn't say anything. I had tried to tell Jennifer not to do anything wrong because it would happen back to her; she started getting interested in my father in 1981 and now it was happening back to her. She was still mixed up but was slowly coming out of it, and I wasn't lonely anymore and missed being single but still wanted to help her.

After Boxing Day, I brought my truck to a service station in Agassiz for a tune-up; but while it was on the hoist, it slipped and punctured a tire, so the owner said I could buy another tire and he would reimburse me for it. I phoned all over Chilliwack and couldn't get another Bridgestone tire the proper size, so we went to Laughing Raven and phoned all over Mission and Abbotsford. We couldn't get another tire and would have to wait until Tuesday or Wednesday at the earliest. I didn't want to miss two or three days of work and didn't want to drive back to Kamloops in the winter without a spare tire, so a dealer sold me a different make of tire. It would be adequate as a spare to get us back to Kamloops.

We went to Laughing Raven, and that was the first time we went there since the summer. And Geraldine asked me for some matches to light her cigarette, so I gave her some. She noticed they were from a restaurant in Vancouver, so she asked me where we got them from. I didn't really answer her or tell her we stopped visiting because of the way she was always criticizing Jennifer.

Chapter 6

1984

When we got back to Kamloops, there seemed to have been much violence during the holidays. Allan Casimer got his wrist broken by one of his workers because he was mad about not being able to cash his check until after Christmas. Allan's glass frames probably saved his life because he had a metal plate in his head and was hit by a belt buckle, so I wondered if the fellow who did it had a chemical imbalance in his brain that's why he was so violent, because I heard other stories about him. Allan had told me about the violent life he had led in the past but had no regrets about what he's been through; his home life was violent, so the residential school was no big deal to him. Henry thought Allan did something wrong in the past and is now suffering for it. As I was driving to work one morning, the roads were icy and I was still rather angry at David for how he was trying to treat me. As I was getting off a side road and onto the Yellowhead Highway, the truck started sliding onto the main road. Luckily, there wasn't any traffic coming, so I told myself, "Don't think evil thoughts!"

I had to make two more trips to the Kootenays, so I told Jennifer to pack more clothes, but she wouldn't because her nerves were getting bad again. I stopped to relieve myself on the way, and as I walked back to the truck, she had a really cranky look on her face. I often wished she wouldn't get like that and wondered what caused it. The roads were icy, and just outside Creston, I hit an icy patch and the truck spun right around and stopped just before a rock bluff. Jennifer got really scared for me and started crying because she was worried that if something happened to me, she wouldn't have anyone to look after her; so I tried to calm her down and assure her everything was all right, but it was hard to do.

I had three reserves to check the projects on—one in Creston, one in Invermere, and one in Cranbrook—and hurried to get my work done this time so we could spend more time in Lethbridge. We got the work done early and got to Lethbridge by Wednesday night. Brenda worked as a janitor and Alvin worked during the day at Canada Packers, a meat-processing plant, and we usually helped Brenda with her work so she could get off early. The next day, we went to shop around and I said to Jennifer, "I wish my parents would listen to my opinion!" Other people just happened to hear me and automatically thought I was just spoilt because young people often get stereotyped and not listened to. We were sitting around the house the next day, and Jennifer said, "I have a feeling we should go downtown." So we went downtown again and I found the book *Murphy's Boy* by Torey Hayden and was happy about that. I knew it would be a good book because I read an article on it in the *Reader's Digest,* and it hadn't reached British Columbia yet.

We went down the bars that night with Brenda, Alvin, and Shirley, Alvin's brother's girlfriend. We were sitting there laughing and having a good time, not bothering anyone, when a huge Native fellow went over and joined us. I could see right away he just wanted a few free beers, so we let him have one but weren't ready to let him have any more. He was going to use his size to force the issue, but Alvin said to him, "I'm a pretty big fellow myself!" so Alvin wasn't scared. Then he pulled out a folding knife and thought he could scare us with it, but I told him I had a knife too and was also wearing a thick woolen mackinaw, which could prevent cuts better than his nylon windbreaker could. I learned some knife fighting in the training I did and this was a chance to let out my anger because of how my family was treating me. I thought to myself, *If I win, I win. If I lose, I won't have to put up with how my family is treating me anymore.* It's a terrible thing to say, but that's how I felt.

We all shook hands, then he walked away; but he turned around and angrily said to Alvin, "I'm going to remember you!" Later on I realized I was lucky he was just bluffing because I didn't know my knife was rusty and couldn't get it open.

We went back to British Columbia and stopped and checked the projects in the Okanagan; that way we spent the same amount of time travelling if we left from Kamloops. Jennifer kept reading the book *Hope and Help for Your Nerves* and was slowly getting better. I read the book *Murphy's Boy* and couldn't believe what he went through but came out of it because one person believed in him and was willing to go through what it took to help him come out of it. After I finished it, I suggested to Jennifer that she read it; and once she started reading it, she could barely stop until she finished it.

One day as I was folding up a blanket, we got into a big argument; so I went, "Ole!" and it surprised her so much she didn't know whether to laugh or get mad. She decided to stay home one day when I went to Enderby, so after filling out my report, I was going to call Robert Hill to go for a cup of coffee again; but it felt like Jennifer was starting to get worried or depressed again, so I thought maybe I better just go home. When I got home, she said she was cleaning up the apartment and saw a worm and that's what scared her.

Vivian asked me if I could use the truck to help her move to another apartment one weekend, so I agreed, but Jennifer was too nervous to go and her wrist was still too weak. Vivian had a number of books, and the novel *Aztec* was one of them, Phaye told me I was an Aztec in a past life, and that was the first time I saw the book; so I told myself, "I'm going to buy it."

Looking after Jennifer was extremely difficult, so I was willing to do anything if it would help her get stronger. I read the book *The Silva Mind Control Method* by José Silva and liked it; the book mentioned courses to learn the techniques used in the book, and I thought it would be interesting to take. I was looking through the ad section of the paper one day and it mentioned a course being held in Kamloops, so Jennifer and I went to the meeting. The course was expensive but 100 percent guaranteed; if we weren't satisfied, we would be fully refunded. It was a struggle to save that much money, but we still went to the first half of the course. The course was okay, but we weren't learning enough to spend that much money, so we dropped out and were fully refunded. There was some interesting people there though; one fellow was close to retirement age and his job didn't have a pension plan, so that made me think I better find a job with a pension plan or save in Registered Retirement Savings Plan, RRSPs. He also mentioned reading the book *The Power of Your Subconscious Mind* by Dr. Joseph Murphy and said it was a good book. Another fellow said he was taking the course out of curiosity because his wife took it then divorced him, so he wanted to find out why.

We went back to the coast one weekend, went to the flea market, and I saw the book *Aztec* and bought it for 25¢. I tried to tell Dad about Kevin Richter, the boy from the book *Murphy's Boy* who was an elective mute and his father made him eat mush that was green with mold and his own puke and killed his sister with a frying pan in a drunken rage. Dad knew I was trying to tell him indirectly that Jennifer's father is a sick man, but he refused to listen and continued to pressure me to leave her. Dad talked about following his hunches and realized they are usually right, so I told him about the fellow who almost got his head sliced off when I was logging. He didn't believe me and acted like he wanted me to believe he was right. I also bought my parents a copy of *Murphy's Boy*, but they did little more than look at the cover. Then we went to visit Phaye again and she asked me if I was protecting someone. I said "Jennifer," and I wondered why she didn't figure that out earlier.

I was asked to put on a forestry workshop at Alkali Lake, an Indian reserve near Williams Lake, and Harry Spahan put on a slide show on forest pests. While we were there, Klaus Berger, another worker for WIAC, said to Harry, "Harry's never gone hungry. He doesn't eat the core of the apple." Then he said, "I almost starved to death during the Second World War that's why I bought a farm. I made sure I wouldn't starve again if I went through hard times." People usually don't forget hard times very easily, especially if they ever went hungry. People my parents' age seemed to be jealous of Dutch people but didn't realize the hard times the Dutch went through during the war, so when they got an opportunity to work, they prepared for hard times.

When we were in Williams Lake, Harry asked me to go to Prince George and Burns Lake for him and do reports on projects for him; he didn't want to go because his wife was about to have a baby. I agreed to go and Jennifer said she kept wishing and picturing in her mind that we go to Prince George; now she got her chance on that trip. I also bought the book *The Power of Your Subconscious Mind* while we were in Williams Lake. I started reading it and thought it was a very good book. The author said the subconscious mind is like a machine: It doesn't think; it only acts on what the conscious mind is thinking. Some people call computers idiots, but they're only machines that do exactly what the programmer tells it to do, no more, no less; so I thought perhaps that's why something bad happens to people when they think evil thoughts. The subconscious mind is acting on what they're thinking about.

Jennifer and I went to Prince George to get the maps of the Indian reserves in Burns Lake, and when I called DIA, the lady in charge of forestry kept expecting me to make sarcastic remarks because of whom she works for. I didn't because I knew it would happen back to me; only if I had a specific, legitimate complaint, then I would have said something. In Prince George we stayed at a motel I spent the night in many years earlier; Prince George had expanded greatly since 1975. On our way to Burns Lake, I showed Jennifer the bar in Endako where I used to go when I worked on the railroad. We got to Burns Lake rather late in the day, and a fellow in the office knew we were going, so he waited for us.

I had to make one more trip to the Kootenays, so that meant another trip to Lethbridge, and Alvin asked us to bring them some salmon. When we were in Creston, Jennifer got mad and wanted to sleep in the bathtub; but I was scared she might try to do something to herself, so I tried telling her to go to sleep in the bed. She got mad and started hitting me with an ashtray, which didn't hurt; then I felt something dripping on my T-shirt. I thought it was water, but it was blood. She insisted I go to the hospital emergency room even though I didn't want to, and the nurse on duty asked me what happened. I didn't want to tell her, so I said I went to the bar and someone threw an ashtray and hit me, but she looked like she knew what really happened.

I did my work, and when we got to Lethbridge, I asked Alvin if he ever went down to that same bar again. He said he did but he didn't see that big fellow there. It wasn't too bad of a visit, but we left a day early for British Columbia; and when we got back to British Columbia, I noticed I forgot my credit card in one of the stores. But luckily, I still had some money on me. I had just enough money for a motel room that night, and the room we got had free instant coffee; but when I got up in the morning, the water was turned off because the civil servants were working on the pipelines. I felt a little annoyed, but when I went out to the woods, a stranger on the project shared his lunch and coffee with me; I seemed to be lucky. This was before Interac was available.

I started thinking about getting Jennifer into the cooking course at Cariboo College in Kamloops and she agreed, so we applied for admission and to her band for funding. We weren't sure where we were going to be, so we had our mail sent to Rosedale. I had about six weeks of work left, and Jennifer decided we should move downtown because she never lived in town before and wanted to see what it was like. I wished she didn't do that because my job wasn't going to last much longer and it was going to cost us to move. We moved downtown but had to buy a new bed because the new apartment wasn't furnished. Jennifer wanted a twin bed because she was nervous and wanted me to be as close to her as possible. I was getting worried about spending so much because my job was going to run out soon. I still had one more truck payment to make and my insurance would be almost due; but on several nights as I was sleeping, it felt like a spirit was holding me up, comforting me, telling me, "Don't worry. Everything will be all right." I was told I could take a day off to look for another job if I wanted to, so I asked WIAC for more work, but there weren't any jobs I was qualified for. There was one job opening, but it was given to Harry Spahan. I went to CEIC one afternoon to look for work and saw a job opening in Nova Scotia. I talked to the clerk there and was going to apply for it but it was closing time, and I really liked the idea of getting that far away from everyone.

Jennifer and I went to Sto:lo Eagle that weekend, visited Wylma for a tarot-card reading, and she advised us not to unpack our things because something was coming. I worked until the last day and didn't take any time off; then just before it was time to take the truck back to Vernon, Harry said he would meet me there and give me a ride back to Kamloops. On the last day of work, I had to bring the truck back but couldn't see any point in rushing; so I took my time leaving, had coffee, and visited people in the office. Then just as I was leaving the office, Graham Go, the financial manager from Spallumcheen Indian Band in Enderby, went in. He said, "I have some money that has to be spent for sent back. Why don't you come and work for us for a month or two. You can take a week off and we'll negotiate. I have to go to a meeting right now."

I was so relieved to hear that! I brought the truck back to Vernon and Harry picked me up. Phaye had told me I would be talking to Harry about something, and we talked about the Nicola Valley Institute of Technology, a postsecondary institution in Merritt; I was curious about the forestry program there.

Jennifer and I went to Enderby and found a place to stay there. It was a bit of a problem, but we eventually found one, then we took a week off and went back to the coast. The night before we moved to Enderby, I asked Jennifer to go to a cabaret that night. She didn't want to go because she thought people might harass her, so I told her that usually if you just sit there and mind your own business, people leave you alone. We went to the cabaret, and there was a couple of big fellows sitting at the table next to us with their wives. I got up to go to the bathroom and she didn't want me to go, but I went anyway. Then when I got back, I wondered why she was scared and the fellows at the table next to us were acting rather guilty. Jennifer said, "Those guys are laughing at us! Come on, let's go!"

We went back home, and it took Jennifer a long time to calm down and tell me one of the fellows at the table next to us slammed his hand down on the table and said what his name was. I knew he just did that as a joke, but he didn't know Jennifer was afraid of her own shadow and we couldn't go back so he could apologize because she was too scared to go back. I almost didn't write this incident into my life story but people told me to do it so, after writing my life story out six times I finally wrote it in.

When we were ready to move our belongings, I tried to get Vivian and her boyfriend to help us because we were both sick and Jennifer's wrist was weak. I couldn't find them or Calf-eye, so I asked Allan Casimer to help us; and just when I parked the moving truck, a heavyset fellow, Dennis, went by and offered to help us. Allan and one of his brothers stopped by and helped a little, but they promised to take their kids to a carnival, so they couldn't stay long. I thought the fellow who stopped by to help us was retarded, but Allan said he got several diseases all at once and suffered brain damage. Dennis looked like an alcoholic, but he said he couldn't even get a job washing dishes because he didn't have his grade 12. He had worked for a moving company before and showed me how to move furniture around stair corners, then just when we got the furniture loaded, Vivian and her boyfriend showed up and offered to go to Enderby to help us move. I thanked Dennis and gave him $21.00 for two hours of work, and he was really happy about that because good-paying jobs paid $10.50 an hour.

Jennifer and I were both sick because we had a virus. I went to the doctor for medication, but she wouldn't go because she didn't want to live anymore, and I couldn't try to force her to go because it wouldn't do any good. When we got to Enderby, I was told what my responsibilities were, how much I would be paid, and the band had enough money to keep me employed for two months. One day in the office, I heard someone say, "I know that guy from somewhere." I didn't know he meant me, so he said it again; it was Gary Abbot, the alcohol-and-drug counsellor from Lytton. He left Lytton and was now working in Enderby, and one day after a staff meeting, he told me why he didn't help me with Jennifer's depression in Lytton. He said, "Everyone's life is laid out for them. I could see it was your responsibility to look after her. Are you mad at me for that?"

I said no, and I was beginning to see why things happened the way they did. We exchanged stories and experiences and he recommended I read a number of books on Indian medicine men. I told him about some of my psychic experiences and how life seemed to go in cycles. Gary also told me some of the symptoms of people contemplating suicide: They may gain or lose a lot of weight, they're depressed for a long time, and then all of a sudden, they're really happy. The decision has been made. They give away their most personal possessions; they don't need them anymore because they're not going to live much longer.

Many people on that reserve kept to themselves, but I didn't mind because Jennifer was too nervous to meet people, so I had to close myself off anyway. I had to go to the doctor again for more medication for the virus, but Jennifer still refused to go. One of the workers there, Nathan Kinbasket, was very outgoing though and told me he had two offers to write a book on his life. He went to jail as well as the Indian residential schools and said life was better in jail than it was in school. Nathan was only eight to ten years older than I.

One of my tires started to wear out and I had to wait several days to get another tire, and when I got it, the tire cost me $175, so the bank doubled my spending limit on my credit card so I could pay for the tire. One week later, a worker was supposed to tell me to wait by the road but told me to drive through the brush instead. I drove a little ways and punctured my tire, putting a big hole in it; now I didn't know if my tire would work as a regular tire or not. I never thought the tire could have a warranty on it because I couldn't think clearly and missed obvious things because looking after Jennifer and the pressure my parents were putting on me to leave her were getting to be too much. I also didn't want to get a phone because Jennifer would keep calling her father, and if he said "Come down for the weekend," she would drop everything and go.

Sometimes when we went to the coast, Dad would tell me I'm getting old and haven't had a girlfriend yet. I didn't answer but thought, *Perhaps I am, but I have to look after Jennifer. If I don't do it, no one is going to do it.* I continued working in Enderby and Jennifer drove me crazy with her spending habits. I tried to get her to slow down, but she wouldn't; luckily, the band kept extending my job. Jennifer insisted on phoning her father on his birthday, and I was tired of the way she catered to him so much and got mad at her while she was on the phone. I knew I shouldn't have done that because my instincts told me not to, and ended up suffering. She went into a fit of depression, went home crying, and cut up one of her expensive winter coats with a knife. It also took her a long time to calm down, so to try and make her feel better, I finally agreed to have a phone installed.

I didn't drink very much, so we didn't have much to do on weekends except go to garage sales and flea markets. Liz and Jeremy decided to get married, so we helped Liz buy a dress and bought a new dress for Jennifer and Desiree, the maid of honor. Jennifer felt really sad about it because she thought the closeness between them would never be the same, but Liz said it would always be like that; they would always be close. Jennifer spent a week with them before the wedding to help make preparations, and it was a welcome break for me. Liz also knew there would be a good chance her father wouldn't show up for the wedding, and when the big day came, Henry didn't show up. Later on he said he knew he wouldn't enjoy himself so he didn't go. When the bride was about to throw the garter belt, Jennifer told me to get in there because we're not married; so when the belt was thrown, we all dove for it and were all scrambling around on the floor and a really crazy guy named Franklin Brown caught it.

I was starting to be able to drink more and more without getting drunk because of the stress of what I was going through. We all had a good time at the wedding, and I went back to Enderby the next day. I continued working and they kept extending my job, but the stress I was under was getting unbearable, so I had to keep some beer in the fridge at all times. Eventually it got to the point where my chest would hurt if I even felt the slightest bit of anger, so I went to the doctor and had to go on a special diet for three days then not eat or drink anything after eleven o'clock at night the day before I went for X-rays. I also had to take time off work. The doctor said I had an inflamed esophagus and asked me how I got it, and I said it's because of the way my parents are treating me.

"Do they treat the rest of the family that way?"

"No," I said and was given some medication for chest pains, but I also had to keep a supply of Rolaids at all times because if I felt the slightest bit of anger or worry, my chest would hurt or I would get indigestion. One day, a professional forester, Mark Atherton, from the Canadian Forest Service, stopped by to see how the project was going. Since many of the band members kept to themselves, they just sneered at Graham Go when he tried to tell them something, so Mark got the opinion I couldn't handle a crew very well because I was too passive.

The band hired a registered professional forester (RPF) as a consultant because it was one of the clauses for getting funding for the projects. His name was Bob Robertson, a very good forester with over twenty years' experience. He had worked for the British Columbia Forest Service for many years then went to work for a forestry consulting company, then when the consulting company went bankrupt, he went into business for himself. Bob was very knowledgeable about forestry and showed me things I was doing wrong and how I could do my job better. I asked him to sponsor me as a reference to get into the pupil program with the Association of BC Professional Foresters and he agreed to it right away. I was happy about that because I was anxious to see what I needed to become an RPF.

The band asked me to try and get a woodlot license, but each time I tried, I failed. They asked me to try and get one near an area on their reserve, but after I looked the area over, I advised them not to get one there. They would have too much road to improve, which would be extremely costly for the amount of timber available, and much of the land was labeled environmentally sensitive. Bob took me to a timber sale and showed me how to read the forms; even though the basic sale price was high and the market conditions for lumber were poor, the bid price seemed to skyrocket, and I could see the tension on the faces of the people doing the bidding. I brought this to the attention of the band and advised them to avoid timber sales for now and gave recommendations I thought they could benefit from and avoid spending money unnecessarily. A fellow working with raising cattle told me how they could raise more livestock, so I put it in my weekly report.

It rained heavily that year, so the roads were often muddy. I got a flat tire one day when I wasn't feeling well and didn't tighten the wheel nuts enough; I just got off a muddy road and was heading home for lunch and thought I would take my time. Then I heard a thump, thump, thump, thump and thought it was just mud; so I didn't check it out. And the next thing I knew, I saw my tire rolling down the road. Nathan Kinbasket was driving behind me and saw what happened, so he drove me to a garage and I picked up some more wheel nuts. I couldn't get metric wheel nuts, so I had to get imperial wheel nuts, which have a different thread. I phoned home and told my mother about it and she got scared for me and said, "Baxter! You could have lost your life!"

"You sure like to make it miserable for me!" I replied.

I had to go to the Forest Service in Salmon Arm one day, so Jennifer went along with me. My truck started acting up and I knew it was the carburetor, so I went to a garage and told the mechanic. He refused to listen and did a number of things to the truck before he finally agreed it was the carburetor, so he just charged me for parts, not Labour. He didn't have time to fix it, so I had to bring it to a garage in Enderby. Jennifer missed physiotherapy for her wrist because of that and the physiotherapist automatically thought my truck was an old wreck, so I told her I bought the truck brand-new, but I don't think she believed me.

Now that we had a phone, Henry could call us whenever he wanted, and that's exactly what I didn't want! He always went to the canoe races in Lummi, Washington, and asked Jennifer to go down for the weekend and stay with her mother while he was gone even though Ryan lived right next door to him. He still had control of her, so she was always doing things for him, so we went to Sto:lo Eagle even though I didn't want to. We spent the weekend there and Jennifer wanted to take her mother everywhere because her dad never took her anywhere. I tried to tell her it's not our responsibility, but she was taught to be that way. On Sunday night I kept telling her we have to get going because I had to go to work the next day, but she wouldn't listen; she wanted to wait until her dad got home, and I couldn't leave her there with her father.

We left late at night, and it was a long drive back. We were still driving at the break of day and still had to drive farther, but I got back just in time to go to work. Jennifer slept part of the way back and went to bed as soon as we got back. I worked all day, and when I got home, she was well rested and wanted to go to Vernon to buy a Raggedy Ann doll. I tried to tell her I needed my sleep, but she wouldn't listen and wait until the next day, so we went to Vernon; and when we got there, the store was closed. I had to do all the driving since she couldn't drive a standard truck and had a cup of coffee before driving back. I hated the way she didn't care about me or how I felt, but I knew I couldn't get anyone interested in me no matter how hard I tried. Usually as soon as we would break up, my family would start trying to force me to find someone else; I felt like I just couldn't win for losing!

Jennifer showed me a magazine article titled "Beware of the Helpless!" mentioning people who don't want to do or try anything for themselves because they're afraid of being criticized if they do something wrong. One or both of their parents was always criticizing them as a child; people go along and do everything for them, believing they are doing the right thing, but it just makes the helpless even more helpless. The helpless can be some of the most powerful people because they can get others to do everything for them. After reading it, I just thought, *Jennifer wasn't just criticized for making a mistake. She was beaten and also put down if she did things right. The best thing I can do is keep encouraging her to do things for herself.*

I went out to the woods with Jennifer one day to check out some timber to apply for a woodlot license, and she slowed me down, which was annoying. Then when I got a little ways from the truck, I heard something sneeze; so I looked up, and a mother bear and her cubs went running by. If Jennifer didn't slow me down, they would have run right into me and the mother bear may have attacked me to protect her cubs, so I went running back to the truck as fast as I could! Jennifer was lying back on the seat and heard a thump, thump, thump, thump; and when I jumped in the truck, she asked me, "What happened?" I was too scared to answer at first then told her what happened!

Jennifer's application for the cooking course was accepted and her band was willing to sponsor her, but our mail was sent to Rosedale. Isaac moved when the mood moved him, so by the time we got our mail and contacted Cariboo College, she lost her seat in the course. His stubbornness was very annoying at times. We went back to Sto:lo Eagle one weekend, and Henry wanted Jennifer to see Isadore Tom because her wrist wouldn't heal. He wasn't available on the weekend, so I had to miss a day of work and make up for it on the weekend.

Henry pulled his "I'm too broke!" stunt as usual and wouldn't help pay any expenses, not even for his own coffee. Isadore worked on Jennifer and said, "Two evil spirits were eating away on her wrist. I can cure some things that the regular doctors can't cure and vice versa," then he told some of the stories about people he's healed.

Jennifer's wrist got better for three weeks then got bad again and we started going to Vernon on Friday and Saturday nights to go dancing. I was surprised I was able to drink up to four glasses of beer and still drive home like nothing happened. It rained hard until the end of June that year, then it got incredibly hot. My job kept getting extended, but Jennifer kept on spending because it was her way of trying to make herself feel better. She was getting over her desire to commit suicide though, and I thought I would rather spend than see that happen.

My job was drawing near an end, and Jennifer started talking separation. She had been the only woman in my life, I had been pretty well the only man in her life, and neither of us had much of a teenager's life. I tried to tell her we should stay together until she gets a career of her own; that way she'll be able to look after herself, but she still said no. I felt rather happy about that because her irresponsibility was annoying and my parents were always pressuring me to leave her. My chest still hurt if I wasn't careful, but I could live my own life now. Just before I got laid off, Gary Abbot said, "Terry Hale, your friend from Strathcona Park Lodge, said he was going on a backpacking trip up the Stein Valley and asked if you would like to go along." I really wanted to go badly, but my job wouldn't end in time; and I kept wishing I could go.

One weekend, we went to the coast and were on our way back with Liz, Jeremy, and Gordon. I thought I should check our tire; the new tire was going flat and wasn't good for anything but a spare. Not only that, the wheel nuts were stripping. I didn't know what to do because it was late at night and we were just outside Boston Bar, twenty minutes from Lytton; so I drove slowly to a garage, explained the situation, and asked if he had any wheel nuts.

He just snapped, "I can't do anything for you! We're closed!"

All I asked for was wheel nuts, so needless to say, I never stopped at that station again. I didn't know what to do because I still had to go to Enderby and go to work the next day; then I had an idea! Take the stripped nuts off, use good nuts around from the other tires, then we can at least get as far as Lytton, where Liz and Jeremy live. I called the band the next day and told them what happened. I didn't know what to do because I couldn't get any wheel nuts in Lytton. Then I realized I only needed enough nuts on the wheel to hold it in place and it would be safe until I could get more.

Jennifer stayed in Lytton, and later on, she told me she kept wanting to spend more time there; things were happening just like it said it would in the book on the subconscious mind, so I thought perhaps that's what people are actually doing when they pray. Jennifer decided not to take her birth control pill anymore because she had too much trouble remembering to take it and I felt really depressed about that because I had been trying for years to get her to go on it. I mainly wanted it for her own protection, but now I finally gave up on trying. We bought a couch set at a garage sale, then I was told I would be laid off in two weeks. We were still talking about separating, and Jennifer started getting interested in Ted, the fellow who broke my canopy window. He was living in Enderby now and I thought he was a nice guy.

When I got laid off, Liz said we could store our furniture in their basement, so we moved everything to Lytton; and when we got there, Terry Hale said he postponed his backpacking trip up the Stein because he was sick and asked me if I still wanted to go. I was really excited about the trip and Jennifer wanted to go too, but Liz talked her out of it because her bones were too weak and I would have to carry everything for her. I had kept wishing strongly I could go and got to go; now I thought perhaps the subconscious mind did work that way.

Terry, his coworker and I took four children, aged twelve and thirteen, with us. I enjoyed the trip with the kids, but we went down a day early because of weather conditions. My chest still hurt if I wasn't careful, but I was happy Jennifer was talking separation because of how everyone was treating me. On our way back to Lytton, Terry said he used to work in a group home and the kids there weren't stupid; they just never had to think for themselves. Some of them decided to go into prostitution, so they called in a pimp then robbed the pimp; instead of leaving, they just sat around drinking. The pimp called the cops. They denied everything and the two-by-four board was right there. When I got back to Lytton, I went to the bar and got drunk because I could feel intense stress building up. Jennifer's wrist still wouldn't heal and she developed eczema on her hands, so we went to the doctor and got some medicine, but it didn't seem to do anything for her.

We went back to Rosedale one weekend, and Uncle Ted asked my dad to go on a camping trip with him up Lillooet and Merritt, and my mother told me to go too because I knew the back roads in Lillooet from when I used to work there. I enjoyed trips with Uncle Ted because he always laughed or made a big joke of everything. Jennifer wanted to go too, but she had to register for her upgrading classes. When she went to the outreach worker and applied, he asked her if she was applying because she wanted to attend or because Baxter wanted her to. She said she wanted to attend and had to stand up for herself without me there; it was a small step toward independence but an important one. We all drank the first night of the trip, and Dad was still pressuring me to leave Jennifer. I tried to tell him he shouldn't be mad at me because I didn't want a girlfriend in the first place; he saw the fights Mother and I had. I stopped going home altogether and I almost flunked out at college, but he just wouldn't listen. My chest still hurt if I felt any anger at all and had to keep a supply of Rolaids for indigestion. I could feel Jennifer's moods, and once when she got extremely depressed, Uncle Ted asked, "What's the matter?"

Dad thought I was just doing that for attention, but I knew I couldn't tell him I can feel Jennifer's moods because he would just say "Where's your scientific proof?" then not listen to anything I had to say.

When we got back to Rosedale, I went back to Lytton to see Jennifer. Jeremy's family was jealous of us staying there even though they knew we had done much to help them in the past, and wondered how much we were going to pay for room and board. Jeremy's family didn't seem to do anything for them when they needed help, so Liz and Jeremy asked us for $100 each a month and we had to take her to Kamloops or Lillooet each month to do their grocery shopping.

Jennifer changed her mind about separating and got $70 a week, $140 every two weeks for upgrading since I was unemployed. Then she firmly said, "Your dad gave you free room and board, so I get free room and board!" We went to Sto:lo Eagle one weekend; and when we were in Agassiz, she decided she needed some new pants, so she bought four pairs of jeans then firmly said, "You're supposed to look after me, so you're paying for it!" I was going to tell her I always bought my own clothes, but I decided not to because she never had an opportunity to work and make money like I did.

At first we slept in the basement, and Jennifer called me from upstairs one day and I thought, *Oh no! She wants my attention and I want to read my book!* so I didn't answer her. She called me again and I still didn't answer, so when she went downstairs to look for me, I hid under the bed. Jennifer and Ryan's daughter Shannon went looking for me and wondered where I went. They went upstairs then went back down and couldn't find me, so she thought maybe I went downtown, but my shoes were there.

Then Shannon put her hand over her mouth to suppress her laughter and pointed under the bed. Jennifer said, "What?" and Shannon did it again; then Jennifer saw my legs and knew where I was. She looked down and said, "Ohhh, there you are!" and I started laughing.

Jennifer's upgrading classes were a few miles out of town and transportation was provided, but she wanted me to drive her. I wanted to help her with her studying anyway and was glad she changed her mind about separating because I wanted her to get a career first. My instincts told me I could get interested in someone now and they wouldn't run around on me, but there didn't seem to be anyone interested in me, so I didn't bother looking; and Jennifer also said she was getting over her desire to commit suicide. One of the ladies in the class lived across the road from us and asked to ride with us. It wasn't a problem because we were going that way anyway. Her name was Veronica and she told us about part of her life, how it affected her, and she was getting over the problems of the past. Since she was catching a ride with us, she offered me some books to read. I had already read some of the books she offered, but she loaned me the original writing of the book *Sacajawea*. The author had to rewrite the book because she was charged with plagiarism, and when Veronica found out, she purchased the original volume. Casey stopped by to say hi one day and told me he was attending the alcohol- and drug-treatment center at Round Lake, and I heard some people say he won't be able to stay dry for very long.

My chest healed and my parents eased off on how much they were pressuring me, but they still wanted me to leave Jennifer and refused to listen to anything I had to say. We went back to the coast one weekend, and I found out I was accepted into the pupil program with the Association of BC Professional Foresters. I was really happy about that and my parents were also happy for me, but I was a little disappointed because I may not be able to work on it. I was twelve courses short and may not be able to study because Jennifer always wanted my attention. The tension between me and my family was building up more and more, Jennifer's wrist still wouldn't heal, and her eczema was still bad. I developed a sore throat from having to put up with the way everyone was pressuring me, and David and I still didn't get along. The doctor gave me some medication for my throat, but it wasn't doing any good, so I tried telling my dad about when that guy almost got his head sliced off as he was walking toward the lines and the voice saying "Tell him to stop!" even though it looked perfectly safe. He firmly said he didn't believe that, so I told Tony the same thing, and he didn't believe me either. Now Tony, Isaac, and my dad all wanted me to believe it didn't happen; yet there's no reason why I would make up something like that.

While Jennifer was in classes, I read the book *Sacajewea* and couldn't believe it because Sacajewa's life and personality seemed to parallel Jennifer's life in many ways, it was like I was reading about her in a past life. When Lewis, Clark, and the other explorers came to the west coast, they ended up living mainly on salmon for the winter, so I thought it must have been normal for the Indians because they grew up that way. I asked my parents, and they said they grew up eating mainly salmon; it was hard for them to adjust when we moved to Merritt, and I thought I would like to try eating mainly salmon to see if I could adjust to it.

We decided to visit our clairvoyant one weekend and took Henry along. Phaye said I was in a fight with another fellow over a woman but we would meet again and be friends this time. I told Henry it was just a drunken brawl and he sneak-attacked me then ran off even though I was just joking around. When I called him back to fight, he wouldn't go, and I knew I couldn't catch him. I was mad about it but let it ride because we were both drinking at the time. Then Henry and Jennifer both wondered, "Did it happen back to him twice as hard?"

"Yes. I was drinking in the bar a few months later and saw two guys getting punched out outside the bar. He was standing there grinning away and I thought that's not very nice, so I used that sneak attack as an excuse to pick a fight with him. He knew that as long as I knew what I was doing, nothing would happen, so he said, 'Well, hit me then if it'll make you feel any better!' Just before he said that, my mind went blank, so I hit him and my mind cleared up just in time to see him drop the case of beer he was holding, so I must have hit him hard."

Later on, Auntie Jeanette told me one of her nieces went missing and was found murdered. Everyone knew her husband was involved, but it couldn't be proven in a court of law, so there was nothing they could do about it. Naturally she was upset about it, so I told her, "You don't have to worry because if you sit back and watch, you'll see that when people misbehave, something will happen back to them." Then I told her about that drunken brawl over a woman I got into, and that calmed her down right away.

Before I met Jennifer, my body was very sensitive to alcohol and caffeine, but now I was able to drink coffee and tea all day and night and go to sleep like nothing happened. I went to the doctor again about my throat, but there was nothing he could do but give me antibiotics. Dad said he ran into Henry one day when he was grocery-shopping and he looked much happier than before. Dad thought he was a fool to listen to what I had to say because it's not scientifically proven and even thought I should give up what I learned over the years because it's not scientifically proven. Usually when I went home, Dad would start slamming things around, expressing his anger at me for staying with Jennifer. I kept telling him I didn't want a girlfriend in the first place, but he refused to listen, so finally I said, "Okay! I'll stop coming home then!"

Jennifer continued to study, and I helped her as much as I could. Her eczema finally went away after three and a half months, but her wrist was still very weak. Liz and Jeremy both decided they wanted a baby, so when she got pregnant, we had to drive her to Kamloops for tests.

Christmas was coming, and Jennifer bought many presents as usual, but I didn't have to buy very many because my family just drew names. I went to the doctor for the third time for my throat, but the doctor just told me to relax. It wasn't that I couldn't relax; it was my family continually pressuring me to leave Jennifer. I finally started thinking about giving up on looking after her, but when I did, a fellow driving by gave me an angry look as if to say "*Asshole!!*" We went to the Canadian Tire store in Chilliwack, and the clerk looked at me as if to say "*Asshole!!*" and was ready to start giving me a hard time. Then when I stopped thinking about giving up on her, right away he went to the other extreme and thought, *Such a nice fellow!* I knew full well that if I gave up on looking after Jennifer, she would commit suicide, but looking after her was hard enough even if my parents weren't pressuring me to leave her. We spent Christmas in Sto:lo Eagle again because my parents went to Chetwynd to see their grandson. I didn't want to, but I didn't have a choice.

Chapter 7

1985

After Christmas, Henry asked Jennifer to sell some smoked salmon for him so he could get some money for his truck insurance. We couldn't get very many people in Lytton to buy it because salmon was readily available, so we decided to go to Merritt to sell it on the weekend. We went to the public library one afternoon after class and I ran into Dave Driedger, the school librarian in Merritt in my last year of high school. He remembered me and said he was of the opinion I was the first Native to take my studying seriously. When the weekend came, we went to some of the Indian reserves in Merritt and I ran into many people I went to school with and was surprised some of them still remembered me. Vivian was going with Calf-eye at the time and we ran into them in Merritt and went to the bar with them that night; he was lots of fun. He was born on April 1, April Fools' Day, and called himself king of the fools! They said we could spend the night with them at Vivian's mother's place, but we got a motel room because Jennifer was still too nervous to meet people. We went over and had breakfast with them the next day though and visited some of Vivian's family. We still had more fish to sell, so we went to another reserve and sold the last of it. Henry said we could use some of the money to pay our expenses, but Jennifer sent it all back to him and said she would use her money from upgrading to pay the expenses.

Jennifer had spent much money on Christmas presents and was relying on her money from upgrading to pay it back, but we were getting on each other's nerves where we were staying. No matter how much we tried to work together, we would eventually have to move out; and very often when things start to get too difficult for me, a change comes. Sure enough, when we couldn't stay in Lytton much longer, I got a job in Cache Creek. I would be working with the Indian band there as a technical advisor on a forest-improvement project. The crew worked Monday to Thursday for ten hours a day and took Fridays off. I was told I would be sitting in the canopy of a truck, full of power saws and gas, since they didn't have room for me in the cab; but since we would be driving on icy roads and there was two feet of snow on the ground, I offered to use my own truck even though I was told I wouldn't get paid for it.

Jennifer and I were going to stay in a motel in Cache Creek, but that was too expensive; so we got an apartment in Ashcroft, a few miles away. The job started in February and would end March 31, so I had to buy new boots for work because that would have been easier than driving to Rosedale to get my old ones. I also bought Jennifer some new clothes so she could go to work with me. I enjoyed working with the people there since they were all very outgoing and always joking around. The snow was deep and it was hard for Jennifer to follow me, but being the clown and fast thinker she was, she surprised me and passed me by rolling on top of the snow.

The first time we got Friday, Jennifer and I drove to 100 Mile House to look for more work. I enjoyed the drive and hoped I could at least get a summer job with the sawmill or in forestry, but I was too late; they had already hired their summer crew and there weren't any other places to apply. When we finished the work that was high up, we moved to lower ground because the snow would melt during the day and freeze at night, making it dangerous to drive. We went to Sto:lo Eagle one weekend, and I asked Henry if the Indian Dancers still wanted to initiate him. He said, "No. They just stopped."

Later on I told him, "Your kids were doing everything for you and you would beat them if they made a mistake. They were scared of you, and something was happening back to you for doing it."

I enjoyed working there, but I was beginning to feel incredible stress, so I started to drink and couldn't understand why I was starting to feel that way. Sometimes Jennifer's depression got bad, but she was getting better all the time; then just before the job ended, I was offered a job piling lumber at the sawmill in Lytton, but I still had a week's work left in Cache Creek. The job in Lytton couldn't wait and I never quit a job once I signed on, so I had to turn the job down, but I was lucky I did that because I was offered two job interviews that week. One was with Corrections Canada as a forestry officer, taking inmates out on work release, and the other was with the National Indigenous Development program. The National Indigenous Development program was to get more Natives working with the federal government, our wages would be subsidized by another department, and it would be used as a training program; but I had to quit my job two days early for the interviews though.

I went home and told Jennifer we had to pack up and go back to the coast because I had to be at Elbow Lake Institution at eight thirty the next morning for a job interview. I had another interview the next day in Vancouver, and on Friday, we had to be back in Lytton so she could write her tests for her grade 12. As we were packing, I went outside to throw the garbage out; but when I went out to the bin, the door closed behind me and locked me in. I couldn't climb out because it was covered with chicken wire and the boards were too close together to get my hand through to unlock the gate. It was dark, there was no one around to let me out, and I knew Jennifer would be wondering what happened to me but she would be too scared to go out and see. It was a funny situation, but I had to prepare for the job interview the next day, so I didn't know whether to laugh or get mad; finally I decided I had no choice but to break part of the door so I could get out. The locked opened up after I kicked it a few times, and when I got back, I told Jennifer what happened; she said she was wondering what happened but was too scared to go outside and look.

We hurried to pack our things and clean up the apartment so we could be there on time. I thought we would have to make another trip back for our things, but Jennifer managed to get it all packed in one load. We unloaded our things in Lytton then went to Rosedale that night, got up early, and went to Elbow Lake Institution for the interview the next day. The interview went well and I was accepted on the eligibility list of applicants, but when we got back to Rosedale, my dad got mad at me for using my truck on the job without getting paid for it. I tried to tell him that was better than riding in the canopy of a truck full of gas and power saws over icy roads, but he refused to listen. He even got mad at me for that trip to 100 Mile House and thought Jennifer talked me into it, but the drive was to look for work.

Jennifer and I went to Vancouver the next day for the other interview. Phaye predicted it would be very informal, and it happened exactly the way she said it would happen. Many people were interviewed, but there were very few job openings because of the recession. We went back to Lytton that night so Jennifer could write her exams the next day, and while she was writing them, Liz asked me to take her to Lillooet to do her grocery shopping. When we went out for lunch, I saw Roger Adolph, a fellow I knew, and asked him for a job.

He said, "If you have your RPF, I can give you one." I didn't, so he couldn't give me a job.

After writing her exams, Jennifer and I drove around applying for work wherever I could; but there was just nothing to be found, and many places weren't even taking applications. I was trying to get our bills down before my UIC ran out, but Jennifer kept spending. She filled out a questionnaire on shopping from a magazine one day and answered yes to most of the questions, so it meant she was a compulsive shopper. My parents continued to pressure me to leave her, but I knew I couldn't do it; and she finally told me she would have committed suicide a long time ago, but she hurt me once already and didn't want to do it again. I thought that was a small price for her life. I walked into a bar in Chilliwack one day and saw Auntie Mary Anne, Uncle Percy, and some family friends there and told them Jennifer tried to drown herself when I was working in Lillooet. They must have told my parents because it was around that time they stopped pressuring me to leave her.

Although Jennifer is seven years younger than I, she said when she was growing up, Indians were always made to look like bad people on TV and in the movies. She saw it so often she started to believe it, and I told her that's the way it was when I was growing up too. I got a letter from the BCIT Alumni Association that year asking where I was and they said they would pass it on to my classmates and asked for donations to help other students with their education, but I don't think many people who went through what I went through would answer a letter like that. Most people don't believe in buying friends either, so I wouldn't send anything if I had it.

We still kept driving around, spending a few days in Laughing Raven, Sto:lo Eagle, Rosedale, and Lytton looking for work, I could still feel incredible stress coming on and couldn't understand why, so I started drinking more beer to relieve the stress and keep from going crazy. I wondered why I felt that way because my parents stopped pressuring me to leave Jennifer, yet if I didn't drink, stress would build up to the point it would affect my driving. Jennifer felt the same stress too and we drove around all over looking for work, usually with a bottle of beer in our hand but always staying completely sober when I applied for work. Then when we ran out of money we sold our bottles and bought more beer or used my credit cards. On our way to Lytton, we stopped at a rest stop and Jennifer got sick and started throwing up then started crying, "Don't hurt me, Baxter! Don't hurt me! Don't hurt me!!" After she calmed down, she said, "I was drinking with my dad and got sick. He said, 'What did you get sick and waste all that beer for?' and started kicking me in the legs. Then he just stopped." I didn't say anything, but I think he realized I was just protecting her from him.

Henry only drank on Christmas Day, so when we went there, we didn't drink; we were only there a few days then were almost at each other's throats because of the stress buildup. As I was standing in the yard, Henry was talking to someone when a lady used their driveway to turn around. She smiled at me as she was turning around and Henry just thought, *He wants to get Jennifer a career* and acted like it was nothing.

We left and did our own thing, and I just couldn't understand why I felt so much stress. We went back to Lytton, and when we were there, Dad phoned me up and said I had a check for $900 there. I got it for using my truck in Cache Creek. Then he thought, *I guess that proves what you put out in life is what you get back.* He would say things like that, but if I said it, he would try to drill into my head I was wrong. I went back to Rosedale; and Dad was cooking when I walked in and he was ready to jump up for joy because he knew that if Jennifer committed suicide, because no one would listen, there was no way I could forgive them. I would have gone away for many years and not go back, but unfortunately, much tension had built up between Jennifer and my family before they found out why I stayed with her.

I started reading the novel *Aztec* by Gary Jennings and was very surprised the main character sounded exactly like me; the only difference was he had poor eyesight and I've got very good eyesight. Toward the end of the book, it was all what we learned in history classes in grade 5, so I was going to stop reading it; but when we went to visit Wylma for a tarot-card reading, she told me to read the book right to the end. Wylma said she would be moving soon because their house had been sold; she and her husband didn't know where they were going, but they would leave a forwarding address at the post office. When the logging camp where he was working shut down, he couldn't transfer to another camp because Wylma was in a wheelchair with multiple sclerosis; now they were losing their house and didn't know what they were going to do except take that problem when it came.

Jennifer and I continued to drink heavily for over two months; then finally our stress level started going down. One evening we went to a bar in Agassiz for a few beers and ran into Tom Frey, a fellow I went to BCIT with. He suggested I go to the Forest Service and get a list of spacing contractors and apply for a job because they might be happy to hire an Indian forest technician with my experience. When I went to the forestry office the next day, Alan Bond, another fellow I went to BCIT with, was there and suggested I put my name in for firefighting. I didn't expect to get anything out of it, but I put my name in anyway. I continued looking for work and couldn't find anything at all but slowed down on how much I was drinking and was getting concerned because I owed a lot of money and my UIC wasn't going to last much longer. There was a large fire in the Kootenays, and I almost felt like going over there to look for work, but that would be a long way to travel to take a chance on not getting a job. It was a bad year for forest fires because of the hot, dry weather.

Liz bought Henry a birthday present that year; and as he was opening it, he said rather sarcastically, "She's the only one who cares!"

I didn't say anything but thought to myself, *Did you ever do anything for your kids on their birthday? They learned from you!* She bought him a plaque that said, "Anyone can be a father. It takes someone special to be a dad." I didn't think it was appropriate, but it wasn't up to me to decide.

When I was in Rosedale one day, I loaned Terri Dargatz two of my books on the subconscious mind. Dad was sitting there and wondered, "Where's your scientific proof?"

I told Terri, "I would like to hear a psychologist's or psychiatrist's opinion on those books. They're trained in that field and make a living at it," but Dad just shook his head and disagreed.

Then I started withdrawing again because I knew I couldn't get anyone interested in me no matter how hard I tried. Jennifer's depression caused her to spend to make herself feel better, and there didn't seem to be anything I could do about it. A lady I took an interest in many years earlier could see I was withdrawing again and tried to stop me, but anger was building up inside me, so it was hard not to withdraw. When my UIC check went in and I deposited $200 in the bank in Lytton to wait for my Visa bill to go in and sent out my UIC cards again, Liz was due to have her baby, so we went to visit her at Ashcroft Hospital and she had a baby boy and they named him Allan after Jeremy's father. After visiting her in Ashcroft, Jeremy went back with us to Lytton and started drinking again. I was tired and wanted to spend the night in Lytton, but we didn't want to be around him when he was drinking and Jennifer said she had a feeling we should go back to the coast, so we went back.

I was waiting for my Visa bill to go in, but I got called out firefighting the day after we got back to Rosedale, so I was lucky I listened to Jennifer's hunch. I had kept wishing I could put $400 down on my Visa account that month and thought, *Perhaps now's my chance!* Jennifer also bought a necklace that I was supposed to pay off in two months and I didn't know how I was going to do it. I was having enough trouble trying to get my bills down; now I kept saying "I hope it lasts a week!"

I heard stories of people working on fires and not getting anything to eat for a long time, so I stuffed myself as I rushed to the airport. When I got there, there were a number of people waiting to go to work and all we did was fly out to a logging camp at the end of Harrison Lake. Then we ate supper, had a meeting on who would be a crew boss, were all assigned to a crew, then we went to bed. The next day we were all taught helicopter safety then flew out to the fire on helicopters. I enjoyed working there, but I had to leave Jennifer behind and knew she would be depressed because I was gone.

We almost got the fire under control on the second day, but all the pumps stopped working, one right after the other, within half hour of each other. The next day was spent hosing down a large area across the gullies on each side of the fire; then in the afternoon, a back fire was lit and it jumped the guard. Then to try and steer the fire, a broadcast burn was lit, so I knew I would have a job for some time to come. I worked for two days as a firefighter, two days as a pump operator, then was promoted to crew boss. Virgil Diamond, a good friend of mine, was also working there as a crew boss.

One night after work, a bunch of us were having coffee in the cafeteria and there was one heavyset fellow who said he was an Indian from Ontario, but I didn't believe him until he showed me his Indian status card. He told us he wanted three women at once one night but he had to get them drunk enough to go along with it, and I thought it was funny the way he described drinking them B-52s. Then he brought them up to his room, but just before he got to his room, his mind went blank. Everyone burst out laughing, and one crew boss who was always cracking jokes, kept saying to him, "How do you know anything happened?"

Then he said, "That was okay. The chambermaid came in and gave me a blow job the next day."

I worked for fourteen days then took two days off, put $400 from my UIC check on my Visa bill, and left $200 in my account in Lytton; now I had over $300 in that account, which I could save for emergency purposes. When I went out, I paid bills, went to the bars, and visited Jennifer and my family. We worked long hours, so I was happy to take two days off and left Jennifer $100 spending money when I went back to camp. Some people in camp thought I was depressed, but Jennifer was depressed because I was gone and I could feel her moods and wished I could get her a job there, but her wrist was too weak. The days were long and we were working long hours, but it was starting to slow down; and at the fire, I ran into Charles, the Native fellow I was timber-cruising with for DIA. He was from a reserve near the logging camp, so I asked him if the fire was on Indian reserve and he said, "Are you kidding? Most Indian reserves are so tiny!"

I worked for thirteen days this time and took two days off, and there were many fires in British Columbia that year, but I stayed right where I was because I had the comforts of a logging camp and knew Jennifer was safe. I thought Jennifer would be happy to see me when I got back, but she was depressed because she didn't like me only going home for two days then going back again. She thought it would have been better if I either stayed away or stayed home. She got so depressed she lost her appetite, and when she went to the A&W, she could only eat ½ a teen burger.

I didn't like seeing her depressed like that, but there weren't any other jobs available and I was hoping that if I stayed on, I may be able to get a job with the British Columbia Forest Service. One fellow with the Forest Service, Pat Hayes, was really happy with my work; and when he got back to Duncan, he recommended to DIA that they hire me if a job opening ever came up. But unfortunately, the government was cutting back on spending. I stayed in town for two days then went back to camp, and Jennifer kept wishing it would rain so I would go home, but I was just happy to be working because I couldn't find anything else. Although the excitement had died down and many people were quitting, I was just happy to have a job. It rained rather hard one night, and the next day, twenty-two people quit, but a fellow from the Forest Service said it wouldn't have much effect on the fire because it takes a great deal of water to get down into the hot spots. Some people worked three weeks straight then quit, but I preferred to pace myself to last the whole summer. There's a restaurant in Hope that served very good Chinese food, so I thought I would like to take my mother there some time and kept picturing it in my mind without realizing what I was doing.

I worked for two weeks again and the job was winding down. We should have had another month of work left, but the British Columbia government had overspent their firefighting budget, and money from constructing the Coquihalla Highway was being used for fires. Since I was first in seniority, I was told I couldn't take any more breaks. I either had to quit or stay until the end. I had already worked two weeks and was ready for a break and knew if I kept on working, I might have an accident from overwork, so I thought I might as well quit. When I got back to town, I caught a ride to the forestry office in Rosedale; the people I went with went to the bar for a few beers, then they gave me a ride home. Jennifer was in Lytton visiting Liz and Jeremy, so I phoned her and told her I'm back and wasn't expected to go back to camp.

Jennifer caught the bus back, and around five o'clock, she phoned me from Hope and said she was at the police station because she got arrested. I didn't believe her at first and she couldn't really understand or explain why she got arrested and a cop said he couldn't say anything over the phone. I couldn't believe she got arrested, so my mother had to drive me to Hope to pick her up because I had been drinking. We met Jennifer at the bus depot then went for Chinese food. Jennifer said some girl stole $1,000 from her sister-in-law and she got arrested because the police thought she may have been an accomplice but if that didn't happen I couldn't have taken my mother for Chinese food in Hope.

We went back to Rosedale and I thought I would have to start looking for another job, but the next day, the Forest Service called and asked if I wanted to go back to work. One of the crew bosses was offered a job as a warehouse man and quit and they wanted me back because I knew the area and all the people. Jennifer said she had a feeling I was going to be going back to camp; there was only a week's work left, but I went anyway. The Forest Service was really happy because I would be saving them lots of money. I worked on the fire for seven more days and most of it was gathering equipment and checking a few hot spots; and on the last day of work, we checked the tool boxes, counted the equipment, then drove back to Rosedale. I was hoping the Forest Service would be happy with my work and offer me a job, but no such luck; there just weren't any jobs available. Some job openings came up in various locations in British Columbia with the Forest Service, so I applied for every one of them and didn't get a single interview. It was very depressing because I had worked so hard to get a career and couldn't get a job anywhere.

After firefighting was over, we made a trip to Salmon Arm to visit Phaye, and I had set money aside in case I had to move to another job. Jennifer started spending again because of her depression, and I had to close down my home-ownership savings plan that year and was determined not to touch it, so I opened a new bank account to deposit it in. I didn't have any insurable work weeks, so I ended up moving back to Rosedale again. We took Henry with us to see Phaye, and he pulled his flat-broke stunt again; he never ever offered to pay anything, and as long as Jennifer was willing to spend our money on him, he took it, no matter how angry I was getting. We treated him to many things and he never ever paid a single cent of the expenses, not even to tip the waitresses if we went out for something to eat. Jennifer started looking very happy now, but I knew that was only on the surface; underneath she was still extremely depressed. People thought she was over her depression, but I knew she was far from it. Henry said he was the one who broke her depression, but he was the one who caused it and Ryan said he could have broken her depression, but he was drinking too much. He sometimes asked me what she had to be depressed about, and neither of them knew how hard it was just to take her that far.

I ran into a friend's wife in the grocery store one day and we told her about the stress we went through in the springtime and she said it's because I was used to working but then I couldn't find any work. I kept applying for jobs and looking for work and didn't have any luck at all; now my only alternative was to go back to college. I applied for Jennifer and me to get into college in Chilliwack and for funding from our bands. We both got accepted in the college and our funding was approved. I wanted to try and get into UBC and become a registered professional forester.

Henry always dropped everything for a week in the fall to go hunting. Not many people would go with him, so he went with Andrew that year; and when he got back, he said they shot two moose but he didn't have them with him. Hunters were only allowed to shoot immature bull moose that year, but he and Andrew shot a full-grown bull and cow moose and got caught by a game warden. Henry said, "They're going to do a ballistics test on my gun and they'll find out it was me who shot the moose," so I immediately told him, "I'm not going to help you! You knew the chance you were taking! You knew something would happen back to you for misbehaving!"

I continued looking after Jennifer and looking for work, but I didn't have any luck with anything and started getting depressed and withdrawn; then eventually I had walls around myself and had a hard time not feeling that way. I started taking Jennifer to a drop-in education class to learn more math, and things seemed to be getting worse and worse; everything seemed so hopeless. We went to Sto:lo Eagle one weekend, and the weather was getting cold and windy. Jennifer was in a bad mood and said to me, "Get out of my sight!" I didn't do anything to aggravate her, so Henry Jr. and I went duck hunting. We went to Weaver Creek then Seabird Island Indian Reserve. I was having so much fun I didn't want to stop and didn't realize how late it was getting, so when it started getting dark, we decided we better go back. Just before we got to the bridge over the Sto:lo Eagle River, we passed Henry and stopped to see where he was going. He said Jennifer got scared for us and asked him to go looking for us, and when we got back, she said she didn't mean for us to stay away that long.

I was always close to one of my aunts because we were always visiting her when we were growing up. Her oldest child, Eddie Dale, and I grew up together and he usually went to Merritt and spent the summer with us; he was almost like a brother to me, but we drifted apart as we got older. She passed away that fall, and when we went to her funeral, I was one of the pallbearers. I always wanted to see a full-contact karate tournament but decided to give the money to the funeral instead; it wasn't much, but it was all we had. There was a dinner after the funeral and a family gathering at her house. I had a feeling something wasn't right, so I said, "Why do young people always get blamed when things go wrong?"

Dad got mad and thought, *Oh no! Not that again!*

Auntie Pat said, "Young people do come up with good ideas and opinions." But something just didn't seem right to me.

Christmas came and Jennifer overspent as usual. I tried to get her not to spend so much, but she wouldn't listen and would just say, "I don't mind suffering." But it was I who always suffered. She bought many gifts, so most of the money she would get for going to college was spent. I wanted her to take driving lessons, but she couldn't because she had already spent her money. Then right after Christmas, Liz called and asked us to go up there because Allan was sick and in the hospital in Kamloops. She wanted us to go up there and drive them to Kamloops to visit him, but luckily I had a little over $300 at the bank in Lytton for emergencies.

We went to Lytton and took Liz and Jeremy to Kamloops to visit Allan; after visiting him, Liz decided to go for Chinese food, so we went to a Chinese buffet. After dinner, Liz said she wanted me to pay for it; so later on I told her that if she wanted me to pay for dinner, she let me know when the bank is open. I didn't mind paying for it, but I was trying to get my Visa bill down. We made several trips to Kamloops; then Jennifer decided she wanted a turkey, so I bought a small one because it was all we could afford. After Allan got better and went home, Liz felt guilty about spending all our money and wondered how she could pay us back, so I told her not to worry about it because that was an emergency and that's what the money was there for.

The day before we were ready to go back to Rosedale, Jeremy's niece went over to visit and asked Jennifer and me to go to the bar with her. We went down the bar for a little while then went to visit some of her friends, had a few more beers there, then I fell asleep on the couch. When I woke up, she had her head on my lap; so I moved over, and she put her head on my lap again. I had spent many years trying to get Jennifer a career, and now she's starting college, so I didn't want to jeopardize it or give up now. That would have made all those years of trying to help her do something for herself a waste of time, so I didn't do anything.

Chapter 8

1986

Jennifer and I both started college. She was taking college preparation courses and I was taking sciences. Most of her classes were during the day, and two of my classes were at night from seven o'clock to ten o'clock. One of the night classes was in Abbotsford, so we had to drive there two nights a week. We started classes at eight thirty in the morning and didn't get home until ten thirty in the evening, and Jennifer wanted me to sit with her in her classes; but the instructor, Theresa Neel, wouldn't let me. I was happy about that because it gave me time to do my own studying and I wanted her to become more independent. Jennifer took a math course even though she knew she wasn't very good at math, but luckily, that instructor let me sit beside her and be her tutor. She wrote her first exam and passed it but didn't do very good, got discouraged, and wanted to give up after she wrote her second test; so I told her if she didn't do very good, she could drop the course. But surprisingly, her marks went up. Jennifer also took an English course where she had to write an essay a week, and I helped her with the writing and encouraged her to keep trying when she wanted to give up. Her English teacher thought that was very good of me and eventually called me tutor extraordinaire, which made me feel good about trying to help her.

I had tried to take chemistry in high school and college, but nothing seemed to work out; so this was my first chance to take chemistry, and I couldn't believe how simple it was. I only studied a little bit before the exams and averaged 90 percent. I could have done better, but I had to help Jennifer with her studying even though she always acted like I wasn't important and my needs and responsibilities weren't important. If I wanted to do something for my interests, it didn't matter; we always had to cater to her father first. Henry's house was being renovated, so we helped him move his things out one weekend. I wanted to do my studying, but I knew I had to go along with helping her father because she would have found a way to get her own way or she would have stressed me out to the point where I couldn't do any studying. She told Henry we bought a turkey for Liz and Jeremy, and he got mad because he thought we should have bought him one too and actually believed he did a whole lot for us and all the things we did for him were nothing.

Henry smoked salmon with his brother Junior that year. Junior was an Indian Dancer who enjoyed drinking and gave most of the smoked salmon to the Indian Dancers for their ceremonies. Henry was really mad about that but he never let it show in front of me and knew I had money in my checking account because I had my bank statements sent to Sto:lo Eagle and was jealous of how much I had saved. He said, "How many thousands have you got in there now?"

"Not nearly enough!" I replied and tried to tell him I was saving it to buy a home, but he wouldn't listen. I was getting mad at my family again because they always tried to tell me finding a girlfriend would take my mind off my studies. I kept telling them all it ever got me were setbacks, and when I found someone, she slowed me down and interfered with my responsibilities; then they blamed me for things going wrong. Now I was being slowed down again and no one seemed to care; the tension between me and my family was increasing.

Jennifer's math teacher didn't believe she was going to make it through the course at first and treated her that way, but her marks kept getting better and better; and at the beginning of the semester, he said he had a PhD in math and math makes you think logically. It snowed quite hard one day and we couldn't get the truck started, so my dad had to give us a jump start. Jennifer was a half hour late for her exam, and when everyone left, the instructor yelled, "Jennifer! Do I have to get my sleeping bag?"

Jennifer almost started crying, and I felt like saying, "It's not our fault it snowed and we couldn't get our truck started! If math is supposed to make you think logically, it doesn't look like it made you think logically!" I wanted to say it but thought he would kick me out and not let me tutor her anymore.

Classes, studying, travelling, and helping Jennifer with her studies were taking their toll on me; but when I wanted to give up, her mother was right there encouraging me to hang in there. One afternoon we went off to an empty room to study and were there for several hours working on her math. It was getting hard on me and she was getting cranky and jabbed at me with her pencil when she couldn't understand something; then I finally decided to take a break and go for a cup of coffee. I felt like giving up again, and as I was thinking of giving up, the song "Against All Odds" by Phil Collins came on the radio. That song was word for word what Jennifer and I went through; I was the only one who really knew her at all. Take a look at her now; if I hadn't been there to look after her, all that would be left is the memory of her face. There would have been an empty space. For me to wait for her to come back was against all odds, but that's the chance she had to take. I was the only one who believed in her and tried to help her do something with her life, so I knew I couldn't give up after all we've been through.

Jennifer's marks in math kept going up and finally peaked at 96 percent on her exam; she couldn't believe it and was so ecstatic. In her English class, they had to write one long essay, and the teacher was going to keep the two best essays. The essays were marked, sent back for rewriting, then marked again; and the teacher kept Jennifer's because it was one of the best. In her other class, everyone thought she had great potential for public speaking after each student gave a presentation, and I thought I had been through a lot and could write a book on my life. Jennifer was starting to feel better about herself and I was starting to come out of my shell and no longer had a wall around myself, then things started to go wrong. Angie, David's girlfriend, was cut off funding for postsecondary education and was pregnant at the same time. David's car broke down and he wasn't making much money at work, so they had no choice but to move back to Rosedale with our parents. Isaac was living there and he never did any housework; and Francie, my cousin whose mother just passed away recently, was also staying there. When David and Angie moved back home, there was eight people living there. Jennifer and I were the busiest ones there, yet we still did the most housework.

This was getting Jennifer down again and she started getting depressed, so her marks started going down; she also suffered from chronic envy, but I didn't realize it was that bad. Henry always talked highly of other children, but nothing his kids ever did for him was enough; he always called them down and criticized them, and now he was telling them they were obligated to him because he looked after them when they weren't old enough to look after themselves and still sometimes beat them or hit them. Henry told Jennifer to apply for a house on the Sto:lo Eagle reserve, and since she was always too scared to say no to him, we applied; but I wasn't worried because I thought it would take four or five years to get a house.

I took Canadian history for one of my classes since I couldn't get all the courses I wanted, and there were some questions I wanted to ask the instructor when it became time for the lecture on WWII but ended up missing that class because I had to bring Henry's TV to the repair shop. Jennifer offered to do it, and if I didn't go along with it, she would have done something to interfere with my studies or not bother with her own. I caught the teacher after class but only got to ask him about one issue. "Canada did their share of fighting in WWII?"

"Yes. We also helped out economically too."

"On the fortieth anniversary of the D-day invasion, the *Province* newspaper said what each country was contributing. When it came to Canada, it said, Canada—coffee and doughnuts. Why would they print that?"

"I don't know."

I didn't get to ask him how the Allies treated their prisoners of war yet we often hear of how the enemy treated their prisoners of war. Would he be willing to bet his life savings that the Allies weren't guilty of atrocities too? Many things were kept secret and many things probably still are.

Jennifer and I bought Henry Jr. a coat just before our classes ended, and when we gave it to him, he said, "Good! Now I won't have to freeze next winter." His father could have bought him a coat, but he just wanted everything for himself. The semester was almost over and Jennifer's depression was getting extreme, so we went to the doctor. He knew her history of depression, so he had her admitted to the psychiatric ward and I went to see Theresa Neel. Theresa was on the phone and didn't know I was just outside and she was talking about when she wouldn't let me sit in the class with Jennifer, Jennifer started opening up and had such a potential for public speaking and such a sense of humor.

I went to one of the student counsellors who help guide students with their career goals and what courses they would need and heard her talking to the student ahead of me. She had lots to say to him about a career in chemistry, but when I got in, I told her I was very good at chemistry and wondered what kind of career I could get. She just said "I don't know" and pretended her mind went blank. She was a blond girl about my age.

Jennifer signed herself out of the psychiatric ward to write her final exams, but it wasn't very long and she went back in again; and while she was in there, Dr. Ryan, a psychologist, asked her if she hated her mother. I knew he asked her that because sometimes when a child is badly abused by one parent, they hate the other parent for not protecting them, but Jennifer said she didn't hate her mother.

I was going to have almost no income soon and I didn't know what I was going to do. I didn't get taxed while firefighting, so I owed the Internal Revenue Service money, and jobs were hard to get. I went to Vancouver for a job interview with DIA, and the job was in Hazelton; it didn't pay very much, and I wouldn't be able to take Jennifer with me. I told her I probably wouldn't take it if it was offered, but the hospital staff told her she shouldn't hold me back like that, so she told me I could go if I got the job.

I applied for more funding to go back to college in the fall, but there was a new lady in charge of education who told me I couldn't go back because I had used up all my student months and wasn't eligible for any more funding. I tried to tell her I wasted my first two years at college because DIA tried to make us give up and failed two times at BCIT for medical reasons, but she didn't seem to listen. Luckily, I knew someone above her in Administration that I used to play soccer with, a Native fellow who knew what the Indians went through, so I phoned him and he told me to go down for a meeting with him. I was offered the job with DIA but kept telling myself, "I don't want to go!" It didn't pay very much and I didn't want to leave Jennifer behind in her condition; then just before I was supposed to go, I got called to Richmond for a job interview with the British Columbia Forest Service. If I got the job, it could turn permanent, so I turned down the job with DIA and arranged to meet with my friend in Administration on the day of the interview so I wouldn't have to make two trips to Vancouver. When I met him, he told me where to apply and on what grounds then said, "You don't know me."

"Sure thing!" I replied.

I thought I was well prepared for the interview, but I failed it miserably because there were many questions I didn't know they would ask. Of all the times I applied when job openings came up, this was the first time I even got an interview. Now I was even more concerned about going back to college because I wanted my RPF, then made out a letter and sent a copy to various people in DIA administration, and my application was accepted before I even sent a copy to the lady who tried to cut me off.

Jennifer went out of the psychiatric ward again for a few days then went back in again. I got depressed, so I bought a case of beer and went to visit Terri Dargatz and no one knew where I was and Dad said someone called for a forest technician, so I missed the job. Everything seemed so hopeless. I went to visit Jennifer in the hospital one day and stayed for a long time. I was hungry, but all I could afford was a cup of coffee. I didn't even ask for help and the nurses were ready to buy me lunch, but I just thought, *I'm overweight, so it won't hurt to miss a meal.* Then I didn't pay my income tax until the last day because I found a tax loophole and used it to defer paying my taxes. I knew I may have to pay it eventually, but at least not right now.

Jennifer wanted me to take Henry to see Phaye again, but I told her we couldn't afford it, so she told me to ask for a reading and we could pay for it later. Henry and I went to see Phaye and he pretended he was flat broke as usual and wouldn't help pay for the trip at all. I was tired of him doing that to us, but Jennifer was always taught to treat him that way and he always went along with it. When Jennifer got out of the psychiatric ward, the staff told her she had the mind of an eight-year-old and would have to get over her problems from the past or she would stay that way for the rest of her life.

I continued looking for work and couldn't find anything at all; then when we were in a tobacco shop one day, we bought a newspaper from Edmonton, Alberta, and Winnipeg, Manitoba. There was an ad for a job with Indian Forestry Development in Kenora, Ontario, so I applied for it. I thought I've got nothing to lose by applying and didn't even expect to get an answer, but surprisingly I got a letter back asking me to go to Kenora for an interview. I was to keep all my receipts for my expenses because I would be reimbursed, so I was really happy about that because not only did I have a chance of getting a job, I could also move away from our families. I was doing my best not to touch my home-ownership savings, but now I felt I had to; and if I got the job, it would be worthwhile. Luckily, Greyhound bus lines had a special deal that year: people could go anywhere in Canada for $99, so Jennifer and I were both able to go.

Jennifer was still seeing a social worker at the hospital for counselling and she told Jennifer she wasn't obligated to her father for raising her as a child because he chose the responsibility of raising a family. She also told Jennifer we shouldn't help Henry with his court case for shooting those two moose illegally because that would encourage him to do it again and rely on us to rescue him. He knew the chances he was taking and should suffer the consequences of his actions.

It was our first trip across Canada and I enjoyed it even though we were on the bus for two days and two nights. It was a long bus ride, but it was an opportunity to see more of Canada. When we got to Kenora, I phoned Meredith in Dryden, the next town past Kenora. Kirby and Meredith had left Merritt and moved to Dryden, Ontario. I told Meredith we were in Kenora for a job interview, so she asked if we were going to go over and visit. I said we would after the interview.

I went for the interview the next day and it seemed to go quite well; and I was asked off the record what I thought Indian self-government meant to me, but I didn't know anything about it. I knew DIA tried to hold us back when we tried to do something for ourselves and made it look like we have everything given to us on a silver platter, which was probably more than most people knew about how the Indians of Canada were treated. We were told we were rated on a point system and the person who scored the most points would get the job; then I was told I got the interview because of my work experience, not my ethnic background. Two days later, I called them back to see how I did and I almost got the job but missed by one or two points.

After the interview, we went to Dryden to visit Kirby and Meredith and they were happy to see us. When I got there, I was surprised to see a fellow who looked just like Meredith's brother Chester and ran into people I went to elementary school with in Merritt. We visited Kirby and Meredith for a week because my family was always close to them. Dad taught Kirby to be a professional tree faller and Meredith sometimes stayed with us when we were growing up, so she was more like a sister than a cousin. We all went to town one day, and as we were standing around on the street, some people were looking at me like

I was too lazy to go to work even though the country was in a deep recession and jobs were very hard to get.

Kirby was in the business of catching minnows for tourists who used them as bait for sport fishing, so I helped him while I was there; it was lots of fun and seemed like a good way to make a living. Kirby seemed to be doing quite well, but he said it was quite competitive and the resort business was even more competitive, but after a week, we had to leave. I told Kirby that when we went to visit them in Merritt, Jennifer got so nervous she peed in her pants; now her nerves were starting to get bad again, so we had to leave. We tried to go back through Lethbridge so we could visit Brenda and Alvin, but the clerk said we couldn't go that way. We went back on the bus again and enjoyed the trip, but I wouldn't want to do it that way too often; and when we got back to Rosedale, I missed a call to a forest fire by one day. Jennifer's depression was getting bad again, so we went to the doctor and there was nothing we could do about it. I couldn't find work anywhere and my family was driving her crazy. Expo '86 was in Vancouver and we couldn't afford to go.

One of my cousins in Bellingham, Washington, was getting married, and we were invited to the wedding; so I told my uncle we could go to the wedding, but we didn't have any money to buy them a gift. But he said, "That's all right! Come down anyway!" It was the second week of June, the same weekend as the annual canoe races in Lummi, Washington; but just as we were leaving, Geraldine phoned and asked us to go visit her. We had stopped visiting her altogether because Jennifer couldn't take the way she was always putting her down; we stopped off in Laughing Raven for half an hour but told her we were on our way to Bellingham for a wedding and didn't have the money to go and visit that's why we didn't go around.

She said, "You could afford to go to Ontario and you couldn't come and visit us!" When we left, she said, "See you next year!" and Amanda, her ten-year-old daughter, said the same thing.

I told Jennifer, "We may not see them until next year. When we go back to college, we probably won't have time to visit them."

"Yeah! You're right!"

We went to the wedding and had a good time with my relatives, and when we were talking to some of the people, one of them stereotyped me because I was young; and Dad told him, "Don't criticize him. He has a lot of get-up-and-go." I stood up for someone like that before, and now I was noticing that everything I was doing in life was happening back to me, even trivial things.

The day after the wedding, we went to the canoe races. Henry always enjoyed travelling to the canoe races and Jennifer's brothers were competing in the races, and I was getting extremely depressed and withdrawn because of the way things were going. Now it was even hard for me to get excited by anyone; even if a model or someone outstandingly beautiful walked by, it would have been hard for me to get excited. I often noticed ladies like that usually wouldn't go out with me if they never had anyone, so I usually gave up without trying. I studied Indian spiritualism and enjoyed reading books on Indian medicine men and met one of Jennifer's uncles down there and told him, "I'm going through a very hard time right now. Everything seems to be going wrong."

Her uncle was an Indian Dancer, knowledgeable about Indian spiritual values and traditions and studied Indian medicines as a hobby and kept telling me, "On July 6th, things will pick up for you."

I said, "Oh yeah." July 6 was three weeks away and seemed like a long time to wait.

We went back to Rosedale after the wedding, and Jennifer's depression seemed to get worse, but there was nothing I could do about it. We went to the doctor again and he said, "Girl! What are we going to do for you? Is it possible to transfer to another reserve?"

There was nothing I could do but stay with her and support her. I got called out firefighting for one day and found out I missed two weeks of work. I wished I could have worked there right from the start, but it may have been too hard on Jennifer for me to go away like that. On the fire, the sector boss said he worked for years in a shake mill and had four kids, then when the recession came, everything he had worked for all his life slowly slipped away. He sent two people to check out a hot spot, and as we were driving away, he noticed one fellow standing around. When we drove back, he was still standing around; and I forgot what he called him, but we both laughed. Then I told him about two fellows I was firefighting with at the end of Harrison Lake last year. The Forest Service hired a helicopter from Global BC news to fly the crew to work, and one fellow said to his friend, "If they start shooting the camera, you better hide because it would be a shock to everyone's system to see cartoons on at lunchtime."

The sector boss said, "What did he say?" so I repeated it and we both laughed.

I earned $100 that day and it helped a little bit with our bills, but we owed too much money, so we couldn't afford to move away. I had applied to many forest companies and tribal councils for summer employment, and most places didn't even reply. I didn't apply to Carrier Sekani Tribal Council in Fort St. James though because I heard a band member there took forestry at the college in Prince George, so I didn't think I had a ghost of a chance of getting a job there. I called Dave Walkem one day and he suggested I apply at Fort St. James because they have a tree farm license (TFL) there; so I applied rather reluctantly, totally expecting not to even get an answer.

Finally the tension between Jennifer and my family got to be too much for her, so she asked Liz if we could move in with them. We didn't have any money, but we could pay her later. Luckily, Liz said it was all right and let us move in with them. We gave Liz what we could afford at the time, and she asked us to take her to Chilliwack to do her grocery shopping. After we got back to Lytton, we babysat Allan while Liz and Jeremy went to work. There wasn't any work in Lytton, so I phoned home every day to see if I got any calls. We went with Allan to a restaurant just outside town along the highway one day for a cup of coffee; and I asked the waitress, who was also the owner, if they needed any workers. She just laughed and said, "No, we don't need any workers."

There was a white couple sitting there who appeared to be in their late forties or early fifties, and the husband thought to his wife, *He had a degree and can't even get a job washing dishes* and felt bad that I was in such an unfortunate position.

Before we moved to Lytton, Liz got involved with a Christian religious group who really took their religion to extremes and were predicting the end of the world was coming. They preached that if something wasn't of the Bible, it was of the devil: music, short-sleeved shirts, used clothing, anything carved or beaded, a deck of cards, dice. Even the children's game of Snakes and Ladders was of the devil because it had dice. You had to believe in God and Jesus Christ or be condemned. Liz told us what she was like before she joined the religious group. When she was happy, she was really, really happy. When she was depressed, she was extremely depressed, and the religious group was what saved her. Liz didn't admit it, but I thought it was her husband's drinking that drove her to that extreme. Now she was totally against drinking and wouldn't allow any liquor or anyone who had been drinking into her house, so I told Liz she didn't realize it but she had manic depression. When people go from extreme happiness to extreme depression, they're manic-depressive and should go for help before it's too late; people may end up committing suicide when they get depressed. She said people can do crazy things when they're on a high too; she gave away many things, even her money when they had bills to pay.

Not long after we moved to Lytton, I called home and Dad said Thomas, from Fort St. James, called for me. He wanted to go on holiday and needed someone to coordinate their tree planting, so as soon as I heard that, I rushed to call him back. If there was a job available, I wanted to get it before someone else got it, so I called him and he told me to go up right away. Jennifer and I went back to Chilliwack to pack up then went back as far as Lytton because it was a long drive to Fort St. James, and I told Jennifer I wanted to leave early the next day because it was a long drive up there. Jennifer took her time leaving the next day because she wanted to spend more time with Allan, so we didn't leave until after eleven o'clock and I got mad at her because she always treated me like I wasn't important. But it was July 6 and things were picking up for us just like her uncle said it would. On our way, we saw an old lady hitchhiking to Clinton, so we picked her up. We didn't know she stank the way she did, so we rushed to Clinton so we could drop her off. Then we rushed to 100 Mile House to get some Lysol spray to get rid of the smell of urine.

Fort St. James is a small town north of Prince George and I knew it would be late when we got there, so I drove as fast as I could without getting a speeding ticket. Thomas said they would have a place for us to stay when we got there, so I phoned him, and he told me where to go and ask. We were to go to Tachie Village, but the house wouldn't be available for a few days. We drove to the edge of town and asked at a house for directions, and the lady told us where to go but that she had never been out there. It was dark as we were driving out of the woods, and it seemed like there wouldn't be any houses out there because it was more like a forest road. When we got to Tachie Village, I went to a log house to see where Jennifer and I were to stay; the lady there looked familiar, and I thought I saw her somewhere before. There were two young fellows rooming together in a house and they let us stay with them until our house was available. One of them was missing his front teeth, so I had to listen closely to understand him. Jennifer noticed right away that the people there seemed to talk a little differently than down south.

I went to the office the next day and was introduced to everyone there, and the people up there seemed pretty nice and easy to talk to. I was also shown their TFL and where I would be working. I was to coordinate delivery with production, make sure the trees were properly stored, supervise the plot checker, and help deliver trees to the crew. The tribal council held a general assembly there for several days, and I saw Linda Pierre there, the first time I saw her in ten years. It never dawned on me until then that she was Thomas's sister. Linda was staying in the same apartment building as my friends were ten years earlier when I was going to college. At that time she was the nicest-looking Native girl I had ever met; after she moved back to Fort St. James, I never heard anything about her and even forgot about her. She was married now, had changed much over the years, and wondered why I never ever tried for her.

I started organizing everything for the tree planting to start and for a band member to deliver some of the trees. Paul Klotz, the RPF working for the company, told me I was managing a $100,000 contract; but the contract wasn't going to start right away, so I did other fieldwork. I went out to paint the boundary for an area to be logged one day, and the insects and devil's club were so thick it almost drove me crazy; and when I got out of the bush, Paul told me I should have worked harder.

Jennifer and I stayed with the two young bachelors for four days before the house was vacant. We slept on a tile floor with our own blankets, got our own meals, and tried to stay away as much as we could so we wouldn't be a bother to them because Jennifer was still sometimes too nervous to meet people. There was another Indian reserve on the way to Tachie called Binchi. One lady there said it's alcohol free; people aren't allowed to bring alcohol in the reserve; and if they do, they're subject to fines, and mentioned how much the people there used to drink. And it was incredible. The lady from the log house who told us where to go went to college when I was there. I was interested in her at the time, but she wasn't interested in me. Now she tried to get me to come out of my shell, but I knew I couldn't get anyone interested in me, so I usually gave up without trying. I knew I was withdrawn and it seemed like I had a mental block. I was aware of things and noticed things, but they didn't always register in my mind. I was aware of being withdrawn and tried to come out of it, but it was hard; then after I met Jennifer, it started going away, but I was still withdrawn.

The tree planting finally got started and the Native crew were anxious to get going and the foreman had been going to the office almost every day. The Native crew and the contractor's regular crew both set up their own camp at the job site. I thought the contract would be done in less than two weeks so we could work seven days a week and it would be done right away. The contract started off rather slowly because the Native crew weren't as experienced or in the same physical condition as the regular tree planters. It was my responsibility to deliver trees from the cache to the planters and I hired a band member to do plot checks to make sure the trees were planted properly. Then just when everything got going good and I was at the point where I could coordinate delivery with production part, the Native crew went out and got drunk. The rule of their camp was "No drinking!" so I had to fire them and start over again, trying to match delivery with production. Things were going slow and I didn't know what to do, but a band member said a group of young people on a training program would be going to help plant the trees. I thought things would start going faster, but they didn't; the young people were beginners and it took time for them to learn.

Jennifer went to work with me and we worked long hours, seven days a week, and I had destroyed my Visa card long before I got this job because we were too far in debt. Since we were working long hours, we didn't have time to go to the bank and ended up eating one peanut-butter-and-jam sandwich for lunch and one for supper. When the crew ate, we usually went somewhere else because we would have felt out of place; but one night they invited us to have supper with them, so we just gorged ourselves because we were so hungry. They thought we kept to ourselves because we went off like that, but we just felt out of place. The planting seemed to go on forever, but when it was almost over, a gap was found between the Native planters and the regular planters; and the regular planters were already planting another block, but we called them back to plant the gap. They were really happy when it was done though because it was their easiest area to plant and they got their best production.

One day, Jennifer and I were driving off a muddy road and I had the hubs turned so I could use the four-wheel drive; as we got off that road, I was thirsty, so I got a drink of water from a small creek and turned the hub on my side of the truck. I thought Jennifer got out to turn the hub on the other side and she thought I turned both of them. We started driving down the road to the other block and heard a thump, thump, thump, thump; so I thought it was just mud because we just got off a muddy road. After we got twenty miles down the road, I discovered one hub was turned in and the other was turned out. I told Jennifer I thought she turned it out, and she thought I turned both of them.

I was slightly annoyed but controlled myself because I had done the same thing when I was sixteen; now fourteen years later, it happened back to me. I was out drinking with some friends, and we found a 4×4 crew cab with the keys still in it, so we took it for a ride. When we needed the four-wheel drive, I turned one of the hubs in; when we didn't need it, I turned my hub out then back in again so one hub was turned in and the other turned out. I left early because I had to go to work the next day, but the others kept driving around. The next day, the driver said he parked it where he thought the police would be sure to find it. They didn't find it for two days, so he parked it sideways in the middle of a road by a sawmill so that it was blocking the road. We thought the police would find it for sure now, but the sawmills were on strike, so it sat there for a week before the police finally found it. Now these things were happening back to me. I was surprised it didn't happen earlier, so I accepted it.

When the job was over and the planters left, I still had to work for two more days before I could make it to the bank. Three of us had to plant some areas that were missed and do some plot checks. We were tired and glad it was over, and I realized I shouldn't have scheduled the work the way I did and should have arranged for a week day off for the crew to go to town. When everything was finally over, I had to wait to get paid; so I offered to take straight time, not overtime, and bank my hours because I had to try and earn enough weeks to draw UIC. Thomas then asked to deduct a week's wages for the slack periods. There weren't any slack periods, and I was too passive and withdrawn to assert myself very well, but I mainly hoped he would give me a job in the future if I did that because I was also in a situation where I was willing to do anything if it would get me a job in the future.

When we left Fort St. James, I felt happy that I had worked but also disappointed about the job. We took our time going back and stopped in Lytton, and Ryan and his family had been in a car accident just before we got there. Ryan and Desiree were in the hospital in Lytton, Shannon was in the hospital in Kamloops, but Sharon and fourteen-month-old Ryan Jr. seemed okay. Liz was still into her form of Christianity that condemned everything if it wasn't of the Bible, and didn't allow alcohol or anyone drinking into her house. We went to the hospital to visit Ryan and Desiree, and Ryan Jr. was immediately attracted to me; the only people he would go to were Jeremy and me, but Jeremy tended to avoid him because he was so cranky, so I ended up babysitting him. When Ryan and Desiree got out of the hospital, we noticed Ryan Jr.'s leg was swollen around the ankle; and I noticed that whenever we put his shoes on him, he would scream, so we took him to the hospital. The doctor X-rayed him and she said that someone was holding him upside down and shaking him, so we told her the family was just in a car accident, but she didn't believe us. Ryan and Desiree couldn't look after him because of their injuries, so Jennifer and I ended up looking after him.

We looked after Ryan Jr. for most of August, and we all stayed in Lytton with Liz and Jeremy. Liz was still heavily into that form of Christianity and almost gave her TV away because they said it's of the devil and preached, "The end of the world is coming! Save yourself! Turn to Christ! The wine people drank in the Bible was just grape juice!"

I noticed everyone there had a severe problem of some kind: The minister and his wife were ex-drug addicts and alcoholics. Liz had manic depression, an abusive father, and an abusive husband. Another fellow who claimed to be a minister said he used to drink and go to the horse races to gamble every weekend; now he gave his life to Christ, so all he wanted to talk about was the Bible. I tried to tell Jennifer not to listen to them because they didn't know what they were talking about, but she wouldn't listen and got extremely depressed. They also told us we were living in sin and should get married. I wanted to use our money for our bills, but we ended up using it for a down payment on rings. We couldn't pay for them in full, so we just made payments, putting us deeper in debt.

We looked after Ryan Jr. until it was time to register for college, then Desiree's brother Dylan started looking after him. Ryan Jr. used to hold his breath until he would faint, but I brought him out of it and thought Desiree would be happy about it, but she thought I was being too strict with him. It was almost time to go back to college, and I thought we would have enough money to get our bills down and live reasonably well; then Jennifer started spending on her parents again. It was driving me crazy, but she wouldn't listen. We took Henry to see Phaye, and he pretended he was flat broke as usual. Anne went along too and Jennifer wanted to treat them to Chinese food and Henry could see he was making life miserable for me, but he still went along with it. Instead of saying "No, you don't have to" or "I'll pay for my own," he just said, "Add it up carefully, Baxter. Sometimes they make a mistake."

Jennifer spent most of our money on her family. We were deeply in debt and living on a low budget again. We also bought Henry Jr. some clothes for school, which I didn't mind because their father didn't do very much for his kids. I just didn't like the way she spent on her father. We got an apartment in town rather than live in Rosedale with my family. I knew I had a rather heavy course load, but I was sure I could handle it, but Jennifer was also going to college and I knew I would have to help her with her math. I didn't want to get married because Jennifer had too many problems to get over first, but we set the date for Thanksgiving weekend. I couldn't get through to Jennifer that the religious group didn't know what they were talking about; but unfortunately, she listened exactly like my parents did, in one ear and out the other, faster than the speed of light.

Linda Pierre and her husband moved to Chilliwack and lived in the same apartment building we were living in, and she still wondered why I never ever tried for her; so I just told her I never saw her for ten years, but she knew that wasn't the reason. There was one very nice-looking Native girl attending college and it looked to me like she was waiting for the right guy to come along and I was sure it wasn't me, so I didn't try for her either. She thought I was doing that because I was hurt that way before, but I just wondered, "Would it do any good?"

She just shook her head and went no. After that, whenever I walked by her, she would just glare at me. I never did know her name, but thought, *Life is too short to waste time flogging a dead horse.*

I thought things were going to go okay in college, but they didn't. Jennifer's depression was so bad she couldn't study and wouldn't let me study because she always wanted my attention. She also couldn't settle down and study because of what the religious group was saying: the end of the world was coming and people have to become Christians in order to save themselves, and Jennifer didn't believe she was good enough to be a Christian. I tried to tell her the worst sinners turn Christian because they can't control their own lives; they drink, fight, beat the kids, run around on their wives or husbands, are crooks or thieves; then they turn to Christianity and are saved. They were saved and believed everyone else should be saved, but she wouldn't listen. She was dragging me down, so I wasn't doing very well in my classes and had to drop calculus and redo my Math 12 because of her. I was getting extremely frustrated and depressed because I wanted to get my marks up so I could get into UBC. Then Jennifer wanted a new TV with a remote control to make her feel better, so I used my savings to buy one and had Cablevision hooked up; but it didn't make her feel any better. I also bought a book shelf and put it together to keep our books organized; she was still depressed and asked me to buy us both bicycles, so I bought them. It didn't make her feel any better and it put us deeper in debt; there was nothing I could do to make her feel better so she could settle down to her studies.

Henry's court case finally came up, and he went to court in Prince George. He got a $400 fine and was ordered not to hunt in the Prince George area for five years but he didn't learn. He was back hunting up there again that year. As usual, he never even saw anything. Then Henry bought a brand-new GMC S-15 pickup and had a lump on his back he thought was cancer, and rather than go to a regular doctor, he wanted to see the Indian spiritual healer in Kelowna Phaye had told us about. Although he was working and had just bought a new truck, he wanted his kids to pay for the trip and said, "None of my kids care about my life!" Not only was Jennifer gullible enough to want to take him, she almost drove me insane with what she wanted to do for him. She wanted to rent a car to take both her parents to Kelowna; pay the doctor, their meals; rent a room; and see a movie in the evening. That would have been extremely costly for us. Time and money we just didn't have. Henry was working and could have paid for the trip himself. I told Jennifer he could go there on his own truck if it's that important to him, but she wanted me to pay for the gas if he did that, but luckily she changed her mind about the whole thing.

I was getting angrier and angrier all the time. My mother had kept telling me finding a girlfriend would take my mind off my studies and wouldn't listen when I told her all she was doing was slowing me down and interfering with my career goals. Then when I found someone and she interfered with my responsibilities, my family blamed me for everything that was going wrong. Often when we went to classes I would have to drive Jennifer home during my breaks because she was so depressed, so I often missed my biology tutorials because of her. Just before my midterm exam in computer science, she wanted to go shopping because she was depressed and couldn't wait one day so I could study, and I ended up failing my exam. My anger and frustration were getting so bad I just about slashed my wrist after an argument with Jennifer one night. I knew that wouldn't solve anything, so I just walked out and went for a walk around the block then finally decided I've been passive and held back long enough! If there's only one way to get people to listen to my opinion, then that's the way it's going to be and felt like breaking my mother's jaw! I passed by her on the road one day and she looked scared. I went back to Rosedale one day and just glared at her, still wanting to break her jaw, give her a karate kick, and break it! My mother was ready to start crying, so I told her to stop telling me to find a girlfriend!

She said "All right!" but it took that much to make her listen!

I had been collecting books on Indian medicine men and was building up a nice collection of books, but the religious group convinced Jennifer they were of the devil, so she got extremely depressed and destroyed them all in front of me because she was trying to save me. She was scared of almost everything, and whenever it became time for her biology exams, she went to the doctor to get a note to postpone it. The doctor finally got tired of it and said he can't keep giving notes whenever she has an exam coming, so he suggested she talk to a priest and made an appointment for us. The religious group was very much against the Catholic church, but we went to a Catholic priest anyway.

The priest, Father Garry, straightened Jennifer around and explained to her the book of prophecies written in the Bible. He pointed out that to the religious group, everything was either black or white to them; if something's not of the Bible, then it's of the devil; if they want to live that way, that's fine. Jennifer finally got her thinking straightened out, but it was too late for me to catch up with my studies. I had to drop my computer science class because I didn't think I would be able to catch up, and we had called the wedding off two weeks ahead of schedule, but we still had to pay for the rings. I decided I had suffered enough because of Christianity. My parents were angry about what they went through in the residential schools run by the church, and I was their scapegoat. Now this religious group slowed me down and interfered with Jennifer and my career goals. I decided if people want to be a Christian, that's up to them! I'm not a Christian and damn proud of it!

I kept studying in my remaining classes though and helped Jennifer with her studies. She slowed me down so much I didn't know if I would pass my chemistry course even though I would have normally found it incredibly easy. The students closed me off in that class except for one girl who would talk to me, but it didn't matter because I was having too much trouble with Jennifer's depression. After a long, stressful day, we would always sit up and watch *Maude*, a comedy series on TV before we went to bed. She always made us laugh and feel better before we went to sleep. Then Linda Pierre finally realized I never ever tried for her because I knew she would say no. Later on I told her she would have treated me like poison ivy anyway.

I had read the book *How to Foresee and Control Your Future* by Harold Sherman before Jennifer destroyed it. It mentioned that people reap exactly what they sow in life, and I started to notice even trivial things I was doing were happening back to me. While visiting Sto:lo Eagle one weekend, Henry Jr. went out to the river to check the nets. It was close to getting dark, so Jennifer got worried and sent me out to look for him, and I knew exactly what was going to happen. We would run into him just past the bridge and he was having so much fun he didn't want to stop. That's what I did the year before, and now it was happening back to me. I was getting back exactly what I was putting out in life.

Henry's house became infested with fleas, and he said to me, "It costs $40 to fumigate the house," and held out his hand like I was going to give it to him. He seriously believed he did everything for us and we were obligated to him, but I wouldn't have given it to him if I had it! Later on I told him, "My bills are going up!" and held out my hand like he was going to help me out. When the semester was almost over, the lady in charge of education said she didn't know if I would be able to attend college the next semester or not. I told her again why I wasted my first two years at college and failed at BCIT two times for medical reasons, but she still didn't seem to listen; so I thought, *It's a good thing I'm not living at home! I would have shown my parents what a black sheep is!*

Wylma had done a tarot-card reading for us in August and told me I would be offered a job in December and I should go for it, and I kept hoping she would be right because Jennifer had run our bills up quite high. I phoned her up one night to see how she and her husband were doing and asked her about the book *Aztec*. She said the main character in the book sounded exactly like me, or someone very much like me.

We finished the semester off and I passed biology, chemistry, and math but had to drop computer science; and Jennifer repeated the same math course she took in the spring even though she did quite well the first time. That religious group really caused us a lot of damage. I still didn't know if I could attend college in the spring yet, and even if I could, all my classes were in Abbotsford. I owed too much money on my credit cards, so I didn't know what to do; but just when my classes ended, CEIC referred me to a job on an Indian reserve in Sardis, a suburb of Chilliwack. I went for the interview and was told it paid $500 a week, which was good money at the time. The job was a project that was supposed to start in October, but luckily for me, it didn't start until mid-December. Robin Norwood's best seller *Women Who Love Too Much* became available in Chilliwack that year and Jennifer was always after me to buy it, but we couldn't afford it; then finally I broke down and bought it, but I didn't have time to read it until later.

Classes were over, Christmas was coming, and I started work right away; but it seemed like I was even busier when classes were over. As we were doing our Christmas shopping, both of us came down with the flu, and that was the sickest I ever got in my life. My temperature went up to 102 degrees Fahrenheit and I would have gone to the hospital if it went up one more degree. Christmas day came and Henry drank on his one day of the year. I didn't know if I would be better by then, but I was starting to recover. I had a week off between Christmas and New Year and was ready to go back to work after that.

Chapter 9

1987

I went back to work after the New Year, and Jennifer's depression was coming out more and more; sometimes she insisted we visit her family in Sto:lo Eagle and didn't care if I made it to work on time the next day or not. She continued spending our money on her father, and there was nothing I could do to stop her. I started reading the book *Women Who Love Too Much*, but she didn't want to read it because it brought back too many bad memories. When I was working in Enderby, the public-health nurse working for the Indian band had been trained as a psychiatric nurse and said women who have been beaten and abused as children often put themselves back in the same situation because that's what they're familiar with and it takes an awful lot to change their way of thinking. Now a book was available, which was readable to the average person, explaining the problem and how to deal with it. I found the book quite interesting.

I enrolled Jennifer in a speed-reading and study skills course at the college because I thought one of her problems is that she's a slow reader and she could attend classes while I was working. She attended some classes but soon stopped because she just couldn't get herself to do anything. The job wasn't too bad, but I thought at least I'll get enough weeks for UIC because there are very few jobs available in forestry. I didn't get a chance to specialize in anything when I was younger, so I couldn't go into business for myself.

Liz and Jeremy owned a car and went down to visit because they were going to Abbotsford to buy a truck, and we went along with them because I was thinking of trading my Datsun in for a domestic model.

The Ford dealer in Abbotsford offered me $3,000 for my Datsun, and they wanted to know if I would still be employed after the project was over. I hesitated, and they immediately offered me $3,500; so I figured if I hesitated more, I could get even more for my Datsun. I asked the chief and band manager if there was a chance the job would last longer, and they said they applied for another project but wouldn't know if they would get the funding for some time. The Ford dealer then offered me $3,750 for my Datsun, but I still hesitated; then they offered me a little bit more, but I wasn't sure if I wanted to buy another truck yet or not.

We decided to check the car dealers in Chilliwack first, but the head gasket went on my truck at work; it was blowing a cloud of white smoke for one hundred yards, and I didn't know what was wrong with it. I went to a mechanic and he wouldn't touch it; he said, "It could be the head gasket and a warped planer head. Take it back to the dealer to repair it. You could end up with a $1,100 or $1,200 repair bill." I didn't think that old truck was worth spending that much money on, so we went to the Ford dealer in Chilliwack to see what we could get for it. I told the salesman the dealer in Abbotsford offered me $3,750 for it but I would be willing to go down to $3,500 since there was something wrong with it. The salesman agreed but had to get permission to do so and had to wait for financing to be approved and asked for a copy of my résumé.

I rode my bicycle to work for several days. Then Jennifer said we should check the dealer where her father bought his truck, and the salesman there immediately offered me $4,000 for my Datsun, but I still had to give $1,500 for a down payment. My savings were going down and I hoped I wouldn't have to take any more out of it. I was taking a big chance that I would be able to find work long enough to pay for it. The truck cost me $18,500, quite a sum then.

Jennifer wanted to take guitar lessons, so I bought her a guitar and signed her up for lessons because if she took an interest in something, I always tried to encourage it to try and make her feel better about herself. I took music in high school for two years, so I was able to give her some help to get started. She was often irritable, cranky, and so depressed at times she didn't want to go anywhere or do anything; so I enrolled us in night classes for meat cutting and taking care of horses because I wanted her to try out different things. She didn't attend very many classes at meat cutting, but we attended all the horse-care classes, and her depression got so bad at times I almost couldn't function properly. I was happy to be working though because I wanted to help coach minor baseball that year; she also thought it was a good idea, and I would finally have a chance to do something for my own enjoyment.

Jennifer continued spending even though I tried to get her to slow down because my job was only going to last six months. I just bought a new truck and hadn't even made our first payment on it yet, so we decided to destroy our Visa card again so we wouldn't be able to use it anymore. The next day I went to work and the band manager called me into her office, so I knew something was wrong; she told me I was being laid off because I was too indecisive and was given two weeks' pay in lieu of two weeks' notice. I felt totally devastated and couldn't understand why I was being laid off, because I tried to be a good worker, follow orders as best I could, and do a good job. I had just bought a brand-new truck and didn't even know if I was eligible for UIC or not. I thought everything was going fine. I was working, and Jennifer was finally making an effort to do things on her own; now I was laid off when I owed a large amount of money.

Strangely enough it was Friday the thirteenth, the day before Valentine's Day; so I went to the bank then went home, and a lady standing on the street saw me and wondered why I was so depressed because usually I was always smiling. When I got home, Jennifer was practicing with her guitar and I told her what happened and she almost didn't believe me. Then we went to McDonald's for supper, and I bought two cases of beer. I had to relieve the tension somehow because I knew we would end up moving back to Rosedale with my parents. Luckily, the manager of the apartment building said we could move out in two weeks, which saved us a month's rent.

Jennifer got go depressed she couldn't do anything anymore and started buying coats and things to try and make herself feel better again. Whenever I tried to gather boxes to pack up, she would get extremely depressed and didn't want to do anything. I often wondered why she was so depressed and what I could do about it because it seemed like no matter how hard I tried, I couldn't do anything for her depression. I went driving down a street one day and there were three white guys standing by their cars. They were rather nice cars, not luxury cars like Lincoln Continentals or Cadillacs, and all three of them were looking at me like I was too lazy to go to work even though

I was driving a brand-new truck. One day when I went home to visit, I was told Isaac's girlfriend, Helen Fruman, was six months pregnant; no one even told me he had a girlfriend.

Finally the end of the month came and we had to pack up and move. We got boxes from a moving company, and Jennifer insisted we keep out only what we needed. Everything else was to be stored at the moving company and not in the basement of my parents' home, so it cost me to have our things moved and stored. When we moved back to Rosedale, the stress was incredible, almost unbearable. Jennifer suffered from chronic envy because people always told her she was overweight, and she envied David's girlfriend because she was so slim. She tried to be perfect, so she started going to electrolysis to have her hair permanently removed from her legs. Her depression and envy were really taking its toll on me, and Dad finally realized the damage he was causing me by trying to drill into my head my opinions were always wrong. He did untold damage by putting me down just for being young all those years, yet he continued to be obnoxious and still got mad me for everything I did. He would always say, "Where's your scientific proof?" then wouldn't let me get a word in edgewise to explain myself. The tension between me and my parents was getting unbearable even though my instincts told me it was better that the band laid me off. I often felt like beating my mother up, but my dad was going to protect her, and it still seemed like something just wasn't right.

After I got laid off, I started sending out letters of application for work and reluctantly applied to Fort St. James but never even got an answer. I started reading some of the books recommended by Robin Norwood in her book *Women Who Love Too Much*. One book I read mentioned people with a low self-esteem often group together because they can relate to each other on how they feel about themselves, like alcoholics and drug addicts tend to conform with each other. Then I finally realized why Ryan started dropping by to visit when Liz was going with an alcoholic and living with us. It mentioned that addicts aren't necessarily addicted to the alcohol or drug itself; it's the escape from reality that they want, a fast release or quick fix, and the key to overcoming addictions is to mature.

David and Angie often asked us to babysit Deidre, their daughter; and each time we did that, David would buy us a case of beer. But even drinking didn't relieve the stress I was feeling, so it wasn't worthwhile for me to drink. I sometimes studied anthropology as a hobby and found Indian spiritualism a fascinating subject. The stress of looking after Jennifer was getting extremely hard on me, so I wanted to shrink my stomach and go on a four-day fast to see what it was like and perhaps find out what was going to happen. Dad was very set in his ways though and believed everything had to be scientifically proven and kept checking the fridge to make sure I was eating. It wouldn't have done any good to tell him scientists haven't proven everything that exists, and I was not doing anyone any harm by fasting because it probably would have taken several years for him to realize that, if at all! Fred Quip dropped by to visit one day and asked if I was optimistic about what I went through, and I said yes; then Dad finally realized how I felt about what I went through, but someone else had to say it.

I kept trying to get into UBC to get my RPF and kept applying and finally got a letter saying I was accepted in the guided independent study program, and Mother wondered why I was suddenly happy when I was usually extremely angry. I didn't know what I was going to do about advancing in my education, so I told Dad, "All those years when everyone was telling me what to do and no one would listen when I told them all they were doing was slowing me down! You did nothing to stop them, and now I can't get sponsored anymore! When things went wrong, even you put all the blame on me! Could you help me with my education now?"

"No. I'm not going to help you!" he said, even though he knew it wasn't fair.

I felt totally frustrated and helpless, like a born loser! I couldn't get a job in forestry because I was only a technician, not an RPF, and couldn't go back logging because of my education and age. I still knew something wasn't right, and a few days later, I was talking to him and the truth came out; he said something the wrong way and I knew he wasn't as innocent as he pretended to be. Jennifer's depression and envy were getting really bad now; she walked out the door one day and it looked like she was going to leave me, so I immediately went into the living room. My mother was lying on the couch, and I said, "I don't want to hear a word out of you!" If she would have said one word about finding a girlfriend, I would have beat her to a pulp right in front of my dad! Usually when Jennifer and I broke up, she would be right on my back telling me to find another girlfriend.

One weekend when we went to Sto:lo Eagle, Henry was getting mad at his kids again. Henry Jr. was helping him build a smokehouse and accidentally got some wood preservative in his eyes, so we took him to Chilliwack to see a doctor even though he said we didn't have to. After seeing the doctor, we took him to an optometrist and found out he needed glasses. David was still working at the brick plant at Laughing Raven and said they may be hiring again; even though he knew I was going through some very hard times, he acted like he didn't want me working at the same place he was working. This was the second time he did that and regretted it later because he knew I would find a way to swing back at him.

I was trying hard to live on a fixed budget so I could get our bills down. I was eligible for UIC but had to wait a long time to get it. Henry Jr.'s class was putting on a dinner to raise money for their graduation and he was asked to bring a fruit salad; his father wouldn't buy him anything, so we had to do it. We also had to buy enough fruit so his father could eat as much as he wanted and there would still be enough left over for his fruit salad. I thought Jennifer and I should have spent the night in Sto:lo Eagle the day before the dinner but didn't say anything, and the next day, Henry made his son work on putting together a drum, leaving him very little time to prepare his fruit salad. I was beginning to think Henry couldn't do enough damage to his kids.

Jennifer's depression seemed to be getting worse, and the way my family was treating me was driving me crazy. She was extremely depressed one day, and nothing I did made her feel better, so I reluctantly offered to take her to Hope for a drive. We went to Hope and looked around in the stores for a little while, but it didn't make her feel any better, so I reluctantly offered to go to Lytton to visit Liz and Jeremy. When we got to Lytton, Liz and Jeremy were preparing to plant a garden and wanted to build a fence around it and asked us to go out to the woods and pick up the fence posts for them and in return they would take us out for breakfast. We picked up the posts and slept in the next day, so we went out for lunch instead of breakfast. I got up to go to the washroom and saw a fellow I knew, John Harrison. John was an administrator for Fraser Canyon Indian Administration and Siwash Silviculture, so I asked him for a job, totally expecting to get turned down; but he said, "Drop by the office this afternoon."

I went to the office after lunch, and he said they needed someone to manage their tree-planting contracts. The job paid $100 a day and was tax exempt because it involved working with Indian bands. He said they had as much work as they could handle then contractors started backing out of their contracts so Siwash Silviculture was then asked to do the contracts and soon had more work than they could handle. They didn't know what they were going to do; then I stopped by. The job started next week.

We went back to the coast to get packed, and Liz and Jeremy owed us some money that we loaned them for their wedding so they were going to let us stay with them for a month free of charge. They couldn't afford to pay us back, so everything was working out great. One night when my dad and I were watching the news, the prime minister said we have to bring in more immigrants into the country because we have a shortage of skilled workers. I wondered, "Why did they hold the Indians back when we tried to do something for ourselves and now they complain about a shortage of skilled workers?"

The prime minister then said something else, and Dad said, "There's your answer right there." I thought that was as vague of an answer as a person could get, but I would never say anything to a politician without enough documented information to write a book.

Geraldine was pregnant again and asked us to babysit their kids while she was in the hospital because I'm a good cook and get along well with their kids. Ben was close to my age and had been a very good boxer when he was younger. He felt guilty about deliberately harassing me when he went out with Jennifer, but I finally got a chance to tell him she would have committed suicide but didn't because she hurt me once already; that was a small price to pay for her life. Then I asked him, "How did the students treat you when you were going to school?"

"They closed us off."

"Even though your name was always in the paper for your accomplishments as a boxer?"

"Yes. One time, a number of them were going to gang up on Buff, but some of us came running up. Some of the other students were going to help us out, but nothing happened." Two days later, I went to the bars with Ben's twin brother, Gerald, and he mentioned the Indians were closed off in school by the other students. Then I wondered why the news anchors were so surprised there had been a big fight with the East Indians after a soccer game the year before; there still seemed to be much racial tension against the East Indians.

Jennifer had a friend in Laughing Raven, Victor, who lived a few houses down the road; he was Ben's nephew and Jennifer went to school with him and they used to play road hockey together. Victor always acted carefree and happy-go-lucky, but I always had a feeling something about him wasn't right. Strangely enough I always got the same feeling whenever I would see the singer Del Shannon on TV. Geraldine had a baby boy they named Ben, after his father, and called him Little Ben. She went home two days after the baby was born because she knew she had to look after the family. Jennifer and I were going through some hard financial times, and that made it rather difficult for us to look after their four children.

We moved to Lytton the day before the job started and left rather late because Jennifer was mad at me for going to the bars with Gerald. The first day on the job, I was introduced to the crew and who would be driving part of the crew to work. I was told where to start, how to look after the trees, and would be given a bonus if I planted trees myself. I tried hard to do the job right, but the crew didn't care and were very irresponsible. They kept coming and going as they pleased, taking days off, and there was nothing I could do about it. There were a number of applicants, but I would call them to work and they wouldn't show up or they were just as irresponsible, so I couldn't fire them because there was no one to take their place. There was a minimum number of trees that were supposed to be planted daily because the trees aren't supposed to be out of cold storage very long and the planting season is short. Some people who applied for work said they were experienced and could plant one thousand trees a day, but when they went to work, they hadn't planted at all; so I had to train them, but I was still happy to be working though and hoped the job would last at least six weeks. I could make larger payments on my bills now and hoped to get enough work weeks for UIC; permanent jobs or jobs that lasted more than six months seemed like a dream.

I didn't mind staying with Liz and Jeremy, but Jennifer started complaining about Jeremy and said Jeremy was driving her crazy. When Liz was growing up, the kids worked and their father got all the benefits; now it looked to me like she was doing the same thing, only it wasn't her father benefiting from her working; it was her husband. I wished I could give Jennifer a job tree planting so she would have something to occupy her time, but her wrist was still weak from when she hurt it five years earlier. I continued working, and the crew was just about driving me crazy because they were totally irresponsible and there was nothing I could do about it. Not only that, after work, if

Jennifer wanted to do something, I had to go along with it to avoid a confrontation; she always found a way to get her own way but always seemed to make the right decision.

I got more phone calls from people who said they were experienced planters, but I was so used to hearing that from inexperienced planters I didn't believe them anymore. Jennifer wanted to move out and get a place of our own, but I didn't want to because of our bills. We stayed there for a month, then Gordon brought a case of beer home. Liz was totally against liquor and phoned him and told him to get out of the house or she'll call the police and have him removed. Jeremy got really mad at her for kicking him out, so he told her he wanted Jennifer and I out of there that weekend! Then he said he wanted us out of there that night! He went down the bars after that, and we packed our things and moved to the Totem Motel, where we stayed before. It was probably better for both of us because sometimes when they went to Chilliwack to visit us, Jennifer said she hated him; now we also had the freedom to do what we wanted to do.

Production of the tree-planting contracts wasn't what it was supposed to be, and the British Columbia Forest Service was getting close to cancelling the contract. The crew knew that if that happened, we may not get paid for the work they've done so far, but they didn't seem to care. I was passive and withdrawn but was being forced to come out of it. I was learning to be more assertive and was coming out of my shell now. I was often worried and depressed about the way things were going; and at the end of the day, Jake Adams, a very good friend of mine, would see me in the mirror of the truck and give me a really crazy look, always making me laugh. I was getting so frustrated I was almost ready to quit but thought, *I've never quit before, so I won't quit now! Besides, even if we lost the contract, the crew may not get paid, but I'll still get paid.*

One fellow on my crew, Albert, was slow, lazy, useless, and a troublemaker who was hired because he had a driver's license, lived the farthest distance out of town, and could pick up part of the crew on the way to town. One Saturday he was supposed to meet me at the job site, but instead of showing up, he took the vehicle and part of the crew to Pasulko Lake and played baseball. Luckily, I had enough equipment for the workers who went with me; and when I saw him at the end of the day, he said the vehicle broke down. When I found out what really happened, I got Derek Kingston to go get the vehicle the next day. Albert appeared at the door, gave me the keys, then disappeared. I didn't know where he was, so I left and went back to town; and when I got to town, another worker quit because he said he was just as guilty as Albert was.

When I got back to the office, Albert's mother called and was extremely outraged at my actions. She asked why I didn't just take the truck away from him when he went to the lake. I replied I didn't have anyone else with a driver's license and I didn't wait for him in the morning because I didn't know where he went. After that, I was going to give Albert the record he fully deserved and recommend that under no circumstances he be hired again unless he had a letter of reference from someone he's worked for saying he's done some growing up and a letter from his mother saying she won't let him hide behind her apron strings and a job with the band isn't good enough! When I got back to work though, Derek, my subforeman, talked me out of it. He said, "You shouldn't be out to break him. He just has some growing up to do."

I reluctantly agreed, but the whole crew was driving me crazy. The Forest Service was almost ready to cancel the contract and I felt like quitting again, but that was when some fast, experienced planters from Lillooet were hired. Luckily, I learned at an early age never to give up; it seemed like something usually happened to make it worthwhile or saved me from being a loser. Now that I had some fast, reliable planters, the crew couldn't play games anymore; so the rest of the crew started pushing themselves for more production and I didn't have to worry about firing anyone because the contracts would still get done. After the fast planters showed up, one of my regular workers showed he could plant as fast as they; he started working faster and did quite well then asked for Friday and the weekend off to prepare for a wedding. I agreed, but when I went to pick him up on Thursday morning, he wanted that day off as well, so I fired him. He was a good worker, but if he didn't want to go to work, that was fine with me.

One Saturday, I was going to divide the crew into two groups for two different contracts. One group was to go to Lillooet and the other group was to go with me. Derek Kingston took the crew to Lillooet, left just before me, took everyone who showed up, and was gone before I had a chance to follow him; so I got the whole weekend off. We went to Sto:lo Eagle for the weekend, and Henry Jr. said his dad was making him train really hard for canoe racing. His arms were sore and he thought he may have pulled muscles, but his dad wanted him to keep training. It looked like Henry didn't want his son to finish high school and used canoe racing as an excuse to interfere with his studies. He yelled at his son, "If you don't want to train, *don't you ever use our last name*!" That evening he told him, "If you're failing at one course, you may as well quit."

Henry Jr. said, "I'm doing all right. I'm going to pass." Luckily, Jennifer talked to him and encouraged him to hang in there.

When the contracts were almost over, John Harrison said we could take the weekend off, so Jennifer and I went back to Sto:lo Eagle to help Henry Jr. rent a tuxedo for his graduation. His father wasn't going to rent him a tuxedo and he would have felt out of place if everyone else was dressed up and he was just in his plain clothes and he told Jennifer he wasn't going to go to his graduation ceremonies because of that. Henry was getting incredibly cranky toward his youngest son and was still treating him like he didn't want him to finish high school. We got ready to take Henry Jr. to Chilliwack the next day to prepare for his graduation, and there was also a full-contact karate tournament on that weekend that I wanted to go to. I always wanted to go to a tournament like that and thought, *Now's my chance! I have just enough time and money to do something for my own interests!*

Henry saw we were going to a karate tournament, so he said to his son, "I want you home by seven o'clock!" deliberately ruining my fun when I was looking after his responsibilities as a parent! I was disappointed about missing the tournament, but at least Henry Jr. was being given an opportunity to do something with his life. It seemed like I could never do anything for my own interests because someone was always ruining my fun! When we took Henry Jr. to Chilliwack to rent his tuxedo, we also went to a photo studio to get his graduation pictures taken.

We went to Spences Bridge one day to visit Dave Walkem and asked him how the students treated him at UBC. He said they didn't know he was Native but mentioned Natives going to school in Kamloops being closed off by the other students and said, "People sometimes get ostracized!" so I finally decided enough is enough! At BCIT, white students smaller than I weren't closed off unless it was by choice; other Natives attending were treated the same way I was treated, so I started withdrawing and keeping to myself. If I knew people before I started withdrawing or if I had to work with them, I accepted them; but other than that, it was hard for me to open up and say anything!

I thought the planting was over at the end of the week; then I was told it would last one more week. We couldn't stay at the Totem Motel anymore because the owners had already rented the room out to someone else, but luckily, Liz and Jeremy let us stay with them for the last week of the job. When I first got the job, I was hoping it would last at least six weeks, and it lasted nine weeks; and when it was over, John Harrison said I did one of the most-difficult jobs successfully.

We moved back to Rosedale again because we didn't have any other place to go and were too far in debt to get a place of our own. Stress and envy were still getting incredibly bad for Jennifer, and looking after her was getting hard on me. She couldn't sit still very long, and it was hard for her to do anything and wouldn't let me go jogging or exercise to keep myself in good physical condition because she always wanted my attention. I still tried to be careful with our spending in case I got another job because it would cost us to find a place to stay and buy groceries until we got out first paycheck. Jennifer would often get so stressed up she would pick things up and start hitting me, so I had to wear long-sleeved shirts all the time to hide the bruises on my arms. I also had to try and think positive all the time or I would get severe indigestion if I even worried slightly, and had to carry a pack of Rolaids at all times for indigestion. I often felt like giving up on her, but I knew I couldn't do that because if she committed suicide, it would hurt many people because of how they treated her.

Since she couldn't sit still very long or settle down and do anything, we were always packing a few clothes and leaving. The stress on me was getting unbearable, but there was nothing I could do about it. I wished Wylma still lived in Harrison Hot Springs because visiting her always made us feel better and would have given me some idea of when things were going to change. We went to Chilliwack one day and Jennifer was extremely depressed, so we phoned Wylma then caught the ferry to Nanaimo to visit her. She and her husband were living in Courtenay, on Vancouver Island. We went to the island and spent the night in our truck in the woods near Cumberland then drove to Courtenay to visit them the next day. Wylma's health was getting worse and Norman couldn't find work anywhere; things were going very bad for them, but they seemed happy enough.

On our way back to the mainland, we missed the last ferry, so we got a motel room in Nanaimo because I didn't want to sleep in the truck again. My instincts started telling me to start coming out of my shell now and start thinking more about romances, but I didn't want to because I preferred to avoid the heartaches and disappointment of looking for someone but noticed some of my relatives were avoiding me like I was starting to keep to myself. Jennifer was twenty-five now, and it was getting very difficult to look after her because her depression was really taking its toll on me now.

When it became time for Henry Jr.'s graduation, Jennifer wanted it recorded on video, so we reserved a video camera for that day but couldn't get it until four thirty; so we had to pick it up in Chilliwack at four thirty, drive to Sto:lo Eagle, get changed, pick up Henry Jr., then drive back to Agassiz by six o'clock for the ceremonies. Henry Jr. had invited as many of his family as he could, his brothers, his sisters and their husbands, his grandmother, and his parents. He was only allowed to invite ten guests, so Jeremy couldn't attend; his parents got a free meal, but the rest of us had to pay $10 each. After we picked up the camera and Henry Jr. and went to the ceremonies, I was hoping Jennifer would record the ceremonies, but she wanted me to do it. I didn't have time to learn how to use the camera and knew something was going to go wrong.

The ceremonies went quite well and I stood near the stage, filming the students as they went up to get their certificates; then when it was almost over, I realized I was filming all the girls from the chin down. After the award presentations, the students did their march through the gymnasium to the hall and there was a dinner and dance at the Harrison Hot Springs Hotel. When we got outside, some parents rented a limousine; one family even rode a helicopter, but Henry wouldn't pay anything!

The dinner was a buffet with all kinds of meats and salads, and there was dancing afterward; and Jennifer said Ben kept looking at us, but I never noticed. After the dinner and dance at the Harrison Hotel, there was a grad party at the Ag-Rec Building in Agassiz; the students were allowed to drink provided a parent or guardian stayed sober to drive them home because this cut down the possibility of accidents. There was music and dancing there, and it looked like everyone was having a good time; and after it was over, we drove Henry Jr. back to Sto:lo Eagle, and he said, "I don't know how I'm ever going to pay you back!"

We both said, "You don't have to pay us back! Just get a career! That's a reward in itself!" We also bought him a sleeping bag and backpack as graduation gifts because we thought they both would be useful when he's out looking for work or working.

I was hoping Jennifer wouldn't want to see the video I made because I didn't want her to know I didn't do a very good job of filming his graduation, but the next day she said, "I want to see the video you made."

I thought, *Oh no!*

We went next door to Ryan and Desiree's to watch it and everyone started laughing. I didn't mean to do it, but I filmed all the girls' chests and rear ends; everyone laughed and acted like I did it intentionally. We left not long after that because we had to bring the camera back by four thirty; after returning the camera, we went to Laughing Raven and Ben could see what I was trying to do. He knew Jennifer and her brothers could do something with their life as long as I didn't give up, so he encouraged me to keep trying. We kept going back to Rosedale, but often we didn't stay very long because Jennifer couldn't stand staying there. I often wished she would do something about her depression, but nothing seemed to work. One evening she started reading the book *The Science of Happiness* by Ken Keyes. I felt incredible relief and thought, *She's finally trying to do something about her depression!*

When I went into the living room, Dad could see how relieved I felt and said, "Are you being religious?"

"No," I said.

"You sure look like it! It's not scientifically proven!"

I couldn't even be happy without him accusing me of being religious! Jennifer's depression and Dad's obnoxious attitude were too much for me, making me wish I could get a job where I could just move away and not go back but had to keep thinking positive to avoid getting indigestion, it just seemed impossible to get a job anywhere! One day I told my dad, "I just seemed to know I was going to do something with my life."

And he just said, "Where's your scientific proof?"

I looked at my letter from UBC again and realized I was only accepted in the guided independent study program, so that meant I was only accepted to take courses by correspondence, which I knew I couldn't do, and look after Jennifer at the same time. One night we went to Sto:lo Eagle and Henry Jr. missed canoe training because he had to study for his final exams, so we stayed there to make sure his father didn't get mad at him for doing it. His father and uncle Junior both walked in and Junior started encouraging him, so Henry started doing the same thing. We went back to Rosedale again but didn't stay long, Dad felt bad about us always leaving and nicknamed us the road runners, and strangely enough, even my truck had *Gypsy* printed on the dashboard by the manufacturer. We were often sleeping in my truck and didn't have a canopy for it yet, so if it rained, we slept in the cab. We didn't worry about eating because Jennifer was too concerned about her weight. I didn't need very much because I wasn't very active and didn't seem to get hungry very often. We went to Sto:lo Eagle again one weekend, and Henry was calling his son down for finishing high school; and I wondered how he could put up with it, so Jennifer told him, "If things ever get too bad for you, you can move in with us."

Since Jennifer couldn't sit still very long, we drove off to Seattle, Washington, and walked around the streets at night, looking in the store windows. I saw a poster of Albert Einstein, and below his picture were the words, "Behind Every Great Mind Are Many Mediocre Minds Trying Violently to Oppose Them." I don't know if I had a great mind, but my family always tried to drill into my head that my opinions are wrong and I couldn't do the littlest thing without them going down on me. We slept in our truck again that night and Jennifer wanted to stay down there longer, but we didn't have very much money or a job to stay down there for. I tried to keep Jennifer occupied so she wouldn't have time to feel depressed, so I enrolled her in knitting classes in Agassiz. She insisted that I enroll with her, but I didn't mind because I wanted to practice working with my hands. We didn't attend very many classes then dropped out.

We had a canopy for our Datsun, so it was hard to get by without one. There wasn't any place to buy one in Chilliwack, so we went to Abbotsford to look for one. We checked the dealers in Abbotsford and couldn't find a canopy we liked, so we ordered one from Rover Recreation. When we got back to Rosedale, my mother said Henry Jr. went by but went for a bicycle ride. He had packed his clothes and sleeping bag in the pack we bought for him and rode his bicycle from Sto:lo Eagle to Rosedale to move in with us, and I was glad he finally moved away from home. Jennifer, Henry Jr., and I then went everywhere together. Although she had her brother to talk to, her stress level was still incredibly high. One day we went to Agassiz and I locked my keys in the ignition; later on that day I went to pay our bill at the storage company and realized I forgot to pay my bill the month before. Her stress was affecting me that much. Jennifer talked about going to the Okanagan Valley to pick fruit but didn't say it was because she wanted to move away. Stress was getting unbearable, so we went to Vancouver to visit Phaye for a psychic reading. I told her I wanted to move as far away from the Fraser Valley as I could get, and she told me I was going to move farther into the valley, so that just made me feel worse.

I often took Jennifer and Henry Jr. to the movies and out for dinner just to get away from home and was getting concerned because our canopy was going to cost $1,200 and our savings were going down. I wondered what we were going to do if I got another job because it would be expensive to move and find a place to stay. Since we had to try and stay away from my parents', place the three of us went raspberry picking. It was only half a day, three days a week, but at least it was something to do. I tried to get Henry Jr. and me a job stacking bales of hay, but there didn't seem to be very much of that available and still had to wear long-sleeved shirts to hide the bruises on my arms from Jennifer picking things up and hitting me. Everything seemed so hopeless. Jennifer seriously talked about having to do something for her father for helping Henry Jr. move out of Sto:lo Eagle, so I told her he wouldn't have a chance in life without us and her father should be obligated to us for looking after his responsibilities as a parent.

One of my aunts went up from California, and there was a family gathering at my parents' place. It was a good family gathering, and I ended up talking to Fred and June after I started getting drunk. Most people thought I had the nicest parents, but I was beginning to hate them with a passion. Fred said he could see how I was being treated because he was right there; he had boarded at our place when my dad was breaking him in to be a professional faller.

Picking raspberries didn't last very long and Jennifer was still seriously talking about going to the Okanagan Valley to pick fruit, and I knew that if we went, I would have to stand right beside her at all times. One of my cousins who had been a heavy drinker and had an addictive personality died in a car accident a few days later. Although he was a black sheep, he was still my cousin, and I attended his funeral. I felt bad that he died, but I couldn't let it show or feel it because I would get severe indigestion. Sometimes when I talked to people, a little while later I wouldn't remember what we talked about. About two days after the funeral though, I got a call from Allan Tweedy, owner of Eagle Timber Management in Williams Lake. He was on his way to Vancouver for a meeting and wanted to interview me for a job. I was really happy about that because if my canopy hadn't been late in going in, I may have missed the job. He said he would meet me at a restaurant just off the freeway in two days at six thirty.

When it became time for the interview, Jennifer took her time getting ready and found every excuse to slow me down, but things always seemed to work out right for her. Sure enough, just as we were pulling off the freeway into Chilliwack, a truck turned off right behind us; and it was Allan Tweedy. Jennifer made the right move again, and we got there just in time to meet him. Allan needed a forest technician for a newly formed company. He owned and operated his company for a year now and it grossed $150,000 in the first year and he was trying to reach $250,000 in the second year. He needed someone to do some timber cruising, but there was a catch; he would only be able to pay me $80 a day. I told him that was fine because I needed a job really badly right now then told him some of my life experiences and about the log rolling down toward my dad and me; then he made me realize how withdrawn I was when I was young. He gave me his business card and told me to call him in a few days after he got back.

I was really happy but still a little concerned about Jennifer, Henry Jr., and finding a place to stay because buying the canopy would take almost the last of my savings. I called Allan two days later, and he said he had quite a house full so I would have to wait until Monday to go up to Williams Lake. I took some of the money out of the bank and left for Williams Lake, leaving Jennifer and Henry Jr. behind, but would have to try and get settled and make arrangements to take them up there. When I got to Williams Lake, the address on his business card was his home address, so I had a little bit of trouble finding it; and when I got there, he wasn't home. His nephew was home though and Allan left word that I would be going.

His nephew and I went out for Chinese food then to the bars for a few beers and I was surprised I was able to drink four glasses of beer, but I didn't want alcohol affecting my work. Allan went home later that night and showed me where my room was. He was going to let me stay at his place so I wouldn't have to worry about a place to stay. The next day we picked up a fellow, Dave Pops, from an Indian reserve just outside town and went timber cruising. I didn't mind timber cruising, although some of the students at BCIT didn't like it very much and I wished Jennifer didn't hold me back when I wanted to keep myself in good physical condition. Even now her depression was also slowing me down because I could feel her moods.

The next day, Allan stayed in the office and Dave and I did the timber cruising. Dave said he went to the residential schools and one girl there had a couple of kids from one of the priests and the priest went on to become a bishop. Many people who attended were too ashamed to say anything about what happened to them. Things started to slip up a bit on the job, so I sat down and tried to figure out what to do. I knew I could do it, but it seemed difficult to use my own initiative because I was used to everyone trying to drill into my head my opinions were wrong, but I figured out the problem right away and it worked out. I sometimes studied anthropology when I had the time and started wondering if I could adjust to living more on fish than on meat. A novel I read said it was hard for the explorers to live on fish all the time when they first came to the west coast, but the Indians were used to it. My parents grew up that way and said it was hard for them to adjust to not eating fish all the time after we moved to Merritt, so I decided to try eating more fish than meat to see if I could adjust to it.

I continued working on the timber cruise until the weekend then went back to Chilliwack to get Jennifer and Henry Jr. I knew I couldn't leave them there by themselves because Jennifer was getting too depressed and wanted to go with me even though she knew she may end up staying in a campground. We packed up everything we thought we would need then went to Lytton and visited Liz and Jeremy. Liz helped us out as much as she could because we were preparing to live in a campground if we had to. Henry Jr. also had his learner's license and could drive if I got too tired to drive. When we got to Williams Lake, we couldn't find a campground close enough to town where we could stay. Jennifer and I didn't know what to do, so we asked Henry Jr. what he wanted to do and he said, "Let's just keep looking." Luckily we found a cheap motel with a kitchen unit, which only cost me $150 a week to stay. We didn't have much money for any luxuries, but at least we had a place to stay.

Jennifer often acted very immature, like a child; but surprisingly she grew up considerably after Henry Jr. moved in with us, almost overnight. One time when we were in Lethbridge, we went out for coffee with Brenda and she started playing around; so Brenda said, "Oh, Jennifer! Act your age!"

Living in Williams Lake wasn't too bad even though we didn't have much money for luxuries or entertainment. I finished the timber cruise and drew it up in the office, but it didn't seem to work out right, so I had to spend extra time in the field. After the timber cruising, I did a slashing contract with another fellow then worked in the office, putting bids together on another timber-cruising job. The cruising job was in Quesnel, and if we got it, we would be living in a camper. Allan didn't have any more work for me, so I was laid off temporarily and he said I could take some time off but he had a hunch we would get the job in Quesnel.

I was happy to have some time off because Henry Jr. had to register for college and arrange for his funding. The day before we left, we spent the night in the woods to complete some fieldwork, and on our way back, Henry Jr. told me he had an appointment to register in college the next day. I was surprised he didn't tell me earlier because now we had to rush back to the coast. I was tired that night; it was a rather long drive back to Chilliwack and I almost fell asleep at the wheel without realizing it, so I let Henry Jr drive. I told him if he got too tired, just to pull off the road and sleep for a little while, but he drove all the way back to Rosedale.

Henry registered in college the next day, then we had to go to Sto:lo Eagle to arrange his funding and help him find a place to stay. After seeing the home school coordinator about funding, we still had to find a place for him to stay so he would know how much money he would receive. We went back to Chilliwack to look for a place for him and looked at a number of places, but none of them suited his interests, and I didn't want to get impatient because I thought he's already been through enough. My check from the slashing contract finally went in, so I went to the bank to cash it and pay bills; and while I was standing in line, a white fellow ahead of me was ready to pay his credit card bill and looked at me and thought, *All you have to do is go to work!* White people were always looking down on me like I was too lazy to go to work, but I was just between jobs; now I was starting to withdraw even more.

It took several days for Henry Jr. to find a place to stay that he liked and could afford. After he found a place to stay, he told us not to tell his dad where he lived; but when we went back to arrange his funding, we ran into his father on our way back to Chilliwack. He found out where his son would be living even though we did our best to avoid him.

Whenever we went back to Chilliwack, Jennifer would get incredibly stressed out and I would forget things I went down for. This was getting extremely hard on me. Allan Tweedy called me back to do the timber cruising in Quesnel, and just before we left, all three of us came down with the flu. We were very sick and the doctor was very busy, but he managed to squeeze us in. Jennifer then insisted we buy some Tylenol and drop it off at her brother's place before we left. On our way back to Williams Lake, I realized I forgot my work boots and heavy sleeping bag at home. The stress got so bad I forgot it, and Jennifer wanted to avoid my family like the plague, and I often wished she would treat her father that way. When we got to Williams Lake, she insisted on cleaning up our truck completely. It was late and I wanted to get to bed early, but she insisted on cleaning up the truck first. It was very annoying, but there was nothing I could do about it because I knew I had to look after her no matter how hard it got.

The next day, Allan said Jim Rowed was going to be doing the timber cruising with me, and Jim was fast in the woods, so I hoped I could keep up with him because I didn't keep myself in good physical condition. After I met Jim, the three of us loaded a camper onto Al's truck and we got ready to go out to the woods for two weeks. I told Allan I forgot my work boots at home, so he told me I could use his; but I grabbed his nephew's boots by mistake, which were too big on me, but I had to use them anyway.

After we were packed, Jim, Jennifer, and I drove to Quesnel to the forest company to get the maps, air photos, and a copy of the cruise plan. The job was west of Quesnel, about one hundred miles out of town. It was a long drive to where the work was, and the roads were rather muddy. We almost got stuck and spent the first day trying to figure out where we were then walked a long ways in when we thought we were in the right area, and I had trouble keeping up with Jim. My legs were getting tired, but I didn't say anything and kept pushing myself to keep going. We found we were in the wrong area the first day, found the right area the next day, and it was getting late; but we managed to put in some plots anyway. It was close to getting dark, and just before we were ready to head back, I looked up and there was a trail cleared straight in the direction we were heading. A gas company had done some exploration in that area and left a line cleared almost back to the truck.

The weather was rather cold in Nazko where we were working, and I didn't have a proper sleeping bag. It took an hour and fifteen minutes of steady walking to get from the truck to where we were working, and I wasn't able to work as well as I could have because I wasn't getting enough sleep at night. We worked for several more days; then Jim phoned Allan to go and help us for a day or two. He went out from Williams Lake on my truck and worked for two days then went back; we worked for a week longer then were given a few days off.

Jennifer and I went back to Sto:lo Eagle as usual, and incredible tension built up by going back to the Fraser Valley; but while talking to Henry, he mentioned Henry Jr. having trouble lifting some of the fish out of the water. I realized he had been telling his son to go home on weekends and help with the fishing, deliberately interfering with his studies, like he didn't want his kids to do anything with their life but cater to him! He was also mad at Jennifer for helping him move out and said, "She planned in all."

I told Henry, "You better stop interfering with your son's studies or I'm going to move back and put it to an end!" Henry wanted Jennifer and I to move back but not under conditions like that. I had gone well out of my way to help his kids do something with their life, bought them clothes when they were going to school, and Jennifer spent much of her money from upgrading on them. I paid for his youngest son's graduation and helped him get into college, which was Henry's responsibility as a parent, and he didn't even thank me at all! All he did was deliberately ruin my fun, so I thought to myself, *I held back in the past on what I could have said to him and that was a mistake! If he thought I was outspoken before, he's going to find out what I'm like when I don't hold back!*

Jennifer told her father we were working in Nazko, and he said it's grizzly bear country, but I wasn't worried because the chance of seeing one is so remote it's not even worth thinking about.

When we got back to Williams Lake, I asked Allan Tweedy if I could buy a pair of work boots on his Visa and he could deduct it from my paycheck. He agreed, so I bought some; but when I got back to the woods, we worked for several days. Then I realized one boot was steel toed and the other one wasn't.

Allan had a Native fellow working in his office for him named Otis Guichon. Otis was younger than I and said he couldn't speak English when he first went to the residential school and was beaten just for speaking his own language. He went to a school reunion, and a number of former students were just laying for a Christian brother, but he wasn't man enough to show up. A brother is a man dedicated to the church but doesn't have what it takes to become a priest. After timber-cruising for several more days Jim Rowed had to go back to Williams Lake to teach a timber-cruising course, so Otis took his place and I had to drive back to Quesnel to get him.

It was getting to be a longer walk to the back end of the block where we were working; usually, first thing in the morning, Jennifer and I would go to the creek to get water to cook breakfast and have our morning coffee. Otis was shorter than I and was able to sleep comfortably in the cab of the truck. There were two days of work left, and Jennifer and I got up and went to the creek for water. After breakfast Otis opened the camper door and was looking down, I was looking up, and there was a huge bear sitting on the road a little ways from the camper. I knew right away it was a grizzly bear but didn't say anything because I didn't want to scare Otis or Jennifer. Then Otis looked up and whispered, "There's a bear! A grizzly bear!" then quietly closed the camper door.

We stood in the camper and watched the grizzly bear do its thing for half an hour, and it looked so peaceful and contented I wondered how people could invade their territory and shoot them. I was still scared though because my rifle and shotgun were in the cab of the truck. Otis said he heard something moving around during the night, and Jennifer and I were lucky he didn't see us when we went for water that morning. After watching it for half an hour, we decided we better get to work. It walked up the road and started walking back toward us when it heard us get out of the camper and move into the cab. Then as soon as I started up the truck, the bear ran away, right into a pond, and started swimming away.

After we parked, Jennifer decided to stay at the truck because she was too scared of the grizzly bear, and I took my 30-30 rifle to work. A 30-30 is a rather light rifle for a grizzly bear, but it was all I had; so if I had to shoot the bear, the shots would have to be well-placed. Otis grew up in the Chilcotin area, was good in the woods, and said a warning shot would probably attract a grizzly bear more than scare it away. When we got back from work that day, the truck was turned around. Jennifer said, "Some hunters came along and turned the truck around for me. I read the manual several times and practiced driving it back and forth. One of them got scared when he heard about the bear, but the other one said, 'Don't let an old grizz scare you!'"

She was too scared to go outside, so she crawled through the window; and I thought, *That must have been a tight squeeze. Those windows are rather small.* Jennifer and I got a motel room that night, which I paid for at my own expense, because I knew that if we went back to Williams Lake, she would insist on going back to Sto:lo Eagle. She would have been too nervous to stay at Allan Tweedy's place and it wouldn't matter how tired I was; she would want to go back to the coast.

We went back to Williams Lake the next day to drop off the truck and pick up our own truck; but when we got there, Jim Rowed said we were going back Quesnel to do a silviculture-surveys contract, and I couldn't get any time off because we had to start right away. That night, Allan called me into his room for a private talk and said he wasn't going to fire me because I'm rather slow in the woods but my opinion of myself had to change. I should have a better opinion of myself. I didn't tell him it was Jennifer's depression that was dragging me down and I had no choice but to look after her.

Jim told me what the contract involved and what I would be expected to do, but I had to take Jennifer along even though she slowed me down. He talked about asking a motel if we could use one of their rooms free of charge during the day so we could prepare for the contract, but I suggested we go to the library. There were many problems with getting organized before starting the contract. Jim was still teaching the timber-cruising course, and I had just gone out of the woods doing a job. He had asked the company for some time off and to start the contract after the course was over, but they wanted him to start right away. That left only one day to get everything ready to start the surveying, and maps of the proper scale weren't available.

We went to Quesnel the next day on the camper and to the library to look at aerial photographs of the areas to survey. I wasn't sure what to look for because it was rather new to me. We did as much as we could until the library closed then spent the night in the camper. The next day, Jim and I started surveying one of the blocks and he showed me what to do. I had done some silviculture surveys many years earlier, but things had changed. We did some plots and took soil samples, then Jim had to go back to Williams Lake. That night, Jennifer and I went to Provincial campground to spend the night and she kept me awake because she was scared of another grizzly bear going around, so I told her it's only in the parks that you have to worry about bears. People sometimes feed them and treat them like pets, so they lose their fear of humans.

"But this is a park though!" she said.

"It's only a picnic ground," I replied. "It's the big parks like Banff and Jasper that you have to worry about bears." But she wouldn't listen, so I didn't get a very good night's sleep again.

I went to work the next day, but I was still tired from the night before. Jennifer went with me and was extremely nervous, so I had to carry my rifle with me because she was scared of bears. There was a herd of horses grazing on the block I was working on and they were making her nervous. I wasn't worried because they weren't doing anything, and she wanted me to fire a shot in the air to scare them away, but I wouldn't do it. I didn't think a shot would scare them away, and she hung right on to me. I finished my strip line and started working on the second. I could use my compass to go in a straight line, but I had a tendency to angle off to the right and couldn't understand why. I was getting depressed because of the way things were going, and she was slowing me down even more because of her depression. Everything seemed to be going wrong.

I worked for a week and didn't get very much done because I wasn't getting enough sleep at night and Jennifer was always depressed. After a week, I got a motel room in Quesnel, so I could get cleaned up. I wanted to have a bath and sit in a tub of hot water, but the room only had a shower. Then Jim suggested I take some time off because I had been working almost three weeks without any time off, so we went back to the coast, and she always insisted we visit her parents. When we got to Sto:lo Eagle, a heavy-equipment contractor was clearing land on the reserve, so Henry said we should get him to clear a lot for us so when our application for a house goes through, our lot will be cleared. And the land was near the store, so it was a prime location.

I didn't want to because we were already having enough trouble paying our bills. I was working, but my money wasn't going in regularly, and one credit card company was phoning me up about it. Now we were going to go deeper in debt, but Jennifer couldn't say no to her dad because he had too much control over her. Time off was just building up more tension and making me feel worse. After we measured the width of the lot and started ribboning the boundaries, I was too upset to care how they were laid out. I just tied the ribbons as I walked along, not caring if the boundary was straight or not; and Jennifer got mad at me for doing that, but I just didn't care! We talked to the contractor and he agreed to clear the land, but I thought to myself, *I wouldn't move back without a large guard dog to protect her because I never know where or when I'll be called off to work.*

That night, Henry said to us, "When people help you out when you're in trouble, be sure you're around to help them out!" referring to when we stopped by to visit him when I was unemployed. He acted like he did everything for us and we were obligated to him, totally ignoring all the things we did for him. He didn't even thank me for paying for his son's graduation and helping him get into college.

I replied, "We've already done too much for you! We're not going to move back just to be on call for you!"

Later on, Jennifer told Henry we were staying at Sylvia's Café, west of Quesnel. He knew where it was because he went hunting up there quite often. When we got back to Quesnel, so much tension was building up I couldn't sleep very well at night and was starting to wake up in the middle of the night feeling extremely depressed. Henry called us one night and said he was going on his hunting trip and would stop by and stay with us, but I said, "You can't stay with us. We don't have room for you."

After he hung up, I told Jim about it and Jim said, "No. We don't have room for him. He just wants a place to stay free of charge."

I was glad we didn't have room for him because he would have meals and try and get me to pay for them no matter how bad things were going for me. We worked for a few more days, then Jim said he was going back to Vancouver to pick up another worker, Mike Sawyer. After he left, I continued working by myself, and Jennifer went to work with me. I normally work hard, but I just couldn't get myself going. I was getting too depressed because nothing seemed to be working out. I wasn't told I wouldn't be paid regularly and I used my credit cards as if I would be. Now a card company was calling me and I could never get time off work to call them back.

On my way to work one day, Jennifer decided she wanted to go back to Sto:lo Eagle. I didn't want to take her to town, but my truck door got stuck and wouldn't close. I called Allan Tweedy and he told me just to take my truck back to the dealer because it was still under warranty. When I took my truck to town, I took Jennifer to the bus depot. She went back home and got Ryan to pick her up on the highway turning off toward Sto:lo Eagle. I continued working for a few more days, then Jim called me to pick him up at the airport; and when I got there, he was showing Mike Sawyer how to use a compass to take bearings. Mike seemed like a very nice fellow and had been working for a large tree-planting company and just got laid off. I accompanied Mike and Jim the next day when Jim showed him how to take soil samples and do plots, then we were each given an area and went to work.

I thought I would work better now that Jennifer was gone, but my strip lines continued to steer off to the right and I couldn't understand why I kept doing that. I was making some rather costly errors, and Jim was getting mad. Finally, Jim and I were talking and we mentioned what I was doing, so we both took a compass bearing on the same location from the same spot and got two completely different readings. Then Jim realized I was holding my compass in my right hand and looking with my left eye. I told him I was meant to be left-handed but my dad always made me use my right hand because he said, "It's a right-handed world. Everything is made for right-handed people." Then I told Jim about some of the things I went through as I was growing up and why it was very difficult for me to speak up or use my own initiative.

Jim thought I should see a psychiatrist, but I thought the doctor would just say I was stable enough and could also see that Jennifer had a very hard life too. We never said very much about her life, but he could see that nobody wanted her and people were always mean to her. Then he said, "The helpless can be some of the most powerful people because other people do things for them and think they're doing them a big favor."

I said, "Jennifer's father didn't just criticize his kids for making a mistake. He would beat them."

I phoned Jennifer one night; and she said her father was away on his hunting trip, the contractor was clearing the land, and she was the only person there to tell him what to do. She said he cleared quite a bit of land because she didn't know how much to have cleared, so I started getting scared because I didn't know how much it was going to cost. I was getting more and more depressed and it was getting so bad I could barely plod along at work. Jim was also getting depressed and starting to have nightmares too; he woke up in the middle of the night, groaning, "Awe, come on now, you guys!" and was standing near the door before he realized it was the middle of the night.

The way the contract was going and the way I was working were really getting Jim down, and he was ready to fire me. Finally, I just snapped myself out of it and told myself, "I'm going to live my own life! Just because other people can't see things that are right in front of them and refuse to take the time to look doesn't mean they don't exist! They can live in their own little world if that's what they want. They don't have to hold me back!" I snapped myself out of my depression and started working harder and faster. I started feeling better and tried to enjoy my work more then had to miss a day because I had the flu.

It was usually cold in the morning then got warm later in the day, so I took my coat off and left it beside the road. I was going to pick it up later but forgot it, and when I went to pick it up the next day, it was gone. Mike, Jim, and I continued working; then Mike decided it was time for him to go back to Vancouver. Jim and I worked a little while longer then decided to take some time off. Jim caught the train back to Vancouver, and I stopped off in Williams Lake at Allan Tweedy's house. I phoned home, and Dad suggested I stay there for the night because traffic would be heavy because of the long weekend. I was lucky I did that because I didn't realize how tired I was. I got paid for doing the timber cruising but never got paid anything for the silviculture surveys, so I didn't know what I was going to do. I had bills to pay but couldn't pay them!

Jennifer wanted me to go get her now that Henry was back from his hunting trip. He and Andrew had gone all the way to Fort Nelson; and as usual, Henry said, "We never saw a thing." He was also mad because we wouldn't let him stay at our place, and said, "I'll never ask anyone for help anymore!" and said that two more times later on.

Henry owned three spaniels, two males named Charlie and Snuffy and a female named Kayla. I always thought Charlie was a really loveable little dog, yet one of Henry's neighbors shot Charlie and Snuffy. Now I knew that Jennifer wouldn't be safe in Sto:lo Eagle even if we owned a dog because someone could shoot the dog, and I didn't trust her father either. I wasn't too worried though because I thought it would take a long time for us to get a house. I spent the weekend in Sto:lo Eagle, then Jennifer went back with me. She didn't tell Henry she was leaving until just before we were ready to go, and his face just dropped with disappointment. He didn't want her to go, but he was already driving her crazy. I knew I could work better without her, but she had no place else to go, so I had to take her with me. I picked Jim up at the train station in Quesnel, and we continued working on the contract, trying to get it done before it snowed and we wouldn't be able to work.

The credit card company finally tracked me down to Sylvia's Café, where we were staying, and told me to send the card back. I was over my spending limit and couldn't afford to pay the amount over my limit. I had always been a good customer, yet they wouldn't give me a chance to catch up on my payments. But I had another credit card from another company, and they raised my spending limit when I hit hard times because I had proven to be a good credit risk. I was rather happy to lose that one credit card though because I should have stopped dealing with that company many years earlier.

Jim and I continued to work and try and get the contract completed; things weren't going very well, but we did the best we could. We kept working day after day, then Jim suggested we take a whole week off because he hadn't spent much time at home and probably needed the time off. Jennifer and I went back to the coast and stopped off in Rosedale for a brief visit. Applications to carry the Olympic torch had been sent out, but I refused to apply and threw the application straight in the fireplace! I always thought I was a nice guy; but I often get closed off, so I thought, *That's fine! I'll keep my distance!*

Jennifer insisted on going to Sto:lo Eagle because she didn't want to stay in Rosedale. Henry didn't drink, and I felt like I needed to unwind, but I didn't drink in there because of him. I tried to tell Jennifer we should go to Laughing Raven since she didn't want to go to Rosedale, but she just acted like I wasn't important then. Finally, near the end of the week, we went to Laughing Raven. I was very stressed out and didn't get very much of an opportunity to relieve my tensions. We only spent one night in Laughing Raven, then it was time to go back to Quesnel. Time off always made me feel worse, and even my own family treated me like I wasn't important.

Jim and I went back to work and finally finished the contract. It had been a nightmare for both of us. Many things didn't go right, and I thought most of it was my fault. We had worked hard for another week, gathered everything up, then went back to Williams Lake and stayed at Allan Tweedy's house again. The next day, Jim and I had breakfast; and after Allan went to work, Jim told me about a letter the Indian band in Sardis sent about me. It was really bad and said I couldn't even take orders very well. I was shocked because I had tried to be a good worker when I was there, but Jennifer kept holding me back. She had told me not to put them on my résumé, but I did it anyway because I was trying to be totally honest. I didn't listen to her again and ended up regretting it.

Jennifer was feeling extremely depressed and wanted to see a doctor. She wanted me to unload Jim's things from the back of my truck, but I thought I had lots of time to do it later, so we drove around town then walked around for a while. Then when I wanted to take Jim's things back but she wouldn't let me because she wanted me to stay right beside her, finally she decided to go to the doctor. The doctor referred us to a mental-health specialist. Usually it takes a long time, several months, to see them; but she got to see her right away. The doctor told her we were both brilliant, and it made me feel good to see that I wasn't the only person to believe Jennifer is brilliant. I never thought of myself that way though. The mental-health therapist diagnosed Jennifer as someone who had been molested as a child. They talked for a long time, and I should have brought Jim's things back, but I didn't want to leave her. The therapist said we could get a room at the Indian friendship center and see her again. Social Services and Housing could help us stay there until my UIC was transferred from Chilliwack.

Jennifer didn't want to stay at Allan Tweedy's again that night, so we got a motel room. Allan had invited us over for supper that night, but Jennifer was too nervous to go. She eventually settled down though and stayed at the shopping mall while I went to Allan's for supper. I finally unloaded Jim's things and he sorted them out, but he was concerned about catching his plane that night; and while we were eating, Jim said, "Canada is a very racist country! It's just that the racism was hidden!"

"I was logging with a fellow in 1979. He said he was ashamed to admit he was an Indian because of what he went through in the residential schools. He was an alcoholic and I thought that was just drunk talk."

"That wasn't drunk talk," Jim said.

After dinner, I drove Jim to town to the bank machine before driving him to the airport, but there was an old man using the bank machine ahead of him, and it took him a long time to finish. By the time Jim got his money and rushed to the airport, it was too late; he couldn't catch the plane that night. I brought Jim back to Allan's house then picked Jennifer up and went to our motel room, but I had to be up early the next day to drive Jim to the airport. It was a weekend now, so Jim had to pay more for his flight home and I felt guilty about it. I should have listened to Jennifer again but didn't. Usually, good luck follows me and things seem to work out right for me, but it seemed like I brought Allan and Jim nothing but bad luck.

Jennifer decided we should just head back to the coast, and I agreed; even if my UIC was transferred from Chilliwack, it wouldn't be enough to live on because we were too far in debt and I didn't know when we were going to get paid. When we got back to Rosedale, David and Angie had moved into their own house, but envy was still bothering Jennifer; there was still much tension between her and my family, making it hard for her to stay in Rosedale, so we went to Sto:lo Eagle. The land was cleared and the brush was piled where we were supposed to be building our house and Henry told me I should go and burn the brush. I told him, "It's still green and should dry out first." I didn't tell him I didn't want to burn it because I didn't want to live there. Henry was persistent though and kept telling me to go burn the brush, so I reluctantly left, only because I figured Jennifer would want me to listen to him.

As I was trying to light the fires, Henry Jr. went out to help me. He said, "Dad said they can do it themselves, but I came out anyway."

We got the fire going a little bit after trying for several hours; then we went back to the house, and Jennifer said we should leave, so we went to Lytton. She was crying and said her father had touched her the wrong way. He was trying to stick a candy in her mouth. It was late when we got to Lytton, so we spent the night in a campground, slept in the truck that night, and went to the hotel the next day to visit Liz. She said it was okay for us to go to their house, and after she went home from work, Jennifer told her what their father did. It was hard for us to stay anywhere on the coast, so we left. The next day, Gordon brought a case of beer up to their place when Liz was at work; so Jennifer and I left, went to the hotel, and told Liz. She phoned home and really blew up. She told Gordon to take his case of beer and get out or she was going to call the police. Then she told Jennifer, "I think you guys better leave now. Jeremy's really going to be mad now!"

We had no place to go, so we spent the night at the campground in our truck again. We didn't have very much money and didn't want to go back to the coast, so our only alternative was to go look for another job. So the next day, we drove to Merritt then to Princeton. I didn't think it was worth applying at any of the sawmills in Merritt because there wasn't much going on during the winter and they're usually laying off forestry staff that time of year. When we got to Princeton, we drove to Keromeos and went to the Indian band office and applied for work. The people there seemed fairly friendly, and I went to a coffee shop with a band member for an interview. He looked at my résumé and said most of my jobs were just a couple of months here, two months there, so I told him that was the only work available. When I went for some interviews, I was told I was luckier than most forest technicians. My luck ran out in 1984, but most technicians' luck ran out in 1982.

Jennifer was looking around in the shops while I was being interviewed, then we left. I told her there might be a job available there but finding a place might be a problem, then we drove to Penticton. There was a trailer parked on the street, selling french fries, so I bought an order of fries and shared it with her. That was our first meal in two days. We slept in the truck again that night and drove to Kelowna the next day. We were drinking lots of coffee rather than eating and didn't have any blankets, so we used our coats to stay warm at night. When we got to Kelowna, we went to a shopping mall to walk around, and both of us went to the washroom to wash and get cleaned up.

I called the tribal council in Kelowna to see if they had any jobs available, but there wasn't any, so we drove to Vernon. As we were looking around in the stores, I ran into Raymond Joe, one of the fellows from the crew I worked with in Enderby. He said to me his band may have a job available and I could call the chief or band office to inquire, so I called the band office the next day and spoke to the band manager. She told me the job involved teaching the band members woods skills and training a band member to be their supervisor and I was to work myself out of a job in three months. That sounded like a job better suited for Jim Rowed because I was still too withdrawn to be a teacher; the chief wasn't going to be back for a couple of days, so I could just send him a résumé.

We drove to Kamloops that night and slept in the truck again. The next day I went to the Kamloops Indian band office to visit Allan

Casimer. Kamloops didn't have any work available, so I reluctantly went to the Shuswap Nation Tribal Council office in the building next door and was getting extremely depressed about not finding any work. I went to the office and asked the forester, Terry Chow, if there was any work available for forest technicians. Terry told me to go for an interview the next day because he had too much work to do to interview me that day, so we got a motel room that night because I wanted to get cleaned up and rested for the interview the next day. Jennifer also said she kept picturing in her mind she wanted to stay at that same motel again; now she was getting what she wanted.

I went for the interview the next day, and Terry told me the job was in Cache Creek, then said, "Did you know that band is $350,000 in debt?"

"No, I didn't know that. Isn't my résumé still on file from before?"

"Yes, it's on file, but Mark Atherton said he had reservations about you because you don't know how to handle a crew very well."

I didn't tell him that was because I had health problems at the time so I had to stay calm at all times or my chest would hurt. I also changed since then, but it would have been disastrous for me to move to Cache Creek and get laid off because I was already far enough in debt. I also got the feeling it wouldn't do any good to tell him about it anyway. Terry said, "I originally got a degree in agriculture, but many of the courses are the same for forestry. Now I'm taking on some forestry courses towards my RPF. Do you think it would be worthwhile for me to go back to college and get a diploma in agriculture?"

"Not really," he said, "the Department of Agriculture is very small, and it's very hard to get a milk quota for dairy farming. I also have to interview more people before I can decide who to hire. I can't hire anyone after interviewing only one person."

After the interview, Jennifer and I went back to Rosedale. There were only two jobs available, none of them worth getting excited about; both of them were only three months long, but it would have been better that living in the truck that winter. I had to get my truck serviced again and pick up my UIC, so we stayed in Rosedale for two or three days. Then Jennifer couldn't take it anymore and we had to leave, but this time we took a sleeping bag with us. Jennifer said I didn't have to go with her and I could stay there with my parents if I wanted, but I told her I was going with her anyway. She couldn't look after herself and could easily become a victim of people who prey on runaways. We didn't know where we were going or what we were going to do and left on such a spur of the moment that I wished I had packed some food.

We went back to Kamloops again but didn't stop in Lytton, and when we got there, we tried sleeping in the woods; but Jennifer was too scared of the dark. I would have preferred sleeping in the woods because I didn't want people to see we were living in our truck. It was December now and the weather was getting cold, so I always made sure we had lots of gas in the tank in case it got too cold. Jennifer wanted to go to Cranbrook, but I thought that was too far. I didn't want to go that far to look for work because I knew my chances of finding work there weren't very good. I also knew the tribal council there had hired a full-time forest technician and Industry probably wouldn't be doing any hiring; most of them would be laying people off now. As I was walking around the streets one day, I ran into Jennifer's half sister Rhonda. She was always funny and said, "I went to Sto:lo Eagle to visit Dad. My father was his usual cantankerous self, so I guess everything is normal."

She told me where she lived and asked us to go visit, but I had to go back and see Jennifer because I didn't want to be away from her too long. Then I told her what Rhonda said, and Jennifer said, "I finally realize my dad is always cranky."

Jennifer was too nervous to go visit her and wanted to keep living in our truck even though we were only having one meal a day. I called Department of Mental Health again the next day, and the receptionist said it would take six months before we could get an appointment; unless it was an emergency, we would have to wait. I don't remember what happened, but we saw a lady at the mental-health unit right away. Jennifer talked to her for a little while, then she told Jennifer to go to Social Services and Housing for help and she would tell them we were going. After her appointment, we went to Social Services and Housing, but by the way the clerk acted, it didn't look like she was told we were going; but if I worked there, I wouldn't believe very much either.

I didn't really want to move to Kamloops because I knew my chances of finding work there weren't very good. Jennifer was always taught to cater to her parents and would still have tried to do things for them. We didn't really look for a place to stay and continued living in our truck, having one meal a day. There was a travelling Elvis Presley museum at the KXA grounds, so we spent the day there. There were a number of other displays there and a lady who did tarot-card readings, so I decided to get a reading. She gave me a short reading and didn't charge me. Then she gave me her card and told us to go over to her house for a reading; that sounded okay to me because we were really down on our luck and I couldn't see any way out of the situation we were in. I also thought that would give me an idea of what's coming in the future because I was at the point where I was willing to try or do anything if it worked.

She told us all kinds of negative things and that Jennifer had a curse on her but she may be able to break it. I was to wrap an egg in some dollar bills, wrap it in a black cloth, and place it under our bed. Jennifer should also hang a cross above her and we should drop by the next day, so we bought the eggs and cloth and did what she told us. When we got back to her place the next day, she told me to leave the room and got Jennifer to smash the egg; then she called me back, and there was some gooey brown substance and what looked like hair in the egg after it was smashed.

I wondered how she did that. Did she replace the original egg with another egg with something in it? I also wondered how she got the substance inside the egg. I enjoy watching magicians on TV and knew even amateur magicians could probably do a trick like that and make it look like something was actually inside the egg. The lady said one time she did that, she pulled out a snake; someone put a curse on her and she may be able to break it. Jennifer should also change her name because all the people from the Bible with her real name were bad. She would have to burn a large sum of money, $2,100, to break the curse; but she could help us out with a few hundred if we needed it. Then she told Jennifer to get holy water from seven different churches, drink some of it every day, and say a number of prayers.

Jennifer told her we were living in our truck, we didn't have a place to stay, and were only eating one meal a day. She was surprised and told us to go stay in a hostel. It was mid-December and cold out, so they won't turn us down. She knew we were that far down on our luck and she still asked us for a large sum of money. Some people will take advantage of others no matter how far down on their luck they are. Jennifer went to a women's shelter that night, and I went to the men's hostel. She didn't want to be apart from me, but they were separate units. At the men's hostel, I was required to take a shower before going to bed, but it felt good to be clean again. I was only given one blanket, and it was rather cold in there. I had my coat, but I wished I had brought my toque. We were in a rather large room with a row of beds on each side of the room like in a residential school. I listened to some of them talk as I lay there, and they were homeless with no place to go. For breakfast the next day, we had toast, porridge, and tea; we were given fifteen minutes to eat until lunchtime, then we had to leave. One old man talked like he had been living like that all his life and talked about riding the trains like people did in the hungry thirties.

I picked Jennifer up after breakfast, and she said she was given a large bowl of chili before she went to bed. She didn't want to eat that much and only ate it because she was expected to. I told her lunch was at noon and dinner was at five o'clock, but she was too depressed to go back and wanted me to stay right beside her. We didn't eat anything for the rest of the day and slept in the truck again that night. We sometimes went down to Riverside Park and sat in our truck. We stayed in the truck again the next night, and when I went to a convenience store to buy something to eat, Jennifer told me to buy her some razor blades. She didn't say it was to commit suicide, but I knew that's what it was for. I went in and bought something to eat and told her the store didn't have any razor blades. We slept in the truck again that night because she didn't want to go back to the women's shelter and said I could go back to the hostel and she could sleep in the truck by herself, but I wouldn't let her sleep in the truck by herself. We looked around in the stores the next day because it was a place to stay warm and get out of the truck for a little while. I couldn't find work anywhere, and now it was time to go back to the coast again. I didn't want to go back, but it looked like we had no choice. I was beginning to feel like Gray Wolf in the book *A Good Day to Die*, starved into submission.

I decided to get a motel room that night so we could get cleaned up and get a good night's sleep because I didn't want anyone to ask or find out what we were doing and it was time for my UIC check to go in. When we got as far as Hope, I could feel the tension building up again. We only stayed in Rosedale for one or two nights then left. We just said we were going Christmas shopping and tried to stay away from Sto:lo Eagle as much as we could. When we were shopping in Agassiz one afternoon, we ran into Henry and Andrew. Henry was working at the time and said we should go for something to eat. When we got to the restaurant, I immediately told the waitress, "Put ours on a separate bill." Henry was slightly surprised because he was used to us paying his expenses for him. I didn't want to go to Sto:lo Eagle for Christmas, but I knew we would end up going there.

Henry and Andrew left to continue their shopping and Jennifer and I went back to Rosedale. The next day, we went to Chilliwack, then to Abbotsford; and Jennifer was getting so depressed she couldn't get herself to do anything. We went to one of the shopping malls and looked around for a little while, and it looked like we were going to sleep in the truck again; but luckily, a couple from Laughing Raven saw us in the store and asked us if we were going to visit Ben and Geraldine. Jennifer said yes only because they would have told them they saw us and thought Ben and Geraldine would be mad or disappointed if we didn't stop by.

We went to Laughing Raven and spent the night but didn't want to stay long because they have five kids to look after. We left the next day and went to Surrey because Jennifer always talked about running away to Surrey. We drove toward Surrey and stopped at a service station for gas and directions, and the attendant said we were in Surrey. We drove around then spent the night in the truck near the Surrey Inn. It was getting colder, so we both slept in the sleeping bag, using our body heat for warmth. The next day, we drove around and looked around in the shopping malls. Christmas was coming, the stores were getting busy, and I wished I could get away from her for just a little while and go for something to eat; but she wanted me to stay right beside her.

After the stores closed, Jennifer wanted me to look for a hostel for us to stay in, so I looked in the Yellow Pages; the nearest one was in Vancouver, so I told her I didn't want to go that far. I was actually hoping she would get tired of the way we were living so we could go back to Rosedale, but we stayed in Surrey for several more days then went to Vancouver. It was cold out and there was about a foot of snow on the ground, but we had no place to go. Jennifer often got cranky at me, and I wished she wouldn't do that, but I knew I had to stay with her in spite of what I had to put up with. We usually drank coffee rather than eat and went to a White Spot Restaurant for coffee one night. The waitress serving us mentioned going home then sensed we didn't have a home, and as we were walking out, some Indians who were well dressed and appeared to be doing quite well for themselves went walking in, so I wondered what they did for a living. After everything

I went through to get a career, I couldn't find a job anywhere. I tried to go back logging and couldn't because I'm a forest technician. It was hard to get a job in forestry because I'm not a registered professional forester, so I felt like a born loser! When we were living in Vancouver, I kept calling Jim Rowed to see about the contract. If he needed any help with the mapping, I would have helped him out; but each time I called, all I ever got was the answering machine.

Jennifer said, "I hope he didn't commit suicide!"

"I hope so too!" I knew we brought him and Allan a lot of bad luck.

We slept in the truck on various streets in Vancouver now and started buying Christmas presents but still only eating one meal a day. We went to the shopping mall in North Vancouver one night, and there was a group of people singing Christmas carols. They had put a hat out for donations, but it didn't look like very many people were donating. There was a recession and many people weren't doing very well. We did most of our shopping in North Vancouver and Surrey, then we finally went back to Chilliwack. Jennifer finally decided to go to the doctor for help, but we had to go to the emergency room because it was late Friday night. We told the doctor where we were living, where we were from, and what we were doing; but the doctor said it wasn't a very good idea to go to the psychiatric ward right now. First of all, it was full, and the staff couldn't do anything for her because it was a weekend, so he gave her some pills and asked us to go back on Monday.

Jennifer felt really discouraged after that. She couldn't go back to Rosedale or Sto:lo Eagle, so we ended up sleeping in the truck again that night. It was cold, there was a foot of snow, and the wind was blowing; but we were all right. We stayed in the truck the next day and tried to avoid seeing anyone we knew and avoided places where people who knew us might see us. Jennifer was given enough pills to get through the weekend but got extremely depressed that night and took them all, hoping it would kill her, before I could stop her. Right after she did that, I rushed to the emergency ward and told the nurses what happened, but they said it wouldn't do her any harm. Finally on Christmas Eve, we went to Sto:lo Eagle; unfortunately it was late at night and all the lights were out at her parents' place. She didn't want to wake them because her father had complained about us stopping in late at night. The lights were still on at Ryan's place next door, but

Jennifer didn't want to go there because Henry got mad at her for going over there too often, so we drove off and spent the night on a side road by a farmer's field. It was cold, but we used our body heat to stay warm.

We finally went to her parents' place on Christmas Day, and I was happy to at least have a place to stay temporarily. Jennifer was very worried about her weight and didn't eat very much; she had lost fifteen pounds and I lost twenty. The day after Christmas, she wanted to move away, but her grandmother passed away that day. I was sad but also relieved because at least we would have a place to stay for a few more days. Someone called Brenda, so she caught the bus from Lethbridge to attend the funeral; then Jennifer, Henry Jr., and I started baking pies while Henry and Andrew helped make preparations for the funeral. When Brenda arrived Jennifer slept with her so they could talk, and I was happy to have some time alone.

Henry was always cranky and criticizing his kids and still sometimes beat them for no reason; nothing they ever did for him was enough. The next day, we were all sitting at the table having breakfast; but Jennifer, she was in the living room, crying. Everyone was quiet around their father, Andrew was cooking, and Henry said, "Crybaby Jennifer! I wonder why she's not eating."

I said, "People said she's overweight, so she believes she's overweight."

"Who said that?"

"*You!*" I replied rather loudly. "And my aunt from Ohio." I had told myself I'm not holding back anymore and I meant it!

Everyone was surprised and looked up, then Andrew thought, *She can't take Dad's criticism!*

I stayed right beside Jennifer or kept a very close eye on her at all times. I wasn't going to leave her alone with her father again because I suffered enough already because of that. Jennifer slept with Brenda, and I enjoyed some time alone. My instincts were telling me to start coming out of my shell and start thinking more about romances, but I didn't want to! I missed being single and doing whatever I wanted to do; it seemed like I could never do even the littlest thing for myself or my own interests. Before the funeral, Jennifer started giving away her most-personal possessions; she gave Brenda a ring she really liked and wanted for a long time and tried to give Liz her watch, but she wouldn't take it. I knew it was a symptom of someone wanting to commit suicide; people who have made the decision feel they don't need their personal possessions anymore because they're not going to live much longer. I had to make sure Jennifer wouldn't do anything!

We went to the funeral, and at the dinner afterward, I noticed one of my cousins and other people avoiding me. Even while Christmas-shopping, it was the same way; relatives were treating me like I was keeping to myself, so I thought, *Maybe it's because I'm not following my instincts.*

Brenda went back to Lethbridge after the funeral, and Jennifer and I went to Henry Jr.'s apartment; he said we could stay at his place, but Jennifer just wanted to stay there until he went back to college. He said we could have whatever we wanted to eat, but we didn't touch anything. The first day, we didn't eat anything at all; then the second day, I bought us something to eat at 7-Eleven. I was hungry, but I went along with what she had to say. We spent New Year's Eve watching TV in Henry Jr.'s apartment. We were hungry, but we still didn't eat anything.

Chapter 10

1988

Henry Jr. came back to college and said we could stay there with him, but Jennifer thought we would be too much bother for him. I called the Shuswap Nation Tribal Council about the job in Cache Creek, but it was given to a fellow from Lytton, so Jennifer and I moved out and lived in our truck for two more days and nights. We didn't eat anything on the second day because we ran out of money and I had to make sure we had enough gas in the tank because it was getting colder. We made an appointment to see her regular doctor because he knew her history of depression, but when it was time for her appointment, she just got out and went walking down the street. It was cold out and she wasn't even wearing a coat, so I ran after her and got her. She tried to change her mind about seeing him, but I made her go. She told the doctor our situation, what was happening, and that we were sleeping in our truck. It was cold, the wind was blowing, and there was over a foot of snow on the ground; so the doctor asked, "Did you keep the motor running all night?"

"No," I said rather quietly.

The doctor immediately called the hospital and had her admitted to the psychiatric ward. The ward was full, so she got a bed in another unit. I brought Jennifer to the hospital and waited until she was admitted; and the first thing they did was give her a bed, some pills, and put her to sleep. I was feeling quite stressed out after that but didn't want to go home right away, so I walked around town for a little while. I ran into one of my cousins and her boyfriend in the bar and had a couple of beers with them. They needed a ride back to Rosedale, so I gave them one; and when we got to Rosedale, they invited me in for supper and a few more beers. I was hungry, so I really heaped my plate then went back for seconds; so my cousin said, "You sure ate a lot!"

"That was my first meal in two days. Jennifer and I slept in our truck last night."

My aunt said, "It's cold out there! You could have froze to death! You could have spent the night here!"

I didn't say Jennifer would have been too nervous to stay with anyone though and spent the night there then had breakfast the next day. I didn't want to go back to my parents' place, but now I had no choice; and when I got home, Dad got mad and asked me, "Were you fasting? You've lost so much weight!"

I just said no and didn't want to tell him what really happened.

"It's not scientifically proven!"

I just sat around for the rest of the day and wished I could move away, as far as I could go, but I was forced to go back. The next day, I went to visit Jennifer in the hospital; although she had lost so much weight, she still believed she was overweight and was trying not to eat very much without the hospital staff finding out about it. I knew she was anorexic, but there was nothing I could do about it. If I tried to make her eat more, she would just take more ex-lax or laxative; so all I could do was stay beside her, be her support, and keep hoping she would get stronger. She snuck some ex-lax into her room without the staff knowing about it and told me, but I didn't say anything because I wanted her to believe she could trust me. Another girl in there was also anorexic, but she wouldn't be allowed out until she started eating, so Jennifer started eating just so she could get out sooner. One day when I was visiting her, she told me, "One of the nurses told me I was trying to live everyone else's life. I told the social worker I always wanted a dad to love me, and he said, 'Well, Jennifer, you have to grow up sometime.'"

When her parents heard she was in the hospital, they went over to visit, and Henry said, "You can move home when you get out."

Jennifer said, "No. I'll have to go for day care therapy." It was a small but important step for her to break away from her father's domination, but it made her feel good. After a week and a half in the hospital, Jennifer was told she wouldn't be allowed out until she found a place to stay. Social Services and Housing would get her a place to stay, and I would only be allowed to visit her once in a while, so she signed out on day pass and we looked for a place to stay.

There was a small run-down house behind an apartment building and Jennifer seriously talked about renting it out, but I said, "No, you wouldn't be safe there. The parking lot would get dark and people would know you're there by yourself. There's too much chance of something happening to you." We looked around for a couple more days then found an apartment behind the post office. It was rather small but affordable, and an apartment like that was much safer than a small house in a dark alley. We went back to the hospital for her to sign out and arrange for day care therapy; then we went to Social Services and Housing and the Social Worker had made arrangements for her to get a security deposit, her rent, and money for groceries.

She moved in to her apartment in the middle of the month, so I took our things out of storage and moved them in then stayed for two days to help her unpack and get settled. I had a phone installed so she could call me if her depression got too bad, and she was on a new drug for treating depression called Prozac. Just before she got out of the hospital, the first murder of the year took place; and when I went to leave her apartment, I found a note on my windshield. I never thought anything of it until I read it, and it said in big block letters, "YOU SICK BASTARD! YOU ARE AN IGNORANT TRESPASSER! COLLECT YOUR BAG OF GARBAGE AND GET OUT! GET OUT BEFORE I KILL! I HAVEN'T KILLED BEFORE BUT THERE'S A FIRST TIME FOR EVERYTHING! I KNOW IT'S YOU, YOU BASTARD!"

I got scared and didn't know what to do. Jennifer got even more scared! We didn't know the people who committed the first murder of the year were already in jail, but I went home for a couple of days anyway then showed it to my dad. He read it then told me to go to the police, so I went to the police station, showed one of them the note, then told him, "Jennifer just got out of the psychiatric ward. That note scared her even more because of the recent murder."

"Was there someone in the ward who may have fallen in love with her?"

"I don't think so."

"I know where those apartments are. The landlords had trouble with one of their tenants recently. We had to go in and evict them."

I told him as I was leaving, "Jennifer would have committed suicide years ago, but I was there to look after her."

Jennifer phoned me the next day and said it was a senile lady who wrote the note. She didn't remember doing it, but she was evicted anyway. Luckily, the landlords didn't charge Jennifer for her first month's rent because she moved in at the middle of the month. Henry Jr. wasn't able to pay for his graduation pictures and his father wouldn't pay for them; he just brought the bill over to his son, so as broke as we were, we still had to pay for his graduation pictures. Jennifer went to her day care therapy and called me up whenever depression got to be too much for her. All we owned for furniture were a twin bed, table and chairs, and TV and stand. If she wanted to watch TV, she had to sit on a kitchen chair. Living at home with my parents almost drove me crazy, so I was happy when Jennifer called me to go see her. Sometimes she was hallucinating, and one time she said she saw a hat floating in the air. Another time, she saw a boot floating in the air, bobbing up and down; and once she was home by herself, and the TV went on by itself. She may have accidentally turned on the timer but didn't know it.

I visited Jennifer quite regularly because of her nervous condition and was happy Henry Jr. lived a little ways away and could help look after her. She often went shopping as a way of forgetting her problems but often found good buys on things that were necessary or useful for her apartment. When she first moved back to Chilliwack, she hated it and wanted to move away. She hated all the bad memories from the past and seeing people from her reserve who were mean to her as a child. She was still thin from all the weight she lost from living in our truck, yet she still believed she was overweight and wanted to lose more weight. We ran into one of her aunts when we were walking around the streets, and her aunt commented on how skinny she was, yet she didn't think so. It was still cold and there was still snow on the ground, so I had to drive Jennifer to her day care therapy, and she also went to Community Services and started seeing a sexual-abuse therapist, Dawn Barr. Things weren't going too bad for us, but it was still difficult to look after her because she felt really bad about herself and believed she looked like the beast in the weekly television series *Beauty and the Beast*. She also believed she had a stamp on her forehead that said "*Incest!*"

I didn't know how to convince her that it wasn't her fault for what happened in the past and didn't know why victims blame themselves for what happened. A good friend of mine from Lytton committed suicide that spring, and I couldn't believe it because he always seemed so happy-go-lucky! Jennifer complained about sitting on our chairs, but I couldn't afford a couch, so I told her she would have to wait until I got a job somewhere. So I went to an auction to see if I could get any furniture we could afford, and ran into another fellow from Lytton. I wondered why Pete committed suicide, and he said Pete was molested by one of the ministers in the residential school. When his case went to court, he couldn't take the memories of what happened and committed suicide, but I still wondered why he did that because it wasn't his fault that he was molested.

I noticed I wasn't sleeping very well at night, and when I went to the band office to photocopy my résumé to apply for jobs, I noticed my cousin Chester was avoiding me again. He thought I was withdrawing and wondered what was happening, then after I started following my instincts, I started sleeping better and relatives stopped avoiding me. Now I knew I should start thinking more about romances.

Sometimes, jobs can be extremely hard to find, so I went to CEIC and got some pamphlets for people looking for work. The pamphlets mentioned people who can't find work start to think, "Is there something wrong with me? I can't find work anywhere, and I keep applying!" and that's exactly how I felt. Jim Rowed phoned me up unexpectedly one night. He was attending Simon Fraser University (SFU) and needed help mapping the contract we did. I was happy to hear from him and more than willing to help with the mapping because it was our last chance to save the contract. I wasn't about to give up without a struggle. I rented a VCR for Jennifer so she could try and keep herself entertained. We had bought some Jane Fonda exercise videos previously, and now she could exercise without anyone seeing or criticizing her.

I packed a lunch and some clothes and met Jim at SFU. I didn't know how long it was going to take to do the contract because we still had to do the statistics. When I saw Jim, he asked me what happened because I had lost so much weight. I told him I wasn't anorexic; we just had a run of bad luck and ended up living in my truck for a month and a half. Working on the contract turned out to be a slow process; it looked like nothing had worked out when we did our plots, and Jim wondered if I could ever do anything right. The first day wasn't too productive and very stressful, so I took a break and went to the pub for a beer. I only asked for a small cup but was given a large one and barely felt any effects from the alcohol.

Jim lived in a part of Vancouver known as Kitsilano, out toward UBC. I gave him a ride home then went to North Vancouver to my aunt and uncle's place. We both worked hard, day after day, trying to save the contract. I have never given up when things got hard and wasn't about to give up now, but it was harder on Jim because he also had to keep up with his studies. He wanted to get out of forestry and become a speech therapist, so we worked steady for a week; then Jim said we should take a break. I went to visit Jennifer and Henry Jr. was there and they were both baking and I thought, "That's good! Maybe she'll learn to have more confidence in herself!"

I took several days off then went back to Vancouver to work on the contract again. Up in Quesnel, Jim suggested I see a psychiatrist and suggested a very good one; but I couldn't afford to see him and still thought if I asked a doctor for a referral, they would just say I was stable enough. I made five trips in total to Vancouver to work on the contract; each time we worked four or five days then took a break. It was a lot of work, but we kept trying. We worked until late and were often exhausted at the end of the day, so I usually gave Jim a ride home in the evening. Jennifer got tired of sitting on the kitchen chairs, so she put a small down payment on a couch-and-chair set at a secondhand store. I didn't know how we were going to pay for it because I was barely keeping payments on my bills, but luckily, Jim gave me $200 for using my truck and the trips to Vancouver, so I used it to buy Jennifer her couch-and-chair set.

Before we completed the contract, Jim said the company called and threatened him with no payment and he was given a deadline to have everything in. I still didn't know if we could do it, but I wasn't about to give up. The British Columbia Forest Service brought out a policy that year that people doing silviculture surveys had to be certified or working on the same block with someone who was certified. There was a course available in Surrey at the end of February, so I applied to take it and was accepted. Jim talked the company into giving him an extension on the remaining blocks we had to do and loaned me all the equipment I needed to take the surveys course. Then I wrote to Allan Tweedy to apply for a job again and asked him for a chance to prove myself as a worker. I told him 1987 was a very bad year for me and things got so bad we ended up living in our truck for a month and a half in November and December. I didn't get anyone to type out the letter because I didn't want anyone else to read it; he didn't answer and I didn't blame him.

After Jim and I completed the contract, my UIC had run out and I was able to start the silviculture surveys course; so I called my cousin, Lori Anne, in Aldergrove to see if I could stay at her place while I took the course. Lori Anne said I could but didn't tell me she had no heat and was a vegetarian. I didn't have very much money, pack any blankets, or have time to pick up my last UIC check but had no choice but to attend the course anyway.

Ludmilla Kelderman and her friend Maureen (Moe) Dehaan were also at the course and were two of the few people who would associate with me at BCIT. Ludmilla (Lud) was in business for herself; and when I told her I wasn't working, she said she may have some work for me, so I gave her my parents' and Jennifer's phone number so she could call me if she had any work. The course was rather intense and the instructor was good, but it would have been better though if the manual followed the course rather than move around from chapter then back again, but I didn't say anything. When the course was over, everyone wrote the test. The test wasn't very difficult, but I had froze and starved all week and knew I may not pass the course.

When I got back home, Lud called Jennifer the next day; but she was too angry at my family to tell me Lud called, so when I called Jennifer, she told me Lud called and wanted me to call her back. I called Lud, and she wanted me to go to Squamish that night and start work the next day. I was to do plot checks of juvenile-spacing contracts and quality-control work on a chemical brushing and weeding contract. As I was getting ready to go, it finally dawned on me that working for Indian bands was walking a dead-end street. Most reserves are so small that I would be lucky to get work that lasted six months. I wasn't learning anything. There was practically no chance for promotions and people never knew when DIA would cut off funding to hold the Indians back and I would be unemployed again. Working for tribal councils was steadier, but I wasn't an RPF; the money earned would be tax free, but that wasn't any compensation for what I would have to put up with. I would always be travelling, packing up, and looking for another job and realized that it was better that the band in Sardis treated me that way or I may not have realized it.

I came to Squamish and spent the night at Lud's place. She showed me what kind of work I would be doing and how to do it. I got up early the next day and had to drive to Pemberton then to the logging camp at the end of Harrison Lake. I enjoyed staying in the logging camp after freezing and starving at my cousin's place. The food was great and I was happy to be back working. I worked for two weeks; then things slowed down. I was supposed to call Lud at the Birkenhead Lodge but forgot to, probably because I was getting more concerned about how Jennifer was doing. Lud had more work for me, but she already had someone to take my place. But it was probably better that I did that though because I didn't have any spiked boots, so I had to borrow my dad's. They were one size too small for me, so my feet were usually sore by the end of the day. I didn't bother asking to borrow any money from him to buy new work boots because I gave up asking him for anything.

I took a few days off then went back to camp again. The brushing contractor had to slow down because they couldn't work in the rain and the spacing contractor, Karl, only worked with one or two people. I worked for another week and the brushing contract was finished, then Lud didn't have any work for herself, so she laid me off. Karl's crew didn't show up, and he couldn't work out the woods by himself. He said he only hired people with their power saw and Workers' Compensation Board (WCB) number, but he didn't even know if his crew was going to show up. It was close to Easter, and the fellow he called wanted to spend Easter with his family before going back to work. I was out of work now, so I told him I could fill in for him. I had never spaced before, but I knew how to use a power saw. Karl told me he would be making the deductions he was paying for and it would be a long time before I would get paid, but I thought that was better than nothing. I would be sleeping in my truck again, but at least it wasn't as cold as last winter.

We worked four or five days then got snowed out, so I thought I better go back through Pemberton because there might be too much snow to go through Harrison Lake. There was heavy snowfall through Whistler, and traffic was stopped for two hours to clear the roads. I was hungry by the time I got to Squamish, but I only had enough money for gas to get home. I tried calling Lud to stop by and visit, but she wasn't home, so I just had a cup of coffee then drove back to Chilliwack.

I had several days off, then Karl called me back to work. I only had enough money for gas to get to the end of Harrison Lake, so I had to rely on Karl to provide my lunch and pay for my supper at the logging camp. I was sleeping in my truck again and wasn't sleeping very well because my sleeping bag wasn't warm enough. I only worked for four days then cut my leg, so I had to stop working; but Karl's crew showed up that day, so I may have saved his contract. I went to Chilliwack along Harrison Lake, which was a two-hour drive, but I enjoyed it. I stopped off and visited Jennifer's family in Sto:lo Eagle on my way back, and after lunch, Henry told me I better go to the hospital. It was a Saturday afternoon, so I had to go to the emergency ward. The doctor said it looked like a power-saw cut, but I just told him I was cutting firewood.

I called Jennifer up, and she was depressed again, so I was glad I cut myself because she needed me beside her again. I didn't have an income now, so I visited her more often. She said someone rang her buzzer and she asked who was there. They said they had flowers for her, but she didn't believe them and went up the stairs and checked the other entrance to see who it was. It was two young boys, but they went away. I started visiting her more often now because it was hard to live with my parents and finally realized that everything I went through had prepared me for what was coming, just like with Annie Sullivan, the teacher in the movie *The Miracle Worker*. I knew I was extremely withdrawn when I finished high school. When DIA tried to make us give up on our postsecondary education by forcing us to take a special program where we had nothing to do but sit around all day, I learned to open up and talk to people, but most Native students gave up. I did a year of physical education and took swimming as one of my electives and saved Jennifer and Jimmy from drowning because I knew what to do.

It seemed like everything I tried failed, but I kept trying anyway; eventually I learned everyone has the potential to do something with their life if they don't give up. When I got sick and flunked out, I was so close to getting my career I couldn't give up because that would have made all those years of studying a waste of time; all I had to do was go the extra mile. When I finally got my career, I thought my hard times in life were over, just like with Annie Sullivan, at the beginning of the movie. But my hard times in life were just beginning because I applied what I learned about life to helping Jennifer and her brothers to try and do something with their life. Even being closed off by the students at BCIT helped prepare me for looking after her; she was too nervous to meet people, so I had to close myself off, which didn't really bother me because I was used to being closed off.

Now I finally realized that if I didn't go through what I went through and if Jennifer hadn't been the only woman in my life, I couldn't have broken her depression. I may not have known what to do, or I may have given up because it was too hard. I never had a girlfriend yet, so I had nothing to compare; even so, it totally exhausted me and it looked like I lost everything I had worked all my life for, but my instincts told me it was almost over. I just wished that my parents had listened to me and didn't treat me the way they did. To give up now would make all the work I've gone through a wasted effort, so I just couldn't give up now! However, I didn't like the way the Indians in Canada were treated. When we tried to do something for ourselves, we were held back by DIA then stereotyped as being "too lazy to go to work"! It seemed like a "No win!" situation; therefore, I continued to stay withdrawn. I never made much effort to meet people or talk to people, and whenever I went to the banks or grocery stores, I wouldn't talk to the clerks. Some of the clerks were outstandingly beautiful, but they didn't excite me because I was used to ladies like that not being interested in me. If I knew people before 1987, I accepted them; but other than that, it was hard for me to say anything and didn't tell anyone why I was withdrawing.

Brenda phoned Jennifer one night and said, "Listen to this guy! Doesn't he have a nice voice?" like she was insinuating, "Forget about Baxter and come meet this guy!" In 1984 she called her father and said I was an alcoholic. I was the only good thing to happen in Jennifer's life, yet her family didn't want us together even though I was trying to get her a career. I didn't realize it until many years later that her family was jealous of her getting ahead of them.

I applied for UIC again but didn't know if I was eligible for it or not and needed a separation slip from Jim Rowed, but he was hard to get a hold of. He said he would get it for me and then he would go off on a job and I wouldn't hear from him; he also said he had an old tape in his answering machine, so messages weren't coming through very clearly. I had rented a VCR for Jennifer for two months then decided rather than rent it again for another month, it would be better to buy one on a purchase plan. The cost wouldn't be much different, and it would be ours in twelve months. Jennifer agreed because it would only cost $3 more a month to buy one. Jennifer also decided she was tired of keeping her clothes in a suitcase and laundry basket, so she bought a dresser and didn't have much money left for groceries, but she was used to living that way.

Jennifer sometimes said she saw men and just felt attracted to them, but I didn't get excited over anyone because I was used to getting turned down. She told Dawn Barr about being attracted to other men, and Dawn said it was to put herself back in a situation she's familiar with, an abusive relationship. I went to visit Dawn Barr one day, and she said, "People who sexually abuse their children are insecure and want total control of everything, even their children's sex life." I told her how Henry hated me, but she said, "He didn't hate you. He wanted to have control over you." I realized a little bit more about why people molest their own children; often they were abused and molested and become abusers. When I mentioned to Henry that he touched Jennifer the wrong way, he just gave me a strange, rather puzzled look; so it made me wonder if something takes over him and he does what he does.

Jennifer's depression was getting bad, so I started spending more time with her, but I was happy to do it because my family drove me crazy when I spent too much time with them. When I found out I failed the silviculture surveyor's course, my mother said, "It's because of Jennifer! She never listens!"

"She listens just like you and Dad!" I yelled back, wishing Dad were there listening. If he said, "All I ask for is scientific proof," I would have said, "Bullshit! The answer could be laid out right in front of you and you never listen! Why don't you just go look for your scientific proof yourself and stop being so obnoxious!" Unfortunately, he wasn't there though.

A contractor in Richmond called me for a job interview, but I couldn't take the job because I didn't pass the course and Jennifer was also having too much trouble with depression, so I was glad I failed it. Her parents weren't visiting us as much now, and she got concerned about it and asked Dawn Barr why they were doing that. She said Henry was losing control of her, so he wasn't stopping by as much. Dawn moved to another town, so Jennifer stopped her therapy; a new therapist took her place, but Jennifer didn't go back. I checked into my UIC again, but I still needed a separation slip from Jim Rowed. He said he would send me one but went away on a job again.

I was living without an income now and owed much money. It was hard, but there was nothing I could do about it. We always had enough to eat though because Jennifer grew up eating salmon most of the time and I taught myself to live more on fish than meat a year earlier; now it was paying off. We were so poor we did everything we could to save money; most of the time I had to bake our own bread, but I always enjoyed baking, and now I had no choice. I let Isaac use my freezer even though it was too small for him; it was better than nothing until he could buy himself one. The weather started warming up, but I couldn't afford another coat. I was cold without a coat and too warm with my winter coat.

Lud asked me to go to a timber-cruising seminar with the British Columbia Forest Service in Rosedale one day and said I may meet someone who may be able to offer me a job. I attended, but there wasn't anyone looking for a forest technician; and when I got back, Jennifer was standing in a corner of the bedroom, crying. Her parents had stopped in and Henry was criticizing her and Jennifer said, "Why does he do these things to me?" I didn't know why he did those things, but I had to try and make her feel better. We weren't doing very well financially, but at least we weren't living in our truck having one meal a day.

Liz and Jeremy stopped by, and Liz was laughing about her childhood and mentioned that when they were picking strawberries in Lynden, Washington, they ate the other picker's lunches because they were hungry. Then I said, "Your dad made you work and go hungry just so he could drink!"

Liz realized what happened then said, "We ate bacon grease in our sandwiches. It tasted good."

I didn't say anything but thought, *Anything will taste good when you're hungry.*

They left, and Jennifer's parents went over again. Jennifer always tried to go out of her way to make them happy, but I got really mad and started yelling at her. Henry just sat there quietly because he knew I was really mad at him, not Jennifer. Emily actually thought I was mad at Jennifer, and I wondered how she could be so naive. The next time they stopped over, Henry was feeling rather guilty because he realized he had made his kids work and go hungry just so he could drink.

On the front cover of the *Reader's Digest* one month, the main story read, "Please Don't Give Up on Me!" Jennifer said, "That's how I feel now. Please don't give up on me!" That made me feel really good because I was winning the struggle to break her depression. I knew I could do it now and wanted to get her a career of some kind. Then in May, Brenda and Alvin moved back from Lethbridge, Alberta. Alvin said Canada Packers was lowering their wages and he didn't like waiting around wondering what was going to happen, so he just quit and moved back to British Columbia.

I still kept trying to get a hold of Jim Rowed for my separation slip, but all I got was his answering machine, or he would be off on a job. We were in a very difficult situation, and it looked like I could even end up losing my truck. Everything I worked for all my life was slowly slipping away. Now we were offered a house in Sto:lo Eagle because our application had gone through faster than I had expected, so we went there for a meeting to discuss what type of house plans we would be allowed, but I felt depressed about it. We went to Jennifer's parents' place and spent the night, so I told Henry, "You were jealous of the money we had saved for a home! Now we're getting a home and we have nothing!" He didn't feel very good about that, but he got what he wanted!

Liz started stopping by more often and said the Lytton Band hired a social worker, Jan Moore, to work with victims of incest and sexual abuse. Jan got Liz to see therapists in Surrey who specialize in sexual-abuse therapy, so Liz wanted Jennifer to go for therapy too. Liz talked about seeing the therapist and what she had to go through, and it was very difficult for her to go back and relive the memories of what she went through as a child. Now I was beginning to realize victims of child sexual abuse often blame themselves for what happened. That's why Peter committed suicide, and I started to wonder if my ex-foster brother, Wesley Pierre, had been molested in the same residential school. If he was molested, he carried that secret with him when he committed suicide.

One day when Jennifer and I were walking around in a drugstore, I started looking at the books and the book *Men Who Hate Women and the Women Who Love Them* by Dr. Susan Forward and Joan Torres just arrived in Chilliwack. I read the cover and told Jennifer,

"That sounds word for word like your father." Henry was really jealous and possessive of his family. He liked attending the canoe races and usually called us to spend the weekend with Emily when he went away. He called us up again, so we went to Sto:lo Eagle; but this time we didn't go there until late Saturday afternoon, spent the night, then left right away after breakfast the next day. I was happy about that because Jennifer was breaking away from her father's domination.

We went to another meeting about our house and chose a house plan we liked, but I was having second thoughts about moving there because it's an isolated reserve and we would need a reliable vehicle. If I couldn't find work nearby, I would have to leave Jennifer home by herself, and I didn't want to do that. We looked around a little bit for furniture, drapes, doors, and such but didn't look very hard because we didn't really want to move there. Finally we decided we just didn't want the house and didn't want to move to Sto:lo Eagle. I couldn't trust leaving Jennifer home alone; her father would try and get us to be on call for him. I didn't trust her to be alone near him, and we couldn't get a guard dog because someone might shoot it. We called the housing coordinator and told him we didn't want the house and apologized for the trouble we caused him. We figured Henry would get mad because we weren't going to move there, but he didn't say anything.

Liz and Allan dropped by to visit one day on their way home from therapy, and Liz said when they were younger, their dad would drink. He claimed to have been a boxer, and they would get used as a punching bag. In 1984, Alvin said he saw Henry back down before; so I said, "To who?"

"To a golden glover."

I didn't say anything but thought to myself, *He used his daughters for a punching bag, backs down from someone who can fight back, then calls himself the man!*

Liz also mentioned, "You watch him. When he buys something, he's really slow to take his wallet out." Liz was really down on her luck and struggling to pay her bills and wanted us to read the book *Men Who Hate Women and the Women Who Love Them* and *The Spirit Weeps*. She wanted us to read them so bad she even wanted to buy them for us, but I told her I would buy them when we could afford them. Everything was still going bad for us when I finally contacted Jim Rowed and he had my separation slip. He was going off on a job and told me to meet him at a restaurant in Sardis. My insurance had run out on my truck, and I couldn't afford to insure it again, so I was riding my bicycle everywhere; even if I had insurance, we didn't have money for gas.

Henry went to the canoe races in Lummi Island, Washington; and when he got back, he said we should have gone too. All it takes is a tank full of gas. I told him we didn't have insurance on our truck and couldn't afford the gas, yet he acted like we should have gone anyway. Henry went to more canoe races the next weekend and left Emily home alone. That night, Ryan called us up and asked us to go over and stay with her. Jennifer answered the phone and told him, "We can't afford the gas."

I thought, *He lives right next door to his mother. If he's so concerned, he could just go over himself.*

Liz kept attending her therapy and eventually brought her father to the therapist to confront him about how he treated her. She also wanted Henry to go for therapy, but when she got back, she said he couldn't go because his mind had deteriorated so much it wouldn't do him any good. On one visit, Liz said Albert from Lytton tried to commit suicide but failed in his attempt. Jennifer and I continued to go through hard times, but my instincts told me not to worry, and I bought the book *Tough Times Never Last, But Tough People Do!* by Robert Schuller. He mentioned people setting high goals for themselves and the five stages they go through to reach them. If what he said was right, then I was at stage 4, very close to reaching my goals.

Previously when we were driving to Richmond for a job interview, Jennifer said she wanted to stay at the Sheraton Villa some time, so I thought, *Jennifer, you've got very expensive goals. Right now, even hamburger and wieners are a luxury.* Eventually, Liz and Allan stopped by; and she wanted me to drive them to Vancouver so Allan could see a speech therapist, and they would be staying at the Sheraton Villa. I drove them to Burnaby and was prepared to spend the next two days sleeping in my truck canopy, but the desk clerk said we could sleep in the room with Liz and Allan. In the evenings, we went swimming in the pool and enjoyed the trip. Jennifer got her wish again.

One afternoon, Liz called us to go to the Seabird Island Cafe in Agassiz because she was going to a sexual-abuse workshop on the Indian reserve there and arranged for her father and Ryan to attend. When we got to the cafe, I wanted to wait outside; but Jennifer wanted me to go in, so I went in with her. We were so broke we couldn't even afford a cup of coffee and were taking a chance driving without insurance. As soon as we walked in, Henry immediately pulled his "I'm too broke!" stunt. He was eating, and Ryan was just having a cup of coffee. I knew Liz was paying for his lunch, and didn't want to ask her for anything because I knew the hard times she was going through. After all the things we did for Henry, he wouldn't even buy us a cup of coffee when we were really down on our luck. After leaving the restaurant, we went to the preschool where the workshop was being held. Everyone was just sitting around, but I knew Jennifer would get things going. At the start, everyone introduced themselves and Liz said, "I'm a survivor!"

Henry just said, "I don't know what I was called here for."

Allan was wandering around and playing with toys, so Jennifer asked me to take him to my parents' place. I was feeling really stressed out because of the way Henry was always treating us; the stress was so bad I started drinking my dad's rye but only drank enough to relieve the stress. When the workshop was over, Liz drove Jennifer to my parents' place; and Jennifer said, "Everyone was just sitting around, not saying anything. I said, 'Where did the abuse start?' And that got everyone going."

The next time, Liz went to Surrey for therapy and stopped by to visit; her parents were there to visit us and they bought her a cake because it was her birthday. Andrew was with them and he got into a big argument with Liz when they were outside; he was extremely mad at her and said, "Dad doesn't need therapy! Everything at home is just fine! You're not living at home! You don't know what it's like!"

I don't know what Liz said to him, but I wished I had been there because I would have told him his father got Jennifer and me apart and touched her the wrong way! Because of that, we ended up living in our truck for a month and a half in the middle of the winter! If I didn't stay right beside her and support her, she would have committed suicide. He would do something to his daughters if he got the chance!

When Liz went in for cake, she asked her father, "Why did you wait so long?"

Looking after Jennifer was hard because of her nervous condition and would often get very irritable, often for nothing! She got so crabby I nicknamed her Crackerby, insinuating she's a crab. She is also very dominating, and I don't like being told what to do, but I had no choice but to put up with it so often when she told me to do something, I would answer, "Okay, Crackerby!" If she got really irritable, I would answer, "Okay, Crackerby Crab!"

General Motors called me up one day because I wasn't keeping up with my truck payments, and the lady who called me just happened to catch me when I was in a bad mood; so I yelled at her, "When one of my payments was late, I was told I now have to make my payments at the dealer! I got my payment in right on time and you tried to draw it directly from my account again! I had more than one account at the time and your mistake cost me $10!" The lady froze up then hung up.

We continued going through hard times and living more on salmon than on meat; so when I got my income tax return, it cost me $276 to defer my truck payments, so now I would have to make fifty payments instead of forty-eight. I was finally able to insure my truck now, so at least I could use it if I found a job or was offered a job. After that, we bought groceries—sugar, potatoes, etc. The only luxury item I bought was a book from a used-book store. I knew it was possible I could still lose my truck, but my instincts kept telling me not to worry and told Jennifer, "If we lose everything, we still have each other. Think of all the rich people who can't afford to eat as much salmon as us." Times were hard, but I didn't bother asking my family for anything other than salmon. I didn't visit David at all because he wanted me to keep my distance; now he was getting what he wanted.

One day when we were doing some shopping, I ran into a friend from firefighting in 1985, Virgil Diamond, and he had a girlfriend named Susan. Susie was from a reserve near Williams Lake and had a daughter named Angela. Virgil was very outgoing, and he and I got along well together. Susie and Jennifer also had much in common, so they became good friends, which I thought was good because most people were out drinking, but they didn't drink, and Jennifer and I hardly ever drank. Often they would invite us over to play cards or they would go over to our place. I enjoyed cooking and we ate the same traditional foods, so I often cooked for them, and it felt good to spend time with people with whom we shared the same interests.

Our hard times carried on, and I missed eating fresh vegetables the most. I was taught to eat everything, but we couldn't afford fresh vegetables very often. I wasn't much for eating fruit, but Jennifer enjoyed eating fruit. I was starting to fall behind on my bills because

I had no money going in and had applied to go firefighting again, but I didn't have any luck with that either. Henry and Emily stopped over and asked us to go to the country fair with them. We barely had enough money to pay the entrance fee, but we went anyway. As we were watching the rodeo, Emily asked me to go get them a hot dog and pop then asked if we wanted one too. I agreed because we couldn't afford it and Henry gave me a surprised look like he didn't want to pay for it, but I told him, "You should do something for us for once."

Later on, I heard Henry had said, "My kids are starting to take advantage of me!"

When I told Liz about it, she just said, "Poor thing!" On one visit, Liz mentioned how much her father beat up on Ryan. Many years earlier, 1980 or '81, Jennifer mentioned he used to beat up on Ryan the most because he was the oldest and that Ryan bought his mom and dad a brand-new fridge. Liz said that after beating on him, he would be all smiles when Ryan was paying his room and board, then said, "Dad is rotten to the core!"

Geraldine and her kids went over to visit one night, and her third child went running around a corner and into a window and was cut up quite a bit, so I had to bring her to the hospital emergency ward because she required a number of stitches. That night I got called to a fire and was to be at the British Columbia Forest Service at five thirty the next morning, I didn't have any bread baked, so I had to spend the night at my parents' place so I would have a lunch the next day. The landlords told Jennifer she would have to pay for the window and she would have seven days to get the money to them, so I wondered, "What did I ever do to deserve this?" and hoped the money I made at the fire would be enough to pay for it.

I was the pump operator at the fire, so I sat back by myself for most of the day; and near the end of the day, two fellows went down to eat their lunch by the creek. I automatically thought they didn't want to associate with me, so I started moving equipment back to the road. They looked disappointed that I didn't stay and talk to them, so I went back and talked to them. The fire was out by then, so I was told to walk up the hill and see if any more work had to be done; and most of the crew was sitting around by then, so I started talking to them. Eventually I found out they were inmates from Elbow Lake, a minimum-security institution; they said they just wanted to be thought of as normal people who misbehaved and got caught. I told them I heard of a successful businessman from the town I grew up in who died of cancer, and after his death, it was rumoured he was one of the biggest drug dealers in town. When I was logging in Pit Lake, people would go and drink with us on movie night, and I just thought they were tree spacers. It wasn't until just before I left that I found they were inmates, but they didn't act differently from anyone else.

Firefighting only lasted one day, so I used the money to pay for the window. I was falling behind on my credit card payments, and one of them was ready to close my account. I wasn't able to make another truck payment and accepted that I may lose it. When Jennifer told me to check the UIC office again, I didn't want to; but she insisted I go, so I went. I talked to a fellow there, and he explained why my claim was delayed. They could begin processing my claim, but if there was an overpayment, I would have to pay it back; so I agreed then left. I didn't get too excited though because I had already been waiting four months, but at least now I knew I had some hope of not losing my truck.

My UIC cards finally went in, seven of them all at once. Usually, people get their checks a week later; but I still had to wait two weeks, so we had to live on salmon for two more weeks. But when I got my checks, it was time to send my cards out again. We immediately paid bills then went grocery-shopping, and as soon as we got home, we started eating as we were unpacking our groceries. It was good to have a change of diet from fish and frozen vegetables to meat, fresh vegetables, and fruit. Then right after I got my checks, I got offered a contract monitoring cone collecting for the British Columbia Forest Service. I couldn't believe it. It was August 15, 1984, when the bad luck started; now on August 16, 1988, my luck picked up again, exactly four years to the day.

I enjoyed monitoring cone collecting and was working for Ludmilla again; that way I could draw UIC when the job was over. It wasn't steady work, but at least I was doing something. I had spent years getting my diploma, and sometimes it seemed like it was all a waste of time and effort; now it was paying off again! I made a trip to Boston Bar and went to Ainslie Creek, and if I had to go to Lytton, I tried to take Jennifer along so she could visit Liz. I stopped off to visit my parents one day, and Dad finally realized I could never do anything without them getting mad at me; that's why I was so withdrawn. I worked part-time cone collecting, then CEIC called me up. There was a temporary job opening for a forest technician at Elbow Lake Institution and the job could turn permanent. The hours were seven thirty to three thirty, Monday to Friday, with a pension plan.

I was so excited I couldn't sleep the night before the interview and had the usual nausea about whether or not I would get the job or be able to do it properly, but I also had bronchitis and was on medication. I knew I still had a problem with communication and asserting myself because of the way my family treated me, but I didn't want to go through any more hard times, so I was anxious to get the job. I went for the interview, met the staff, was given an orientation of the place, and was told how to deal with some situations and what my responsibilities would be. As soon as I got the job, I applied to go on the National Indigenous Development program; that way, DIA would subsidize my wages and I would be guaranteed a year's employment because I wanted to work as long as possible.

The second day at work, I had to go to Port Coquitlam with George York taking a crew of inmates to do some roadside brushing at Buntzen Lake. On the way, there an elderly man, Woody, who was sitting in the front with us and said, "I haven't worked since 1953. Whenever I needed money, I would go out and rob a bank. I've been across Canada nine times. I got so used to robbing banks I got careless and got caught. I've got my future secure! I'll have free room and board the rest of my life!" Then he proudly said, "Who says crime doesn't pay!" He also did other things, but I didn't write them in because I don't want to give anyone any ideas.

We went to Buntzen Lake, dropped the crew off, then picked up the chipper. It took the chipper a while to warm up, so we had coffee. After the chipper warmed up, the crew started working and George showed me how to do the timekeeping, then it was lunchtime. After lunch we went for a walk up the road to see how the crew was doing, and it was time to go back. It seemed like we didn't even do anything and the day was over. The next day I went out with Al Wannamaker's crew; they were working near the institution, preparing stream beds for salmon enhancement. Our job was mainly to sit back and supervise the inmates and it almost drove me crazy to just stand around most of the day, I felt guilty, like I would be fired and definitely didn't want that to happen. After a three-day orientation to the job, I was assigned to take a crew to Buntzen Lake. I was a little nervous at first because they were inmates, but George had told me most of them were immature.

Since it was a long drive to Buntzen Lake, I was soon put on a condensed workweek starting at six thirty, working until four thirty, and got Fridays off. I had to leave home at five thirty each morning, but I liked it that way. When we left the institution, we would call our vehicle number on the radio that we were moving out. The trucks were given a letter, either *T* or *P*, and a number. Since *T* could easily sound like *P* over the radio, I started using phonetic alphabet that I learned in army cadets. I called tango 6 or whatever the number was, or if the vehicle letter was *P*, I called papa 6 or whatever the number was. The other forestry officers started doing the same thing, and later on I found out I got everyone else doing the same thing.

I was still withdrawn and unsure of myself, but the crew I worked with was good. The crew may not have been working very hard, but the job was getting done. I wasn't sure if I should tell them to work harder or not because they were only getting $20 a day, and with free clothing and room and board, it was all spending money to them. The job almost drove me crazy because I knew I was withdrawn and lacked assertiveness. I hated going to work and not doing anything and not knowing if the crew was working hard enough or not. Sometimes the stress would get so bad I couldn't wait to get off work and go for a beer and sometimes went to the bars, but I usually preferred to drink at home. One night I bent the key to my truck without realizing it when I went to unlock the door. Now I was glad I didn't get the job in 1985 right after my interview in spite of the hard times I went through because I was still too withdrawn and passive to handle a crew of inmates until now. I kept working at coming out of it, but it was hard and took time.

I needed a class 4 driver's license for my job, and the institution paid for me to take the test. I still hadn't been paid yet, and all I used for work was a worn-out denim jacket, so people sometimes thought I was an inmate or too lazy to go to work because of the way I dressed. Some of my socks wore right through on the heels, and I almost didn't throw them away because hard times are hard to forget. My paychecks finally started going in after six weeks, and I was able to buy myself some new clothes. I also got my class 4 driver's license, was able to take a larger crew to work, and had to take a first aid course one weekend as a safety factor for working with the crew. The course was on a weekend, so I would be allowed time off, so I thought I would take time off between Christmas and New Year. I didn't like working at Elbow Lake very much, and I wondered why this was happening to me. I told Virgil about it and said, "Maybe it's just a test of my patience," and he agreed.

On Thanksgiving weekend, we went to Sto:lo Eagle for turkey dinner. Henry Jr. took his father's truck to the service station for repairs, so when Henry had to go to the store for groceries, I drove him. I helped pay for some of the groceries; but as I was paying for them, I told Henry, "You can take as much time as you want taking your wallet out. I'm only paying for my own!"

When we got back to the house, Henry got mad at his son and said, "What took you so long? I almost had to walk!"

Henry Jr. said, "They were busy at the station! Besides, Baxter was here!" Henry even got mad at his kids for things that couldn't be helped.

Eventually we all sat down for dinner, and Henry was sitting near me. As I was serving myself some cranberries, he looked at me rather angrily and thought, *You're supposed to save it for me!*

I just thought, *There's lots of it there. There's more at the end of the table. It's home cooked, but it's easier on your diabetes.*

The staff at Elbow Lake was good to work with, and the job at Buntzen Lake was well-done and completed on time. After that job was over, my crew got a job doing roadside brushing for the Forest Service and we went back to a regular workweek. The brush had to be cut ten feet from the edge of the road and moved out of sight so it would look better to the tourists and the slash wouldn't create a fire hazard. I was to keep track of the time worked on each half-kilometer strip and who worked on each section. I was mostly just sitting in the truck, driving back and forth once in a while; if a man got hurt or needed gas or oil, I was there to supply it or apply first aid. Not long after I started the roadside-brushing contract, a new inmate was put on my crew. Woody mentioned him and said, "He's nervous because he doesn't know what jail's all about. He's only in for impaired driving."

His name was Jerry, a heavyset tall fellow. I thought he was okay to work with, although I was still learning how to handle a crew.

I got up to go to work one morning and my truck was gone. I couldn't believe it at first, so I walked around and looked for it; but sure enough, it was gone. I went back inside and told Jennifer, and she didn't believe me until I phoned the police and they knew all about it. Someone tried to steal it but one of the tenants opened their window and scared the thief away just before the police arrived. He got the truck running but broke the steering wheel right off. I couldn't go to work that day because it was too late to catch a ride with someone else. It was Friday morning, and I couldn't see ICBC until Monday morning, which meant I would miss two days of work; and when I got back to work, I was told there wasn't any compensation for such things. Now I was going to lose two days of my time off I wanted to take at Christmas. I was disappointed, but I thought about the time we took that truck for a joyride when I was sixteen. The crew probably missed two days of work because of that; now it was happening back to me sixteen years later. All the bad things I did in the past were eventually catching up to me.

Jennifer was still worried and upset about her weight and went back to the psychiatric ward again because her depression was getting bad, but she didn't stay in very long and got out. I couldn't visit my family very often because of all the tension between them and Jennifer, but I often wished she would stop visiting her father and doing things for him. She even talked about me going on his annual hunting trip with him. We went to Sto:lo Eagle one weekend and I drove Henry to town and back. It wasn't very far, and he was already getting on my nerves. I thought, *If I can't stand driving him just to town, how could I stand hunting with him for a week?*

On our way back, we stopped at a service station and the attendant said to him, "You never stop smiling!"

That was far different from what he was like six years earlier, and Henry just said, "That's because I don't have anything to cry about!" He went on his annual hunting trip and never saw a thing.

Jennifer asked me if I hit her on the shoulder when we were standing on the sidewalk when we were living in Lytton, and I told her I didn't do it, but she wasn't sure if I did it or not. Liz mentioned when she was growing up, her friends would say, "My daddy's logging. What's your daddy doing?" It was embarrassing to answer because he didn't work. He was a band counsellor, so she would answer, "He works in the band office."

I started getting used to the job, but I didn't like remembering what I went through. I tried not to think about it, and if I did, I would go home and drink a few beers. Fortunately, I have a very low tolerance of alcohol and didn't drink more than four bottles of beer. One of the staff, Bernie Kucheran, tried to ask me about my past; but I couldn't answer him because it would have brought back memories I didn't want to think about. I sometimes stopped at a hotel in Agassiz after work for a cup of coffee or something to eat. It was hard for me to say anything, so the staff just served me and left me alone. I usually only talked to people I knew before I started withdrawing or the staff at Elbow Lake.

Susie's daughter, Angela, started going over to visit us. She was about twelve years old, but I enjoyed her going over to visit. I liked kids, but if Jennifer and I had any, I would have had to be the father and mother at the same time. Not only that, we couldn't afford to support a family because it was often very hard to find work. People sometimes said I looked parental and wondered why I didn't have any children of my own. On my birthday, Jennifer, Angela, and I went to a restaurant for dinner. The waitress was Kim Loren, a young lady who used to work at a restaurant where my mother used to work. She was interested in me when I met Jennifer, but I was concerned about Jennifer's depression, so I thought I better stay with Jennifer until she feels better about herself.

I was finally able to pay for the land clearing on the Sto:lo Eagle reserve; and Mike, the contractor, said it was all right because he knew hard times are part of life and only charged us $300. He also said he may have a job for me falling timber in February or March. If he got the contract, he would need a faller and was willing to hire me. I was also finally able to pay Dad back the $200 I borrowed from him two years earlier but didn't try to tell him I couldn't pay him back earlier because of the hard times I went through because he never listened to anything. I also bought thirty sides of wind-dried salmon, our traditional food, because if I got laid off, I wasn't going to go hungry again. I didn't go home very often, but when I did, I would just stuff myself because that's what Dad wanted so bad; so that's what he was getting.

Christmas was coming and I kept hoping if I would get the brushing contract done before we got snowed out; then one of my best workers got drunk and sent back to a medium- or maximum-security prison and was replaced by another worker, Geoffry. Geoffry was a young Native fellow who didn't push himself to work very hard and had a rather cocky attitude. I didn't like having him on my crew very much, but I didn't have to fire him because he went to a Christmas dinner on a temporary leave and didn't go back. Then an Italian fellow named

Donovan asked to go with my crew after that. I had an opening, so I said he could go with my crew.

Henry stopped over to visit two times before Christmas; and each time, he said, "I make my truck payment. The rest of my money goes just like that," and he would snap his fingers.

I just shrugged it off because I knew better than to believe anything he said. While we were doing our Christmas shopping, I noticed a very nice-looking Native girl in the store one day and almost got excited; but she had a man's name on the sleeve of her jacket, so I gave up. She thought that was no reason to give up, but I didn't answer. That was harder than I usually tried. As Christmas was approaching, we went over to Sto:lo Eagle as usual. Henry's job usually started in September and ended in December, so he was going to work and doing his Christmas shopping after work. When he went home for lunch one day, Jennifer and I were sitting there; and he said, "I'm flat broke now. I'm $3 short of buying Gloria a gift." Gloria was his brother Junior's wife, but I just ignored him and continued eating, and he realized I wasn't going to give him anything. On Christmas Day, he said rather calmly, "Christmas cost me $1,000 with all my travelling to Chilliwack and my meals over there."

I didn't like spending Christmas in Sto:lo Eagle, but Jennifer always found a way to get her own way. After Christmas, I went back to work for two days then took my one day off.

Chapter 11

1989

After New Year, I went back to work at Elbow Lake. The roadside-brushing job was shut down because of heavy snowfall and there weren't any other contracts available, so we did some volunteer work cleaning up a United Way children's camp. We worked at the United Way camp for two days and then the job was done, but George York wanted me to go back for one more day and burn some slash, so we went back. Unfortunately, I was still too withdrawn and soft-spoken; so sometimes the crew didn't hear me when I gave instructions, and Donovan took a tire to go light a fire. I didn't instruct him properly but thought the other inmates could tell him, and right after the crew went to work, George York drove up to check up on us. Just then I heard there was an accident! Donovan had burned himself trying to light a fire and was cooling his face off in the lake when I went over to see what happened! I thought the best thing to do was rush him to the hospital. George was on a separate vehicle, so he took Donovan to the hospital. I felt very bad about what happened and hoped he wasn't hurt too bad.

We continued working for the rest of the day then went back to the institution; and when I got there, an LU (guard known as a living unit officer), Ken, called me into a private room to investigate the accident. When he asked me what happened, I got scared and thought I was going to lose my job for sure. I didn't lie to him because I knew it's always best to be totally honest, and after talking to Ken, he wrote down everything I said; then I signed the report.

I knew I was withdrawn and had trouble with communication and handling a crew before I got the job, but the hard times I went through before I started here were almost too much for me. My family always tried to drill into my head my opinions were wrong, nothing was ever enough for them, and now a man got hurt and I could lose my job because I was never allowed to express an opinion! I felt extremely depressed and felt like a total failure in life! I tried so hard to do something for myself, but it seemed like nothing was working out; then I thought, *If I lose my job, I could still go falling for Mike Smith, and when that was over, I could try and go contracting for the BC Forest Service again. It wouldn't be steady work, but at least it would be work.* I couldn't wait to get home and start drinking again because alcohol would relieve the tension for the evening, then I could decide what to do; but as I was driving home, I kept getting behind a slow driver and couldn't pass. When a passing area on the road came up, traffic would go in the opposite direction, so I was forced to take my time going home and thought, *Perhaps something is saying, "Don't worry about it!" Everything is going to work out!*

When I got home, Virgil and Susie were over visiting; and I told Virgil about the accident and he said, "What then?"

"I could lose my job!"

"What then?"

"I could find a better job." I was used to everyone putting down my opinion, so I acted to the situation the way they expected me to, but deep down I was optimistic. I started feeling better even though I never had anything to drink, and sat back on my La-Z-Boy and tuned my mind in to see if I could see what was going to happen, and I couldn't believe that my intuition told me I was going to be extremely successful in life. Jennifer wanted to go shopping that night, so I had to drive her to the mall; and on the way there, I stopped at the hospital to see how Donovan was doing. He said he had no hard feelings toward me and everyone enjoyed working for me. The temptation to ask him to lie for me was great, but I knew it was better to be totally honest. I didn't ask him to lie and was glad to see that at least he would recover. I was just the victim of two very angry parents.

After that I started to speak out louder and clearer to my crew. I told them that if they were caught lighting fires with fuel other than burning mix, they would receive a suspension; if they did it again, they would be fired. Ken told me we have to lead them by the hand because some of them may have fried their brains from all the drugs they've taken. It's a good idea to treat them all that way because if an accident happens, at least they were given instructions on what to do. After the church camp, we started doing maintenance work for the Department of National Defence (DND). We were hired to maintain fences, clear the brush along fences, and clean up some of their property. I did everything according to how I was shown during my orientation, but I still wondered if I was going to lose my job because of the accident. The institution now bought new yellow containers for diesel and burning mix, but it took me several tries to get the proper mixture of gas to diesel for lighting fires.

Jennifer went back to the psychiatric ward again because she was anorexic and only ate because she had to, so the staff would let her out on passes. I didn't try to get her to eat even though she seriously talked about trying to get her weight below ninety pounds.

One day, an inmate told me I was going to get put on the logging crew and I was surprised and happy, because I thought I was going to get laid off. Phaye had told me I was going to get put on the National Indigenous Program several years earlier; now it was coming true. We were still working for DND when one of my power saws went missing. I was doing everything the way I was shown during my orientation, but I wasn't sure what to do now because I was tired and had bronchitis at the time. I searched all over for it, checked everywhere; but sure enough, it was missing. I still wasn't sure what to do, so I waited a few days then finally reported it to George York. Power saws are expensive and easy to sell to people on the street, so if a saw goes missing, it's a major catastrophe. Then my crew got shut down for a week, and it ruined George's plans for how much work was going to be accomplished; he was mad at me, and I felt very guilty about what happened.

While my crew was shut down, I had to help lay out the roads and landings on a timber sale; but in the meantime, I came up with an idea on how to prevent any more saws from being stolen. I bought a day journal and recorded everything: where I went each day, the vehicle I drove, and if an inmate did something wrong. The saws were all numbered, so where each saw was placed was recorded. If I moved some or all of them from one vehicle to another, it was recorded. If another forestry officer borrowed them, they were put in the saw shop or in my spare lockup; it was recorded. If I was asked where any of my saws were, I could just give them my journal and they could find my saws, if they weren't there I did everything I could to look after them.

Jerome, a stocky, powerful Indian fellow, was put on my crew. He had a sense of humor and was always giving me a hard time, but I warned him, "You better get off my back or I'm going to get you back!" One day the crew was cutting and limbing trees that were blown over by the wind on DND property. Jerome pretended he got his saw stuck and told another inmate, Pete, to jump on the log so he could get it out. Pete started jumping on the log and Jerome said, "Keep jumping! I almost got it!" Pete kept jumping away, then he saw Jerome laughing and knew it was all a joke.

I went to work one day and found out one of the forestry officers had been fired. Not very much was said about it, but Jerome said he was reading letters that were supposed to be in the mail. Eventually I learned that the inmates got to know him, got him talking and recorded what he was saying, then got him fired. After I learned what happened, I was standing in line at the bank; and a Native lawyer, Steven Point, was standing behind me, so I told him what happened. And as soon as I found out, I felt like transferring to another department.

I finally started taking the logging crew out, and the block was mostly standing timber, so the fallers had to go in first to fall the timber and the right-of-way where the roads and landings would be located. The ground was too muddy to build the roads, so that would have to wait until the weather warmed up; then once the roads were built, we could bring in the yarder and start yarding the logs. I had to talk to my crew before we started work, so I asked an Indian fellow, Harvey, how much experience he had. He just turned around and said, "None at all!"

Often when I tried to be serious, something funny would happen. Harvey was merely doing time for impaired driving. There were five fallers going to work with me. Harvey usually sat next to me in the crew cab and would hear me when I would mumble things to myself. Some inmates were taking an industrial first aid course, and someone in the crew said, "One of those things for breathing."

I mumbled to myself, "A plastic doll." Harvey heard me and burst out laughing. One day after work, Jerome asked for some paper towels; so I said to myself, "Now we know who shit their pants." So Harvey heard it again and burst out laughing. One morning when I brought the crew to work, everyone left; but Harvey was still in the truck, so I asked him, "Do you ever watch WWF wrestling?"

"Oh yeah."

"Do you know an old man named Felix Victor?"

"Yeah, I know him."

"One of his sons is kind of tall, slim, curly haired, dark complexioned, wears glasses, and conceited, so he got nick named the Slickster. Even his boss at work, Larry, was going to buy him a dark brown suit to go to work in."

We both started laughing loud and hard; and Ken, a tall, thin white fellow, was standing by the back of the truck and said, "Are you playing favorites again?"

The weather started warming up and the roads were finally built. The fallers continued working and Ken showed them all the proper way to fall trees to make yarding them more efficient, but I wasn't experienced enough to know these things. When I got home from work one day, I noticed a bump on my Achilles tendon. It was getting large but didn't have any feeling, and I would have had to squeeze it with a pair of pliers before I would feel any pain. Jennifer got scared that it could be cancer, so she made me go to the doctor, who looked at it then sent me to a bone specialist. The bone doctor had me get it X-rayed then said, "It's just a pump bump. I'm going to have to remove it and smooth the bone out. You're going to have to miss a month of work and probably give up some of your annual leave."

I didn't want to miss a month of work or give up part of my holidays, so I said, "How about if I miss two weeks of work then take it easy for two weeks?" The doctor agreed and I was happy about that.

As I was working, Bernie Kucheran tried to ask me about my past, but it was too painful to think about; so I just told him, "I would hate to see anyone go through what I went through."

I was surprised at how fast I was able to get in to the hospital for my operation because I heard of people complaining about the British Columbia medical system, but I never had any problem with it. It seemed like a simple operation. I went to the hospital in the morning and was out in the afternoon. Jennifer and I were always helping Susie and Angela out, so she was happy to drive me home from the hospital. Sometimes if Susie had to go somewhere or do something and needed a ride, I would drive her; and other ladies were often looking at us, wondering, "What's going on there?"

It was humpback year again that year and many couples were separating. Susie and Virgil had broken up, and I wondered if Jennifer and I were going to stay together. I usually did Henry's income tax for him, so I went to Sto:lo Eagle to do it for him; and when I saw his tax statements, I knew from the interest he earned that he had over $8,000 in the bank. After all the things we did for him, he wouldn't even buy us a cup of coffee, which only cost $1, when we were really down on our luck.

I had time off for recovery from my operation, but it wasn't really a holiday for me. In my second week off, I went to an intertribal forestry meeting in Vancouver that Dave Walkem had told me about. I met Mark Atherton, Thomas Pierre, and many other friends at the meeting. Mark felt rather guilty about giving me a bad reference about not being very good at handling a crew. Thomas Pierre realized that cutting back part of my earnings wasn't a very nice thing to do, and I didn't work with Indian bands anymore. I didn't admit that to him though. I only attended the meeting for two of the three days it was on because I didn't think it was important to me.

Andrew had a girlfriend in North Vancouver, was working for the CN railroad, and had to wait six weeks for his first paycheck. I looked at his work boots and knew they wouldn't last until he got paid; so I gave him a brand-new pair of steel-toed work boots that I got from work because our feet were almost the same size, four pairs of work socks, felt insoles, a can of boot grease, and Jennifer loaned him $100. I didn't mind doing it because he had a chance of making a career out of that job and knew his father wouldn't help him but he would be right there to take his money from him.

After the weekend, it was time to go back to work again. The yarder had been moved to Sumas Mountain and the crew started logging. I usually just sat in the truck while the crew worked and had gone back to working on a condensed workweek, ten hours a day for four days and taking every Friday off. I enjoyed logging but couldn't do anything because of my operation, but when the weather started warming up and my foot healed, I started logging with the crew.

Liz continued to go for sexual-abuse therapy and often stopped by to visit and wanted Jennifer to go for therapy too, but Jennifer was too scared to go. When she asked her doctor for a referral to see the therapist, he wouldn't give her one. He looked at the business card and didn't know if they were legitimate or not and said, "They didn't put their qualifications on the card. There could be fraud involved, so I'm not going to give you a referral," so she was happy about that.

Jennifer continued to go for day care therapy three times a week and people said she was getting better and she decided she wanted to go to work. She was often cranky and depressed at night, and I had to sit up and talk to her. It didn't matter how tired I was or that I had to get up at five o'clock and leave at five thirty to go to work; I still had to sit up and talk to her. It got hard on me, so I was always happy when Friday came and I could sleep in. One time, she said, "It's hard to face reality because it's so scary."

When Jennifer decided she was ready to go to work, I thought she should carry on with her day care therapy, but I wasn't going to hold her back. She got a job dishwashing at a hotel and often worked nights, which gave me a break from looking after her. She continued to visit her parents and spend our time and money on them. I tried to get her to stop, but she wouldn't listen. When I tried to get her to stop spending on her father, she used her mother as an excuse to spend on them. She said, "My mother gets bored and depressed because Dad never takes her anywhere."

We picked them up one weekend and took them to Lytton to visit Liz and Jeremy. It was Easter weekend, so we spent two days there then drove to Merritt. We drove around Merritt and visited some of my friends then drove to Princeton and stopped for coffee. Henry pulled his "I'm too broke!" stunt as usual and wouldn't even pay for his own coffee. When we got to Princeton, he said, "I just found seventy-five cents in my pocket," as if he really was that broke. We went to Sto:lo Eagle again one weekend to visit, and Jennifer asked me to go to town to rent some videos. She wanted me to take her dad and said, "Let him choose some of them."

Henry choose the tape *Kickboxer* and thought, *Choosing that tape should make up for the karate tournament you missed.* Then he walked out, leaving the videos on the counter for me to take out to the truck.

I wondered, *How could that make up for the tournament I missed? We're paying for them and he won't even carry them out to the truck!* Jennifer seriously talked about me going on his annual hunting trip with him again, but I wondered, *I can barely stand driving him to town and back! How am I going to stand hunting with him for a week?*

I finally started visiting David now. He wanted me to keep my distance, so I didn't visit him for a year and a half; if he wanted me to stay away longer, that was fine with me. Jennifer was working, and I picked her up after work. There was some heavy lifting involved and the cooks wouldn't help her, so when she got off work, she was tired and cranky. She hurt her wrist one night when she was throwing out the garbage and ended up taking time off and going on worker's compensation. I wondered why she didn't get physically stronger no matter how hard she exercised, so I wondered if she had osteoporosis.

Liz and Jeremy stopped by one day on their way home from therapy, and Liz said, "I want a divorce!" Jeremy just sat there and didn't say anything.

We went to the canoe races at Harrison Bay in June because Jennifer liked to watch her brothers and cousins race. Henry always dropped everything to go to the canoe races and sat at the end of the dock, working as a judge. When he went walking back, he had a really guilty look on his face when he saw me; and when he went for something to eat, he did the same thing as I was sitting down the table from him. He knew he had pushed me too far now and something was going to happen. I often noticed people who are greedy like him just don't know when to stop; greed seems like a disease because people don't know when to quit and can make some bitter enemies.

Donovan was finally out of the hospital and back at Elbow Lake, so I tried to apologize to him and explain why it happened; but he just cut me off and said, "It could have been worse! At least I didn't lose my life," and was released a short time later.

Harvey quit the logging crew because he wasn't making enough money; and another inmate, Karl, was put on the logging crew to work in the landing. Karl was a bit taller than I, a very powerful fellow and a very good worker. I liked working on the logging crew because I worked with them. With my logging experience, I could fill in if we were short of experienced workers because like any other job, safety was the main concern. I was slowly starting to open up and show that I had a sense of humour. I didn't visit my parents very often, but when I did, I would just stuff myself. Dad didn't like it, but I kept doing it anyway. He was getting angrier and angrier and was almost ready to say something, but I blew up first and said, "Well, you shouldn't be so obnoxious all the time!" Then Dad finally realized just how obnoxious he really was.

Logging shut down because the landings were full, and the contractor was having trouble getting logging trucks to haul the logs out, and the market for hardwoods wasn't very good, so he was having trouble finding a buyer for his logs. Much of the timber was fallen and most of the roads were built, but it wasn't worthwhile for us to go to work since there weren't any trucks and no market for the logs. Sometimes we ended up working on other contracts such as slashing or roadside brushing, but the logging crew seemed to have the most breakdowns. We did some brushing and slashing to open up a recreation vehicle park. Jerome was still giving me a hard time again, and I had warned him to stop or I would get him back. When we were clearing the recreation lots, there was a large cedar tree that was leaning heavily and appeared to be rotten near the stump; so I told the owner of the property it could be a safety hazard, and he agreed it should be cut down. I was going to get a logger to fall it, but most of the good loggers were busy training for the firefighting-unit crew; so I decided to wait, but Jerome said he wanted to do it. After it was cut down, the owner said he wanted it cut into two-foot lengths for shakes. We didn't have anything to measure it with, but Jerome said, "I have something! It's six inches long!"

"Do you want my knife to cut it off?" I replied.

"I'll stand there and hold it!"

Karl was standing there, laughing away; and I said, "So he can cut it with a power saw?" Jerome started fuming, but everyone else was laughing.

Not long after Susie and Virgil broke up, she and Angela moved into an apartment around the corner from where we lived. Susie said she had a feeling she should move out of the apartment where she was living, and I wondered if Jennifer and I were going to make it.

There was a new book on the market titled *Feeling Good* by Dr. David Burns. It was a way of treating depression without drugs known as cognitive therapy. Jennifer found out about it while watching TV, so I bought her the book. In the book, there was a questionnaire testing a person's level of depression, and Jennifer's was extreme, almost to the point of suicide. She tried working on her depression through cognitive therapy for a little while, but it didn't seem to be having any effect. Looking after her was extremely hard on me, but all I could do was keep trying to make her feel better about herself. We were having trouble with our relationship because she kept complaining that I wasn't affectionate enough, and I kept telling her she always treats me like I'm not important and she's always pushing me away. "I'm working long hours because of all the driving to and from work. When I get home, I'm tired and you don't care! You keep me up until all hours of the night because you're depressed! By the time you get over your depression, it's late, and I have to be up at five o'clock in the morning to go to work! Everyone else's needs and interests are more important than mine! If I wanted to do something for my own interests, it's not important. We always have to try and live your family's life!" I argued with her about that, but it didn't do any good. I just wasn't important to her!

Henry Jr. bought his parents an automatic washer and dryer and hoped everyone else would chip in, but Jennifer was the only one who did. She gave him $200 even though I didn't want her to do that because I thought her father should have paid for it. One night, Jennifer went to bed and I sat up and drank a few beers. The next day, she said, "Do you remember what you said last night?"

"No."

"I was laying there sleeping and you came in and touched my ass and said, 'Here, Crackerby. I'll cover you up.' I said, 'No, Baxter! I'm too warm!' You said, 'Yeah, but your ass is cold.'"

The weather started getting warmer and there were more forest fires, but I missed some because Jennifer couldn't stand staying home waiting. She said, "Daddy always made us stay home all the time. Now I can't stand staying home very much." In my opinion, Henry made life miserable for everyone. Jennifer went out to a cabaret one night with one of her cousins and didn't go home until the next day and was really cranky and wanted some more beer, so I bought her some. At first I thought it was because of her depression, but eventually she opened up and told me she had run around on me again and was feeling guilty about it. The man she went out with was a truck driver, getting a divorce, and was down on his luck; so after she told me, I threatened to leave and said, "You can have everything!"

"No, you can have everything!"

"Well, give it to that useless piece of shit over in Sto:lo Eagle!"

"Okay, we'll stay together, but we won't see my family anymore."

I agreed to stay with her on the condition that we don't see or do anything for her father anymore. I knew from reading the book *Women Who Love Too Much* that she was attracted to dysfunctional men and bored with me. A few days later, I stopped off to visit my parents after work and looked at the mirror on the living room wall. There were pictures of my brother's girlfriends and my nieces and nephews, and my mother got mad again because I accepted that most women weren't interested in me. It was still hard for me to get excited by anyone.

I went to work one day, and two inmates on my crew were laughing and asked for my autograph. They were on their way to a movie and heard on the radio that Donovan was suing me for $100,000 and said something about making a movie about it. To the inmates, something like that to a Corrections employee was a big joke. We did more ground maintenance for the DND, and at the end of the day, I had a scythe in my hand and told the crew it was quitting time. Jerome was sitting on the grass with his legs spread apart and said, "Come here!"

I made a swift motion like I was going to use the scythe, and everyone burst out laughing; it always made my day to get the better of Jerome. Crew weren't allowed store stops on their way to and from work anymore for about three months. Later when we were allowed one store stop on the last day of the week and I didn't know it was only one day a week until I attended a staff meeting, before that I was stopping every day. The inmates got mad about it, but I told them I didn't ask. Tom (the superintendent at Elbow Lake) mentioned it at the meeting. Jerome kept giving me a hard time, trying to get me to make more store stops, but I wouldn't give in. I only stopped at the end of the week at the approved store stops. He said he could have my job, but I just said, "Go ahead! Arrange a meeting with Tom!"

Jerome talked about alcoholics who quit drinking then start going to bingo: no matter how broke they get, they can still afford their bingo. They still spend just as much time away from home and the family still suffers just as much. Another Indian fellow on my crew said, "In the residential schools, we were hungry, while the priests and nuns were living like kings!"

Jerome was a very good worker and the life of the crew, but he was also a troublemaker. When his troublemaking almost got unbearable, he slipped away at work, bought a case of beer, and carefully hid it so I wouldn't catch him. When we got back to Elbow Lake, he got called into the office because he was on the inmate committee; and the girls in the office noticed right away that he was drunk, so he got sent back to a medium-security prison.

Liz, Jeremy, and Allan stopped by one day after therapy; and Jennifer and I were still fighting about her running around on me again. Liz tried to ask what the problem was, but I just slammed a book on the table and said, "I don't want to talk about it!"

They left a little while later, and a week later, they stopped by again and it looked like they were getting along okay. But the next day, Liz and Allan went back; and she said, "Jeremy and I just broke up."

We let them stay with us because she was filing for a divorce, and Jeremy had put her so far in debt she didn't know what she was going to do! I was happy to have them stay with us because she was close to Jennifer. Jennifer was off work because she hurt her wrist, so now she had someone to talk to and it gave me a break from looking after her. Now I could give Liz some money and a grocery list so she and Jennifer could do the grocery shopping. The manager of the apartment also said it was all right because she knew what it was like to be down on her luck and going through a divorce. One day, Jennifer and I went out; and when we got back, Liz was sitting in her truck, crying. We asked her what was wrong, and she said, "I'm so far in debt I don't know what I'm going to do!"

We both said, "Don't worry about it! We'll help you! You don't have to worry about paying us back until you can afford it." So we loaned her $400 to help her pay bills, and that made her feel better.

Liz got a job cooking in a restaurant in town, and Jennifer looked after Allan until her wrist healed; then Jennifer went back to work for two weeks then got a better job in another restaurant, so she quit and went to work there. As Liz was staying with us, she and Jennifer started talking about what life was like when they were living at home in Sto:lo Eagle and the sexual abuse. As they were talking about what it was like, it sounded to me like Henry was in love with one of his daughters, Brenda. As soon as I started wondering, Liz said, "It looked like he was actually in love with her!"

Liz didn't work there very long, then she quit because of the emotional stress of her sexual abuse and going for therapy; then a few days later, she got a job cooking in the restaurant at the Kent Hotel in Agassiz. She moved in to her uncle Bruce's house in Sto:lo Eagle, two houses down from her father's place. He told her she didn't have to pay him anything until she was in a better financial position, but she still went over to visit us regularly and she either got Desiree or Henry to babysit for her. After the way Henry treated her as a child, he was still charging her for babysitting. We sometimes spent the night there, and I was happy about not having to drive so far to work in the morning. The British Columbia Forest Service had to burn some slash after logging a block, so the crew from Elbow Lake was hired to put it out after burning. We worked the weekend, so I took Jennifer to stay with Liz while I was away.

One night when we were visiting them, Bruce went over and talked to us about Henry and said everything was the exact opposite of the way Henry said it happened. He said, "Henry was always lazy and useless. He wouldn't even get the land cleared for his house. Someone else had to do it for him. Our father didn't beat us. He beat one of the kids once when he was drunk but apologized for it the next day. Mom and Dad bought a car and he talked Junior into taking it because they both had the same name."

"Why did he hate his parents?" I asked.

"That was a deal over cows. Mom wanted her car back, so he asked for two of their cows and he would return the car. Mom agreed and Henry took two cows, but they wouldn't breed."

"Did the Indian Dancers really want to initiate him?"

"No. If they wanted him, they would have got him a long time ago."

I wondered about that because he was always down there drumming and singing for them, so they could have easily initiated him then. Many years earlier, Henry talked about how hard he worked to buy a car and his parents took it away from him. He also mentioned buying Ryan a truck, but Ryan told me he was the one who bought his dad a truck. I wondered if Henry was telling the truth because I never ever saw him do anything for anyone else.

Jennifer asked me to buy a Nintendo game for her so she would have something to do while I was away on fires, and Angela liked to go over and play Nintendo too and I would walk her home at night, but I enjoyed her going over. One evening, Jennifer called me from the hospital and said she hurt her back and was in the psychiatric ward. I went to visit her then left when visiting hours were over. That night, George York called me to go firefighting and to pack enough clothes for a week; but as I was packing and doing my laundry, he called back and said I would only be gone overnight.

I drove back to Elbow Lake and helped load equipment, then we drove to Pemberton that night. The forestry officers were going to be making extremely good money in overtime and one of them wondered why I didn't show any jealous reaction, but Jennifer was back in the psychiatric ward, so I was better off not to go. People are more important than money. Jennifer was in the psychiatric ward for depression and also had a bad back, but the doctor didn't check her back for a week. He knew her history of depression, so that's probably why he did that, but Jennifer could barely walk around. On the weekend, I rented some videos; and as I was sitting back, watching them, an LU called from Elbow Lake and said there was a fellow there who wanted my address and phone number. The staff wouldn't give it to him, but they called me to talk to him on the phone. The fellow said, "I tried to locate you, but your name isn't in the phone book. I have a writ of summons here for you. Donovan is taking legal action against you. Can I meet you somewhere?"

"How about at the Kent Hotel restaurant at four o'clock?"

"That's kind of late and I have to get going. How about meeting me at McDonald's in Chilliwack at one thirty? You'll know me because I have a white car and there will be a little kid in it."

I agreed and met him at one thirty, and he gave me a writ of summons stating the charges against me. The case was going to the Supreme Court of British Columbia and the Supreme Court of Canada. I didn't hear him right and thought it was only going to the Supreme Court of Canada. Several months earlier, there was a letter sent to the institution, stating Donovan was taking legal action against me and the institution because of the accident. I got scared and didn't know what to do, so I called Jennifer in the hospital and told her what happened. She got scared too, and we both wondered what we were going to do! I called Elbow Lake and they gave me Tom's home phone number, so I called Tom, told him what happened; and he said, "Don't worry about it. You're not alone in this, Annis. Just photocopy it and leave a copy on my desk on Monday morning."

I was still scared and didn't know what to do! I knew it was a result of my family always putting down my opinion and trying to drill into my head I was wrong. I had tried to move away many years earlier but couldn't. Now I felt very angry at my parents because of how they treated me, so I called Phaye and told her my situation and asked her if she could tune her mind in and give me some idea of what is going to happen. She said, "Well, it's not something that happens regularly. It only happened once. I can't really see anything now."

I went to work after the weekend, and we got called out to fight a fire in Hope, and Jennifer was still in the hospital, so it was all right for me to get home late. We were still working on the fire when Jennifer got out of the hospital, and Liz moved back to our place for a few days when she got out. After working for several days, some of the inmates took some time off. Three forestry officers showed up for work, but there weren't enough inmates left to form three crew, so I had to stay in the office that day. It seemed rather unfair, but I tried to be optimistic about it.

I sat in the office for a few hours then finally worked up the courage to talk to Tom because I was feeling guilty about the accident and all the trouble I had caused the institution. If I thought about or was reminded of the things I went through, I would often have a few beers to relieve the stress of remembering it. One night, I almost destroyed my gold St. Christopher's medal even though it cost me $300, because of the damage done to the Indians in the residential schools run by the Christian churches. Tom and another supervisor, Ram, a fellow from Fiji, was also in his office; and Tom said they were both psychologist enough to understand why people behave the way they do. He said I have to get rid of the ghosts from the past and gave me the address of Dr. Clare Brant, a Native psychologist in Ontario. Then when I went to lunch, the ladies from the office got excited because they could see I was finally starting to open up. I sat with Bernie Kucheran at lunchtime and he tried to ask me about my past, so I just told him, "I'm a miracle worker," but didn't say what I did. That afternoon, I wrote this letter to Dr. Brant:

> *Dear Dr. Brant:*
>
> *I am a Native forest technician in British Columbia working for Correction Services Canada as a work supervisor. I had a problem with communicating with others because I was my parents' scapegoat, and whenever I did anything, they either laughed at me or tried to convince me that I was wrong. Consequently, I learned to withdraw and not say anything because they would get angry or laugh at me and make me feel humiliated.*
>
> *I moved away from home after completing high school and gradually learned to open up and speak up more. I learned much about life and went through a lot before I finally got my diploma. But I continued to be my parents' scapegoat. They always tried to convince me my opinions were wrong.*

Even if the answers were laid out in front of them, they still continued to press their opinions on me. I could never do anything without being laughed at. My father used to put me down just for being young, even though all I did was stay home and study. This went on until I was twenty-six years old. I'm thirty-three now and my father didn't realize I could never do anything without him and my mother getting mad at me until last year.

I wasted my first two years at college when Indian Affairs tried to make us give up and failed two times for medical reasons at the British Columbia Institute of Technology. Therefore, it took me eight years of studying just to get a two-year diploma. I had no regrets because of what I learned about life and the good times I went through. My parents told me I was being religious and completely insisted they were right. It took years to get through to them that I was only being optimistic about the situation.

During those years of studying, my mother was trying to get me married off and wouldn't listen when I told her all she was doing was slowing me down and interfering with my responsibilities. Even when I almost failed at college and it may have affected my ability to transfer to other institutions, she was still telling me what to do. We had many heated arguments over that, some I didn't know about until several years later.

I never had any luck with finding girlfriends, but I knew things seemed to work out right for me. After I finally found someone, she slowed me down and interfered with my responsibilities. My parents wouldn't listen when I tried to tell them I was her only alternative to suicide. She wouldn't go on the pill because she wouldn't remember to take it, didn't know how to say no, and was scared of trying anything because she was used to being beaten or criticized if she made a mistake.

My family wouldn't listen when I tried to tell them why I stayed with her and was so protective of her just because she ran around on me once. My parents almost disowned me. They pressured me so much to leave her I developed health problems and had to take time off work to go for X-rays. When I first met Jennifer, she seriously talked about going to jail so she wouldn't have to worry about being pregnant. My parents knew she had a nervous breakdown and was afraid of her own shadow, but they still pressured me to leave her.

I told my parents she's very intelligent and I wanted to help her do something with her life. They disagreed and thought someone else could do it for her and laid all the blame on me because things were going wrong. I tried to tell them her father is a sick man, a child beater with incestuous desires, but they wouldn't listen. They wouldn't listen with a direct approach, so I tried an indirect approach. I bought them the book Murphy's Boy *by Torey Hayden to give them the hint Jennifer needed someone to protect and look after her. They refused to do more than even look at the cover. At one time in 1981, Jennifer was going into fits of depression where she was just screaming. The only thing I could do was be there when she came out of it. If I tried to slap her out of it, she wouldn't have felt it and it would have made the situation worse.*

After I put Jennifer through upgrading until she got her grade 12 and got her into college, people realized she's very intelligent. But we were together for five years, off and on, before my family somehow found out I was her only alternative to suicide. By that time, much damage was done to both of us and a lot of tension was built up.

Jennifer and I went through some very hard economic times because of the recession and sometimes had no choice but to move home with my parents. At the time, it was hard for me to understand why victims of child abuse and incest blame themselves for what happened. Since she had such a low self-esteem and because of problems in the past, it was very difficult to live with my family. The stress got so bad in 1987 that if my mother said one wrong word, I would have beat her to a pulp right in front of my father. The years 1985-87 were very difficult to find work, and we often had no choice but to move back with my parents.

In 1987, the stress was getting so bad that it was affecting my ability to work properly when I found a job. We hit a run of bad luck in the fall of 1987 on a silviculture-surveys contract, and I didn't get paid. When we went back to the coast, Jennifer's father got us apart and touched her the wrong way. We tried to move away but couldn't find work. We ended up living in my truck for a month and a half in November and December. We didn't have any money for food, so we only ate one meal a day and sometimes one meal every two days. I lost twenty pounds and Jennifer lost fifteen pounds.

I couldn't find work, and we had no choice but to move back to the Fraser Valley. I felt like Grey Wolf in the book A Good Day to Die, *starved into submission.*

We moved back to the Fraser Valley and went to Jennifer's parents' place for Christmas. I wouldn't let her out of my sight while we were there, not even in the same room as her father. I felt sad but relieved at the same time when her grandmother passed away and we stayed there for four more days rather than sleep in the truck again.

After the funeral, we moved into Jennifer's brother's apartment for two days until he went back. We lived in the truck for two more days and didn't eat anything at all. I finally got her to go to the doctor, and he put her in the psychiatric ward because he knew her history of depression.

I then met one of my cousins and spent the night at my aunt's place, having my first meal in two days, before moving back with my parents. My father got angry at me and asked if I was fasting because I study Indian spiritualism. He still doesn't know what happened and tried to convince me I'm wrong most of the time.

In January 1988, Social Services and Housing got Jennifer a place to stay so she wouldn't have to put up with family members. It was a very difficult year for me because my UIC was delayed by four and a half months. It looked like I was going to lose everything I worked all my life for. I tried to forget what I went through because I didn't like remembering all the extreme anger and frustrations I went through. Sometimes when I think about it, I have a few drinks to relieve the stress.

After my UIC finally went in, I got a part-time job doing contract work with the British Columbia Forest Service. Then a job offer came up with Corrections Canada. I didn't want to say I had a problem with being withdrawn, because I thought they wouldn't give me a job and I didn't want to go through any more hard times.

As a result of my being conditioned like Pavlov's dog, I didn't train my crew properly and a man got hurt. He is now taking legal action, and I hope things work out for both of us. I wish I hadn't been so conditioned and perhaps this wouldn't have happened. Right now, all I feel I can do is be optimistic and hope for the best.

I would like to know if you have any suggestions such as books, courses, etc., that I can refer to to break my habit and come out of my shell. I've read many books to help Jennifer and to keep myself from losing my mind. I find working here had helped, but I finally forced myself to talk to the warden. He gave me your address and suggested I get a referral to a psychiatrist for therapy.

One thing I learned about life from the movie The Miracle Worker is that when it looks like something is going wrong, it could be better that it happened that way. It was hard to write this letter, but I'm glad it's over.

Yours truly,
Mr. Annis Alex

I photocopied several copies of it before I mailed it, but after writing it, I couldn't wait to get home and start drinking. When I got home, there were five bottles of beer in the fridge, so I drank them and still wanted more. Jennifer and Liz were out somewhere; so I went out for dinner, had two beers with my dinner, and stopped at the bowling alley for a pint of beer. I felt like I only drank two or three beers and thought to myself, *Now I see why victims of child abuse have trouble talking and writing down what they went through!*

A few days later, I drove to Pemberton with Tom to pick up the crew who had been out firefighting; and as we were driving, he said, "Sometimes after talking to you, I would wonder, did I get through to that guy?"

"My family was always putting down my opinion and tried to convince me my opinions were wrong. Consequently I learned not to say anything, I always had to keep my opinions to myself," I replied, then showed him the letter I wrote to Dr. Brant.

After reading it, he said, "You're right! It would be hard to write a letter like that. This Jennifer, are you still with her?"

"Yes, I am. She's getting better, but she still has trouble with depression. My uncle was the administrator at St. Mary's residential school in Mission before it closed down. He told my mother, but I don't know if he told my father he had to bring in a special counsellor just for her." The way I said it, I let him know I was used to my mother not listening to anything at all, and he wrote something down but wouldn't show me what it was. After driving a ways farther, I told him, "My father was a faller before he retired and cut his arm at work one day. He needed a number of stitches, and I think he had to take a few days off work because of it. When I found out he was mad at me for staying with Jennifer, I should have known right away, but I didn't figure it out until a year later that he was thinking of me when it happened. He didn't deny it, but he still wouldn't listen to anything I had to say."

Tom wrote something down again and wouldn't show me what it was. I think he thought you have to be psychic to know how to do that, but it was hard for me to speak up, so I didn't tell him how to do that.

"Your parents are very dogmatic!" he said. "You should go see a psychiatrist! Open up and tell him everything!" Later on he asked, "Has Jennifer ever thought about what she's going to do with her life?"

"She's thinking of becoming a nursery school teacher. She seems to relate well to kids."

"Good!"

We picked up the equipment and crew and stopped at McDonald's in Squamish on the way back and George York bought everyone a milkshake and everyone was happy because of the money they made. The next day, I went back to Elbow Lake, and we did our paperwork and sent our bills to the Forest Service.

Liz and Allan were staying with us again, and Jennifer babysat Allan during the day. Liz found her own way to work in the morning and I picked her up on my way home since her truck needed repairs; and as we were driving, I said, "I would hate to see anyone go through what I went through!"

"Even my dad?"

"Yes, even him. Would you like to see the letter I wrote to Dr. Brant, a Native psychologist in Ontario?"

"Yeah, okay," she replied and read it.

"Other things happened, but I didn't write them all down."

"Well, you can't write everything down in one writing. It would be hard to write a letter like that. Did your father hate you?"

"I don't know! I don't understand why he treated me like that. He says I look just like him when he was young."

When Liz got paid, she said, "My boss paid my truck-repair bill, so when I got my check, I just signed it and gave it back to him."

Jennifer was good with kids and seemed to get along well with them, so I thought she would make a good nursery school teacher. I looked up the prerequisites and required courses to see if she could take some courses before applying for the program, so I registered her in one course and hoped she would be strong enough to be able to do some studying. Liz talked about attending Nechi Institute in Alberta for alcohol and drug treatment in January and February with Jennifer, so I told her I could make her truck payments for while they were there. That would also give me a break from looking after Jennifer, and hopefully she would come out stronger because of it.

As I was walking down the street one day, I ran into Charles, the Native fellow I worked with up in Smithers, so I stopped to talk to him; and as we were talking, the clerks in the bank wondered why I talked to the Indians but wouldn't talk to them. I just pretended I didn't realize what I was doing because I didn't want to tell them why I had withdrawn the way I did. Kim Loren eventually got a job as a cashier at Save-On-Foods, so I talked to her whenever she served me. One night when we were grocery-shopping, I was standing in a lineup and a clerk asked me to go to the express aisle and the customer behind me politely said, "This is the express aisle, you know."

"I know," I replied. "One of the clerks told me to come here." Kim was working at that till and the clerks knew I liked talking to her, so they sent me there.

I finally went to the doctor in Agassiz to get a referral to see a psychiatrist. My regular doctor was away and there was a substitute doctor taking his place, so I told him the stress I was going though because I have a court case coming up is quite unbearable and I don't know what to do!

Right away, he said, "Do you want to go on pills!"

"No, I don't think I'm that bad." Then I showed him the letter and said, "There was more than that. Sometimes when the feeling came over me not to say anything, I couldn't say anything no matter what the circumstances." Then I told him about out the log rolling down toward my dad and me as we were walking in for lunch, so he quickly gave me a reference to see a psychiatrist; but most of them were booked up, so I got a referral to see Dr. Ryan, a psychologist. I was glad I was able to see him because he had worked with Jennifer for a little while in 1986 and he would understand the stress I was under.

I gave Dr. Ryan a copy of Dr. Brant's letter and told him everything I went through and learned over the years, and on my second visit, he said I could write a book on my life. I taught him how I learned to tell when people were thinking evil thoughts, what they were thinking about when it happened, and what I accomplished with that little bit of knowledge. I almost got into a car accident one time when I was thinking evil thoughts, but there seemed to be an invisible wall protecting me. He wondered why I wasn't angrier after everything I've been through, but I didn't know what to say. After I finished seeing him, he said he learned a lot from me, but I was going to have to get stronger than my father and make him realize what he's doing to me.

It was a hot sunny day after the Pemberton fires were over, and the logging crew went back to work. We were allowed a store stop that day, so Karl said, "Alex! Why don't you buy us all a pop!"

"Well, I didn't put in twelve days on the fire! By the time you get paid, you'll be wearing dark glasses to hide the dollar signs in your eyes!"

The crew burst out laughing, but Karl usually just liked to get in the last word and said, "Yeah, but I'm thirsty now, not three months from now!" I bought the crew a pop anyway because we were all hot and thirsty.

Jennifer started attending classes for the course I signed her up, but it was hard for her to concentrate on anything. I tried to help her as much as I could, but it was no use. She was still too depressed to study. The fire season was drawing to an end, so things were getting back to normal and the crew went back to doing contract work. Jennifer had a hard time staying home because she was forced to stay home so much as a child, so I missed some fires on weekends and some overtime. It was frustrating, but she got very depressed when I was away too much; and usually if I didn't listen to her, I ended up regretting it. We didn't go to Sto:lo Eagle anymore, and I hardly ever visited my parents; so Dad knew that when I did that, something was bothering me. I couldn't stand his obnoxious attitude, and now I had a court case against me because of him. I stopped off once to pick up some smoked fish, and he started getting on my nerves after half an hour, but I stayed longer because Freddie and June stopped by. Freddie was always laughing and joking, so most people enjoyed his company.

Liz and Jeremy got back together eventually because Jeremy promised to quit drinking and go for therapy, but I still wondered how long Jennifer and I would stay together. She still complained that I wasn't affectionate enough, yet when I tried to hug her, she pushed me away emotionally, I told her, but she still wouldn't listen. We didn't visit Jennifer's parents for three months, then finally near the end of September, we visited them. I didn't say very much to Henry because I was tired of trying to entertain him and be responsible for him. Then as we were eating breakfast, he was still telling his boring jokes when I said to him, "*You make my life miserable!*"

That hit him like a blow between the eyes, so he went and sat down in the living room. He was preparing for his annual hunting trip and said, "I thought you were going to say if you get something to give half of it to you!"

I just frowned, and Andrew could see I didn't like his dad and didn't make any attempt to hide my feelings. Then Henry said, "Do you want to come on my hunting trip?" making it perfectly obvious I had to pay my own expenses.

"*No*, I don't want to go on *no hunting trip* with *you*! You never come back with anything!"

Henry felt depressed again then thought, *I'll make sure I get something this year! I'll give them some of it!*

We didn't stay long, and I was happy to get away from him because he was always trying to take advantage of us. He went on his annual hunting trip a week later and stopped to visit Liz at the Kent Hotel. She was mad because he expected her to pay for his coffee. Brenda and Alvin had moved to Chilliwack in July and not many people would go with Henry on his hunting trip and his kids said he got too crabby. One of his nephews, the only person who ever seemed to go with him, was working; so Alvin went with him. I didn't know Alvin went with him until they got back. After Henry was gone for a few days, I got the feeling he changed his mind about giving us anything, but that didn't matter because I didn't think he would go back with anything. When they got back, Alvin said, "I went with Henry on his hunting trip. I don't know what he took me along for! I know he hates my guts!"

"No one told you he never comes back with anything on his hunting trips?"

"We saw a cow and bull moose, but they got away before we had a chance to shoot because our shells were in the back. It was illegal to shoot them though. Maybe it's better that we didn't because of all the traffic on the road."

I thought Henry would have learned from the last time he shot two moose illegally. It cost him $1,200 for a lawyer; he got a $400 fine, and that didn't include the cost of commuting to Prince George; and after all that, he never even got any of the meat. I was also surprised when Alvin said Henry insisted on paying for some of his meals on the trip because after all the things I did for him, he wouldn't even buy Jennifer and me a cup of coffee.

After Liz and Jeremy got back together, they moved to Forks, Washington, where Jeremy got a job logging and she got a job cooking; and about two weeks later, Jennifer's high school friend from Laughing Raven, Victor, committed suicide by hanging himself. Although he seemed to act carefree and happy-go-lucky, I often had a feeling about him that something wasn't right and got the same feeling when I saw Del Shannon, the singer, on TV. He also committed suicide. I didn't attend the funeral, but I should have because Jennifer wanted me beside her for emotional support, but I couldn't get the time off work because he wasn't a close relative. After work, I went to Laughing Raven to visit, and Jennifer was falling behind on her studies. Everyone was drinking, and Geraldine kept calling Jennifer to go talk to her. I told her to let Jennifer sleep because I wanted her to catch up on her studies, but she wouldn't listen, and Brenda kept walking in and was too drunk to listen when I told her to stay out. I got mad at Geraldine the next day, but she just snapped, "Don't give me shit for that right now! I'm not in the mood for it!"

I felt like throwing something at her but just told her she was causing me trouble and I didn't think Jennifer would be able to catch up on her studies now; she felt guilty about it, but it was too late now. If Brenda needed her sleep so she could catch up on her studies Geraldine would have guarded the door and made sure no one disturbed her but it was Jennifer so she didn't care!

Jennifer went to Laughing Raven again two weeks later, and I would get there later because a friend had asked me to help her move that day; and when I got to Laughing Raven, Jennifer was depressed because Elbow Lake had called me to a fire. I was excited about the overtime, but she was depressed because I would be away. I called Elbow Lake, and George York asked me if I wanted to go work on a fire in Ainslie Creek; and when he started to tell me where it was, I told him I already know where Ainslie Creek was. We worked on the fire for several days, then two other crew were available from Elbow Lake. On our way out, Burt Duncan, the Works supervisor, said on the radio, "George, be careful when you drive through Boston Bar. I heard the police are pretty strict there."

"That's okay! We're only following Annis."

Burt always had a sense of humor and said, "In that case, we'll get a ticket for driving too slow." Even the inmates used to joke about how I drove because I rarely drove over the speed limit. They sometimes jokingly said, "He's trying to set a record! He passed two cars today!"

Burt and George worked there for two days then got called out to another fire. When the fire was out and all we had to do was look for hot spots, a process called cold trailing, I said to the crew, "All right! You all know what cold trailing is!"

"Yeah!"

"You stick your dink in! If it's hot, you know it's a hot spot!" When the fire was completely out, we packed up the equipment and left. There was another fire in Barriere and the Elbow Lake unit crew was called in again, so I drove the delivery truck with Tom. I was going to tell him how I knew my dad was thinking about me when he cut his arm at work, but we kept falling asleep when we weren't driving, so I didn't tell him.

Jennifer went to Forks with Liz and Jeremy on one of their trips down, and I was to pick her up on the weekend. Jeremy only worked a few more days then got laid off because the season was ending and other workers had more seniority. Liz had asked us to move down there because living there seemed easy, but I didn't want to leave a job once I had one. I went to work one day and wanted to get in early and phone Jennifer. I was still very angry at Henry and knew I shouldn't think evil thoughts toward him, but it was hard not to. On our way back, we stopped to relieve ourselves; then the truck wouldn't start, so I radioed Elbow Lake and they said George York was the only person who knew where we were and they couldn't get him on the radio. It was late when they finally contacted him and he drove up to where we were to give the truck a jump start. On our way down, he got a flat tire and didn't have a spare tire, so he rode back with me to Elbow Lake; and as we were getting things ready, I grabbed my flashlight from my own truck. It was getting dark and George said we wouldn't need it, but I took it along anyway. It was fairly dark when we got back to the other vehicle, so it was a good thing I brought my flashlight along. We didn't get back to Elbow Lake until ten o'clock that night, and it was another hour's drive home. I guess I shouldn't have been thinking that way toward Henry because the overtime I got didn't make it worthwhile.

I suppressed the memories of what I went through then wondered why I stood up to that huge fellow for a knife fight, then I read the letter to Dr. Brant again and the feelings came back. I called Jennifer the next day and told her what happened. She said that was all right but wanted me to drive down there and pick her up. I asked her just to borrow the money off Liz and Jeremy and take the bus back, but they didn't even have that. On the weekend I drove down to Forks, Washington, to pick her up; and when I went for something to eat, the waitresses got crabby because I wouldn't talk to them. I was rather surprised because I thought surely other people keep to themselves.

Liz caught a ride back with us, and I was still mad at Jennifer for the way she treated me, but knew I had to keep looking after her. I was still having trouble getting her to go on the pill to protect herself, and she was still trying to put herself in dangerous situations because it felt normal to her. We never said anything to Liz about the trouble we were having and dropped her off in Abbotsford so Geraldine could pick her up, then she jokingly said, "You're dropping me off like a sack of potatoes."

Jennifer needed new shoes again because she always wore them out fast and wanted to see a tarot-card reader because she was worried about being pregnant, I felt like giving up on her again and didn't know what to do. We went to Vancouver, the Kitsilano area near UBC, and bought her some shoes and looked in a bookstore that had many books on Indian spiritualism and other religions. There was a tarot-card reader there, so I got a reading. Jennifer wanted to sit in the room with me, but the lady wouldn't let her. I could see she was good, but not as good as Wylma; and when I got my reading, she mentioned a death. But I was told previously that it was just the death of a situation, so I wasn't worried. Seeing her didn't make us feel much better. When we got home that night, we started arguing again, and I stood up with my fist clenched like I was ready to hit her and said, "If you're so damned attracted to abusive men, then I'll start being abusive! Maybe you'll finally care about how I feel!" I knew I couldn't hit her anyway, and life had swung back at her for what she did wrong.

Liz went back to Lytton and got her job back at the hotel. A few days later, Jeremy went back and got a job logging in Lytton. Thanksgiving was coming up, and I was thinking of taking a week off to go hunting with Jeremy. We could leave early in the morning and Jennifer could spend the day with Liz and Allan. Liz and Jeremy still had to move some of their belongings back from Forks and were going to bring them back on the weekend. We had already done so much for her that she didn't feel right asking us for any more favors; then we got a call late that night. The phone wouldn't stop ringing, so I finally got up and answered it; it was Jennifer's mother! She said, "Jeremy was in a car accident and Allan's in the hospital! They don't know if he's going to recover or not!"

"Where's Liz?"

"I don't know!"

I immediately woke Jennifer up and told her what happened, and she got scared and wondered where Liz was, so we phoned the hospital in Hope. She wasn't there, but Jeremy was rushed to the Royal

Columbian Hospital in New Westminster, but Gordon and his wife were there in the hospital. We phoned Royal Columbian Hospital to see if she was there, but she wasn't, then they said Jeremy just passed away. We got even more scared, so we phoned their place in Lytton, but there was no answer. Then we phoned the police in Hope, and they said there had been a car accident that night. Jeremy had the right-of-way when a truck tried to pass another vehicle. Jeremy pulled to the right, but the other driver pulled off the road at the same time. It was right against a rock wall with no place to go, so there was a head-on collision, but they didn't say what happened to the occupants. Finally, we phoned Ryan and Desiree; and Ryan said, "Liz died right away in the accident!"

News of that hit us like a ton of bricks; neither of us wanted to believe it, and wanted to believe it was a mistake! She always made Jennifer feel better and now she was gone! We didn't want to believe it, so we immediately drove to the hospital in Hope. Jennifer waited in the admitting room and I walked in. The nurses said there had been a car accident, but all of them said Liz wasn't brought in but I could go down the hall and ask Gordon. On my way down, I asked a doctor in the hall where she was. He said, "There wasn't any Liz brought in."

I asked Gordon, and he said, "Liz died right away in the accident."

It was confirmed. I didn't say what happened to Jeremy because there had been enough tragedy that night. I held back my tears because I didn't want anyone to see how I felt; and when I told Jennifer, she started crying loudly and said, "It's a mistake! It's a mistake!" Then we drove to Sto:lo Eagle, and she kept crying, "It can't be! It's a mistake!"

When we got to Sto:lo Eagle, Henry was out hunting with Andrew, and no one knew where they went or how long they would be gone because Henry never ever phoned home when he went on his hunting trips. It was late Friday night, so I phoned Elbow Lake and told them I wouldn't be back at work next week because of what happened. Then around nine o'clock Saturday night, Henry and Andrew went back and we told them what happened, so I gave him a hug to let him know I cared about him even though I was very angry at him. We couldn't do anything about funeral arrangements until Monday, so I went to visit Ryan and Desiree the next day and said, "How much is Henry going to put down for the funeral?"

They both got mad and said, "This is no time to worry about that!"

The next day, we called Henderson's Funeral Home in Chilliwack to make arrangements; and as we were getting ready to go, I said to Henry, "How much are you going to put down for the funeral?"

"This is no time to worry about that!" he said.

"I wouldn't put it past you if you never put anything down for your own mother's funeral!"

He didn't say anything, but when we got to the funeral home, Desiree and I were standing in the parking lot and he said, "I don't see any point in buying an expensive coffin because the body's just going to rot anyway."

I said, "When your time comes will be the happiest day of my life! I won't be at the funeral because I'll be too busy celebrating!"

Complications arose because the bodies were in Vancouver and we had to wait for them to be brought back to Chilliwack, so we all went back to Sto:lo Eagle to make arrangements for pallbearers, funeral, dinner, etc. The next day, we went back to the funeral home and I donated $1,000. Henry Jr. left right away and we went to ICBC and they said to just send the bill to them. After that, we all decided to go for a Chinese buffet for lunch. Brenda ended up sitting beside me, and I very angrily said, "Henry Jr. was the only one to finish high school, and he called him down for making it!" Henry was sitting at the end of the table just glaring at me! He was always trying to get us to pay his way for him; so when we finished eating, I said, "Oh! You don't want us to come around anymore!"

There was nothing more we could do, so we all went back to Sto:lo Eagle; and one of Jennifer's cousins went over to visit and I thought ICBC was going to pay for the funeral, but I wasn't worried about the money. Henry said, "You're going to lose your $1,000."

"How would you know?" I asked.

He jumped up and clenched his fist, ready to start hitting me, and said, "I've been in this death business long enough to know!" I realized that what I did to Jennifer was now happening back to me. It scared her, but when Henry sat down, I walked out and went next door. I hated that man! There were still problems with funeral arrangements; and by Thursday, Henry had missed four days of work and grumbled, "We should hurry and get this thing over with."

I was asked to be one of the pallbearers and readily agreed. Arrangements were finally made, and they were to be buried on Saturday in Lytton. The funeral home delivered the bodies on Friday and was on a fixed schedule because it had another funeral to go to the next day. After everyone got up and had breakfast, I started trying to get the pallbearers together; and as I was asking them to get ready, Henry thought, *Now's my chance!* and said, "Why don't you do that yourself?"

"I'm already getting things ready," I politely replied.

"Don't you snap at me! I'll snap right back at you!" I just walked away and carried on trying to get things ready so the funeral people could go to their next funeral. After the bodies were laid and prayers were said, people started burying them. Eventually I was the only one who kept working, but I could understand people being too upset to continue; then the flowers were placed. As people started leaving to go to the hall for the dinner, Henry was one of the last people to leave. His truck wouldn't start and Andrew tried signalling us to give their truck a jump start, but we didn't see him. When we got to the hall, Henry Jr. went over and joined us; and when I heard about what happened to Henry, I wondered if he pulled the stunt I thought he was going to pull. As someone was announcing what people were donating, I could see Henry would get extremely mad if I listened to see what his contribution was, but I wasn't worried about it because the truth usually comes out.

After dinner, everyone went home and Jennifer asked me to take some time off work to stay with her. I agreed and called Elbow Lake and told them I would be working Wednesday to Friday that week. Luckily I was only working four days a week but long hours. When I was ready to go back to work, Jennifer asked me to spend more time with her; but everything was already arranged with the crew, so I had to go back to work even though I was still devastated by what happened. Liz had wanted Jennifer and me to be Allan's godparents, but Jeremy wanted his sister Gladys and her husband to be his godparents. I thought, *Perhaps it's better that way because Jennifer and I didn't have much of a relationship and she has too much trouble with depression. Now her depression is even worse. I also heard people say it's not right for parents to stay together just for the children.*

I took the crew out logging again and Karl mentioned having acted in some plays previously. One day, a log he was standing on rolled and he fell, aggravating an old injury. It was right at quitting time, so I loaded everyone up and left. As we were driving away, I tried calling Elbow Lake on the radio to let them know what happened; and when George York heard me calling, he knew something was wrong, so he asked me what happened. I told him Karl hurt himself when a log he was standing on rolled so I was bringing him to the hospital in Mission. Al Wannamaker heard us on the radio and said he could bring the rest of my crew back to Elbow Lake. After seeing the doctor, Karl's arm was put in a sling and he was given some painkillers. We were rather late getting back and he and Ken were the last to eat, so I filled out an accident report; and instead of asking him to sign it, I said, "Since you've been into acting 'Can I have your autograph?"

Ken laughed and thought, *He never misses an opportunity to tease us!* but Karl just said, "Everyone is funny today!"

Winter was coming and the logging crew was shut down because there wasn't any market for the logs. There weren't many contracts left for the crew, but there was a little bit of work left with DND. One day as we were leaving the yard, I heard on the radio that the probation officers were on strike and weren't letting us leave the yard to go to work. When all the forestry vehicles met where we could get turned around, I said to the crew, "Probation officers put up picket lines and aren't letting us leave the yard to go to work! But that's okay! You guys can get out and rumble with them!"

Everyone burst out laughing, then Al said, "Annis! You don't have a stretcher!"

"Well, we have to go back and get a stretcher anyway!"

"What do we need a stretcher for?" an inmate asked.

"You might need it when you're through rumbling with the guys on the picket line!"

There wasn't very much work with DND after that because of cutbacks in their budget. We did some small contracts for ski resorts, but after that, there wasn't very much to do at work. But I was still happy just to have a job. Christmas was coming and Jennifer spent on presents to try and make herself feel better. We usually spent Christmas in Sto:lo Eagle, but I was tired of it, so she went to Sto:lo Eagle and I went to Rosedale and took time off between Christmas and New Year.

When I got to Rosedale, I drank a few beers, then Angie invited me to spend the night at their place because my parents had a house full. I told Angie how I learned to tell how people were thinking evil thoughts and how David tried to treat me in the past. If I tried to treat someone that way, I would have been surprised if they didn't get violent. Then I told her all the bad things that happened to me when I was thinking of taking a round out of David, and she said, "You should have learned after you blew a tire!"

Then I showed her the letter to Dr. Brant because it was easier for me to open up and talk after a few beers, and she was quite surprised at some of the things that happened. After Christmas, I went back to Sto:lo Eagle because I didn't trust leaving Jennifer alone with her father. I wanted to go back to Chilliwack because I didn't like staying there, but she wanted to stay. I told her, "It's no holiday for me if we just stay here! If I knew we were going to do that, I would have kept on working!" but she wouldn't listen and we ended up staying there.

Chapter 12

1990

After New Year, it was good to get back to work. And sometime between Christmas and New Year, the apartment building Susie had been living in was completely gutted by a fire; and if she hadn't followed her hunch to move out, she could have lost everything. I kept trying to get Jennifer a career, and nothing seemed to be working out. She wanted to take a hairdressing course in Chilliwack, so I called CEIC and booked an appointment for her to see if she could get sponsored. It snowed rather hard one day I asked for a day off. George said it was all right, and Jennifer was happy I was able to go there with her. The next day, CEIC called and tried to postpone her interview because the person to see her was sick, but I said I just took a day off work to bring her in, so they said she could see someone else. When we got there, the receptionist said I couldn't go to the interview with her; she would have to go by herself. When she got out, she was disappointed because CEIC no longer sponsored students for hairdressing because too many people take the course then drop out of it, so I told her she can still apply to her band and hope for the best.

I knew my court case would be coming up, and I was worried about how I was going to pay the legal fees and the financial settlement. The only way I could think of was to write my life story and hope it sells, so one day when no one was in the office, I started writing my memoirs. It was hard to find time to write because I wasn't allowed to do it in the office, and when I got home, Jennifer always wanted my attention; but I also didn't want her to know I was writing an autobiography.

One night, Andrew called and said they just took their dad to the hospital because he had a stroke, so we went to visit him the next day; and he couldn't talk. He could only mumble. He stayed in the hospital for two or three weeks then was brought home, and I started getting blood in my feces after bowel movement; so I told Jennifer, and she made me go to the doctor. He told me I would have to go on a clear-liquid diet for three days then get X-rays, so I knew I would have to live on apple juice. We went to Sto:lo Eagle again, and I put my juice in the fridge that night; and the next day, Andrew cooked breakfast and gave Henry a drink of my juice. I told Henry I was on a liquid diet because I had to go for X-rays, and after breakfast, he was watching TV and asked for another drink of my juice. Even though I couldn't eat solid foods, he still wanted a drink of my juice; so I said, "No, you can go buy your own juice."

He got mad at me for that because of how laid up he was and eventually got better but was slow and walked with a limp. His speech was more clear now, and when we went to visit him, he was talking to the boys and strongly emphasized "My pop!" I didn't hear what he was saying, but I knew he didn't want me to drink any of his pop, but I didn't care because I hardly ever drank pop. I continued working, and we were visiting Sto:lo Eagle more often now. One night I went over to visit Ryan, and he said, "Dad never put anything down for Liz and Jeremy's funeral. I have a list of what everyone donated." When I heard that, I thought he had a lot of nerve getting mad at me at the funeral.

One of Jeremy's sisters called one day and said they were going to lay the headstones on Thursday, so I asked them to wait until Saturday so everyone else could show up. I always did Henry's income tax for him, and when I looked at his income statements, I knew he had well over $10,000 in the bank; yet he wouldn't put anything down for his daughter's funeral. He knew I didn't think very much of him after that, and I said, "Something's going to happen back to you for doing that, you know!"

"I've had nothing but bad luck all my life! Do you think I'm worried about that!" he responded. It was a sunny day when the headstones were placed, and we couldn't have had better weather. After they were placed, Henry knelt down in front of them and cried a river. I wished he really did care that much, but his money was more important to him!

Now that the snow was gone, contract work was becoming available for the inmates, and we got a contract with Department of Highways cleaning rails and sidewalks on bridges and in tunnels between Hope and Boston Bar. On our first day, John Blades, a Highways employee with quite a sense of humor, said to Harvey, "Oh, Harvey! They finally caught you!"

I asked Harvey about it, and he said, "John used to own a restaurant in North Bend. I ate there while I was logging and didn't pay my food bill."

At that time, a Sikh who joined the RCMP was allowed to wear his turban on the job. We were required to wear hard hats and Harvey was always wearing a baseball cap, so I said to him, "You will wear a hard hat! And take your turban off because you're not in the RCMP!"

One day when we were cleaning in and around a tunnel, Harvey was standing at one end of the tunnel, holding a rake; so John said, "He's a rake foreman!"

It was a long drive to Boston Bar, so I always stopped so the crew could relieve themselves. One day when we stopped, I said, "All right, animals! Get out and mark your territory!" Most of them laughed, but no one would get out after I said that.

We finished cleaning a tunnel early one day, so we cleaned up a picnic area. When we finished, everyone was standing around except one inmate, OB, who kept gathering and burning leaves; so John said, "He's an arsonist!"

After the Highways contract was finished, we got other contracts; and one day as we were leaving the yard, OB was standing by the duty office and Ken waved and said, "OB."

I said, "He's an arsonist! Works half an hour past everyone else! Lighting fires with a gleam in his eyes! Doesn't realize everyone's already quit working!" Then Ken repeated it to him out loud, word for word.

Easter weekend was coming and four of my cousins from the same family were celebrating their twenty-fifth anniversary. We were invited, so Jennifer and I agreed that she would drink that night and the next day we would go to Laughing Raven then I could drink. We had a good time that night, and the next day, we went to Laughing Raven for Easter dinner. Henry, Emily, and Andrew were already there; and I had a few drinks. I must have been tired because I got drunk rather fast, and the last thing I remembered was I wanted to give Henry a good kick in the groin then do a *war dance* on his head because of how he treated his kids and wouldn't put anything down for his daughter's funeral. I probably would have done it, but Emily got scared for him. That was the last thing I remembered, and when I woke up, they were gone and I was back to my normal self. Geraldine said I was fucking this and fucking that, and later on I heard Jennifer offered to get him a plate of food, and I said, "No, Jennifer! He can fucking well get up and get it himself!"

She said, "I'll get it for him if I want to get it for him!"

In the kitchen I said, "Here! Give him that!" and wanted him to eat the grease out of the pan while everyone else had ham and turkey. A few days later, Jennifer told me to go to Sto:lo Eagle after work and apologize to him, so I went to Sto:lo Eagle after work; and he was in the backyard, talking to Andrew. He started walking away with tears in his eyes when he saw me going, and I said, "Well, aren't you going to say hi?"

He couldn't walk very fast because of his stroke and said, "Oh, I thought that was Henry Jr." I didn't remember doing what I did, but I didn't apologize to him because I thought it was justified. Henry and Andrew came over to visit, and when they left, Henry got mad at me because I wouldn't help him get up; then when he got outside, he felt bad that I wouldn't help him get into his truck either.

Since I was working and had money in the bank, I thought Jennifer should get her learner's driving license and take driving lessons because if she had her license for a number of years without an accident, she may be eligible for a safe-driving discount on her insurance. It was hard for her to concentrate on any one subject for very long, so it took her a while to feel confident enough to write the exam. After she got her learner's license, I looked in the Yellow Pages for driving schools and called one that advertised, "Nervous Drivers Are My Specialty." I made arrangements for her to take driving lessons but thought, *I hope he doesn't regret placing that ad. Jennifer's real nervous.* When the driving instructor came to our apartment to pick her up, I thought, *He's a tall fellow. I hope Jennifer doesn't get scared!*

Jennifer took her first lesson and said she scared the instructor; then after taking another lesson, we drove around so she could practice her driving. She was really cranky and was always getting mad at me, drove where she would have to drive for her test, and said, "You're supposed to watch for traffic! We're going to keep doing it until we get it right!" Even though I was tired, I knew it would be worthwhile in the long run.

Jennifer had to go to the doctor one day, and her regular doctor was away; so she saw his replacement, who was familiar with Martens and Associates. So he gave her a referral to see them for sexual-abuse therapy. Now that she had a referral, I called and made an appointment for Friday because I was working on a condensed workweek and got every Friday off. Jennifer was scared to go and I had to argue with her to get her going, and when we got to Surrey, I had a hard time finding their office because I didn't know my way around. When we got there, we met Hubert Smith, the therapist Liz was seeing and talked about. He said he would have to see both of us individually so he would know what kind of conditions Jennifer was living under, but first we would have to fill out a questionnaire. That was all we did for our first session, then we booked an appointment for the following week.

At our second appointment, I told Hubert I was working on an autobiography but haven't done very much writing yet because it was hard to find time to write, so he photocopied all my writing to date then took me to a private room where I could write while he talked to Jennifer. Jennifer was told to start writing about her past and get her feelings out, but it was very stressful for her. During the week, I would tell her to work on her writing, but she wouldn't do it. She always said she wanted to visit Brenda, her mother, or her brothers or found some other excuse not to write. Then when it became time for her appointment, I had to argue with her to go, and she tried using the excuse "Hubert's going to be mad at me because I never did very much writing!" but I would force her to go anyway. My own writing was going rather slowly, but I got as far as 1980 when her desires to commit suicide started coming out and I tried to find a psychiatrist for her to see. That was the last paragraph I wrote; and when I showed it to Hubert, he said, "Keep writing!"

Jennifer eventually got her driver's license, and I was told I may get laid off soon, but hoped it would be at the end of the summer, when the fire season was over. I wasn't sure what to do because I didn't want to be unemployed again and end up living in my truck, so Tom suggested I apply to become a prison guard. I didn't really want to do that, but it would have been better than nothing, so I applied.

A psychologist went to Elbow Lake to talk to the staff, and they suggested I attend because I had applied to be a guard. He talked about pedophiles and how they put themselves in positions where they can molest kids, such as Boy Scout leaders, camp counsellors, etc. Kids are often attracted to them because they have the mind of a child, and there is no cure for it. I didn't say anything but thought it would have been more appropriate to say a cure hasn't been found for it yet. He said one father had three daughters who would play cards to see who would go to bed with him. I found it hard to believe that he could have so much control and brainwash his daughters to that point, but it happened. Just before he left, he said we all have sexual desires, and a lady there felt frustrated because she knew I didn't have any. When I told Jennifer about the daughters playing cards to go to bed with their father, she said it's to see who's his favorite.

A couple of months after I applied to be a prison guard, I got an interview and answered all the questions with total honesty, which may have been a mistake because I got turned down. My family and I were happy about that though and I didn't really want the job anyway. Not long after I got turned down, there was a helicopter escape at the maximum-security Kent Institution in Agassiz that happened just like in the movies. A helicopter was hijacked, landed in the prison yard. Two inmates escaped and a guard got his knee cap shot off in the incident, so now I was even happier that I didn't get hired.

I continued working and taking Jennifer to therapy on Fridays. She had to relive many traumatic memories and would often go out crying. As I was sitting in the waiting room, I noticed many of their patients were Native and sometimes went out crying, so I asked Hubert about it, and he said 85 percent of their patients are Native. It's well-known many Indian reserves have alcohol problems; and I read an article by Ruby Dunstan, the chief of Lytton Band at that time, saying people have a drinking problem, go to treatment centers for help, then go right back to drinking again. Several years earlier, a friend from Lytton, Casey, went to a treatment center because he had a problem with alcohol; and people said he won't be able to stay off drinking for long. After Jennifer started going for therapy, I realized the impact sexual abuse can have on the victims. My ex-foster brother and a friend who both committed suicide mentioned having attended the Indian residential school in Lytton. It was said that one of the ministers was charged with molesting the Indian children in the residential school there, and after everything he did, all he got was two years in jail. I'm sure there were other children that he molested and drove to addiction and suicide!

Since I missed some fires because Jennifer couldn't stay home, I rented a pager so I could still be called, but it rained hard most of the time. I continued working, taking her to therapy, and started applying for other jobs because I didn't know when I would get laid off. A temporary job came up at Canadian Forest Products in Harrison Mills, so I applied for it. I got an interview, but unfortunately, another applicant was more qualified than I was. An opening came up with the British Columbia Forest Service in Lillooet, so I applied and had to go to Kamloops for the interview. I wanted the job even though Jennifer didn't want to move there, and didn't get the job again. Then I applied for a job opening in Pemberton and had to come to Squamish for the interview. Jennifer had gone on a spending spree because she thought I would be going away on fires, but it continued to rain, and I kept hoping my job would last until the end of the summer so I could get some overtime to pay off my bills.

I kept taking Jennifer to therapy even though she would be depressed and often cried after reliving what she had gone through, but she felt a little better after each time she went for therapy. I was eligible for holidays but didn't want to take time off because I had been unemployed too long. If I got laid off, I would still be given my holiday pay, which I could live on temporarily. I went to the interview in Squamish, but I didn't think I had very much chance of getting on there; then an opening also came up in Rosedale, so I applied there and hoped I would get that job instead. I was allowed a new pair of work boots each year; so when I went to get some, they said, "No. You're going to get laid off next week. Since you didn't get a new pair this year, you can keep your leather caulk [spiked] boots."

I didn't know whether to get excited or depressed. I didn't like working there but could have adjusted to it. My bills had gone up, and now I was getting laid off before I had a chance to get them down. I wasn't sure what I could do now except work to the very last day. One day I was going to tell Tom how I knew my dad was thinking about me when he cut his arm at work; but he was in Ottawa, Ontario, for a week. Then just before I was to be laid off, a permanent position came up at Elbow Lake for a forestry officer, and I was eligible to apply because it was an in-service job and I was still working for Corrections. I applied even though I would have preferred to work somewhere else;

and as my job started winding down, an LU said, "That smile gets bigger every day!"

I wanted to keep working, but I couldn't see very much future in this job. If I got laid off after ten years, I wouldn't know very much because I would be too used to doing nothing. Then two days before I got laid off, I got a call from the Forest Service in Squamish. I had won the competition, could start right away, and it was a permanent job with a pension plan. But it was in Pemberton, a long way from where I was taking Jennifer for therapy, so I wasn't sure what to do! I had been through some extremely hard times, and now I was offered a job I wanted for years, so I asked for a few days to think it over.

I was in a very difficult situation now. I had an opportunity for a job I always wanted, but it took me a long time to get Jennifer into therapy. I knew she had to continue her therapy because I saw what sexual abuse does to the victims, but I also owed very much money on my credit cards. Then I remembered an old proverb that used to be advertised on TV, "If you put people ahead of things, everything will find its place." I often ended up in lucky situations by trying to help Jennifer do something for herself; if she committed suicide because of what happened, she can't be brought back. You can always get another job, but you can't bring people back once they're gone, so I told the Forest Service I couldn't take the job because Jennifer needed her therapy. This was a very difficult decision to make, and it was also very hard to get her into therapy; so I kept hoping I would get the job in Rosedale, but didn't get it.

Right after I got laid off, the rain stopped, the weather got hot, and the fire-hazard rating went up. I couldn't get my UIC right away because I took holiday pay rather than time off and was offered to have my superannuation (pension fund) paid out or deposited directly into my RRSP. I knew I could get my bills down with it, but I still chose to put it into RRSP so it would always be there. As the fire hazard started getting worse, I suggested to Alvin, Andrew, and Henry Jr. that we all put our names in for firefighting. It didn't pay very much, but at least it would be a chance to earn some spending money, so I helped them all put in applications and hoped we could at least get some temporary work.

There was an ad in the *Province* newspaper one day for forest technicians to become timber cruisers with International Forest Products (Interfor), and I thought, *Now's my chance! If I can get the job,*

I would specialize for a minimum of two years and monitor everything closely: travel time, weather, terrain, camp costs, etc., and if I got laid off, I would have enough knowledge to go contracting on my own. I didn't specialize when I was younger and realized that was a mistake.

I continued taking Jennifer to therapy once a week, then one night, I got a call to go firefighting. They also asked for Alvin; but when I called him, one of his uncles just arrived for a visit, so he couldn't make it. So I called the Forest Service back and told them to call Andrew. It was six o'clock Friday night and there wasn't much daylight left and the fire was just past Sto:lo Eagle near a lake, so we picked Andrew up along the way. We worked until it was dark. Then we were supposed to be back early the next morning, so I decided to just stay in Sto:lo Eagle that night; and the next morning, Henry Jr. gave us a ride to the junction where we would be picked up. It was a small fire, but the area was rocky and it was rather difficult to walk on the huge boulders. We worked all day. Then Andrew and I were asked to go back the next day to control hot spots when they flared up, and I was asked to use my own truck the next day, so I went back to Chilliwack that night.

We went back the next day, and Andrew and I were asked to patrol the fire for a few days and call for help if it flared up. Having us there was cheap insurance if they could get the fire under control right away if it started up again. Andrew and I were getting tired, but when everyone else left, we were asked to stay for another hour and watch for hot spots, but we were still happy just to be working though. I went home that night and told Andrew I would pick him up in the morning and told Jennifer what we were doing and she could go along if she wanted. We drove to Sto:lo Eagle the next day, picked up Andrew, and drove to the fire. We left some equipment there and found a hot spot and put it out as soon as we got there; then we sat around, waited, and patrolled the fire every two hours. It was so small it didn't even take ten minutes to walk around it.

We worked ten hours each day, but that included our travel time to and from Chilliwack, and after the first day, we decided to bring lawn chairs and fishing tackle to help pass the time. When we picked Andrew up, Jennifer told me, "Don't just take the lawn chairs. Ask Dad if we could use his lawn chairs." Even though he couldn't walk, I asked him and didn't think I should have to, yet still he got mad and thought, *He wants to borrow my lawn chairs, yet he won't even buy me a cup of coffee!* I didn't think what he did was justified, so I took them anyway, and Andrew took an inner tube along and went swimming.

We put out two hot spots that day and radioed the Forest Service each day on how things were going. One night, I got a letter from Interfor for the timber-cruising job and left Andrew and Jennifer on site the next day when things were calm to arrange for an interview on Monday morning. As we were walking around on the boulders, Jennifer slipped and fell on her knees, and I didn't think she fell very hard, and it wouldn't bother her. The next day, we went out again and Jennifer's knees were weak and she was having a bit of trouble walking around. I thought her knees were just slightly bruised and she would get better right away. We thought we would only be there for three days, but we were asked to go out on the fourth day. On the fourth day, there weren't any hot spots, and I thought the job was over; but we were asked to go back again the fifth day. We were getting bored with it and started wishing it would end, but at least we were getting some spending money. Then on the fifth day, we were asked to be back to the office by three o'clock. When we got back to the office, I turned our time sheets in and Andrew gave them a hard-luck story and got his check right away. I tried to get mine right away too, but they were too busy.

Then a staff member called me in to another room and asked me if I wanted to work as a fire warden and patrol the Coquihalla Highway. I would be working ten hours a day, paid more than I did in firefighting, given a day rate for my truck, and reimbursed for my gas. I was to post signs prohibiting fires on all picnic areas except provincial parks and walk around making sure no one was lighting any fires and would have a magnetic sign for my truck saying "FIRE WARDEN." I accepted the job but told them I couldn't work on Monday because I had a very important job interview to go to. Then I told Andrew about my new job and my interview, and if I got the job with Interfor before the patrolling was over, I would try and pass it on to him. When we got to Chilliwack, Andrew cashed his check and took us out to McDonald's to show his appreciation for helping him out; then he went out to the bars and cabarets with his friends, and Jennifer and I went home.

The next day, I took Jennifer along with me to post signs and watch for people lighting fires. We drove all over, posting signs where we thought people would be camping or picnicking; drove up the Hope-Princeton Highway as far as Manning Park; had coffee; then drove up the Coquihalla Highway. We drove around a bit more; then it was time to drive back. I had a radio and called the Forest Service to tell them where I was at what time. Jennifer and I went out to patrol again, but her knees were still weak and she was beginning to have trouble walking around. Even though it was a weekend during the summer, there were very few people out and about.

On Monday morning, Jennifer and I drove to Vancouver for my interview and left early to avoid rush-hour traffic to go for coffee. At the interview, the lady looked at my résumé and asked why I took such a variety of courses at college, so I told her we were forced to take certain courses because the government was trying to make us give up on our postsecondary education. Then when I got to BCIT, I failed there two times for medical reasons, so it took me eight years of studying just to get a two-year diploma. I'm interested in timber cruising because I want to specialize in one thing. I've done everything from tree planting to high-lead logging and never had a chance for a permanent job because of the recession of the eighties.

After the interview, she introduced me to a forester who was several years younger than I who said they have to hire a certain number of women and wondered why they were stereotyped. I said it was probably because of the movies we watched as children and the roles they were expected to play at our parents' age could have stayed with us subconsciously; then he realized that the movies always made the Indians look like bad people and that I had been closed off in the past.

I really wanted that job badly, and when I went back to Chilliwack, I picked up my check for firefighting. Someone at the office got mad because I was supposed to be out patrolling, but I told him I specifically asked for that day off for a job interview. I continued patrolling the Coquihalla Highway, and Jennifer sometimes went with me, but her knees were getting worse. She was having trouble walking, and I couldn't understand why she was like that, so I thought maybe she had weak bones. That job lasted a week; then it rained, so Jennifer and I went out and took the signs down. I had worked two weeks now, so I wouldn't get any UIC.

I was off work for another week; then someone called looking for Andrew. There were only three people with that last name in the phone book, so he called us. I didn't know if he was looking for Jennifer's brother or Andrew from Sardis. The fellow on the phone said he was looking for

Andrew from Sardis because they needed a logger, a chaser, for one day this week and two days next week. So I told him I could chase, so he told me where to meet him the next morning. I got so excited I couldn't sleep that night. Here was a chance for a job that could extend until we got snowed out. I showed up the next day, and the logging contractor picked me up. He only needed me for one day, but that was all right. When I phoned him up a week later, he didn't need me, but I could pick up my paycheck at the same place; and when I picked up my check, one of the crew said to him, "Doesn't he look like he's done something great with his life!" That sure made me feel good.

After I got paid, I bought Jennifer some vitamins and calcium tablets because I thought her body lacked calcium that's why her bones were so weak. Sometimes when Angela would ask to go over, Jennifer would say, "No, Angela! I'm having too much trouble with depression right now," and I wished she wasn't like that because I enjoyed it when Angela went over to visit.

In an Indian newspaper, *Kahtou*, Thompson Highway, an Aboriginal author and playwright said out of two hundred Indian students, he started out with two of them who graduated from high school in the residential school. That meant 1 percent of the Indians got their grade 12, so I wondered if blacks in segregated schools in the United States ever had dropout rates like that. Natives younger than I said the residential school was like a prison and thought Tomson Highway must be at least ten to fifteen years older than I. Not long after I turned the job down in Pemberton, the Oka crisis in Ontario started and the Mount Currie Indians from just outside of Pemberton put up a roadblock. Sometimes people are jealous of us, and many people don't understand why the Indians are the way they are. If people knew the truth about how the Indians have been treated and what they went through, they may be surprised such things didn't happen much earlier.

I still didn't know how much I was going to get on UIC because I never got a full check from them yet, and Jennifer said, "I'm not going to move back with your family!" Just before the end of the summer, Jennifer's family held a family gathering for Allan at Brenda and Alvin's; and when no one was listening, I said to Henry, "I think you should eat what your niggers had to eat!"

Henry cried and thought, *My kids had to eat the grease out of the pan.* Then when he was leaving, he felt really bad because I wouldn't go help him get into his truck. His coordination was off because of his stroke, but Alvin wouldn't help him either.

In the spring, Jennifer had applied to her band for her to take a hairdressing course; her funding was now approved, but they wouldn't give her anything for room and board. They only paid her tuition. One of her uncles was now interested in the land we had cleared; and since we turned the house down, I thought, *If we sell the land, it will pay for the clothes you need to take the course.* We both got excited and went on a spending spree but were careful not to spend more than $400. After we bought the clothes, we called her uncle, and he agreed to buy the land for $400. We were all excited, but I hoped her knees would be strong enough for her to take the course. When she was ready to start the course, I went with her on the first day and she was told she needed a kit. Kits cost $500, and we didn't have it. The instructor said she could apply for a student loan to purchase one, which would take two months, but she couldn't start until then. We didn't have $500, and I didn't want to ask my family for help. Not only that, Jennifer didn't want to ask them either, so she said she could ask her dad; but I knew he wouldn't help her, but didn't say anything.

We went to Sto:lo Eagle to ask him for help, but I knew it was just a waste of time. Jennifer asked him if she could borrow $500 for her course and she could pay him back when her student loan went through, and I thought even if he told us not to pay him back, that would have been nothing compared to what we've done for him. I knew Henry had lots of money in the bank, yet he wasn't going to help us out; and he said to Andrew, "How much money have I got in the bank?" Andrew didn't answer, then Henry said, "I don't know. That's quite a lot. We're going to go hunting." He could barely walk, yet he said he was going hunting and wouldn't help her.

Jennifer realized he wasn't going to help her, so we left. I felt like picking up a case of beer and getting drunk, but my instincts told me everything was going to work out. Jennifer got extremely depressed and started crying, but before we reached Agassiz, she said, "Now I finally see my father for the greedy man he really is!" I felt so much better when I heard that; and when we got home, instead of going out for a beer, I went out for a cup of coffee. It was a disappointment turned into a victory! Not long after Henry turned us down, he wound up in the hospital again because his stomach was manufacturing too much acid. I knew something would happen back to him for the stunt he pulled.

Two weeks later, the hairdressing school called and said Jennifer's band paid for her kit and I thought, *She's finally going to get a career of her own. Even if she changes her career goals, at least it's a stepping stone.* We were both excited, but her knees were still too weak to walk very good, so we had to postpone her start-up until her knees got stronger. Her knees kept getting weaker and weaker until her knees got so weak she couldn't walk. She couldn't even lift her knees half an inch from the linoleum to the carpet. I kept taking her to sexual-abuse therapy in Surrey every week and had to carry her or help her as much as I could. She wanted me to rent her a wheelchair, but we couldn't afford it. Usually after therapy, she liked to walk around Guildford Town Centre to relieve the stress from therapy, and I started wondering if she was going to be like that for the rest of her life.

Even though Henry wouldn't help Jennifer with her career goals, she insisted on visiting him in the hospital, and I knew it would be hard for her to break away from him from all the research I had done. Usually when she went to visit him, I tried to go to a waiting room and read or do something else because I couldn't stand him. One day when we went to visit him, some of his nieces and nephews were there and brought him some fruit. He couldn't talk very clearly but was mad at me because we wouldn't bring him anything, so I said, "I don't care if you're bored or not! You've never done anything but make life miserable for me and been a useless mooch ever since I met you!" I had promised Jennifer I wouldn't ever tell him he's never been anything but a burden to us, so I said everything else. I kept my promise.

Henry felt bad that I said things right out loud in front of his family, but eventually, he began to realize he was suffering for everything he had done wrong in the past, for molesting his daughters, and for not helping Jennifer with her career goals. Now it was all happening back to him. He finally started to realize he didn't treat me very well after all the things I did for him and started trying to be nice to me, but it was too late; he had pushed me too far.

One night I got a phone call from people who were doing a survey on the British Columbia medical system and they asked whether I thought it was good or not. I told them I thought it was very good; I've never had any problems with it; everything I needed I got; and even when I needed an operation on my ankle, I got in right away. The only problem I found was there wasn't enough sexual-abuse therapy available. Then I told them what happened to my ex-foster brother and my friend from Lytton and the impact sexual abuse has on the victim. When I tried to find sexual-abuse therapists for Jennifer, they were very few and far between. She's seeing a therapist in Surrey, and people go all the way from Lillooet and Keromeos every week for therapy. Several months later, I saw on the front page of the *Province* newspaper, "There's Not Enough Sexual Abuse Therapy in BC"; but I was too shy to see if my name was mentioned.

Jennifer started seeing physiotherapists in Abbotsford, but her knees seemed like they wouldn't heal, so she started worrying that she might have Lyme disease; but a bone specialist said she didn't have Lyme disease. He said she would need cortisone shots, which we would have to pay for ourselves because the British Columbia medical system didn't pay for them, but we asked Indian Health Service to pay for them and they agreed. When Jennifer got her cortisone shots in her knees, she just screamed, and the doctor got annoyed and thought she was acting like a baby. After we left the office, she said it reminded her of when her dad was kicking her in the legs; that's why she screamed.

I called Corrections Canada about the job I applied for and they said the interviews will be held when the fire season is over because staff are too busy working on fires. Then I asked who was being interviewed, and when they told me, I knew who was going to get the job; but the lady on the phone got really mad and wouldn't let me say, "I'll go for the interview, but I know who's got the job!" Now I wished I had applied for work with Canadian Forest Products in Harrison Mills or with the British Columbia Forest Service in Rosedale when I was attending BCIT, but I couldn't stand living that close to my family. I was beginning to think that was a mistake and felt like a born loser again. I went to the interview anyway and didn't get the job but was rather happy about it because I didn't want to work for Corrections for the rest of my life. I could have adjusted, but I wouldn't have been happy.

I continued taking Jennifer to therapy in Surrey and physiotherapy in Abbotsford, but her knees were still weak. She had to prepare to confront her father on why he treated her that way, and it was extremely hard for her to do. She needed me right beside her for support, so I thought, *Maybe it's better that I'm not working right now!* The cortisone shots didn't seem to be having very much effect on her knees, and the physiotherapy didn't seem to be helping either, so I still wondered if she was going to be like that for the rest of her life.

We went to Laughing Raven to visit Ben and Geraldine one weekend, and I apologized to Ben for the trouble I caused on Easter weekend, but he said he didn't remember because he was too drunk. That night, Ben and I went to town to pick up some beer. And on our way back, I told him why I gave Henry a hard time in front of everyone, and Ben said, "Henry should have just stayed home and saved his money."

It was hunting season again, and I knew I was going to miss it. I always enjoyed hunting even when I didn't get anything. Doe season would be open for a week in November, and I was hoping I could get a deer that year because it would help with the grocery bill since I missed the fire season. I heard it had been one of the best fire seasons ever. Then just before doe season opened, Andrew fell asleep while driving his father's truck and totalled it. Henry always taught his kids, "That bed is the worst place for you! You have plenty of time to rest when you're in your grave!" That's probably why he pushed himself that far.

I wanted to spend some time hunting up Mount Cheam, near my parents' place, but Jennifer wanted to go to Sto:lo Eagle and said, "Andrew may be suicidal because of the accident. We should go over there and see him. I'm going to give him a rosary and a Bible. It might make him feel better." I knew there would be no point in arguing. It seemed like I never get to do anything for my own interests. It was frustrating, but I was used to it because that's the way it was when I was growing up. I didn't put myself back in a situation I was familiar with. Everything I went through had prepared me for what was coming. I had no choice but to put up with what I was going through.

Sometimes over the years, Ryan would ask me what Jennifer had to be depressed about if I mentioned her depression. Usually I didn't say anything, but this time I said, "Victims of incest and child sexual abuse often blame themselves for what happened. That's why Peter and my ex-foster brother committed suicide. After my foster brother moved out, all he ever did was drink. He cut himself up with a knife twice! Then he committed suicide when he was twenty-two!" Ryan never said anything; and later on in the week, I told him, "Ben thought your dad should have just stayed home and saved his money at Liz and Jeremy's funeral." Ryan gave me an angry look for telling Ben that but didn't say anything.

We stayed in Sto:lo Eagle for a little over a week then went home. Doe-hunting season was over by then, so I missed it again. I went for a walk to visit Alvin one morning, and as I was walking by the hospital, Ryan and Desiree were there to pick Henry up. I helped them move his belongings but wouldn't help Henry move out; and when we got to the car, Desiree thought, "Baxter hates him!"

I continued taking Jennifer to therapy every Friday, and although I was on UIC and owed much money on my credit cards, people who drove by me in a Mercedes or Corvette would sometimes look at me like I should be driving one too. I thought that was far different from people looking down on me as too lazy to go to work. When I was working, I had money deducted from my checks and put into Canada Savings Bonds. I got my bonds in November and saved them for Christmas; that way, Christmas wasn't a problem.

Henry's health continued to get worse; he could barely walk across the room by himself, but I wouldn't help him because he never did anything for us in spite of all the things we did for him. We went to Abbotsford to do some Christmas shopping one day then to Laughing Raven to visit. We were drinking in the evening and somehow they started talking about Henry, so I said, "Oh, fuck him! I hate him! He's wimpy!" Jennifer and Geraldine both got mad, so we left. Jennifer was really uptight and drove around for a while before we went home, and when we got home, she grabbed our kitchen knife and wanted to scare me with it. She had chased me around the apartment with a knife several times in the past when I didn't even do anything, and this time I didn't know what she was going to do! I was cornered against the wall in the kitchen, so I tried to grab the handle. Instead of grabbing the handle, I accidentally grabbed the blade and cut my fingers; so she told me to go to the hospital, but I said, "It's all right! I usually heal fast!"

She wouldn't listen and called a taxi for me. I think she was too mad at me to drive herself, so I went to the hospital emergency ward and ended up getting four stitches on two of my fingers. When they asked me what happened, I told them my girlfriend cut me with a knife; later on, Jennifer said Brenda laughed when she heard on the radio someone was in the emergency ward because his girlfriend knifed him. After I got my stitches, I asked the receptionist to call me a taxi; but when I got outside, Jennifer was sitting there in our truck and said, "I wasn't going to do anything!"

We went to Sto:lo Eagle a week before Christmas because Jennifer's family didn't have a vehicle to get around on, and when we took them to Chilliwack, I charged them for gas even though my instincts told me I didn't need the money. On Christmas Eve, there were three cases of beer and a bottle of wine at Henry's place, and I hoped it would be saved for the next day. Brenda and Alvin were there, and Alvin and Andrew were sipping the wine and wanted me to drink with them. I drank rather slowly because wine sometimes seemed to bring out the worst in me. After drinking the wine, we started drinking the beer, so I knew something could go wrong; and when the beer was finished, Andrew and I got into an argument. Jennifer wasn't drinking; and when she heard us, she went into the kitchen, got mad at everyone, and told us all to go to bed. I went into the room where we were going to sleep and Andrew went in. We shook hands, hugged each other, and I said, "I heard we got into an argument!"

"We never got into an argument!"

Everyone started getting ready to go to bed, and I went into the living room and waited to use the bathroom. As I was waiting, Brenda went in and said, "I heard about Laughing Raven and I don't like it!"

"If you don't like it, wake him up and ask him what it was all about!"

Brenda knew I would have started beating her dad up, so she said, "Well, his mind is going. He won't remember."

Even with four stitches on two of my fingers, I would have just wailed on him! The next day, I said to Alvin, "What were Andrew and I arguing about?"

"You said something bad about the man."

"What did I say?" Alvin wouldn't answer. It may have been bad, but it was probably the truth. Christmas went by rather uneventfully after that; there was the usual family gathering and Christmas dinner. The next day, Ryan and Desiree asked me to drive them to the bar because they wanted to drink and needed a driver to stay sober, so I agreed and went with them. When we got to the bar, I told them, "I helped Henry Jr. finish high school and paid for his graduation. Your father never gave me any thanks at all! All he did was deliberately ruin my fun! Henry had over $10,000 in the bank and never put anything down for Liz and Jeremy's funeral! When the kids were young, they went picking berries and he took every cent of what they made, then they stole the other picker's lunches because they were hungry!"

"That was a long time ago though, Baxter," Ryan said.

"Would you make Shannon and Sharon work and go hungry just so you could drink?"

"No," he replied, shaking his head.

"He didn't lose his daughter! He lost his nigger!"

"Lost his what?" asked Desiree.

"Lost his nigger!"

I really got cranky that night when I told Ryan and Desiree how I felt toward Henry, but it appeared to me that what Henry was doing felt normal to them. I only drank a little bit in the bar and waited until we got back to Sto:lo Eagle before I drank. Jennifer and I left the next day, but just before we left, I told Henry, "I didn't want to come here!" He got mad because he had tried to be nice to me, but nothing anyone ever did was enough for him; now it was happening back to him. We visited my family in Rosedale for a little while then went back home New Year's Eve. It looked like everyone was out somewhere and we were the only ones staying home.

Chapter 13

1991

Jennifer continued going for therapy and prepared to take her father to Surrey to confront him on why he treated her that way and said it felt like doomsday was coming; I wrote down everything she wanted to say to him then photocopied it, and we put it together in the order she wanted to tell him. It was very stressful for her and she got really cranky, but I put up with it because I wanted to be as supportive as possible. She thought her knees were finally strong enough for her to take her hairdressing course, so we called her band to sponsor her; but the money was already spent on another student, so I felt defeated again and wondered if she was ever going to get a career of her own. It was getting cold out, so I asked my mother if I could trade her vehicles for one day. I thought she would agree, but she said, "There's going to be a lot of tension built up between them. Wouldn't it be better if they rode apart?"

I felt disappointed again; my parents do everything for my brothers, but when I ask for something, they just automatically say "No!" Eventually toward the end of January when we had everything ready to confront Jennifer's father, we went to Sto:lo Eagle to get them, and I helped Henry put his socks and shoes on to get ready. Henry Jr. was watching me and thought, *It must be important! Baxter's even helping him put his socks and shoes on! Normally, he doesn't even help him walk across the room!*

I loaded a number of blankets onto the back of my truck so Jennifer and her mother would be comfortable because Henry usually sat in the front, and before we left, I told Jennifer to make sure they brought money for their lunch because I was tired of providing everything for them. When we got to Surrey, Jennifer talked to her father in another room. Hubert put it all on videotape, and when it was over, she said her dad cried when she confronted him. After therapy, we went to Church's Chicken for dinner then drove home. Henry Jr. went back to college to take his math course again because he wanted to get a better mark before advancing further, and when he needed help, he would stop over to visit so I could tutor him. I enjoyed it because I wanted to see him get a career and do something with his life.

I sometimes got lonely while looking after Jennifer, but usually, no one was interested in me. Now that she was getting better, I noticed that some ladies were getting interested in me. It didn't matter though because I had given up too many years of my life to give up looking after her. Jennifer asked me if I ever felt attracted to anyone, and I told her there was one lady I liked, but I wasn't going to do anything about it; she was a Native girl, but I didn't have a preference for Native girls.

We continued going to therapy every Friday, and one day, Hubert told me to go into a room and do role play and I was to pretend Jennifer was my mother. It came completely unexpected, so I asked if I could review my notes and prepare for it, but he said no. When we got into the room, Hubert set up the video camera, and I couldn't believe how much anger I had in me. The trouble started the summer I went haying; after working ten hours a day, seven days a week for four weeks, I was only allowed one day of rest. I didn't mind doing the housework, but I didn't like getting up early and having nothing to do for the rest of the day. She drove me to drinking then I got punished for doing things I was too drunk to remember doing!I didn't make many friends when I was younger because I was continually teased; often it was just for being young, then I went on about the trouble she caused me all those years when I was going to college and BCIT and being forced to give up what little free time I had after seven years of studying just for her. If she had been there and tried to argue, I would have gotten violent! I just had no choice!

At the next session, Hubert told us to watch the movie *Something about Amelia*. It was the second time I saw it, but I took notes on what I saw.

- Father gives image of being the ideal father. He works and provides a comfortable home for the children.
- Rather possessive of daughter, thirteen years old, plus doesn't want her going out on dates.

- Dominates wife, puts down her opinion, makes her feel worthless.
- Amelia goes out on date plus keeps her boyfriend at a distance.
- Father seems jealous over Amelia, had a tradition of going bowling every Friday, wants her to find a better boyfriend.
- Amelia doesn't believe she's pretty.
- Mother tried to soothe Amelia's feelings when she's upset; father doesn't want her to.
- Father wants Amelia to watch football rather than visit her friends; younger daughter offers to watch the game with him.
- Jennifer saw Amelia get jealous of her younger sister sitting beside her father. I couldn't understand her feeling that way because I thought Amelia was happy to get away from her father but didn't want her sister to go through the same thing.
- Both parents are working, giving him a chance to be alone with his daughter.
- School counsellor is worried about Amelia, her marks are going down, and he tries to ask her about it, but she can't talk about it,
- Amelia admits it to counsellor, who tells her mother. Mother doesn't believe it or want to listen to her counsellor.
- Mother doesn't want the police to remove the children from the house, stands beside her husband.
- Amelia believes she is the criminal and may be charged.
- In therapy, Amelia tells how she was manipulated into believing it was her fault and felt really bad about it, how she was told not to talk about it.
- Younger sister doesn't want to believe it happened, just like Jennifer did.
- Younger sister is angry at Amelia for having father taken away, believes Amelia was lying.
- Mother scolds Amelia; why did she let him do it? Why didn't she stop him? She was forced.
- Mother called father to talk to him, tells him she's on tranquilizers, says she knows Amelia is telling the truth.
- Father starts making excuses for his actions.
- Mother seeing a psychiatrist; he asks, why did she let it happen?

- Father doesn't believe he can tell his daughter he loves her.
- Marriage is on the rocks. Psychiatrist recommends the father go for sexual-abuse therapy.
- Psychiatrist explains how Amelia feels about the situation.
- When father was ordered to stay away from home, he felt lonely when watching Shirley Temple on TV.
- This is the second time I saw this show, but I got much more out of it this time.

At the next session, Hubert told me to write a letter to each member of my family and tell them what I thought of them. Here they are:

February 8, 1991

Dear Tony:

I'm glad you finally settled down and started to do something with your life. You have a lot of potential but were wasting it going down a dead-end street.

Looking back through your childhood, I guess everything came too easy for you, so you created your own excitement. You weren't taught to be as responsible as the rest of us and eventually ended up being totally irresponsible.

All those years when you were totally irresponsible, it was annoying, sometimes very annoying to everyone else. However, bad situations can often be turned around into good ones. It looks like you're using your experiences to prevent others from following the same path.

I kept wishing you would settle down and do something with your life. To me it looks like all those years are being turned around for your own benefit, helping you to help others following the same path. Congratulations.

From
Baxter

February 20, 1991

Dear Dad:

Jennifer's sexual-abuse therapist told me to write a letter to all members of my family. I know you had a difficult life, having to look after your brothers and sisters, the way you were treated in the residential schools, and not being able to get what you wanted out of life.

I appreciate how hard you worked to support us and provide for us, but I wished you didn't put me down so much and tease me all the time. I was very withdrawn, and it took me a long time and much effort to come out of it. But I always tried to be optimistic about whatever situations I met in life.

I know you are knowledgeable and well-read in many subjects, but I wish you would stop putting down my opinion. I will always be younger than you, but that doesn't mean I don't know anything.

I often say or do things that you do, and you try to convince me that I'm wrong. Nothing was enough. I usually couldn't get a word in edgewise to explain myself. Sometimes it was "Do as I say, not as I do!"

I never really knew you when I was growing up because usually you were away working. When you were home, you were usually fixing power saws, doing books, or rounding up a crew. Making the most of the situation, I learned to be more independent and self-going. If I needed something done, I had to do it myself since there was no one around to help me or show me what to do.

I guess you know the worst thing you ever did was not to stop people from trying to run my life when I was working on my career and not listening when I tried to explain why I stayed with Jennifer.

Even after you found out why I stayed with Jennifer, you tried to run my life. You acted like it was sacrilegious to do things that weren't scientifically proven. Scientists readily admit they can't even explain the human brain.

Everyone has a brain and their own unique talents. People also have feelings and instincts, things that exist but can't be felt, touched, or seen. Most scientists work on physical things in their labs.

You follow your instincts and realize they're right because you sometimes talk about it. I do the same thing, but I also did much research on the subject. I also studied how scientists and inventors came up with some of their ideas and followed the same techniques.

I wish you weren't so obnoxious and tried to tell me I was wrong all the time. I have a court case going to the Supreme Court of Canada because of that.

I'm trying to be optimistic about the situation, and it forced me to come out of my shell. It also inspired me to try writing a book on my life to prove that nothing is impossible. You keep saying it but turn around and tell me I can't do it.

From
Baxter

February 20, 1991

Dear Mother:

After seeing Hubert for a while, he told me to write a letter to all members of my family. Right now, I feel the time is right to write a letter.

I know both you and Dad had a difficult childhood, and I appreciate you not wanting us to go through what you went through. The schools for the Indians are something many white people wouldn't want to see their children go through.

However, I just wish you didn't try to run my life, my free time, the way you did. I wish you would have listened when I told you I wanted to stay single all those years when working on my career. I also wish you didn't pressure me so much to leave Jennifer and treat her the way you did. Looking after her was hard enough without you making it worse.

But this isn't the main reason for writing this letter. From the research I've done and from what I learned at Jennifer's sexual-abuse therapy, I get the opinion things in your childhood weren't right. It's not my intuition saying this, just an opinion from things I've seen and books I've read.

I'm sure you and Dad have memories of things you don't like to talk about. I could never express my opinions because no one ever listened, or even my brothers tried to convince me I was wrong. I had to keep everything to myself and be seen and not heard.

From
Baxter

February 20, 1991

Dear David:

Looking back over the years, I guess your older brothers had a tendency to spoil you, but we weren't mature enough to know better. After moving back to the coast, I don't think Dad realized how hard it was for a young child to live way out there by himself after growing up in the middle of town.

Dad can be very naive at times, and he usually doesn't listen to us. When people get so bored, they almost go crazy they start misbehaving for something to do.

We all noticed how fast you changed when Jimmy Stewart moved in with us. You needed someone your own age to associate with.

While living out there, you had many things given to you and you took it for granted. You made money fishing at an early age, and things went easy for you. Luckily though, you weren't as spoilt as much as Tony and didn't end up like him.

After all the things I did for you and all the running around you did on my truck, you refused to do the littlest thing for me. I tried to tell you that something would happen back to you for being that way, but you refused to listen. You knew everything.

You claimed to be a good mechanic, but after buying that car off Gary Victor, I guess you proved otherwise. Before you treat someone in any way, you should keep in mind it's going to happen back to you. You used to put my opinion down, but you had already proven that your mouth is bigger than your brain.

I'm glad you've grown out of it, but you could learn to be more flexible and open-minded.

From
Baxter

February 22, 1991

Dear Issac (Arthur):

I was told to write a letter to all my family members on how I feel toward them. In some ways I wish I had some of your stubbornness and perhaps I could have handled the situation with my parents better. But too much of everything can work against you.

We all have our own unique personalities, attitudes, and opinions. Your stubbornness caused you to drop out of college when Indian Affairs tried to make us give up. I was more flexible and learned to take the good with the bad.

Although you are a good person, you never showed any consideration for other people's needs when we went to college. I don't mean the first time, but the second time when we were rooming with Eddie Dale. You know I was trying hard to succeed, but you did as you pleased without caring about how your interests were interfering with my studies.

I tried to tell you to stay home and study and secure your future, but your stubbornness ruled your life. Another thing that really bothered me was that year I almost failed at college because of everyone trying to run my life. You had to be obnoxious and tell everyone I would have failed anyway. I did everything to get everyone off my back. I stopped going home altogether. I went up north every chance I got and didn't apply for jobs close to home so I could get away from them. Nothing was enough until I was at my breaking point and almost had to get violent.

One thing you should try and learn is to have more patience and more understanding. I don't mind checking the net, but you got too cranky and impatient. You don't realize I never had as much experience as you and David.

You are a good person, but you should try and control your obnoxiousness. Especially in matters dealing with career goals because that's a person's future security. If you're too dense to realize that, you probably won't reach your full potential in life.

From
Baxter

I tried to get my bills down, but it seemed like something was always going wrong, and it was also costly to take Jennifer to the therapy. Sometimes when it was cold and windy, Angela would ask me to drive her to school; her mother didn't own a car and her parents were separated, so I drove her. I tried to tutor Susie in her upgrading classes, but she didn't seem to be able to concentrate on her studying; then an opening came up for Natives to take a one-year course to become a sexual-abuse therapist, so she applied and we drove her to Vancouver for her interview. When we got back to Chilliwack, she was all excited about the course. I was hoping it would help her get a career of her own because she had a very hard life and education is the key to breaking the welfare cycle the Canadian government tried to keep the Indians on.

Susie got accepted in the course, so I offered to help her find a place to stay since I know Vancouver quite well. She also had a friend in Vancouver who was willing to help her out. We all expected to have a hard time finding a place to stay and weren't looking forward to it. We visited her friend in Vancouver, had coffee with her, then I went to the store to get a newspaper to check the ad section for apartments. Surprisingly, we found a place right away; we only checked two apartment buildings and found a place right across the playing field from her friend's place. After putting down a damage deposit, we went back to Chilliwack. Susie rode in the front seat for a little while, and other ladies watching us thought, *That friend he likes to drive around with.*

Henry finally got his insurance settlement for his truck after Andrew totalled it, so Jennifer and I drove them to Chilliwack to buy another one. The truck they wanted wasn't available right away, so they were given a courtesy car; and when their truck arrived, we went to the dealer to visit them. The insurance settlement was used for the down payment, and Andrew said he was going to make the payments. Henry Jr., Andrew, and one of their cousins went hunting in Boston Bar two weeks later because the Indians are given permits to hunt for food and ceremonial purposes. Henry Jr.'s truck broke down in Boston Bar and they called and asked me to pick them up on their dad's truck and Andrew said I could ask his father for money to put some gas in the truck. I told Henry, "Andrew and Henry Jr. broke down in Boston Bar. They want me to pick them up on your truck, but I need money for gas."

Henry didn't answer and just sat there hesitating like he didn't want to give me any money to pick them up. I wasn't going to use my own money because I've already looked after enough of his responsibilities and never got any thanks at all, but luckily, Emily had some money and gave me $12 for gas to go pick them up. When I got there, a cop was checking their deer permits. He was just doing his job, but white people are sometimes jealous of us and think we have everything given to us on a silver platter. Henry Jr. had shot one deer for each permit he had and rather reluctantly gave one deer to each member of his family, and everyone was happy about that.

Henry Jr. was still attending his math class, and when I went to butcher my deer, I had to rush with it because I had to help him prepare for an exam. It was my first time butchering a deer, so I wasn't really sure what to do; and Ryan said some of my packages of meat were rather large for just Jennifer and me, but I was in a hurry. I saved some of the meat to grind up for hamburger because my dad had an electric grinder and said I could use it, and when I went to a meat shop to get some beef fat, the clerk asked me, "Is that to feed the birds?"

"No, I'm making hamburger," I replied, then she sort of slapped it at me. It looked like she was jealous of our right to hunt for food, but I wondered if she would feel that way if she knew the truth about how the Indians were treated.

Things were going along okay even though Jennifer had trouble working on her sexual-abuse therapy. When I tried to get her to work on it, she used the same excuse not to work on it; and when it became time to see Hubert, she would say, "He's going to be mad at me because I never did very much writing!" and I would have to try and force her to see him anyway.

While I was unemployed, I began to realize the unemployment rate on most Indian reserves is phenomenal. It wasn't in our culture to sit around and do nothing, because we had to live off the land; if we just sat around and did nothing, we would have starved to death long before the settlers came. Now, very few of us even know how to speak our own language, let alone how to live off the land. As I was walking down the street one day, I ran into Dave Walkem. He was on his lunch break and asked me to go for lunch with him, so we went for Chinese buffet. As we were eating, I mentioned it to Dave and told him something had to happen to make us like that.

He asked, "What happened?" but I didn't know.

The waitress serving us was a very nice-looking girl and thought I only went out with Indian girls; she thought she would have a chance for me because people thought she looked part Indian. In reality, looking after Jennifer was my first priority; once that was over, she could decide whether we stay together or not. If she decided she wanted a life of her own and we separated, I wouldn't go out with Indian girls only.

My court case was finally drawing near and Tom called me and asked me to go to Vancouver and meet my lawyer, so I took my writings along and hoped it could be used as part of my defense. I asked Tom if he wanted to read it, but he said, "No. It can contain some highly personal material."

I met my lawyer; and a very nice-looking lady, Karen, who was training to become a lawyer, interviewed me; and Gerald Donnegan interviewed Tom. Gerald told her, "This will give you some practice on what type of questions to ask."

Karen interviewed me and asked a number of questions about where I worked and what type of work I do and asked me to go into detail about how much supervisory experience I had. When we finished, I told her I had problems with communication and was well aware of it; a psychologist and Jennifer's therapist can verify it.

"What do you think would have happened if you weren't like that?"

"This accident wouldn't have happened."

"Well, that wouldn't stand up in court."

Before Tom and I left, Gerald said the federal government was paying my legal fees and financial settlement, so I felt incredible relief! After all that worrying, writing, seeing a psychologist, and therapist, it was a total waste of time and effort. I didn't have to write a book to try and pay my legal fees and financial settlement! I hadn't even finished writing up to when I finished BCIT and found out I had nothing to worry about, but decided to keep writing my autobiography anyway so other people could learn from my experiences and because Hubert had told me to keep writing. If I made any profits, it would be appreciated, but I didn't get my hopes up too high because I didn't know what to expect; writing also made me feel better about myself.

We continued seeing Hubert and Jennifer's physiotherapists, so I didn't have much time to write. I was kept busy looking after her, but she was getting better after each visit with Hubert. We would often walk around in shopping malls after seeing him, and when we went by a T-shirt shop, I wanted to buy my dad a T-shirt that said, "When I Want Your Opinion, I'll Give It to You!" And on the back I wanted to print in big block letters, “Mr. Obnoxious,” but Jennifer wouldn’t let me.

I made another trip to Vancouver with Tom to see our lawyer. The lawyer asked me questions to prepare me for my court case, and I told him a little bit about my personal life and that I was writing an autobiography. After meeting with Gerald Donnegan again, we had to meet with Donovan and his lawyer. The lawyers were gathering evidence for the court case, and each person’s lawyer had to present what evidence each other had. It was called an examination of discovery and was held at the courthouse on Nelson Street, just up the street from the bar where I used to drink many years earlier. On our way to the examination of discovery, Tom said he may be able to hire me for three months during the summer; it wouldn’t be anything long-term, but at least I could get the fire season. He also said Donovan had three seasons of high-lead logging experience, one of which was out at the Queen Charlotte Islands, first-year sciences at UBC, and a degree in economics at Simon Fraser University. He’s been a longtime junkie, heroin addict, and may be just looking for a way to support his habit. When we got to the courthouse, we went into a separate room and a court reporter recorded everything that was said. When Donovan told his story about how he got burned, I put my hand over my eyes and probably looked like I was depressed, but I was trying to keep from laughing. Then Tom accidentally nudged my foot, so I straightened out but held a straight face.

After it was over and we were on our way back, I finally opened up and told Tom how I knew my dad was thinking about me when he cut his arm at work. I taught Henry how to do that; then he stopped beating his kids when he realized he was doing something wrong and it was happening back to him for doing it. Then I told him I learned to do that when I was training in unarmed combat to take a round out of my ex-landlady’s son even though I knew something would happen back to him for misbehaving. The beatings I took in training weren’t what stopped me, even though I almost got knocked out when I took a good blow to the chin while boxing. I noticed what would happen whenever I would start thinking about it. It was almost like something was saying “Don’t do it! They’ve suffered enough!” I guess it sounded funny and people would think I was joking when I would say, “Were you thinking evil thoughts?” but actually I was quite serious. After that I told him how David tried to treat me and all the bad luck I had when I wanted to take a round out of him. When I told his girlfriend, Angie, about it, she said I should have learned after I blew a tire. Tom was surprised when I told him all that and thought, *I finally found out what goes on in that mind!*

It felt good not having to worry about my court case anymore and knew that no matter what happens, it's always best to be totally honest and tell the truth; the temptation to lie was great, but I knew it could only make things worse. We went to Laughing Raven again one weekend, and I talked to Harvey about my parents because he was close to my dad's age. I told him, "Everyone thought I had the nicest parents, but they were very dogmatic. Sometimes it was 'Do as I say, not as I do,' and I would try to tell them, but they wouldn't listen. They were always right and I was always wrong. I could lay the answers out right in front of them, and if it sunk in at all, it would take several years. Usually I couldn't get a word in edgewise to explain myself".

"They got that way from the residential schools. It was a way of coping with what they were going through." Harvey was a residential-school survivor.

"I spoke to a fellow from Gold River on Vancouver Island and he talked about going to the residential school in Kamloops. My aunt from Seabird Island also went to Kamloops, because I can remember visiting her as a child."

"The government tried to keep the Indian children away from their parents."

I spoke to another fellow from Laughing Raven that weekend about the schools; he was a drunk and drug addict and said, "The only difference between jail and school was there was bars on the windows in jail."

I always wanted to learn the Indian language, but the Indian children were usually beaten for speaking their own language in the residential schools even though some of them couldn't speak a word of English; now the languages are almost lost. Uncle Joe was teaching the Indian language at the school at Seabird Island Indian Reserve, so I asked him for tapes to learn the language. As I was growing up, I always thought the word *Xwelitem* meant "white people," but my aunt said it actually meant "the hungry ones." I heard vague stories that some of the settlers wouldn't have survived if the Indians didn't help them out.

I continued helping Henry Jr. with his math, and sometimes after class, he would pick me up and I would go to Sto:lo Eagle to help him study. I enjoyed it because it gave me a break from looking after Jennifer and a chance to do some writing. He said some of his classmates asked why he was doing so well, and he said he had a friend who helped him with his math. One time, he took his truck to a service station to get some work done on his truck; they did some work without his authorization and he was mad about it! He said he could have taken his truck to his brother-in-law's and fixed it himself. I was his friend, but Alvin was his brother-in-law. Everything was going along smoothly until he smashed up his truck going home from a cabaret one night. His truck was totally demolished, he lost all the money he put into it, and now had to find a way to get to classes; so I told his father, "You were jealous of him owning a truck and now it's totalled! You got what you wanted!" and his face dropped with remorse.

I had applied to many places for work, but most of them didn't even answer. I applied for a job with a small forestry-consulting company in New Westminister and got interviewed but didn't get the job. I thought I may not have been able to take it anyway because I had to look after Jennifer. Her knees were still so weak she sometimes couldn't walk, and I kept hoping I could get a job in Chilliwack or Rosedale so I could help Jennifer and Henry Jr. with their career goals. Jennifer had applied for a student loan to take her hairdressing course, but it hadn't gone through yet when I got a call from the Forest Service in Squamish. There was a job opening there, and they wondered if I would be interested in it. I was a little undecided at first because I was helping victims of child abuse do something with their, life so I asked my mother. She said, "I'm not going to try and change your mind, but you have to start living your own life sometime."

I told Jennifer the job could turn permanent and had a pension plan, so we wrote down all the advantages and disadvantages and decided to move. I called Stephen DeMelt and told him I was interested in the job and arranged for an interview. The job sounded like what I was interested in. I would start April 15 taking a silviculture surveys course in Mission then start work in Squamish. This job could turn permanent, so I decided to open up and not be so withdrawn anymore even though I knew it wouldn't be long and the staff was going to close me off. I was offered the job because I won a competition last summer and they needed someone with field experience.

When we went grocery-shopping, I ran into Kim at the cash register and told her, "I've got a job in Squamish now!"

"Where's that?"

"Up past Vancouver!"

"Are you going to drive up there every day?"

"No, I'm going to move up there. The job could turn permanent and has a pension plan. I'll be working Monday to Friday, eight thirty to four thirty." I was all excited about that. It seemed to bother the clerks in the grocery store that I wouldn't talk to them, but two Native girls were hired just before I left and staff seemed to close them off. I found that confusing.

I had heard about how to tune the mind in to remember anything you wanted to remember from books I read on the subconscious mind and finally figured out how to do it. I channelled my energy to the left side of my brain and kept picturing in my mind what I wanted to remember; it worked if I forgot where I put something and didn't have to search all over for it. I had taken the silviculture-surveys course once before and failed it because I was too cold and hungry to study. Now I was taking it again, but luckily, I was only allowed to audit the course because my home life wasn't conducive to studying. Jennifer was going through too much because of her sexual-abuse therapy, and I had to drop everything to try and calm her down. I finally made the last payment on my truck and thought, *Now I can start getting my bills down and save for another vehicle.*

The course was intense, and when it was finally over, I felt totally burnt out; so we went out to a cabaret that night and got drunk in a public place for the first time in a long, long time. The next day I had to get my tires rotated and the truck tuned up, but when I went to get the tires rotated, the mechanic said the upper and lower ball joints were gone and had to be fixed right away. I also had to pay for it right away because the mechanic at the garage where I had an account was going to a wedding and would only be working half a day. I had to be in Squamish the next day and start work on Monday, so I thought, *There goes all my savings!*

Our apartment wasn't going to be available for a week, but luckily, Ludmilla Kelderman said we could stay at her place since we didn't have enough money for a motel. Jennifer only stayed there two nights then started going crazy because she was still too nervous to meet people, so she went back to Laughing Raven. Ben had a twin brother named Gerald, and Gerald's wife passed away suddenly and was to be buried in Aiyansh, a town north of Terrace, British Columbia. Ben and Geraldine needed a babysitter while they attended the funeral, so Jennifer babysat for them. She couldn't cook very well, so I went back on the weekend to help look after the kids.

It was quite a struggle to pay our bills now. We were over our limit on our Visa, but luckily, the bank we dealt with was known to give people a chance to pay their bills when hard times came. I couldn't get reimbursed for the tuition fees for the surveys course until I got the receipt, but the receipt was mailed three times before I finally got it. After that, it still seemed like a long time to get reimbursed. Our truck insurance was going to be due soon, I had to try and save for it, and my income tax refund was also delayed because their workers were on strike. It seemed like nothing was going right for us, but I thought, *Maybe there's a reason why things are happening this way.*

Ben and Geraldine's fourteen-year-old daughter, Amanda, sometimes acted like she was interested in me; but I wanted to help Jennifer get a career. I sometimes wondered what was ever going to become of her because it appeared to me like she had no goals, no direction in life, very little guidance, and very little discipline. I would have liked to do something about it, but looking after Jennifer was hard enough. Three weeks after we moved in to our apartment, we went home one night and Brenda called and said, "Amanda committed suicide last night! She hung herself!"

"Oh no!" I said. "Why did she do that?" As soon as I said that, Jennifer knew something serious had gone wrong! I told her what happened then said, "Pack up and go to Laughing Raven! I'll gas up the truck and catch the bus on the weekend!" She was scared to drive the Squamish Highway by herself especially at night, but this time she had no choice. We lived close enough to the office, so I could just ride my bicycle to work.

I worked until Friday then caught a ride to Vancouver with a staff member. I had asked Stephen DeMelt for a day off for the funeral, so I caught the bus to Abbotsford; then Jennifer went to pick me up. She said she was so stressed out that when she got there, she locked the keys in the truck and someone had to go in through the canopy. The next day, Ryan and Desiree went with their kids. Ryan said they had to gather their bottles to have enough gas to get there and didn't know if they had enough gas to get back home, so I gave them $22 and $4 in coupons so they could get $26 worth of gas.

That evening, we were drinking and I tried to tell Ryan and Desiree to just let Henry stay home and save his money. They knew what I was trying to say, so they kept cutting me off then Jennifer got mad at me because she thought I was making a fool of myself even though I wasn't loud, just trying to stand up for what I thought was right. My income tax refund went in just before the funeral, and my parents didn't know Amanda committed suicide until I picked it up, so I donated most of it to the funeral and thought perhaps it was delayed because I would need it for the funeral.

The day before the funeral, I was talking to a fellow who worked as an alcohol-and-drug counsellor who studied Indian spiritualism and had attended the Indian residential schools. I had been taught to be a Christian as a child, so I knew what they were taught, and we talked about growing up Indian and Catholic. When we were children, we were taught it's a sin to eat meat on Fridays; if we did, our souls would be condemned unless we went to confession and apologized. We were taught to think of people who weren't Christians as pagans and they usually insinuated people from the South Seas, but when I looked into the meaning of the word *pagan*, it meant people with little or no religious beliefs, and realized people with different religious beliefs aren't pagans. We were always taught to think highly of people who spent all their time praying; now I wondered if people who did that had an addictive personality. The movies always made the Indians look like bad people, so as children if we played cowboys and Indians, we always wanted to be the cowboy because we didn't want to be the bad guy and didn't realize we were Indians ourselves.

After the funeral, I was talking to one of my cousins from Rosedale, Eleanor Douglas, and asked her, "Why did you attend the residential school when you lived so close to town?"

"They still had the dreaded Indian agent!"

I was in elementary school at the time, and they were only a few years older than I. I heard about her and her sisters quitting school as soon as they were old enough, and I wondered why they did that. Now I realized it was because they attended the residential school and probably couldn't wait to get away from there!

I was going to leave early the next day to go back to work, but Jennifer asked me to stay there with her; so I phoned Squamish to let them know I needed another day off, but Stephen DeMelt never got the message somehow and was mad when I got back. I went to work with him and other staff members that day to prepare the unit crew for the fire season; and at the end of the day, I told him, "It was a suicide. She was only fourteen years old." Jennifer was going to stay in Laughing Raven for two weeks because she knew the family was depressed, but Geraldine started criticizing and putting her down again, so I had to pick her up on the weekend.

I started working on juvenile spacing contracts, which were direct award contracts to Indian bands to get them to become contractors, thinning dense young stands of trees so trees left behind would have less competition for nutrients, water, and light and will grow better. Lyle Leo, a fellow I used to play soccer with many years earlier, was from one of the bands I was working with and was taking forestry at BCIT; so I asked him how the students treated him. He said, "They didn't know I was Indian, because I could pass for Spanish or Italian. Some of the students talked down on us as being too drunk to go there, but when they found out I was Indian, some of them apologized." Lyle's wife had been seeing the same therapist Jennifer and I were seeing, and he said, "When she didn't see him for a while, she would wake up in the middle of the night screaming."

Since I was an auxiliary employee, I had to work extra hard to make up for the time I took off for Amanda's funeral. I also tried to build up time so we could see Hubert, but every time we tried to get an appointment, something would go wrong. Hubert was at a weeklong meeting about the residential schools, and the next time, the staff were on holiday; so it seemed like nothing was going right for us. Jennifer's knees were still very weak and her left wrist still bothered her, so she was almost totally helpless. I didn't know if she was going to be like that for the rest of her life, but she finally made up her mind; she was now forced to work on her therapy.

It was quite a struggle to try and get our bills down, and after Amanda's funeral, it looked like we just didn't have enough money to pay our bills. Then just when I felt defeated, I got a check for travelling to Vancouver for my court case, which was more than I needed to cover my bills; not only that, Donovan had settled for an out-of-court settlement. Jennifer's depression would sometimes get extremely bad, and I would have to take her for a drive so she could cry and scream as loud as she wanted without anyone hearing her. Sometimes she would cry and scream for an hour, crying, "Mommy, help me!" Sadly, no help came. Fire season was coming, but I hoped I wouldn't have to go away for any fires because I didn't want to leave Jennifer in her condition even though we owed so much money. Stress was now getting so bad I developed severe acne on my cheeks for the first time in my life.

As I was looking over the forest-cover maps, I again noticed how small Indian reserves are. I don't know what it's like in other provinces, but most Indian reserves in British Columbia can be covered with a postage stamp on a 1:20,000 scale map. What little the Indians were cut off with, BC Hydro took part of it back by putting their lines through the Indian reserves. On the maps it appeared to me like BC Hydro made sure they went through the Indian reserves. The government says if Indians make any money on reserve land, they don't have to pay tax on it; but most Indian reserves are so small there's nothing there, so in most cases, the tax-free money isn't even worth the paper it's printed on. Canada is one of the largest countries in the world, and the Indians were cut off with next to nothing. The government makes it look like we have everything given to us on a silver platter, but it's more like we had everything taken away from us and were held back when we tried to do something for ourselves.

There was an employment-equity workshop that all the staff were required to attend. We couldn't all attend at once, so we attended in small groups; and the district manager, Paul Kuster, attended at the same time I attended. The lady giving the workshop said Indians often know what's going on but are slow to speak up; that was the second time I heard people say it. She also said it was in writing that Indians weren't allowed high positions anywhere except in the most-remote areas. Even though Paul Kuster had been with the Forest Service for twenty years, he looked like this was the first time he heard about it.

Then we were given a comment sheet with some people's opinions and were asked to write our own comments and opinions. On the sheet, it said that some people believe all Indians are too lazy to go to work. I wrote: "The unemployment rate on most Indian reserves is phenomenal, yet it wasn't in our culture to just sit around and do nothing because we were living off the land without a beast of burden. If we just sat around and did nothing, we would have starved to death long before the settlers came. Now, very few Indians even know how to speak their own language. People are told if we work on the Indian reserves, our money is tax free. What they're not told is how small Indian reserves are; what little the Indians were given; part of it was taken back with hydro lines, railroads, and highways; so the tax-free money earned on the Indian reserves usually isn't worth the paper it's printed on. A clear-cut example of how the Indians were held back from doing something for themselves can be found in the student newspaper in the fall of 1973 at Vancouver Community College, Langara campus."

We tried to make time to see Hubert, but things still seemed to be going wrong. Allan went up to visit us for a week, so Jennifer had to hold everything in; she couldn't cry and scream anymore because she didn't want Allan to see how she was really feeling. Then the day before we were to see Hubert, she decided to clean out the apartment. I told her we didn't have to do it that night and it could wait until after the weekend, but she wouldn't listen. To me it seemed like she was trying to avoid seeing him. I was rather happy to take Allan back even though I enjoyed looking after him, because Jennifer couldn't let out her feelings when he was there.

We saw Hubert then went back to Sto:lo Eagle on the weekend the canoe races were held. One of Henry's friends and his daughter, Shelley, stopped over after the races. Andrew took an interest in Shelley and they started going out together. Previously we had made several trips back to Chilliwack and Sto:lo Eagle after moving to Squamish, and Jennifer wasn't very happy here at first and wanted to move back, but I told her we're lucky that I was even able to find work. Then just before we left Sto:lo Eagle, Desiree asked if her daughters, Shannon and Sharon, could come and visit with us for a week. I enjoyed having them come, but I knew it would be hard on Jennifer because she would have to hold her feelings in again for another week. We took them out to Alice Lake for a picnic one night then went to Whistler for a drive to look at the houses, and I wondered what people who owned houses like that did for a living. After we brought Shannon and Sharon back to Sto:lo Eagle, we found out Andrew and Shelley were going to get married. It surprised most people, and many thought it probably wouldn't work out because they had only been going out together for a short time.

In June my work pants wore out and I needed a new pair of rubber caulk boots really bad. I was going to use my faded jeans, but Jennifer threw them out even though I told her I needed them for work and couldn't afford any new work pants; but at the end of June, I got my holiday pay and was able to buy what I needed. When my truck insurance became due, I could only afford six months insurance because the hard times we were going through just seemed to keep getting worse. Luckily, a permanent job opening came up with the Forest Service, so I applied for it. There were several positions available and I got one of them. I would have to stay in Squamish for two years, but I was happy about that because I knew I could stay in one place long enough for Jennifer to finish her therapy.

We were still struggling with our bills and I finally got the major repair bill on my truck paid off, but now we had to prepare for Andrew's wedding. Jennifer needed some new clothes. We shopped all over Vancouver for something for her to wear to the wedding, but surprisingly, we found something in Squamish. My truck had been acting up again, but I didn't think it was anything serious. I also wasn't worried because I had bought a five-year unlimited-mileage warranty that wouldn't expire until February 1992, five years after I bought the truck. On the wedding day, the weather was sunny and warm, a perfect day for an outdoor wedding. Just before the wedding, I was talking to the priest and told him, "It seems like whenever things get too unbearable for me, a change comes."

"You'll never be given a cross you can't carry," he replied.

After the wedding, there was a dinner and reception at the hall in Sto:lo Eagle, and I was surprised Shelley's father wasn't at the wedding. We had a good time at the reception then went back to Jennifer's parents' place. The next day, Jennifer, Henry Jr., and I went back to the hall and cleaned it up. It was a long weekend in August, so we spent the weekend in Sto:lo Eagle.

We went to therapy as often as we could, and my truck continued to act up, so I asked other people what could be wrong with it; but no one seemed to know. Finally, we took it to the service station in Agassiz where I had an account, and if it cost me too much, I could make payments on the bill. When I brought my truck to the service station, the mechanic put it up on the hoist and took the transmission case off; it did not look good because there were iron filings in the transmission oil, but I told them I bought an extended warranty and to charge it to them. It would take several days for my truck to be ready, and I had to go back to work, so we caught the bus back to Squamish. A few days later, I called the garage and they said the transmission was gone and my warranty had expired in May, so I wondered what they were talking about because the warranty was supposed to be for five years and I hadn't even owned the truck for five years. I told them to go ahead and fix it because I needed my truck, but I had to wait until the weekend to see what was going on with my warranty.

During the week, I asked John Harkema if he could give us a ride to Vancouver again. He said he could, but I was worried about Jennifer's knees because they were still very weak and she wouldn't be able to walk very far. When the weekend came, John was late getting out of the woods, so we just took the bus to Vancouver; it was better that way because the bus went straight to the bus depot and Jennifer didn't have to walk very far. We took the bus to Chilliwack and spent the night with Brenda and Alvin. Alvin gave us a ride to Rosedale the next day to pick up my truck, and I checked the warranty. Sure enough, the warranty had expired. They started the warranty before I even bought my truck. I didn't know what it was going to cost for repairs, but I knew it would be expensive.

After I got back to work, I asked people in the office if they ever bought an extended warranty on their vehicles; and of all the people I asked, only one person was happy with buying an extended warranty. When I got my bill, it cost me $1,200; so I decided the next time I buy a vehicle, I won't buy an extended warranty. The only way I would buy one is if the dealer lowered the price of the vehicle by the price of the warranty and I would reimburse them up to the maximum cost of the warranty for repairs; that way, if it's nothing but a scam, it's the dealer's loss, not mine.

Jennifer's depression continued to be bad and her knees just wouldn't heal. She had to prepare to confront her father again, and I wondered if I would have to go through the same preparation as the last time. Then she finally admitted she internalized the pain from the sexual abuse so much that it came out on her body; that's why her body wouldn't heal no matter what the doctors and physiotherapists did for her. She was scared because she was also going to have to confront her mother as well and thought she was going to hurt them by confronting them and talked about moving back to Sto:lo Eagle for a little while after the confrontation. When I went home for lunch one day, Jennifer said the pain felt so bad it was like her father killed her four times over; it felt like he drowned her, knifed her, axed her, then shot her.

I had to keep going out to the field to check my contracts and to build up enough hours to take her to see Hubert and often worked all day without taking any lunch or coffee breaks, so I could get my work done without leaving her alone for very long. The stress on me was so incredible I developed severe acne on my face and it just wouldn't go away. On our way to see Hubert one day, we picked up a hitchhiker who was a French Canadian from Quebec. He said he grew up with the Indians back east and knew most of those who participated in the Oka crisis even though they were wearing a mask. He said the French people in Quebec were oppressed but most people didn't hear about it, so I told him all we hear about are the good things the government does for the East and it's the same with us Indians. We were oppressed, and the government made it look like we have everything given to us on a silver platter. When I first went to college, the first thing Indian Affairs did was try to make us give up; and when I went to BCIT, the students wouldn't associate with us, which surprised him.

Jennifer and I went to West Vancouver one night to do some shopping and I decided to call Susie to see how she was doing while Jennifer was looking around in the stores. She said, "I'm doing all right. I'm healing more and more and don't feel the same need to lash out and hit Angela. I'm also starting to attract healthier men than before. I used to always attract dysfunctional men."

I felt like I had helped accomplish something again. Susie was healthier now and had gotten over much of what was plaguing her from the past. It was well worth the effort I went through to help her and thought, *Maybe if she goes back to school, she'll be able to concentrate more on her studies.*

After talking to her, I went back to see Jennifer because I knew I couldn't stay away from her for very long. She asked me what I did and I said, "I called Auntie Pat." Then I said, "No. I called Susie to see how she was doing." Jennifer got really mad and went storming out to the truck because she didn't want me to call her right now and started crying and screaming again, so I drove off to an isolated street so she could scream without anyone hearing her. She cried and screamed for over an hour, and I didn't know what to do except stay beside her until it passed.

Jennifer often cried "*Mommy! Mommy!* Help me! Help me!" Then she would cry, "*Why! Why! Why* are you doing this to me!" After she came out of it, she said, "I tried to make enough noise to wake Mom up when Daddy came to get me. She wouldn't wake up!"

When I took Jennifer to her next appointment with Hubert, I told him what happened, so he gave us his home phone number and told us to call him at home if things got really bad. Things were getting hard on me, but I knew I couldn't give up. I had to carry Jennifer through what she was going through. We continued writing and preparing for when she was going to confront her father again. The stress on Jennifer was incredible, but it was also hard on me. As she told me what she went through as a child, I had to write everything down; then we put it in the order she was going to tell him, and we were up until all hours of the night getting ready. The day she was to confront him was September 13, surprisingly, Friday the thirteenth, considered an unlucky day to some.

The day before Jennifer was to confront him, we were up all night getting things ready; after we got it all ready, I had to rewrite it clearly and double-spaced so she could tell him everything she wanted to say. I told Jennifer to try and sleep for a couple of hours while I rewrote it. I was getting tired from all the late nights and knew I wasn't going to get any sleep that night. When it was time to go, I was extremely tired and had to keep drinking coffee to keep myself going. I knew it was going to be a long day and I could end up so tired I couldn't sleep that night, so I bought some beer.

After we left, Jennifer started looking over the notes I had written. I was so tired I left some information out and had to stop so she could prepare the notes and fill in what I left out. She wanted to stop and see Hubert about her notes before picking her parents up, but I told her that would have take too long and Hubert may have been too busy to see her. As we were driving toward Sto:lo Eagle, I knew we wouldn't get to our appointment on time; so we stopped to call Hubert to tell him we would be late, and he said it was all right, so we kept on driving. When we got to Sto:lo Eagle, we talked to her parents for a few minutes then asked them to go to Surrey with us; and Jennifer told Henry, "Make sure you bring money for your supper."

I laid a plastic tarp and some blankets in the back of the truck so they could go. Jennifer and her mother rode in the back again, and Henry rode in the front. When we got to Surrey, I helped Jennifer and her parents get out of the truck and wait by the elevator, rushed upstairs, and took the elevator down to pick them up because Jennifer's knees were still very weak. After Jennifer and her parents were in Hubert's office, I went back to the truck to go to sleep and time just flew by; before I knew it, Jennifer was standing by the truck, waiting for me. She was mad at me for not going to get her, but I needed some rest. After that, we went for supper. Emily wanted to go to Church's Chicken again, so that's where we went. When we got there, I got up and placed the order and as we were eating Henry said, "I want a corn on the cob."

Jennifer said to me, "Why don't you get it? It only costs $1."

I said, "That dollar is more than he's ever spent on us!" but paid for it anyway. That didn't make Henry feel very good, but it was the truth. After supper, we did a little bit of shopping then went back to Sto:lo Eagle, spent the weekend there, then came back to Squamish. Jennifer now had to prepare to confront her mother.

We had to live on a fixed budget every week so we could keep payments on our bills, but I also needed a new winter coat now. Not only that, I had to start saving for Christmas because my truck insurance would be due right after Christmas. I continued to drink whenever the stress got too unbearable and continued to do my own writing whenever I found the time. It was getting hard for me to write my memoirs and relive what I went through but thought it must be even harder for Jennifer.

My job kept me busy working with Indian bands, and I became friends with some of them because we could relate to what we've been through. I didn't know that at one time, Indians needed a pass to leave the reserve, until I read about it in the book *The Dispossessed* by Jeffrey York. Lawrence, the foreman for the Mount Currie Indian Band, said, "In my day, the Indians still needed a pass to leave the reserves. The schools we went to were just like a concentration camp! All we had to do to get beaten was speak our own language!" Eventually I found out Lawrence was only ten years older than I.

Ludmilla Kelderman won the bid to administer some of the contracts I was working on, and when we did the contract viewing, she thought I had a preference for Indian girls. I didn't think so, but I guess it looked that way; so I asked her, "Do you remember students laughing and yelling out, 'Up in Lower Post, they put up eight-foot fences to keep the Indians out!'"

"Yes, I do."

I just thought if it appears that way, I was forced into it; she only saw part of what I went through.

The Mount Currie Band got going on their second contract and Jennifer continued to prepare to confront her mother. She said, "It's almost as hard as preparing to confront my father! Why didn't she protect us?" I continued to help Jennifer with her therapy. Luckily, I have a low tolerance of alcohol and usually only drank twelve bottles of beer a week to keep my stress level down. I also had to work long hours so I could get time off to take her mother to Surrey.

At last the big day was approaching. It was one month to the day after she confronted her father, and Stephen DeMelt asked me to work Friday, but I had to take time off for what was coming. Jennifer sometimes seemed slow to get ready for things like this because it must have been incredibly hard for her. I was often tired and sometimes forgot things, but finally we were all ready and started rushing toward Sto:lo Eagle. It was Thanksgiving weekend and traffic was heavy. I tried to rush, but we just couldn't seem to get going. If that wasn't bad enough, the Service Engine Soon light on the dashboard went on; everything seemed to be going wrong! When we got to Mission, we phoned Hubert and told him we were going to be late; but he said, "That's all right. You can bring her in on Monday at two o'clock."

That was a big relief to us, so I thought Jennifer must be one of the worst patients he's ever had! He gave us his home phone number in case things really got bad for her; now he's opening his office for her on Thanksgiving Day! His office is in Surrey and he lives in Richmond, a forty-five-minute drive on a normal workday.

Brenda and Alvin were also in Sto:lo Eagle that weekend. They had moved to Gibsons in September so Alvin could take a course in salmon enhancement. They wanted to have Thanksgiving dinner on Sunday so they could miss the rush at the ferry; so when they went in, I asked Henry, "Are you going to tell Alvin to save the cranberries for you?"

Henry got mad and thought, *He's always ruining visits with my family!*

Henry was always making life miserable for me, so whenever I had the chance to do it back to him, I did it! When we were eating, Alvin didn't sit near Henry, but he knew I would be watching to see if he was going to treat Alvin the way he treated me. Brenda and Alvin left that night, and the next day, we brought Henry and Emily to Surrey. I knew I would have to drive them back to Sto:lo Eagle then drive back to Squamish that day, but at least I wasn't too tired. I sat in another room while Jennifer confronted her mother. I heard Emily crying for a little while, so I was glad Hubert was there to calm things down.

After it was over, Jennifer said, "Mommy cried and I had to stop for a while. She said she didn't know Dad was molesting the girls."

I wondered, "How could she not know? Wasn't that why she sent Geraldine to live with her aunt and uncle?"

"I think she's in denial."

It's hard to believe people can deny something that much, but it's true; people can deny things to the point where they don't know or believe anything happened. After we left the office, we went to the White Spot for lunch. I didn't eat very much because we were expected at my parents' place for another turkey dinner. We paid for the meal at White Spot, but when we got back to Sto:lo Eagle, Henry insisted on paying us back; that was the first time he had ever done that since Jennifer and I met. We left Sto:lo Eagle and went to Rosedale but didn't stay long because it was getting late.

I continued working on Native initiative contracts and toldLawrence, "When I was at BCIT, the students wouldn't associate with us."

"None of them got the lucky breaks you got though."

I thought, *He's right. Many students would probably just love to be closed off and get the lucky breaks that I got.*

Lawrence had some old-time loggers on his crew and said, "The logging companies wouldn't break us in to run machinery. White people who weren't there as long as us were broken in, but they wouldn't train the Indians to run machinery," and all the ex-loggers agreed. I had heard rumors of that many years earlier from one of my cousins, Sidney Douglas. Sidney said white people in Pemberton didn't like to see Indians get ahead of them. One fellow worked behind a Cat for fifteen years because the company just wouldn't break him in to operate it. I couldn't believe Sidney was saying that because he was always so open-minded, and thought, *I guess there must have been more reasons for the Mount Currie roadblock than most people realize.* When I mentioned the fellow who worked behind the Cat for fifteen years to Lawrence he said it was his brother-in-law.

Jennifer and I went back to Sto:lo Eagle just before I started the fertilization contract. I was to be out in a logging camp for a week, so we brought Henry and Emily back to Squamish with us. I didn't want to take them with us because I knew we would have to babysit Henry; even if I didn't have to, I preferred not to be around him. They stayed in Squamish for two days; then Jennifer wanted to take them to Gibsons to visit Brenda and Alvin, so I told Jennifer Henry would have to give her $20 for the ferry crossing. I didn't want him to visit his kids at our expense, even though I was happy to get rid of him. They went back on Friday so they could pick me up when I got out of camp. Jennifer still felt responsible for entertaining them, so we stopped for coffee on our way back. I didn't want to, but I went along with it anyway. After taking them to Sto:lo Eagle, we stayed one night then went to Rosedale. And when we got to Rosedale, I noticed my mother's car was gone, so I thought she went somewhere; but she was home. I walked in and said, "I thought you were gone because your car's gone."

"Tony used it to take his AA friends back to Vancouver." When she said that, she realized she would let Tony use her car to take his AA friends to Vancouver but she wouldn't trade vehicles with me to take Jennifer's parents to Surrey for her therapy. AA is Alcoholics Anonymous, a group that helps people stop drinking. That was nothing unusual though; my parents do things for my brothers but don't do things for me. I decided once Jennifer finishes her therapy and gets a career of her own, I would try and move to Vancouver Island to stay away from my family!

Jennifer often watched TV talk shows during the day, and as she was watching TV one afternoon, Phil Donahue talked about "the fantasy bond." When children are badly abused by their parents, they tend to fantasize them as ideal parents because it's a way of coping with what they're living through. I thought, *It must be an incredibly strong bond. After what Henry put his kids through, they still do everything for him. It doesn't happen that way in every case though because very few things ever work out exactly the same in situations dealing with the human mind and body. Some kids are driven to the point where they kill their parents because they have no choice then automatically get blamed for what happened. Perhaps that's why Bruce said they weren't beaten as children.*

We went to therapy as often as we could, and I tried to get our bills down; but when our bills finally started going down, Christmas was coming. I had set money aside for Christmas, but our truck insurance was due at the same time. I was only going to pay for six months' coverage again, but the rates were going to go up 19 percent in February, so I decided to buy insurance for a full year. Then on the first weekend in November, there was a fire on a Friday afternoon, which surprised everyone. Someone was burning a slash pile in a landing and the fire got away; we had to work the weekend, but everyone was happy because we were getting some overtime just before Christmas. I wasn't allowed to take holidays and had to take holiday pay instead, but I got my holiday pay just after Christmas, in time to pay my insurance; so I guess I was lucky I could only afford six months' insurance and could avoid the 19 percent increase for a year.

Before Christmas I was invited to a party for the silviculture staff. I wanted to go but knew Jennifer wouldn't want to go, so I didn't say anything. There was a staff party a week later and I bought two tickets, but Jennifer got depressed again, so we didn't go. It was annoying, but I was used to not being able to do anything for my own interests. We usually spent Christmas in Sto:lo Eagle, but after we did our Christmas shopping, Jennifer decided not to go there this year; and when we got to the turnoff to Sto:lo Eagle, we stopped and let them know we weren't going until after Christmas. I was really happy about that because she was finally breaking away from her father's control; she was breaking the fantasy bond and starting to see reality. When we got to Rosedale, everyone could see I still had severe acne; and Dad said, "It's just nerves! You should just try and relax more."

I didn't say anything but was very annoyed and thought to myself, *When I was younger and optimistic about hard times, you said I was being religious! Now that stress is so bad it's affecting my complexion, you're telling me to relax!*

After Christmas, we went to Sto:lo Eagle; and when we got there, one of Jennifer's cousins was visiting Ryan and Desiree. Jennifer said she never saw her before in her life; and when her cousin and I started talking, she said, "Not many people are going to be sorry when Henry's time comes! My mother made us stay there for two weeks when we were children and we're still mad at her for doing it! At mealtime, all we would get was a small, little serving!"

"And he made sure he got as much as he wanted!" I said.

"Yes! Emily would sneak us a jam sandwich when we were in bed and said, 'Don't tell Father, or he'll get mad.' Henry also used to go hunting with my relatives from the interior, and they would get a moose every year." The interior is the Interior Plateau of British Columbia. I didn't believe her because he only got something once in all the years Jennifer and I were together, but she insisted, "They got a moose every year! Henry wouldn't share with the other hunters, so eventually, no one would go with him."

"Where did you go to school at?"

"I went to the residential school in Kamloops."

"Then you probably know some of the Indians I went to school with in Merritt."

She named some people I knew then said, "There was a fellow named John. He was so friendly. He had kind of a round face. Where is he now?"

"He committed suicide many years ago. Some of the other Indians turned into drunks and alcoholics. Of all the Indians I spoke to who went to the residential schools, only two of them said life in school was better than life at home because their parents drank too much." I only had five days off, so we had to go back to Squamish. Normally, the field season would have been over, but my contracts extended into the winter. I was happy about that though because I could still get time off to take Jennifer to therapy.

Chapter 14

1992

It was a mild winter that year, and the crew on my contracts was able to keep working but sometimes got snowed out. Jennifer continued to work on her therapy and was slowly getting stronger, but I still had to take her out for a drive so she could scream and let out her pain. Sometimes when she would scream, she would say, "*Why! Why!* Why are you doing this to me!" Then she would say, "I hate you!" I also continued to do my own writing, and it was getting harder. I didn't like reliving what I had gone through but felt better after writing it down. Now I could understand what she was going through; it must have been harder on her because what she went through was far worse than what I went through. At least my parents encouraged me to get a career and didn't beat me for making a mistake. One night, I was sick, on medication, and had to be up at six o'clock in the morning to do my fieldwork. I was writing what I went through in 1987 and the stress of reliving when my parents pushed me right to my breaking point and would have beaten my mother to a pulp right in front of my dad if she had said one wrong word was incredible. I got so mad I wanted to destroy all my writings but knew that would only make things worse, so I decided to have a few beers instead. I thought I only drank four bottles of beer, but when I looked in the fridge the next morning, I had drank six. The stress was worse than I thought it was.

When I took Jennifer out for a drive so she could scream and let out the pain of the abuse, she said, "The abuse comes out when it wants to come out. I have no control over it." I finally realized that's why she would often get cranky for no apparent reason over the years. I was glad she was getting better because at least when the abuse came out, her fits of depression didn't last as long as they used to. I continued writing, but sometimes it was hard to look after her at the same time, so I enjoyed spending the night in Pemberton for work now because I could write without any interruptions.

Henry Jr. went back to college again to get more math and science courses and was happy he took some time off because now he was more mature and determined to get a career and knew he wanted to get into salmon enhancement. There was a staff curling bonspiel one weekend and I signed up to participate. I was excited about it because I had never tried it before and beginners were encouraged to participate, but just before the bonspiel, Henry Jr. asked us to go to Chilliwack to help him with his math. I thought, *He never had a chance in life and won't unless I help him. \once he gets a career of his own, he's set for life. Missing a bonspiel is a small price to help him get a career*. So I said, "We'll be there Friday."

Jennifer and Henry Jr. got along well, so I was happy to visit and help him with his math. At first we missed living in Chilliwack, but now we were breaking away from our families and living our own lives. While I was helping Henry Jr. with his math, I started looking through a continuing-education booklet from the college in Nanaimo. There was a weekend course for people who wanted to publish their book in Canada, so I thought, *Perhaps there's a similar course in Chilliwack or Abbotsford.* I picked up a course calendar from the college, and sure enough, there was a course offered in Abbotsford; so I rushed to apply so I could register before the course filled up.

On the day of the course, there were a number of people there and the instructor was an author and he asked everyone to introduce themselves and say what kind of book they were writing. Some people were writing their life story, cookbooks, children's books, etc. One fellow, Reverend Brown, was writing books on theology; and I wondered if he had a son named David Brown, a fellow I went to elementary school with. The last person to enter the room was Debra Cressy, a lady I went to school with in Merritt from grades 8 to 12. I was just as surprised to see her as she was to see me. This was the second time I saw her since we finished high school, and during our breaks, we managed to talk a little bit about what we've done since high school. She said she wanted to write children's books, and I told her part of what I went through, and she said she would like to read my book. I asked her if she went to our tenth-year high school reunion and if she went back to Merritt very often. She said, "I didn't go to the tenth-year reunion. Going back to Merritt just brought back bad memories. My father was an alcoholic and died when he was thirty-seven."

"I grew up in the middle of town, so I never felt different until I got older. After everything I went through to get a career, there were some years I couldn't even get a job washing dishes, yet some people looked down on me like I was too lazy to go to work. Many Indians are on welfare, but it's because of the way we were treated."

"My father was raised by the Indians in Douglas Lake. He taught us you can't blame them for being alcoholics. I would like to read your book when it comes out."

I didn't have very much time to talk to her because she was in a hurry to go and I couldn't leave Jennifer for very long because of her knees; if she wanted to go anywhere, I had to be there in case her knees gave out on her. My stress level continued to be high and still drank more than I usually do, yet my acne stayed on my face. I began to realize Jennifer and Henry Jr. both may have been born losers if it weren't for me. I had tried to tell Andrew to go back to school, but he was indecisive about it. Their father was a very mixed-up man and acted like he didn't want his kids to succeed in life, yet when they worked, he expected them to spend their money on him. Sometimes I thought he acted like he couldn't do enough damage to his kids.

Jennifer was getting better and told me I didn't have to go to his funeral if I didn't want to, and I thought, *She's finally breaking the fantasy bond! She has a right to be that angry at her father!* Jennifer decided she wanted to go home and visit her mother, so I told her she could take the truck and pick me up at the bus depot in Chilliwack on Friday. When she picked me up, I bought some Chicken McNuggets at McDonald's, and we went back to Sto:lo Eagle and ate them. As we were eating, Emily wanted to give Henry some of them, but I wouldn't let her. I didn't say anything but thought, *He can go without! He usually gets everything and everyone else gets little or nothing!* So we ate them all without giving him anything.

The next day, Jennifer said, "Daddy fell and hurt his leg. I took him to the emergency ward in Chilliwack. They let him go and said he was all right. I think we should bring him back."

I didn't answer, but I didn't want to take him there because I wanted to give him as much as he's ever given us! Not only that, I was still mad at him for not putting anything down for his daughter's funeral after the way he treated her. We didn't do anything for him on Saturday, and the next day we decided we better take him to the hospital, but I still wouldn't take him. Jennifer said we should take him to the hospital, but I just said, "Maybe he should go in Ryan's car."

When Ryan finally got home, we told him he should take his father to the hospital because his leg didn't look very good. Ryan said, "You can take him there in my car. You'll have to put some gas in though because I don't have enough gas to go over there."

"Hold on," I said. "I'll get some money." And went back in the house. Emily gave me some money for gas, so I made Henry pay for the gas to get to the hospital.

As Henry was getting into the car, he said, "It hurts so damned much!" Ryan and Desiree were both tired, but they drove Henry to the hospital anyway. Emily went with us, and we followed them. After they dropped Henry off, they left right away and didn't stay around to take Emily home.

Jennifer got mad at me and said, "You should have listened to me when I said to take him to the hospital! After we dropped him off, we could have drove back to Squamish!"

"Yeah, you're right!" I just didn't want to do anything for him. Jennifer settled down right away though and wasn't even mad at me for doing that. Then we drove Emily home and drove to Vancouver. Hubert had moved his office to Richmond and we didn't know the area very well, so we practiced driving over there from North Vancouver. Jennifer practiced the drive several times so she could get there by herself if I was working. It was late by the time we got back to Squamish, and I was tired. Jennifer knew her father may not last much longer and talked about pulling the same stunt he pulled at Liz's funeral. We were only going to buy flowers and not make any donations and threw out everything he gave us or reminded her of him. She even threw out the cup that read "I Luv My Dad" because it reminded her of him.

I continued working and taking time off to take her to Richmond. Usually after therapy, we would do a little shopping or driving around before coming back to Squamish. I asked Hubert if Jennifer was his worst patient so far, but he didn't answer. Two weeks later, he said Jennifer wasn't his worst patient so far and my file wasn't the thickest; then he showed me a thicker file. We stayed in Richmond until after dark one night, and on our way home, Jennifer's depression started going out again. We had just gone off Granville Street Bridge on a one-way street and she started screaming, "*Help me! Help me!* Help me! Why! Why! Why are you doing this to me!" so I turned the radio on loud so no one could hear her because I thought people would get scared for her and call the police.

It was Friday night and the streets were busy, traffic was heavy, and there were many people walking around; so I hoped I could get on a deserted street or to Stanley Park as soon as possible, but couldn't. We kept hitting red lights and had to wait, people were in their cars beside us and walking across the streets, and I didn't know if they could hear her or not. When we got near the turnoff to Stanley Park, there was a car blocking the road, trying to get into the other lane; but traffic just wasn't letting him in. When he finally got into the other lane, I drove to the parking lot and tried to park as far away from other people as I could so no one would hear her scream. I wondered if I would hear police sirens at any minute or not as she continued to scream, "*Help me! Help me!* Help me! Help me! Why! Why! Why are you doing this to me!" There were other people parked there even though it was dark, and I kept hoping no one would hear her. She cried and screamed for an hour and toward the end she cried a little quieter, "I hate you!"

Jennifer was breaking the fantasy bond with her parents and was beginning to see them as they really are. A few days after Henry was taken to the hospital, he had to get part of his foot amputated; his foot still wouldn't heal, so he had to get more of it amputated. When I told Hubert what I did, the therapist in training with him felt bad that I hated him that much. Henry was in the hospital, so we went to visit him because Jennifer thought he may not live much longer; but apparently, he appeared to be doing quite well. Then I told him I wouldn't drive him to the hospital and even made him pay for the gas, and he knew it was justified. There was an ad in the paper in Squamish for a woman's support group for victims of sexual abuse, so Jennifer started attending those meetings. I was glad she did because it gave me some free time to do some writing.

Spring was coming, and we were preparing our contracts for the year. I still had two contracts from the year before still ongoing and it was interfering with this year's work, and I got sent to Victoria for three days for a writing course. I realized I was writing my reports without giving much thought to properly communicating what I was writing. It was an interesting course though and I got much out of it. The following week, I went out the field for three days because my two contracts were completed and I had to check the access to my new contracts. I didn't get as much work done as I had planned and felt extremely frustrated. When I got back, I realized the mistake I made and how it could have been avoided. Steve was under much stress and started going down on me. Then suddenly, one morning, my back started hurting. It was so sore I could barely bend over to shave. I thought it was just a cold in the back, so I took some Tylenol for the pain and rubbed my back with Vicks VapoRub. It didn't seem to do any good, but I continued working anyway.

A lady in the office, Carolyn Wold, suggested I see a chiropractor; so I agreed and made an appointment in the afternoon. I called Jennifer and told her what I did, and she really blew up at me and said, "No, you're not going to see a chiropractor! You're going to see a doctor first! I'll call and make an appointment for you!" She drove me to the doctor at lunchtime; and he told me I had muscle spasms in my back, wrote a prescription for some pills, and made an appointment for me to go for physiotherapy. Jennifer then drove me to the drugstore for my prescription and back to the office. I had some work that had to be done right away because it was near the end of the fiscal year, told Steve the doctor told me I may have to take two weeks off work. I took two pills the first day for pain then went home. Later in the afternoon, I went to physiotherapy; and the physiotherapist said, "You can see the spasm all up your back" and almost said, "I haven't seen one that bad before!"

I thought this could be because of all those years of being under incredible stress from looking after Jennifer, and it was almost over and may need time to adjust to not being continually stressed out. For the first four days, all I did was sleep. The time off was good for the first week, then I wanted to go back to work. My back gradually healed and I ended up missing twelve days of work, so someone else had to do my contract viewings for me. The contracts seemed to start off okay and Jennifer wasn't shopping as much to try and pick herself up. I continued to take her to therapy and didn't have to take her for a drive as often; once or twice when I took her for a drive, she didn't really cry at all.

When we went to Chilliwack, one weekend on the front page of a weekly newspaper, a Merritt man was charged with sexual assault.

I knew this fellow was David's age, and he had an older brother who was my age. When I was twelve or thirteen, it was rumoured that the older brother and a friend of his had molested his sister. My friends and I wondered how he could do that to his own sister. Normally they can't stand each other, but we were too young to realize the seriousness of the situation. I never thought about it until now and started wondering, "Maybe the children thought, 'Daddy does it, so it's all right.'"

When I told Hubert, he said, "It didn't have to be Daddy. It could have been an uncle or relative."

Sometimes when I would open a cupboard, an insect would go running off at an incredible speed, and didn't really think very much of it; so I never said anything to Jennifer. Finally, one night we went home and saw an insect and sprayed it with Raid. It still ran behind the fridge, so we sprayed around the fridge then moved the fridge to find the insect. We kept spraying it with Raid until we were finally able to catch it then put it in a plastic bag. It was a cockroach. We told the manager, and he said he would have the apartment fumigated; the fumes would be strong, so we would have to stay away for six to eight hours.

We went to Richmond that day to see Hubert and stayed away until midnight, and the fumes were still strong, so we slept in the back of the truck. I had to be up early the next day because I volunteered to help with National Forest Week in Whistler, and Jennifer was allowed to go with me. It was raining and blowing that day, yet many people turned up. That night when we got home, Jennifer said the fumes were still too strong for her, so we called a number of people who said we could stay at their place if the fumes were too strong; but no one was home, so we slept in the truck again.

We opened the windows to let the fumes out, but fumigating didn't kill all the cockroaches because they're incredibly hard insects to kill. Scientists believe that even in the event of a nuclear war, cockroaches will still survive, so we asked the manager to fumigate the apartment again. While the apartment was fumigated, some people asked us to stay at their house while they were away on holiday so they wouldn't have to worry about burglars, so we stayed there until they got back then went back to our own apartment. Jennifer was still scared to go back, so she took my truck and drove around while I was at work. She was just about losing her mind, and I thought she better go see

Hubert. I was glad the time was coming for us to see him again, but whenever I tried to phone for an appointment, the phone number was no longer in service. I got scared and thought, *Maybe his business went bankrupt! Now I'm really going to be in trouble unless he moves back to Surrey!*

I called his home phone number to see what happened, but there was usually no answer; finally, I called in the evening and his son answered, "The building the office was in burnt down, and everything was destroyed."

Oh no! I thought. *It seems like something is always holding Jennifer back from her therapy and seems like it's going to go on forever! But that's also how it felt when I was getting my career. In the end, it was better that it all happened that way.* I eventually talked to Hubert, and he told me the police wouldn't let anyone in the building, so he didn't know how many files were destroyed. By Friday I had the day off and Jennifer's nerves were getting bad again; she got really cranky and we got in the truck and she just kept on driving. She wouldn't answer when I asked her where we were going, but we finally ended up in Richmond and had a look at the building. I didn't think anything could survive a fire like that, so we drove around Richmond for a little while then back to Squamish.

Jennifer didn't want to go back to the apartment and wanted to go back to Vancouver and said, "We could sleep in the truck again. We did it before."

I didn't want to live in the truck anymore because I had enough of that, so I said, "Why don't we just go to Laughing Raven for the weekend? The kids would probably be happy to see us."

She was undecided but finally agreed. The kids and everyone else were happy to see us. I thought it was better than living in the truck even though it may have cost less for gas and meals if we went to Vancouver.

When we got back from Laughing Raven, we decided to get a new place to stay. I didn't want to but thought I better do it for Jennifer's sake. We went out and found a place right away, but we couldn't move in until the end of the month. I went to work the next day and Jennifer picked me up at lunchtime. She was almost losing her mind, and I didn't know what to do! I missed lunch that day, and at the end of the day, we picked up some boxes for moving. The next day, she asked me to stay home after lunch, but I didn't think I could take time off even though I was very concerned about her. I was drinking cup after cup of coffee to cope with the stress, and finally, Carolyn Wold told me I could ask for special leave. Steve said I could take some time off, and when I got home, she was almost losing her mind. She got rid of most of her clothes and our groceries, even our canned food and food in the freezer. Then I got so mad I phoned home, and Dad answered; so I yelled, "Tell Mother if she ever tells me what to do again, I'm going to break a bottle over her head!" then slammed the phone down.

Jennifer was almost losing her mind in that apartment, and we couldn't move until the end of the month, so she decided to go to Gibsons for a week to visit Brenda. She almost didn't go because of me, but I thought she better go rather than lose her mind because it would have been too hard on me to go to work and try and look after her at the same time. I sent Jennifer across on the ferry that night and went back home. I lived on sandwiches for the week because she had thrown out most of our groceries and our pots, pans, and dishes were all packed up; but it was a welcome break from what I was going through. At the end of the week, we were allowed to move into our new place, so I went to Gibsons on Saturday to get her. I picked Jennifer up, visited with Brenda and Alvin for a few hours, then we came back to Squamish. We moved the rest of our belongings that night and cleaned up the apartment the next day. We moved into a basement suite, and Jennifer was happier. I didn't mind living there even though it was rather small because at least she wasn't losing her mind, and the first thing we did was cover all the holes; so hopefully, cockroaches wouldn't get into the cupboards.

People in that part of town didn't like other people renting out part of their house; the way this family was doing, I didn't mind living there because it was a little cheaper than the other apartment, so I paid more on our truck-repair bill. Jennifer got worried her father may not live much longer, so she took the truck to Sto:lo Eagle to visit her family. I enjoyed it when she went to visit them because it gave me a break from looking after her and a chance to do some writing. I finished writing the rough draft as far as I could go, so I started to rewrite, put the story, and put it in the order that it happened. We continued to struggle with our bills and things continued to go bad for us; we still couldn't afford another couch and Jennifer had sold our bed to Henry Jr. We were going to buy a bed from Sears, but she changed her mind and decided to buy a bed from the Brick, a major chain furniture store in British Columbia. We chose a bed but only used it for a few days. Then it sagged to one side, so we returned it, but we still had a foam mattress I bought from Sears and that's what we slept on.

Jennifer was getting better now, and I didn't have to drive her off very often to scream her anger out. Sometimes when I drove her off, I had to ask her to hold it in until we got out where no one could hear her and think she was in danger. I usually drove toward Whistler, but now I sometimes drove toward Vancouver because I didn't want to go through any stop lights with her screaming because people may call the police thinking she was being kidnapped. Jennifer decided to go to Gibsons again to visit Brenda, so I drove her to the ferry terminal at Horseshoe Bay. She stayed there for a few days then asked me to go over and get her. She had bought a foam mattress for us to sleep on and wanted me to go over and pick it up. I went over for the weekend again and realized the mattress would have been far too heavy for her to pack by herself. While visiting, Alvin started telling me how much Henry had spent on him over the years; and on his hunting trip, I was surprised because after all the things I did for him, he wouldn't even buy me a cup of coffee, never mind the fact that he knew I literally went through hell to save his daughter from suicide! Then he said he did everything for us and we were obligated to him!

Henry was in the hospital for a couple of months, then one of his brothers took him back to Sto:lo Eagle, but I thought Henry should have been left in the hospital because no one was around to look after him. Ryan and Andrew had their own family to look after. Emily was too old and not healthy enough. Henry Jr. couldn't be around all the time and Jennifer and I lived in Squamish.

We continued struggling with our bills and trying to get them down, but very little seemed to be working out. It was a wet summer again, and I wasn't getting any overtime from fires. I continued working and taking Jennifer to therapy whenever we could. I enjoyed working, but I was still drinking a case of beer a week and still had severe acne. My acne got so bad that for a week, I went to work with a trickle of blood running down my chin because I would cut myself shaving. Jennifer finally got tired of my acne and made me buy a bar of special soap for acne from the drugstore. The soap cost $15 a bar, but I knew I had to do something about my acne. My acne started going away, then I developed a very large pimple on my right cheekbone. It was so large I couldn't lie on the right side of my face because it would hurt, and it took a long time for that one pimple to open up and drain, but my acne finally went away. After two and a half months of sleeping on a foam mattress on the floor, Jennifer decided we should buy a bed. After seeing Hubert, we searched around Richmond then decided to buy a bed at the Brick so we wouldn't have to pay for it until next year. The bed couldn't be delivered to the store right away, so we had to wait a week to ten days.

A Japanese student from UBC was working with us for the summer and administering a juvenile-spacing contract in my work zone near D'Arcy. I told him the government did things to keep the Indians from doing anything for themselves and made it look like we have everything given to us on a silver platter then showed him some of the houses on the Indian reserve compared to houses off the reserve. The difference between the houses on reserve to those off the reserve was like night and day, like there's an invisible wall at the edge of the reserve and people often stereotyped us as being too lazy to go to work. Then I showed him some houses on the Mount Currie Indian reserve and told him that's what most reserves looked like in the 1960s and '70s.

On one visit to Sto:lo Eagle, I told Henry, "After all the things we did for you, you got mad at me for borrowing your lawn chairs! If it was Alvin, you would have helped him carry them out!"

"I couldn't walk then!"

"You would have helped him anyway!" Then he realized that was how he treated his kids and that was how I was treating him.

We went to Laughing Raven one weekend, and Geraldine suggested her kids go visit with us for a week. Isabella didn't want to go, but Layla and Little Ben went, I enjoyed having them with us because I like kids; and when people in Squamish saw me with them, they wondered if they were my kids. The summer was almost over, and the summer students who were rooming together invited everyone over to their place for a barbecue, so I offered to bring a salmon. I told Jennifer I wanted to go, and she agreed at first; but when the time came, she raised hell about it, so I decided not to go. She kept saying "Go!" then "Don't go!" and got me so uptight I just didn't want to go; then she got worried about Layla and Little Ben getting bored at a party of grown-ups. Then finally she decided just to drop me off and take the kids swimming. I wasn't going to drink at the party, but

Jennifer got me so uptight that when I got there, all I wanted to do was drink even though I was used to not being able to do anything for my own interests. Jennifer sent Layla in to get me around nine o'clock; and when I got out, Jennifer said she left the side window open and someone stole her cut-offs, which cost us $50, and broke the latch in the process.

There was a heavy lightning storm the next day and it was the end of the week, so we decided to bring the kids back that night; the lightning was so close and loud it was scaring us. When dropped the kids off then came back to Squamish. Our bed was ready to be picked up in Richmond the next day, so we waited until noon for fire calls then left. I didn't want to go because there was still a chance of a fire call, but Jennifer insisted we go. She had insisted on buying a queen-size bed, and it sure felt good to sleep on a bed that size after sleeping together on a twin bed for many years then on a foam mattress on the floor. When I got to work on Monday, other staff asked where I was because there was a fire on the weekend; everyone got called out and made good money in overtime. I was disappointed about missing it because I could have paid off my truck-repair bill sooner. The summer was almost over now and I knew there wasn't much chance of having any more fires. Since I didn't have much training in firefighting and the weather wasn't very bad, I only got one weekend of standby.

Near the end of August, I was looking forward to hunting-season opening; there seemed to be lots of grouse that year, and I was anxious to go hunting. I went to work one day and didn't realize I was sick until I got out of the woods. I had forgotten my lunch and work boots at the office, so I did whatever I could and had two days of work planned. When I went to get a room at the Pemberton Hotel, there weren't any rooms available in town because a film company was shooting a movie there. I felt really sick but had to drive back to Squamish anyway. My throat was sore and making me feel nauseous, but I thought it would go away in a few days. I didn't get better, so I went to the doctor and he gave me a month's supply of pills. I was to take two pills a day for fourteen days then one pill a day. When hunting season finally opened, I told Jennifer I wanted to go hunting and she raised hell about it; then finally, we went. We didn't go out very far because of our financial situation and I was sick, but I couldn't enjoy myself very much by then, so we just went back.

I took two pills a day then started taking one pill a day, but I wasn't getting any better and still needed to take two pills a day. I went back to the doctor again and he gave me a three-month supply, taking two pills a day. I didn't think I had a disease or infection of any kind. I just thought it was a stress-related syndrome. All the stress I've been through since finishing high school seemed to be winding down, and I thought it was taking time for my body to adjust to not being under such incredible stress. Jennifer was getting better now and didn't need to drive off and scream her pain and anger anymore. She had thrown out her winter coat, boots, and most of our clothes because she was so scared of cockroaches; now I had to replace them before the weather got cold. I only got one weekend of standby, and it was on Thanksgiving weekend, so I calculated how much extra money I would be getting and told Jennifer it would be $200 and she could use it to buy a new winter coat.

Since we were living in the basement of someone's house, Jennifer got tired of always trying to be quiet and scared of people complaining about illegal suites; she was also scared to make noise because her father used to beat the kids when they made too much noise and thought we should move. She went to visit Brenda again and asked me to look for another place to stay, so I gave notice that we were leaving and found another place to stay closer to town with a convenience store right next door. It wasn't laid out very well, but it was an ideal location and the landlord was a very nice fellow from Iran, so I took it; and when Jennifer got back, she agreed it wasn't laid out very well but it was an ideal location.

We packed and moved our things when I was on standby, and it was cloudy and drizzling slightly, so there wasn't much chance of a fire call and to me it was like being paid to move. I didn't get any overtime yet, but there was still a chance I could get some when the fertilization contract starts. I had booked my holidays so I could do a week of hunting before the fertilization contract started. Lyle Leo was going to go hunting with me. Unfortunately, the company doing the fertilizing decided to do the work a month ahead of schedule, and part of it was done when I booked my holidays, so I only got a few hours of overtime. I would have preferred extra pay to time off for holidays because of my financial situation, but that wasn't allowed, and the fellow I was going to go hunting with couldn't afford to take a week off because he wanted to pay his vehicle off right away. I didn't have any money to go anywhere, so we just went back to Rosedale.

We spent one night in Rosedale then left the next day because Jennifer still couldn't spend very much time there. Then we went to Hope to visit Jennifer's grandmother; her grandmother was an old lady who lived by herself, yet she seemed incredibly healthy and active. The only health problems she seemed to have was she walked with a crutch and was rather hard of hearing. We stayed in Hope and visited for a few days, bought her grandmother a smoke alarm, and put some storm windows on her house. I was hoping I could still do some hunting, but I was sick and forgot to refill my prescription before we left Squamish. After visiting with her, we went back to Chilliwack and spent a few days with Brenda and Alvin. They had moved back to Chilliwack after his course was over. I knew Alvin enjoyed hunting, so he and I went duck hunting in Agassiz one day. He shot two ducks and retrieved them, and I shot two ducks; but the water was too deep and muddy to retrieve them, so I didn't shoot any more. We drove around the reserve behind my parents' place and didn't see anything, so we went back to Chilliwack. Alvin was too busy to do any hunting after that, so we just visited with them and Henry Jr. and spent the last of my holidays in Laughing Raven because I didn't want to go to Sto:lo Eagle. My time off wasn't too bad, but I didn't have very much money to do anything and I was still sick.

I was scheduled to take the silviculture-surveys course again that fall, but I cancelled it because there was too much chance I would fail it because I was still sick. I signed Jennifer up for a one-day course in traffic control and flagging, hoping she would have a better chance of getting a job when her knees got better. She passed the course but knew she wouldn't be assertive enough to do the job, and it could be dangerous because of careless drivers. We continued seeing Hubert as much as we could, and I told Jennifer to shop around for a new winter coat. She couldn't find one she liked in Squamish or North Vancouver, so she looked around Pacific Centre Mall in Vancouver. She found a coat she liked and put it on hold until we could pick it up. The coat she chose was originally over $300 but was now on sale for $220. We saw Hubert a week later then stopped off on our way home to pick up her coat, and as we were walking down the street toward the mall, I picked up a $5 bill on the corner of the street. Other people probably saw it too, but I got it first. When we bought her coat, the store gave her a $50 gift certificate that she could use at any branch of their store. Christmas was coming, so she saved the certificate for Christmas presents; and I thought, *Maybe my luck is finally picking up again.*

It was November now, and we finally got our truck-repair bill paid off. The field season was over now, so most of the staff were busy catching up with office work. We were receiving a year's retroactive pay, which was good because Jennifer needed new winter boots and my truck needed a new muffler and brake work done. I booked the rest of my holidays at Christmas so I could take two weeks off and hoped the college would offer some vocational training in January that Jennifer could get into, but the town was too small to offer very much. My acne had gone away for two months then came back again on and around my nose. I was still under incredible stress because of our financial situation, Jennifer's therapy, and trying to get her a career.

We started doing our Christmas shopping, and Jennifer was getting better, but she still had all-or-nothing thinking. When she bought presents, she was either extremely frugal or too extravagant. I didn't want her to do either, but I couldn't stop her. Fortunately, I got a raise in pay late in the year, so I applied to have money deducted for Canada Savings Bonds. The amount deducted wouldn't be enough for me to miss, and when I got my bonds in the fall, I would have money for Christmas.

Jennifer got bored one weekend and wondered what to do. I told her there was a staff party in Whistler that night but I didn't buy any tickets; she asked why, and I said because she always starts a big fight when I want to do something for my own interests. The silviculture staff also had a Christmas party and I was told to bring some swimming trunks for sitting around in a hot tub afterward, but she started a big argument before going, so I forgot to bring them. We went to Laughing Raven for a few days to visit Ben and Geraldine, went to Chilliwack to visit Brenda and Alvin, then to Sto:lo Eagle. I didn't want to spend the night in Sto:lo Eagle, but Henry Jr. and I were going to go hunting the next day; but it was raining too hard, so he didn't wake me up. I went back to Rosedale and Jennifer didn't want me to go there, but I didn't want to stay in Sto:lo Eagle.

My parents had a house full, so my mother asked me to spend the night at David and Angie's. David was working that night, so I showed Angie the letter I wrote to Dr. Brant and she was quite surprised at what I went through to save Jennifer from suicide. Then I told her about Henry asking me for a drink of my juice when I was on a liquid diet because I had to go for X-rays but I wouldn't give him one. I also told her Henry knew what I went through to save his daughter from suicide, yet all he did was mooch off us and make life miserable for me then said he did everything for us and we were obligated to him. When we were really down on our luck, he wouldn't even buy us a cup of coffee and he had over $8,000 in the bank.

Then I told her how Henry treated his kids when they were young. He wouldn't even look after his responsibilities as a parent. The kids even had to put his socks on and shoes off for him, and he would beat them if they made a mistake. The kids went picking strawberries in Lynden, Washington. In their sandwiches they had to eat the grease out of the pan, and he took every cent of what they made, then the girls stole the other pickers' lunches because they were hungry. When Liz and Jeremy were separated and she was really down on her luck, he was still charging her for babysitting for her; and when he stopped off for coffee where she was working, he even expected her to pay for it. When Liz and Jeremy both died in a car accident, the first thing I asked him was how much was he going to put down for the funeral? He had over $10,000 in the bank and all he did was buy flowers, so why didn't he just stay home and save his money?

Angie said, "*Yeah, right!* He had a lot of nerve asking for a drink of your juice!"

I went back to Sto:lo Eagle after Boxing Day, and she said her and Henry Jr. had piles and piles of dishes to wash. I told them Tony got Helen's name in the draw and put a note under the tree, telling her where to look for her present. When she got there, there was another note telling her where to look; so she ended up looking all over the house before finding her present, so Henry Jr. did the same thing to Brenda.

It was also Ryan's birthday, so Jennifer bought him a cake; and I had to renew our insurance, but it had snowed too hard to get back to town for a few days. Brenda and Alvin were over visiting, but I made a doctor's appointment for Jennifer to get her prescription refilled and renew my truck insurance at the same time; but when we got to town, Jennifer was really mad at me and started a big argument because she wanted the whole family to sing "Happy Birthday" to Ryan because he's never had it done by the whole family. I asked her if that was more important than our own responsibilities and got me so uptight I couldn't think straight again, so when I paid my insurance, I randomly choose June 4 as the time to renew my insurance. After paying for the insurance and going to the doctor, Brenda and Alvin drove up just as we were on our way back to Sto:lo Eagle. They were on their way back to Chilliwack and stopped to buy things and talk to us. While we were in Sto:lo Eagle, Jennifer was always renting videos and buying snacks even though it drove me crazy. I didn't mind doing it for her brothers, but I hated doing anything for her father. We went back to Sto:lo Eagle that night then went to Laughing Raven the next day; and I thought, *This is supposed to be my holiday, but I would rather have not taken time off at all*," and spent New Year's Eve in Laughing Raven.

Chapter 15

1993

We left the next day and drove back to Squamish even though it was Friday and I didn't have to go back to work until Monday, but it was a good thing we went back early because it snowed rather heavily and we may have had trouble getting back. It was nice to get back to work again because of our financial situation, and we wouldn't be spending as much. Jennifer bought a few more things then realized how far we were in debt and decided we should destroy all our credit cards. I thought it was a good idea, so we wouldn't be tempted to use them anymore.

Straight office work was boring for most of the staff, but we were preparing for the coming field season; we had new contracts to put together and had to project how much work we were going to do that year. Since I wasn't doing any fieldwork and still had to take Jennifer to see Hubert, I had to use my vacation time. I booked one day a month from January to March, but she was having stomach problems, so I had to use more vacation time to take her to Vancouver to see a specialist and go for X-rays. We finally started getting our bills down, and I felt good about that because after two years of working, we were still just as far in debt. I told Jennifer what we pay in interest every month could pay for a brand-new couch in a year. I had tried to set our budget so we could make large payments on our bills and save for our truck insurance, but things seemed to keep going wrong. I had booked a day off work to see Hubert, but earlier that week, my aunt from North Vancouver passed away. Her funeral was on the same day that we were to see Hubert, but luckily, he said we could see him on Saturday morning.

When I got back to work, Stephen DeMelt called me in to his office to discuss my work plan for the year. He mentioned when I was on medication and wondered if it was substance abuse because I would be really sick then I would feel better a little while later. I told him I was on prescription medication and thought it was a stress disorder because everything I had been going through since high school was winding down and it could be taking time for my body to get used to not being under so much stress.

Jennifer started getting bored, and I hoped it was an indication she's getting better. She still needed her math to get her grade 12 certificate. I enrolled her in upgrading classes, but she was too scared to attend classes without me and said she couldn't really understand the teacher, so she gave up. I signed up to participate in the staff curling bonspiel, but she started getting depressed again; she said it was all right for me to go, but when I got home, for lunch she was incredibly cranky again. I didn't know if I would be able to go back for my next round of curling, but she picked herself up and let me go. I was finally able to do something for my own interests but didn't go to the dinner and dance that night. Jennifer started getting more and more depressed and started talking about suicide again. I went home for lunch one day, and she had my shotgun loaded because she wanted to see what it would be like to point a loaded gun at herself. I had a bit of a struggle taking it away from her because I was scared she would actually pull the trigger, then I took all the shells and put them in the truck so she couldn't do it, but she promised to call me if she got too serious about committing suicide.

I got worried about her and didn't know what to do. I tried calling Hubert, but each time I called him, all I got was the answering machine. We were only allowed one day off a year for domestic emergencies, so I thought I better save it for when she calls. I thought Jennifer was getting better, but she wasn't; things got so bad we had to drive off to an isolated area so she could scream again, but at least now when she screamed, it only lasted twenty minutes to half an hour and was happening less and less. Luckily, Jennifer's thoughts of suicide didn't last very long. I tried teaching her how to handle finances and now she got obsessed with trying to pay our bills off. She added everything up and spent time trying to find the lowest prices in the grocery store. When I set our weekly budget, she made me put anything we didn't spend on to our credit cards.

We went back to Chilliwack one weekend and stopped at a nursery on our way back and bought some house plants. I had bought Jennifer a book on plants just before Christmas to try and encourage her to develop hobbies and interests. After buying two plants, she went to extremes looking after them and buying fertilizer and insect sprays; she always had to be obsessed with something. She started getting more and more interested in plants and asked me to buy her another book on plants. I thought it was good to encourage her because she might decide to become a horticulturist or go to work in a plant shop. When I bought her the book, she was reading it constantly, and her friends were also giving her plants; then we were always going back to the nursery to buy flowerpots, insect sprays, and soil for plants now. The plants seemed to be growing good, but some of them developed spider mites, so we bought some spray for them; then we were told it would be impossible to get rid of them on some plants, so she threw them out. I accidentally bumped a plant and some leaves fell off, so she got mad and threw it out. Her obsession with plants didn't last very long.

Jennifer got more and more obsessed with our bills when I tried to let her handle the finances. She stocked up on things and bought many bulk foods, but after she tried eating them, they seemed tasteless compared to name-brand products; so she realized that wasn't the way to save. She needed more clothes now, so I bought her some shirts; and she usually wore her shoes out rather fast, so I always had to buy her expensive running shoes so they wouldn't wear out very fast.

We went to Chilliwack again one weekend to visit Brenda and Alvin, and when we got there, Jennifer and Brenda went shopping on my truck. I was feeling rather stressed out, so when Alvin asked me to chip in and buy a case of beer, I went along with it. I didn't know she was planning on going to Rosedale that night because she never said anything to me, and when she got back and saw I was drinking, she got really mad and drove to Hope to visit her grandmother. I didn't even know she left and got back early in the morning. She was still mad at me the next day, and when we tried to leave, the truck wouldn't start; and if that wasn't bad enough, someone slashed one of my tires. I couldn't get the wheel off because one of the wheel nuts stripped and wouldn't turn. We tried for a couple of hours to change it then finally called Henry Jr. to see if he had any tools to try and change the tire, but his tools were at his cousin's place, so he had to go get them.

Nothing we tried worked; then a neighbor went out and helped us. He said he was happy to help us because many farmers on the prairies helped him out in similar situations.

After we finally got the tire changed, the truck still wouldn't start, so I had to call Stephen DeMelt and tell him I couldn't make it to work because my truck broke down. I called the auto mechanic I used to deal with quite regularly, and he told me to have my truck towed to his garage the next day. It took just about the whole day to get our truck fixed, cost us $200, and when it was ready, the gas gauge didn't work because he forgot about the send-back unit. It was late and he had more work to do, so he said we could bring it back and he would fix it free of charge. We drove back to Squamish that night, and the next day, I reported it to ICBC and it still cost me $143 to replace the tire. I was hoping we could save for our insurance, but every month, something seemed to be going wrong.

The field season was starting, so I was going out to the woods more often. We had some road opening to do for one of our contracts and I had to be there to supervise and monitor the work, so I had to spend a few nights in a logging camp. Jennifer started doing volunteer work at the mini-flea market during the day then applied for work at a local restaurant that just opened up. The restaurant couldn't afford to pay her, so she just worked there as a volunteer dishwasher and the cook showed her some cooking skills. I was glad she found something to keep her occupied because it gave me some free time even though I had to buy her some new clothes for work and pick her up later. Jennifer got some of the waitress's tips because the waitress and her husband were the new owners of the restaurant. She was starting to get better now and was realizing we would never get anywhere if she kept spending the way she used to. Now she gave me all the extra money, and whatever we didn't spend out of our weekly budget was put on credit cards.

Jennifer did volunteer work for a couple of weeks then decided it was taking up too much of her time. She was still going for therapy and didn't have time to do her writing, so she decided to quit. Quitting seemed to take much of the stress off her mind because she knew she would have to confront her father again for her therapy. We continued seeing Hubert, and she finally worked up enough courage to confront her father again; so Hubert said if we couldn't take him to Richmond, he could go to Sto:lo Eagle and she could talk to him there. Jennifer decided it would be better to talk to him there because of his health, so she set a time and date with Hubert to confront him.

They chose the same weekend we were having National Forest Week in Whistler, so I couldn't volunteer that year. I forgot how stressful it would be for her and booked an appointment to have our gas gauge fixed in the morning and she could confront him in the afternoon. I thought we could spend the night at Brenda and Alvin's then leave early in the morning. As we were packing to leave Thursday night, I told Jennifer I made an appointment to get the truck fixed, and she got really mad at me for not telling her earlier! This was an important event for her and very important for her therapy, and I realized it was very naive of me to do that. We drove to Chilliwack that night and Jennifer decided she didn't want to see anyone that night. I offered to get a room so she could prepare what she was going to say, but she didn't want to because we owed too much money on our credit cards. She was also mad at me because she needed time in the morning to prepare what she was going to say. Since Jennifer didn't want to get a room, we decided to just sleep in the truck. We weren't prepared for it, but it wasn't too cold out. The next day, Jennifer was really cranky because of all the stress she was under; so I offered to cancel our truck appointment, but she said, "No!"

I called the mechanic, but his helper forgot to book the appointment, so he told me to just go over. I didn't think it would take very long to fix, but he said it would take a couple of hours; so I said, "Can I bring it back some other time?"

The mechanic enthusiastically answered, "Don't break my heart!"

I told Jennifer, "I cancelled the appointment because it would take a couple hours to fix it and we don't have the time."

"I knew it would. What did he say?"

"Don't break my heart!"

We drove off to where we wouldn't be disturbed, and she wrote and prepared what she was going to say to her father. When she finished, she decided I needed a new pair of shoes and insisted I buy some, so we went to a shopping mall and had to put it on my credit card because I needed them right away. After that, we drove to Agassiz and waited at the turnoff to Sto:lo Eagle for Hubert. He arrived around two o'clock, and we drove to her parents' place. At first we just went in and had a cup of tea; then Jennifer showed Hubert around the house and yard. Henry Jr. was there, but he stayed in his room while Jennifer confronted their father. Jennifer talked to him about how he treated her and how she always wanted a father just to love her. I was glad Hubert was there because Henry tried to deny everything, but Hubert said, "You admitted doing it at my office, Henry."

Henry didn't like being confronted like that then stood up and said, "I'm gonna go check up on Emily!"

Hubert stood up and said, "I'll go check up on Emily."

Jennifer was crying and said, "The least you could do is give me an apology!"

Henry hesitated then reluctantly said "I apologize!" but didn't sound like he meant it at all, so I felt like just wailing on him! In spite of how I felt toward him, I just sat through the whole ordeal and didn't say anything because I knew that was the right thing to do. It didn't take very long, but it built up a great deal of stress preparing for it. Jennifer wondered why her mother left, but Hubert said it was too painful to hear what was going on, so we stayed in Sto:lo Eagle for the weekend then came back to Squamish.

I continued working on my contracts, and work was starting for the field season. Jennifer told me to go to the doctor to treat my acne, but I wouldn't go because I thought it was just stress from what I was going through. One night when I was in the logging camp, the cook said I should go to the doctor for medication to treat my acne or I could end up with permanent scars. He had the same symptom many years ago and said it was rosacea. When I got back to town, I went to the doctor and he agreed it was rosacea and gave me some pills; then Jennifer said, "Now, who was right?" I didn't listen again and regretted it.

I continued working then finally got a day off to get the gas gauge fixed. I was lucky the mechanic was able to fix it rather than spend $400 plus Labour for a new part. We thought the truck was working fine now; so Jennifer said she wanted to go to Lynden, Washington, for a drive then to Sto:lo Eagle for the weekend. We drove to Lynden, looked around for a little while; then as we were driving, the truck started powering out again. Jennifer thought I was just doing that, but the fuel pump wasn't working again. The truck finally stopped completely, so I got Jennifer to steer it while I pushed it. There was no shoulder on the road to let traffic by, so I had to push it into someone's yard.

Lynden is a farming community and there were many farms along the highway, so I hoped the people who owned the house were farmers and could help get my truck working again. A fellow, Ron Hendriks, and his son went out of the house; but he owned a clothing store and didn't know anything about mechanics. He was a very nice fellow though and let us park our truck in his yard and invited us in for a cup of tea. He said we could call Jennifer's sister in Laughing Raven and even called a tow truck operator to see how much it would cost to have our truck towed to the border. It would cost us U.S. $100 to tow it that far, and Geraldine was in town shopping with the kids. Luckily, Ron said we could just leave our truck there and they could drive us to Laughing Raven. They were a very nice couple and didn't want us to give them anything for helping us out, so I mentioned that when we helped an elderly couple when they broke down on the freeway, we drove the wife right to their house but the husband wouldn't leave their van.

When we got to Laughing Raven, Ben's brother-in-law, Harvey, was there and he mentioned a mobile mechanic who only charged $15 an hour, kept his tools in a van, and could drive right to the site and work on it. We called him up, and he said he could fix it in the morning. I told him I thought the fuel pump had gone on it from the way it sounded. The mobile mechanic picked us up the next day then drove us to the border, but it took a while to get across the border because we were checked thoroughly. After crossing the border, we went to where the truck was parked and Mrs. Hendriks was there and let us use her phone again. The mechanic called an auto-parts store, and they had a fuel pump that could be installed under the hood of the truck; so we drove to Lynden, picked up the part, then went back. Mrs. Hendriks was very nice about helping us and brought out a cup of tea and cupcake for all of us, then she had to leave. The mechanic fixed the truck then offered to buy the fuel pump off us when we got our regular fuel pump fixed because it was handy for his business, so I agreed.

On our way to the border, I kept hoping the truck wouldn't break down again; and after we got across the border, I felt safer, but the truck seemed to putter along without getting any power. I thought it might stall, but it kept going. We drove to the same garage, parked the truck, then called Brenda and Alvin to go pick us up. They went and got us, but we had to wait until Monday before the mechanic could start working on the truck. I knew it was the fuel pump again and wished they were mechanical rather than electrical because I could have fixed it myself; now it's a major job to replace them.

I called Stephen DeMelt and told him I couldn't make it to work because my truck broke down again. The mechanic was busy with other vehicles before mine, so he couldn't start working on it until late in the day. He couldn't get it fixed that day, so I had to miss another day's work, and I was getting concerned because I was supposed to be taking a course and had to prepare for the exam. When my truck was finally fixed, it was late Tuesday afternoon, so I didn't have time to get my books from the office to prepare for the exam. We sold the fuel pump to the mobile mechanic on our way back, and when I got back to work, I went to classes for one day then prepared for the exam the next day. I passed the course, but I only got a one-year certificate and missed the five-year certificate by 4 percent.

Things seemed to get back to normal again, and we decided to go back to Chilliwack for the weekend two weeks later. I didn't want to go to the canoe races at Cultus Lake that year, but we went on Saturday, the first day of the races. Alvin stayed home, so we went there with Brenda and the kids. I didn't mind it too much, but I knew Jennifer would want to take her parents there and we would have to look after them. I felt really irritated about that because it took all the fun out of going to the canoe races. I liked walking around and talking to friends and relatives I don't see very often. Sure enough, Jennifer suggested we take her parents to the lake the next day but said I wouldn't have to help look after them. I agreed even though I didn't want to, because I had already done enough for them and never got any thanks at all. Fortunately, one of my mother's uncles passed away and there was to be a viewing before he would be cremated; that gave me an excuse not to go to the lake with Jennifer's parents.

We went to Sto:lo Eagle that night; and the next day, Geraldine, three of her kids, and a friend went over to take their dad to the lake because they knew it could be the last time he ever went. They stayed and visited, helped prepare some food to bring over, and just before everyone was ready to leave, Brenda called and told them not to forget the lawn chairs. Henry never showed any reaction, but I got mad at him and said, "I knew you wouldn't get mad at Alvin for borrowing your lawn chairs!" Then Jennifer passed him a small dish of potato salad to try it out, and I said, "I'm not touching it! You'll say you did everything for us and we're obligated to you!"

Henry just glared at me and noticed I refused to eat anything. I only drank coffee and tea. When everything was ready and packed up, Henry knew I wasn't going because I couldn't stand him. Jennifer dropped me off across the road from my parents' place then went to the lake. A few hours later, she stopped by and visited with my family, then we came back to Squamish. As I was rewriting my autobiography, I told Jennifer, "I'm dreading the thought of reliving 1987 again! It was the worst year of my life!"

"I never noticed that it was hard because life has always been hard for me."

"When your dad wanted to see an Indian doctor in the Okanagan because he thought he had a cancer on his back, you were driving me crazy the way you were talking. We were deeply in debt, didn't have very much money going in, and barely getting by. You wanted to rent a car, pay the doctor, rent a room, take your mother along, pay for their meals, and take them to a movie in the evening."

"It's hard to believe I was talking like that."

Jennifer did some more volunteer work at the restaurant then got a job doing janitorial work. It paid $8 an hour and she almost quit, but Brenda told her she was lucky to have a job that paid that much. She needed my truck to go to work, so I had to ride my bicycle in the afternoons, which was okay because it was only a ten-minute ride; and with her working from five o'clock to nine o'clock, I had a break from looking after her. She worked for a few more days; then I went home from work one Friday and there was a note on the table, saying the truck wouldn't start again. I went outside and tried to start the truck, but it wouldn't start. The fuel pump went on it again and we couldn't get it fixed until after the weekend. We couldn't go anywhere or do very much without our truck, so we just did a little grocery shopping and our laundry that weekend. On Monday morning, I rode my bicycle to work and booked an appointment to get the truck serviced, and I thought we were lucky it broke down there because I could push it to the shop and save towing charges.

When I got home at lunchtime, Jennifer was really cranky because the abuse was coming out again. She was still cranky as I was pushing the truck and some clown yelled out, "Come on! Push a little harder!" I started laughing, and a young boy walking by offered to help but I was already near the repair shop, but I thanked him anyway. It was getting late. The staff seemed to be taking their time and Jennifer wanted me to take a taxi back to work, but I rode my bicycle. It was harder pushing the truck than I thought it would be, but at least I saved the towing charges. I knew it was the fuel pump again and it would cost me another $200 to get it fixed. I went to the shop after work, and it wasn't ready yet. Jennifer was worried about going to work, but someone else picked her up. Then when the truck was ready, I drove it to where she was working and rode my bicycle home.

I took Jennifer to see Hubert in Richmond again and told her we had to leave at two o'clock because I was on standby for fires and she had to go to work. I thought she was progressing well in her therapy, but she got really mad at me afterward and went on a spending spree. Then while we were driving back, she started crying and screaming again as we were driving through Vancouver, so I had to close the windows and turn up the radio so no one would hear her and think I was kidnapping her. Fortunately, it didn't last very long and she was able to go back to work. Things seemed to be going quite well for us although Jennifer wasn't really too happy with her job, but at least now she knew it was important to have a job that paid well because jobs can be very hard to get. She called Sto:lo Eagle one day and talked to her dad and was surprised he was talking really positively to her and was encouraging. Jennifer was doing more driving on her job, was gaining more confidence, and becoming more sure of herself. She started talking about separating after she helped me go out of debt because she realized she ran our bills up that high, but I suggested she get a career first.

One of my cousins who was a year ahead of me in high school stopped by to visit one night. He was working for British Columbia Telephone Co., now Telus, and had graduated computer technology. He said he wasn't going to go to BCIT but thought, *If Annis can do it, then I can too.* It sure made me feel good to know that I was his inspiration.

Some new job openings for aboriginal forestry advisors were coming up in various forest districts in British Columbia and paid more than I was earning as a technician, so I thought it could be a chance to transfer to an area where I could put Jennifer back in school since Squamish didn't offer very much. I applied to several districts, but just before the interviews, we got reclassified and a raise in pay; so the job wasn't worth transferring to. It still paid more, but I would have lost too many benefits I enjoyed being a technician, but I went to three interviews in two days and they were very stressful. I didn't know what to prepare for these interviews and what the job would involve, so I didn't do very well in the interviews and was happy I didn't get any of the jobs though because I decided I wanted to stay a technician.

A week and a half later, I went for an interview for a technician's job in Chilliwack. I didn't really want to transfer, but I wanted to put Jennifer back in school and help Henry Jr. with his studies if he went back to college. Jennifer was really stressed out the weekend before the interview, so we ended up partying Friday night and all day Saturday. She drank on Sunday, but I knew I had to slow down if I wanted to pass the interview, but someone else got the job anyway. Even though I didn't do very well in the interview, I started having second thoughts about moving because I liked Squamish forest district and didn't really want to leave; not only that, Jennifer decided she wanted to take her hairdressing course in Vancouver rather than in Chilliwack. Jennifer decided she wanted me to get used to us being separated, so she moved all her things into the living room. I knew this would happen eventually but didn't expect it to come so suddenly. Jennifer was healing her wounds from the past, and now she wanted independence.

We went to Laughing Raven one weekend then to Sto:lo Eagle the next day, and Brenda and Alvin were there. I didn't want to spend the night there, but I knew most of my family would be at my cousin's wedding. Henry couldn't get around by himself, so if he had to go to the bathroom, someone had to help him. Alvin was sitting right beside him and he looked like he expected me to walk across the room and help him. Later on in the day, I fell asleep on the La-Z-Boy, and Henry usually sat in the chair beside it. I woke up just as he was being helped back from the bathroom and he thought, *He won't wake up and help me out.*

"You can ask your favorite," I replied. Alvin never helped him get around, so why should I? He treated Alvin a whole lot better than he treated me in spite of all the things I did for him, never mind the fact that he knew I literally went through hell to save his daughter from suicide! Henry Jr. started to notice that I wouldn't help his dad do anything, not even sit up straight when he slid down his chair. He felt rather annoyed about that and started wondering if he should pay me back for his graduation, but I just told him, "He treats me like shit and he treats Alvin like gold!" but I helped him a little bit the next day though.

Jennifer's job and the idea of separating was putting a great deal of stress on her, so we started going to the bars. I usually just sat there and drank pop while she drank a few beers. When the last long weekend of the summer came, we decided to just stay home for the weekend and went to the bar on Friday night. Just as we sat down, a young lady went up to me and asked if I wanted to be an extra in a TV movie; at first I thought it was just a hoax, but I went outside so she could take my picture anyway. Then I gave her my home phone number and my number at work. There was another girl sitting with her, and they said the company would be filming on Thursday and I would know by Tuesday if I got the part. They said the movie involved a strike by angry miners during the Depression and they wanted some Indians on the set because the mines hired some Indians at that time, but I didn't really believe them. They said I could also pass for an Asian immigrant from Northern Siberia and asked if I knew any Indians with short hair who could be used as extras and asked me not to shave or get a haircut until after filming. I still thought it could be a hoax, so I asked for a business card, so she gave me one. I told her I could be available Thursday afternoon but I would have to think about whether I would be available for the full day or not. After we got home, Jennifer and I talked it over and she thought I should go for it; our clairvoyant said this would happen, and it did.

Then Jennifer said, "See! If we didn't go to the bars, this wouldn't have happened! Now I get half of what you earn!" The next day, Brenda called and said Henry Jr. didn't go back to college, so I thought it's just as well I didn't move back to Chilliwack because I enjoyed working in Squamish, housing was expensive but working conditions were like heaven.

On Monday night I was asked to go to Britannia Beach for filming on Thursday; and on Wednesday night, I was called and told to be at Britannia Beach at six thirty in the morning, so I went to bed early that night. The next day, Jennifer drove me to Britannia for filming. She waited around for a little while then left because she needed the truck for work. There were many people there working as extras, and the first thing we did was get clothes to wear and fill out forms. Some people there were trying to make a living at acting and helped get things organized. We were given instructions on what we had to do, and if we left to relieve ourselves, we had to inform the workers first. Since we were supposed to be a group of angry miners in the 1930s going on strike, some people put hair grease or makeup in our hair then rubbed a mixture of lotion and charcoal on our faces to make us look like coal miners. After that, we had to rehearse the scene a few times before the director started shooting the camera, and I was surprised at how friendly the stage directors were and took time to explain how they wanted things done. Sometimes on TV they're made to look like cranky, miserable people who like to yell at the actors.

After the first scene was over, it was lunchtime, and we were provided a lunch; and after lunch, some people were asked to do another scene, but not all of us were needed. About an hour and a half later, we had to do another scene, acting like a group of miners at a secret union meeting. Another fellow was there with speaking parts in both scenes, but no one seemed to know he was actually the star of the show because he just played his role and made suggestions as things went along. It was getting warm in the afternoon and most of us were getting tired, but it was finally over, so I caught a ride back to Squamish with someone else. The next day, I told a lady in the office about standing in a crowd of angry miners with a club on my shoulder, trying to look mean. On some takes, I thought everything was over, so I started standing around; then I would hear the director yell "Cut!" Another lady who couldn't help but hear me was laughing because she knew it was hard for me to hold a straight face right through.

Even though I was faithfully taking medication daily for my acne, it was still coming back. I was feeling stressed out again and couldn't understand why. After the weekend, I started the second half of a large contract and found out I was making many mistakes, forgetting many things without realizing it and couldn't understand why. That afternoon I realized I was feeling extremely sick but had much work to do, and it was too late to get someone else to take my place. I had to go out to a logging camp that night and start two contracts the next day. For the next two nights, I woke up several times during the night feeling cold, yet my T-shirt was soaked with sweat. I had much fieldwork to do, but fortunately, most of it was driving from place to place. I stayed in camp one night, at the Pemberton Hotel for two nights, then called Jennifer and asked her to make another appointment with the doctor for me because my throat was bothering me again. After three days of fieldwork, I was finally able to see the doctor and he gave me some pills to take for ten days, which I took faithfully and on time. I worked for two days in the office the next week and realized I was still making mistakes and wasting other people's time. My sore throat seemed to numb my brain to the point where I couldn't think, so I decided I was doing more harm than good by going to work.

I took one day off then went out of the woods the next day because I had an appointment with a client. It was a long day for me because of the long drive, and I was slow because I wasn't feeling well. I decided to just stay home for the weekend to rest up and hope I would get better when the duty officer called me on the radio and asked me to go on standby for the weekend. I gladly accepted it though because it was nice to sit around home like I intended to do and get paid for it. There wasn't much chance of a fire starting, but I would have gone anyway.

I took all the medication the doctor prescribed, but it didn't do anything for me, then went to another doctor; and he said it was a flu that would have to run its course. I talked to Stephen DeMelt one afternoon and told him Jennifer and I were in the process of breaking up; not only that, I felt sick all the time and couldn't seem to concentrate on my work. He said he noticed I'd been starting to look run-down for over two months now and asked if I wanted to see a counsellor through the employee assistance program. I agreed and he called the counselling service for me.

I went to the counsellor, Mary Anne Rolfe, and told her a few things about myself. She questioned me about drinking, how much I drank, and if I had a problem with alcohol. I told her I didn't have much of a teenager's life because I was teased so much as a child and was always staying home babysitting my younger brother while everyone else was out having fun. I showed her some of my writings and told her I would probably be up to chapter 12 if I didn't lose part of my writings in a fire. She suggested I go to a treatment center for repressed anger because treatment centers aren't only for drug and alcohol addictions. She could make arrangements for me through the drug and alcohol counsellors from the Squamish Indian Band, so I agreed then told her we could book another appointment to see each other again.

I went to work for a week but still wasn't functioning as well as I should have been because of my throat and started looking forward to time off now and still wondered if it was because my stress level was going down. On my days off, Jennifer and I were supposed to see Hubert, but she was stressed out, so we left late. I wanted to see him too, but he had another appointment, so we went to Laughing Raven after seeing him. I was going to visit my family for a week and Jennifer was going to go back to work in Squamish on Monday, but when we got to Laughing Raven, she forgot her driver's license. Ben said he was going to have a barbecue next Saturday because it would be the last of the good weather and we were invited, so I only visited my family for a couple of days then drove Jennifer back to Squamish.

The next day I decided to see a doctor in Agassiz, so I called home and asked my dad to make an appointment for me and went to the doctor the next day, and he told me to take two pills two times a day for two weeks. If my throat didn't get better, I should get some lab tests done; so I took the pills, but they didn't do anything for me. I continued to feel sick and tired most of the time and was glad I took my holidays when I did. I just laid around and rested because I felt so tired all the time.

I stayed home for a few days, then Tony gave me a ride to Laughing Raven for the salmon barbecue and Jennifer would drive down and meet me the next day. I went in the house and some of the kids were there and Geraldine was in the kitchen, cooking. I felt sick and tired, so I just went into a bedroom and laid down. I had bought a twenty-four-pack of canned beer, but I just left it in the bedroom. A couple of hours later, I started to feel better, so I tried to do some writing but couldn't concentrate. Ben was home from work by then, so I went outside to talk to him and one of my cousins. They were having a few beers and talking to people as they were passing by. I wasn't feeling well, but I had a few beers anyway. Jennifer went the next day for the barbecue, and most people sat around and drank a few beers. It would have been enjoyable if I wasn't feeling so sickly. We stayed there again that night, and I went to Rosedale the next day.

After Thanksgiving dinner, we usually drew names for Christmas presents, but Jennifer stayed in Laughing Raven. I picked her up and we came back to Squamish. I went to work the next day and was told I would be going out to a logging camp to monitor the fertilization contract. The starting date was changed again, so I only had one day in the office. I didn't have time to do any grocery shopping for Jennifer because I was given such short notice. Although we were in the process of breaking up, I was still supporting her. I was looking forward to going out to camp because I knew it would be very relaxing. You go to work, go home, and a terrific meal is waiting for you. I would only be there long enough to enjoy it then leave before I get tired of it.

The contract went well though, and I enjoyed spending time in camp. I wanted to prepare for the silviculture-surveys course that was coming up, but I was usually too tired and sickly to do very much studying in the evening. I missed the first course because the fertilization contract didn't finish on time and the second course was cancelled, so I had to take it at a later date on Vancouver Island. I was happy about that though because I would have more time to prepare for it. When I got back to town, I went to see Mary Anne again, and she referred me to see a psychiatrist, I happened to see some of the notes she wrote about me, and she thought I was a potential time bomb. The psychiatrist diagnosed me right away as having a chemical imbalance caused by repressed anger and told me to start taking Prozac.

Jennifer made another appointment to see Hubert again, and he said he had a hard time diagnosing me but finally figured me out. Most people who went through what I went through explode and get violent and aggressive; rather than exploding, I held everything in and imploded. I asked him if the psychiatrist could give me a referral to see him, but he said he wouldn't be around long enough to council me because he was moving to Alberta but could try and give me a referral to see one of his ex-associates if I was willing to travel that far. I agreed, but I was going to Vancouver Island for a week, so he said he would call the Squamish Indian Band for me to attend their group therapy sessions. I told him I would give Jennifer a number where I could be reached, then we came back to Squamish.

I took Jennifer grocery shopping the next day so she would have something to eat while I was gone, and as we were shopping, I began to feel myself slowing down because I wasn't feeling well. Jennifer also noticed it and mentioned it to me. I wasn't feeling well and still had to drive to Parksville that night, so this would be a long day for me. I had to pass the course this time because my job could depend on it, and I hadn't been doing my job properly because I was feeling incredibly sick. I wanted to leave rather early so I wouldn't have to rush, and be well rested the next day; and when I got to Parksville, I got a room where the course was being taught and called Jennifer to let her know I was okay. I was hoping a friend from the office would go too, but he had a job interview to go to, so he couldn't take the course. After I got a room and made arrangements for a wake-up call, I went out for a six-pack of beer. I was feeling rather stressed out, so I decided to have a couple of beers. I sat down and watched TV then went to bed, and when I got up the next day, I realized I drank all six beers. I was far more stressed out than I realized.

I knew the course was intense and didn't want to fail it due to burnout, so I studied before going. The first day of classes was the usual introductions of people and to the course. I had more woods experience now, and the bad memories of doing surveys in Quesnel no longer bothered me. Jennifer was stronger, and I felt better after writing my memoirs. After classes, I went my room and went to sleep for a couple of hours, went for supper, and after supper, did some studying and watched TV. The people taking the course were all pretty nice, and some of us would go to different restaurants or stay in the hotel for lunch. I was much more relaxed now than I was the last time I took the course. I wasn't under as much stress from looking after Jennifer, and my future seemed much brighter now.

The course seemed to be going well and some of us met in the morning for breakfast and most of us went out two nights in a row for a buffet dinner. I was still feeling sick and taking one pill a day, but I wished I could take more so I could get better faster. Ludmilla had to renew her certificate that year, so she showed up for the last two days of the course and she helped me along. We did the field test and wrote a written exam on the last day of the course. We had to stratify an area after it was logged and the trees started growing back then do five plots. Most of it went well except I made a mistake in some of my plots and had to do them again. By the time I finished and started heading back, it was late, so they left without me. The instructor had told them to go and she would give me a ride back. When we got back to the hotel banquet room, we had to compile our data and do the paperwork that goes with surveys, and it took me a long time to do the paperwork because of how I was feeling.

After the course was over, I drove to Nanaimo to catch the ferry back. I may have been allowed to stay one more night, but I was getting tired of restaurant food. I was tired and burnt out from all that studying but had to wait until I got home to do anything, and picked up a case of beer on my way home so I could unwind when I got back. Jennifer knew I was tired when I got back, but she wanted to go to the bars, so I told her she could go but I was too tired. We weren't together, but we were still living in the same apartment. She went out and went back a little while later and said she was going to visit some friends she met in the bar and with a fellow who seemed interested in her then took my beer, but I told her to be careful though.

I knew she was still attracted to dysfunctional men, and to break away from that kind of thinking was extremely difficult because it felt normal after being badly abused as a child. Looking after her all these years was extremely difficult, and it was taking its toll on me. I didn't mind being single again and was actually looking forward to it. There may have been some ladies interested in me, but I never really noticed.

I thought we may get back together again because it didn't seem like the time was right for me to look for anyone. I also wanted her to get a career, and the only thing available in Squamish was a course in long term care aide. It wasn't what she wanted, but it was all that was available; so I thought, *Perhaps there's a reason why things are happening this way.* I checked into the course and found out students needed a first aid course and CPR certificate first, so I signed her up for the courses that would qualify her for entry. She would also have to write an English placement exam, which I was sure she would pass because she's good in English.

I had a few beers then went to bed, and the next day, Jennifer phoned. I told her to be careful when she's drinking because she lets her guard down and could get taken advantage of and told her many times that after food and shelter, the sex drive is one of people's strongest drives. She said the truck was parked in town and I could go get it because she knew better than to drink and drive. I was just lazing around because I didn't have the energy to do very much but eventually went to town to get my truck.

I stayed home and rested again the next day and was slowly getting some of my energy back. It was my birthday, but I didn't feel like going out to eat anywhere because I was tired of eating in restaurants. I watched TV and slept most of the day then went to work on Monday. Jennifer went back and was upset and crying. She said she was taken advantage of again while drinking and didn't know if she was pregnant or not. She finally realized she couldn't handle alcohol, but it took a catastrophe to realize it. She had gone off the pill for a month because she forgot when to start it while I was on holidays. I didn't remind her because I was tired of looking after her every need and thought she should start looking after herself and being responsible for herself.

I didn't know what to do except wait and hope for the best. She didn't know what to do either and was extremely worried. She had wanted to get her tubes tied, but I wanted her to get stronger in the mind before making such a major decision. Now she was mad at me for not letting her do it. She wanted to move out on her own, but I wanted her to get a career first so she could support herself. I also didn't think she was strong enough to get out on her own yet. She asked if she could move back and was worried that I would say no, but I told her she could move back. I told her she could stay with me and we would see what happened. We'd go to the doctor, she could explain the situation to him, and he could tell her what her options were. I don't believe in bringing a child into the world unless you can give it a loving, stable home. We went to the doctor and he thought her chances of being pregnant were very low, then she went to Alcoholics Anonymous (AA) meetings to see an alcohol-and-drug counsellor. The counsellor she was seeing was Mary Anne, so I thought, *Good! Now she'll have a good idea of what I'm going through.*

We went to Sto:lo Eagle Friday night after Jennifer got off work, and Brenda and Alvin were there. Alvin was already in bed, and all of a sudden, Henry started screaming because of stomach pains, so we called an ambulance. Jennifer had a fluorescent vest in the truck she used for work, so I put it on and went outside to signal the ambulance where to stop. When the ambulance got there, they put Henry on a stretcher and carried him out; and as they were carrying him out, he was surprised that I was just sitting there like nothing was happening. Henry Jr. rode with him in the ambulance to Chilliwack and Jennifer and I followed to take them back if he didn't have to stay in the hospital. He was taken to the emergency ward and was still screaming; but finally, the pain went away and the doctors couldn't find anything wrong with him, so we took him back to Sto:lo Eagle. Jennifer and I slept on a mattress on the living room floor, and when Henry got up for breakfast, he was mad because he knew I wouldn't do anything for him when Alvin was there. Later on, I told Henry, "I knew you were psychosomatic. We took you to the doctor and there was nothing wrong with you."

Henry realized he had said the same thing to Jennifer when she had torn ligaments in her knee and was in severe pain, so now it was happening back to him. Everything he had said to Jennifer, I was saying to him. Several weeks later, Henry realized he wouldn't even buy Jennifer and me a cup of coffee yet he spent all kinds of money on Alvin, and looked like he was so depressed he was ready to cry but that didn't mean anything to me. He cried a river at Liz and

Jeremy's funeral, but I don't think there was anything anyone could have said or done to make him put anything down for their funeral. After that, he tried to be nice to me, but it was too late now. Too much damage had been done for me to forgive him, and eventually he was able to get into an old-age home where he could get twenty-four-hour professional care.

Jennifer continued to worry about being pregnant, but her period came a few days before her first aid course. She continued working and started studying her first aid book, so when she took the course and wrote the test, she did quite well in it. Christmas was always stressful for her, making it stressful for me. She decided to just buy a gift for the whole family that year rather than buy each individual a gift because she finally realized she wasn't responsible for them. We drove to North Vancouver and she did most of her shopping in one weekend but wanted to buy individual gifts for her mom and dad. She was also in a name draw at work and wanted me to buy birthday presents for Andrew and Ryan and bought gifts for the names I drew for Christmas.

I was still rather stressed out because we were getting ready to break up, but I wanted her to get a career or at least some job skills so she could support herself. I was also trying to get my bills down so I could trade in my truck and decided to save my bonds for emergency purposes though and let me bills go up a bit. Since Jennifer was working, she had her own money for Christmas.

I was slowly starting to feel better but still felt sick and dragged out. I still had severe acne, and it got worse when I didn't use special soap. Jennifer wrote her English placement exam but didn't do very well in it and said she didn't want that kind of job because she had to look after her parents for so many years. She was driving me crazy but was trying to find a place of her own; she couldn't afford very much because she was only working part-time, and the course was coming up soon. I thought if she moved out then went back right away, it could get expensive for me, so I kept hoping she wouldn't find a place to stay until she found out if she was going to take the course or not. Jennifer had to work until just before Christmas, and I booked my holidays at Christmas, so I had to let her use my truck for work. I didn't want her to drive to Sto:lo Eagle by herself in case the roads were bad or the truck broke down, so I stayed in Squamish for a few days then caught the bus to Chilliwack since she used my truck for work.

My acne was getting bad again and Jennifer quit drinking, so I didn't drink because I didn't want to get her started. When I got to Chilliwack, I bought a six-pack of beer then called for someone to pick me up. I never drink and drive, so I waited until I got home before I drank anything. I drank again that day and just let myself relax. My acne cleared right up in two days but came back when I came back to Squamish.

Jennifer and I drove to Sto:lo Eagle when she got off work and her father was out of the old-age home for a few days. I left a little while later because I couldn't stand him and was tired of spending Christmas in there. Henry Jr. looked disappointed that I was leaving, but I couldn't stand his father even though he was trying to be nice to me.

I picked up two cases of beer before going home and started sipping when I got there. My cousin from North Vancouver Richard Band, Tony, and his new girlfriend and two of her kids were also spending Christmas there; so my mother asked me to spend the night at David's. The next day, I showed Tony's girlfriend some of my writings and she showed me some of hers. We agreed to keep it a secret though because we were both writing a book on our lives, and I told her even my family doesn't know some of the things I've been through. I told Richard about the college newspaper article, saying, "There's a high dropout rate of Native students. Perhaps Natives can't handle post secondary education." He said, "Many of them can't because the quality of education they got in the residential schools didn't prepare them for postsecondary education."

I drove to Sto:lo Eagle that day and opened my presents from Jennifer's family and spent the night there. We drove back to Squamish the next day so she could go to work that night. I spent a couple of nights there with her then decided to go back to Rosedale to visit my family. Jennifer said she would be all right, but I made sure there was food available that she could cook for herself.

I caught the bus back to Rosedale again and borrowed my dad's truck to go to Agassiz for a haircut and pick up a case of beer. The barber appeared to be about twenty-five, and I told him I grew up in the middle of town in Merritt and my dad was a logging contractor; so the barber said, "Then he chose to be a white Indian." I felt like punching him in the head, but he just didn't know how we've been treated. Several years later, I told that to a George Christopher, a black my age; and he said, "You mean you have to be white to go to work!"

I stayed there for a couple of days then walked down the reserve to visit Isaac and Helen. They had invited some friends over for New Year's Eve, so he asked me to go to the store and get some cabbage. When I got to the store, I picked up a weekend advertiser and there was a continuing-education calendar for people to take courses on weekends and in the evenings. I started looking through it out of curiosity and noticed there was a short-order-cooking course offered on weekends in Abbotsford and thought it would be a good course for Jennifer to take because it's offered on weekends and it's an opportunity for her to learn how to cook. If she liked it, she still had time to apply for a full-time cooking course and apply for funding from her band or CEIC. I spent New Year's Eve sipping a few beers and talking with Isaac, Helen, and their friends. Isaac developed diabetes and couldn't drink anymore, but he didn't really like drinking anyway. I stayed there one more night then caught the bus back to Squamish, and Jennifer said she went to an AA dance on New Year's Eve.

Chapter 16

1994

When I got back to Squamish, I told Jennifer she would have to write the English placement exam again and told her about the short-order-cooking course. I kept trying to convince her that the long term care would give her an opportunity to work and save for a career she enjoyed, but she still didn't want to take it. It was getting difficult to live with her. I kept trying to help her find a place to stay that she could afford and was starting to feel better but was still slow at work and couldn't think very well. I also had to leave the office right at four thirty so she could use the truck for work because it was too cold and dark to take a chance riding my bicycle.

I heard about a karate club that trained at the elementary school close to where we lived, but they hadn't opened yet. Then when the recreation guide came out and the karate club would be starting the next week, with training on Monday and Thursday evenings so I thought that was great. The evenings I would most likely be able to make it fit right in with my work schedule. On the first night, Jennifer's boss travelled to Vancouver, and I had to sit by the phone in case she broke down. It was disappointing because I had been waiting for a chance to do something for my own interests, but I was also used to it. I hoped she would enrol in the course and change her mind about not taking it, but it was getting late; the course would start in a week, and she still wasn't accepted. Finally, at the end of the week, she wrote the test and said she tried her best to pass it. I started training in karate and enjoyed it because it felt good to get out and meet people and keep myself in good physical condition.

When the course in long term care started, Jennifer wasn't called, so she asked me to hurry and register her in the cooking course. I thought I would have to go to the college and do it directly then remembered I could do it over the phone and just give them my credit card number. I called the college a number of times before I finally got through to get her registered and it cost me $200, but we had to wait and see if the course was going to be offered or not. I continued trying to get psychological counselling, but payments had to be approved through Medical Services first.

Jennifer told her boss when she would be starting the course and wouldn't be able to work weekends after the first week of February; then five days before the course was to start, the college called and said the course may be cancelled if there weren't enough participants. This caused her a great deal of anxiety because her present job was stressful enough; now she would have to wait until Thursday to find out if the course would be offered or not.

Jennifer was getting extremely worried; but finally, two days before the course was to start, she got called and told the course was being offered. Then Ricky's Restaurants called her to go to work that morning as a dishwasher. Now she worked some days as a dishwasher and every night for four hours with the janitorial services. I told her to try and get a good night's sleep before going to class, but she couldn't sleep very well because of her nerves and the usual anxiety people have when starting something new. We got up early to be there on time, and she knew the course was important because it would give her job skills that could get her a full-time job.

I wasn't feeling very well, so I went to the student lounge to sleep and checked the cafeteria once in a while to have coffee and see how she was doing. I slept most of the day, and the instructor let people leave early because he could see they were all tired, the anxiety of starting the course. We came back to Squamish that night because Jennifer was tired and didn't feel like seeing or talking to anyone. I was glad she would be resting up the next day because on Monday and Tuesday she would be working all day washing dishes and four to five hours in the evening doing janitorial work.

I continued to feel sick and tired most of the time and knew it was affecting my work. There had been a mix-up on whom the doctor sent my referrals to, so I still wasn't able to go for counselling. I was still trying my best at work but couldn't control how I was feeling.

When the weekend came, I drove Jennifer to Abbotsford Saturday morning and slept for most of the day again; and after classes, we went to Sto:lo Eagle and spent the night there. I wanted to go to Rosedale, but Jennifer wanted me to visit with Henry Jr. because she said I was like a father to him, so I told him I saved Jennifer from suicide and his father wouldn't even buy me a cup of coffee. Then he realized why I was so angry at his father and figured I wouldn't even be going to his funeral. We were going to go to Chilliwack to visit Brenda and Alvin the next day, but they went fishing, so we left rather early. I was happy about that because she had two long days of work ahead of her and I had karate classes on Monday and Thursday evenings. Sometimes I felt too tired to go to karate but went anyway because I always felt better afterward.

Jennifer started drinking again but was learning to drink moderately and not let herself get carried away and was told there would be a small apartment in town available at the end of February, two weeks away. She went out Thursday night, so I rode my bicycle to work on Friday. I was feeling sick in the afternoon and kept phoning her so she could pick me up, but she didn't go home, so I rode my bicycle home after work then walked to the bank to get some spending money and pay some bills. I picked up a case of beer on my way home, and two of her friends stopped by, so I had a few beers with them. Jennifer went home and wanted to go out again, so I reminded her to get home early and get lots of rest before her classes. She was still attracted to dysfunctional men and abusive relationships and I didn't know what to do about it. I kept hoping Hubert would go back and talk to her, but we never heard from him since he moved to Alberta last October.

Jennifer was tired the next day when I took her to Abbotsford, so I told her to sleep along the way and was still tired when we got there. I was tired too but didn't sleep as much as in the last two weekends. I ate breakfast, but food didn't usually stay with me. On our way back, Jennifer decided we should look for a new TV and VCR for me. The Brick had a "do not pay until next year" deal, so that's where we shopped. I didn't really want to, but she talked me into it, and it was near the end of that promotional deal. We looked around, compared, then decided what we should buy and bought it.

When we got home, Jennifer called Ricky's to see when she had to go to work because they tried to call her that day. They wanted her to work at three o'clock because one of the dishwashers couldn't make it, so Jennifer told them she couldn't work on Saturdays because of her course. We were both tired, so we went to bed around eleven o'clock that night; and the next day, Ricky's called at seven thirty for her to work from ten o'clock to three o'clock. I took her to work then went home. She wanted me there at three o'clock sharp, so I was there on time, but she didn't get off work until four o'clock. It had been a busy day at the restaurant, so she was tired and anxious to get home.

Jennifer moved into her own apartment and I helped her as much as I could. She took our old TV and VCR and I let her use the vacuum cleaner and helped her wash the walls. On our way home from her next cooking class, we stopped in Surrey to pick up the new TV and VCR. It was a stereo TV, and Jennifer noticed the difference in sound right away. Jennifer continued working part-time at two jobs and taking her cooking course on the weekend. I hoped it would lead to a career goal for her, but she said she didn't think it was her line of work. Working at two jobs was getting hard on, her but she wasn't getting enough hours dishwashing to quit the janitorial job. Hubert still never went back from Edmonton, and we both wished he were around to help Jennifer with her problems.

I continued going to work trying to get my contracts ready on time and help Jennifer get settled. The snow was melting, and I had to check the access to the roads to the blocks we were going to space that year. I was in charge of getting roads opened that were washed out, but the stress I was feeling was incredible. Even though I was training hard in karate and drinking on weekends, I still had severe acne. When I worked in the woods I worked hard and sweated profusely, but it still didn't do anything to clear my acne. I enjoyed living alone, but all I was doing on weekends was staying home after drinking Friday night, which was relaxing; and I thought I could get out and do more when I felt better and Jennifer didn't need to use my truck.

After Jennifer's cooking course was over, she started getting more hours dishwashing, but it was getting hard for her to keep two jobs at once because she was now working sixty hours a week. She gave two weeks' notice that she would be leaving the janitorial service but was replaced after a week because she wasn't available on Saturdays. She was relieved about that because she wouldn't be pushing herself as hard now. Nothing very eventful happened in April, but Jennifer continued to use my truck to go to work. She started going out to the bars and cabarets more often, so I warned her to be careful so people wouldn't take advantage of her. She started seeing a fellow named Aaron; she was attracted to him, and I told her it was because he was like her father. I still wished Hubert would go back and finish her therapy so looking after her wouldn't be so hard on me.

I was slowly starting to feel better but was still taking medication, and in May we did our grading in karate and I earned two green stripes for my belt. I was really happy about that and hoped I could keep working where I could keep training in the same style of karate. I was living alone now, but I didn't look for anyone or feel lonely. I was still having a hard time trying to get my bills down because something was always going wrong with my truck. I was still affected by the chemical imbalance, so I finally just called the psychologist and started seeing Dr. Friedenburg in North Vancouver.

Jennifer started drinking more and more. I hardly ever saw her, but I let her use my truck whenever she needed it for work. Eventually she told me she tried cocaine a few times and even bought some herself; it was expensive, but she liked it. I got really scared for her because I knew she could easily become addicted to it because of all the pain and anger she still had in her, so I warned her it can be addicting and to try and find another way to relieve her stress. Most of the inmates at Elbow Lake were in on cocaine charges because they got addicted to it and ended up robbing banks to support their habit.

I usually just stayed home on weekends and let Jennifer use my truck, so things were rather uneventful. I continued going to work and picked Jennifer up after work if she worked in the evenings. She couldn't handle her finances very well and often borrowed money off me, sometimes even to pay her rent. I started getting concerned about the way she was spending money on cocaine, so one weekend I took her shopping to Whistler. I knew she would enjoy shopping and buying herself some new clothes would make her feel better, so we spent $300 to $400. She felt better afterward, so I told her the next time she was depressed and wanted cocaine, we could go shopping again; if we didn't buy her clothes, we could buy clothes for me.

Geraldine tried really hard to get a hold of us one weekend and called all over for us. When she finally got a hold of us, she said Jennifer's daughter had written them and wanted to meet her real mother. Her name was changed from the names Jennifer gave her, and she wanted to spend the summer with Jennifer. Jennifer didn't know if that was a good idea or not because her apartment was so small and she was still having trouble with depression. She didn't know what to do, but her daughter changed her mind about going down from up north, where she was living.

Things weren't going very good on my contracts because the administration contractor was having problems with her crew, which was affecting her job performance. My home life wasn't going very good either because something was always going wrong with my truck, so I couldn't get my bills down. I wasn't counting on overtime from fires because there were very few fires since I started here.

We didn't go to Chilliwack or Sto:lo Eagle very often because we were trying to be careful with our spending. Jennifer was also attracted to another fellow because he was dysfunctional and controlling, just like her father was. People also told me it could be because she could focus on his problems so she won't have to think about her own. We went back on the July 1 long weekend, and I dropped Jennifer off in Sto:lo Eagle then went to Rosedale to visit my family.

After the weekend we came back to Squamish and back to work. Jennifer hurt her shoulder at work and ended up missing three weeks of work and going on worker's compensation. Her physiotherapist said it happened because of her poor posture and she would have to use tape to help her stand up straighter. It was hard for her to do because she was used to being scared all the time and didn't feel very good about herself. I continued taking medication and seeing Dr. Friedenburg every two weeks and told him about when I got so mad in 1986 I almost slashed my wrist and how I reacted to the situation. He made a tape like hypnotherapy for me to listen to; it hypnotized me and I fell asleep the first time he made it for me. I listened to it every night and realized I still had very much anger that I didn't know I had toward my parents.

I usually just stayed home on weekends, but one Saturday, I decided to go to the bar for a few beers; and a girl there with one of her friends went and joined me, but I didn't get too excited. I knew she had a drinking problem and I was tired of getting disappointed, so I hardly ever got excited anymore. We had a couple of beers there, then I invited them over to my place for a few more; and when we got there, she was hungry and asked for a sandwich, but I suggested we all have a steak. After having something to eat, we took a taxi to the civic center for a dance. Her friend went off to talk to some other people, and we mostly just sat there and drank. It could have been boring, but I was used to being treated like that; then at the end of the dance, she went to talk to some other people and her friend said I could go home by myself. I wasn't disappointed though because I didn't get excited, then I realized it had been many years since I got excited by anyone.

The weather started getting warmer. I continued working and slowly feeling better. My acne went away temporarily and I thought my stress level was going down, but it came back. I had to go on standby for fires the next weekend, so I had to stay home and not go to the bars again. My prescription for Prozac finally ran out, so I went to the doctor for more medication for my acne at the same time. I was getting better all the time but was still slow and not my usual self. I finally started feeling well enough to start writing again and was able to rewrite my writings that had been lost in the fire, the notes that were lost were just before Liz and Jeremy died in the car accident and up to the next summer when I got Andrew a job firefighting. I thought I had let out all my anger toward Henry, but when I started rewriting, I realized I still had very much anger in me toward him, writing it down again seemed to get it out and I felt better.

There wasn't any fire calls on the weekend, but the fire-hazard rating was going up, so we were told to stay in the office when we got back to work in case there was a fire. We were on standby after work, and there had been many lightning strikes that night, so we were asked to go to the office at six thirty the next morning. Jennifer still had my truck and I couldn't get a hold of her, so I rode my bicycle to work. Then around ten thirty, the three-man initial attack crew I was assigned to got sent out to check a fire report. It was a rather long drive in; and when we found the fire, it was a long way up the hill, so we needed a helicopter to fly us in. Since there were so many lightning strikes and fires to check, we couldn't get a helicopter for several hours.

Finally, when a helicopter arrived, it dropped us off well above the fire and we had to walk down to find it; and when we got there, the ground was incredibly steep, so the helicopter had to sling in our equipment on a long line. Luckily, we found a small trickle of water just large enough for a small pump to pump water. We worked until we decided it was getting too dark, then had to walk down while there was still enough daylight. We got in late, and the next day, we had to leave at six o'clock in the morning and we got the fire out early in the afternoon. When we got that fire out, we had to put another small fire out before it spread. It didn't take long to get that fire out, but it was still a long drive back to the office, so we got in at eight o'clock that evening.

After all the fires were taken care of or people were working on thefires, I was able to get back to my regular work. I worked four days in the office then took Friday off to see Dr. Friedenburg again. He asked me if I ever got lonely, and I said, "Not really. I haven't been excited by anyone in almost nineteen years. I never seemed to have much luck with finding girlfriends, and I'm tired of getting turned down." He suggested I check the personal ads in the paper and look for someone, so I checked the personal ads but never really gave it much serious attention. I just thought, *Perhaps the time isn't right that's why things are happening the way they are.*

I added up how much I would be earning in overtime and was happy because my take-home pay would be at least $1,000. That would really bring my bills down when it went in. I worked two days in the office and planned on going out of the woods on the third day when Jennifer called me early in the morning and said the truck broke down. She didn't know what happened or why, but she was extremely depressed about it and threatened suicide; so I told her not to do that and if she felt that way, call me. Then I told Stephen DeMelt about it, so I would be staying in the office all day.

Jennifer called again and told me where the truck was, so I called the GM dealer and asked them to tow the truck in for repairs. I called Jennifer, and she said she would meet me after work and we could see what was wrong with the truck. When we got there, the mechanic said the engine has gone down and it would cost about $2,000 to put another engine. I didn't think it was worth it so we asked what we could get for it and considered buying another truck. He didn't have very much in stock since it was a small dealership, so we test-drove a truck the same size but was a two-wheel drive. I sort of liked it, but it cost more than we could afford, so we bought a small car called a Sunbird. I always liked them and definitely wanted a four-door so people could get in and out of the backseat without anyone moving. The owner had to leave to meet another customer, so I said I could go back on Friday or Saturday because I was going to Pemberton for the next two days.

I stopped at the Pemberton field office the next day to call the dealer and asked him to make arrangements for me to buy the Sunbird. He was busy with another customer again, so I waited around for him to call back. As I was waiting, the duty officer called and asked me to go on standby that night and for the weekend, so I agreed because now I not only had my credit cards to pay off but also a brand-new car. I went out to the woods and got back a little earlier than I expected, and there was a fire call that afternoon. It was a good thing I was there because only a few people could go out until someone showed up with an industrial first aid certificate, so I had to wait at the office until the first aid attendant showed up then drove the suburban to the fire. We needed the suburban because a stretcher could be placed in it if anyone got injured.

It was getting dark by the time I got to the fire, so I just had to sit and wait on the road. I couldn't find any headlamps for the crew, so they had to quit working and come down before it got too dark. The days were long, so we worked as long as we could and got back to the office at ten thirty in the evening, then we were up at five o'clock the next morning because we had many things to prepare and to get to the fire as early as possible. It was just a small fire caused by lightning strikes, but we had to put it out before it spread. It was on steep ground and there wasn't any water nearby, so we had to bring water in a bladder bag by helicopter.

A crew of Indians from D'Arcy were brought in to work on the fire and we got it completely out but left some hand tools there for someone to go back and inspect the fire. When the crew left, Yves LaForest, a coworker, and I went back to Pemberton and got ready to inspect another fire that the same crew had put out the day before. After checking out the other fire down Lillooet Lake Road, I drove back to Squamish and got in at ten o'clock in the evening. I had worked two long days but was happy for the overtime.

I was on standby again that weekend and finally bought my car. I finished my acne medication and it went away, but my face was still red. Jennifer got into an argument with one of the cooks because she wasn't being treated fairly, so she walked off the job. She went back to work for the janitorial services and applied for a job cooking at the Dairy Queen, got hired a week later, and was now working at two jobs again.

I continued doing my regular work and made an appointment to see Dr. Friedenburg on Friday but was asked to work on a fire for the weekend. The fire was on a logging setting where most of the fallen timber was burned and had spread into the standing timber where we had to put out hot spots. We worked on the hot spots then waited around to see if more of them would flare up. It was a rather quiet day, so we quit early so the crew could make it to the bank. We left early the next day; flew over the timber, checking for hot spots; put them out; then sat around, flying around every two hours looking for hot spots. Around three o'clock, people started thinking about heading back to town; but an hour later, hot spots started flaring up, so they had to be put out right away or they could flare up, spread, and start a major forest fire. It was rather late in the afternoon, so we didn't get back until nine o'clock that night.

The weather started cooling off and rain helped lower the fire hazard, so I continued doing my regular work and being available to help Jennifer if she needed me. The Labour Day long weekend was coming and I couldn't go anywhere because my money hadn't gone in, so I just stayed home for the weekend. Jennifer called and said she was tired of being scared of Aaron. I was happy about that because I thought she was getting better. After the weekend, I was only allowed to work two days because I had accumulated too many hours and had to take time off, so I saw Dr. Friedenburg again and went on standby again for the weekend. Jennifer stopped by and said she was getting tired of her relationship with Aaron because it was all give and no take.

While waiting in Dr. Friedenburg's office, I read a magazine article by an East Indian about living in Merritt. He mentioned it was bad for fighting with the Indians, but I was living in Merritt when it started. The East Indians picked fights with the Indians, so the Indians retaliated and fought back. Many years later, I learned the East Indians were very bitter about the way they were treated by the British, so they picked fights with the Indians like we had something to do with it. They didn't realize that we were also colonized by the British and weren't treated any better than they were.

I kept trying to get Jennifer to see a sexual-abuse therapist, but she insisted on seeing one of Hubert's ex-coworkers. I kept calling them; but usually they were out of town, on holidays, or just didn't have time to see her. Finally, in the second week of September, Kerri Mackenzie called and said he would be away for a week but I could call him on the weekend. I was happy to finally be able to talk to him and hoped Jennifer could finish her therapy. I called Kerri as soon as I could, but he wasn't seeing any new patients because he was traveling too much and couldn't see people on a regular basis, so I told him Jennifer had been one of Hubert's patients and was almost finished her therapy; so he said he would call her later.

The next day, Ryan called and said their father was in the hospital because he fell and broke his hip and couldn't take medication for pain because his heart was too weak. When the weekend came, we went to Sto:lo Eagle and took Jennifer's mother to the hospital to visit him. We came back to Squamish and Jennifer was extremely depressed over how her father was doing. We worked the week then went back to Sto:lo Eagle because Jennifer wanted to see her father again.

I was on annual leave that week, so I didn't take Jennifer back to work until Monday morning. The next evening, Kerri called and said he could see Jennifer the following Saturday. He was on the verge of closing down his office, so he could only see Jennifer for one appointment. I hoped Jennifer could finish her therapy, but he just didn't have time for it. We went to the appointment then went to Sto:lo Eagle and visited Henry in the hospital the next day. I had to outright tell him that the issue between us was that I didn't like the way he treated me when he knew I literally went through hell to save his daughter from suicide, then he glared at me when I told him he sure didn't mooch off Alvin and make life miserable for him.

I drove Jennifer and her mother back to Sto:lo Eagle then went to Rosedale to visit my family. I spent the night at David's, and he thought I was turning into an alcoholic; but I told him I spent many years babysitting him and staying home studying while everyone else was out having fun, so now I'm making up for what I didn't do. Many people could see I was treated differently from everyone else.

It was Thanksgiving weekend, so after I got back to work, I had to stay in the office for two days for a course. I was falling behind on my fieldwork and knew I would have to work extra hard now. I called a contractor and told him I would meet him out on the job site Thursday morning, but when I got up, my back was so sore I could barely put my socks on. I thought it would go away; but when I got to the office, I couldn't bend over, so I called Jennifer to book an appointment with the doctor for me. And I wanted to be at the start-up of another contract, but she told me just to take time off. When I went to visit her, she looked at my back and thought it was rather bad.

I went to the doctor that afternoon as soon as I could get in, and he gave me some medication and sent me for physiotherapy. I missed work again the next day because of my back and stayed home all weekend. I was getting bored with drinking, so I didn't drink that weekend. Since I hurt my back, I just went to the office and tried to keep myself busy with office work. The fertilization contract was supposed to start early that week, but there was too much fog. A new girl started in the office and was paid by her Indian band to work there and learn about forestry, so I took her out to one of my spacing contracts with me one day because I wanted to get out of the office. When we got there, we walked along a road to see how my back would take it; but it started to hurt, so I thought I better now take any chances and make it worse.

The fertilization contract started the next day and I wasn't sure how to monitor it properly except watch them from a distance and was scared of injuring my back again, so I didn't want to walk around in the woods and hoped that filling out daily reports at the end of the contract would be enough. Henry Jr. called that night and said their father wasn't expected to live through the night, so I gave Jennifer $50 and my car and told her to drive to Chilliwack. Henry died the next day at 10:40 a.m., but I had to work until Monday night before anyone would be available to take my place. Jennifer called and said the funeral would be on Wednesday, so I told Dairy Queen that Jennifer would be away for a week.

I left a note on Steve's desk Monday morning, worked all day, and tried to get back early enough to show whomever was going to take my place what to do. I walked home that night and caught the earliest bus to Chilliwack the next day. Jennifer met me at the bus depot and said she was so tired she had to turn on the air-conditioning to stay awake. She still had to get flowers and try to get back to Sto:lo Eagle by four thirty when her dad would be brought home. We rushed around to all the florist shops until she finally decided what to buy, then we went to Sto:lo Eagle. She fell asleep on the way back, so I took my time and drove slowly so she could get as much sleep as possible. When we got to Sto:lo Eagle, there were people in the yard but, fortunately, not very many cars. We went inside and sat around for a little while then started preparing for supper and prayers. Everyone ate. Then a priest and some nuns went in and said prayers, and Jennifer told me where I could sleep, so I went to bed; but she stayed up all night talking to her brothers. Since there wasn't a church on the reserve, funeral services were held in the smokehouse. I was surprised at how many people were there, but many people knew him from helping out at canoe races and attending Indian dances.

It was raining rather hard that day, and Jennifer's mother rode with us in my car, so it was a good idea I bought a car instead of another truck since my car was needed for her family. One of the pallbearers couldn't make it, so my cousin Sidney was a pallbearer; but not one of his son-in-laws would be his pallbearer, and Sid seemed rather surprised because he knew me all my life and he's never ever seen me get mad. Alvin and Ben stayed in Ben's van, and I got out and took pictures but wouldn't offer to help with the burial. After the burial, everyone went back to the smokehouse for the dinner. Jennifer sat with other members of her family, and I sat on the benches with one of my cousins. Usually after funeral dinners, people get up and talk about the person who passed away, and when it was over, we went back to the house and I waited around for a few hours then drove back to Squamish. I had to finish the fertilization contract and go back and pick Jennifer up on the weekend.

I drove to Pemberton the next morning and worked on the fertilization contract. Every method of monitoring the rate of spread I tried previously didn't seem to work, so I just resigned myself to watching them from a distance to make sure they were doing everything properly. It was Thursday, and the fertilization wouldn't be completed until Sunday. On Saturday there wasn't much work left to do, so I left that night and drove to Sto:lo Eagle because I didn't think it was that necessary for me to stay.

I spent the night in Sto:lo Eagle, then we drove back to Squamish the next day. We both went to work on Monday, but Jennifer almost cracked up over losing her dad, so I took her to the doctor the next day. The doctor said she was reacting to this in a normal way but suggested she take two weeks off work.

A farmer in Pemberton complained about fertilizing a block where a creek flowed into his water license, which watered his livestock. Stephen DeMelt got concerned about it and asked for my documentation of the contract work, but I didn't document anything, and the contractor had all the papers. Not only that, I didn't monitor them on the last day. He got really mad at me and asked me to sign my performance management plan review stating that I didn't do my job properly and could get terminated. He knew I was on Prozac and got word that I was often in the bar in Pemberton until closing time, but luckily, he decided to put me on probation instead because I volunteered a weekend of my own time to help out with National Forest Week.

I felt like a born loser in life again! I had tried so hard to do something with my life, overcame many obstacles I wouldn't wish on anyone, and now I could lose a job I loved at my age. I felt extremely slow and tired all the time even though I had been going to bed at nine o'clock in the evenings and had an appointment with Dr. Friedenburg that Friday, so I took the day off and showed him the first two chapters of my writings. My back was still sore, so I had to get back to Squamish right away to see the doctor. Jennifer wanted to go back to Sto:lo Eagle that weekend but changed her mind, and I realized that alcohol was slowing me down, so I had to quit drinking if I wanted to keep my job. I was very close to becoming an alcoholic. I continued working and tried to improve my job performance. Jennifer was feeling extremely stressed out and wanted to move to Sto:lo Eagle to be with her mother, so she borrowed $20 off me to go to the bar, and the next day she said a fellow she was talking to in the bar talked her out of moving back to Sto:lo Eagle. She went to the doctor again, and he said the same thing and told her not to quit her job.

There was a very early snowfall that year, so we couldn't accomplish all our goals. I did as much as I could in spite of the snow then settled down to office work. On Friday, Jennifer didn't make it to work and thought she could be fired, but I called Dairy Queen and straightened it out. Jennifer felt down again on Monday, but I called her and told her to go to work because people were depending on her. Then on the first weekend in December, Jennifer and I went to Sto:lo Eagle to take her mother Christmas shopping. I missed the cargo space in a truck, but the passengers were more comfortable.

I continued training in karate, working in the office, staying off alcohol, and felt better now that I quit drinking and taking medication at the same time. After I quit drinking, I started going out for coffee on weekends. When I was drinking, all I was doing was staying home, not going anywhere or doing anything, just wasting my life away by staying home all the time.

Jennifer wasn't able to work steadily after her dad died, and had trouble paying her rent; and she thought she could get evicted, but

Aaron talked to the landlady and straightened everything out. I started my two weeks' annual leave and wanted to go to Rosedale, but Jennifer wanted me to stay in Squamish. I called home one day, and Tony wanted him and me to take Dad hunting for a few days in Merritt, but I ended up staying in Squamish. Jennifer was asked how much time she wanted off at Christmas, so I suggested she only take the day after Boxing Day off; she agreed but later changed her mind and took the whole week off between Christmas and New Year.

I ended up staying in Squamish all week, and on Friday night, Jennifer called me from the hospital because someone slammed her hand in a car door. I got scared she may not make it back to work because it could take her a long time to heal because she was often slow to heal when she got injured. We finished Christmas shopping the next day and drove to Sto:lo Eagle. I didn't want to stay there for Christmas, but Jennifer said I should because her dad died and it could make her mother feel better, so I stayed. Christmas was rather uneventful, and we had the usual dinner and opened presents.

The next day I went to Rosedale to visit my family, and my cousin Richard was there. Everyone was over visiting by then, so I mainly stayed at my parents' place. I only stayed two days and wanted to stay longer, but Jennifer was worried about the things in her apartment, so I went back to Sto:lo Eagle. She said Aaron called that day and was going to a treatment center to get off cocaine, so she was worried about the things in her apartment. We bought another turkey, cooked it the next day, then came back to Squamish; and Henry Jr. appeared to be getting cranky and seemed to feel better that we were leaving. Jennifer said she was glad she didn't quit her job and move back to Sto:lo Eagle now. I didn't really want to go back that soon, but I went anyway. I was getting bored and wanted to go back to work; now that I quit drinking, New Year's Eve was uneventful for me even though I hardly ever did anything on New Year's Eve.

Chapter 17

1995

Jennifer spent the night at my place before she went back to work, and I couldn't sleep, so I turned the light on and read until I was tired enough to go to sleep. The next day she was cranky because she was kept awake by me reading. I thought this was an indication she was getting better because before she couldn't sleep in the dark; now she can't sleep with the light on. I called the counsellors at Mental Health to see if Jennifer could start seeing someone for counselling, but they were fully booked; and Aaron called Jennifer from the treatment center Victoria Life Enrichment Society (VLES). I continued seeing Dr. Friedenburg every two weeks and was worried about losing my job. Now I had a new car to pay for and still owed much money on my credit cards, but I signed up for karate anyway. I knew I had to do something constructive to release my tensions and was feeling like a loser again.

When Aaron got out of the treatment center, Jennifer threatened suicide, so he had the cops take her to the hospital. It was a Friday night, and she called me the next day to pick her up at the hospital. When I picked her up, the hospital staff wanted her to stay there and talk to a doctor; but she left anyway, so I made an appointment for her to see a doctor on Monday and went with her. Then after work, I took her to see a priest because she felt guilty about being mad at her father, but the priest told her anger is a natural defense mechanism.

Jennifer almost cracked up again the next day, so I called Mental Health and made an appointment for her and left work at two forty-five to take her to the doctor and to the psychiatric ward at Lions

Gate Hospital in North Vancouver. I thought she would be in there for two weeks and I would have to pay her rent again, which stressed me out, but fortunately, she called me the next day and said she was ready to go out; she just had to see a counsellor and wrote a letter to her dad then started feeling better. She said she felt his presence and how he fought to the bitter end, and the doctors were surprised he lived that long, and that made her determined to get better. Now she wanted to go home. I told her to wait until tomorrow because I had to see Dr. Friedenburg anyway, so I picked her up the next day then went to karate in the evening. I noticed my back was sore and I couldn't bend over as far as I usually could.

On the weekend, I went to the staff curling bonspiel and to the dinner and dance in the evening and left right after the gift exchange because my back was getting stiff. My back felt even worse the next day, but I tried to ignore and hide it. Jennifer and I did our laundry, and she was really crabby toward me; but at the end of the day, she saw my right shoulder sagging and realized I had a bad back. When I woke up the next day, I could barely bend over to put my socks on. I felt okay lying down; but when I tried to get up, my back felt incredibly sore, so I called in sick and made a doctor's appointment. I couldn't get in until four o'clock and could barely walk around the house, but Jennifer's crutches were there. I used them to walk around but thought if I fell, I may not be able to get back up. I went to the doctor, and Jennifer met me there. She got my prescription filled out then drove me home. I also got medication for my acne and was told I had a pinched nerve in my back. The next day I had to find out how I could move without feeling any pain and Jennifer thought I should go to the hospital because she wasn't available to look after me.

I ended up missing two weeks of work and still worried about losing my job; then I started thinking ahead and realized that if I lost my job, I could move back to Chilliwack and get Jennifer a career. Then I would look around for other opportunities to do something with my life. After two weeks, my back was still sore, but I went back to work anyway. While preparing our silviculture plans, I knew where much of the work had already been done and the conditions of many roads, which really saved time in planning; and Stephen DeMelt realized it's lucky he didn't let me go.

Jennifer eventually got word that her daughter, Roberta, was in an alcohol treatment center in Calgary, Alberta, and thought she developed a drinking problem because she was depressed that her natural mother didn't try to contact her; so Jennifer called the treatment center, but they wouldn't let her talk to her. I called Brenda for Roberta's address, but Brenda got mad at me and wanted Jennifer to agree that I write to Roberta first. Then I wrote this letter but didn't mail it until a week later because I wanted Jennifer to read it first; she read it and said it was okay, so I sent it.

> Dear Roberta:
>
> I guess I should have written to you sooner and told you about your mother, but I wasn't sure how much she would want me to say. Not only that, I was suffering from a chemical imbalance caused by stress and have been taking Prozac for over a year and a half.
>
> I hope you're not mad at your mother for not writing to you, because she's still mixed up and going through a hard time. She's had a very difficult life, but she's getting better. I also had a very hard life and went through hell to get a career because of the way the Indians were treated. Fortunately, I got stronger because of it and it prepared me for what was coming, looking after your mother.
>
> When I first met your mother in 1980, she was such a nervous wreck everyone thought she was beyond recovery. I sometimes thought so myself, but all I could do was keep trying to make her feel better about herself and trying to help her out. Obviously she wasn't beyond recovery because she's still here. Now she's cooking at the Dairy Queen and had a place of her own, but I still do what I can to help her survive.
>
> Jennifer started going for therapy in March of 1990 and went for three and a half years. Unfortunately, her therapist moved to Alberta before your mother finished her therapy, and we haven't heard from him since. I tried to get her to see other therapists, but she wanted to see his ex-coworkers. I tried to arrange for her to see Hubert Smith's ex-coworkers,

but they were in the process of closing down their offices and weren't taking any new patients.

Jennifer tried to see counsellors at the Department of Mental Health here in town, but she was always just put on hold. Finally, this year she ended up in the psychiatric ward in North Vancouver for a couple of days and they started treating her.

I'm in the process of writing an autobiography on what your mother and I went through. If no one beats me to the title, I'm going to call it *Almost a Born Loser!* I know how I want to end the book, so I'm waiting for these events to happen. Jennifer could probably write a book on how things were for her, but we agreed not to read each other's writing without permission.

Most people know me as Baxter Aleck, but my real name is Annis Aleck. If my book gets printed before you meet your real mother, you'll know she was the victim in it. If you wish to write back to me or ask me anything, my address is there. I hope you start feeling better about yourself and don't feel angry that your mother hasn't tried to contact you.

From
Baxter (Annis) Aleck

We had a violence-and-harassment workshop at work, and everyone in the office had to schedule a time to attend. When the instructors asked for reasons why people don't report sexual harassment, I said to the fellow next to me, "It could be the boss's favorite doing the harassing, so people would hesitate to report it. Why don't you tell them?"

He just said, "It's your idea! Why don't you tell them yourself!" So I ended up telling them myself. At the end of the session, we were asked to write our comments on a Post-it, so I wrote, "Sexual harassment against the males could be more than what's reported." I never thought of males sexually harassing other males though.

I was told what the goals were for the year, so I set up my contracts accordingly; and the plans kept changing, so I kept changing my contract packages. After changing my contract packages several times, the plan was finalized and we were only spacing one hundred hectares that year. I was tired of changing my contracts, so I chose to just space one block and save work. Then Mike Fidgeon, the silviculture planner, asked if it was a high-priority block; but I forgot to check. After the fertilization contract was finally approved, the block I chose for spacing fit in perfectly with fertilization. To do things properly, a block should be spaced just before fertilizing, then we gain maximum benefit. Jennifer went out to the bars one night because she said Aaron was too controlling and it was stressing her out. It looked like she was getting better, and she talked about moving away and getting another apartment. Jennifer got a note from her doctor in April for her to go to a treatment center, VLES in Victoria, the same treatment center Aaron went to. She wanted to go in on April 23, so I checked with Darlene, her counsellor from Mental Health; but Darlene said the paperwork wasn't completed, so she may not go until May. One of my cousins had just passed away, but I missed the funeral because I flipped a coin and it said "Don't go." Luckily, I didn't go because I had to help get the forms filled out, but they couldn't be sent out until next week. Aaron had gone back to Vancouver Island, so I looked after Jennifer all weekend. I missed another day of work because of a sore back, and the doctor told me to start going off Prozac and only take one pill every two days.

Jennifer decided she wanted a better guitar, so I put a down payment on one for her birthday. We went to Sto:lo Eagle that night and I went to Rosedale the next day. I felt okay until I got there then realized how stressed out I was, so I bought a case of beer and drank it all that night. I went to karate when I got back to Squamish but left after an hour because my leg hurt too much. I still felt stressed out, so I bought a bottle of whiskey for the first time in years.

Jennifer got accepted at VLES, so Aaron made arrangements to get her a ride from Nanaimo to Victoria, and the next day, she called because she was worried about funding and didn't really think she should be there. I called Mental Health as soon as I could and funding for her was arranged; then I also ended up seeing Darlene as a patient. After the first week, Jennifer called and said the program was very good and I should go there too. I continued seeing Darlene every two weeks, and after two weeks, Jennifer came back to Squamish for the weekend and said she learned over here that she's too dependent on other people. She was getting better, and we went out for coffee; then I drove her to Tsawwassen Ferry Terminal the next day to catch the ferry back to Victoria.

In the middle of the week, my back was hurting again, so I could barely tie my shoes. So I drank that night then drank again the next night because drinking seemed to relieve some of the pain. Jennifer went back from VLES the next day, and we went to Sto:lo Eagle the day after she got back. She finished the program at VLES and started seeing an AA counsellor. I went to Rosedale to help Isaac with my niece's birthday party and didn't drink. All my nieces were happy to see me because I hardly ever went back to Rosedale and they know it's because of the way everyone treats me.

I was still having trouble with my back and woke up at three o'clock one morning and couldn't sleep, so I worked on my writing; writing seemed to make the pain go away for a little while, but it usually came back. I often felt tired most of the time and often slept at lunchtime, then I somehow pulled a muscle in my groin, so I missed some karate. Hubert called me at work one day, but I missed the call and he didn't leave a return number. I finally finished rewriting my life story to the end of 1994 but couldn't start typing it because my typewriter wasn't working.

Geraldine called one weekend and said Roberta was going to meet her in Laughing Raven, which got Jennifer all excited and stressed out because they could only stop for an hour. Jennifer didn't want to miss any time seeing her and stressed me out driving to Laughing Raven, but when we got there, Roberta hadn't arrived yet and Ryan and Desiree were also there to meet her. Then I saw a white car going down the road. I knew it was her, so we went outside to meet her; she asked me if I was Ben's brother, but I said, "No, I'm Baxter." She got the letter I sent her. I just sat in the living room while Jennifer and Geraldine talked to Roberta and her adopted parents; since she would only be there a short time, I thought Jennifer should talk to her.

I continued taking Prozac and finally went off it at the end of June. Jennifer was having health problems and often went to North Vancouver to see a specialist, so on one trip I got Aaron to drop my typewriter off at a repair shop. Jennifer and I both continued seeing Darlene for counselling, but I still felt incredible stress. Stress got so bad my teeth started to ache, so I drank two nights in a row then started editing and typing my writing.

Near the end of July, Jennifer told me Harold, a fellow from Laughing Raven, committed suicide by jumping in a river and they couldn't find the body. Jennifer also told me how Aaron treated her, and I thought, *That's how she treated me, and now it's happening back to her. I hope she learns to start treating me better.*" Jennifer also told me Brenda called when she was drunk and threatened suicide; this all stressed me out, so I went out for a few beers in the evening.

In early August I finally realized the source of much of my stress was holding on to anger from past injustices. I knew they suffered for what they did wrong, so it was time to forgive them; then I started feeling better. I decided I should slow down on drinking now that my stress level was going down; but a week later, I felt stressed out again, so I missed karate and drank. I went to the bars the next night and ended up drinking most of the weekend with a couple from Squamish. His wife was from a reserve near Hope and she knew my dad when he was still single. I drank most of the weekend, but by Sunday I decided I had enough and walked home. When I got home, Jennifer said she got worried about me because she didn't know where I was and if I was all right, so she took my car to Vancouver and bought some cocaine. After talking to me, she said she was going to quit coke and drinking but called me at five o'clock in the morning for the next two days.

I realized stress was affecting my work, and I had already considered going back on Prozac, but I just relaxed and tried to get more sleep. When the weekend came, I decided to just stay home, relax, and watch TV for the night. Later on, a neighbour went over and asked to use my phone. She left; then her twin sister, who lived downstairs, and two other girls went to visit. They left, then I drove one of the girls and her young son home. Later on, Lois went back and I slept with her without a condom. We both made sure neither of us had HIV, but it was still a disappointing experience to me. The next day, Jennifer got mad at me for going out with her and threatened suicide, but she calmed down eventually. She said I should have used a condom, because she worried about me, and was going to move back in two weeks. That night she borrowed $20 off me and went to the bars. Her shoulder was hurting, but when she drank, the pain went away, so I told her she needed to do more writing; but she said she couldn't seem to do it with Aaron there.

I mostly just stayed home that weekend, went out for coffee, baked cookies, and did laundry. I tried to relax so I would do better at work, but when I got back to work, I was stressed out by three thirty. I couldn't think, so I went out to the woods to check roads that were to be opened. The roads were more brushed in than we expected, so I had a machine brought in to open up the roads. I had to be out there to monitor the machine while it was working, and I was glad to be where I didn't have to do any thinking and could sleep off and on. The stress I was feeling was incredible, so I was glad the road opening lasted four days. It was close to the end of August now and I still felt incredible stress for some reason. I often went to bed early and still felt slow and tired the next day and didn't know what to do about it. I felt that way through much of September and wished I had booked my holidays earlier. I still saw Darlene every two weeks but was too stressed out to do any writing and often slept most of the day on my days off and still felt tired.

Lois called on my buzzer late one night and asked if I wanted company, but I told her I was too tired. She rang the buzzer again later that night, but I didn't answer because I felt I still had to look after Jennifer. The next day I drank a few beers then went out for breakfast, but Jennifer called before I left and said she wanted to leave town. I told her she should work on her problems first because she may just end up putting herself in a worse situation. I told her about Lois calling then slowed down on drinking but couldn't seem to do any writing yet. The next day I finally felt well enough to vacuum my apartment but still couldn't seem to do any writing. That night I drank a six-pack and barely felt anything. Finally, by the end of September, I started feeling better. I was still tired most of the time and usually slept at lunchtime, and after work, I started feeling better now but decided to wait before I did any writing so I didn't make too many mistakes.

I finally decided to go to the doctor by the third week of September, but he was booked up. I felt stressed out again but didn't drink very much because my body started rejecting it. Lois tried going by at one thirty in the morning, but I was too tired; she always went by late at night. I didn't drink the next day because I wasn't stressed out but still couldn't do any writing, so I just started reading books. The next day, I helped Jennifer do her laundry, relaxed, and read all day. By the middle of the week, I started feeling stressed out again, so I bought a six-pack and a bottle of whiskey and drank some of the whiskey and five cans of beer that night. I felt incredibly stressed out again the next day and could hardly wait to get off work, so I could drink again. I worked long hours that day and got everything done, so now I would have two days off.

I took Jennifer out for lunch the next day and stayed sober for karate. I sort of got interested in a few girls, but they had boyfriends, and I realized I still had to look after Jennifer. I decided not to look for anyone and finally started feeling well enough to start writing. I think my instincts are telling me to stay single, but it doesn't bother me because I'm used to it. Jennifer went over to visit on the weekend and was really cranky. She wanted to get a new place to stay but couldn't find one; then finally, around noon, we went to Vancouver to do some shopping. I tried to go to a boxing tournament in the evening, but it was postponed; and Brenda Billy, my neighbour, borrowed the money off me. I finished typing chapter 4 the next day and found writing exhausting. I seemed to get hungrier writing than working out in the woods and sometimes felt burnt out and tired after typing only two pages.

My holidays were coming up and I was getting stressed out and drinking. At the end of the week, I was tired when I got home and didn't feel like cooking, so I was glad Brenda Billy asked me over for supper. After eating, I drove her to the liquor store and she bought me a six-pack, so I drank a few beers with her and her sister; then she started coming close to me. She invited me downstairs, but I told her to go to my place, but she went home and passed out.

I was on my holidays now and Jennifer was crabby and threatening suicide, so I decided not to go to Rosedale until Tuesday morning. Eventually she started feeling better, and I told her things could be happening to her because of the way she treats me. I drank with Brenda again that night but hoped she wouldn't get interested in me because I knew she had a very hard life and a drinking problem because of it. I didn't want to be a rescuer again. I stayed in Squamish for karate again then went to Rosedale to visit, helped take my nieces to Abbotsford swimming, then to Sumas to buy dancing shoes for their classes. I hardly ever see them, so they enjoyed spending time with me, and I left around three o'clock the next day so I could go to karate again.

I also had an appointment with Darlene, and she said Jennifer will have to learn to draw boundaries because moving out of town or kicking Aaron out isn't the answer, as she could end up with someone worse. I was finally able to see the doctor and found out I also had beaver fever from drinking contaminated water; that's why

I felt tired all the time. I was going to take Jennifer to Sto:lo Eagle that night; but we stayed in Squamish, went to Bellingham the next day, then to Laughing Raven. Jennifer and Geraldine drank most of the day, then I drove them to Sto:lo Eagle that night. Jennifer wanted me to stay the night, but Geraldine told her I have to visit my family too. Thanksgiving dinner was pretty good the next day; but on the way back to Squamish, Jennifer got stressed out about going back because of Aaron, so I told her I would help her find a new place to stay.

I didn't intend to drink the next weekend, but Jennifer's depression was rubbing off on me. She borrowed some money off me again, so I had a few drinks. That night she tried to buy some coke for Aaron, but the two fellows just took her money and ran off. She chased after them and fell on the sidewalk, hurting her wrist and knees. The next day, I took her to the hospital emergency ward and now she couldn't work and the doctor asked her and me about drinking. I talked to her boss, Janelle Smith, at the Dairy Queen and told her a little bit about Jennifer's history of depression and her problems then told her about Hubert giving us his home phone number and opening his office on Thanksgiving Day for her. Then Janelle said she wanted to talk to Jennifer at four o'clock.

Jennifer now stood up to Aaron and told him to stay off cocaine (coke) or she'll move out. She was learning to draw boundaries now. I wanted to leave early the next day for Rosedale but waited for Jennifer. Finally, around three thirty, she decided not to go to Sto:lo Eagle; so I went to Rosedale. The next day, I went to Sumas with my mother to visit my aunt from San Diego. They played pull tabs and I got bored with it, so I drank a few beers. I took the next day off work to visit with my aunt but came back to Squamish for karate. When I got back, Jennifer was worried because Aaron owed the coke dealers $200, so I loaned her the money. She said she'd pay me back and asked me not to give up on her. I knew she was getting stronger because I could feel her moods, and I was getting over the urge to drink.

Toward the end of the week, I felt tired and didn't feel like going out the woods; but I flipped a coin and it said to go, so I went. When I got out there, I found an excavator working near where we had to open some ditches, so I made arrangements for the machine operator to do some work for us the next day. Luckily, I did what the coin told me to do. At the end of the week, I felt burnt out, so I went home and drank. On Sunday, Jennifer said she did some cocaine the night before and I got scared for her and suggested she move back to my place even though she drove me crazy. Her wrist was still too sore to go to work, and she thought about moving into the apartment down the hall from her place if it became available.

At the end of the week, I took Friday afternoon off but didn't do any writing. I often felt tired in the afternoon, but I did my grocery shopping and Jennifer and her friend Vern went over to visit in the evening. The next day I started getting bored with staying home; so Jennifer, Vern, and I went to North Vancouver to shop around. I bought Jennifer some vitamins from a health-food store, hoping it would help heal her wrist so she could go back to work on Monday. I didn't drink that night because I wasn't stressed out, woke up rather early the next day and did some writing, then took Jennifer out for coffee. I brought her back home, did some more writing, and wanted to watch the football semi-final games; but she called me back to go for a drive. We didn't go very far though, and she didn't cry or scream, and realized she may have been holding too much pain in that's why she was always getting hurt.

Jennifer went back to work on Monday, and on Tuesday she bought me a great big ice-cream cake because it was my birthday. I was now forty years old. Very often after work, I would feel like having a few beers; but I would just have cake and coffee, sleep for an hour or two, then I would feel better and not want a drink. The next weekend, Jennifer said Aaron wanted to marry her if he could get his act together by the end of the year. She said she couldn't say no to him, so she agreed but thought their relationship may not last long as far as she was concerned. I still like the single life, but I guess I should look for someone unless Jennifer still needs my help.

I still felt tired most of the time and usually went to sleep at lunchtime and after work. Sometimes I wished for a beer after work but usually got over it after having a piece of cake then going to sleep for a little while. This went on until I almost finished the cake then Jennifer threw the rest of it out because she said it was going stale. At the end of the week, I drank with Brenda and her sister again, and Jennifer got mad at me for doing it; then she tried to buy some coke, but luckily, the drug dealer wouldn't sell her any. We went to Bellingham on Saturday and I bought her some boots, spent the day shopping around, and spent the night at my place.

I told Jennifer about a cooking course being offered in Squamish, and she was interested in taking it, but it was only available to UIC recipients. But people couldn't quit their present job to go on UIC to take the course. I still sometimes buy her groceries because I can't see her going hungry, which probably still feels normal to her. She went to work one day then went home because she was worried about Aaron. She told him she was moving out, so he said he called the building inspector; and she got worried about that too, so I told her to call me from now on rather than go home from work and I'll try and help her out. I'm finally learning to relax and not worry so much about my bills. I went to the bar one day because life is today. I'm paying for yesterday and saving for the future.

Jennifer still wanted to leave town and thought about training for a career, so I looked into it for her. I told her quitting her job and leaving town weren't the answers; she had to work on the cause so she wouldn't put herself back in the same situation. She wanted to get into the cooking course, so I called her band to see if she could get funded through them. Capilano College called her and said she couldn't take the course, but she asked if she could get accepted if she could get funding from her band, so her name wasn't taken off the list.

When I started my annual leave, Jennifer and I took Aaron to a detox (detoxification) center in Vancouver then went Christmas shopping. The next day, Jennifer said she felt empty inside because she really missed Aaron even though he drove her crazy. We looked at the book *Women Who Love Too Much*, decided to buy it, then Jennifer bought a notebook and pens and brought them to Aaron at the detox center so he could write out his feelings. I wanted to go to Rosedale and visit but stayed in Squamish to try and get Jennifer into the cooking course. I worked on my writing in the meantime and writing seemed to be getting easier, and the next day, her band called and said they didn't have money for her to take the course.

Jennifer had an appointment with the specialist in North Vancouver toward the end of the week, so I drove her there and picked Aaron up from the detox center. The next day we drove Aaron to Horseshoe Bay so he could go to Qualicum to his parents' place for Christmas. He wanted to leave Squamish right away to avoid the temptation to drink again, and Jennifer and I went to Sto:lo Eagle that night. The next day we took her mother shopping in Chilliwack and I spent the night in Sto:lo Eagle. Jennifer and I went shopping in Chilliwack again the next day, then I took her to Sto:lo Eagle then went back to Rosedale. I didn't like going to Sto:lo Eagle very much because Henry Jr. was starting to make me feel unwelcome.

Christmas was okay, and I didn't drink because I didn't feel stressed out; normally, I drank heavily on Christmas Day because of stress. The day after Christmas, I just played cards and didn't drink; then the next day, I finally went back to Sto:lo Eagle and Henry Jr. was sick, so Jennifer and I came back to Squamish. She wanted to go to her own place but fell asleep, so I just let her sleep at my place. The next day, we just lazed around and I bought her $100 worth of groceries. She went home and cooked a large pot of chicken soup and was going to give me some; but she had too many visitors, who all had a bowl of soup, so there wasn't any left.

Toward the end of the week, we went to North Vancouver to do some shopping then decided to go to Sto:lo Eagle; but on our way there, we decided to go to Laughing Raven, so we only stayed in Sto:lo Eagle for a few minutes then left. When we got to Laughing Raven, Ben was sleeping, and I wasn't stressed out but drank a few beers anyway. Geraldine wanted to go the flea market the next day, but it was closed; she bought some beer, but Jennifer and I didn't buy any or drink that night even though it was New Year's Eve. Nothing eventful happened that night, and I was getting restless and anxious to go back to work.

Chapter 18

1996

Geraldine was tired from drinking the night before, and I got up and had coffee with Ben and one of my cousins. My holidays weren't too bad, but I didn't get to do very much that I wanted to do. When we got back to Squamish, Jennifer was scared to go home and realized her problems but had a hard time working on them. Then I finally realized that if I got any of the jobs I applied for after leaving Corrections, I wouldn't have had time to take her to therapy. I signed up for karate again; but one night after karate, Jennifer stressed me out, so I drank when I got home. I went in the staff curling bonspiel again and had fun while Jennifer drank in the bar all day. The next day we shopped around North and West Vancouver and she started feeling better. I thought about coaching minor baseball that year because I like kids and told a fellow at the karate club because he's involved in coaching sports, but he never called me back.

I drove to North Vancouver one weekend to get a new typewriter ribbon and my green belt for karate and dropped Aaron off at Horseshoe Bay because he wanted some time to get his act together. Jennifer called me at three o'clock the next morning to borrow some money because she wanted to buy some beer, but the next day she said she bought cocaine because she was depressed over Aaron leaving. She thought he wanted to break up with her, and I told her it may be because she was getting stronger and he was losing control of her. She drank a few days later and was late for work the next day; now she's admitting she had a drinking problem and it's the first drink that gets her drunk, like she was told at AA meetings. Jennifer wondered why Aaron wanted to go back to the island so fast and if he was seeing someone else. On the weekend we shopped around North Vancouver, Richmond, New Westminister, and Guildford before going to Sto:lo Eagle.

Jennifer was extremely depressed, so she laid some flowers on her father's grave the next day and cried with grief at first then with anger like he was molesting her, crying, "Why! Why are you doing this to me!" After that we went to Hope but couldn't buy flowers anywhere, so we went to Lytton and cleaned off Liz and Jeremy's grave. We did laundry in Chilliwack on our way back and got into an argument over her doing a workout when she got home because I knew it would be late then went out for Chinese food, so she had a couple of beers with her meal. After I got back to work, I didn't feel tired and sleepy at lunchtime for the first time since September but felt stressed out in the evening, so I drank a six-pack after karate.

I drove Jennifer to Horseshoe Bay the next day and loaned her $30 so she could see Aaron in Qualicum, stayed home most of the day, then went to a going-away party for a staff member. I stayed home again the next day, waiting for Jennifer to call, but she didn't call until nine thirty in the evening. I picked her up at Horseshoe Bay and hoped she would break up with Aaron and find someone more responsible. I felt stressed out again, so I drank a six-pack. In the middle of the week, Jennifer went to the bars then went over at six o'clock in the morning. She had tried to buy some cocaine, but the fellow took her money and didn't go back; but luckily, he did that or she wouldn't have made it to work and probably would have gotten fired. She's admitting alcohol is a problem with her, but she won't do any writing. Alcohol and cocaine are a fast relief from the pain she feels, but she can't seem to focus on the consequences of her actions.

I did some writing and drank a six-pack in the evening the next day, but I wasn't stressed out and was getting tired of drinking. It was a weekend, so I took Jennifer shopping in North Vancouver and Metrotown Mall, but we didn't drink in the evening. We went shopping again in Vancouver the next day, and I started taking medication the doctor recommended from the health-food store. It seemed to work because I felt better than I usually do. I still sleep at lunchtime and often don't realize how tired I was until I wake up. In January I applied for a course in modeling and acting but didn't think anything would come of it; now I got a call for an interview in two weeks and Jennifer strongly recommended I go for it.

I was still seeing Darlene for counselling, and on the weekend, I took Jennifer to Port Alice at the north end of Vancouver Island to see Aaron because he was working there. I didn't want her to travel alone and wanted to see the nearby town of Port McNeill. Port McNeill seemed like a nice town, but I wouldn't want to move there. We left later than I wanted to the next day and it snowed heavily part of the way and we almost missed the last ferry, but my instincts told me things were going to work out.

The next weekend I went to the acting agency for an interview, and it was going to cost $525 for a basic acting course. I was hesitant about taking it because of the cost but decided to take it mainly to build up my confidence and self-esteem. My instincts also told me to take it in Gastown in Vancouver, not Squamish; and it seemed to make me feel better about myself because the next morning, my back wasn't hurting as much as it usually did. My back was still hurting but not enough to feel uncomfortable, and Jennifer said Roberta called and wanted us to go to Whitehorse and visit her, so I phoned Roberta about going up north to visit her. Jennifer got her holiday schedule agreed by her boss, so now we could visit Roberta in June and Brenda and Alvin in October. On the weekend, I drove Jennifer to Sto:lo Eagle, went to Rosedale; then Aaron went back from Port Alice the next day, so we picked him up at Horseshoe Bay.

On Easter weekend, I took Jennifer and Aaron to Laughing Raven, spent the night there, took them to Sto:lo Eagle the next day, then went to Rosedale. We all came back to Squamish Sunday night because Jennifer had to work the next day, and Aaron went over to watch TV and videos because he was evicted from Jennifer's place. In the evening, I gave Jennifer $20 to join baseball, and she asked me to buy her a glove; so I hoped it would help keep her away from drinking by having fun to relieve tension.

At my next appointment with Darlene, I talked about Henry. I told her Henry said Isadore Tom said he was a man without a spirit, but I'm sure he meant he was a man without a conscience. Isadore was an old man and may not have been able to speak English that well. Darlene said he was a sociopath because he couldn't have lived after all the things he did wrong if he had any conscience at all.

I tried to take Jennifer to a steak dinner on her birthday because it was also my fifth year with the Forest Service, but she went out drinking instead. I was going to go to Rosedale for the weekend because I had a new niece born on Jennifer's birthday, but she talked me into staying in Squamish. I also had second thoughts about spending too much time with my family because I would be coming back to Chilliwack for a course. I called Roberta in Whitehorse and told her we may be going up in the last week of June. I went to a three-day course in Chilliwack but spent the nights in Rosedale visiting my family and my new niece. It was an interesting course and I really enjoyed it. I answered half the questions that were asked and was only wrong two times. One fellow there used to be the Chilliwack forest district manager, so I offered to let him answer some questions, but he just let me carry on.

After Jennifer moved out, she sometimes asked me why I didn't find a girlfriend, but I just asked her if she knew anyone interested in me. I helped out with National Forest Week in Whistler again, and at the barbecue, I saw a very nice-looking girl there who was single; but she thought, *I know he's single, but there's something about him saying I should turn him down.* So I didn't try any harder. I believe things happen the way they do for a reason and I rather like the single life.

I started getting sick, so I went to the doctor for medication for my cough and acne because I had severe acne again, and the doctor suggested I quit drinking. I also started rewriting my memoirs for the fourth time but was careful of what I wrote and my spelling. I figured I would end up writing my life story at least four times. Jennifer got depressed again one day, so I had to leave work at ten o'clock because she asked me to take her to the hospital; so I took her there, to the doctor, then to see Darlene. Darlene told her how to tell Aaron to move out, and in the evening I took her for a drive where she cried and screamed for an hour.

I enjoyed taking acting lessons. The other people there were pretty nice; and the instructor told me I was improving and talked me into taking advanced lessons, which I signed up for, but it cost me $725. I missed the last lesson though because I wanted to take Jennifer to Whitehorse to visit her daughter. I called Roberta and her mother said it's okay for us to go up there. We drove to Prince George the first day, and I knew I would miss grading in karate, but it couldn't be helped. That was disappointing because I had trained so hard and only missed three classes since January. We drove to Fort Nelson the next day and spent the night at the Fort Nelson motor inn. It was a long, exhausting drive, but Jennifer got to visit places her father talked about when he went on his annual hunting trips. We arrived in Whitehorse rather late and decided not to visit until the next day and slept in the car, and surprisingly, I slept very well. I had called Roberta from Teslin, and they said she was busy, so I figured she had a boyfriend.

We shopped around most of the day then finally went to see her, but she just went upstairs and said she was busy, so we went to sleep in the TV room. Her stepfather, George, went home for a little while, talked to us, then left; and Jennifer didn't like being ignored after travelling that far, so we left and went for a beer. At dinner we met her boyfriend, and they went to a movie in the evening. Roberta's mother was a social worker, but she talked to us though. We shopped around again and Roberta didn't say very much to us again, but I just thought she's a teenager in love; so that song "A Teenager in Love" kept ringing through my head. We decided to leave the next day, and that night, Sandy and George took us out for a drive sightseeing in Whitehorse and Jennifer told them we would be leaving the next day. Sandy and George took us out for breakfast the next day with Roberta, but she was still rather quiet. Sandy told us she's very shy, but I just thought she's in love. We drove a long ways that day, stopped in Dease Lake for a beer, then drove to Meziadin Junction; and both places had changed tremendously since I was there in 1978. It was late when we got there, so we just slept in the car.

We woke up early the next morning and drove to Kitwanga. Jennifer wanted to go to Terrace, but I told her that would take too long and we had a long ways to travel; and we argued about it, but it was better that we didn't go. We drove to Prince George, got a room, then went for supper. I fell asleep for an hour, then we went for a walk and ran into a fellow who used to cook at Ricky's when Jennifer was there. He said Jennifer's a lot livelier now; back then she was very quiet and withdrawn. Then at about two forty-five in the morning, some lady was pounding on my door, so I thought it was an emergency, but she was looking for someone to sell drugs to. I was the wrong person, so she ran off like a rabbit before I could report her. The next day we shopped around Prince George for a little while before driving back home. Jennifer bought some clothes in Williams Lake and we stopped for a couple of beers in 100 Mile House. Then I bought her some beer to drink on the way home and drank when I got home. I was stressed out, and Jennifer ended up going over. Aaron went over a little while later and spent the night. I drank a few more beers then went to bed.

I felt incredibly stressed out again the next morning; so I had a couple of beers, did some grocery shopping, cooked for Aaron and Jennifer, then went to sleep. I felt like drinking again by supper time, but I ate heavily so I wouldn't feel like drinking. I slept in the next day and felt stressed out but didn't drink. Jennifer said the trip did her a lot of good because it made her want to slow down on drinking. Seeing Roberta and her family in what appeared to be a normal family made her want to slow down on drinking. I also enjoyed the trip, and it made me feel like moving up north. She stressed me out, but watching the movie *Braveheart* made me feel better. I felt rested up now, and it seemed like Jennifer is finally getting better.

A week later I felt stressed out again because the stress of looking after Jennifer was getting bad again. During the week, the three of us went fishing in Whistler; then Aaron took us out for dinner and started drinking, so he suggested Jennifer spend the night at my place. The next day, Aaron asked Jennifer to take him to Horseshoe Bay so he could go to the island, but he changed his mind when he got there. Karate was over for the summer now and Jennifer was stressing me out, so I started drinking more. I tried to slow down, but Jennifer was stressing me out too much. During the week, I went to Vancouver for karate one night and felt better, so I didn't drink. I was still seeing Darlene for counselling every two weeks and getting over problems I never knew I had.

On the long weekend in August, I took Jennifer shopping then went to Laughing Raven to visit. The next day, I took her to Sto:lo Eagle then went to Rosedale to can some salmon, and Mom and Dad both went out of their way to help me. I sometimes write up to six pages a day now but drink when too much stress builds up. One Sunday I felt stressed out, so I bought a six-pack, and Jennifer said she wanted to move out of where she was staying. Actually, she wanted to move away from Aaron. The next day I felt stressed out and was looking forward to karate, but it was cancelled; so I did some writing but finally gave it up because I felt stressed out to the point my chest was hurting, so I drank. Surprisingly, I drank eleven beers.

After I finished chapter 7, I read over chapter 8 and felt angry when I read it. A couple of days later, Jennifer borrowed $20 off me to go to the bars; then at two o'clock in the morning, Aaron called me to go get her because she was depressed. I took her for a drive then to my place for something to eat and back home before seven o'clock the next morning because I had to leave early to get my fieldwork done.

We had a staff barbecue before the summer students went back to university, and we had hired a young first-year forestry student from BCIT. He said it's easy to get a job if you have lots of woods experience, but it didn't dawn on me until then that I probably had more woods experience than most of the other students did, yet no one would hire me. I only got a job because someone else turned it down because he had already committed himself to another job. But I got a job where I wanted one the most. I made more money than the other students did. It was all spending money, and I had so much fun I didn't want to go back. I'm sure most of the other students would have been happy not to get a job until the last minute for conditions like that. Perseverance pays off!

I had Friday off because of the long hours I worked; and at two o'clock in the afternoon, Ailsa Siemens, the receptionist called, and said we won $1,700 each in our office lottery pool. The next day I took Jennifer shopping in Vancouver then drove to Sto:lo Eagle. She said Aaron kept her from seeing her family very often. That's what she did to me and now it's happening back to her, which I tried to tell her, but she denied it. The next day, we took Emily out for Chinese food then to Bellingham, Washington, to do some shopping. It was a long weekend, and the next day, Jennifer said Aaron held her back from doing anything. Now she's concerned about gaining weight and being out of shape, exactly what she did to me many years ago. Although it was a long weekend, I almost booked in sick when I got back because I felt so stressed out; but eventually, I started feeling better, so I was glad I didn't. A week later I took a late lunch break to see Jennifer at the doctor's office. She was really stressed out that day, so I hoped she would feel better by the end of the day.

After I finished chapter 8, I read over chapter 9 and it stressed me out; but a couple of days later, I drank a cup of coffee at night and it kept me awake, so I hoped it was an indication my stress level was going down. I decided to stop writing for three weeks until after my holidays because my left arm would often stiffen up so much it was very hard to type anything. I called Phaye to arrange for a reading when we went on our holidays then went to Dairy Queen for lunch, and Jennifer told me if she was late for work one more time, she was fired. I took the morning off work on Friday because we were not allowed to build up too many hours, and Jennifer was really cranky and said she wanted to move away from Aaron and got cranky with me too, but at least I got her to work on time.

I started advanced acting lessons that weekend, and there were only six people in the class. Two of them were thirteen; one, sixteen; one, eighteen; one, twenty-six; and I was the oldest one there. A couple of days later, Jennifer threatened suicide again; so I talked to her, told her her options, then she spent the night at my place. The next day Jennifer had to see a specialist in North Vancouver and Aaron inquired about the apartment below my place but was turned down. She got me so stressed out I drank a six-pack that night and said she'd probably move back to my place so she can save money. I thought if she did that, I would have to try and get her into hairdressing so she won't drive me crazy, then arranged for a time to see Phaye in Vernon.

We stayed in Squamish so I could go to karate on Monday night, and the next day we went to see Phaye. She told me I'll be moving to the Sunshine Coast next year, which surprised me because I didn't intend to move for a few more years. After seeing her, we went to Kelowna to visit Brenda and Alvin, stayed in Kelowna for a few days, then went to Sto:lo Eagle. I didn't stay there long then went to Rosedale and had Thanksgiving dinner there the next day.

A week later I watched part of the documentary *The Irish in America*, but Jennifer was cranky and wouldn't let me watch all of it. I felt stressed out a few days later, so I went to the bars for a few beers and a lady there tried to go out with me, but she was ugly and I didn't want to be a rescuer or do anything wrong to Jennifer. The Irish were very badly treated by the English, but a soap commercial used to mention an expression called luck of the Irish. Ailsa Siemans was from England and she said they have an expression called luck of the Irish. At one time in Canada and the USA, women were discriminated against by law. They didn't have the right to vote, weren't allowed in the bars without a man, and often didn't get equal pay for equal work; but we have an expression called Lady Luck. It appeared to me that when people are badly treated and discriminated against, life seems to reward them if they have the drive and perseverance to succeed. Although I went through hard times I wouldn't wish on anyone even before I went to BCIT, I eventually got lucky breaks that made everyone else envious of me. Even as a child living with my parents, I didn't get equal treatment that my brothers got, but I seemed to get lucky breaks that they didn't get. After all the hard times and unfair treatment I got, the best thing I feel I can do is play the system so hopefully, I can get the things I want out of life after being severely slowed down by things beyond my control.

On the weekend I was called to Gastown for an assessment of my acting classes and was asked to go for field film placement studies, which would cost $2,000. I would have said no, but they offered to pay half the fees, which would be paid back when they found me work. I didn't believe they would do that unless it was legitimate, so I reluctantly agreed. That night we drove to Pemberton to bring Aaron some sandwiches and lend him some money so he would have groceries for the rest of the week while working there. The next day I felt stressed out over the money I've been spending and the running around I've been doing, so it affected my acting lessons, but I felt better in the evening.

On Thursday I took Jennifer to see a specialist again and she couldn't make it back to work until Monday. I went to work, and in the afternoon during my coffee break, I called Sue and she told me I should drop the acting lessons where I'm at because her daughter had taken lessons at the same place and got nothing out of it; so I called them up the next day to tell them my intentions and sent them a registered letter telling them I'm dropping out. I wanted to go right to the office and get my money back but was asked to work the weekend, and they called me back to reconsider my decision, but I told them I'm dropping out. I went there to get my money back, and on my way out, I met my cousin Prescott Shackelly from Merritt. He said his daughter had taken lessons at the same place but he put a stop to it and sent her to another agent. I phoned him up a few days later; and he said they used the same sales pitch on him, "She's doing good, but she needs more training," so I knew I had to give up completely with that agency.

I continued working on my writing but got a sore throat, so I went to the doctor. He told me to take the same medication I was on before, and I still had some left, so I used that. My acne was also starting to come back, so I hoped it would keep it under control. My back started hurting again, and often, my left arm and shoulder would stiffen up so much when I wrote my memoirs that I could barely move my hand to finish typing two pages a day, double-spaced. Sometimes I would stiffen up right to my cheek.

I tried to go out the woods to finish some fieldwork, but I was asked to be in for Safety Day and missed most of it to take Jennifer for X-rays. I tried to go out to the woods again two days later, but I had to be in the office to hear about downsizing in our district. Twenty-two positions were slashed from our office, and the Pemberton field office was going to be closed down completely.

A week later I picked Jennifer up after work to see Darlene, and she was depressed, so I missed karate to spend time with her. I also realized my left shoulder was stiffening up because of anger toward my parents, and the pain started going away when I started forgiving them. I took Jennifer to Vancouver on the weekend and she talked me into missing my acting classes because she was depressed. She was sick with the flu, but in the evening, she said she had to do some writing. Christmas was always stressful for her, but she was also depressed because her dad wouldn't be there, and was still sick the next day; so I missed karate to look after her. I started feeling better toward mid-December, but I still tried to sleep at lunchtime. Sometimes I would lay down and one-half hour would pass before I even knew it. Jennifer also stressed me out again one night after karate, so I drank a six-pack.

I took Jennifer shopping in Vancouver the next evening and we got in rather late; then the alarm went off in the store below where I lived, so we were awakened at four thirty and stayed up until five forty-five. We did more Christmas shopping the next day in Vancouver, but we were quite tired, went shopping again in Vancouver on Sunday; and Jennifer was getting extremely stressed out and depressed.

I worked in the office for two more days then went on annual leave. There was a staff Christmas party at the office two days later, but I missed it for karate and because I had been drinking too much and thought I should slow down. I often missed staff parties because no one wanted to associate with me, then some of them would say I did that for attention. We stayed in Squamish for two more days waiting for Aaron to get paid, but he didn't, so we went to Sto:lo Eagle. Then I took Jennifer and Emily shopping; then after bringing them back, I rushed to Rosedale because I was worried about snow and road conditions. Christmas was uneventful and Jennifer was sick the next day and asked me to bring her back to Squamish, but she was better by the time I got there, so we stayed in Sto:lo Eagle two more nights. We drove back to Squamish on Saturday even though it was snowing and blowing, because more snow was predicted for Sunday and I was worried about the roads closing down because the roads between Chilliwack and Abbotsford were closed down. It was snowing rather hard, so we had to drive rather slow at times, but once we got past Vancouver, it was okay.

I wanted to do my laundry the next day, but it snowed too much and my car got stuck, so I walked to town and bought a shovel to dig my car out. There was so much snow I couldn't drive anywhere until the snow was cleared. Jennifer didn't want to go to work the next day and Kelly Smith, the owner, called and told her not to go to work because there was too much snow. I drove to town to pay some bills and buy groceries and did some writing in the evening; writing was getting easier all the time. The next day was New Year's Eve and I took Jennifer to work and she was told to take the rest of the day off. The snow was melting, but it was still hard to find a parking spot at my place, and I went to the bar in the evening but didn't go out of my way to party.

Chapter 19

1997

On New Year's Day I did quite a bit of writing, and the more I wrote, the more I was able to forgive Henry. Previously, I just couldn't forgive him for the way he treated me when he knew I literally went through hell to save his daughter from suicide as well as treat him to all kinds of things and look after his responsibilities as a parent. I just couldn't swing back at him hard enough even though I clearly saw the things I was doing to him happening back to me. I knew he suffered for everything he had done wrong; but I couldn't see it, even when he broke his hip and couldn't take medication for the pain because his heart was too weak, because I was blinded by anger. Now, after writing everything out four times, I finally saw the suffering he went through before he passed away.

I went to work the next day and Jennifer stressed me out, so I drank a few beers when I got home. I started karate again the next week, but Jennifer kept me awake one night because she was worried about the medication she was taking. It seemed to make her hallucinate slightly and alter her heartbeat. There was a staff lunch for people who were going to be leaving Squamish, but I didn't go. When I first got this job, I knew it wasn't going to be long and staff were going to close me off, so I often missed staff luncheons like that. Even at our monthly staff meetings when we went out to the woods, everyone tried to avoid me and didn't want me to ride with them, but an East Indian wasn't treated that way. I was happy to have a permanent job though, and a feeling like I was thinking evil thoughts very strongly said, "Don't think about it!" And I knew I sometimes let it bother me more than I should have.

A week later, Jennifer was depressed and cranky, so I missed karate. She was sore all over from working and when she fell down and bruised herself. We drove around for a while then parked in the civic center parking lot, where she cried and screamed for an hour, then said it was like her dad was kicking her legs and wouldn't stop, then said that wasn't her real dad because he was never there. After she stopped crying, she said nothing could have hurt worse then said there's something that did hurt worse.

Toward the end of the month, I was going to take Jennifer to Sto:lo Eagle; but she got depressed, so we didn't go. I took her shopping in Vancouver the next day and to Whistler the day after that because we were bored with staying home. At the end of the month, I had an appointment with Darlene, and when I got home, Jennifer was depressed because she almost got fired for being two minutes late for work again. She argued, cried, and stood her ground for twenty minutes; so Kelly finally let her stay. If she was late one more time, she would be definitely fired.

We went to Sto:lo Eagle one weekend and Henry Jr. told us that Charlie stole a car and ran it into someone's porch. Then he ran through the brush to his dad's house and hid but forgot to close the front door, and the police got a tracking dog and tracked him down. He wanted to go back to jail though because that's where all his friends were. Jennifer said she had a crush on him when she was eight years old and still does. I knew why Jennifer was attracted to him, and if she went to jail, it could have easily institutionalized her mind and it would have felt normal to her. If Jennifer had got together with Charlie and they acted out their anger, they could have become another Bonnie and Clyde, notorious bank robbers and killers in the 1930s whose lives were made into a movie.

I wanted to do some more karate training in Vancouver as well as Squamish, but I started having trouble with my back again so I ended up going for more physiotherapy. In the second week of February, I missed karate one night because Jennifer was depressed. We argued slightly then went for a drive where she cried and screamed for an hour and cried, "I didn't want to hurt you, Dad! I didn't want to hurt you, Dad!" Eventually she cried, "I just wanted you to see how you hurt me! I love you, Dad!" After she settled down, we were going to go for coffee. But I mentioned using karate to cope with what I'm going through, and that set her off again, so she cried and screamed again but eventually settled down and went home and did some writing.

I felt stressed out a couple of days later, so I bought a six-pack even though I flipped a coin and it told me not to drink; and the next day I forgot about Jennifer's appointment with Darlene, so I should have done what the coin told me to do. I went to a boxing tournament and it made me want to participate in karate tournaments, but I missed karate again a week later because Jennifer was depressed. It was disappointing because I hate giving up my fun for other people and don't seem to get any appreciation for it. It's been like that all my life! I felt stressed out again but didn't drink. Near the end of the month, Aaron came back from Port Alice because his back was hurting too much to continue working. Jennifer picked him up at Horseshoe Bay, and they spent the night at my place.

In early March I didn't think I was very tired and laid down at lunchtime. Before I knew it, one-half hour had passed and it was time to go back to work, so I thought I still needed more stress medication from the health-food store. I also got an e-mail from Wilma Robinson, a Native girl from Bella Coola I went to college with in 1973. I had an appointment with Darlene at the end of the week, and all she talked about was for me to look for someone. I'm still used to getting turned down and tired of looking for anyone even though I don't remember the last time I asked anyone out. Near the middle of the month, I had a course in basic law training. I took my books home to read but felt too stressed out to read, so I worked on my writing. Then I woke up in the middle of the night and couldn't sleep, so I knew I would be tired the next day. On the weekend, I took Jennifer to Sto:lo Eagle because she wanted to get away from Aaron. We got there late and Henry Jr. was crabby, so we left and slept in the car by the Husky station in Chilliwack. We were going to go to Laughing Raven, but Jennifer decided she didn't want to go there, so we did some shopping then came back to Squamish. I felt stressed out again, so I drank that night.

In early April, I felt stressed out and drank a little bit, but I tried to be optimistic and think positive about what I was going through. Darlene kept telling me to look for someone, but there didn't seem to be anyone interested in me. Dad called me early in the morning on Jennifer's birthday and said they'll be passing through Squamish with Auntie Tilley and Uncle Sal from San Diego, so we went out for dinner with them, but Jennifer was still too nervous around my family and couldn't eat very much. They said Tony wasn't doing very well. He was back on drugs, hadn't been seen or heard from in a week, then borrowed Dad's truck and didn't return it; so Dad had to track it down.

A week later I tried to go to Vancouver to train in karate, but Jennifer slowed me down and it stressed me out, so I drank instead. I was not as tired as I usually was and didn't sleep as heavily at lunchtime as I usually did, so I hoped it was because Jennifer was getting stronger. She went to the bars that night then went over to my place and kept waking me up off and on during the night, so I was tired the next day. I tried to take Jennifer to Sto:lo Eagle to get away from Aaron, but she didn't want to go there, so we just slept in the car by a farmer's road. I took her to Bellingham the next day to shop around; then we came back to Squamish. She was getting stressed out over the extra money she was going to get and what to do with it so Aaron wouldn't spend it on her. I took her shopping in North Vancouver the next day, and she slept while I did the laundry; then I felt rather stressed out in the evening, so I drank a few beers and was slightly hung over the next day, so I thought I better not drink anymore if I have to work unless I'm stressed out. I felt good about it though because my stress level may be going down, but my acne is still coming back.

I felt tired and slept at lunchtime the next day, but I think it's because I should have gone to bed earlier the night before. I still felt tired and slept at lunchtime and after work; but in the last week of April, I was doing late check-in, so I had to stay awake until everyone checked in. My acne also seemed to be getting worse again. I took Jennifer to Sto:lo Eagle on the weekend and spent the night there. She wanted to take her mother out for lunch because it was Mother's Day, so we took her and Henry Jr. out for Chinese food. Henry Jr. traded the truck in this year, bought an extended-cab three-fourth-ton four-wheel drive, and didn't want me to ride in it, which I could understand because it's a very expensive vehicle.

After coming back to Squamish, I drove to Vancouver to train in karate and really enjoyed it. I still felt tired most of the time and liked to sleep at lunchtime, but I didn't feel as tired as I used to; but after our next night of karate training in Squamish, I still felt stressed out, so I drank a six-pack. Around the middle of May, I started waking up rather early for a few days and usually only felt tired when Jennifer kept me awake at night. Even after work I didn't feel as tired as I usually did. I took four days off work in holiday time after the long weekend in May to go to Kelowna because Jennifer's niece, Cheryl, was graduating from high school; so I missed out on National Forest Week. Brenda didn't realize why I was so angry at her father for calling Henry Jr. down for graduating high school, until her daughter graduated; then she realized it was important.

At the end of May, Darlene told me Jennifer's problem was more than addiction to suffering and people who went through far less than what she went through have been in and out of mental institutions. Then I realized she was totally brainwashed into believing suffering is normal. After writing out my life story four times, I told Darlene about visiting Veronica in the hospital when she was having a baby and Veronica said it was like the whole world was against Jennifer, then I asked her if I should write that into my life story. Darlene wouldn't answer and just said, "What do you think?" I also realized the seriousness of not wanting to go home after living in my truck and not eating at all for two days when it was that cold out and got really depressed.

I participated in a karate tournament that weekend and enjoyed it. On Monday, Aaron dropped by for lunch and I didn't feel tired, but I lay down and my timer seemed to go off immediately. Even though I went to bed at eleven o'clock and got up at seven o'clock, I was still tired. I bought a six-pack in the evening and only drank three beers but felt better. The next day I slept at lunchtime because I was tired from drinking, but I also got stressed out from not doing my job properly even though I was doing my best. I drank coffee in the evening, which was a mistake because it kept me awake at night, so I drank two beers to put me to sleep. I feel like my stress level is going down because I can't drink coffee at night anymore.

My acne started going away in early June and I decided I better not drink unless I'm stressed out. In the middle of June, I went to bed early and had a hard time getting up, so I knew I was burnt out; so I bought a case of beer in the evening. Near the end of the week, Jennifer got depressed, so she went to the bars; then Aaron and I tried to pick her up at ten thirty, but she got ugly and stayed in the bar. On the weekend, I felt bored, so I drank and realized I was stressed out. When I got back to work, I still felt stressed out, so I had a glass of beer after work then went to karate for grading. Eventually, I found out

Jennifer was stressed out, and I could feel it. She went to the doctor the next day and he said her health problems were caused by incredible stress. Two days later, I found out I didn't do very well in my grading in karate, which was depressing because of all my dedication, and thought it could have been from drinking; then as soon as I decided to only drink when stressed out, my acne started clearing up. Later on I was glad I made that decision because I know if I'm not stressed out, my body can be very sensitive to alcohol.

On the first weekend of July, I studied at home for the basic law enforcement course again. It was a subject I didn't find very interesting and studied to the point my chest was hurting, so I bought a six-pack and drank it. My acne seemed to come and go, but I hoped Jennifer was getting stronger, and I still slept at lunchtime even though I was not very tired. After the course, studying and worrying about the exam burnt me out, so I drank in the evening. The next day I went to Vancouver to train in karate and really enjoyed it even though I was slightly hung over.

A week later I felt like having a beer after work, but I flipped a coin and it said no, so I had a cup of coffee instead. The next day I found out I failed the law exam again, which stressed me out, so I drank a six-pack in the evening. Near the end of July, I still slept at lunchtime but I was not very tired and my acne still came and went. I wanted to go to Vancouver for karate but was worried about Jennifer, so I didn't go. I had a few beers in the evening because I was stressed out, but it would have been better to go to karate than drink.

At the end of July and early August, I still slept at lunchtime, but I was not as tired as I usually was. Near the end of the first week in August, I had a rather hard time getting out of bed one morning and thought I would be tired at lunchtime. I tried to sleep at lunchtime but wasn't tired, so I hoped I was getting better. I went to sleep after work though, and Jennifer was stressed out about her chances of getting an apartment above the post office. The next day Jennifer got a place above the post office, where she always wanted one, but she had to borrow $300 off me for a security deposit. I told her she could have the love seat because I wanted to buy a new couch; then Roberta called that day and said she and her mother will be stopping by in Squamish on Monday.

The acting company called the next day and asked for a film assessment of me, so I told them I would go as long as it didn't cost me anything. I didn't trust them because of how much money Sue spent on Amanda there and didn't get anything out of it. Aaron also went back from working in Pemberton and borrowed $100 off me even though he had made good money there.

When Roberta and her adopted parents stopped by, they were on their way to California. She talked about getting married and I told them about writing my life story. I was on my fourth edition and set my goals at typing a minimum of two pages a day. It was hard to do even that much because my left arm would stiffen up so much I had to use my other hand to push the keys down; then she and her stepmother both thought it must be quite a story.

I had a hard time sleeping that night, and at four o'clock in the morning, Geraldine called and told me my cousins Cindy and Darwin and another fellow all died in a car accident. Jennifer called me at six o'clock to pick her up and thought I would be mad at her, but I was glad she called, so I could tell her what happened. She went out drinking again a couple of days later and asked me to pick her up at four thirty in the morning, depressed and crying because people kept telling her there's no hope for Aaron, he'll never change, and he's beyond recovery.

Ron Gabriel came to Squamish for a meeting, and after work, I talked to him in the parking lot. Ron said when he first went to the residential school, he couldn't speak a word of English, was severely beaten and didn't even know why, and eventually found out it was just for speaking his own language. He only went as far as grade 5 and left as soon as he could because he couldn't stand living there and wouldn't let his kids go to the residential school after what he went through.

By the third week of August, I wasn't sleeping as much at lunchtime; so I hoped I was finally getting over the chemical imbalance, but drank on Friday night because Jennifer stressed me out over not being able to pay me all the money she borrowed. On the weekend, I went to my parents' place to can some fish but didn't drink, got back rather late Sunday night, and Jennifer was in the bar. Aaron and I tried to get her to go home, but she got ugly and went back, so I picked her up later on and couldn't sleep from drinking coffee. I went to bed early the next night and still had a hard time getting out of bed in the morning. I didn't think I was still tired, but I slept at lunchtime. Two days later, Aaron gave me $20 for helping him out, so I bought a six-pack. It wasn't enough, so we chipped in and bought another case of beer. I was more stressed out than I realized.

We just stayed home on Labour Day weekend and didn't do very much; but by the middle of the week, I felt stressed out, so I drank. I went to Vancouver for karate the next day and really enjoyed it, and Jennifer didn't give me a hard time about going. There was a going-away party the next day for Stephen DeMelt, and Jennifer didn't give me a hard time about going there either. A staff member was moving the next day and I wanted to help him move, but Jennifer's nerves were getting bad again, so I forgot about helping him; so we just went to Vancouver, did some shopping, then went home. I didn't always sleep at lunchtime now because I was not always tired. I wanted to go to Vancouver for karate after the weekend, but Jennifer stressed me out, so I didn't go; but I was also feeling rather sick that day, so it didn't bother me.

In the middle of September, I almost started feeling sorry for Henry because of all the bad luck he had before he died, but he knew he was making life miserable for me when I was literally going through hell to save his daughter from suicide. He didn't care, so it still feels hard to forgive him completely. Jennifer went to the bars the next day and I couldn't sleep very well because I was worried about her spending all her money, but luckily, her bank card wasn't working. She wanted me to move in to her apartment with her, and I considered it because of mistakes I made in the past from not listening to her, and it would also help me get my bills down so I can buy a truck. The next night, I couldn't sleep for two and a half hours in the middle of the night because it seemed like my instincts were telling me not to move in to her place. I went to see Darlene at the end of the week and felt stressed out after seeing her, so I went for a few beers then to Dairy Queen for lunch. I bought a six-pack then another case of beer in the evening and still felt stressed out in the morning, so I had a few more beers then went out for breakfast. I've been feeling incredible stress again.

I took the basic law enforcement course again and passed it this time, and on Friday, Jennifer called Henry Jr. and he said it was okay for us to go to Sto:lo Eagle to visit. We owed Emily some money and couldn't pay her right away, so we just took her and Henry Jr. out for Chinese food. The power went off in the evening and Jennifer wanted to take Emily to the Seabird Island Cafe for tea, but I thought that was too far to go. Jennifer started getting depressed on Sunday, so we left at noon. I started driving toward Mission, but she didn't want to go that way, so we turned around and went through Chilliwack. As we were driving, she cried and screamed for one and a half hours; and when we got home, she said she woke up at four thirty and couldn't sleep for an hour because that's what time her father would go and get her. I felt stressed out but didn't drink because I flipped a coin and it told me not to. I was lucky I did that, because I would have regretted it the next day.

The next weekend I took Jennifer to Vancouver shopping and she stressed me out, so I drank a case of beer in the evening. She and Aaron went out partying that night and ended up taking drugs as well as drinking. She said she would have gone to my place, but I was drinking, and now she wanted to start going to AA. I had a week's annual leave, so I went to Rosedale; then after Thanksgiving weekend, Jennifer went over to my place one morning and said she wanted to quit drinking and putting herself in dangerous situations. I hope I'm now winning her battle against depression and straightening out her way of thinking so she'll realize suffering isn't normal or healthy. Near the end of the third week of October, Jennifer said she was getting stressed out because that's the month Liz and her dad died. She stressed me out, so I drank ten beers and thought I better go to bed so hopefully, I would get enough sleep.

On the weekend, I wanted to go to Rosedale because Auntie Tilley from New Mexico and Auntie Deedee from Ohio were supposed to be going, but we got as far as Burnaby then turned around because Jennifer wasn't feeling well. The next day she got up before I did and was really cranky and wanted everything hers moved into her own place; then she decided she wanted to visit her mother, so I drove her to Sto:lo Eagle then went to Rosedale. When I got there, my aunts had just decided to spend the night in Everett, Washington, which I tried to find out if that was going to happen before going all the way back to Rosedale; but it was a good excuse to stay away from Sto:lo Eagle. Although I saved Henry Jr.'s sister from suicide and tried to help him get a career, he sure didn't make me very welcome when I took Jennifer to visit her mother; but when Alvin visited, no one in that family could do enough for him.

When we got back to work, Jennifer stressed me out and I got stressed out over missing karate; so I told her the next time she was stressed out to try and let me know well ahead of time so I won't be disappointed over missing out on my fun for other people. At the end of October, Darlene told me to start letting Jennifer be responsible for her own actions, so I told Jennifer and she liked the idea. On Sunday, Jennifer was getting better, but she still stressed me out. I wasn't really sure why I was stressed out, but I bought a six-pack and drank it.

On November 5 our band was having elections for chief and council, and Isaac was running for chief and asked me to vote for him. I agreed, so I took the afternoon off and thought I could stop by at Langara College and get copies of the student newspaper from when I attended as a student. I went to the Langara student newspaper to get copies from the fall of 1973, when DIA segregated almost all first-year Native students, but only one of the two front-page articles was available. The article titled "Native Students Angry at Segregation!" was missing. Before that article came out, I noticed a Native student sitting back by himself looking like he was lost, and other Native students said the same thing about him, so I went over and talked to him; and he said he was from Whitehorse, up in the Yukon Territory. I was sitting in the cafeteria one day; and a white fellow, probably from DIA, and Gary went and sat across me. He said, "I saw one Native student looking like he was lost."

Gary said, "We should have put him on these Native group studies then eased him into a regular program," and sounded like segregating us was the best thing he could ever do for us. One example of how Gary was treating the Native students is a fellow who wanted to be a teacher. He went to the regular college counsellors, did his first-year arts, then went to Gary, who just put him on the teacher-aide program. The student got frustrated, quit, then joined the RCMP. Unfortunately, much of this couldn't be documented; and even if it were, it would be hard to trace and probably very well hidden.

Although James was two and a half years older than I, he graduated from high school a year after I did. James told me about going to the Indian residential school in Port Alberni and running away. After he got caught, Gary drove him back to Bella Coola and didn't give a single word to encourage him to stay in school, but I'm sure Gary was merely doing what he was ordered to do. Gary tried screwing me around then gave me a hard time over what happened, but when I gave him a hard time right back, he wouldn't go near me. After he got fired, he went and talked to me in the cafeteria because he was taking some college courses and even had a beer with me a couple of times. He was all right in the cafeteria but was rather arrogant when he had a beer with me. One of the times he had a beer with me was in the Nelson Place, a pub on Granville Street in downtown Vancouver, when that was where the Indians hung out. Eventually, I realized we didn't even ask him to go and join us, he just went over and started talking to us. That's also why I believe he was only following orders when he was deliberately trying to make the Native students give up on their postsecondary education.

Two days later I took Jennifer to Yic's, a Chinese restaurant in North Vancouver, for dinner because it was my birthday; but the food wasn't very good this time. I took her to Sto:lo Eagle the next day, and on Sunday, Henry Jr. asked us to leave and Jennifer said he's still hurting over losing his father. Jennifer and I both had Monday off, and on Tuesday, Remembrance Day, she stressed me out; so I had a few beers and watched a Remembrance Day special on the horrors of war. Several days earlier, a war veteran could see I was bitter about how the Indians were treated when they got back from fighting in the war and offered me a poppy free of charge, but I wouldn't take it. It hurt to see what the soldiers went through, but it hurt even more to realize the Indians went through the horrors of the residential schools as well as the same horrors of war and how they were treated when they got back. I went to the beer and wine store to buy a six-pack, and a white fellow who walked in behind me seemed a little annoyed that I was buying beer on Remembrance Day; but he sensed that if he said anything, I would have called him out. I wasn't doing anything he wasn't doing.

On the third weekend of November, I went to bed rather late and had a hard time going to sleep until I started thinking about sex, then I went to sleep right away. I realized I should start opening up more and perhaps even start looking for someone. Nothing eventful happened in December except that I was kept busy looking after another staff member's contracts while she was away on courses. In the second week of December, I went to karate and still felt stressed out afterward, so I bought a six-pack and drank it. I still felt stressed out again the next day, so I bought a case of beer and drank eleven bottles. That night, Jennifer said she missed work because she was sick, and I took the next day off work because I'm not allowed to build up too many hours.

On Saturday I kept trying to call Jennifer, but there was no answer, so I knew she was depressed; and in the afternoon, she finally answered her phone. The next day she was depressed and wanted to move back in with me so she would have more spending money. I agreed then she said she was depressed because she and Aaron were arguing. Eventually she said they were doing cocaine the day before and that's why she missed work on Thursday. A week later, Aaron's father and sister picked him up and took him back to Vancouver Island. Jennifer called him in the evening, and it sounded like his family was finally being good to him. Previously it sounded like his family treated him like an outcast.

The next day I took Jennifer to Sto:lo Eagle then went to Rosedale. Christmas wasn't very eventful except Tony borrowed my car, dented it up slightly, and was drinking at the time; so my insurance wouldn't pay for it. It cost me $1,250 for repairs, and I had enough cash to pay for it; but it drained my finances even though I got a good deal on the repair work. Now I was forced to move in with Jennifer for financial reasons even though Tony said he would pay me back, but I knew he never would. Eventually, I realized Tony sensed I had money to enjoy my time off and was jealous of seeing me have fun! He was always like that; his social life was his only concern, but he was jealous of seeing the rest of us have fun, especially me! Many Indians said they didn't know how to parent because of what they went through in the residential schools, so we're still feeling the spin-off effects of what they went through.

Chapter 20

1998

Jennifer got a gift certificate for the Bay from the Dairy Queen and bought some perfume with it. She was going to go to the island to visit Aaron, but she overspent, which stressed me out even though my instincts said everything would be all right. We ended up in a big argument and she got too depressed to go visit him, so I decided, "That's the last argument we're going to get into because of how my family always puts down my opinion! If they want to think negative and be miserable, that's up to them! They're not going to drag me down anymore!" I drove Jennifer to Horseshoe Bay the next morning, and she went to Qualicum to visit Aaron. Jennifer wanted me to move in with her so she could save money and Aaron told her to do it, so she was finally listening; but it stressed me out to think of moving in with her, so I decided I should try and transfer to Port Alberni if she could get a career there.

I felt tired the next day at work, so I went to sleep at lunchtime and tried to go to bed early; but Jennifer kept me up until eleven o'clock, but my intuition also told me she may start her career soon. I called a moving company to move my things over to her place because I didn't own a truck and couldn't move anything heavy because I had a sore back. After they moved my things, I took Jennifer to Sto:lo Eagle to visit her mother and felt rather good about moving in with her as long as she didn't get crabby and hoped I could get my bills down.

I started karate again, and on Friday I took Jennifer to the ferry terminal at Horseshoe Bay so she could visit Aaron and the next day I had to get my right front bearings fixed, which cost me $270. Jennifer was sick when she got back, so I took her to the doctor and the hospital the next day and missed karate to look after her. Jennifer missed work all week because she was sick, and on the weekend, I took her to Sto:lo Eagle to visit her mother. Henry Jr. had gone to Saskatchewan, so we just stayed there for the weekend.

Henry Jr. went hunting in Saskatchewan. They got three moose, and the people he went hunting with said he could take it all because they could get moose whenever they wanted. It was just him and his mother at home and they eat lots of salmon, so one moose would have been more than they could eat. I grew up eating moose and deer meat but never had time for hunting since high school because I was getting my career and Jennifer always held me back; in spite of everything I did for that family, Henry Jr. only gave us three packages of moose hamburger.

During the week, Jennifer got extremely depressed over having to go for an operation, so I missed another night of karate to stay with her. The next week on Monday, I had to take her to North Vancouver for her day surgery (biopsy and scraping). I got sick and missed two days of work, but Jennifer also wanted me to stay home and look after her because she was depressed. At the end of the week, I wanted us both to go to a mood-disorder-group meeting; but I figured she would be too tired, so we didn't go. She did some writing that night and started to feel better. In February I still sometimes felt tired and forgetful and had to take my car in for repairs because the radiator was leaking. It would take a couple of days to get fixed, so I had to ride my bicycle to work and stay in the office at lunchtime. While I was in the office, I phoned Jim Rowed because he was working with First Nation people who succeeded in life, and they all told the same story: they wouldn't give up.

One day as I was on my way back to work after lunch, some news reporters from a Vancouver TV station were in town interviewing people about a juvenile who murdered a young girl over twenty years ago; but the reporter didn't talk to me because she sensed that I would have asked, "Why don't Indians get hired?" If what she went through to get her job was such a ordeal, I would have said, "Where's your life story? Would it be highly justified to say Canadian film companies need not apply?"

In early March we had a meeting with Paul Kuster, the district manager; and he talked about how badly the forest industry is doing, how many big companies are downsizing, and our own budget is going down dramatically. Before starting with the Forest Service, I had applied to many forest companies and couldn't even get an interview; now it seemed like it was a good thing they wouldn't hire me because I could have ended up unemployed again.

On the first weekend in March, I went to a karate tournament in Steveston with Jennifer but wished she would have gone somewhere else that weekend because I knew she would stress me out. Sure enough, she stressed me out so much I almost didn't participate in the tournament after we got there. She eventually calmed down though, and I enjoyed competing in the tournament, but I was ready to quit karate altogether because it seemed like I could never have fun without someone stressing me out first. I took Jennifer shopping in Vancouver the next day but felt so stressed out my heart was hurting, so I drank a case of beer in the evening and missed karate the next day though because I was too tired from drinking the night before. The next day, Jennifer went home from work and said staff were starting to treat her better, so I hoped that was an indication she was getting better. I got sick and missed the second night of karate that week, but Jennifer and I went to Vancouver to see the movie *Titanic*; it was a very good movie.

On the weekend, Jennifer went to Vancouver Island to see Aaron; and when she got back, she said he wanted her to move over there. But I tried to tell her to get her career first, but she wouldn't listen. I also told her that in Squamish she has a good job with good hours and security, over there she would lose all that, it's out of town, it could be hard to find work, and she could go hungry, but I also knew that would feel normal to her. I hoped she would get better by May because she talked about moving there in June. The next day, Jennifer considered seeing a psychic to see what she should do; and when I got home from work, she was stressed out over having a big argument at work. She almost walked off the job, but it didn't seem like she would be staying there much longer.

I was still seeing Darlene for counselling and I mentioned when I first met Henry, his youngest brother lived right next door to him and his wife would have nothing to do with him. Henry said he would ask to borrow something and she would just give a short, sharp "No!" with no explanation; then it finally dawned on me that she may have been protecting her daughter from Henry, a well-known child molester.

Toward the end of March, Jennifer started thinking about going into long term care aide and Darlene thought that would be a good idea because she was always trying to do things for other people and now she would be getting paid for it. Darlene also wondered what Aaron's sister was going to do when his UIC ran out: would she let him stay there if he had no income?

I wanted to compete in another karate tournament at BCIT on the first weekend in April, but I couldn't get registered on time for sparring; and when Jennifer got home from work, she said, "Let's go to Qualicum!" So we drove to Horseshoe Bay. While we were waiting in line for the ferry, the lady parked in front of us looked familiar, so I started talking to her. It was Patricia Kelly, a girl I worked with in Mission in 1983. Patricia told me she was working on a degree in media and communications, so I told her why it took me eight years of studying just to get a two-year diploma and I'm writing an autobiography; then as soon as I said that, she said, "Can I edit it for you?" Many years earlier, Phaye told me that when my book is almost finished, someone I know will be there to edit it for me. I wondered how that could be because I don't know any authors or publishers; now I hoped I would be able to finish my book soon.

I took Jennifer to Sto:lo Eagle the next weekend and visited my parents because it was Easter weekend, but we came back on Sunday night because Jennifer had to work the next day. We went to Qualicum again the next weekend and I didn't really want to go, but Jennifer got really sick, so it was better that I went and looked after her. Jennifer was too sick to go to work the next day. I missed karate to look after her and had to convince her not to go back to work until she felt better, so she missed two days of work. Auntie Tilley was visiting from New Mexico and I didn't have time to go visit her, so I called her at my parents' place after work. She said when she was eighteen, she tried to get a job, but no one would hire her because they wouldn't hire Indians. Years earlier, my dad said something similar. He never saw any Indians working in restaurants, cafés, stores, etc., that's why I didn't believe Indians were hired to work in the mines when I was asked to be an extra in the Highlander series.

On Friday, Jennifer and I were both sick, so we planned on staying home for the weekend and work on our writing; but the next day, Aaron called and asked us to go over and help look after him because he wasn't feeling well. The next day, I decided I better not go to work if

I was too sick. I missed four days of work that week because I was sick and worked on my writing but couldn't do any writing in the evenings because Jennifer always wanted my attention. Jennifer talked me into going to Qualicum again the next weekend, May 1, to visit Aaron. She talked about moving to Qualicum, but I hoped I could make her realize it was the wrong move even though she's tired of working at Dairy Queen. I helped out with National Forest Week again the next weekend and really enjoyed it, and when I got home, Jennifer decided she wanted to visit her mother, so I took her to Sto:lo Eagle. I wasn't feeling well and didn't know if my being around would stress Henry Jr. out, so I went to Rosedale; that was another spur-of-the-moment trip and was enjoyable.

I went to Nanaimo for a course on Monday, so I missed karate and felt stressed out the next day, so I drank a few beers. Jennifer didn't like it, but she didn't realize how much she stresses me out. Jennifer then decided she wanted to buy an $800 bicycle, but I suggested she shop around first, and that threw her into a fit of rage because she knew Aaron would get her to spend all her money on him and it would be lost. I tried to take her to Horseshoe Bay to visit him, but I got a speeding ticket along the way, so she was too late to catch the ferry. Then I took her to Horseshoe Bay the next day and patrolled the campsites around Cat Lake in the afternoon and evening with a young female RCMP constable named Allison Good. I told her about one of the laws that still existed that was clearly discriminating against the Indians when I was a child and the police still had to enforce it. The penalties were pretty stiff, and she asked me what the penalties were, but I wouldn't tell her because it's written in my life story. Then I told her I often get closed off by non-Natives and she asked me why I would get closed off. I said that's how Natives usually get treated but said it very calmly like it didn't bother me.

I tried to do some writing the next day, but Jennifer was stressed out and I could feel it, so I bought a case of beer and drank it. The next day was the Victoria Day holiday, so I picked Jennifer up in Horseshoe Bay. She was really cranky because she spent all her money on Aaron, so I realized I shouldn't tell her what to do, just let her take the consequences of her actions. Jennifer ended up buying a bicycle on credit and had it delivered to an Indian reserve so she could save the taxes. We put a down payment on it and intended to pay the rest in two to three months. The next weekend I took Jennifer to Qualicum for Aaron's birthday and missed a staff member's going-away party. She was the aboriginal forestry advisor, so I opened up and told her a few things. She may have thought I deliberately missed her party because at staff parties, it was nothing unusual for everyone to close me off; but it was also my niece's birthday, so that was one weekend I would have been committed anyway.

On the last weekend in May, I went to a film forum in Whistler hoping I could get some part-time work to get my bills down; but Jennifer stressed me out before going, so we had a big fight and she started destroying things. I missed quite a bit of it and we just walked around Whistler for most of the day. I felt like no one liked to see me have fun without stressing me out first, but Jennifer had much anger building up inside her, and it was set off by the slightest thing.

I normally don't take my holidays until the fall, but this year, I took the second and third week of June off because Jennifer was getting stressed out over the way she gets treated at work. We stayed in Squamish until Sunday then left for Sto:lo Eagle and stopped at a store in Deroche and ran into Ron Gabriel. He said the doctor told him he had to quit logging in 1976 or his back was going to give out on him. When he was logging, the companies had to pay him an extra $20 a day more than the union wage rate before he would work for them because he was a very good logger. That was lots of money back then. He also mentioned Indian students weren't allowed to take academic subjects in high school, and as we were talking, a white fellow driving by in a minivan thought, *All you have to do is go to work.*

I responded, "*Stand toe to toe and say that!*" He wouldn't do it because he knew I would have beaten the shit out of him!

We stayed in Sto:lo Eagle a couple of days, then Henry Jr. asked us to leave, so we went to Kelowna for a few days; then Jennifer decided she wanted to go to Qualicum, so we drove around Merritt for a little while then went to Qualicum. I was only going to stay until Tuesday but stayed to drive Aaron to Courtenay to see about getting a job on Wednesday; then on Wednesday, Jennifer stressed us all out before we left. In 1977, Sue was pregnant with Tony's child when they broke up. She had a baby girl who was given up for adoption and is now living in Prince George. I sometimes phoned her and wrote to her to arrange for her to meet our family. She went down that week, but I didn't have the money to go back and meet her, so I just stayed in Qualicum so I could bring Jennifer back to Squamish.

I went back to work on Monday even though my back was incredibly sore. In early July, I worked and spent the night in Pemberton at the Mount Currie Bed and Breakfast. The owners, Bob and Jolene Green, moved to Merritt the year before I left; and I graduated with their daughter. Then Bob asked if I was automatically put in the class of slow learners because it appeared to their children that Native students were automatically put in the class of slow learners. That was in Chemainus, on Vancouver Island. I said, "No. We went by our grades. My friends said one fellow's father wanted his son put in the class of slow learners and even went to the school to try and force the issue, but the principal stood his ground and made him go the regular route."

The next time I stayed there, there was an Australian couple there and the husband asked me why there was so much unemployment on the Indian reserves when we were living off the land before the settlers came. Of all the non-Natives I've spoken to, he was the first one to ask me that question. I told him the Indians were forced by legislation to go to the Indian residential schools, where they were very badly treated. Indians older than I said life in jail was better than in school, and Indians younger than I said it was like a prison. Indian children were beaten just for speaking their own language even though some of them couldn't speak a word of English; then when we tried to do something for ourselves, we were held back by the government.

That night, Aaron went over from Qualicum to go to work again for Beaverfoot Resources, a company he had previously worked for in Squamish. A week later, Jennifer was stressed out and really wanted to go back to school, so I told her to start saving her money to go back. I know that when she gets obsessed with something, she doesn't rest until she gets it. Now I hoped she would get obsessed with getting a career, so I wrote to her band to apply for funding for her course in long term care aide. On the weekend, I took Aaron and Jennifer to Qualicum to straighten out his UIC and his employment with New Forest Opportunities Ltd. (NewFOL). I don't mind helping people out if it's for work.

I felt stressed out again the next weekend, so I drank at home and Jennifer and Aaron went to the bars and ended up taking drugs as well. She asked to borrow some money off me, but I wouldn't do it because my money was set aside for bills. The next day, Jennifer decided she wanted to visit her mother, so I took her to Sto:lo Eagle then went to

Rosedale; and when I picked her up on Sunday, Henry Jr. thought I was avoiding him, but I told him I knew he was just having emotional problems. He actually asked me to leave a bit too often, so I preferred to stay away as much as possible. I was starting to get tired of drinking, even on weekends, but I drank a little bit one weekend because I was bored. Jennifer wasn't only drinking; she was also taking drugs and was at the point where it could get bad, so I thought I better slow down on drinking if that was her excuse. Aaron finished his job the next day and they went out partying, so Jennifer ended up spending all her money drinking and taking drugs. I tried to warn her about spending all her money, but she said Aaron seemed to get her to spend it all the time. Then two days later, I loaned Aaron $20 so he could go back to Vancouver Island.

On the long August weekend, Jennifer and I went to Loggers Sports for a little while; then we drove to Chilliwack. We were going to go to Sto:lo Eagle, but when I phoned to ask if we could go over, Henry Jr. said it wasn't a good time to go there. It didn't bother me though because I didn't really want to go there anyway. Jennifer then wanted to go to Kelowna, but we couldn't get Brenda and Alvin's number and I forgot I had it in my packsack, so we just went out for dinner then drove back to Squamish. The next day, I took Jennifer shopping in North Vancouver, then we went back to Loggers Sports. She got mad at me then left to visit one of her friends because I asked her if the popsicle I bought her was all right. Often she got mad or blew up at me over the littlest thing. On my way to Loggers Sports, there was a semitruck parked just outside the gate with "Vancouver Community College, Langara" written on the side and when I thought to myself, "Not a nice experience" and the driver felt bad that the Indians didn't get treated very well.

Aaron called the next day from Nanaimo for us to pick him up in Horseshoe Bay. His UIC had run out and he didn't know if he had an income now. The logging camp at Spring Creek was shut down for fire season and we had much work to do near the end of Harrison Lake, so I and a summer student camped out there for two nights and three days, and I really enjoyed it. I worked all the next week and on Friday I was stressed out and wanted to take the day off, but I had to go in for a course and was lucky I did that because I got standby for fires for the weekend. I drank that night because of stress and Jennifer borrowed $100 off me, money I had set aside for my car payment;

but she got paid on Monday, so I thought it was all right. On Sunday I still felt stressed out to the point my heart was hurting, so I bought a six-pack and drank it but was still stressed out, so I bought another six-pack and drank five more beers. I was tired the next day and went to bed early, hoping I would get a good night's sleep. Jennifer stressed me out because I knew she would spend all her money. I didn't know if I would get my car payment in on time and knew what she and Aaron were doing. On Tuesday, Jennifer called in sick and Aaron said he would put $200 in my bank account on Wednesday. I didn't want to take it for granted that nothing would go wrong, so I borrowed $100 on my Visa and put it in my account for my car payment.

The next week, I started feeling sick but went to work anyway. I knew Jennifer could probably write a book on her life, but it only dawned on me now that her life story could be very inspirational to other people who have literally been through hell and are still surviving. I called home that night, and my mother finally realized I travelled as much as I could when I was younger to get away from home because of the way she was always treating me. I felt sick all week with a sore throat, so I went to the doctor and he took a swab to send to the lab for analysis. The results came in a week later and were negative, so I wouldn't need antibiotics, so I figured I could be sick from stress again. In mid-September, there was a going-away party for a staff member, so I donated some salmon and went to the party. I had a good time and people talked to me rather than just ignore me like they did at previous parties. Toward the end of September, I still felt sick and had to go out the woods one day. I wanted to buy some pills from a health-food store, but I got in late because of a flat tire. On Saturday we went to Sto:lo Eagle for a dinner and gathering of friends and relatives for Jennifer's grandmother. I wanted to get some information from some of the people there, but we got there rather late, so I didn't get to talk to the people I wanted to see. Brenda was also there and Henry Jr. let her help herself to as much moose meat as she wanted.

I often felt stressed out and sometimes had a few beers to relieve the stress. Although I was kept busy at work and enjoyed it, the month of September seemed to just drag by because I wasn't feeling well most of the time. We had Pizza Day at lunchtime one day, but I missed it because I had to view the fertilization blocks, but I usually don't go to staff lunches like that anyway.

Jennifer took the first Friday of October off to go to Oregon with Ryan for an Amway meeting, and he tried to get me to go too; but I didn't think I would enjoy it, so I didn't buy a ticket. Then Jennifer changed her mind about going the morning she was supposed to leave, and I was glad about that because I was worried about what to do if something went wrong. We started the fertilization contract the next week, so we were putting in some long hours, but on Tuesday I had to take Jennifer to Capilano College in North Vancouver for an information session for her course. I didn't bring the letter saying which room it was in and there were no directions in the hallways and all the information booths were closed. It was frustrating to the point I wanted to give up, and when we found the room, there were so many people there I wondered if she would even be able to get into the course; but I thought we should try anyway.

I got to work two days on the weekend, and it was Thanksgiving weekend. I always used this overtime money for Christmas and took Jennifer to Sto:lo Eagle after work and spent the night there. The next day, Thanksgiving Day, I went to Rosedale for the turkey dinner and Mother told me there was going to be a big announcement. I figured David and Sandra were planning their wedding day and that was what it was.

I had to take Jennifer to Capilano College again the next day for her reading and assessment test and interview at four o'clock. We left at noon, but she insisted on buying new clothes for the interview since she always had to wear poor clothes and wanted to look more presentable. This took time, which also stressed me out, but she was also stressed out about the test and the interview and was still stressed out when it was over, so we went out for dinner. I went to work the next day and wanted to stay overnight in the logging camp, but it was shut down, so I stayed in Pemberton. I still felt sick and wished I had booked in sick. That night at dinner I had three beers and went to bed at nine thirty, woke up at six o'clock to go for breakfast, and still felt tired; so I took some pills from the health-food store. I had enough hours built up to take the next day off, so I drank in the evening because I felt quite stressed out. On Saturday I wished I didn't get stressed out because I don't really enjoy drinking and usually have a cup of coffee after work because it makes me feel better. The next week I had a cup of coffee, worked out in karate, and still couldn't sleep until three o'clock in the morning; so I hoped that was an indication my stress level was going down.

Near the end of October, Jennifer got a letter from Capilano College saying she wasn't accepted in the residential-care-attendant program because her English skills weren't good enough. I was surprised because Jennifer is usually very good at English. That got me extremely depressed and I wanted to go out and drink but decided to go to Vancouver for karate instead. Not only that, my instincts told me that it's better that it's happening this way. The drive itself often made me feel better, and I usually felt even better after the workout. That night I sparred with the higher belts and the black belts and really enjoyed it. After karate I went out for something to eat, then finally at two o'clock in the morning, I had a few beers. Jennifer and Aaron went out and got back at three o'clock. I had the next day off and an appointment with Darlene. I told her about Jennifer getting turned down; and she suggested we appeal it, ask where she went wrong, and see if she can write the test again. I called the college and all I got was an answering machine, so I asked the lady to call me back, but she didn't.

On Saturday, Jennifer got really depressed and raised hell with Aaron again and told him to move out. She wanted him to stop taking drugs and said that was what they did on Thursday night. I know Jennifer is still hurting badly inside because of what happened in the past. Drugs are a fast way to forget the pain, and Aaron also has problems from his past. It was also a big disappointment for her when she was turned down for the course because she wanted to get away from Dairy Queen. In November, Jennifer and Aaron went out two nights in a row; and on my birthday, Aaron got really sick. Jennifer was supposed to take a CPR course for the resident-care-attendant program, but she didn't bother going.

My cousin Richard Band used to be a teacher at a university in California, so I called him and asked for information on when the Indians got the right to vote and where I might find the missing college newspaper article. He told me to call the college library because it should be in the periodical section, so I called the library at Langara College the next day while at work and staff were listening, so they knew something was up. The lady at the library was sure they still had a copy of the student newspaper dated November 2, 1973.

On Tuesday, Aaron was sick and Jennifer and I went for a run in the morning. At lunchtime, Aaron seemed to be feeling better; but that night, we took him to the hospital for X-rays. Wednesday was Remembrance Day, so I had the day off and had built up enough hours to take Thursday and Friday off as well. On Thursday I went to the library at Langara College to get the student newspaper article, but it wasn't there. There were articles going back to the '60s, so I searched for two and a half hours for the article titled "Native Students Angry at Segregation!" but it wasn't there. Then I went out for a Chinese smorgasbord then to karate. From studying Indian spiritualism, my instincts told me I was going to learn something in my search.

On Friday I finally made it to the doctor because I was feeling sick, so he gave me a different type of pill and sent me for X-rays on my stomach and throat. When I got back to work, I called Joy Hall to see if she kept the newspaper article I was looking for because she was a journalism student when it happened. I also asked if she knew where Roberta Smith, another journalism student at that time, was because I thought she may have been the person who wrote it. She didn't know, so I asked where I could find Samantha. She didn't know that either, but she gave me Samantha's oldest sister's phone number. Samantha had married one of the instructors, so I thought either her or her husband may have thought of keeping it.

On the weekend, Jennifer was signed up for a first aid course, but she went to the bars the night before and didn't make it. Then on Monday I called Stan Dixon, who owns *Kahtou*, an Indian newspaper based out of Sechelt, British Columbia, to see if he knew Roberta Smith or where she was. He didn't, so we talked about the letter I sent him in May, and he asked me to fax it to him. He wanted to put it into the next issue of his newspaper because someone may have kept the article I was looking for. He also wanted to meet me in Vancouver at the Hotel Georgia to talk about my life story and told me to be optimistic about it, but I told him that's what kept me going through everything I went through to get my career.

I went to the doctor again on Thursday the next week and he gave me a three-month supply of the same pills and said my stomach was manufacturing too much acid. That was what was making me nauseous and causing me to have a sore throat. I went for X-rays again the next day, saw Darlene at eleven o'clock, and drove to Vancouver to meet Stan Dixon at two o'clock. I got tired of waiting, so I went across the street for a cup of coffee. When I got back, we missed each other by two minutes; so I called him in the evening when I got home and he said his staff had already put that letter in the newspaper.

On December 1, I got a letter from the Aboriginal Employees Association (AEA) and phoned a lady involved, Susan Kelly. I got an e-mail from them and found out things that are going on, what some people are doing, and what some people have done to succeed in life. Wednesday, December 2, was the last day of karate in Squamish for the year and I thought I would get stressed out again. Jennifer usually stressed me out at Christmas, but she didn't stress me out this year. On Monday after work, I was feeling rather stressed out and was thinking of drinking when Ed Dorosh called and said Eric Puchmayer; his father, Vic; and I could all grade on Thursday. So that really picked me up, but it wouldn't disappoint me if I didn't get my brown belt. The next day I took Jennifer to shop in Vancouver while I trained to prepare for grading. On Thursday all three of us went to Vancouver to grade and had quite an intense workout. The instructor, Allan Chan, said those who came from Squamish were all doing extremely well. I didn't know how well I did because I didn't have to spar with him and he wouldn't let me pay him right away. Usually we have to spar with the instructor and it costs more to grade when we advance to a higher belt.

There was a staff Christmas party on the weekend, but I didn't go. It also looked like I wouldn't find the missing newspaper article I was looking for, but I thought Samantha may have been mature enough at the time to keep it, but her husband had passed away several years earlier. I called Brad (her brother-in-law) and her oldest sister; but neither of them would give her number to me. They both just said they would give her my number and she could call me. Samantha never called, so I thought I would go to a shopping mall in West Vancouver, where I sometimes run into her. It's on Indian reserve, so anything we buy is tax free, so Indians often go shopping there. I ran into her while Jennifer was doing some Christmas shopping, and Samantha said she first went to college when she was eighteen, a year before I went there. She said Gary sent a letter to the Indian agent, telling them not to sponsor her anymore because she was too young to continue. She had worked for DIA during the summer, came across that letter, and kept a copy of it; and it was in her apartment somewhere, but she couldn't remember where she put it. Then she told me I might find the information I'm looking for at a certain library at UBC because she sent her husband's information there after he passed away.

Gary's own daughter was in college when I was doing my second year. She was eighteen and just out of high school. She mentioned not being nineteen or old enough to go to the bars, and from talking to her, it sounded like she wanted to get married right away. She was a non-status Indian because Gary had given up his Indian status, known as enfranchising, so she wasn't funded by DIA. She was discouraged because of one of the assignments in her course, and I tried to tell her not to give up; but she wouldn't listen, and I never saw her again.

I went back to work, and on Wednesday I found out I got my brown belt, so that really made my day and my Christmas. I phoned the library at UBC and asked what days and hours they were open, so I planned on going out there next week when I was on annual leave; Tuesday would be the best day to make it. On Saturday morning, Jennifer's mother called and asked us to take her shopping because Henry Jr. was working, and I was rather happy about that though because Jennifer could visit her mother. We took her to Chilliwack and didn't get back to Sto:lo Eagle until eleven thirty that night. Andrew went over at six thirty the next morning and was in a hurry to get going to work. He saw my car but forgot it was there and turned as he was pulling out. He was used to turning before leaving the yard, but my car was there; and he backed into the passenger door, putting a big dent into it. I was still in bed when it happened, and he went in and told me about it. I went to visit my parents and report the accident to ICBC. My radiator also started leaking, so that stressed me out even more. It was Sunday and the office wasn't open until noon and the earliest appointment I could get was on Tuesday. The next day, I had the cooling system checked and the soldering done in February that cost me $400 was coming undone. I called the car dealer where I got the work done, and they said they could fix it on Wednesday morning.

On Tuesday I took my car to ICBC for an assessment then took the form to an auto-body shop. I wanted to go to UBC to look for some information that day but couldn't because of this appointment. On Wednesday I took my car to the mechanics and was told my car was under warranty, so it wouldn't cost me anything. Then I took Jennifer shopping in Squamish, but we had to walk around until my car was ready. It was only fixed well enough so I could go to Chilliwack for Christmas, and I would have to bring it in again after Christmas;

but as we were walking around, people thought we were "too lazy to go to work!"

On Thursday we wrapped presents, then I took Jennifer to Sto:lo Eagle. The roads were icy and slippery between Squamish and Vancouver, so I had to drive slowly. We got to Sto:lo Eagle about seven o'clock in the evening and I left right away because I was worried about the roads turning icy and slippery. I'm usually quite stressed out by Christmas Eve, but this time I wasn't too stressed out. Not only that, my Uncle Ted, Richard's father, from North Vancouver, had passed away two days earlier and the funeral would be right after Christmas. Christmas was on a Friday that year and it was rather quiet. I didn't drink until the evening because I wasn't stressed out.

On Boxing Day I went to Sto:lo Eagle and Jennifer was really stressed out and cranky; she even kicked me a few times. Then we laid some flowers on her father's grave. When we left for Squamish, she was still cranky; and by the time we reached Abbotsford, she finally broke down and cried and screamed off and on until we reached Squamish. When we got back to Squamish, she still cried and screamed, so we drove around and parked off and on for about forty-five minutes before we went into the apartment, where she still cried off and on; but eventually she calmed down. Nothing happened the next day, Sunday, except Jennifer, Aaron, and I went out for steaks.

On Monday, Jennifer wanted to go to Sto:lo Eagle to visit her mother, but I had to take my car in to get the radiator fixed; so I took her to the bus depot in Vancouver and she got really cranky but eventually calmed down and got on the bus. I went to North Vancouver to Uncle Ted's place and his nephew left me there by myself, and his other nephew (Al Band) and his wife went over eventually. Al is a dry alcoholic, and we talked about addictions, reasons why people drink and use to justify their drinking. I told Al about drinking heavily and taking Prozac, and he said I was living pretty dangerously.

I felt rather stressed out the next day, so I went to the bars for a few beers; then on New Year's Eve, Aaron and I picked Jennifer up at the bus depot in Vancouver. She was hungry, so we went to the Swiss Chalet for something to eat. We all ordered, then she got really cranky and walked out of the restaurant just before the meal came. We didn't know where she went, so Aaron and I ate then took her order to go. We waited around outside for about fifteen minutes, then Aaron went for a walk down the street to look for her and I waited at the car. He went back one-half hour later, then he waited at the car while I looked for her. I tried checking the Avalon Hotel Lounge and Pub, but they were charging a $10 cover charge to get in, so I knew she wasn't in there; so I walked around there a bit more. Then I finally saw her walking back to the car. She was still depressed and slightly crying but seemed to be feeling a little better. She had gone for a long walk down Marine Drive then went back.

Chapter 21

1999

We didn't really do anything for New Year's, and I had decided to slow down on drinking. Jennifer and Aaron went to visit one of Aaron's friends and they did a little bit of drugs and Jennifer got really uptight about it. I had gone to bed early to get a good night's sleep and was woken up at two o'clock because Jennifer was mad at Aaron. She went back to the bar and Aaron ran after her then returned. I went looking for her because she didn't have a coat on, and Aaron went looking for her again. When I ran into her, we walked around the dock behind our place, looking for Aaron, then got home just as Aaron was getting back. I told him to just go to sleep and I would look after Jennifer, so we walked around the dock again for a little while. Eventually, around three o'clock she went home and went to bed, but I sat up for another hour to make sure she was all right. The next day, Jennifer and Aaron were still arguing; but eventually, Jennifer and I went to Vancouver to do some shopping. She said she was stressed out because of how Kelly treats her at work, so she bought a Sony Game Boy to help keep her mind off her problems, so I agreed to pay $100 out of the $250 it cost.

On Monday when I went back to work, I was usually anxious to get back, but this time I wished I had more time off. Other staff members felt the same way, and I could understand why Paul Kuster previously said, "No matter how much time you have off, it's never enough." Some even wished they could retire, and Micheline Bell said her husband is starting to get tired of his job. He works for the Parks Board, and the novelty is wearing off. The next day I felt stressed out to the point my heart was hurting, so I went to Vancouver for karate and my brown belt certificate; but I was still stressed out when I got home, so I bought a six-pack and drank it.

Jeff Fedyk, my former boss, said he sold Wayne Sakamoto a laptop computer that he doesn't use anymore and may be interested in selling it to me. I got excited because I wanted to put my writing on a computer disc.

I had joined the Aboriginal Employees Association last December and found out through e-mail messages and websites about organizations I didn't know existed. One was the National Aboriginal Veterans Association and decided to write to them for some information and wrote a rough draft but stopped to look after Jennifer because she was sick. On the weekend, Jennifer was still sick, but I took her to visit her mother because Henry Jr. asked us to go there and visit. I hoped he was getting over his emotional problems because he usually asks us to leave when I take Jennifer to visit her mother. I also took Jennifer to a drop-in medical clinic and she was diagnosed with acute sinusitis, so I missed karate that week because she was sick; then I got sick toward the end of the week. Aaron was working on a forestry job in Chilliwack, went back on Tuesday, and went to the bars that night. Jennifer got mad because she wasn't feeling well and thought he would want to spend time with her, so we went for a drive later in the evening, and Jennifer only cried slightly; then we went back home.

On Wednesday I typed out the letter to the National Aboriginal Veterans Association during my coffee break, and the staff knew it was a very serious letter, one of many letters that I would write. Jennifer called me in the morning and said she wanted to break off with Aaron. I went to work in the morning then stayed home after lunch because I was too sick to work and missed karate again. On Thursday Jennifer was still sick and cranky but went to work anyway. In the afternoon, Aaron left to get his money, paid bills, and visited friends. He was late getting back, so Jennifer and I went looking for him. When we found him, he said he had some money for us and was just on his way back and Jennifer told him to pay his bills then have his fun; if he was doing drugs, she wanted him to move out.

On Friday, Jennifer was still sick in the morning; but when she went home for lunch, she was happy and feeling better. On Saturday I slept in, had breakfast, and watched videos. In the afternoon, I drank two cups of coffee and couldn't sleep that night, so I thought I better not do that again. Aaron and I both noticed Jennifer wasn't flipping out like she usually does, so I hoped she was breaking her addiction to crisis. I started feeling more energetic, but I was bleeding heavily after bowel movements, so I thought I better see a doctor. I took Jennifer to North Vancouver shopping, but on our way back, my windshield wipers stopped working just past Britannia Creek. It was dark and raining hard, but I was lucky I have very good eyesight.

I was finally able to start karate, but the workout wasn't very intense; so I went home, did some writing, and that week, Wayne Sakamoto sold me his laptop computer for $100, a very cheap price at that time. At that time, laptops cost $2,200 brand-new and used laptops usually cost $1,100. I wanted to play with it but felt too nauseous and thought that could have been from the bottle of castor oil I had to drink before going for X-rays the next day. I was late from getting my X-rays, so I only saw Darlene for fifteen minutes, but it was a good visit; but after lunch, I felt sick again and thought it was still from the castor oil. Then I realized I had the flu.

I went to the staff curling bonspiel at the end of January and thought it was fun and wanted to go in another one on Valentine's Day, but I flipped a coin and it told me not to go. On Monday I wanted to go to karate but felt stressed out to the point my chest was hurting, so I went to the bar for a few beers instead. Normally I just like to drink at home, but I decided I should start going out more often. I still had severe acne, and the next day, the doctor gave me acne medication and told me to go for X-rays in six months. I still slept at lunchtime and didn't understand why because I was starting to feel more energetic.

Jennifer's left-handed and said it felt easier for her to read things from left to right, so I told her she had to learn to read from left to right because that's probably why she failed the English assessment test. If she had trained herself to read properly, she could be in the course right now, so she started trying to learn to read properly; but Henry wouldn't let his kids read. He said that was being lazy and wanted them to pay attention to him. In the second week of February, I felt sick at karate; and the next day, I slept right through my alarm and realized I was sick, so I booked in sick. On Valentine's Day I helped Richard move Uncle Ted's things out of the house, then he treated us to Chinese food. Jennifer went to the bars that night, got stressed out, then got the police to drive her to Tina Harry's place. Both were female and Allison Good was there and the other one seemed to wonder about me.

I couldn't sleep very well the next night and woke up early, so I was tired at work; but when I started thinking more about romances, I settled down and relaxed more. Jennifer also said Kelly is starting to treat her really good now. I still slept at lunchtime because I was tired and my throat was still bothering me. One night I was stressed out to the point my heart was hurting severely, so I bought a case of beer and missed karate. I sometimes went to bed earlier than I usually did and still felt tired at lunchtime, but my instincts tell me there's nothing but good things to come now. Jennifer seriously talked about moving back to Chilliwack, but I didn't do anything to discourage it. I thought more about helping her move there. She said Kelly was starting to treat her better, but it was too late now. She still wanted to move.

Toward the end of February, I was finally able to get a hold of Art Eggros of the National Aboriginal Veterans Association of Canada. He didn't get the letter I sent him because I wrote the wrong address on it. It wasn't returned, so someone else may have gotten it; so I sent him another copy. Jennifer inquired about low-income housing for Natives in Chilliwack, and it finally dawned on me that there probably isn't any other ethnic race with an unemployment rate in Canada as high as that of the Native Indians, yet people still believe we get equal treatment. In the first week of March, I went to work on Monday morning and left after two hours because I was sick. I wanted to compete in the Steveston International Karate tournament on the weekend and paid my fees but was too sick to go. Early the next week, I was stressed out to the point my heart was hurting severely again, so I drank. Aaron asked me if he was the cause of it, but it was Jennifer flipping out and my trying to look after her when it happened. She also wanted to give her notice that she was leaving Dairy Queen, but I suggested she look at the job market first.

Toward the middle of March, I was still feeling tired at lunchtime and the doctor's offices were shut down for a week, so I had to wait to get more pills for severe acid indigestion (acid reflux). At the end of the week, I was stressed out to the point my heart was hurting, so on Friday night I bought a case of beer. I wanted to take Jennifer to Sto:lo Eagle, but we had to wait for Aaron to get back from his job. I still felt stressed out the next day, so I bought another case of beer and drank it, but it's unusual for me to stay stressed out like that. When the doctor's offices were opened the next week, I got medication for acid reflux and was given two different types of pills.

Near the end of March, Jennifer gave Kelly her notice that she would be leaving Dairy Queen on May 14. I wasn't feeling well but still made it to work all week, and on the weekend, I took Jennifer to Chilliwack to apply for work. We were going to go to Sto:lo Eagle, but she decided she wanted to come back to Squamish. She kept saying she wanted to get away from Aaron; but when she got away from him, she wanted to go back. I think she was still addicted to suffering but she was starting to break away from it. On our way back, she decided to go to the bar that night and Aaron joined her. She borrowed $40 off me and they ended up doing drugs like I knew they would; then the next day, Jennifer and Aaron argued over doing drugs. She wanted him to stop taking drugs completely and not tell her to take drugs when she said "No!"

On Easter weekend I drank on Thursday night because I was stressed out and the next day I was going to take Jennifer to Sto:lo Eagle then go to Rosedale, but I ended up drinking again and eventually went to the bars. When I woke up the next morning, my wallet was gone, but my instincts told me not to worry; and when Jennifer and Aaron got back, she had my wallet and they took $400 out of my account to buy cocaine. I was mad even though Aaron said he would give me his whole next paycheck, so I told him he had to stay off cocaine now or move out. Then I took Jennifer to Sto:lo Eagle and ended up spending the night there. My family was going to have dinner on Monday; so Deidre and Sarah, David's daughters, would be there. Brenda and Alvin were also in Sto:lo Eagle and were well treated by Henry Jr. I had a hard time going to sleep that night, and I decided Aaron wouldn't be my roommate on an equal basis because he's not very responsible. I was only helping him while he was down on his luck. There was an Easter dinner there the next day, then I brought Jennifer back to Squamish so she could go back to work on Monday. I had a hard time going to sleep again and had to be up rather early the next day.

On Monday I got up, did some laundry, went out for coffee, and helped Jennifer get ready for work. She was cranky when I dropped her off at work; then my mother called while I was gone, so I called her back, and she was mad at me because I didn't call her when I was in Sto:lo Eagle. She said Sandra and my nieces couldn't make it and it would be lots of driving for me to go there for dinner, so it wasn't worthwhile for me to go. I did most of my laundry and went out for coffee while it was drying. I only drank three to four cups of coffee, and it made me shaky, so I knew my stress level was going down. When I went back to work, I felt sick most of the week and didn't dilute my coffee. I drank it strong, just like Aaron's was. By Friday I started feeling a little bit better but still liked to sleep at lunchtime and slept quite heavily. I missed a day of work the second week of April and went to the doctor. He said I had a throat infection and put me on pills for ten days. Dairy Queen in Chilliwack also called and wanted Jennifer to go for an interview Saturday at ten o'clock. It was Jennifer's birthday the next day, so I took her and Aaron to Yic's in North Vancouver for supper. Jennifer had lobster tail and Aaron and I had Chinese buffet. I felt good that she's now thirty-seven and didn't think she would live to be twenty-five when I met her.

The next day, a message was sent out to all staff regarding budget cuts and staff reductions. There would be a total of 338 positions cut, 256.7 in operations where I work. I got excited rather than depressed because I thought I could get a transfer to a place where I can get Jennifer a career and keep up with my karate training. Either that or take a transfer for someone who doesn't want to leave Squamish for recreation because their spouse is working and can't leave their job or like one co-worker, who wants to live near his son. If I was able to transfer, I hoped it would be to Campbell River because it's got a college, a karate club, and an outdoor recreation center half an hour away.

On Saturday I took Jennifer to Chilliwack for her interview at Dairy Queen then took her to Sto:lo Eagle and left right away because we were having a burning at my parents' place. A burning is an Indian ritual for family members who have passed away. There's a family gathering and a plate of food is burned to feed their spirits. It was a good gathering. Not a single person had a drink, and I enjoyed it. I picked Jennifer up the next day and we shopped around Abbotsford and North Vancouver before coming back to Squamish. I still slept heavily at lunchtime; and when I finished the pills the doctor gave me, my throat was still sore, like an infection.

Aaron went out to a logging camp for a tree-planting job; and my throat still bothered me, and I often felt stressed out. In early May I took Jennifer to Chilliwack to look for a place to stay. There were many places vacant, but the managers weren't there to view the apartments, so we came back to Squamish. Aaron called that night at ten forty-five and said he was on the ferry from Duke Point, so I knew he wouldn't get in until two o'clock in the morning. Jennifer wanted me to watch the story about Noah's ark that night, but I got bored with it; so I started making phone calls, which stressed her out, because she thought I was calling down Christianity and that's what saved her from suicide, so she went to the bars. I missed karate the next day because I wasn't feeling well, and Aaron gave me the $400 he owed me; then he and Jennifer went to the bars.

I helped out with Arbor Day in Whistler again and was glad I did because not many people showed up. Most of the regulars who helped out before had other commitments that year. Jennifer was also worried about finding a place to stay in Chilliwack, and it was stressing her out quite a bit. There were several apartments available where she wanted to live, so she found a place right away. Now she wants to go back to school so she can earn more than minimum wage.

I was still feeling sick most of the time and went to the lab for blood tests. I missed three days of work in the second week of May; and when I tried to go back to work the next week, I was still sick, so I went home after two hours. I went to the doctor again, and he found I had severe acid reflux and the medication for it had to be approved by DIA; so I still missed work all that week and started spitting up yellow goo, usually an indication I'm getting better. Jennifer and Aaron went to the bars and ended up taking drugs again; then she got mad and raised hell with him over taking drugs. Approval for the medication didn't come right away, so Jennifer called the drugstore and the pharmacist said I could get some medication right away then get the rest of it when payment was approved. I did that and started feeling better as soon as I took the medication, but I was still too sick to be concerned about her and Aaron taking drugs or even talk to them about it. I didn't realize how sick I really was until I got the right medication for what was wrong with me.

I took Jennifer and Aaron out for breakfast the next day and wanted to go to Rosedale for Ashley's birthday but was too sick to go. I was still sick but was getting better. I was glad it was a long weekend, so I could rest up before going back to work. I went back to work in the morning but took the afternoon off because I was still sick. I only missed half a day of work, but at the end of the week, I was still spitting up yellow goo. Jennifer asked Henry Jr. to help her move and said Saturday was the only day he could make it. Then Jennifer stressed me out Friday night because she was stressed out, so I drank a few beers. Hubert once told Jennifer her health problems were from anger leaving her body, so I wondered if that's what was happening to me.

On Saturday, Henry Jr. and their cousin Jerry helped Jennifer move to Chilliwack. Then we took them out for lunch, arranged for her to get a phone, visited their mother in Sto:lo Eagle for a little while, then came back to Squamish. On Sunday I still felt sick, but at least I stopped spitting up yellow goo. On June 1, Aaron and Jennifer took my car to Chilliwack to move furniture and apply for UIC, but the lady hadn't moved out yet, so they had to stay for one more day. Jennifer couldn't move into her apartment until the third and Aaron and I both told her to try and look into job training. I stayed in the office at lunchtime and slept right through my lunch hour, and the next day, I was still tired at lunchtime even though I had gone to bed early.

On the weekend, I bought Jennifer a used TV from a repair shop, which seemed like a good TV, then took her to Chilliwack. We went to Cultus Lake canoe races and to Save-On-Foods in Sardis on the Indian reserve, and Natives working there appeared to be accepted by other staff. On Sunday I took Jennifer to Sto:lo Eagle for a little while then went back to Chilliwack and bought her some more groceries at Save-On-Foods in Chilliwack, and Kim was still working there. There were Natives working there as well, and they seemed to be accepted by the other staff; for years it was extremely rare to see Natives working in the grocery stores, and clerks wondered why I would talk to Kim but not the rest of them.

When I went back to work, I was going to bed early and sleeping at lunchtime, yet Jeff Fedyk said I still looked tired. On the weekend I took Aaron to visit Jennifer then visited my parents, and the next day I helped Jennifer get settled and look for work. I didn't realize how stressed out I was until I got back to my parents' place. On Sunday I helped Jennifer look for work again and Tony gave me $200 for damaging my car, but the wheels started squeaking.

When I went back to work, I sometimes didn't think I was tired, but I still slept at lunchtime. On Tuesday I got my brakes fixed, and Aaron and I drank a case of beer. We were still stressed out, so I bought another case of beer, and the next day there were only three bottles left.

I was feeling a little bit better by the middle of the week and thought it was emotional stress making me tired. Jennifer called in the evening and said she got a part-time job at A&W. I thought it was close to where she lives, but it was in Sardis. By the third week of June, I wasn't sleeping as heavily at lunchtime as I did, was feeling more energetic, and Darlene said I was starting to look better.

July 1, Canada Day, was a statutory holiday and landed on a Thursday. I had saved enough hours to take Friday off, and we had rehearsals and photos for David's wedding; then he and Sandra got married the next day. On Monday I only slept lightly at lunchtime, and it seemed like it was time to forgive David for what he did to me. I did a contract viewing the next day and put in some long hours, so I drank a cup of coffee before leaving Pemberton so I could drive safely. I couldn't sleep because of that when I got home, so I went for a couple of beers to relax from the caffeine. I still had trouble going to sleep, so I knew my stress level was going down because my body was getting sensitive to caffeine again. I still sometimes felt tired and slept heavily at lunchtime but not all the time like before. It was time to go for X-rays again and I didn't want to go, but I started bleeding heavily after bowel movements again, so I thought I better go.

Jennifer called and said she wanted to see the band Aerosmith in concert if they ever came to Vancouver, so I called Vancouver Ticketmaster to see when they were coming. The clerk didn't know, so she told me to check the *Georgia Straight*, a free weekly entertainment newspaper; so I picked one up and a lady chuckled slightly when she saw me picking it up. In the paper, the Vancouver Film Fest was coming up; and one of the films was titled *Unwanted Soldiers*, about Chinese Canadians wanting to go to war for Canada in WWII but were continually turned down because the Canadian government thought they would demand the right to vote when they got back. Finally, the British government stepped in and realized they would be useful for dangerous commando work behind enemy lines because they could blend in with the population. I wanted to record that documentary but didn't know when it would be broadcast or on what channel, but the first thing I wondered was, "What kind of benefits did they get when they got back?"

In the last week of July, I still slept at lunchtime and felt quite stressed out, so I thought I should get more medication for acid reflux; and my instincts were now telling me my hard times in life were almost over. I sure hoped so. The doctor wouldn't give me any more medication though.

The course calendar for the University College of the Fraser Valley (UCFV) wasn't available until August 10, so Jennifer wasn't able to find out what she needed to go back to school until then. I couldn't get the hours in to take any time off, so I couldn't help her out until she got the course calendar. She found out the seats were filling up fast for the resident care attendant (RCA) course. She may not have all the necessary prerequisites and needed to do thirty hours of volunteer work first. I started thinking about applying for a promotion in Chilliwack because of that, and there's better karate training there. I also wrote a letter to her band to apply for funding for her course. I managed to get enough hours to take one day off in the second week of August and wanted to go to UBC to look for some information, but I thought I better help Jennifer get registered instead.

When I went back to work, I got some job postings on my e-mail from AEA for Fisheries and Oceans. I called Henry Jr. and asked if he would be interested in applying, and he called me back in the evening and said he was interested. I told him if he got the job, he could make $20,000 in six months, so the next day I sent the job postings by priority post to him and Isaac. It would get there by Thursday and would have taken just as long and cost me more to send it by courier. I started wishing someone would help me out the way I help Jennifer and her younger brothers out, but then I realized I wouldn't want to go through what they went through. I had booked some holiday time in the last week of August and planned on going fishing in Port McNeill with my cousin Dean Shackelly, but Jennifer needed me to drive her around to get her paperwork in place so she could do her thirty hours of volunteer time in a resident care facility. It was hot and would have been lots of work if I wasn't there to drive her around, so I booked my holidays at the right time.

While I was off, I phoned Cariboo College in Kamloops and asked for Jennifer's GED transcripts from her upgrading. They didn't have a record of it and told me to phone Victoria. I called Victoria but had to wait until next week to get through because of the shortage of staff due to holidays. When I got back to work, I called the education department in Victoria for Jennifer's transcripts for her upgrading, but they couldn't find them. I got really depressed because I thought they may have been thrown out because it was a long time since she did her upgrading; now I wondered if I would ever be able to get her a career! I called Victoria again the next day then realized Jennifer took adult basic education (ABE), not GED. I didn't know there was a difference, so I called Jennifer and told her to fax Cariboo College in Kamloops and ask for her ABE transcripts. She sent the fax to Cariboo College the next day, and I told her if she didn't get accepted, we'd try and get her into something else. The day after her request was faxed, she called me in the afternoon and said Visa rejected the charge. I called Cariboo College and had to keep trying over and over to get the right person because they were busy with the fall semester registration. Then when I finally got it straightened out, the lady said she would send it out in the morning.

In April, the Mount Currie Indian Band had applied for a logging cutting permit and part of the application to log a four-hectare patch of timber on the Indian reserve, but it had to be approved by DIA first. It didn't get approved until near the end of August, and Lyle Leo said they had lost $20,000 due to changes in market prices, and I didn't know how it could take that long to approve cutting such a small patch of land by DIA.

I wasn't really feeling well that week but had to go to work to try and get Jennifer's transcripts to her. I took Aaron to Chilliwack Labour Day weekend to visit her, and nothing eventful happened that weekend. When I got back to work, I decided to break down and buy a typewriter because I knew I would have to write out my life story at least two more times for stress management.

On Friday night I didn't feel stressed out but drank a few beers because I had nothing else to do. Aaron went out and didn't go back that night. I woke up early the next day and couldn't sleep when he knocked on my bedroom door. He had been up all night drinking and was worried he could get fired; he had a great job and still screwed up. I told him to call Rob Carrico, tell him he was too sick to go to work and I would take him to a medical clinic in North Vancouver. When he got to the clinic, he found out he had asthmatic bronchitis, would have to take medication and a few days off, and if he hadn't caught it, it could have turned into pneumonia and he could have wound up in the hospital. There was also a typewriter repair shop just down the street from the clinic, and I got a word processor for $35. That was a pretty good deal since I had considered buying one a few years earlier for $300; luckily, none of the salesmen would serve me.

In the third week of September, I was often tired, slept heavily at lunchtime, and had a sore throat. I went to the doctor on Thursday and he said there weren't any signs of an infection, so we both figured it was from emotional stress. Since I wasn't feeling well, I took the afternoon off; and New Forest Opportunities Ltd. (NewFOL) called Aaron for a job in the logging camp at Spring Creek, the north end of Harrison Lake. I always told him to turn the answering machine on when he leaves the apartment, but he sometimes forgets; he forgot to that time, but I was home to take the call.

Jennifer hurt her back that day and went to work for an hour the next day then went home; so Aaron and I went to Chilliwack to help her out, and I took her to the doctor the next day. She couldn't sleep on the couch because of her back, so on Sunday I bought her a bed. I was lucky I was able to get her a double bed with a firm mattress that was good for her back for $150. Karate finally started up again when I got back to work, but it would be shutting down in early December. I felt quite stressed out again by Thursday, and on Friday I felt sick but hung on till lunchtime then took the afternoon off. That afternoon I watched a program on near-death experiences, and strangely enough, Jennifer watched the same program. The lady said when people do wrong, they see what they did wrong before they reach heaven. Phaye said Henry made it to heaven but had trouble getting there. When Henry passed away, he had a wooden marker for his grave; and although it was treated with preservatives, it turned black in less than a year except for a slight ring around the outside edge. I wondered if he still suffered after he passed away but didn't take a picture of it because I didn't want anything to do with him. Most people who've had a near-death experience tell the same story; even a hit man for the Mafia told the same story, so there could be some truth to it.

Aaron and I went to Chilliwack to help look after Jennifer because of her back, then on Sunday she decided to come back to Squamish for better physiotherapy, and I could look after her. Aaron also had to go to Pemberton the next day for his job at Spring Creek, so Jennifer had to drive him to the bus depot the next day and probably had trouble getting back up the stairs. Aaron didn't have any money set aside for bus fare, so I had to lend it to him, and I missed karate that night because I had to look after Jennifer. I went out the woods on Wednesday but had to be back on time to take Jennifer to physiotherapy. I knew I would miss karate again and had been looking forward to some time alone, but Jennifer hurt her back.

There was a message sent out by e-mail to all British Columbia Forest Service employees from Lee Doney, the deputy minister of Forests, about an "employment equity and diversity action plan." The message was the following:

—Original Message—
From: Doney, Lee FOR:EX
Sent: Monday, September 20, 1999 5:15 PM
To: FOR ALL Forest Employees
Subject: 99/00 Equity and Diversity Action Plan

Since the introduction of the Equity and Diversity program in 1990, the Ministry of Forests had made progress towards achieving a workplace, at all levels, that is reflective and welcoming of the population we serve.

To date our efforts and our successes have been largely focused on how we can increase awareness and, to a lesser extent, how we can increase representation. We support and promote provincial and local equity and diversity advisory committees and their initiatives; and, we meet goals for mandatory equity and diversity training; and, we regularly find ways to experience and celebrate the diversity of cultures among us, particularly during multiculturalism week.

Although we must continue to build on creating awareness and build upon successes, the expectation upon us as an employer is to increase designated group member representation. The means by which the ministry will be evaluated on, and our reputation as a leader in equity and diversity initiatives maintained, will increasingly depend upon the extent to which the composition of our workforce, at all levels, reflects the population we serve.

With the current financial restraints placed upon us, we continue to be challenged in our ability to increase representation levels. However, we still see small successful steps being made. The key to our success will be to act upon any opportunities made available to us; to continue to integrate equity and diversity objectives into the day to day operations of the ministry; and, to remember that equity and diversity is a strategic plan of the ministry that can not be completed overnight. While we may have some setbacks due to current restrictions, I believe that ultimate the ministry will be successful in reaching it's equity and diversity objectives.

I am attaching the website address for the 1999/00 Equity and Diversity Action Plan to this message. The plan is a rollup of all submitted division and regional action plans. You are encouraged to review the plan and determine how you may contribute to the ministry's success in this area.

Questions about any of the initiatives, or the plan in general can be direct to Sharon Stewart, Manager, Equity and Diversity, Human Resources Branch at 387-8756.

Lee Doney
Deputy Minister
Ministry of Forests

I wrote out a response and typed it out; but just before I sent it, Paul Kuster came along, so I asked him to read it. He said he would read it but told me I was supposed to send it to Sharon Stewart, the manager of Equity and Diversity, Human Resources branch, not Lee Doney. Paul looked over the note and was still in the office the next day when I went out of the woods, and he told me to add some positive notes to it, so I adjusted it slightly and sent the following response:

In response to your equity and diversity action plan, I would like to know if any aboriginal employees are RPFs with LSO jobs or exactly how many Natives in British Columbia and Canada are registered professional foresters.

It was drilled into our heads that everyone in Canada gets equal treatment here, yet the unemployment rate on most Indian reserves is phenomenal. Before the settlers came, we were living off the land without a beast of burden, and that's definitely not a weekend camping trip. Now very few of us even know how to speak our own language, let alone how to live off the land. Of all the people I've spoken to, only one person has asked me why's there's so much unemployment on the Indian reserves when we were living off the land before the settlers came, and he was an Australian fellow.

Canada is one of the largest countries in the world, yet most Indian reserves in British Columbia (I'm not sure about other provinces) can be covered with a postage stamp on a 1:20,000 scale map. What little the Indians were given part of it was taken back with hydro lines, railroads, and highways. The general public is told that if we work on the Indian reserves, the money we make is tax free. But most reserves are nothing more than a useless, isolated rock pile; so in most cases, that tax-free money isn't even worth the paper it's printed on.

I was born in 1955 and went to college right after finishing high school in 1973. I was proud to be Canadian because we were continually told all people are equal and treated as equals here in Canada, so I couldn't believe how we were being treated in college. Department of Indian Affairs (DIA) segregated almost all first-year Native students and forced us on to a Mickey Mouse program that for most of us had nothing to do with what we were there for. There were two write-ups in the college newspaper, the first one titled "Native Students Angry at Segregation!" In that article, the exact words said by Gary, the counsellor from DIA, a federal government employee, were, "There's a high drop out rate of Native students. Perhaps Natives can't handle post secondary education."

It was well-known among Native students that Gary was deliberately putting students on the wrong programs and giving them courses they didn't want or need, making them waste their time there so they would get frustrated and quit. I was seventeen years old when that happened, so I was too young to think of saving it. I went back to Vancouver Community College (Langara campus) to get it, but it was missing.

The second article was titled "Native Students Cite Segregation!" which was still available, so I took a copy of it and showed it to various influential people.

I'm strongly of the opinion Gary was only doing what he was told to do when he was screwing the students around to try and make them give up, but I'm keeping that to myself. The reasons for it are in my life story, which I hope to publish soon. So far, only Paul Kuster (the district manager) and a coworker know why I believe Gary was only following orders. In my life story, I changed his name to Gary; I didn't give his real name.

Perhaps outright segregating the Native students was an isolated incident, but screwing them around or holding them back to make them give up probably wasn't because there are very few Natives over forty years old with successful, educated jobs that didn't take special programs for Natives. I spoke to other Natives who were held back from doing something for themselves by DIA, and it wasn't Gary that did it to them.

Many Natives told me stories about applying for work and just being ignored in spite of their qualifications and then white people would walk in behind them and get hired on the spot. Many times I've applied for work and couldn't even get an interview even though I have a diploma in forestry and years of woods experience. If that's not bad enough, it's nothing unusual for us to be closed off like condemned criminals by staff members when we do get hired. I've often been the only Native there and been closed off by everyone, but I try to be optimistic about it though. Fortunately, I've never really heard of Natives being harassed without just cause, and working here in Squamish has been a positive experience for me. I was still shy and withdrawn when I started here, but supervisors and staff encouraged me to speak up and gave me recognition and credit when I gave positive suggestions. Also, staying in one place and getting to know the district really well is an added bonus because in many cases, it saves time and money. When I'm assigned work, I often know if the work should be done or not; what the access is; and if arrangements should be made for road opening, helicopter access, etc.

I wasted my first two years at college because of DIA, attended for two more years, then transferred to BCIT. I knew I would be closed off by the students before I went there, but I was determined to get a career and not let anything stop me. Then I failed there two times for medical reasons, so it took me eight years of studying just to get a two-year diploma.

I've been through hard times I wouldn't wish on anyone, but eventually, something good came of it. What's most annoying though is being called "Too lazy to go to work!" more times than you can shake a stick at. I knew something was wrong when for a number of years after I left Merritt, the town I grew up in, every time I heard about that place, one of the Indians I went to school with died or committed suicide. Now I'm writing an autobiography, and if no one beats me to the title, I'm going to call it Almost a Born Loser!

Although I was born in 1955, one law still existed that most people don't believe ever happened in Canada. Retired RCMP constables knew about it because they had to enforce it, but they also told me the exact year it was modified then completely removed. When people say "Proud to be Canadian!" they forget to say "Since I'm not French or Indian!" If Canada is everything it's made out to be, it would be interesting to find out why Quebec wants to separate.

One possible solution to increase the number of RPFs is those aboriginals who have been employed by the MOF for at least five years and intend to make it their career should be encouraged to go on the pupil program.

I took Jennifer to Chilliwack the next day to pay her rent and vacuum the hallways in the building she lived in, and she also got a letter saying she had all the prerequisites for the RCA course. Then she came back to Squamish again for physiotherapy and so I could help look after her. On Monday I sent the response about equity and diversity to Sharon Stewart, the manager; Sally Prowse, Equity and Diversity advisor; and Bertha Elliot, AEA. I didn't get an answer from anyone but didn't really expect one.

Looking after Jennifer and taking her to physiotherapy was stressful, but she got lots of writing done while Aaron was in camp. On Friday I wanted to go to UBC to look for some information but decided to have a day of rest. I drank that night, and the next day I took Aaron and Jennifer to Chilliwack and spent the night at her place. I felt stressed out and worried because of the way Jennifer drained my finances, so I drank again; then Jennifer also got a letter from the college saying she hadn't completed her thirty hours of volunteer time. Jennifer gave up her job vacuuming the hallways in the apartment building because it was getting too hard on her back. It was Thanksgiving weekend and I booked a week of holidays, so I took Aaron and Jennifer to Sto:lo Eagle for Thanksgiving dinner then went to Rosedale. Dinner at my parents' place was a little bit late, but it was still a good dinner; then I had to bring Aaron back to Squamish to arrange his ride back to work. We got in about ten o'clock, just in time for him to arrange a ride.

Jennifer saw a doctor about her back to apply for UIC, and I missed karate for three weeks, but getting Jennifer stronger was my main priority next to my job. I wanted to go to UBC on Thursday but had to look after Jennifer, so I took her shopping in West Vancouver. Her back was getting better, but her cheek was hurting from her dental work; and she forgot her purse in one of the stores, which stressed me out. So I drank two beers at home then went to the bars for two more. I was going to take Jennifer to visit her mother on Saturday night, but she thought Henry Jr. was crabby, so we just stayed home and went there the next day. I told Henry Jr. how his father said he did everything for us and we were obligated to him, so I refused to do anything for him, and he realized what I did was right.

I went back to work and usually slept heavily at lunchtime. Aaron finished his job on Wednesday, went home Thursday morning, and asked to go back for more work; but other people were chosen. I couldn't sleep very well Thursday night and was surprised I wasn't tired the next day and only slept lightly at lunchtime. Jennifer completed her volunteer time but couldn't bring her letter of reference to the college because they were shut down for Pro-D Day. She came back to Squamish for physiotherapy, and on Monday I mailed her letter of reference to the college at lunchtime. Jennifer finally found a doctor who would listen to her and put her on intravenous injections. The next day I felt stressed out to the point my heart was hurting, but surprisingly, I felt better after only four beers; and on Thursday, Jennifer had an appointment with Darlene and she said Jennifer had post-traumatic stress disorder.

Although Halloween was on a Sunday, I still volunteered to take Ashley and Nicole, Isaac's daughters, out trick-or-treating; so I got back to Squamish rather late. But surprisingly, I woke up early the next day and couldn't sleep. Jennifer called A&W and said she won't be back to work next week either. I slept at lunchtime but not very heavily, and on Tuesday I felt stressed out but only drank a few beers because I've been slowing down on drinking. A week later, I took Jennifer to visit her friend Tina Harry and saw *Unwanted Soldiers* would be aired on Remembrance Day, but it didn't say what channel or time. I called the college the next day to see if Jennifer was accepted, but all I got was an answering machine.

Thursday was Remembrance Day. I had enough hours saved to take Friday off, and a female police constable noticed I outright refused to take part in the Remembrance Day ceremonies and felt bad about it because she knew it was justified. Our band also had elections the next day, and Isaac was running for chief but didn't make it. After Remembrance Day, I found out *Unwanted Soldiers* was broadcast on VTV, a Vancouver television station; so I e-mailed VTV for a copy of the film and they said I could get it from the National Film Board (NFB), so I phoned NFB and ordered the video. Before I ordered the video though, I phoned Veterans Affairs Canada (VAC), told them about Chinese Canadians being unwanted soldiers, and asked, what kind of benefits did they get when they got back? The fellow answering sounded like an elderly fellow and couldn't give a definite answer, so I thought it might be mentioned on the video. He also didn't know the Indians didn't get any benefits white soldiers got and about a law that still existed when I was a child.

The next day, Jennifer found out the RCA course was filled and there were a dozen people on the waiting list to get in. We didn't get our hopes up too high because we didn't want to get too badly disappointed, but I tried to be optimistic about it and went out for a cup of coffee. I took the last week of November off for holidays and had hoped to go hunting but just felt too tired and drained of energy. I called Glen Shackelly, and he asked me to go hunting with him, but

I just didn't have any energy. Hilda Gosselin, a lady who lived down the hall from Jennifer and was a retired nurse, said her daughter was twelfth on the waiting list for the RCA course and still got in. That picked up our hopes and made us feel better, but we still didn't get our hopes up too high. My week off wasn't too bad, and I felt rested up and started feeling better.

In the second week of December, I still felt tired most of the time and slept when I got home from work. I went to Vancouver for karate one night and really enjoyed it but still felt stressed out when I got home, so I drank a six-pack, I missed the staff Christmas party on the weekend, but I guess I should have gone. On Saturday I phoned Jennifer and she wanted me to go visit her, so I went back to Chilliwack and she came back with me on Sunday. Jennifer and Aaron went to the bar the next day, and I got scared for Jennifer because she doesn't seem to know when to stop drinking and may get in trouble. She borrowed $50 off me and I knew what it was for, and I tried to say no, but she was too persistent.

I've been writing ever since I bought my word processor and could now type four to six pages before it started to get to me. It actually made me feel sick; then I felt better afterward. The next day, Jennifer said she wanted to go to AA now because when she drank, she wanted to do cocaine. I wanted to go to Vancouver for karate, but it snowed, so I thought I better not go. I did lots of writing, six to eight pages. It still stressed me out to relive what I went through, so I drank a six-pack. On Wednesday I didn't think I was tired, but I slept heavily at lunchtime and after work. I felt really tired most of the time during the summer and fall and didn't even have the energy to spar in karate.

The staff had a Christmas party at the office, and each person was expected to bring a non-perishable-food donation for the food bank; so I brought a cake mix, icing, and Jell-O. I had them in my cupboard and wouldn't be using them. Then after donating them, it dawned on me that it's important for kids to have luxuries like that once in a while, especially if they're from a very poor family; and all other staff members agreed. Some people are so poor they can't even afford a cake mix.

Jennifer asked me to call AA for her and find out where and when the meetings were held, and she met a lady who was eleventh on the waiting list for the RCA course and still got in, so that made her feel better. I had enough hours to take the next day off, so I went to UBC

First Nations House of Learning, and the lady there wasn't going to let me search the archives and said I could leave a note for someone else to look for it. When I started writing down what I was looking for, she opened the door and let me search before I even finished writing. The other lady, Anne Doyle, wouldn't be back until after the New Year but may be able to find it; but I also had to be back to Squamish by five o'clock in case Aaron's paycheck went in.

I had taken the bus to Vancouver to avoid heavy traffic, especially at Christmastime; and when I got to the bus depot, I was going to eat there but decided to wait until I got back to Squamish. Aaron's check didn't go in, so I flipped a coin to try and decide where to eat. The coin said to go to McDonald's, so that's where I went. When I got to McDonald's, I saw someone who looked familiar, and he said hi to me. It was Russel, Jennifer's cousin from Sto:lo Eagle; so I joined him, his wife, and two of their grandchildren. I talked to them about my job, the issues I brought up, what I've been through, and eventually we talked about Henry. I told Russel about how Henry treated me and he said Henry's mother was also like that. Then Russel's wife said Russ's grandfather went after Russel's father with a gun. Andy, the grandfather, beat the kids; and both parents made the kids and grandkids work and give them all the money, and Russel's parents did the same thing to him. Andy was originally from Musqueam but left because people wanted to put him in the smokehouse for misbehaving. Russel said he picked cascara bark, maple buds, and moss for money; cut firewood for the grandparents; and they still took all his money. At dinner time, the uncles sat on one side of the table and the grandchildren sat on the other side. Yeast bread was baked, and a dish of butter went down the uncle's side of the table then stopped. Russel served himself a little bit of butter out of the dish beside him, and Andy said, "That's mine!" and kicked him off the table. One of his aunts even had an abortion from one of Henry's kids. Russel said, "Henry's my uncle, but that's all I have to say about him." I figured Jennifer's uncle Bruce may have been in denial, a coping method for severe abuse, and fantasized his parents as ideal parents. That's probably why his story was different from Henry's.

Four days before Christmas, I brought Aaron back to Squamish so he could pick up his check, and wanted to pick up the video I ordered from the NFB so it wouldn't get sent back while I was on holiday. Aaron wasn't in Squamish long and felt he had to leave because he had money and would be tempted to do drugs. I watched the video in the evening but kept getting interrupted, and the issue I inquired about before ordering the video wasn't mentioned, so I would have to check into it when I got back to work.

Nothing eventful happened up to Christmas Eve, but Jennifer had to go to work on Boxing Day, so I let her and Aaron take the car to Sto:lo Eagle. We stopped at my parents' place to drop me off, and my parents were happy to see her. Jennifer had bought flowers for her dad and wanted to leave early enough to place them on his grave, but we didn't get the gifts wrapped on time. Henry Jr. also bought flowers for their father's grave, so they both placed them on Christmas Day. I felt proud of myself for my accomplishments but finally realized eight years is a long time out of a person's life to get my career, a two-year diploma. After Christmas, Jennifer stressed me out with her spending habits and we got into a big argument. She got over it right away though and said it was because she missed her sister Liz.

Chapter 22

2000

On New Year's Day, Jennifer had most of her family over to her place for a turkey dinner, and it was a good family gathering. On Sunday I was feeling rested up and knew if I had more time off, I would start getting restless, but wasn't anxious to go back to work though because there wasn't very much to do at work. I still had Monday off since New Year's Day was on a Saturday; and I took Jennifer, Aaron and Henry Jr. out for a Chinese buffet for lunch. Then Aaron and I came back to Squamish because it was snowing and we were worried about road conditions.

Getting back to work was all right; then I noticed an e-mail for field operations supervisor (FOS) training, so I decided to apply for it. I thought it would be hypocritical of me not to apply because I kept bringing to the government's attention what kind of jobs aboriginal employees have. Then I couldn't sleep at lunchtime that day because I was too excited about applying for training to get a promotion. I told Paul Kuster about the documentary *Unwanted Soldiers*, and the first thing I wondered was, "What kind of benefits did they get when they got back?" and he said, "*Way to go, Annis!*"

Aaron wanted to borrow my car to go to Vancouver that day to go to a bank and pick up some money, but I didn't trust him to go that far with my car, so I drove him. After he picked up his money, I drove him to the bus depot then went to the Renfrew Community Centre for karate and was surprised Shihan Yabanaka, a seventh-dan black belt and the head instructor of Canada, was there. By helping Aaron out, I helped myself out again. When I got home, I was surprised I couldn't sleep until I did some writing and searching for information on Chinese Canadian WWII veterans, and slept heavily the next day at lunchtime, probably because I went to bed rather late. After work, I didn't think I was stressed out, but I flipped a coin and it told me to buy a six-pack. I drank five beers then realized I was quite stressed out. On Friday I asked the Chinese Cultural Centre Museum and Archives for the information by e-mail then worked on my writing in the evening. It stressed me out, so I drank seven beers and woke up sitting at the table.

On Saturday I worked on my writings but took a break after each hour of writing. It was less stressful that way, but I was still mad at Henry for how much appreciation he showed me for all the things I did for him as well as saving his daughter from suicide. I was finally able to let go of more anger because I knew he suffered for everything he did wrong and saw many of the things I did to him happen back to me, but it was still hard to forgive him. Writing and reliving what I went through was still stressful, but I knew I had to do it again for stress management. I thought I would get stressed out reliving 1987 again, but after reading it over, I felt proud of myself for what I went through and wouldn't give up. When I got back to work, I called the Langara College newspaper and asked if those articles from 1973 were on microfilm. I got referred to the library and was told the archives weren't open to the general public, so I asked for a certain article on a specific date; staff were listening and I was told it's not there but it might be at the main library at UBC.

Aaron went to visit one of his brothers on Vancouver Island, and I started sleeping more lightly at lunchtime and felt more energetic. On Thursday night I didn't feel like cooking just for myself, so I decided to go out for supper. I flipped a coin and it told me not to go to A&W or Dairy Queen; then I remembered I had Burger King coupons, and the coin told me to go there. When I got to Burger King, Sharon Malleappah was working there. She graduated high school in 1999, so I asked her if schools still drilled into everyone's heads that everyone gets equal treatment in Canada. She said they did, so I told her a number of reasons why nothing could be farther from the truth. I told her about the size of Indian reserves; where they're located; the unemployment rate is phenomenal, yet we were living off the land before the settlers came; and now very few of us even know how to speak our own language, let alone how to live off the land. Then I told her what I went through to get a career, being closed off, and Natives not being hired in spite of our qualifications then being labelled "too lazy to go to work"! Then I told her there are also many funny stories that can be told.

I slept lightly at lunchtime again the next day but didn't visit Jennifer because it was snowing too hard. I did some writing off and on the next day, and it felt really good to write now. I feel proud of myself for what I went through and wouldn't give up. On Sunday I did more writing and went to bed when I felt tired but couldn't sleep, so I got up and finished writing "1987." My car wouldn't start the next day, so I had to get someone to give it a jump-start; then I couldn't get it started at lunchtime, so I had to get a mechanic to go get it and knew I would have at least a $500 repair bill. I drank that night because I was too stressed out to do any writing, probably because of all the writing I did the day before, so I had to learn not to push myself so hard. For two nights in a row I slept well at night and woke up early; perhaps I was feeling better because I was letting go of anger.

Jennifer and Aaron went out drinking one night, and I missed karate to study for the FOS exam so I could apply for a promotion. I also did some writing because it made me feel better, like it took some weight off my chest. I wrote the exam the next day and didn't think it was hard. It was long, but I enjoyed it because it felt mentally challenging. A few years ago I would have been too stressed out to apply for a promotion. I drank in the evening because the exam burnt me out, but I felt really good about trying to advance now; the job was in Chilliwack. At the end of January and when I got home from work one day, Aaron asked to borrow $2 off me to go to the bar for a beer. I didn't want to, but when he got back, he said he got a job from someone in the bar. He would have missed it if he didn't go to the bar, but I didn't know if he was telling the truth or not, until someone called for him.

I woke up at four o'clock the next morning and couldn't sleep and figured it's from not thinking about sex; normally, I don't think about it because I'm used to getting turned down. I trained in karate the next day and still felt stressed out, so I bought a six-pack and drank it, still felt stressed out, so I bought another one; but I didn't know why I felt that stressed out. I got another video I ordered from the NFB, *Forgotten Warriors*, the story of Canada's aboriginal war veterans but was too stressed out to watch it. I still felt stressed out when I got home the next day; so I drank my last beer, slept for a little while, did some writing, then watched my video. Then the video made me anxious to write my life story to expose more of the truth about Canada.

The next day I had a good visit with Darlene and she made me realize how my anger toward Henry was affecting me. She told me to pretend he was there and say what I thought of him and how I felt toward him. I knew he suffered for what he did wrong, but it was still hard for me to forgive him. I went to Chilliwack that night and drove Jennifer to work the next day; then after dropping her off, I went to visit my parents and told my mother about Jennifer eating wild plants and stealing from the store because she was hungry and being beaten for making a mistake, the littlest excuse or for no reason at all. Geraldine mentioned how hungry the kids were but the food had to be saved for *Old Useless* (Henry). Then my mother finally realized why I tried so hard to look after Jennifer and help her get a career. I knew I was doing the right thing but still worried about doing too much for her.

I missed karate when I got back because I was stressed out and drank a case of beer and didn't know why I felt that stressed out though; but on ThursdayI didn't feel like going to karate, went anyway, and felt better afterward. I was starting to get my energy back but still slept at lunchtime. On the weekend I went to UBC main library and checked their special collections; they had copies of newspapers from Langara College, but the article I was looking for wasn't there. Now my only chance to find it might be the Union of British Columbia Indian Chiefs (UBCIC) or ask a former student if they kept it. On Monday, David Haffey, an RPF from Interfor, went to the office and did some work with me. He knew I was just a forest technician and realized there are many issues people should consider before they say, "Everyone gets equal treatment in Canada!" He was only the second non-Native Canadian to say that to me, so I mentioned him later on in letters I wrote to influential people.

On Tuesday I thought I could finish typing "1990" but was too stressed out, so I drank, and the next day I realized it could have been from all the writing I did. I called UBCIC research department, and they didn't have the missing article either. I doubt if I'll find it now, unless some other student thought about keeping it, so I'll have to try and look them up. I tried to do some writing the next week but felt stressed out to the point my heart was hurting, so I drank to relieve the pain and still slept heavily at lunchtime.

On February 24, British Columbia got their first Indo-Canadian premier, but many Indians probably wondered when the first Canadian Indian would make premier, and the news station I usually watch knew many of us felt that way too. I had a hard time getting to sleep that night, but surprisingly, I only slept lightly at lunchtime, I got much writing done on the weekend, and it was not as stressful as it used to be. I also felt better when I spoke out and brought issues to other influential people's attention. By the end of February, I slept lighter at lunchtime and sometimes woke up before the timer went off, thinking it was time to go back to work. I did some writing after karate one night and still felt stressed out, so I had a few drinks of rye. I almost finished writing "1993," and it felt good. I hoped to finish it soon so Jennifer could read it before she started classes and I could pass it on to Auntie Jeanette. I couldn't drink coffee at night very much anymore because it kept me awake.

On Friday I decided to just drop everything and take the night off. I did lots of writing the next day and felt really good about it. In the evening I wanted to keep on writing, but Jennifer kept phoning and interrupting my concentration, so I stopped. I felt really good when I woke up the next day and didn't have a sore back. I finished typing "1993," felt stressed out, then went for a walk and ran into Keith Brown and had lunch with him. He said he had some information for me and loaned me the book *Spirit of the Wise*, a collection of stories by upgrading students who interviewed Native elders. I was still stressed out to the point my heart was hurting, so I went to the bars for a few beers. Writing still stressed me out. I worked on my writing again then stopped when I was making too many spelling mistakes, so I thought I better not push myself too hard. At first I dreaded the thought of writing "1994" because I almost got fired that year, but now I'm proud of what I went through and succeeded.

On the second weekend of March, I wanted to go to Chilliwack to visit Jennifer, but Aaron needed my car to go to work. I got lots of writing done that weekend, so that was okay. Writing still stressed me out though, so I had a couple of beers Sunday afternoon and felt pretty good the next day. Writing let out lots of tension as long as I didn't overdo it. I woke up at three o'clock the next morning and couldn't sleep until five o'clock, and Aaron thought it could be from doing too much writing all at once.

That week, Aaron rented a rug shampooer to clean the carpet, and a friend of his helped him but dropped my typewriter on the floor. They were drinking when I got home, so I went to karate then drank when I got home. On Thursday I took the typewriter to North Vancouver to see if it could be fixed then went to Chilliwack to visit Jennifer. She had an information meeting that night; then she came back to Squamish to visit. She was to go for an interview on March 27, and we were excited about that. The next day I found out my typewriter wasn't worth fixing, so I thought I may just have to borrow one to type what's left over. On Saturday I took Jennifer shopping in West Vancouver and was going to look for another typewriter but didn't think I would need one, but on Sunday I changed my mind because I thought I might do more writing later on but decided to take a break first. I've been pushing myself rather hard and drinking heavily as a result; although writing and reliving what I went through was a catharsis, it was still stressful.

I slept well Monday night, woke up early and couldn't sleep, and slept again at lunchtime but not very heavily. I felt stressed out after work though, and Aaron was depressed because a friend of his died in an avalanche, so I loaned him $20 to go to the bar. I was starting to sleep lightly at lunchtime now and Jennifer seemed happier and was feeling better about herself. When I went back to work, I was feeling sick and ended up missing work on Wednesday and Thursday. Jennifer and Aaron both figured it could be from not doing any writing, so I borrowed a typewriter off Keith Brown and started writing "1999." I pushed myself quite hard, drank two beers, then Aaron and Gary Columbus came home with a six-pack.

In March I really pushed myself to finish writing "1999" then had a hard time going to sleep and thought it could be from the stress of reliving what I went through. Aaron's been going to the bars every day for a few days now and Jennifer's been going out quite a bit too. I still worried about Jennifer putting herself in dangerous situations because it felt normal to her, and both of us worried about Aaron getting into drugs. On Friday, Darlene suggested I get into writing because I let her read all the research reports and letters that I sent out to influential people. She said I'm a gifted writer, and I told her I thought about writing some fiction and maybe even some biographies.

Aaron and I went to visit Jennifer, and Aaron stayed in Chilliwack that week. In the first week of April, I felt rather tired, so I decided to work on my writing in the evenings. I felt tired at lunchtime and the timer seemed to go off right after I set it and realized it could be from not doing any writing. I went to karate one evening but should have just stayed home because when I got back, I drank a few beers and didn't do any writing, so I decided to go to Vancouver on the weekend to buy another typewriter then started sleeping lightly at lunchtime again. I figure I'd start feeling better if I did more writing, and got a sore throat again and was sure it was from emotional stress because the doctor said there wasn't any sign of an infection.

I called Jennifer on Friday and she said the fire alarm went off at 2:30 a.m. and she was the only one who responded. There was a man with a knife, threatening to blow the building up and telling her to leave. Aaron went out there and was told the same thing, so she called the police; then about seven cop cars showed up, and the tenants had to wait outside until everything settled down.

On Saturday I checked a pawnshop in North Vancouver for a typewriter and couldn't find one, so I went to Yic's for lunch then checked another pawnshop, and a young Native fellow walked in behind me and said he could sell me one. I took his address then checked an office-equipment store, but they were too expensive, so I bought one off the Native fellow. It worked, but the correcting ribbon didn't. I went to visit Keith Brown the next day, and two female police officers noticed I was going out more often; then I realized I was staying home quite a bit and drinking too much again, so it was time to slow down before it got out of hand. I worked on my writing and felt good about it; phoned Wilma Robinson during my coffee break; and she said when we went to college, that was the first time there was that many first-year Native students, so DIA outright segregated us.

It was Nicole's birthday on Saturday, so I took her and Ashley to Wonderland in Abbotsford since Isaac was working. It was also Jennifer's birthday, but she was working. The next day I took her and Aaron to Hope for a drive; then we went out for a steak dinner, and Jennifer now had all the paperwork in place that she needed for her course.

When I tried to find out information on Chinese Canadian WWII veterans, I started wondering when Chinese women were allowed into Canada. I didn't get any answers anywhere I asked, so I called Citizenship and Immigration Canada. They just told me to fax Public Affairs Canada, gave me a fax number, and said they have a fax but no phone. I didn't believe them but sent the fax anyway and didn't get an answer; that was no surprise. One day after work, I felt stressed out and my instincts told me to go to the lounge for a beer, so I went there and sat at the counter. Another fellow went in and sat at the corner near me and right out of the blue said Chinese women started coming into Canada in 1948. I didn't even mention I was looking for that kind of information. I called Wilma during the week, gave her Gary's phone number, and asked her to fabricate a story to him and try and find out if he kept the missing article from the Langara newspaper and if he would send her a copy. She tried, but all she ever got was an answering machine.

I went to bed early and slept heavily at lunchtime then realized I was sick, so I took Thursday off; and it was Easter weekend, so I had lots of time to recover. When I got back to work, I sent Sharon Stewart a confidential e-mail titled "Final Information" because I didn't intend to let out any more information. Normally, she doesn't respond; but this time she did. She agreed that aboriginal employees are badly underrepresented at the professional level but thought I was extreme in thinking there probably never has been a Native RPF with a professional's job with the British Columbia Forest Service ever since it came into existence. She also told me the Native representation is way too low—1.1 percent of 1,113 professional positions are aboriginal people who identified themselves. Then I wrote another article titled "Lack of Native Professionals" and told her most of the truth about how Indians have been treated and obstacles we had to go through to get a career.

On my next appointment with Darlene, she was late, but it was still a good visit. I expressed my anger toward my mother then told Darlene it was a mistake to buy Jennifer's work clothes when she was working at Dairy Queen because it taught her to be irresponsible, but she told me not to worry because even a trained professional would have made mistakes. In May I started sleeping lightly at lunchtime but still sometimes slept heavily at night. I helped out with National Forest Week, taking elementary schoolchildren on forestry tours, and helped out with Arbor Day in Whistler again. We always give trees away there, so I decided to take some and plant them on my reserve. Since I helped out almost every year, they gave me two boxes of hemlock to show their appreciation. Chris Runnals, a coworker, also gave me some cedar trees; and I managed to get a few fir trees.

Being a pre-award technician wasn't very busy, and there wasn't any fieldwork; then I realized I could work on articles for Equity and Diversity. I was given permission to do it, so I wrote some more confidential articles bringing many issues to the government's attention. I only marked them confidential because it's coming out in my life story. In the middle of May, I started feeling rather stressed out, so I called Jennifer one afternoon and she said she had to go for another interview for her course; that's probably why I was feeling stressed out. On the long weekend in May, Aaron and I planted the trees I obtained on the Indian reserve. We planted on Saturday, took Sunday off, then finished planting on Monday. After planting the trees, the three of us went out for a steak dinner since it was Aaron's birthday.

When I got back to work, I went to a forum on representation of aboriginal people in the public service; there were only eight people there, but some very interesting issues and statistics were brought up. I told them some of the things I went through and suggestions to remedy the lack of Native professionals and didn't realize until then that one of my last major obstacles was just to get a permanent job. I went to the dentist the next day at 11:20 a.m., got out early, had lunch, then slept soundly for fifty minutes, twice as long as I normally slept.

One Sunday I took Jennifer to work then went to visit Helen. Jennifer hurt her wrist at work and took a taxi home rather than call me to pick her up. When I got back to work, I was stressed out, so I missed karate and drank; and when I woke up, I realized I drank eleven beers. I missed karate again the next day because I was tired and needed a night of rest but finished typing "1999" and was now ready to put everything on a computer disk. For some reason, I started sleeping heavily at lunchtime again.

Jennifer went for her interview and was told she's been out of school too long and would have to take a study-skills course before getting into the RCA program. The course was to start in July, but now she was told to wait until January, which disappointed her; but she tried to be optimistic about it. I kind of wondered because Phaye said she would be starting her career in January or February; then Aaron and I went to Chilliwack to visit her because we knew she would be depressed. We went to the Cultus Lake canoe races the next day, and I was glad I couldn't finish my life story two years ago because of what I learned since then. Eugene Victor (a fellow from my reserve) and I were talking to an Indian from the Musqueam Reserve in Vancouver, and he said statistics say most Indians commit suicide between the ages of forty and fifty-five. We went to the canoe races again the next day, and on our way back, I was surprised to see a car of nice-looking girls smiling at me. Normally, girls like that just act like I'm not there.

I usually slept lightly but sometimes slept heavily now. On Thursday I went to Vancouver for karate and still felt stressed out when I got home, so I drank. The next day, Darlene asked me to get the reasons in writing why Jennifer couldn't get into the course, then appeal it. I tried to do that, but it didn't do any good; no one would even answer.

Two weeks later, Aaron and I went to visit Jennifer. He was in the bar when I was ready to leave; and when I went to get him, he forgot something at home, so he asked me to get it while he finished his beer. I went to get it and saw Derek Kingston sitting in a restaurant, so I went in and talked to him. Derek was the subforeman on my crew when we were tree-planting in Lytton in 1987; most of the crew were Indians, and Derek said half of the crew is dead now, either from suicide or alcohol- and drug-related deaths. He also said Lytton averaged ten Indians dying a year by suicide or alcohol- and drug-related deaths, and the fellow sitting with him said one year it was as high as fourteen, but things are slowing down now. Even before I left Chilliwack in 1990 a girl from Lytton, Donna Hance, said Lytton's going to become a ghost town because so many people there were dying. The next day I spoke to Eugene Victor about that and what the fellow from Musqueam said. Eugene and I are in the same age group, and from what we've seen, most Indians commit suicide between the ages of fourteen and twenty-five.

The next weekend, Aaron's sister, Deb, had to move out of her place; so Aaron had to move his things. I drove him over there and we spent the night at his brother Jim's place. We came back the next day, and it was a rather nice visit. I did the late check-in when I got back to work, and on Tuesday I went to the drugstore to buy a newspaper, carrying the radio. There were three white people sitting at a table outside a coffee shop, and I heard one of them say, "It's about time some of them went to work!"

I responded, "Only a Canadian would say that!"

The next weekend was a long weekend of July, and I got to put in some overtime patrolling recreation sites. I was going to go to

Chilliwack after work, but Aaron was drinking and we couldn't get his power saw until the next day, and he needed it for a job in Chilliwack. We went to Chilliwack on Sunday, and I caught the bus back to Squamish on Monday since it was a holiday. The weather was getting warm, so I let them use the car, and I rode my bicycle to work.

I had to go back to Chilliwack the next day for a course, stayed at Jennifer's place, and felt stressed out when I got back; so I drank a six-pack. Aaron and Jennifer were drinking when I left, and Jennifer flipped out again; she grabbed a knife and may have wanted to hurt herself, but Aaron stopped her and cut his hand in the process. Both of them ended up in jail. Aaron got a restraining order to stay away from her, and she ended up with a black eye. Jennifer caught the bus to Squamish the next day, and I got scared she would lose her job because she missed work, but Aaron eventually drove to Squamish. I was worried Jennifer may end up moving back in with me even though there was a message on her answering machine saying there was a seat reserved for her in the RCA program in January; looking after her was still stressful.

I had enough hours built up to take the next day off, so we drove to Chilliwack and Jennifer wasn't fired. Aaron had to see a probation officer, then we went to Isaac's place. My cousin Marilyn and her husband, Bob, were visiting from Missouri, a state in the USA; and her mother, Auntie Tilley, and her other daughter, Linda, were also there. Then my mother finally admitted she used to deliberately hold me back from having fun when I was a child and teenager.

Jennifer had Sunday off, and I caught the bus back to Squamish. Aaron needed my car to go to legal aid, see his probation officer, go to work, and had a two-week job on Vedder Mountain near Chilliwack. I stayed home the next weekend and wrote an article to a friend I used to log with in 1979, Harley Wylie. We're in the same age group, so we can relate to what we've been through and the things we saw happen and called it "Grim Reality!"

GRIM REALITY!

Last month, I ran into Derek Kingston, a white fellow who worked on my crew in 1987 in Lytton when I was managing tree-planting contracts. He said ½ the people who worked on the crew are now dead from suicide or alcohol- and drug-related deaths. Derek and his coworker, a contractor, said in Lytton there was an average of ten Natives a year dying either by suicide or alcohol- and drug-related deaths. One year it was as high as fourteen, but things are slowing down now.

One former chief of Lytton Band, Ruby Dunstan, said people have a drinking problem, go to a treatment center for help, then go right back to drinking.

This year one fellow said statistics say most Natives commit suicide between the ages of forty-five and fifty-five. I don't know where he got his information because from what I've seen and other people have seen, it's more like between fourteen and twenty-five.

Everyone thought I had the nicest parents, but when I was twenty-five, I stood up to someone three times my size for a knife fight. I thought, If I win, I win! If I lose, I won't have to put up with how my family is treating me anymore! *I'm now writing my life story out for the sixth time and finally getting over the pain and anger of that incident.*

I went through hard times I wouldn't wish on anyone and did everything I could to cope with the stress. One method was doing research on human behavior and addictive personalities. Native Indians are known to have a problem with alcohol, but after doing some research, I wondered if Indians were drinking because of the pain and anger of what they went through in the residential schools. Eventually I saw Indians interviewed on TV, and they said that was why they drank. When I was told some studies said some Indians said life in the residential schools was better than life at home, there was no answer when I asked, Did those studies say how many people were interviewed and what percentage of them said life in the residential schools was better than life at home?

After what I've been through and seen happen over the years, I'm glad I was able to save one Native girl, Jennifer, from suicide; but that was an ordeal I wouldn't wish on anyone.

One article I read said that suicide is contagious, and from the stories I heard, it's not only contagious to siblings. Sometimes when I asked about people I've met over the years, people say they committed suicide or attempted suicide. They said, "My best friend can do it, then so can I!"

There were two fourteen-year-old girls from Laughing Raven reserve who were close friends and committed suicide in 1991. Later on it was rumoured several of them made a pact to commit suicide. That reserve used to be nicknamed the dog patch because people there drank so much. Now it's rumoured to be bad for drugs.

That was where I met Jennifer, in 1980, the year I thought I was going to graduate from BCIT. I was at the point where I could name my town and there would be a job there. She was staying with one of her sisters, and I thought they would be happy to see her with a successful guy like myself, but they told her to leave me because I was too serious. I moved Jennifer away from the reserve and kept getting her jobs and putting her back in school, pushing her toward independence, yet her family still didn't want us together.

Jennifer's father, Henry, went to the residential school in Mission with my father. Henry was from the Sto:lo Eagle reserve between Mission and Agassiz. He turned out bad, was a child beater, and was really mean to his kids; but I calmed him down without realizing what I was doing. My father thought Henry was a fool to listen to what I had to say because it's not scientifically proven. I guess it was beyond my father's comprehension to realize that just because a scientist can't see something that's right in front of them and won't take the time to look doesn't mean it totally doesn't exist.

Although the Indian residential schools have been closed down for some time, now it looks like we're still feeling the effects of them. Fortunately, there are now healing foundations for people to work on the cause of the problem, not just the symptom.

Once Jennifer gets a career of her own, she'll have a chance to do something with her life rather than just be another grim statistic. She's going for more therapy now, and she should be starting her career in January. After she gets a career of her own, I'm going to wait until the end of the year to see what happens to finish my autobiography. That way, I don't know how it will end, but I've been told it will be inspirational to other people. Hopefully, it can prevent other people from committing suicide or make them decide to do something with their life.

I thought I could finish my life story two years ago, but I'm glad I couldn't because of what I learned since then. I'm still learning more and gathering more information to expose the truth about this totally hypocritical country. I'm still trying to find out if the Japanese were brought in as a source of cheap Labour like the Chinese were. I would also like to know what the entrance requirements were for the Chinese women compared to other immigrants when the Exclusion Act was repealed in 1947. So far, no one will answer.

Being optimistic was what kept me going when I was working on my career goals; and when I finally got through BCIT, I thought I knew much about life, but that was only the beginning. I wouldn't wish the hard times I went through on anyone, but I wouldn't change anything even if I could because something "great" came of it. Once it's over, I can get on with my own life and hopefully advance in my career goals, beyond being a forest technician, where most Natives stop. Looking after Jennifer kept me from trying to become a registered professional forester (RPF), but that was better than letting her commit suicide. She was "almost a born loser"!

Writing brought back many painful memories was healing but stressful at the same time. I wrote twelve pages and got so stressed out I drank four beers and was still stressed out, so I drank another six-pack. That's how much it took me to unwind. When I got back to work, I e-mailed my message to Harley, and he sent me this response.

Harley's Response:

Hello Annis,

A lot of First Nations people from our and the previous generation can relate to the contents of your e-mail, I certainly can. After what I have seen in my lifetime the mortality rate of the crew that Derek mentions it does not surprise me. A majority of the First Nation people I knew as a child and young adult are dead and buried now.

Ruby's observations and comments have some deeper connotations than the superficial observations made. When an Individual confronts addiction/s & problem/s they are usually faced with a multitude of personal issues. Many times these problems and addictions are derived from their Family of Origin. A First Nation individual's Family of Origin will quite often have a history of Residential School legacy and the related effects of that experience; physical abuse, sexual abuse, culture and self esteem destroyed etc. There may be good intentions on the part of an individual and a 12-Step Program but it will normally take more than that to effectively deal with generations of problems, injustices forced on a continent of First Nations. A successful outcome will need more specific professional support and understanding than a 12-Step Program and it's peer support.

One of the federal government's Aboriginal Healing Foundation's funding priorities is for the Intergenerational Effects of Residential School. In 1995/96 when I worked at Min. of Aboriginal Affairs I sat on the National Indian Residential School Task Force. In time the Provincial Residential School Project was formed and the federal Gathering Strength document was developed that recognized the Residential School legacy. Part of the Gathering Strength document brought the formation of the Aboriginal Healing Foundation. I am currently a committee member of the Provincial Residential School Protocol Committee (PRSPC) and have cc'd their Provincial Coordinator, Sharon Thira. Sharon may be of assistance to any enquiries you may have or she may have knowledge of initiatives in or near your community. She is very approachable and supportive in this regard. This may be a more appropriate venue for your information regarding these matters.

I believe a lot of non-Aboriginal people do not understand the full magnitude of what First Nations people have actually been subject to and the intergenerational impact of the Residential School legacy. A lot of First Nations people in the new generation may not be aware of the far reaching effects that the earlier generation had to experience. Those that have become statistics of drug & alcohol related deaths cannot tell any story. The experience of people like yourself is now even more important to leave for posterity.

In September I will be working with Health Canada in Vancouver for a 1 year assignment. My new Director has said it should not be a problem to allow me to continue some of my committee work so I should still be involved with the PRSPC. I will forward my new e-mail address to you when that takes place and would be happy to get together at some point to discuss these issues and your autobiography.

Thank you,
Harley Wylie

The next weekend, I went back to Chilliwack to Tony's place because that's where Aaron was staying. He wanted to go to the bars, so I took him there then picked Jennifer up after work. She told me to go look after him, so I sat in the bar with him and Marge, Tony's girlfriend. Aaron wanted me to drink, and we could take a taxi home; but he got kicked out, so we went to Tony's place. I drank when we got there, and we sat up and talked to Marge and her friend Sandra. The next day I picked Jennifer up and drove her to work. She was worried about Tony being a bad influence on Aaron because he could get Aaron started on drugs again. Jennifer wanted me to take Aaron to a movie, but we weren't in the mood to go anywhere. Aaron drank most of the day, and we had a good talk with Marge about what our lives were like and dysfunctional families. Marge said dysfunctional families need a scapegoat and it's usually the strongest. I wanted to compete in a karate tournament, but Aaron needed my car; so we picked Jennifer up after work, went to a movie, then spent the night at her place. She was slowly starting to feel better about herself ever since she started cooking, so I wondered if the stress of the job helped break her addiction to suffering.

Near the end of July, I sent another article to Harley titled "Cause of Suicide and Addictions," based on research I've done, my own observations, and stories I heard.

Cause of Suicide and Addictions

I was aware of much of the cause behind Ruby Dunstan's comments. I'm sure Ruby was aware of the real cause of the problem too; she just didn't say anything in that article.

People with problems with addiction also have to work on the cause of the problem, not just the symptom (e.g., alcohol or drug addiction); otherwise, they may give up one addiction for another, like bingo, and the family will still suffer just as much. I heard about people who give up drinking for bingo. No matter how broke they are, they can still afford their bingo. They spend just as much time and money away from home, and the family still suffers just as much (perhaps even more).

Working on the cause can be very stressful and bring back very painful memories, but they'll feel better afterward. I'm writing my memoirs for the sixth time, and it's still stressful. But if I don't deal with the anger, I may develop health problems again or become an alcoholic. I'm feeling better now though, so it's doubtful I'll fall victim to addiction.

Even though I started writing my memoirs in 1990, I've had health problems caused by repressed anger since 1992. By 1994 it progressed to a chemical imbalance and I couldn't do any writing for about a year and a half and was on Prozac all that time. The fourth time I wrote my memoirs, I set my goal at typing a minimum of two pages a day, double-spaced. It was even hard to do that because by one and a half pages, my left arm would stiffen up so much I had to use my other hand to push the keys down. Sometimes I felt the stiffness all the way up to my cheek. Karate also helps with stress management.

One of those fourteen-year-old girls who committed suicide was Jennifer's niece, Amanda. I sometimes wondered what would ever become of her because the way I saw it, she had no goals or direction in life and very little guidance or discipline. Perhaps she just didn't have a sense of well-being.

The cause of the high suicide and addiction rate among Natives may be more than just what they went through in the residential schools; it was the physical and sexual abuse that carried on afterward. Sexual abuse is bad enough without the other things that went on in the residential schools. One of my cousins is seven years younger than I. I was born in 1955, and he went to the residential school in Lytton for a few years. He said the sexual abuse was reported but nothing was done about it.

Being held back when you try to do something for yourself can also drive a person to excessive drinking and contemplating suicide. Fortunately, me and my second-oldest brother adjusted after heavy drinking. He had a log fly over him while logging. Instead of running, he just walked away. Luckily, I ended up quitting the railroad, partly due to heavy drinking, but it was sometimes tempting to throw myself off the motor car as we were driving along. I almost got killed a couple of times from drinking too much, so the best move I ever made was to go back to college and give it one more try.

Getting a career made me feel good about myself because I overcame obstacles and setbacks that I wouldn't wish on anyone. When I met Jennifer and her depression and desires to commit suicide started coming out, I thought getting her a career would make her feel better about herself so she won't commit suicide. I put her back in school and wouldn't let her give up, but eventually I found out she had to work on the cause of the problem, not just the symptom.

I didn't know the impact sexual abuse had on the victim; but when I found out, I finally realized why many of my friends and acquaintances not only fell victim to alcohol, drug addiction, and suicide but would also cut themselves up with a knife. To me it appears the twelve-step program has good intentions, but the victim must work on the cause before they can be fully cured. I've seen and heard of people who go to treatment centers, some of them many times, then go back to alcohol and drugs.

When I tried to get Jennifer into sexual-abuse therapy, there was very little of it available. In a telephone survey in 1990, I was asked about the British Columbia medical system. I told them there's not enough sexual-abuse therapy available in British Columbia and what sexual abuse can do to the victim. About six months later, what I told them was on the front page of the Province.

I was naturally shy as a child and was continually put down just for being young, and my family always put down my opinion. Many bad things happened because I was too shy to speak up, but one incident made me decide to start writing an autobiography. When I got Jennifer seeing a sexual-abuse therapist, Hubert Smith, he was reading my writings. He told me, "Keep writing!" then eventually asked to use some of my writings to work with other patients. I told Hubert I noticed that people who are spoilt rotten as children develop problems with addiction just like with people who are badly abused. He said that's because they haven't developed a sense of responsibility.

Saving one person from suicide (it took me over three years just to realize she wasn't beyond recovery; everyone believed she was and wanted me to give up) can have a positive spin-off effect. Hopefully, it can help give other people some sense of direction in life because it was the movie The Miracle

Worker *I saw when I was sixteen that first helped me learn to be optimistic.*

Since people always tried to drill into my head my opinions were wrong, I learned to have things confirmed by people who did these things before I speak up. That way, I have a solid foundation to back up my opinion. People can't use the most common Canadian propaganda, "Everyone gets equal treatment in Canada!" One lady who graduated in the class of 1999 said they're still taught the same thing in school.

I don't think anyone would be "Proud to be Canadian!" if they went through what I went through, saw the things I saw happen, heard the stories I heard, then got called "Too lazy to go to work!" as many times as I have. I still get called that, but they won't stand toe to toe and say it. It's a direct way of saying I don't like to be stereotyped.

I've seen posters saying "elimination of racism," but I think the best way to do that is to expose the truth so the majority of people will know what made people the way they are.

I sometimes thought about sending an information package to The Oprah Show *after I found the missing article "Native Students Angry at Segregation!" but from what I've learned, even if I found it, I would wait to gather more information. I'm still connecting many of the things I learned and saw happen over the years and still get blown away by some of the things I learn. Sometimes when I ask for information, people either don't know or don't want to answer. Even government departments won't answer some of the questions I ask. Later on I find out and other people act like the information I'm looking for is common knowledge and even tell me more.*

I don't recall if I sent you any confidential information that I sent Sharon Stewart, but some of it may be useful for your job. I wasn't sure exactly what kind of work you were doing, so I didn't send it.

I had built up enough hours to take two days off, so on Wednesday I took the bus to Chilliwack after work since I had to help Jennifer register for her study-skills course. I spent the night at Tony's place so I could drive Aaron to work and use the car the next day, but when I picked Jennifer up after work that night, she was really cranky. I took her to the college at seven forty-five the next morning and people were already lined up to register and she was told if the class is full, she should contact the instructor and ask if another student is allowed in. A lady ahead of us said there were nine people on the waiting list to get in, and she got really depressed because she didn't think she would be able to get in. I looked at the list and realized that was for the Abbotsford campus. There were only four on the waiting list in Chilliwack, so she still had a chance to get in.

Aaron and I spent the night at Jennifer's place, and I drove both of them to work the next day; then Jennifer stressed us both out, so we went to Tony's place and drank. Aaron was scheduled to work the next day, Saturday, but was asked to work Sunday instead. Jennifer was cranky again after work, so Aaron stayed at Tony's place; then he suggested we all drive to Squamish the next day because both he and Jennifer had Monday off. I drove Aaron and Jennifer to work again on Sunday, and when I picked Aaron up after work, I ran into Patricia Kelly. She was visiting her sister in Rosedale and thought I should send an information package to Oprah, a popular black American talk show host.

Aaron's check was more than he expected, and I slept heavily at lunchtime. I had done much writing on the Indian reserve and it stressed me out, so I bought a case of beer. Jennifer went to the bars after she got back to Chilliwack and didn't remember where she was then took a taxi to Rosedale to see Aaron. The next day Jennifer had to do an eight-hour shift with a hangover, so she decided to quit drinking. I used to worry about her because when she drank, she didn't know when to stop; not only that, being scared and in dangerous situations still felt normal to her.

I pushed myself to do lots of writing and it was stressful, so I drank a beer or two during my breaks. I was starting to sleep rather lightly at lunchtime, and it was great for stress management. The next weekend was a long weekend and I had booked four days of annual leave, and by the end of the week, I started feeling rested up and was ready to go back to work. The more writing I did, the more I was able to see the suffering Henry went through, so I was able to forgive him even more. When I got back to work, I forgot to bring the timer with me, and at lunchtime I lay back at my desk as usual and went to sleep. I thought I only slept for fifteen minutes, but slept for fifty minutes. I had really pushed myself to do more writing, so I drank a six-pack in the evening.

On Wednesday, Aaron drove back to Squamish because he had a few days off and said the first aid instructor had a stroke and it was pain he would never want to go through again and wouldn't wish it on anyone. I finally realized Henry must have suffered incredibly when he had a stroke, so I was able to forgive him even more now. Previously I just saw him sitting there doing what he always did and having a good time. Aaron and I went back to Chilliwack on the weekend, and Jennifer talked about wanting to move to Quesnel, so I told her I thought about it too and was applying for a promotion there.

I hardly drank at all on the weekend but was stressed out when I got back to Squamish, so I went to the bar for a few beers then had a few at home. I wanted to watch the National Black Belt Championships in Richmond but couldn't because Aaron had my car; that was about the only other time I missed my car. The next weekend was Labour Day weekend and Aaron had four days off, so he came to Squamish. I got some overtime on Saturday; then we went to Chilliwack to drive Jennifer to work. There was a program on the History Channel about the Scottish settlers being banished from communities when Canada was being settled. Aaron watched it, but I only caught the last minute of it.

On Wednesday, Jennifer was able to get in to her study-skills course and I paid for her books and registration but didn't mind because it's for her career. Jennifer said there were three people waiting to get into the course and were lucky to get in; if everyone who registered showed up, they would have been out of luck. On Friday I slept quite a bit at lunchtime and felt burnt out in the evening; then on Saturday I finally decided to give up on getting my RPF unless I'm bored stiff and have nothing else to do. At my age it didn't seem worthwhile because all my life I've had very little free time to do anything I wanted to do; going on the pupil program and taking correspondence courses to get my RPF would take up too much of my free time. Then even if I got it, I didn't think I had enough working years left to make it worthwhile, so I guess the government succeeded in holding me back in my career goals; and working on my writing still burns me out.

Karate started in the third week of September, and I didn't realize how out of shape I was even though I had been riding my bicycle to work during the summer. On Thursday, Jennifer got mad, quit her job, and caught the bus to Squamish; so I wondered if she's afraid of success. I thought if she quits her job to concentrate on her studies, I'll be even happier that I didn't buy a new vehicle. I talked to her at lunchtime, and we both decided to go back to Chilliwack for the weekend. She would try and catch up on her studies and thought maybe things were happening to her because of things she did wrong in the past. I told her she was a very mixed-up person and should be proud of surviving what she went through. The next day we went to A&W for breakfast with Tina Harry, and an old couple driving by thought I was too lazy to go to work.

We went to Chilliwack; then Jennifer and Aaron came back to Squamish with me the next day. I was feeling tired and nauseous, realized it could be from stress, and ended up closing the bar down. The next day, Jennifer decided to drink and I knew she would get ugly and stress everyone out, so we ended up having to look after her and keep her from phoning the police. She was drunk and disorderly, so I didn't get to bed until two o'clock. I went out the woods the next day and was worried about Jennifer getting drunk again, but she was okay when I got home. She said she wasn't going to argue with me; then she and Aaron took the bus back to Chilliwack. I went out the woods again the next day and worked hard, so I went to bed early, and Jennifer called that night and wanted me to help her study on the weekend. I went to Chilliwack for the weekend, and Jennifer was lucky to get her job back because Aaron talked to her boss and said Jennifer was under all kinds of stress, close to a nervous breakdown; and the way she got bossed around at work didn't help.

I visited my parents, and my mother said my cousin Hank Rosealice died a week ago. They rarely ever phone me or tell me anything; but I sent Terri, his sister, a card anyway. On Sunday, Jennifer was rather cranky and got called to work from six o'clock to ten o'clock, so I waited around to give her a ride home; so I didn't get back to Squamish until one o'clock in the morning. I slept rather heavily at lunchtime the next day and found out I failed the FOS exam miserably, but I didn't really want the job because I find pre-award boring but thought I would like to move to Quesnel. I also thought Jennifer may need me to stay close by to help her study if she got into the RCA program in January.

I had fieldwork in Pemberton during the week, and I ran into Paul Johnny, an Indian from D'Arcy, and he said he wanted to be a draftsman but DIA made him take a welding course even though he was getting straight As in drafting. It was well-known among the Indians right down to my age group that even when we applied to take a trade, DIA would often put us in a different course other than what we wanted or applied for, but I didn't know what their reason for doing that was.

On Friday I felt stressed out after work, so I drank a few beers then went out for Chinese food and didn't feel like drinking after that because treating myself sometimes makes me feel better. I went to Chilliwack the next day because it was Thanksgiving weekend and I had a week off. The next Saturday, Jennifer was stressed out, so I drove her to Lytton to visit Liz and Jeremy. It was almost eleven years to the day since they died. Jennifer was having a hard time with depression and Aaron and I were getting tired of it, but I called Patricia Kelly in the evening, and she thought my book was going to be a good one. I told her it was almost all on computer disk. I kept a journal and still got blown away when I read what I went through at the end of the year. On Sunday, Jennifer finally started feeling better and decided she should do some writing rather than lash out at me and Aaron. I drove her to work, and when I picked her up, she was thinking positive and happy just to have a job and people helping her out.

When I got back to work, I got an e-mail saying there would be an Aboriginal Employees Association (AEA) annual general meeting in Victoria and some very important invited guests would be there. I would also be given fifteen to twenty minutes to talk about issues that I thought should be discussed, so I made a speech bringing up a number of issues but didn't get a chance to speak. I was sick, so I didn't get many notes, but I took the following notes at the meeting from Harinder Mahil, British Columbia commissioner of the human rights. He said there are many inaccuracies about Canada, aboriginal people have ten times the national average suicide rate, and brought up the following issues:

A. Misconceptions of Employment Equity

1. People tend to hire people like themselves.
2. Lack of opportunities in challenging positions.
3. No consistency across government, unfair treatment in different minorities, and target groups encounter harassment and unfair treatment.
4. Indian reserves have 70-90 percent unemployment rate.
5. Twenty-four to thirty-five percent aboriginals graduate high school; seventy to eighty percent of them don't qualify for university entrance.
6. Racism against aboriginals operates in a subtle manner.

B. Solutions:

1. Commitment, no more studies, show leadership.
2. Culture—employment equity process, opportunities equal to all.
3. Employment equity managed by a separate agency.

C. Recommendations:

1. Hiring panels members of designated groups.
2. Process to keep in contact with visible minorities and why they left the public service.
3. Put aboriginal relations into working plan, main theme being education. Aboriginal people's graduation rate in only one indicator. They usually drop out earlier than the majority of dropouts. There should be a public hearing into this issue.

The next week, Jennifer had an interview for the RCA course and a midterm exam. Getting accepted into the course would depend on how well she did on the exam, which stressed me out, so I drank that night. I started feeling more energetic toward the end of the week, and at the end of October, Chris Runnals gave me some fir and cedar trees that he was going to throw away. I was happy about that because I could plant them on the Indian reserve, and on Saturday I helped Jennifer do some research at the library and with her studies. On Sunday I planted some trees, but Aaron couldn't help because he was sick that day. I helped her more on Sunday; then Richard Band passed away that day.

I got home rather late that night, and surprisingly, I only slept lightly at lunchtime and called Gary after work to see if he kept the missing article from the college newspaper, but he didn't think of it. He was rather hard of hearing, but other than that, he was all right and didn't get defensive about what happened like I thought he would. He didn't admit to having worked for DIA and said he worked for Workers' Compensation Board (WCB), he worked for WCB after he got fired from DIA.

There were prayers for Richard on Wednesday evening, but I flipped a coin and it told me not to go, so I stayed home and watched *Unwanted Soldiers* on TV even though I had the video. Then that gave me the idea of calling Alex Louie for information because it was his daughter, Jari Osbourne, who made the documentary and he lived in Vancouver. The next day I arranged to meet my family for breakfast in the morning in North Vancouver; met my family at the Holiday Inn, where they spent the night; and I looked up some phone numbers. My mother wondered who was calling Louie, so I said I was and went to Richard's funeral right after that. After the funeral, I went to a shopping mall and called Alex Louie and asked, what kind of benefits did they get when they got back from WWII? Alex was happy to talk to me and said the Exclusion Act was repealed, so Chinese women were allowed into Canada and they got the right to vote, but the Chinese had to be wounded before they would get a pension. Aboriginal soldiers got the worst treatment because most of them only had a grade 6 education because that was only as far as they could go in the residential schools; then he told me to call Bing Wong, another Chinese veteran.

I called Bing Wong right away, and he said Natives got the worst treatment when they got back. They couldn't get very good jobs because of the poor education they got and didn't know whom to ask or where to apply for pensions and benefits. When Chinese women were allowed into Canada, not many came, possibly because the entrance requirements were prohibitive. In the theatres, Chinese, Japanese, and Indians had to sit on the right side until after the war. He took an accounting course. There were five Chinese and 250 whites, but no one would hire the Chinese. Many Chinese went into business for themselves because no one would hire them. Even as I was getting my career, I noticed many Chinese owned convenience stores in Vancouver; fortunately, major grocery stores closed at six o'clock, giving them an opportunity to operate a convenience store. Then Bing told me to contact Larry Wong for more information and he would send me a copy of the Chinese Canadian Military Museum newsletter. Previously I met a black veteran, Roy Lewis, who I thought was Indian because of his last name. He was born in Canada, but his parents were originally from the Dominican Republic. Roy served in WWII in the Canadian army but didn't get a pension until 1990 even though he was wounded in the knee by shrapnel and it wasn't retroactive.

I went to Chilliwack the next weekend, and Aaron and I planted trees on the Indian reserve. It was a long weekend because of Remembrance Day, so on Monday we took Jennifer to visit her mother in Sto:lo Eagle; then Aaron and I planted some more trees. We planted some trees on my dad's property, and I suggested he get the Indian reserve's tractor to clear the brush on his property and I would plant it with trees. If the trees get established, they could be pruned and it would look just like a park. I felt really good about what I did and hoped to get a crop of trees established. I picked Jennifer up the next day to go to work, and she flipped out again. I felt like giving up on her, but she was all right when she got off work.

When I got back, I called April (not her real name or the month of her birthday) to see if she had kept the missing article because she was a first-year-college student when I was there. She didn't think of saving it either and said Gary took her out for a drink and tried to get her to drink a hard drink; he said, "Drink this or you're not going to get your next check!" April then asked for $30 so she could take a taxi home, and he tried to get her to a hotel room before she called a taxi. Gary then asked her for her address, but she wouldn't give it; then he said, "That's okay! I can get it from your registration."

The taxi driver said she should have called the police! April then went to the DIA office, told them Gary wouldn't give her her check, and they asked, "Why not?" The next time she saw Gary, he said, "You didn't have to go that far! You're not going to get sponsored anymore!"

April then said he tried to do that to Maria, so she dropped out after about a month of college. There was a girl from Sardis, where I worked, who said when she went to Langara College in 1974, she almost had to fight her way out of Gary's office one day too. April also said Gary was arrogant; and June Quipp, the chief of my reserve, tried to find out who gave Gary the orders to try and make the Native students give up on their postsecondary education, but didn't have any luck finding out who it was. I knew that information would be kept very private.

I went back to Chilliwack the next weekend to help Jennifer with her term paper. She wrote a paper titled "Plight of the Native Elders," and I thought I should send a copy to influential people. I had the statistics of the incomes of Native elders compared to non-Native elders from the computer; on the average, across Canada, the income of aboriginal elders was only ½ of that of non-aboriginal elders. I got it during my coffee breaks since no one would let me sit with them. I picked her up after work, so I got home rather late again. I called Wilma Robinson again, and she said Bella Coola isn't bad for suicides but is bad for alcohol- and drug-related deaths. Fortunately, she never heard of Gary trying to sexually exploit the female students.

I felt incredibly stressed out on Tuesday, so I bought a case of beer and drank ten bottles. Jennifer had to do a presentation on her term paper Wednesday, and that was probably stressing her out. She did good on her presentation though and got four out of five marks for it, and although she had three different tutors look at her essay and tell her what corrections to make and she made them, I thought there was still a chance the instructor might fail her miserably.

I went back to Chilliwack again the next weekend, and on Saturday, Tony phoned and said our cousin Beaver died in a hunting accident. Mother would be going down for prayers on Sunday and the funeral would be on Monday, so we took Jennifer to Sto:lo Eagle to visit her mother, then Aaron and I planted some trees at my dad's place. Then we spent the night at her place and planted more trees the next day; but I had to be ready to go to Lummi, near Bellingham, Washington, for the funeral. I went to Lummi with Tony, Marge, and my mother for prayers, which weren't over until midnight. We were up at six o'clock the next morning for more prayers and rituals then speeches about Beaver. There was nothing but good said about him. He was a hunter and always gave to the elders and his sister's families before taking anything for himself; perhaps that was why he was such a successful hunter.

On December 6, Prime Minister Jean Chrétien talked about Natives living in third world conditions, and something should be done about it; although this is his third term as prime minister and he was the federal minister of Indian Affairs at one time, this was the first time I heard him say that. He's a very smart man though, so he probably had a good reason for doing that, and there's a good chance he may have suffered because of how the French Canadians were treated; that's something I've never heard of any prime minister mention.

I went back to Chilliwack again on the weekend and wanted to plant some more trees, but on Saturday, Tony called and said they would be laying Richard's ashes that day; so I caught a ride with them to North Vancouver and thought there would be a large ceremony, but only eight people showed up. The next day I dropped some information off to the chief, June Quipp; but she wasn't home, so I visited with her husband, Fred. I knew Fred had a hard life, and he said he eventually realized he was a racist, but I told him we had no choice; we were forced to be like that. He also said he totally stays out of Indian band affairs, so the chief never shared any of the information I gave her with him.

I had enough hours to take Monday off, so I took Jennifer to the college to see about her course; and she didn't have a TB (tuberculosis) test yet. She wrote her final exam but didn't do very well on her term paper. I sometimes heard about Natives getting failing grades in classroom assignments for speaking the truth and thought it was exaggerated; now I see they weren't exaggerating. I was visiting Jennifer when her instructor called, and she was really mad. She asked if Jennifer was going to take the course or just audit it; and you could almost hear right across the room, and it wasn't a speakerphone! That's how I've sometimes seen Canadians react to the truth when we speak out.

I took Jennifer to Abbotsford for a TB test rather than wait ten days to get it done in Chilliwack, and when we got home, I found out she already had the TB test but forgot to bring in the results. She got depressed and went to the bars, and I had to come back to Squamish. Then she phoned me at three o'clock in the morning, and I was glad she called because I couldn't sleep because I was worried about her. Jennifer called the next day and said she's been accepted in the RCA program but was too tired and hung over to get excited. I called Vivian Ignace because she moved back to Merritt and told her about looking after Jennifer and how her family reacted toward me. She said Jennifer's family was jealous of her because they didn't want her to get ahead of them and Henry hated me because I stood between him and his daughter, so he couldn't lash out his anger on her. I said he also couldn't sexually abuse her either, and unfortunately, Vivian didn't think of saving the missing article either. People didn't realize it could be important later on or that it would disappear, but if I saved it, I wouldn't have learned some of the things I learned.

The next day, Jennifer asked me to call the college to see when registration forms were sent out, and it finally dawned on me that if she got accepted any earlier, she may have still been afraid of success because of her addiction to suffering; not only that, she still needed more therapy. On Friday, Jennifer called again and said she had to register and pay $100 deposit, so I told her just to use my credit card. I called her again when I got back to work, and she was registered in the course now.

I went to the staff Christmas party that night because the staff seemed disappointed that I usually miss the Christmas party. I wanted to go back to Chilliwack the next day, but it was snowing again and I had to wait and see if Aaron's check would come in on Monday. On Monday, Aaron's check still didn't go in, but I wrote a very long letter to the Chinese Canadian Military Museum Society and made a donation. I asked for information on Canada's treatment of Chinese people and gave a $100 donation so I would get a quick response.

Aaron had an appointment in Surrey for funding to go back to school for job training on Wednesday, so I asked him to change it to Tuesday so we would have time to do other things. I went back to Chilliwack in the afternoon because Jennifer had a Christmas dinner with the A&W staff and wanted me to go. The staff were excited about her going for job training; and her therapist, Jane Byra, was getting more and more to the root of Jennifer's problems and healing old wounds. Jennifer told me more about why Christmas was always stressful and depressing for her and wanted to go to Kelowna but changed her mind.

On Tuesday we came to Squamish and to the bars; and Jennifer flipped out, disappeared for a little while, then went back. The next day she told me she was going for more therapy and realized why she always had to be stressed out to feel normal. Things were always tense, then there would only be a calm after a beating; so if things were too calm, she couldn't handle it. Christmas Day didn't change things at all. Henry sometimes got drunk and didn't wake up until two o'clock, and they couldn't open their presents until he got up. Either that or people would go over and party, the kids would have to run for them, a big mess would be made, and the kids would have to clean it up. These were issues that were the cause of Jennifer being the way she was.

On Thursday, Jennifer went shopping with Tina Harry; then we went out for coffee. Jennifer talked about the teacher failing her on her term paper, so I told her some Canadians get really uptight when we start talking about what really happened and how Indians have been treated. On Friday I had Jennifer's apartment fumigated for silverfish because they drove her crazy, and I didn't want anything to interfere with her studies. She flipped out again, probably because Christmas was always stressful for her, but she didn't flip out too badly like she usually does. I knew Jennifer always needed to be obsessed with something, so I thought if she uses that need to be obsessed toward getting her career, she should easily pass the course.

We did the last of our Christmas shopping on Saturday, and while shopping I ran into Ernie Victor, a fellow from my reserve who's fifteen years younger than I. I told him many Indians I went to school with committed suicide or died of alcohol- and drug-related deaths before they turned twenty-five or are just physically existing as alcoholics, drug addicts, or welfare cases; and he said it was the same way with Indians in his age group.

I felt stressed out from shopping and looking after Jennifer, so I drank a few beers in the evening, and Aaron caught the bus to Vancouver then went to Qualicum to visit his family the next day. I drove Jennifer to Sto:lo Eagle then went to my parents' place. Christmas was uneventful, and I picked Jennifer up in Sto:lo Eagle on Boxing Day, then we went to Chilliwack. Aaron came back on Wednesday but went to the bars, so we didn't know he was back until two o'clock in the morning. After Christmas, Aaron bought an eighteen-pack of beer; and toward the evening, I drank with him and the three of us went to the bars. Jennifer flipped out again when we got back, and when I woke up, the kitchen was a mess with broken dishes and cereal thrown all over the floor. A lady down the hall warned us that they can't put up with any more noise like that; one more time and Jennifer would be evicted, so Aaron finally realized he shouldn't ask Jennifer to drink when she doesn't want to. Jennifer felt sick on Saturday, and on Sunday the doctor said she had tonsillitis.

Chapter 23

2001

I had spent New Year's Eve at Isaac and Helen's place, slept in, then eventually went to see Jennifer. She flipped out again but not as badly as she had at other times; then toward the evening, she started feeling well enough to read her module for her course. I came back to Squamish and got in at midnight but couldn't sleep, possibly from drinking coffee. Aaron stayed in Chilliwack. I went to work and still slept at lunchtime and after work. Aaron called that week and said he had interviews to attend in Vancouver for work and going back to school, so he may need to borrow my car. I was only back to work for three days and felt stressed out, so I had a few beers in the evening. I woke up late the next morning because I forgot to pull the alarm button on the clock; even though I slept in, I still slept heavily at lunchtime and thought I may have the flu. Aaron came back from Chilliwack on the weekend to file for UIC, look into job training in meat cutting and advanced training in forestry, then said he would try and get both appointments on the same day.

Karate started on Monday, and on Tuesday, Aaron needed my car to go to Vancouver. I had a hard time getting up that morning and slept heavily at lunchtime even though I was at my desk. After work I felt quite stressed out, so I went to the bars with Aaron and Gary Columbus. Gary said he used to live in Merritt, where I grew up, and thought he remembered me. On Friday, Aaron borrowed my car again to see if he could get into the meat-cutting course; and he needed $15 for registration, so I gave it to him. We went to Chilliwack for the weekend, and I took them out to a Chinese buffet for lunch because it was now twenty-one years to the day that I met Jennifer. My fortune cookie said, "You will soon be very proud of someone close to you!" and the word *very* seemed to stand out. Then we took Jennifer to Abbotsford to buy uniforms for her course but ended up buying them in Chilliwack. She was cranky and not feeling very well the next day, but my instincts told me "something great is coming"!

I went to visit Isaac, and he said I'm not a happy drinker because I had gotten mad at one of his friends on New Year's Eve and told him to *stand up*! Then he warned me that I could get charged if I ever got into a scrap because of all the training I've done. Aaron helped Jennifer get her meals ready for the next two weeks, and we decided to leave in the morning. On Tuesday morning during coffee break, I felt bored, so I started exploring on the computer; then I decided I might e-mail or write letters to influential people. I only wanted to visit Jennifer every second weekend now so she can learn to do things on her own. By the third week of January, I started sleeping lighter at lunchtime; and on Thursday, Jennifer called and said she got forty-five out of fifty, an A on her exam. Now I was feeling very proud of her for doing so well!

I got a response from the letter I sent to the Chinese Canadian Military Museum, and they were happy to answer my questions even though my donation was enough for a lifetime membership. Larry Wong couldn't answer all the questions I asked, but he still wrote a long letter giving me much information. When I first heard about Tomson Highway, a Canadian aboriginal author and playwright, being one of two people to graduate high school out of two hundred students that he started out with, I thought he must be least ten to fifteen years older than I. While exploring on my computer during coffee break, I saw his name under biographies, so I looked him up. Previously when I saw him on TV, I thought he just looked younger than he was; but much to my surprise, he was only four years older than I. He was born in 1951.

Now I'm really glad the staff close me off at coffee breaks because often that's the only time I have to read a book, phone around or write to various influential people, and explore on the computer, either directly searching for information or finding out about organizations I didn't know existed. I thought perhaps that's why my instincts very strongly told me not to think about being closed off by the staff. That day after work, I phoned Harbour Publishing and talked to Peter Robson since Howard White, the owner, was away. Peter thought books like mine would be very good and sell well, then I told him about information I wanted to send to news stations on aboriginal and Chinese Canadian veterans for Remembrance Day, and he said I should give them plenty of time for them to check issues out before they would broadcast it.

I got sick, so I missed work for the rest of the week; and on Wednesday, Aaron borrowed my car go to Vancouver to arrange for funding to try and get into a meat-cutting course. It's not confirmed yet, but it's still possible he might get in. Near the end of January, the governor general, Gloria Makarenko, talked about the extreme poverty in Indian reserves; although it's been that way for decades, people are finally noticing or mentioning it on the news. Although Aaron enjoys working out in the woods, there's very little of that type of work available anymore, so I told him it's a good time to change professions before he gets too old and no one will hire him. Hopefully, he'll find a job with medical and dental benefits.

On Thursday morning, Jennifer wrote an exam and was really worried about how she did on it then called back in the afternoon and said she got 96 percent. Now I was really glad she was taking the course in Chilliwack because I didn't want to be right beside her holding her hand. I wanted her to be more independent and build up her self-confidence. Perhaps I made some mistakes while looking after her all these years, but anyone would do that; and Jane Byra, her new therapist, said after everything Jennifer's been through, she deserved some spoiling. I told her that by doing good in class, it will make her eligible for more-advanced training. She didn't know that because no one had ever told her.

By the second week of February, I only slept lightly at lunchtime; but in the third week, I missed one night of karate and drank because I was stressed out. I called Auntie Jeanette about letting her read a rough draft of my life story because she had been a social worker before she retired. She got really excited and writing, and speaking out made me feel better. I only visited Jennifer every second weekend, and while I was away, she got rid of some of her furniture in a fit of anger; and on one visit, I checked the trees we planted in the fall and they weren't doing very well, but I hoped to plant some more Douglas fir and red cedar in the spring. I drank coffee one night after work and thought a karate work out would wear off the caffeine but it didn't but I was happy about that because I knew my stress level was going down even more. On one visit with Darlene I told her how my family treated me and she said I was lucky I made it that far after everything I've been through.

I still sleep lightly at lunchtime and eventually I didn't go to sleep until I started thinking about *sex*, so it was time to start coming out of my shell and maybe even start looking for someone. In late March, the AEA asked me to send a letter to the prime minister regarding Indian education, so I added some extra information and included copies of letters that I sent to influential people. I didn't expect an answer, but one of his representatives answered a few weeks later and said my letters would be forwarded to the appropriate minister and taken into consideration. Ever since I moved to Squamish, I gathered much information on how minorities, mostly Indians, were treated in Canada then put it together in information packages and sent it to influential people as well as the Southern Poverty Law Center in Montgomery, Alabama, to expose the truth.

By April I thought I was ready to move back closer to where my family lived, but I called a friend in Merritt, Patrick Cullen, during my coffee break. Patrick had been friends with us since we were in elementary school and I still call him regularly, and he said, "Did you know Meredith Hourie?"

"Yeah, she's my first cousin."

"Her funeral was a week ago!"

I had been calling home, and everyone I spoke to said nothing new had happened. We had always been close to Kirby and Meredith, like they were immediate family, so I phoned Kirby to offer my condolences. He was mad because not one person from my family showed up for his wife's funeral; he knew I would have been there, but no one told me she passed away. I thought I was ready to move back to Chilliwack, but now I decided to wait another five years.

I went to Chilliwack for Easter weekend and because it was Jennifer's and my niece Nicole's birthday on Saturday. I went to Isaac and Helen's for Nicole's birthday party then went back to Jennifer's place since my family wasn't having a dinner that weekend. On Monday, Jennifer was cranky, so I left for a little while. She only had five weeks left to finish her course, and it seemed hard to hang on even though my instincts said everything was going to work out. I often felt like giving up on her when she got too cranky, and I swore I would never be a rescuer again! After I got back to work, I started sleeping heavily at lunchtime again, and drinking coffee after work didn't keep me awake at night. Jennifer had been worrying about her exams even though I told her my instincts told me she would pass the course; and in the last week of April, Chris Runnals gave me a box of Douglas fir trees, so Aaron and I planted them on my parents' property. Most of the trees we planted last fall died because they were planted too late in the year and some of them were turning moldy, but we had planted them anyway because it was worth taking the chance.

At the beginning of May, I read over part of my life story, and it was still stressful to see what I went through. Then I bought a six-pack of tall cans of beer and drank five of them and hoped I could get some more seedlings at Arbor Day this year, but it was cancelled due to lack of support. However, Scott Bennet, an RPF from Interfor, said he may have some low-elevation Douglas fir and cedar seedlings for me, which made me feel good because I wanted more seedlings to plant on my Indian reserve.

On the first weekend in May, I took Jennifer to visit her mother in Sto:lo Eagle and Henry Jr. said he had a chance to get on with Corrections Canada at Elbow Lake Institution, where I used to work. The Sto:lo Eagle band was looking into taking it over, and if they did, his money would be tax free; and he wouldn't have been eligible to apply for that job if he didn't have his grade 12 diploma. I thought he would probably prefer forestry or fisheries work or salmon enhancement, but there isn't much work in those fields anymore; then I thought after everything he's been through, he deserves lucky breaks like that.

I took elementary schoolchildren out on forestry tours again because there wasn't very much for me to do in the office and hoped I could get some seedlings to start planting by the weekend, but Scott Bennet said they wouldn't be available until the eighteenth, just when I would be starting my annual leave. On Thursday, May 17, Jennifer called me at home at lunchtime crying and said she didn't pass the practicum because the instructors said she was too soft-spoken and not well organized enough, so I told her not to give up and see if she can do the practicum again. Previously, Phaye Sutton predicted that Jennifer was going to have to write an exam twice but failing the first time would put her in a better position, she would get into her work, and she's going to just love it.

The next day I called Jennifer and told her what Phaye said, and Jennifer said the instructor didn't think she was suited for that kind of work, but Aaron called me at lunchtime and said Jennifer passed her final written exam though. I went to Chilliwack that night and waited around for Scott Bennet to call me and let me know if the trees were available, and he told me to call him on Tuesday night. I had booked two weeks of annual leave for when Jennifer finished her course, but it wasn't happy like I thought it would be because she didn't pass her course. I hoped the band would get a crew to brush out the seedlings we planted last year, but they couldn't afford it; then on Sunday, Tony called and said Sam Douglas, the former chief of our band, drowned in a boating accident on the Fraser River, often just called the river by Indians living in the Fraser Valley. That was the fourth Douglas to die in a few months.

On Tuesday I brought Aaron and Jennifer to Squamish in my dad's truck to pick up the trees Scott Bennet left for me. He said he left twenty-five boxes of trees, and I got really excited. We waited until Wednesday evening to drive back to keep the trees cool though; then on Thursday we planted part of Dad's property, and Jennifer helped us by cutting the brush with a scythe. I wasn't used to physical work, so I thought this would be the last volunteer work I would do for the band. Dad cooked steaks for us because he knew we would be tired and hungry, and I still felt stressed out, so I didn't get much sleep that night. We planted more trees at the back of the reserve again the next day and found out there was better survival of the trees we planted last spring than we expected. On Saturday we planted more trees at the back of the reserve, then I suggested we do more planting on my dad's property. The next day we planted more trees on my dad's property, but we were getting tired because this was my annual leave. Dad was also tired of cooking for us because he's retired now and likes his free time.

Jennifer also had to see the director of her course on Monday and was told she would have to take the practicum again, which would start in late August and end in December. She also had to take a standard first aid course that involved cardiac arrest patients, so I paid for the course. Someone in her class told Jennifer to go to an office called Windows for Women to try and find a job, so we went there and found out there were other courses she could take to help build up her confidence. I signed her up for an Assertive Communications Skills and Remarkable Women-Positive Self-Talk because I knew she lacked confidence and assertiveness.

That night I felt stressed out to the point my heart was hurting, so I bought two cases of beer, which Aaron and I drank; then on Tuesday we went to Kelowna to visit Brenda and Alvin. We didn't do very much, just shopped around a little bit because their son Eugene's graduation ceremonies were that weekend; and on Friday, Aaron, Alvin, and I drove around a bit while Jennifer and Brenda worked and shopped around. Eugene's graduation was on Saturday, so Jennifer and I bought him a stereo for a graduation present because Brenda didn't make very much on her job and Alvin wasn't working, so all they could afford to buy him was a few lottery tickets; then we took them out for a buffet dinner. Although Jennifer and I didn't speak about it, we were both thinking the same thing: buy him a graduation present and take them out for dinner. I somehow manage to be in the right place at the right time when people need my help. We left Kelowna on Sunday. I dropped Jennifer and Aaron off in Chilliwack then came back to Squamish. My two weeks of annual leave was over, but it wasn't as happy as I expected it to be because Jennifer didn't pass her course.

I went back to work for a week then went back to Chilliwack the next weekend for a memorial for Sam Douglas down by the river, and Aaron and Jennifer took the car to Sto:lo Eagle so she could visit her mother. Terri Dargatz was at the memorial, and she agreed that I should try and get Jennifer a career and she also needed emotional and financial support, especially when things get hard and you feel like giving up; otherwise, she would just physically exist with low-paying jobs. After the memorial, I brushed out more of Dad's property to prepare it for planting more trees; and the next day, Aaron and I planted some cedar trees down by the river. If I had time, I thought I would plant more cedar trees down by the river for poles that could be marketable in twenty to twenty-five years, if fisherman didn't use them to hang their nets when they're tall enough.

I went back again the next weekend to plant more trees but knew that was taking a chance because they've been out of the cooler too long. We planted on Saturday and a few more on Sunday, but Jennifer wanted us to go to Sto:lo Eagle to visit. I got annoyed at her for slowing me down again but knew things seem to work out in her favour. On Saturday there was a dinner at the reserve hall for my cousin Johnny Aleck because he just got his degree in business administration. Patricia Kelly was there, so I gave her a copy of my writings that were on computer disk so she could do the editing, and decided I wouldn't be eligible until Jennifer got her career. The next weekend was the July 1 holiday in Canada, so it was a long weekend. I worked Friday and Saturday nights patrolling recreation sites and thought I would just stay home and relax for the weekend, but on Sunday, Jennifer flipped out again and asked me to go to Chilliwack. Monday was a holiday, and Aaron and I were too stressed out to cook, so I took them out for lunch. I had been spending lots of money because Jennifer didn't pass her course and didn't have a job, but I still have a feeling everything's going to work out.

When I went back to work, I was tired and tried to sleep after supper but couldn't because I felt incredibly itchy. Finally I called Jennifer to see what was bothering her. Aaron said she wasn't eligible for UIC anymore because they don't give it to people who quit their job to go back to school. The next weekend I finally got some time to myself; but on Monday, Jennifer called and said she got an interview for a janitorial job, working Monday to Friday, eight thirty to four thirty. She was going up on the bus and would be needing my car. I didn't really need it because I usually ride my bicycle during the summer anyway.

Ryan had given Aaron a referral where he could get a job peeling logs to build log houses, so Aaron checked it out on Jennifer's bicycle, tried it for a day, then got hired. I helped him by buying him a drawknife for peeling logs and was going to buy him a sharpening stone for $40, but Jennifer wanted to look around in a second hand store first and he found the same sharpening stone for $5. The next weekend I caught the bus to Chilliwack, took a taxi to where Aaron parked my car, drove it to their place, then we went to the lounge. Aaron left for a little while to pay a debt, went back, and we had a few beers. We left because Jennifer was passing out, and she argued and screamed on the way home. A cop passing by asked us what was going on, and Aaron said, "Nothing! We're only fifty feet from home!"

The cop sternly said, "*Go home!*"

When we got in the apartment, Jennifer really flipped out, moved things into the hallway, and raised hell with Aaron; so I suggested he go for a walk. Then Jennifer destroyed his dresser. Someone called the police, and when they came, they threatened to take one of us with them if they were called back. Half the building was disturbed, and I thought Jennifer would get evicted for sure! I woke up early the next morning because I was worried about Jennifer getting evicted and the cost of her finding another place to stay, so we drove around most of the day because we were scared to go back. Eventually, Aaron called her on her cell phone and said she wasn't evicted but got a stern warning. I felt like looking after her and trying to get her a career is more trouble than it's worth and wondered if she'll ever get a career!

On Sunday I brought Jennifer back to Squamish with me because I was scared of her getting too stressed out living with Aaron; at least by staying with me, she should start feeling better. When I woke up to go to work, I realized I was sick, so I didn't go to work; and on Tuesday evening, someone from A&W, where she used to work, called and said she could get her job back. Jennifer decided to accept the job and called back on Wednesday, but the boss wouldn't be back until the next morning. Jennifer called again on Thursday and said she could start work on Monday. I finally went to the doctor on Thursday; then on Friday, Jennifer went to the bars, which I knew would be a mistake because when she drinks, she doesn't know when to stop. I went there later on to look after her but had to leave before her because I have a low tolerance of alcohol and was passing out. Then we woke up the next day; we decided we should quit drinking because something could easily have happened to us.

On Sunday I phoned Alvin Tolley in Quebec because he had written some papers on the Indian residential schools in Canada. I sent him a package of information regarding Canada's treatment of minorities that I had sent to various influential people. Alvin and I had a good, long talk, and he said he applied for grants to hold a conference in Ontario and asked if I could be there to speak. The grants would pay my air fare there and back, so I told him I would go if I got the chance.

I told Jennifer to take my car back with her because I wouldn't need it and she would also be working mostly night shifts, so she would have a ride home. She didn't want to take it, but I told her to take it anyway and had to tell her three times to take the car before she would take it. On Monday the doctor phoned in a prescription to the drugstore for me, and I realized I was sicker that I thought I was; then on Tuesday, Jennifer called and said she had done some writing and found out why she drinks until she blacks out. As a child, she used to black out because of the kind of love her father gave her, so blacking out felt normal; that was a way of coping with what she was going through.

I had built up enough hours to take Friday off, so I caught the bus to Chilliwack on Thursday night; and on Friday I helped Jennifer get ready to go back to school, but she was stressed out over work because of people slacking off. I told her laziness catches up on people and she should try to be optimistic. Henry Jr. stopped by to visit Jennifer and started talking about when he drove to Kelowna to take Alvin out hunting. It's about a five-hour drive from where he lives; then he realized he didn't even want me riding in his truck.

When I went back to work, I tried to sleep at lunchtime but couldn't, so I wrote a letter to Alvin Tolley; even if I were at home I may not have been able to sleep. However, the next day I felt stressed out to the point my heart was hurting. The next weekend was the first weekend of August, which was a long weekend, so I patrolled recreation sites on Friday and Saturday night for the overtime pay; then I just stayed home all weekend and had some time to myself. I went back to Chilliwack again the next weekend and brushed out some of the seedlings we planted last spring, and they appeared to be doing quite well. Aaron didn't help me on Saturday because he was drinking, and Jennifer really flipped out again after work. A female police constable went to see what all the noise was about, but Jennifer calmed down and said she was stressed out over going back to school. Jennifer was really cranky again the next day before going to work, so Aaron and I drank a couple of beers before doing more brushing; then I drank eleven beers when I got back to Squamish because I was stressed out from looking after her. The next weekend, Aaron and Jennifer came to visit me in Squamish, and on Saturday we went to the Pacific National Exhibition (PNE). We all had a good time there but I didn't go on any rides because I get motion sickness. They went on all the scariest rides, but it didn't seem to scare or bother Aaron at all, and I hoped this would let Jennifer's tensions out so she wouldn't flip out again.

On Sunday, Jennifer was still stressed out about going back to school, but I told her to try and be optimistic about it then told her to remember what they told her from Positive Self-Talk, "Your biggest obstacle may be your attitude!" I said if I had a choice, I wouldn't have gone through what I went through to accomplish everything I accomplished if there would have been an easier way to do it. That helped, but Positive Self-Talk worked the best. Then Aaron and I went to Rosedale to brush out more seedlings we had planted, but I brought the car back to Squamish because I needed it to carry a radio home after work because I did the late check-in that week. Then I went back to Chilliwack again the next weekend to can some salmon but left the car with Aaron and Jennifer because I wouldn't need it.

It was the end of August now, and the long Labour Day weekend in September was coming. I worked at patrolling recreation sites again and stayed home for the weekend. I called Alvin Tolley again; and he said there would be a conference held in Ontario in December, it would be a two-day conference, it would take a day to fly there and a day to fly back, and he wanted me to speak at the conference. I thought I might have to give up a trip to New Mexico unless I could build up enough hours to go, but I thought the conference would be a good chance to expose my life story and the truth. I went back to Chilliwack the second weekend of September, finished brushing the trees on my dad's property; and Jennifer liked the idea of me speaking at a conference, but I thought she would also do very good at speaking at a conference like that. Uncle Percy Roberts suggested I bring up the issue of different sizes of Indian reserve: some are rather big, but others are incredibly small. Then on Tuesday, September 11, planes were hijacked and flown into the World Trade Center buildings in New York. That was a big shock to everyone!

I went back to Chilliwack again the next weekend because Jennifer wanted me to go to the corn festival in Agassiz with her. On our way there, I stopped at a credit union; and right after I parked, Patricia Kelly went and parked beside me. I told her I intended to send a letter and information regarding Canada's treatment of minority war veterans to two news stations in Vancouver, British Columbia, so she suggested I send it to *60 Minutes* as well. When Jennifer and I got to the corn festival, Brenda, Alvin, and their daughter, Cheryl, were there and we ran into Henry Jr. and their mother. Henry Jr. thought if Alvin did that much for him, he wouldn't be able to do enough for him, yet he treated me like an outcast and my presence still seemed to stress him out!

On Sunday I helped Jennifer practice her scenario roles, getting patients dressed and out of bed, because she would be tested the next day. She was also worried about the USA going to war and the possibility of another war, so I told her to finish her course then advance to practical nursing. Then if there was another war, she could end up looking after wounded soldiers, and she said she would like that. The next day, Jennifer called and said she did quite well on the test and half the class failed it; she may not have done that well if I didn't help her, and that really made her day as well as mine.

I was supposed to start karate that night but felt stressed out, so I stayed home and drank a few beers. I passed out on six beers, so I probably should have gone to karate instead. I started karate on Thursday, and it felt like I had been away for four to six months rather than two months. I stayed home on the weekend and gathered information and wrote the covering letter that would be sent to the news stations with the information on war veterans. Speaking out makes me feel better, so I couldn't sleep very well Sunday night because I was too excited, but I also knew they may not even say anything at all about these issues. I called Alvin Tolley during the week and he said the conference was postponed to July next year because not very many people were willing to fly there because of the airplane hijacking.

On October 1, I mailed my letters to the news stations in Vancouver but got the mailing address of *60 Minutes* in Australia instead of New York. I registered the letters to the Canadian news stations though because if they didn't like what they saw, all they would have to say is they didn't get the letter and I wouldn't have a leg to stand on. I sent the letters early so they could research issues if they wanted them confirmed before Remembrance Day, November 11. The next day, I got the right address to *60 Minutes* in New York and decided to send the same information to *60 Minutes* in Australia as well. The premier of British Columbia was going to bring out a treaty referendum next year, so that gave me the perfect excuse to speak out to the government on aboriginal issues; but I waited until now to include the information on aboriginal and Chinese Canadian war veterans and sent it to Parliament Buildings in Victoria, British Columbia by registered letter.

A fellow from Victoria phoned me up later on and tried to act dumb and asked me what I wanted them to do with that information and said, "Why don't you send it to the Ministry of Multiculturalism?" I said major decisions were going to be made by people who knew very little of the truth of Canada's treatment of minorities; then I talked on and on about how badly the Indians have actually been treated, the stories I heard, and most of what I went through and still going though. I was very angry, and he knew that if we were in the same room and he tried to get that ignorant, I would have told him to *stand up*! Then two days after that, the government issued an apology for how the aboriginal people have been treated.

I had enough hours built up enough hours to take Friday off, so I trained in karate in Vancouver before going to Chilliwack. I did more brushing on Friday and saw there was good survival of the trees Aaron and I had planted last spring. I bought Aaron some tobacco from the band office on the reserve because I could get it at ½ the price it's sold for in stores; then I realized I couldn't have gotten very many trees planted without his help, so I did the right thing by helping him out. It was Thanksgiving weekend in Canada, so on Sunday I took Jennifer to Sto:lo Eagle for the turkey dinner. Brenda and Alvin were there, and her family treated Alvin extremely well; he got the royal treatment! We left rather late, and Jennifer didn't want to spend the night there. I actually wanted Aaron to take her there, but he just wanted to stay home.

Monday was a holiday, so I finished brushing out the trees we planted last spring. It would really make me feel good to try and get a crop of trees established on the Indian reserve. When I went back, Chris Runnals gave me some more trees again; and I knew I would have to try and get them planted right away because it was late in the season, and if they're planted too late, they won't survive. That meant I would have to go back to Chilliwack again the next weekend. I went to Chilliwack Friday night and Jennifer was stressed out because Aaron went to the bars again. On Saturday I took them out for lunch and she nagged him so much he left and went to the bars again. Jennifer then boxed up more of her things and I borrowed my dad's truck and helped her move them into storage.

On Sunday, Aaron said he couldn't take much more of Jennifer's nagging, and I wondered how he put up with her this long. Jennifer went to work; and I planted the trees Chris gave me, filling in where they died in the spring, and I tried to shade out the blackberries. Now I'm really glad I went into forestry because I'm getting something done for my Indian band. If I didn't do the planting and brushing, it probably wouldn't get done for years, wasting many growing seasons.

When I went back to work, I had to get the key to a gate from Gerard Peters because the road goes through the Indian reserve he's from. Gerard invited me in for coffee, and I told him about planting trees on my reserve through volunteer work; and from talking to him, I got the opinion volunteer work is the best way to go. If DIA still existed at harvest time and they tried telling my band what to do, we could tell them where to go because the foresters from DIA did absolutely nothing to get the trees established and the band didn't spend a single penny in the process. There would also be no record of the reserve land being planted.

I phoned Jennifer on Thursday, and she said the nurse said she was doing really well. She was crabby though, but that still made me feel good and went back to Chilliwack again for the weekend. Normally I prefer just to go back every second weekend, but I ended up going back three weekends in a row. Jennifer and I went to the bars on Saturday night, had a good time, and she didn't flip out this time. I went back to work, but I sometimes drink a few beers in the evenings because there's usually not very much to do at work, so I get bored and stressed out.

Near the end of October, *60 Minutes* in Australia thanked me for the story suggestion but said it's not something they would cover since they receive so many story suggestions. I had watched *Canada: A People's History* episode 14, and it mentioned a Jewish death camp in Germany. There was a warehouse full of food that could have saved them from starvation, but they were cut off from it, so they called the warehouse Canada. It mentioned Canada only allowed 450 Jewish refugees into the country during the Holocaust, so I wrote this in another letter and sent it to the two news stations in Vancouver, British Columbia. I mentioned that Canada appeared to be just as much against the Jews as many other countries were but stopped just short of outright trying to exterminate them; perhaps Canada merely left that up to other countries.

I went back to Chilliwack on the first weekend of November, and Jennifer came back with me. She had a week off because she only had to do the practical part of her course. On Monday night she was okay, but on Tuesday night she went to the bars, so eventually I joined her. We didn't get too drunk and she didn't flip out but offered to let two drug addicts move into her apartment to try and recover and get off drugs. I tried to tell her not to do that until she finished her course, but she wouldn't listen. I still felt good the next day though and thought perhaps Jennifer was finally breaking her addiction to misery and stress. She talked to people in Squamish and found out there was a long list of RCAs looking for work there. I had enough hours to take the next two days off though and was anxious to leave and reluctant to answer the phone in case the drug addicts called. We left for Chilliwack, and they didn't call, which made me happy because I didn't want anything to interfere with her classes.

On Saturday morning, Aaron drove me to the bus depot so I could go to Vancouver International Airport and fly to El Paso, Texas, to visit Auntie Tilley and Uncle Sal in Las Cruces, New Mexico. Aaron and Jennifer would be using my car for the week because Jennifer had her classes in Abbotsford instead of Chilliwack. Abbotsford is about thirty miles from Chilliwack, so she arranged a ride with one of her classmates.

Uncle Sal was retired and didn't drink anymore and Auntie Tilley hadn't drank in years. It was a very relaxing trip, and they took me to a number of tourist sites and to two gambling casinos in El Paso. Normally, I drink because of stress while I'm on holiday, but this trip was so relaxing I hardly drank at all and didn't miss it. I stayed there for a week then flew back the following Saturday, and when I got back to work, Barry Caldwell and Ailsa Siemens both told me the news stations didn't say one word about the issues I brought to their attention. That was only a slight surprise but a major disappointment because of all the effort it took to find the truth; they didn't even acknowledge getting the information, a *totally Canadian* reaction to the truth!

I had a bit of trouble sleeping at lunchtime now, but I got bored at work because there was often nothing to do, so I sometimes had a few beers after work. I slept rather lightly at lunchtime though, and one night I missed karate to help Jennifer with one of her assignments over the phone. I stayed home the next weekend, and on Sunday, Aaron called and said Jennifer's uncle Junior died last night. Junior was always lively and had quite a sense of humour. It was sad to see him go, but his health was getting worse, so it may have been an end to his suffering.

I called Alvin Tolley on Tuesday morning and he said he may know a publisher for me and I should send my letters regarding Canada's treatment of minority war veterans to a Native newspaper and to Germany. While I was in college, I heard there was a strong interest in Indian culture in Germany. On Wednesday I called Helen during my coffee break and she said Auntie Beatrice Shackelly in Merritt passed away on Saturday and thought her funeral was today. Her oldest son, Dewey, said he would call me; but he forgot. I had called Dewey on

Monday night but he wasn't home; and his wife, Jackie, forgot to mention it to me. So I called their Indian band office and Roger, the second youngest of the boys, was there. Roger said his mother passed away on Saturday and her funeral was the next day.

Jennifer was in Sto:lo Eagle for her uncle's funeral, so I picked her up and told her I had to go to Merritt for my aunt's funeral the next day. She was depressed, so I didn't go to bed until two thirty in the morning. I had saved enough hours to take time off work for her funeral because I knew she wasn't well and left early the next morning because of wintry road conditions. I had enough hours to take Friday off as well, so I spent the weekend in Chilliwack. Aaron got stressed out though and missed two days of work. In the paper John Les, chairman of the treaty referendum committee, asked the premier of British Columbia for an apology and expression of regret on how Canada's aboriginal people have been treated. It felt good to know some influential people are starting to face the truth.

It was the beginning of December now and Jennifer only had three days of classes left, so I wrote a covering letter for her résumé to apply for work when I got back to Squamish. She knew she would get her report on Tuesday and was worried about how she would do, but she called me at 10:26 a.m. at the office and said she passed the test. That was a big relief since she was so worried about failing it. I also read on the computer that day that John Les recommended a "process of reconciliation" with aboriginals, which would include an "expression of regret" from the British Columbia government about the troubled lives Natives had since the arrival of Europeans.

Wednesday was Jennifer's last day of classes, and she wanted me to be in Chilliwack to help her look for work on Friday, but on Thursday she still didn't seem too excited about passing her course. On Friday morning I helped her get ready for her class evaluation, then we went out for lunch. I wanted to go to Dragon Tower, but we ended up going to Canton Gardens; and when we walked in, I saw Henry Jr. and their cousin Jerry sitting there, so we joined them. Henry Jr. acted like he didn't want us to join them, but we joined them anyway, and he said he just got accepted by Corrections Canada to be a prison guard that day and would be starting a thirteen-week training course in January. I felt really happy for him because after what he's been through, he now had a chance to do something with his life and wouldn't have been eligible for the job if he didn't graduate from high school. Even though we helped him finish high school, paid for his graduation, helped him get into college, and tutored him in math, he still treated us like that!

Jennifer and I then went to the college, and the students were given letters stating they passed the course and their RCA pins. I was the only outsider there; the rest were all students and instructors. Then when Jennifer went up to get her letter and pin, she was given a standing ovation. On Sunday, Jennifer went to work at noon, so I went to a movie and saw *Behind Enemy Lines*. It was a very good movie, based on a true story and I got much out of it. The hero was shot down behind enemy lines and seemed to have an invisible wall protecting him yet he couldn't get rescued until he had the evidence proving war crimes had taken place, it appeared like that was meant to happen that way.

While visiting my parents, my mother told me about sugar-sale restrictions to Indians because of a law that existed in Canada. Most people don't believe that law ever existed in Canada at all, yet it still existed when I was a child. What my mother said didn't sound quite right, so I thought I would check into it when I got back to work. I don't know how, but I often seem to be in the right place at the right time to learn things. It appears to some people that you can't do anything without me finding out, but there will always be some people who won't believe the things I saw happen and the stories I heard. There are many stories coming out that people aren't going to believe.

I wanted to come back to Squamish Sunday night, but Jennifer wanted me to stay for one more day to help her look for work, so I booked a day of annual leave the next day and felt really happy when Jennifer started talking about wanting to live until she's eighty. On Friday I had a good visit with Darlene, and she was really happy Jennifer passed her course. Jennifer was depressed that day though because she forgot to take her cell phone out of her coat pocket before she washed it; now it didn't work, and she also misplaced her registration papers and needed them before she could get her certificate. I tried to straighten it out with the college, but they wouldn't give me any information. Jennifer would have to call them herself. I got worried about her registration papers and hoped nothing would go wrong at the last minute because I had worked so hard to bring her this far. There was nothing I could do until after the weekend, but I would be on annual leave so I could help her out.

On Monday I helped Jennifer get her registration papers filled out at the college, bought her some clothes to get ready for job interviews, then took her to Sto:lo Eagle to visit her mother. I just dropped her off, went back to Chilliwack, picked her up on Thursday, then we did some Christmas shopping. We went back to Chilliwack Monday morning and finished our Christmas shopping. Christmas was uneventful. Jennifer went to Sto:lo Eagle, and I visited my parents in Rosedale. Nothing much happened after Christmas, and on Saturday afternoon, I brushed out more of my dad's property for planting trees.

Phaye said Jennifer would feel good in the fall and it would feel strange to her. For years now I had been wishing it would happen this year, but again, it didn't happen. She also said I would be over my last hill in May, so again I hoped it was next year. Jennifer still had trouble with depression, and looking after her has been quite an ordeal, something I wouldn't wish on anyone! I know some people won't believe my life story, and that was what happened and the way things were, but they have the right to their own opinion. They can do their own research if they don't believe me; maybe they'll learn things they didn't expect to learn like I did.

Chapter 24

2002

Jennifer came back to Squamish with me on New Year's Day for a visit. I went back to work Wednesday, and on Thursday she went back to Chilliwack. She left me a note thanking me for helping her out with everything and said she couldn't have made it through school and gotten a career without my help. I wanted to stay home on the weekend, but she wanted me to go to Chilliwack and help her get a new cell phone; so I went back and got her cell phone activated, which may not have been properly done if I weren't there. Then she got two days off and thought about coming to Squamish again, but when we flipped a coin, it said no. Then in the third week of January, we were told how many jobs from each department would be eliminated, but not many people were specifically told they would be losing their job.

Aaron got his check from income tax, so he drank while Jennifer was working. I picked her up after work and we rented some videos. Aaron was sleeping when we got home and she woke him up, so a big argument followed. Jennifer started screaming and threw things around the room, so the police were called again! Two regular constables and one auxiliary constable went, so I told one of them about Jennifer's history of depression and the physical and sexual abuse she's still suffering from. And a Native constable talked to Jennifer, and eventually, she calmed down; but looking after her is still hard. The next day, Jennifer packed up more of her things and I put them in storage for her. She wanted to move out of Chilliwack, so I told her to be optimistic and try and be happy. I said if there had been an easier way for me to get a career, look after her, and get her a career than what I went through, then I definitely would have done it; so she started feeling better.

I slept lightly at lunchtime now, and by Wednesday I couldn't go to sleep until I started thinking about *sex*, then I was out like a light; so I guess it's time to come out of my shell. I competed in the forestry curling bonspiel again and was glad I went there rather than compete in a karate tournament in North Vancouver because it snowed hard the day before and the roads were icy. That night I got indigestion and thought I might be getting an ulcer again, but it went away when I started thinking about *sex*! Jennifer called me the next morning and was tired and stressed out, but she said she would start to try and think positive and be happy. On Monday we were told the Squamish forest district would be losing four and a half job positions and more would be laid off at the end of June; in November, more staff would be given layoff notice and they would be laid off at the end of March 2003.

I went back to Chilliwack again the next weekend, and on Sunday I took Jennifer to Sto:lo Eagle to visit her mother. It appeared I still stress Henry Jr. out, so I would have preferred to leave earlier than we did. When Henry Jr. saw me there, he was surprised to see me there after how he treated me because previously when I visited, he put the remote control for his satellite dish away then left for the day. Other times he asked us to leave or just went stomping off into the bedroom while I was sitting at the kitchen table, so on this visit I told him I was just taking Jennifer to visit her mother. It was mealtime when I said that and only served myself an extremely small serving because I get treated like an outcast, then he slammed his forearms on the table and went stomping off into the living room! Jennifer finally said, "Next time, just drop me off then leave!"

In early February, I started having trouble going to sleep at lunchtime; and Jennifer went to the bars Wednesday night, which I knew she would do. I still worry about her, but there was nothing I could do, and slept well at lunchtime when I thought about *sex*. I stayed home on the second weekend of February because I only wanted to visit her every second weekend to give some time to myself. I got bored and restless though, and Jennifer called me on Sunday because she was depressed and worried because when she drinks, she doesn't know when to stop. Then she phoned a couple of psychics, asked them some questions, and felt better. Aaron didn't think Jennifer had a problem with drinking, only a problem when she drinks, so I told him she shouldn't drink until she cures her problems that cause her to flip out because something could happen to her.

I went back to work, and on Tuesday I tried to sleep at lunchtime and almost didn't sleep at all; then Jennifer called me after lunch and said she's been evicted because of all the noise they made on February 6. I was feeling happy until she told me that, but I guess life was just too calm for her, so she had to turn everything upside down. I felt stressed out, so I went out for coffee after work then had a few beers. Strangely enough, I felt good on Thursday even though I knew I would have to help Aaron and Jennifer find a new place to stay, and on Friday I had a good visit with Darlene and couldn't sleep at lunchtime.

I stayed home that weekend, and the next weekend, I helped them look for a new place to stay. Jennifer flipped out again on Sunday but not too badly this time, and I was still trying to get her to think positive. She called me the next day and said they got an apartment but needed their first month's rent and a damage deposit, so I had to loan them $450. I called Jennifer on Friday morning, March 1, during my coffee break and she said Henry Jr. dropped out of his course to be a corrections officer and went logging because he needed the money; and I didn't think Corrections would be a very good job for him, but that was only my opinion.

In the forestry news briefs, in the *Nanaimo Daily News*, a Vancouver Island newspaper, Dave Walkem received the Forester of the Year award. Dave is my age, and it said he was the first Native to become a British Columbia registered professional forester and he got it in 1984.

I went back to Chilliwack for the weekend to help Aaron and Jennifer get packed and move on Sunday, and Henry Jr. helped them. I still stressed him out because he was crabby toward me. I didn't think he would get crabby toward me, but he was! I told him two times saving Jennifer from suicide was an ordeal I wouldn't wish on anyone, hoping he would change the way he treated me and at least show some appreciation for what I've done, but he didn't change at all and just said, "*I know! That's all you talk about!*" He definitely didn't treat Alvin that way when he went down, so I decided I would stay away from Sto:lo Eagle as much as possible now.

Although I went to bed rather late Sunday night, I only slept lightly at lunchtime the next day, and Jennifer called in the evening and said Aaron went to the bars and got robbed just outside the door to the apartment building. Three hooded teenagers appeared out of nowhere, hit him on the head with a baseball bat, and wanted his money; so Aaron ended up with eight stitches on his head!

During the week, I often woke up early and just couldn't sleep. It was snowing on Friday and the roads were icy, so Aaron suggested I stay in Squamish and go on Saturday. Jennifer had also been waking up early and couldn't sleep. She flipped out again on Sunday but didn't stress Aaron and me out as much as she usually did. When I went back to work, I only slept lightly at lunchtime and wondered if I should give up karate since I was not too stressed out anymore.

I stayed home for the weekend and only slept lightly at lunchtime during the week, went back to Chilliwack on Friday, and Jennifer had missed work on Thursday. She drank, flipped out again, and stepped on the Game Boy three times as hard as she could; and surprisingly, it still worked. Aaron said the kids lightly stepped on Henry Jr.'s Game Boy once and it didn't work. I brushed out some more areas on my dad's property to get it ready to plant more trees, and there was also a retirement dinner for Uncle Percy Roberts at Uncle Joe's place. The end of March was Easter weekend, so I went back to Chilliwack again the next weekend; but normally, I liked to stay home every second weekend.

I felt rather stressed out during the week and slept rather heavily at lunchtime the next week and ended up going back to Chilliwack again on the first weekend of April because Isaac had planned a surprise dinner for our dad's birthday on Sunday. Ryan and Desiree were also having a dinner on Saturday to celebrate their twentieth wedding anniversary. Jennifer wanted to go but couldn't make it because she was sick. I was happy about that though because I may have had to drive her over, and I didn't want to go because I want as little to do with that family as possible now. On Sunday, Jennifer was really cranky; so when I took her to work, Aaron went to the bars and I went to Rosedale. When I got to Rosedale, I decided to check the trees we planted at the back of the reserve to see how they were doing; and much to my disappointment, many of them were dead or damaged from horses walking over them. After work, Jennifer had a meeting at A&W in the evening, and Aaron finally flipped out! He moved all her things into the extra bedroom, slightly damaging the door and scratching the wall. When I picked Jennifer up, I told her what happened and she was happy about that because she wanted to end her relationship with him. He was passed out when we got home, so I helped her pack and move some more things into storage. I originally thought I was going to leave early but didn't leave until midnight.

I thought I would be tired the next morning, but I woke up early, and Aaron could now understand why I didn't want anything to do with Jennifer's family. They couldn't do enough for Alvin, and no one else is important. Unless you're going with Brenda, nothing you do for them is enough; then if you're with her, they can't do enough for you! Even though I had a good workout at karate the next day, I was still stressed out, so I drank a few beers when I got home. That week I was finally able to get a hold of my cousin Dewey Shackelly in Merritt to discuss restriction of sugar sales to the Indians. Dewey's mother, Beatrice, was very knowledgeable and didn't hold back when I asked for information; but she passed away last fall. Dewey had heard about it, and we had a good talk; then he told me to call Don Moses.

Don Moses is a Native from Merritt, is at least fifteen years older than I, and has a degree in political science and economics. Don mentioned working at Armstrong's Department Store in Merritt in the late 1950s when half the store was a grocery store and the other half was a hardware store. Don mentioned something he had to do about vanilla extract when he worked as a grocery clerk, because of a law that still existed at that time; then that made me wonder if there were very many towns where stores and cafés hired Indians to work for them as late as the 1960s and '70s. I asked around when I did my research for a research paper I titled "Sugar and Vanilla Extract"!

I went back to Chilliwack again the next weekend because it was my niece Nicole's and Jennifer's birthday. On Friday I helped Helen get ready for the party, and Jennifer got off work early but got mad because I wasn't there to pick her up right away. I drove Jennifer around a little bit on Saturday then went to Rosedale to take Helen and her kids, Ashley and Nicole, to a play thing called Go Bananas; and Jennifer got mad because she finally got two days off in a row and couldn't spend it with me. It felt like a rather long day, and Jennifer decided she wanted to visit her mother, so I drove her to Sto:lo Eagle; and the next day, Henry Jr. said he would drive her back to Chilliwack.

I got sick when I went back to work, worked all day Monday anyway, then took three days off because I was sick. There was a going-away party for three staff members on Friday, but I didn't go because I was finally getting a weekend to myself. On Sunday I called Alvin Tolley in Quebec and he gave me more information on "Sugar and Vanilla Extract" and said he would send me some information. I wanted information to send to influential people to expose the truth about Canada and, hopefully, find a publisher for my life story. Jennifer called me in the evening and said her cousin Melody passed away that day. She and Melody were almost the same age and were childhood friends. I slept lightly at lunchtime again the next day, and that night, I called April and she gave me some more information on sugar and vanilla-extract sales.

All week I slept lightly at lunchtime, and on Thursday, Jennifer called and said Melody passed away on Tuesday, not Sunday. One of her aunts got things mixed up, and her brothers were mad about that! On Saturday I took Jennifer to Boston Bar for Melody's funeral but had trouble finding where it was, so we didn't get to the hall until the body was being taken out, but we still made it to the burial. As she was being buried, Henry Jr. finally realized that could have easily been his sister that was being buried but I was willing to go through what it took to save her, and finally started being nice to me, but it was too late now! I showed far more patience than I ever would have ever expected anyone to show and I was still treated like an outcast; now I want to stay completely away from that family!

Sunny Boy and Rosalie were there; and at the dinner, I said to Rosalie, "The bottom line!" Rosalie knew I finally realized she was protecting her daughter from Henry that's why she wouldn't have anything to do with him even though he was her brother-in-law. After the dinner there was a gathering for people to say prayers and for Indians do their rituals for the departed. Some of the people there mentioned when the Indians there grew orchards and could have become self-supporting but the land was taken away from them. I don't know when it happened, but it may not have been that long ago and heard Roy Munro, an Indian from Lytton who was three to four years older than I, died of a heart attack.

On Sunday, Jennifer said she and Melody were close friends as they were growing up until people called her down for associating with her. Then when Jennifer was twelve or thirteen years old, she was taken away from home because Liz reported the sexual abuse to the police, and Henry always blamed Geraldine for planning the breakup of the family and couldn't see what he was doing wrong.

On the first weekend of May, I finally decided I had done as much as I could for Jennifer. There's nothing more I could do now except try and help her get into licensed practical nursing (LPN). I called Jennifer, and she was mad. Last night she went to the bars and ended up in the drunk tank, said she wanted to go to the bars again; and I tried to tell her not to go, but she wouldn't listen. I felt there was nothing I could do about this situation and wished it would end! I was stressed out all day from worrying about her, but she called me later on and said she didn't go to the bars. She said she should start going to AA meetings with her cousin Roger now.

When I got back to work on Monday, I stayed in the office until after five o'clock to send an e-mail to Equity and Diversity titled "Sugar and Vanilla Extract" and had to give them advance notice it was coming because of the title because it wasn't totally about government issues and sent it after five o'clock. I wanted to add something positive to it, so I didn't completely stick to government issues.

I went back to Chilliwack the next weekend and drank a few beers with Jennifer on Friday night. She was cranky the next day, and I was hung over. I was glad she worked from eleven o'clock to seven thirty that day, so I could brush out my seedlings on my dad's property, but didn't get very much done because I was hung over. On Sunday, Jennifer wanted to visit her mother again, so Aaron drove her to Sto:lo Eagle and dropped me off in Rosedale. My mother told me my niece Deidre was suicidal, so she was going to move her out of David and Sandra's place. I got lots of brushing done and was really happy with the survival rate and got back to Squamish rather late but couldn't sleep for some reason.

We had a first aid course on Wednesday and I couldn't sleep at lunchtime. I drank coffee during the day, and it seemed to keep me awake at night; so I drank a few beers to counteract the coffee, but it didn't seem to do any good. Jennifer called that night and said she wanted to go to Sto:lo Eagle on Saturday because Brenda was going down, and I was happy about that because it would give Aaron and me a chance to do our own thing. Since it was a long weekend in May, I got to patrol recreation sites Friday night and wanted to be in Rosedale for the weekend because it was Aaron and Ashley's birthday. On Saturday, Jennifer caught the bus to Vancouver. I picked her up at the bus depot then took her shopping at a large, major shopping mall. Then she dropped me off in Rosedale and went to Sto:lo Eagle.

Jennifer spent the night in Sto:lo Eagle and picked me up the next day before going to work at noon. Then I took Ashley, Deidre, and their friends to the movies in the afternoon; and Deidre was now staying with my parents.

I took Jennifer to Sto:lo Eagle after work so she could visit with Brenda, and Henry Jr. looked crabby and realized he treated me like an outcast and rolled out the welcome mat for Alvin when he visited. I left right away though because I wanted to have a few beers with Aaron and wouldn't even use the bathroom or drink their water. I offered to take Aaron out for a steak dinner the next day, but he didn't want to go and didn't go to work because it was raining. I picked Jennifer up, but she was cranky again. She wanted to come to Squamish but decided to stay in Chilliwack and rest up. I went back to work, and on Wednesday, Jennifer called and said she was coming for the car to go for a job interview on Thursday. I called Vivian Ignace that afternoon, and she made me realize that finding the truth is my passion; then Jennifer called the next day and said ten people were interviewed for the job and she would know on Monday if she got the job or not.

I caught the bus to Chilliwack on Saturday, and Jennifer and I went to a psychic fair and was told this will be a good year for me. I write well and people I wrote to will be answering me. Jennifer was told she'll be taking an eight-month course for her LPN, not the full twelve-month course; then I checked the trees Aaron and I planted down by the river, and many of them didn't survive. It seemed like everything I tried to do for the Indian reserve fell apart, but the trees I planted on my dad's property were doing quite well.

I went back to work, and on Wednesday I got an e-mail asking for submissions from aboriginal writers for a book titled *Gatherings*, to be published by an aboriginal book publishing company in Penticton called Theytus Books. I decided to submit a short outline of my life story and perhaps write an article for *Windspeaker*, an aboriginal newspaper based out of Edmonton, Alberta; and Alvin Tolley had suggested I send the information on minority war veterans to *Windspeaker*.

I went to Chilliwack on Friday so I could take Jennifer to the canoe races at Cultus Lake, the first weekend of June. We went to the races, but I avoided Henry Jr. and walked around visiting and talking to people. Jennifer went to work on Sunday, so I did some more brushing of my seedlings, went back to work; and on Tuesday, Jennifer called and said she had an interview with Sto:lo Tribal Council on Friday. She got stressed out over finding her student card and medical reports for the shots she had to take, but if she got the job, I would have to let her keep the car. Then on Thursday, Jennifer called and said she won a scholarship. At first I thought she was just kidding, but she won a $100 scholarship for her perseverance!

I felt bored at work but thought at least next week I'd be getting some fieldwork and had enough hours built up to take Friday off, so I caught the bus to Chilliwack that night to take Jennifer to her interview the next day. I had made arrangements for her to pick up her guest tickets for the graduation ceremonies before I left for work, but when I got to Chilliwack, she started talking about not going to the ceremonies. I told her that after the run around she got just to get into the course and what happened after she got in, she should go to the ceremonies; then she said, "Look at what you went through, and you didn't go to your graduation ceremonies!" I never ever thought of that until she mentioned it. After eight years of studying, I *totally* refused to go to my graduation ceremonies!

On Friday I got up early, took Aaron shopping for tools, took him to work, then helped Jennifer get ready for her interview; and she was really stressed out about it! She stressed me out, so we had a big argument, but eventually she settled down. She went to the interview and said there were eleven people being interviewed for four job openings; then she wanted to go to Sto:lo Eagle because it was Henry Jr.'s birthday, but I said, "No!" I told her she was tired and had to go to work at five o'clock, so she slept for a while, then I dropped her off at work then went to Bellingham to visit Auntie Jeanette.

I gave Auntie Jeanette a copy of my life story, and once she started reading it, she couldn't put it down. Her oldest daughter, Charlene, stopped over; and Jeanette wanted Charlene to read it too because she's been working with abused children for years. Charlene said she also wanted her daughter, Winona, to read it after her because Winona's working on a master's degree in psychology and then it might be spread to the psychology department. Charlene then worked on me spiritually and told me to get rid of all my negative energy then suggested I contact Sherman Alexie, a Native author, actor, and entertainer to help me get my book published. On Sunday, Auntie Jeanette was sick, so she didn't read much more; then I went back to Chilliwack and Aaron and Jennifer drove me back to Squamish. I let them take the car in case Jennifer got the job and she needed it to prepare for her graduation ceremonies.

I woke up at four thirty the next morning and couldn't sleep, so I started working on my submission for *Gatherings*. On Wednesday I called Aaron and Jennifer. She didn't get the job, so I told Aaron she should try and be optimistic about it because maybe a better job was coming because at least she had her certificate. I took Thursday afternoon off and caught the bus to Chilliwack and bought Jennifer a dress and shoes for her graduation ceremonies. I had booked a day of annual leave for her ceremonies, and she got extra tickets so her mother, Ryan and Desiree, Henry Jr., Aaron, and I could all attend. Jennifer was really happy about graduating, and the ceremonies were held in Abbotsford. After the ceremonies, we went for a lunch buffet, and her family was really happy for her! We went to the bars in the evening, but I didn't drink right away and ended up looking after Jennifer. Usually when she goes to the bars, she doesn't want to leave, and on Saturday, she was tired and hung over and went to work at noon.

Since Sunday was Father's Day, there was another dinner for my dad at my parents' place; then Jennifer came back to Squamish with me and admitted that when she goes to the bars, she doesn't want to leave, so she shouldn't go there. On Monday, Jennifer was in the bars when I got home from work, so I joined her a little while later. We didn't stay until closing time though and went home. She stayed in Squamish for one extra day then took the car back to Chilliwack.

On Friday I woke up at five o'clock and couldn't sleep, so I called Alvin Tolley in Quebec since they're four hours ahead of British Columbia time; and Alvin told me to call Paul Barnsley, the senior editor of *Windspeaker*, and say Alvin recommended him. I had an appointment with Darlene that day, and she was really happy about Jennifer's graduation and her winning a scholarship! Then she got me to read the main points of the outline I was sending to *Gatherings* and told me to say more positive things about myself in it and to write in my life story why I didn't attend my graduation ceremonies from BCIT after eight years of studying.

When I graduated from BCIT, I totally refused to go to my graduation ceremonies even though it was after eight years of studying for a two-year diploma. One reason I didn't go was because I thought I might be working and may not be able to attend, but I also didn't apply because the students closed me off and wouldn't associate with me, so I thought I would be a *good Canadian Indian* and keep my distance! After writing my life story out six times, I finally decided to write that in. Yes, I had lucky breaks that all the other students wished they had, but I went through four years of incredibly hard times I wouldn't wish on anyone before I got those lucky breaks! I also had many things holding me back, and it really slowed me down, and I couldn't go home to take a break from what I was going through! If all that wasn't bad enough, Indians I went to school with were dying and committing suicide left and right as I was getting my career!

Then Darlene told me to read out the comments I wrote on Jennifer's graduation card. I wrote the following message:

> Congratulations, Jennifer!
>
> You finally have a career and a chance to do something with your life! When I first met you in January 1980, you were such a nervous wreck it looked like you were beyond recovery! If that wasn't bad enough, it was like the whole world was against you!
>
> I stood beside you, and together we fought them off and won!
>
> You've proven that there is hope for you and you can do something with your life!
>
> Looking after you all these years was an ordeal I wouldn't wish on anyone! But surviving what you went through would make a very inspirational story!
>
> Keep up the good work and advance to licensed practical nursing. If life begins at forty, the best is yet to come!
>
> Love,
Daddy!

I couldn't read it without crying tears of *joy*! When I first met Jennifer, she was such a nervous wreck it looked like breaking her depression and getting her a career was an impossible task! If that wasn't bad enough, the whole world was against her; my parents pressured me so much to leave her that I developed health problems and had to take time off work to go for X-rays! On top of all that, all her father did was mooch off me and make life miserable for me then said he did everything for us and we were obligated to him! I still wouldn't give up though, and finally, after twenty-two years of hard times I wouldn't wish on anyone, she didn't commit suicide and has a career of her own!

I went back to Chilliwack again the next weekend so I could take Jennifer to get her graduation photos, and there was going to be a surprise dinner for my parents' fiftieth wedding anniversary. Jennifer had gone to Sto:lo Eagle Friday night and took her mother with her to get the photos taken, which slowed me down on what I wanted to do. Then when she went to work, I had to take her mother back to Sto:lo Eagle then go to my parents' anniversary. I got stressed out because I felt like Jennifer was deliberately trying to keep me from having fun again, but I decided I would rather put up with that than see her commit suicide! Suicide is permanent. Her depression won't last forever but sure feels like it's lasting forever! I went back to work, and on Tuesday I woke up at five forty-five and couldn't sleep; so I got up, and Jennifer called me that morning and asked me to help her get some job application letters ready. I got them ready and sent them with some money since her hours were being cut back at work. The next day, Jennifer called and said Andrew offered her a job paying $55 a day babysitting his kids for six months while Shelley, his wife, went to school for a course in early childhood education.

I called Auntie Jeanette again, and she had been sick for two and a half weeks then finally started reading my life story again. I got to patrol recreation sites on the last weekend of June since it was a long weekend and stayed home for the weekend because I was tired of running around all the time. When I got back to work, Chris Runnals gave me some more trees again, so I told Jennifer to come back so I could bring them to Rosedale. On Thursday I mailed the outline of my life story to Theytus Books, and Jennifer came to Squamish on Friday and spent the night. In the morning I looked at her eyes and could see she was getting stronger and will get even stronger. Henry Jr. was at the canoe races at Ambleside Park in West Vancouver and called to ask us to stop by. He may have wanted to see me, but enough is enough. I just don't want anything to do with that family anymore!

We got going rather later because of a power outage and an accident delaying traffic, because we wanted to have lunch before we left. Although it was late when I got to Rosedale, I still got some trees planted and brushed out more areas for planting. I did more planting on Sunday and had enough hours built up to take Monday and Tuesday off, so I did more planting. Unfortunately, on Monday, Jennifer got off work early; so I had to pick her up at two o'clock, which didn't give me much time to get the work done. I wanted to take my time and enjoy myself, but now I had to rush. It was raining rather hard though, so I just brushed out areas so I could plant more trees the next day. On Tuesday, Jennifer started work an hour later than usual, which cut into my time, but I still finished the planting; now all I have to do is keep them brushed out until they're as tall as the competing brush.

For some reason, I often wake up early in the morning and can't sleep. Previously I wanted to use my flex time to meet with Sharon Thira, the program director of the Provincial Residential School Protocol Committee, a healing program for survivors of the residential schools and their children who have been affected by these survivors. While cooking supper one night, I didn't think I was angry but merely thinking about how Henry Jr. treated me and cut my thumb slightly. I realized I have to do my best not to think about it, but I still wanted to stay away from that family!

Balvinder Biring, an East Indian RPF, was transferred from Victoria to Squamish in July due to government cutbacks and put up a plaque in his cubicle, a Golden Award giving him recognition for all the work he had done in Equity and Diversity. I had brought up many issues to the attention of Equity and Diversity, which I thought were being shared with staff doing the same work; so I asked him if he heard about any of the issues I brought up, and he said he never even heard of me.

In the second week of July, Joy Ward, a counsellor on aboriginal problem gambling, sent out a request for feedback on why some people give up alcohol addiction for a bingo or gambling addiction. I stayed home that weekend and wrote a response but wanted Jennifer to read and approve it first because it involved what she had gone through. She read it and said it was okay to send it but wanted her name changed. The response was positive, and at first, Joy thought I was a woman because I have a different name.

On Thursday night, I called April and she said she and one of her sisters was interviewed for a book on residential schools and Indian children being taken away from home and placed in foster homes. Many Indian children were taken away from their parents in the 1960s and placed in non-Native foster homes in what was known as the Sixties Scoop. Some were taken away from their parents for the flimsiest excuses. She said by the time the book was published, there wasn't any truth to what was printed; but after trying to deal with one of the two authors on aboriginal issues, I could believe that.

The next week I called Sharon Thira and made an appointment to meet her on Friday, and she was excited about meeting me because of the articles I wrote and sent to her. I had enough hours built up to take Friday off, so I caught the bus to West Vancouver and met her at her office near a shopping mall. Sharon has a bachelor of science degree in biology, a master's degree in counselling and was from British Guiana. We had a good meeting, discussed many issues, and I gave her more articles I wrote based on my research and observations. I knew that in situations like what Jennifer's been through, the siblings suffer just as much as the victims do, but Sharon finally made me realize that's why Jennifer's family treats me the way they do. My mother had told me we confronted their parents, brought back very painful memories they would rather not face, and now it was finally sinking in. I still thought they should at least show some appreciation for saving their sister from suicide and getting her a career though! If it was Alvin, it would still be a major event and no one in that family would be able to do enough for him even if it was nothing compared to what it took to save Jennifer from suicide and get her a career!

Sharon also said many Indians from Alkali Lake Indian Reserve near Williams Lake gave up their alcohol addiction for bingo. At one time, Alkali Lake was nicknamed Alcohol Lake. Sharon also said she knew Gary, the counsellor from DIA, interviewed survivors of all the residential schools in British Columbia; and they all had horror stories to tell of those schools!

The next weekend, I asked Aaron and Jennifer to come to Squamish to pick up my jars so I could can some salmon. They came on Saturday, and Aaron didn't want to stay in Squamish any longer than he had to because of the temptation to do drugs. It was the long weekend in August, and on Sunday, Jennifer spent most of the day with Brenda since she had gone down to visit. I did some brushing; then Jennifer wanted to go to Sto:lo Eagle, but I wouldn't go because her brothers sure don't make me very welcome, so I spent money taking her out to dinner instead.

I went back to Chilliwack again the next weekend so Aaron could pay me some of the money he owed me and to brush out the seedlings some more. He was crabby though because his paycheck was small and most of it was spent; so he dropped me off in Rosedale, picked Jennifer up in Sto:lo Eagle, and suggested I stay in Rosedale. I had Friday off, finished the brushing Saturday, and Jennifer picked me up because Aaron was drinking. On Sunday I took the bus back to Squamish, but now I was starting to miss my car. Two months was okay, but now it was the third month.

I went back to Chilliwack again the next weekend because Auntie Tilley from New Mexico and Auntie Deedee from Ohio were visiting. I had enough hours to take Friday off again; so I drove Aaron to work, went with Jennifer to her appointment with Jane Byra, then drove her to work. I went out for lunch; but after work, Jennifer was stressed out, so I went to the bars with her. When Jennifer drinks, she usually drinks until she blacks out, so we didn't get home until four thirty in the morning. We had a family reunion that weekend on Saturday, but I thought it was on Sunday, so I missed it.

I'd been putting in long hours at work, so I was able to take the next Friday off as well, so I caught the bus to Chilliwack Thursday night; but Aaron didn't wake up to let me in, so I got Dad to take me to his place. I canned my salmon on Friday and spent the night at my parents' place. Aaron and Jennifer went to the bars in the afternoon, and Jennifer really stressed me out! I often miss being single and wish Jennifer would start feeling happy and good about herself because it still takes its toll on me. It was Uncle Joe and Auntie Irene's fortieth wedding anniversary on Saturday; that's also why I went back to Chilliwack. I did some grocery shopping on Sunday, and a clerk there seemed to be interested in me. Previously, I just couldn't get anyone interested in me no matter how hard I tried; so hopefully, I'm almost over my last hill in life.

I went back to work but got sick toward the end of the week and missed work on Thursday and Friday. I tried calling Paul Barnsley, the senior editor of *Windspeaker*, but he was out of the office. Paul returned my call the next day, but I missed it by eight minutes. I called back right away, but he was already gone. Since it was the first weekend of September, I got some overtime patrolling recreation sites again then took the rest of the week off in annual leave and went to Chilliwack. I called Paul again on Thursday, and he was interested in the information I wanted to send him regarding Canada's treatment of minority war veterans. I was going to mail it to him, but he said he would be in Squamish on September 25 and 26 and we could meet on the twenty-eighth. I offered to write the story, but Paul told me just to give him the information and he would write it on my behalf. Paul said he knew June Quipp, the chief of my reserve, and wondered why Gary was the only person to get fired in 1974; so I told him Gary was probably a scapegoat and Native politicians might be able to explain that.

Jennifer was stressed out all day because of Shelley's crankiness, started drinking, and got really drunk; now I felt more like I didn't want anything to do with her family for the rest of my life! I finally realized Jennifer seems to seek out and dwell on negative issues the way an alcoholic or drug addict goes after their booze and drugs. She does that because it feels normal to her; even an addiction to suffering can be extremely hard to break. I took Aaron to work then went to Rosedale to buy some tobacco from the reserve, visited my family, and my mother told me about a job in the Chilliwack paper Jennifer might be interested in.

On Saturday, Jennifer came back to Squamish with me but was stressed out, so we stopped in North Vancouver and she had a few beers. I only had one because I was driving. She calmed down by the time we got to Squamish and didn't drink anymore. Two times Jennifer said she liked the graduation card I bought her but didn't like what I wrote on it and said it was too negative! I wanted to go hunting grouse on Sunday but wasn't feeling well when I woke up, so I just stayed home and rested; then Jennifer and I went to the office and faxed an application to the job my mother mentioned, but she didn't get an interview.

I was sick all week but worked until Wednesday because I had work to do with a client then took Thursday and Friday off. On Thursday, Jennifer called and said Aaron was drinking, so she was coming to Squamish. She still felt sick and depressed, and I had a hard time going to sleep because I kept coughing. On Friday I made an appointment with the doctor for Jennifer and me. She wasn't only sick; she was also depressed, making me miss the single life again. I needed a car now and thought if Jennifer got a job, she was also going to need a car too; so I had her come to Squamish to sign the Sunbird over to her then buy myself a new Chevrolet Cavalier. It's a rather small car, but if I hit a windfall, I could give it to her. A Cavalier would suit her needs perfectly. I had made arrangements with a car salesman to buy a new car and had $2,600 for a down payment, but when I called the salesman, he said the bank would only take $1,245 for a down payment and my monthly payments would be lower than I expected. On Saturday we picked up the Cavalier, but it wasn't ready until eleven o'clock because it took a while to get the insurance transferred, insure the Sunbird for Jennifer, and arrange the loan. Then I found out the car would be financed over five years instead of four. I was annoyed at first then decided there would be less financial stress and I may be able to make an RRSP contribution when Jennifer paid me back for the insurance.

After that we went to Abbotsford and Jennifer wanted to take her mother to the fall fair in Agassiz but locked her keys in the car, so we had to go to Chilliwack and get the other set of keys from Aaron. Her mother was too sick to go to the fall fair, so Jennifer went to Sto:lo Eagle to visit her and wanted me to go there too, but I visited my parents instead. On Sunday, Aaron's father Don and stepmother, Tina, came over to visit Aaron and Jennifer; and they were happy to see me too. Don was happy for the way I helped Aaron and Jennifer, and Tina thought it was great that I gave them a car to use for work. I told Tina some of Jennifer's friends envied her and wished someone would get them a career. Henry Jr. had gone back and completed his course to become a corrections officer and would be graduating on the twenty-fifth, a Wednesday. He was only allowed to take three guests, but I wouldn't have gone even if I were asked.

I came back to Squamish and couldn't sleep because I kept coughing, worked all day Monday even though I was sick, then stayed home that night. I went back to Chilliwack on Thursday night but stopped in Vancouver for karate; and the instructor, Allan Chan, wanted me to grade in October, and that really made my day because the next grading after that would be black belt! Jennifer was in Sto:lo Eagle, and I thought Aaron would pick her up on Saturday because I had to get the brakes done on the Sunbird the next day, but Henry Jr. took her back to Chilliwack Friday morning. We dropped Aaron off at work then got the Sunbird serviced; previously when I had the transmission oil changed, the transmission shop tried to tell me I needed a $600 repair bill done, but I told them to write what the problem could be and I would get a second opinion. They wouldn't write anything down, and I found out it didn't need any transmission repairs; but it cost me $600 to do the brakes, which I was expecting.

Then I helped Jennifer apply for work with an Indian band and at a rest home in Agassiz called the Glenwood. She got an informal interview at the Glenwood, and the lady was impressed with her résumé. She said Jennifer might get a formal interview the following week, may be on call for training, and start with cleaning. Then we went to Sto:lo Eagle, where Jennifer thought about applying for work there but changed her mind because of the drive over. We peeled apples for baking pies, and I wanted to be gone before Henry Jr. got home; but he arrived before we left, so we visited with him for a little while then left later than I wanted to leave. Jennifer got cranky again on Saturday but calmed down eventually, and on Sunday she talked about moving to Sardis. I mentioned her flipping out yesterday; she didn't flip out like she did when they lived on Mary Street, and at least the police weren't called.

I came back to Squamish and thought I could make it to work, but I woke up coughing heavily. I went to the doctor again and he prescribed some pills for me, said I had an allergic reaction, and sent me for X-rays. On Wednesday, September 25, I still felt sick, coughed quite a bit, and my throat felt like its burning; then I called Paul Barnsley's cell phone, and he was at a motel in Squamish and he would meet me on Saturday. I met Paul and told him about many Canadian issues and had a good, long talk with him. I gave Paul quite a bit of information and told him about Marilyn Chapman being against the Nisga'a Treaty and sending a pamphlet around the office about how much it would cost. Then Marilyn worked with Equity and Diversity and changed completely after I showed her my response to the equity and diversity action plan. Paul didn't believe me, so that was the first article I showed him. Then he advised me to go out of the country to get my life story published; he said not many Canadians will want to publish it because it exposes too much of the truth and suggested I contact Sherman Alexie to try and find a publisher. I mentioned a certain popular TV talk show host and said the way that host interviews all blacks and white and ignores the Indians you'd almost think that host is Canadian. He laughed and said he would send that talk show host an e-mail to that effect. Although Paul didn't read many of the articles I gave him, there were still many things we could have talked about; then Paul said that if Jennifer was to write a book on her life, she would be treated like a hero.

On Monday, September 30, I was still coughing but went to work anyway then finally remembered in 1985 when I was working in Cache Creek, I was told Charles Bara committed suicide! Charles went to school in Merritt when I was there, but I didn't talk or associate with him because he was younger than I. I was still sick on Thursday, so I went to the doctor again. I had enough hours built up to take Friday off, so I left that night. I stopped in Vancouver for karate, and Allan Chan told me I wouldn't be graded because I had been making mistakes in my basics. I didn't know because no one had told me, but it may also have been because I was sick.

When I got to Chilliwack, Aaron was sleeping and Jennifer was in the bars, so I went to see her. She didn't make a fool of herself in the bars but got mad when she got home, so we ended up sleeping in the car by a Husky station truck stop. On Friday morning, Jennifer wasn't too angry, and I went with her to her appointment with Jane Byra, and she started feeling better after seeing her and unpacked some of her things that she previously had packed in boxes. Then I bought them a VCR and Aaron and I watched videos after Jennifer went to bed. On Saturday, Jennifer finished unpacking her things and we watched videos again that night. On Sunday she was rather cranky again, so she bought a bookshelf, then we went to Abbotsford to do some shopping. Jennifer seemed happier now, but Aaron was rather grumpy, so I wondered if he was also addicted to suffering. On Monday I missed karate because I was stressed out for some unknown reason, bought a case of beer, and the clerks at Save-On-Foods were excited about seeing me.

I wrote the covering letter to the information I was going to send to Paul Barnsley and found out my submission to *Gatherings* was rejected because it didn't fit in with the theme of "elders" for that year. They said it was an excellent piece of work though and that was a hard decision to make, but I was optimistic about it. I had an appointment with Darlene on Friday, and she told me I should stay completely away from Jennifer's family now.

On Saturday, Jennifer called and wanted me to take her, Brenda, and their mother to town; but I said I couldn't because her mother's walker wouldn't fit in my car. I went back to Chilliwack because it was

Thanksgiving weekend, and I had booked the following week off for holidays and told Jennifer where I could meet her, but Henry Jr. drove up before I had a chance to sneak away from him. Jennifer's family had their Thanksgiving dinner on Sunday and my family had our dinner that day too, so that gave me the perfect excuse to stay away from Sto:lo Eagle. Jennifer wanted me to pick her up early on Monday to go to Kelowna, but I wanted to try out my new .22 rifle. I tried it out; and when I got to Sto:lo Eagle, Jennifer was stressed out, so we drove to Lytton. She said some things at Liz and Jeremy's grave site; then we went to Spences Bridge, where we used to work. From there we went to Merritt, and Jennifer had a beer in three different bars; then we drove to Kelowna and spent the night in the car since it was late.

We spent the week in Kelowna, and nothing eventful happened. It was a good visit though and we didn't drink. We came back on Friday because Aaron got paid and Jennifer wanted to get the money he owed her. They went to the bars, and Jennifer got me to call Sto:lo Eagle to tell Henry Jr. she was home now. I called and hoped I would get the answering machine, but he answered, and I decided that would be the last time I call Sto:lo Eagle unless Jennifer was there. Then I joined them in the bar. Aaron went home when he had enough to drink; and Jennifer, her friend Susan Adolph, and I went to a cabaret and had a good time. But I didn't drink. The next morning, Jennifer was cranky and mad about the money she spent, but eventually I told her to just accept that she had a good time and should be happy.

On Sunday I called Dewey Shackelly in Merritt and started researching something Gary Abbott had told me about in 1985. In 1985, when I was visiting in Lytton, Gary Abbott told me it was rumoured that at one time, Indian girls were being sterilized. In 1990, Darrel, a Laughing Raven band member, was operating a convenience store out of his basement and said Indian babies were being sold in the USA and who the minister of Social Services was at the time, so it wasn't that long ago. Unfortunately, both of them died before I could get any more information from them, so I asked Dewey about both issues; and he said his mother, Beatrice, vaguely mentioned Indian girls were being sterilized, but she passed away before I could get more information from her. Dewey said Indian babies were being sold in the USA in the 1930s and '40s and now some of them were coming back to Canada, but from what Darrel said, it was still going on rather recently.

On Tuesday night I called Paul Johnny and asked him who it was that made him take a welding course when he originally wanted to be a draftsman. This type of thing was common when Indians right down to my age group tried to do something for themselves. Paul told me who made him take a welding course rather than become a draftsman even though he was getting straight As in drafting, then I asked him about Indian girls being sterilized. He said sterilization was a common practice in the residential schools. Many abortions were performed, and some students just disappeared, and that may have been because they didn't survive the abortion or sterilization. I finally found time to research this very important issue and was surprised at how much he knew and was willing to tell me about it. Paul went to both the Williams Lake and Kamloops Indian residential schools, and I thought he was at least thirteen years older than I from the way he talked about what he went through and saw happen. Later on I found out he was only eight years older than I.

On Wednesday, Chris Runnals gave me some more tree seedlings, so I had to go back to Chilliwack on the weekend to plant them. I wanted to stay home for the weekend, but if I didn't get the trees planted soon, they may not survive. I had enough hours built up to take Monday off, so I knew I would have enough time to get them all planted. I tried to leave early on Friday afternoon but kept getting delayed, so I didn't make it to Rosedale until four o'clock in the afternoon, planted until it was too dark, then brushed out more area for planting trees. I planted trees on Saturday on my parents' property and decided it's finished if these trees survived; then I planted the rest of the cedar trees at the back of the reserve.

Jennifer couldn't find work anywhere, so she went back to work at the A&W and started that Sunday, but she stressed Aaron and me out before she went to work. I phoned Alvin Tolley about sterilization of Indian girls and selling of Indian babies in the USA; he knew about it and said he would send me some information later. Then I called Paul Barnsley; and he also knew about these issues, wrote a report on suspicious deaths that occurred in the residential schools when he interviewed survivors of what was happening, and mentioned why they were scared to report it to the police. Unfortunately, there wasn't enough evidence to lay charges, and this was in the June 1998 edition of *Windspeaker*.

I bought Aaron some tobacco at the band office and was stressed out, so I wanted to get back to Squamish on time for karate. I bought Aaron and Jennifer some groceries, and she seemed to take her time in the store, which annoyed me at first; then when I went to put some gas in their car, I knew it was too late to make it to karate. When I got some gas, Harley Wylie went in behind me and we didn't recognize each other, but we had to sign a sheet with our Indian status number to get a discount on our gas since it was on an Indian reserve; then Harley went running out behind me and asked if I was Annis Aleck, the logger. I wanted to find where he was working so I could research issues, and didn't know where he was after his job in Vancouver was over. Now we ran into each other, and he was working with Indian Health in Vernon, the interior of British Columbia. Again, by helping Aaron and Jennifer out, I ended up helping myself out.

I went back to work, and on Friday I called Isaac's place at coffee time, and their friend Jean answered the phone and said my cousin's fourteen-year-old son committed suicide! I finally got to stay home for a weekend and took a well-deserved rest. On Monday I went to the dentist, got some major dental work done, and missed karate because my teeth were hurting too much. That night on *CBC News Magazine*, there was a documentary about Indian girls in Peru being sterilized, which was condoned by the government, and called it a way to end poverty. The government set quotas where medical staff would get bonuses if they did it to a minimum number of girls.

I got some fieldwork during the week and built up enough hours to take Friday off again. I was cold and wet when I got home from work on Thursday, so I had a hot shower and missed karate, then I drank a few beers. It was my birthday, but I couldn't go out for dinner because of putty still on my teeth after Monday's dental work, went to Chilliwack on Friday, and Jennifer flipped out slightly. We went to the bars that night, but she wasn't too bad and got depressed for a little while before going home though. The next day after work, she started working on her writing; and I thought, *At last! She's finally trying to heal herself!*

It was Remembrance Day weekend, November 11, and I had booked another week of annual leave. I wanted to go to New Mexico again, but Auntie Tilley and Uncle Sal were going to San Diego for a wedding. I came back to Squamish Wednesday night for a dental appointment Thursday, and Jennifer went with me; then we went back to Chilliwack Thursday afternoon. There was another psychic fair in Chilliwack that weekend, and Jennifer and I went there on Saturday when she got off work. She was tired and didn't want a psychic reading, but I got one. Lora Schultz, the psychic, told me I'm highly intelligent, get bored easily, and don't finish everything that I start. Forestry isn't my thing anymore. I should become a therapist or counsellor, and I'd be moving to the Sunshine Coast next year. She also said I'll never get any thanks or recognition from Jennifer's family for what I went through to save her from suicide and get her a career. I didn't think I started very many things that I didn't finish other than buying books that I don't get around to reading.

Jennifer liked my reading, so the next day we went back and she got a reading from Lora too. Lora said Aaron will get another job in April or May and he's really going to like it; Jennifer will get into LPN training and it's going to be a breeze. Working for Corrections will be a good chance for Henry Jr. to let his anger out, and Jennifer should be proud of surviving what she went through! She survived to tell the story like the Holocaust survivors survived to tell the story of what happened.

Working for Corrections wasn't a very good experience for me other than learning to be more assertive, speak out more, and start writing my memoirs. At first I didn't think it would be a very good job for Henry Jr., but now I realized it might be very good for him. When I got back to Squamish, I wrote a rough draft of a covering letter to try and find a book publisher for my life story. It was suggested I contact Sherman Alexie in Seattle, Washington; so I wrote a rough draft of an e-mail for his representative, Christy Cox. The next day, I tried to sleep at lunchtime but couldn't, so I sent some information to Jane Byra. Karate was great that night, and when I got home, I rewrote the letter to Christy Cox. I had the covering letter and all the articles I wrote that I thought would be important ready to send on Friday; then I flipped a coin and it kept telling me not to mail it yet. I wondered why then thought I should talk to Paul Barnsley before I mailed it. I flipped a coin again, and that's what it told me to do.

I wanted to stay home for the weekend, but it was Uncle Percy and Auntie Mary Anne's fortieth wedding anniversary on Saturday, so I went back to Chilliwack. I knew it would be a good family gathering, and Uncle Percy always had a sense of humour. On Sunday I called Uncle Joe and asked about the two issues I was now researching.

He knew a bit about it, and my mother said my picture was in the newspaper, *Windspeaker*. There was also a brief story based on information I gathered. It was a good story, and my mother also said she would pick up the paper for me. I called Roger Adolph again that day, and he said the issue I was researching was called Target Zero or something like that, which was secretly ordered by the government.

I came back to Squamish and called Paul Barnsley on Monday morning before I went to work. Paul mentioned laws that existed in Alberta, interviewed survivors, and wrote a story on it for *Windspeaker* in 1998; then I decided to include this information in the letter to Christy Cox and mailed the letter and information the next day. I was going to go to Bellingham the next weekend to visit Auntie Jeanette, but I phoned her several times on Thursday and there was no answer. Then I called Charlene, and she said they went to Seattle for the weekend. I had a short chat with her, and she was surprised when I told her about a law that still existed in Canada when I was a child and that it even went as far as "Sugar and Vanilla Extract"!

I stayed home the next weekend. It was the end of November. I felt really good for some reason and hoped Jennifer was finally starting to feel good about herself and getting over her addiction to suffering. On Friday, Jennifer called me and asked to borrow some money, so I didn't have time to sleep at lunchtime. That night, the staff had their Christmas party at Joe Clarke's place because Joe would be taking early retirement and leaving the British Columbia Forest Service at the end of March. Joe is Métis but didn't look Native at all, was status Indian, and showed me his Indian status card several years ago. Joe knew about Métis girls being sterilized, boys being castrated, and told me a bit of what was going on with the Métis in Canada. He's the oldest of ten children and said his mother was constantly worried about the children being taken away because they were poor.

Brenda Billy went over to visit one night and we had sex. She used to live in an apartment below where I lived before I moved to this apartment and was working on the weekend, so I didn't call her back. I stayed in Squamish for the weekend, and on Sunday I decided the trees I planted would be a good education fund for grandchildren if I didn't need the money because there's a good chance I might make good money on my life story. I mentioned this to my dad and Isaac. I could use the trees as an education fund for his grandchildren, and they liked the idea.

On Thursday morning, I called Alvin Tolley to keep him up to date on the research I was doing; and he said, "Keep up the good work!" He mentioned what was happening to the Inuit and was surprised when I told him when Indian children were taken away from home in what was known as the Sixties Scoop! He said Paul Barnsley remarked, "The greatest country in the world" is only for white people! Earlier in the week, I had sent out an e-mail to Harley Wylie asking for information on Indian girls being sterilized, Indian babies being sold in the USA, and if anyone in his circle of contacts had any information. Harley replied and asked for an introduction letter stating who I am, what I'm doing and why, what I'm going to do with the information, etc. He said people would want to know these things before they open up and give information and sent me a sample introduction letter. I hoped I could get the letter ready on the weekend and send it out next week, but I would only be in the office on Monday.

I stayed home again for the weekend and tried to get the letter ready for Harley, but Jennifer phoned me at three thirty Sunday morning on her cell phone. She was depressed, crying, and said Aaron gave her a bleeding lip and I should have gotten her out of there a long time ago! She said she destroyed the Christmas tree, the phone, and TV. I know she flips out and almost forces people to treat her badly, so now I don't even want to know that family! I originally wanted to go back this weekend but stayed in Squamish for a course on Tuesday and a dentist appointment on Wednesday; then she hung up and called again and said she destroyed the VCR but not the TV.

Surprisingly, I woke up feeling good on Monday morning and had a hard time going to sleep at lunchtime. I worked in the office then went to the course because changes were coming but left rather late on Wednesday because of the dentist appointment. Jennifer was cranky the next morning and went to Sto:lo Eagle, but I didn't go because I wanted to stay away from her family. I went to visit my parents, and my mother had picked up a copy of *Windspeaker* for me. I didn't know I helped amalgamate the aboriginal and Chinese Canadian WWII veterans to pressure the government to remedy past injustices until I read it in the paper.

Aaron got his UIC check then went to the bars, and Jennifer was cranky after work. She said she felt robbed of a normal family life (e.g., no loving father, grandfather, etc.), so I told her the old Indians said that for every bad thing that happens in life, two good things happen back to them. I was badly treated by my family but often got lucky breaks; she has someone who believed in her and helped her get a career. Then she finally started feeling better. Previously, nothing else, not even what a priest said to her, seemed to work. On Friday I bought Aaron and Jennifer another phone and was going to take her Christmas shopping, but Henry Jr. took her out for lunch. I didn't join them and felt rather bad that he pushed me to the point where I don't want anything to do with that family.

On Sunday I took Jennifer to the bars after work to join her co-worker, Kathy, but didn't drink because I was driving. By Monday I had shopped with Jennifer for three days. We finally had all our shopping done, and I was burnt out. Aaron and I drank a few beers, which stressed Jennifer out, so she went outside and slept in the car. I forgot Christmas stresses Jennifer out because her dad's not there anymore. The next day, the day before Christmas, Aaron drove Jennifer to Sto:lo Eagle then came back; but I didn't go to there at all.

Christmas was uneventful, and Jennifer came back on Boxing Day. She wanted to go to the bars, got Aaron stressed out, and got depressed again. We stayed out until it was late, but Aaron went home earlier and I didn't drink. As we were sitting in the car, the police asked what was going on. I said she was going though depression again but everything was all right. She went to work on Friday, and Kathy said I was a bit eccentric, but Jennifer told her I'm highly intelligent. I offered to buy another VCR that day and felt really good!

I went to visit Isaac and Helen that day; and Gary Victor and his black friend George Christopher, liked to be called Chris, were there. Chris is my age; lived in Ohio; moved to Regina, Saskatchewan; and now lives in Rosedale. He said the only difference between Canada and the USA is racism isn't in words or in writing, so I told them I worked for Corrections Canada taking inmates out on work release before I got this job. We didn't wear uniforms, so people sometimes thought I was an inmate; then they laughed hard when I said that. Then I told them when I was a common Labourer, people accepted me; but once I was above that, I was closed off like a condemned criminal, and Chris said, "You mean you were out of your place!"

On Monday, December 30, the day before New Year's Eve, Jennifer got depressed and wanted to go to the bars after work to celebrate the New Year. Aaron went too, but I didn't drink. She got depressed again but didn't flip out too badly or get noisy when we got home and said she was depressed about losing her sister Liz and not having any parents, but eventually she calmed down and went to sleep. I felt like I just can't have any fun around that family! The next day was New Year's Eve, and Aaron took Jennifer to Sto:lo Eagle and came back. I bought an eighteen-pack of beer and drank at home, but Aaron only had a few beers.

Chapter 25

2003

Jennifer was in Sto:lo Eagle on New Year's Day, so Aaron and I went to the bars because she wasn't there to stress us out; then I picked her up the next day but didn't talk to Henry Jr. I was hung over and he seemed crabby, so I just sat in a chair and slept. He offered me a cup of coffee, but I wouldn't have anything to eat or even use the bathroom then threw up when we got outside. On Saturday, Jennifer was stressed out after work and wanted to go to the bars. She said she was depressed because of her job and because I would be leaving the next day. Eventually she got happy and didn't flip out like she often does when she drinks. I developed a sty on my left eye that day and thought it was an insect bite or pimple. I wanted to leave early on Sunday to see Brenda Billy but left late because I was invited to a staff dinner at the A&W.

I sent some information to Harley Wiley that I was originally going to send before Christmas and was glad I waited until now because I included the news article saying I amalgamated the aboriginal and Chinese Canadian WWII veterans to pressure the government to remedy past injustices. I also called Brenda Billy during the week, but she didn't seem to be very interested in me. I wasn't disappointed though because I was used to getting turned down. On the second weekend of January, I went to Bellingham to visit Auntie Jeanette again; and her oldest daughter, Charlene, still didn't have time to read my book yet. Then I told Auntie Jeanette and her other daughter, Donnelle, about Target Zero and the high suicide rate of Canadian Indians.

I slept rather lightly at lunchtime now and called Rita, a lady who lived across the road from Jennifer's parents. Rita was the president of the Indian Homemakers of British Columbia and was very knowledgeable about Indian girls being sterilized right up to 1972, Indian babies being sold in the USA right up to the late '70s and early '80s and how long it had been going on. Rita also said she felt bad about how Henry treated his kids; then I recommended to Paul Barnsley that he contact her for information and write a story. I had an appointment with Darlene on Friday, and she said I was looking better than when I first met her, said the sty on my eye was caused by stress and should go to the doctor. I've been feeling more energetic and didn't sleep as much at lunchtime.

I went back to Chilliwack on the weekend and nothing eventful happened. On Tuesday morning I called Alvin Tolley, and he knew about sterilization and said Inuit girls were almost automatically sterilized when they came south to the hospital. Alvin didn't know why that was happening and suggested I call Anne Acco, a researcher in Quebec. I called Anne Acco on Thursday morning, and she was very knowledgeable about how Indians were treated; she was rather busy though, so I gave her my phone number and she said she would call me back.

I went to the forestry curling bonspiel on Saturday, and it was lots of fun. After the bonspiel, I went home and watched *Circle of Justice* on Aboriginal Peoples Television Network (APTN). It was about aboriginal girls doing time in jail, and one Indian girl who looked to be much younger than I said, "Jail is heaven compared to the residential school!" Then the sound went off until just before the program was over, so I didn't catch any more. I watched the Superbowl the next day, and as I was watching it, Anne Acco called. Last year when I took Jennifer to Sto:lo Eagle to visit her mother, I watched the first half of the Superbowl and didn't realize until now that when Henry Jr. got home, he changed the channel even though he wasn't even watching TV. I wondered why they were having such a long halftime show and didn't know he changed the channel.

Anne said Nunavut, a territory set up in northeastern Canada for the Inuit people, was set up to fail and told me about racism going on; but it wasn't reported or checked into by the police or Labour Relations. She also said Natives could get educated but no one would hire them, which is something I could easily relate to. Anne said Inuit girls were sterilized because of an interest in the oil deposits in the north and suggested I read the book *Genocide Machine in Canada* by Mark Davis and Robert Zannis.

I had gone to the doctor for medication for my sty, but it just got bigger and hurt more; and a specialist was supposed to drain it if the medication didn't work, but he didn't call. I went to Chilliwack the next weekend and Brenda came down from Kelowna. Aaron took Jennifer to visit her on Saturday and Henry Jr. called right after they left and I answered the phone even though I knew it was him. I got stressed out, so I went to the bar for a few beers; then Aaron and Jennifer picked me up and Jennifer said Brenda was going in the smokehouse to become an Indian Dancer. Jennifer went back to Sto:lo Eagle the next day after work, but I decided I wouldn't answer the phone anymore if I knew it was her family.

On Tuesday, Aaron called and asked me to help him get his power saw out of the pawnshop. I didn't want to, but he wouldn't have been able to go to work without it; and on Tuesday, Brenda Billy came over and we started seeing each other. I called Patricia Kelly two times to get my manuscript and disks back so I could update my story. She was having financial trouble, but I said perhaps she'll have time to edit my life story for a reasonable price. I told her I thought I could finish my life story after I got Jennifer a career but the right events just wouldn't happen then there was more issues to research and expose, so perhaps that's why I couldn't finish my life story yet. I stayed home the next weekend and worked on my writing. Jennifer had told me to work on it because anger was causing me to develop a sty; then the more I worked on my biography, the more my eye healed.

In January, a website came out about a healing program for victims of the Sixties Scoop; many victims suffered incredibly in foster homes, but some said it was better than life at home. White people can also tell horror stories about some foster homes too, but Indian children were sometimes taken away for the flimsiest excuse; Rita was very knowledgeable about this. I contacted the coordinator of this healing project, Scott Stephens, and he knew about the sterilization of Indian and Inuit girls that had been going on; then he e-mailed me a website on sterilization, which was mostly American. Although Canada wasn't mentioned, it had also been going on in Canada; then I found the book *Genocide Machine in Canada: Pacification of the North* on Amazon and ordered it.

I called Lawrenceone evening, and he knew about the sterilization too. Lawrence said he separated from his wife three years ago when the sexual abuse in the residential schools was being exposed, so I told him it's extremely painful to the victims and their siblings, and he suggested she go for therapy; but she wouldn't go. I could understand that because I knew how stressful it is from looking after Jennifer. I called Roger Adolph again the next night, and he knew the sterilization had been going on right up to 1972 and first heard about it in 1979 from born-again Christians. It was done when we were at our lowest point—dysfunctional lives from the residential schools—and done very discreetly, so it would be very hard to lay charges. He never mentioned it when I was working in Lillooet in 1980 or when I would phone him up or run into him over the years, until I asked about it. He was also surprised when I told him I *totally* refused to go to my graduation ceremonies after eight years of studying.

I called Paul Barnsley on Thursday and suggested he call Rita for a story on sterilization and selling of Indian babies in the USA and called Scott Stephens again in the evening and mentioned lynching of blacks. I said either it didn't happen to the Indians of Canada or it just wasn't reported, but he said things were just done in more-subtle methods like dropping people off outside of town in freezing temperatures. Later on I got a website on that; Indians were dropped off outside of town by the police so often they called it starlight drives, and naturally the police denied it happened at all.

I went back to Chilliwack on the weekend; and on Saturday, Jennifer wanted to go to a specialty store, Redwing Shoes, in Surrey, British Columbia for a pair of shoes. We went there and I bought her some rather expensive shoes for work, then we stopped off in Abbotsford at a shopping mall on our way back. Jennifer wanted to buy some earrings at the Bay, and as I was looking at some pendants, I thought about buying a pendant that said "Graduation." Then Jennifer said, "You didn't go to your graduation ceremonies from BCIT!" The clerks heard her and knew I had worked extremely hard to get my career yet refused to go to my graduation ceremonies!

Jennifer wanted to go to Sto:lo Eagle that night to see Brenda at the Indian dances, but I only went to buy Aaron some tax-free tobacco. At the store, someone asked me, "Did you get lost?" I felt bad that I was pushed to the point I didn't want to go there anymore. We didn't know which smokehouse they were in because there were several, so we went home. We went to Abbotsford again the next day so Jennifer could buy some earrings at the Bay, and some ladies wondered why I was so angry that I refused to go to my graduation ceremonies and tried to be nice to me.

As a child, I heard tuberculosis was epidemic amongst the Indians and heard stories about Indians going to tuberculosis sanitoriums; even Jennifer's father and some of my uncles went there. During the week, I went out to the woods near Pemberton and stopped off to see Lawrence on my way back. Lawrence was fifty-seven and said when he was young, he came to Squamish for an eye operation; the operation didn't work, so he went to Coquileetza, in Sardis. Coquileetza used to be a TB sanitorium, then a preventorium, then a residential school, and is now a cultural center. Lawrence wondered if they were being used for medical experiments because they were given many needles, and one pinkish needle he was given really hurt. A former patient he talked to many years later thought the same thing. Lawrence said when he saw the movie *One Flew Over the Cuckoo's Nest*, it reminded him of Coquileetza, seeing patients walking around in a drugged and dazed state; whatever they were given made them act crazy. Then Lawrence gave me some phone numbers and names of people I could phone and interview for stories and information. I phoned them, got more information and more stories confirmed. Lawrence also figured Indians are going to have to learn to work again after several generations of being on welfare.

I stayed home the next weekend and worked on writing out "2002" and got stressed out to the point my heart was hurting, so I drank a few beers. Then I realized I was still angry at Jennifer's family for how they treat me compared to how they treat Alvin! My acne also started to come back lightly. I got red around my nose but didn't break out in pimples very much. I did some more writing on Sunday and got quite stressed out. Brenda Billy came over for the weekend and we talked about what we've been through, and I knew she could still be hurting inside and was told she could write a book on her life.

I got an e-mail about a group called the Coalition for the Advancement of Aboriginal Studies (CAAS) trying to get the truth of Canada's treatment of aboriginals taught in grade school, so I wrote a rather long letter with my opinion titled "Aboriginal Perspectives in the Classroom." I sent it then watched *Rocks at Whiskey Trench*, about Canadians' reaction to the Indians after the 1991 Oka protest in Quebec.

Anne Pohl, a member of the core working group, responded right away and asked if that letter could be put on their website. She really liked what I said, especially the four ways Canadians react to the truth when aboriginals speak out, and said it happens too damned often!

I said she could put it on their website and made a comment about the Oka crisis and *Rocks at Whiskey Trench*. I said if the truth was common knowledge, that protest may not have taken place at all. Usually, when changes are made, nothing is said about why they're justified, causing much resentment and jealousy among non-Natives! She added the first paragraph to the letter and printed it on the website as is shown:

Aboriginal Perspectives in The Class Room!

I think it's very important that the truth be exposed to make some well justified changes without causing too much resentment or jealousy! I watched "Rocks at Whiskey Trench!" the other day and I hate seeing that kind of reaction to well justified protest! If the truth was common knowledge the protest may not have taken place at all or not very many people would have been out there throwing large rocks!

I think it's a great idea that the truth on how Aboriginals and other minorities were treated be taught in grade school as long as it's taught exactly the way things happened! Just don't distort it so much that there isn't any truth to it or minimise it to the point it's barely noticeable!

Canadians have been programmed by schools to believe there wasn't any racism in Canada and everyone gets EQUAL TREATMENT! In reality Canada is no less racist than the USA, perhaps even more racist! Since it's not in words or in writing most Canadians believe it's TOTALLY non-existent! Canadians usually don't say anything at all about what really happens or maximise the good things they do! Even when the truth is brought out it's usually distorted so much there isn't any truth to it! Either that or the truth is minimised to the point most people will miss it! Even in classroom assignments students can get a failing grade for speaking the truth!

Usually when Aboriginals speak out Canadians react on one of 4 different ways in descending order:

1. *They say we get equal treatment then close their ears or run off without backing up their statement at all!*
2. *They automatically think we want special treatment or a handout!*
3. *They just ignore everything or don't say anything and act like it never happened!*
4. *They get really uptight and actually want us to believe nothing at all happened and such things don't happen!*

Now they don't want to hear anything at all!

The truth should start being taught as early as elementary school then more of the truth be brought out as the students get older. The truth on what Indian Residential Schools were really like and the quality of education they got there should be exposed! We were also forced by legistlation to go there, many were sent to schools a long ways from home even when we lived close to town and we weren't allowed in public schools. I asked one of my cousins who's only a few years older than me why she went to Residential School? She said, "They still had the dreaded Indian Agent!" Some Residential School survivors said life was better in jail than it was in school but a much smaller number said it was better than life at home. If this is mentioned students should also be told how many survivors were interviewed and what percent said it was better than life at home.

The Residential School legacy and being held back when we tried to do something for ourselves are very important issues that we are still feeling the effects of and should be exposed! The general public is told that if a status Indian works or buys something on an Indian Reserve it's tax free. What they're not told is most Indian Reserves are usually nothing more than a useless, isolated rock pile that can be covered with a postage stamp on a 1:20,000 scale map. What little the Indians were given part of it was taken back with hydro lines, railways and highways so in most cases that tax free money isn't even worth the paper it's printed on!

On January 25, 2003 on "Circle of Justice!" Aboriginal women in jail were interviewed. Just before the sound went off one girl who appeared much younger than me said, "Jail is heaven compared to the Residential School!" I was born in 1955!

I work for the BC Forest Service and we have an Equity and Diversity Branch so I brought up many issues to their attention. There were laws that existed in Canada that were clearly discriminating against the Indians! Most people don't believe these laws existed in Canada at all yet some of them still existed when I was a child. One article I wrote to Equity and Diversity was titled "Sugar and Vanilla Extract!" so I had to give them advance notice it was coming! That's how discriminating laws were right up to 1964!

One report I read, but I'm sure there's more, said Apartheid in South Africa isn't any different than Indian Reserves in Canada! A Black my age lived in Ohio, moved to Regina, Saskatchewan and now lives in Chilliwack said the only difference between Canada and the USA is racism isn't in words or in writing!

Canada appears to pride itself for helping people in Third world countries yet it often ignores the plight of the Aboriginals. Even when changes are made usually nothing is said about why it's justified making non-Natives believe we're getting special treatment and often causing much resentment!

It can take lots of work to find the truth on how minorities were treated in Canada because Gov't departments often don't like to answer when asked for the truth. If everyone got equal treatment like we're taught to believe what have they got to hide? Even when they answer they don't usually give a straight answer or try to give a response completely off the main issue!

It took lots of work to find the truth on how minority WWII veterans were treated when they got back from the war! I gathered much information and sent it by registered letter to 2 major news stations in Vancouver, BC. Not only was one word not mentioned they didn't even acknowledge getting the information! A TOTALLY CANADIAN response to the truth! I also sent a follow up letter on Canada;s reaction to the Jewish refugees during the Holocaust! Even that letter appeared to be ignored! Then I gave all that information, including a copy of the registration receipts to Windspeaker, an Aboriginal newspaper based out of Edmonton, Alberta. A brief story by Paul Barnsley, the senior editor, was written in the November 2002 edition based on information that I gathered. A longer, more detailed story will come out eventually but will be approved my me first.

In grade school we were told about the Underground Railroad, freeing Black slaves in the South and bringing them to Canada. Canada also had Black slaves and in documentaries about Blacks in Canada they were treated like any other minority. They were forced to live on the edge of town and society and expected to stay there! I heard some stories about how Blacks in Canada were treated but haven't got enough information to speak out yet! That made me wonder if the Underground Railroad was operated mainly by former Black slaves who wanted to free other slaves or were only a few rescued and this was maximised to make Canada look like Goody-goody Two Shoes!

In the book "Ten Lost Years!" by Barry Broadfoot, one person interviewed said the war was just an excuse to take everything away from the Japanese! This issue was reduced to one sentence! I wouldn't be surprised if the author, editor, publisher or all 3 were told a whole lot more but deliberately minimised it to the point it's barely noticeable!

I never heard about Lynchings and thought perhaps it's just not reported but someone said it was just done in a more subtle manner! While in elementary school I read in a major

BC newspaper, the Vancouver Sun that before the war White people wanted to destroy a Japanese village on Powell Street in Vancouver, BC. The Japanese were ready for them, fought them off and won!

I'm trying to research these 2 issues to find the real story but haven't had any luck yet! I would just love to be wrong on these 2 issues though! There's other issues I'm researching but I'm not going to mention them right now! When the truth does come out it should be exposed and taught in grade school!

The truth should also be told about how hard it was for Indians to find work. I don't know about other provinces but I know what Indians did in some parts of BC did for work and what they sometimes did just to get a low paying job! Since most Indian Reserves are just a useless, isolated rock pile there's usually very little, if anything available for work. Even when work was available it was very hard for us to get hired! If everyone's willing to hire Natives and we actually get EQUAL TREATMENT how many Natives have they hired? How old are they, how long have they been working there and what kind of job have they got? Are any Natives over 40 years old in management? If they're over 40 and in management what's their life story like? What kind of obstacles did they have to go through to get there?

Two very important issues that should be brought up are:

1. *The unemployment on most Indian Reserves is phenomenol yet before the settlers came we were living off the land without a beast of burden. That's definitely not a weekend camping trip and now very few of us even know how to speak our own language, let alone how to live off the land. If we just sat around and did nothing we would have starved to death long before the settlers came!*
2. *The suicide and alcohol and drug related death rate among Aboriginals is also incredibly high! At an Aboriginal Employees Association Meeting on October, 2000 the BC Commissioner of Human Rights, Harinder*

> *Mahil, said Aboriginals have 10 times the national average suicide rate and brought up other issues! I wonder if many White Canadians would stand up and tell the truth like that!*

Statistics on Aboriginal suicide usually don't include those that attempted suicide but failed or those Aboriginals that are just physically existing as alcoholics, drug addicts or welfare cases! They're not physically dead, just physically existing! Some Indian Reserves are bad for suicide but others aren't! But even those that aren't bad for suicide are often bad for alcohol and drug related deaths!

I don't want us to be made out to look like Noble Savages! Just normal people who have been very badly treated and oppressed in our own country, "The Greatest Country in the World!" Some people have said the Indians of Canada are some of the World's most oppressed people! Canada is one of the largest countries in the world, rich in resources yet many Indians are still living in third world conditions! Where is all that equal treatment and when did it start? Even as I was growing up many Indians still had wells, wood stoves, outhouses and used coal oil or kerosene lamps for light.

Although I was born in 1955 and didn't attend the Indian Residential Schools I still suffered incredibly because of how the Indians were treated! I suffered because of how my parents were affected by the Residential Schools then went through 8 years of hard times I wouldn't wish on anyone just to get a career and thought my hard times in life would be over once I got my diploma! Unfortunately, as I was getting my career Indians I went to school with were dying and committing suicide left and right before they turned 25!

Then the year I thought I was going to get my diploma, 1980, I met Jennifer, not her real name, a Native girl.`When Jennifer's depression and thoughts of suicide started coming out I thought I better try and save her! If I failed at least I did my best to try and save her! What I went through to get a *career was nothing compared to what it took to save Jennifer from suicide and get her a career!*

I changed the name in this letter because she's still ashamed of what happened to her and what she went through! Paul Barnsley said if she were to write a story on her life she would be treated as a hero! I asked her to write a book on her life but she doesn't feel up to it right now. I don't press the issue very much because I know how stressful it can be!

Now I'm working on an autobiography which is almost finished! When I realised the hard times I went through had prepared me for what was coming, looking after her, is less than 1/2 way thought my life story. Paul Barnsley also told me to go out of the country to get my life story published. He said not many Canadians will want to publish it because it exposes too much of the truth!

I thought I could finish my life story 2 years ago when Jennifer finally got a career but the right events just didn't seem to happen! Then last October I finally found time to research 2 issues I heard about many years ago! There's usually a reason why things happen the way they do so perhaps I couldn't finish it because these 2 very important issues need to be exposed to the public! Writing an inspirational story like mine is one way to get people's attention and get them to listen to the truth! I told Paul Barnsley about a lady who's very knowledgeable about these 2 issues and has much information on them! He's going to try and contact her for an interview so he can write a story for Windspeaker.

If you have and suggestions or connections with American publishers who may be interested in publishing my life story can you let me know? If you want more information on Canadian issues just give me a mailing address where I can send it. I'll also include a brief outline of my life story if you want! My life story is titled "Almost a Born Loser!" and it's open for a sequel! Where did they go from there? Some articles I wrote to Equity and Diversity were marked "Confidential!"

because they're all going to come out in my life story. I want to keep it intriguing and full of surprises so I can hold the reader in suspense! What's going to happen next?

Annis Aleck
Box 2062
Squamish, BC
V0N-3G0

I went back to Chilliwack again for the weekend, the first of March, and Jennifer bought some things for Brenda because the Indian dancing was winding down for the season. She wanted to go to Sto:lo Eagle, but Aaron wouldn't drive her and I refused to go over there, so she drove herself and didn't get home until two thirty in the morning. Then she was crabby the next day, and I was happy she was working day shift, so I would have some time to myself. During the week, I worked on my writings and realized I was still angry over things that happened last year! I was mad at Jennifer for holding me back when I tried to have fun and eventually realized my own family must have been jealous of me because they always tried to hold me back from having fun! They weren't happy unless they were making life incredibly boring for me. Writing was still stressful, but I felt better afterward.

Brenda Billy didn't call me during the week, so I thought she was working night shifts; and I tried calling her, but the number was out of service. She had been having trouble with her roommate, so I thought that's what happened. On Friday I went to the A&W for supper and read the paper to pass time, and in the paper I found out Brenda died last Sunday! I asked her former boyfriend, Gerry, what happened. Gerry said she hung herself because she was into heavy drugs; now I was really happy I was willing to go through what it took to save Jennifer from suicide even though I get practically no recognition from her family! I figured Brenda was still hurting very badly inside because of what she's been through.

I went to the funeral home for prayers Saturday night and asked people for information on sterilization of Indian girls. Brenda's funeral was on Sunday, and I interviewed more people on aboriginal issues. Keith Brown suggested I write a book on stories Indians could tell since I enjoy doing the research; and Harvey Andrews, sixty-years old, was there and had a story to tell me about the residential schools. During the week, a client, Wes Matkovich, was interested in buying some standing dead timber in D'Arcy; so I had to meet him and have a look at it. Wes said he treated Indians as individuals and hired them if they applied for work. He knew Jimmy Fountain, my dad's friend in Merritt, and knew about Indian girls being sterilized but didn't remember where he heard it from and heard about the blacklist.

I kept writing and working on my life story, and the more I wrote, the more the sty went away; not only that, the more I said to myself, "I don't want anything to do with Jennifer's family anymore!" the better I felt. I called Jennifer on Friday morning, and Brenda was still in Sto:lo Eagle; but when Jennifer went to Sto:lo Eagle, she was asked to leave after three days, so I decided I didn't even want to use their bathroom or even drink their water anymore! I sent an e-mail to Anne Pohl and suggested she research and expose the truth of Canada's reaction to Jewish refugees during the Holocaust since she's of Russian-Jewish descent. From documentaries I saw on TV, it appeared Canada was just as much against the Jews as the Germans were but stopped just short of outright trying to exterminate them. Canada probably just left that up to other countries.

I went back to Chilliwack again that weekend to brush out more of my parents' property for planting trees and had indigestion that wouldn't go away until I accepted that I'm going to be a rich man someday. I didn't sleep at lunchtime as much as I used to and just stayed home on the last weekend of March to attend a going-away dinner for three staff members. Then I got a postal note saying there was a parcel for me, and I figured it was the book *Genocide Machine in Canada*!

I went back to Chilliwack again the next weekend to brush out more of my parents' property for planting, got Aaron to help me, and told him I would probably give him the Sunbird when I gave Jennifer the Cavalier for helping me with the planting and looking after Jennifer. We also had a surprise dinner for my dad's birthday that weekend. I had to go back to Chilliwack again, the fourth weekend in a row, to plant the Douglas fir trees Chris Runnals had given me; and Aaron helped me with the planting and with celebrating my nieces' birthday.

On Sunday I took Jennifer to Vancouver so she could participate in the Sun Run, a ten-kilometer run for raising money for charities, then took her out for Chinese food on our way back because it was her birthday. I felt good that she had turned forty-one now, but looking after her was still hard! I went to Chilliwack again the next weekend because it was Easter weekend. During the week, Jennifer called me and said her glasses were stolen off her face. She was still getting drunk and putting herself in dangerous situations because being scared felt normal to her. Last year a fortune-teller said she would change in one and a half to two years, which still felt like an eternity!

I planted some cedar seedlings that weekend at the back of the reserve, and it looked like many were surviving from before. On Monday I took Jennifer to Sto:lo Eagle for their Easter dinner but just dropped her off then left. I didn't even get out of the car or say anything to anyone. I wanted to stay home and rest the next weekend, but the psychic fair was coming to Chilliwack; and Lora Schultz, a psychic we saw, said she knew about Indian babies being sold in the USA thirty years ago. Near the end of April, Jennifer called and said her mother fell on Easter weekend, so she may not be doing very well; then it dawned on me how painful it must have been for Henry when he broke his hip and couldn't take any medication for pain because he had a weak heart. Although he suffered incredibly for what he did wrong, it was still hard not to be angry at him!

I've been sleeping lightly at lunchtime now and sometimes couldn't sleep at all; that was the first time I felt that way in years. I went back to Chilliwack the second weekend in May, and Aaron tried to have a surprise party for Jennifer. She couldn't drink at home though, so I ended up going to the bars with them. Aaron goes home when he's had enough to drink, but Jennifer drinks until closing time or she's cut off, but at least now she doesn't get mad and flip out like she used to. Jennifer was cranky on Saturday and Sunday but calmed down when she got to work on Sunday. I asked her about Henry Jr. and she said he's a full-time corrections officer now but was reluctant to say anything. I'm still glad he's come that far though and is doing something with his life after what he's been through. When I got home, I couldn't sleep and thought it was because I had a cup of coffee in the afternoon; then when I told myself "I'm a rich man," I was out like a light. I went back to work and started feeling sick during the week but didn't go home because I wanted some overtime on the long weekend in May.

I took the next week off because I was sick and watched *Je me souviens* on the History Channel, which was about widespread anti-Semitism that existed in Canada. Mackenzie King was Canada's prime minister during the Jewish Holocaust and wanted Canada to have the worst record for allowing Jewish refugees into the country. Even a priest told his parishioners to boycott Jewish businesses, and a gray-haired university professor said anti-Semitic language was quite common; fortunately, in church, parishioners agreed but still dealt with Jewish businesses.

I went back to Chilliwack again the next weekend to brush out my seedlings and felt good about doing it because they probably won't need much more brushing, then I would have more free time. My sty didn't completely go away even though I finished writing "2002" but went away when I worked on Target Zero. Jennifer called and wanted me to go back to Chilliwack again for the weekend because she would get the whole weekend off and there were the Cultus Lake canoe races. She really flipped out on Saturday morning and stressed Aaron and me out, so I took her to Sto:lo Eagle to visit her mother but came back the same day. I only went to Sto:lo Eagle because Henry Jr. was working; otherwise, I wouldn't have gone there at all. On Sunday we went to the canoe races, but I didn't see very many people I knew; and after the races, we stopped off at London Drugs to do some shopping. Jennifer ran into one of the students who took the RCA course with her, and he wondered why the instructors failed her and said not many of them were able to find work in that field.

I stayed home the next weekend and worked on my research report on Target Zero; by the time it was finished, I had quite a package of information put together and had to do a covering letter. People who worked in Equity and Diversity were given advanced notice, the main letter, then the information package, and sent it off the second week of June but included a paper written by Ralph P. Reed titled "Silent Genocide," written in 1998, although it was American; but I thought it sounded *totally Canadian*!

My sty was still there but appeared to go away more and more when I spoke out to influential people about the truth of Canada's treatment of minorities. In the third week of June, *Unwanted Soldiers* was broadcast on TV again as it had been many times. *Forgotten Warriors*, about aboriginal soldiers, was only broadcast once that I noticed, unless it came on when I was gone because I watched for both of them.

I gave Patricia Kelly an information package on Target Zero and wanted her to look it over and see if I should send a package to the Assembly of First Nations, an aboriginal organization in Canada. The next day, I called Alvin Tolley in Quebec and asked if he knew if any aboriginal soldiers were made commanding officers in WWII. He said that was a good point and told me to ask the Assembly of First Nations. I called the Assembly of First Nations, and Larry Whiteduck confirmed that no aboriginal soldiers were made commanding officers and wives of aboriginal soldiers who didn't come back never got any benefits that the wives of white soldiers got if their husband was killed, and wanted a copy of my research report. I had watched documentaries on the American Civil War, and both the North and South had Indians who were commanding officers. In a documentary on building the Alaska Highway in WWII, blacks commanded segregated black units, but at least they were made commanding officers. The Assembly of First Nations was doing its elections for grand national chief, so I wasn't going to send them any information until after elections. Since improving the living and social conditions of aboriginals was a major issue in this election, when I sent the report on Target Zero, I included some suggestions I thought could improve the living conditions of the Indians of Canada.

I went back to Chilliwack again for the next two weekends to plant some cedar trees on the reserve. I had enough hours built up to take Friday off the second time, so I went there Thursday night. Jennifer was in the bars, so after dropping the seedlings off in Rosedale, I went to the bars to look after her. She got quite drunk as usual and may have been lucky I was there to look after her. We slept in the car that night, and I hoped she would realize she could get in trouble if she keeps drinking like that, but it didn't do any good. I went back to Chilliwack again two weeks later and ended up having a few beers with Aaron and Jennifer; normally, I stayed sober and looked after Jennifer, but she didn't flip out and get mad this time.

I sent the information package to a number of influential people in British Columbia and called Stewart Phillip, director of the Union of British Columbia Indian Chiefs, a provincial Native organization. He was interested in my information, especially after I told him the government issued an apology for how we've been treated after I spoke out on aboriginal issues and how we get treated when the BC premier was going to bring out the Treaty Referendum. He was also interested in my suggestions for improving the social and living conditions of the Indians. Near the end of July, I called Anne Pohl, and she said I wrote really well; other people who read articles I wrote said the same thing.

A week later, Jennifer called me at seven o'clock in the morning, crying hard, and said she destroyed her stereo, broke her glasses, and pulled the cord out of the phone! She had flipped out again really badly, making me wish I was still single! The first weekend of August was a long weekend, so I stayed in Squamish to get some overtime patrolling recreation sites. The sty was still hanging on, so I wondered if I was still angry about things I wasn't aware of. Writing and speaking out to influential people really made me feel good, but the sty just wouldn't go away. That week, there was a documentary, *Tickling the Dragon's Tail*, on the History Channel, about a Jewish nuclear physicist who no one would hire in Canada in the 1930s; so he went to work in Chicago. Then he went on to help develop the atomic bomb and mentioned that anti-Semitism was quite prominent in Canada.

The fire-hazard rating was getting bad, so we got more overtime doing fire patrols, making sure no one was lighting campfires. Dale Feltrin, a staff member who is quite religious, said, "Your sins will be revealed!" Then he said there was a convent where the sewage system was plugged up. When repairmen were called in, it was plugged up with dead babies that were flushed down the toilet. That's when I decided to open up and tell influential people why I figured Gary was following orders when he was trying to make the Native students give up on their post secondary education. I wrote up a covering letter and put the articles that I sent to Equity and Diversity regarding this issue in an information package (titled Orders), so more issues were exposed. Even though I did much writing, finished my report on *Target Zero*, and sent it to many influential people, my sty still wouldn't go away; then when I decided to give out more information to influential people, it went down even more.

Jennifer called me around midnight in the middle of August. She had been drinking, which I knew she would do, and she was sleeping in the park near where she lived. I wished she would work on her anger, but she wouldn't do it even though she knows it makes her feel better. I didn't have to work that weekend, so I went back to Rosedale to can some salmon and ran into Patricia Kelly. She was surprised that I wrote my life story out six times yet didn't mention that my family had made life so boring for me that I barely made it through grade 11.

I stayed in Squamish to do fire patrols again the next weekend and had trouble with indigestion and not being funny; then when I accepted that I'm going to be a rich man, I felt better. The fire-hazard rating got so bad we had a complete woods shutdown. Everyone had to be out of the woods, so we put up cement and wooden barricades on some roads and drove around to make sure no one was in the woods. The first weekend of September was a long weekend, and I got to work the whole weekend. I made good money and told my niece, Deidre, how much I made then told her that's the advantage of getting a career.

I started sending out to influential people information packages on why I thought Gary was following orders when he was trying to make the Native students give up on their postsecondary education, and hoped it would help speed up some highly justified changes. I ended up working seventeen days straight, and we were only allowed to work fourteen, so I took two days off just before the weekend. I went to Chilliwack, and Jennifer still stressed Aaron and me out but I kept hoping it was almost over. Karate started again when I got back to work, and I called Basil Quewezanci at the Assembly of First Nations in Ottawa. He was just reading my reports on Gary following orders and was surprised at what had been going on.

I took a week off, and on Sunday I took Jennifer to Abbotsford with her mother then went back to Sto:lo Eagle with them and was glad Henry Jr. wasn't there. Jennifer was getting better and didn't flip out as much as she used to. She quit drinking for over a week, but I knew it wasn't going to last very long and she was going to get stressed out and start drinking again. During the week, Jennifer stressed Aaron out in the morning, so he went to the bars in the afternoon. When she got off work, she flipped out, went to the bars, and blamed me for stressing her out. She probably would have flipped out anyway, and I knew she wouldn't stay sober for very long; however, my instincts told me everything was going to work out just fine. Jennifer was really cranky the next morning and stressed Aaron and me out. Now I felt like I didn't want to hear her family name for the rest of my life! That family is still *miserable* because of the way their father treated them! Then Jennifer went to the bars and I went with her to look after her but didn't drink. I wanted to visit Isaac and Helen on Saturday, but Isaac was fishing and Helen was sick, so I just stayed at Jennifer's place and wrote a letter to Aboriginal Peoples Television Network (APTN) regarding the police shooting of a Native, Dudley George, in an unarmed protest. They asked if there should be a public inquiry into it. I agreed and stated such:

1. Under freedom of information, the police should say who gave the orders to use that much force and fire that many shots.
2. They should also say how many unarmed non-Native protests they did ever use that much force and fire that many shots.

Then I brought Jennifer her lunch at A&W and ran into Mark Point. Mark is the principal of an Indian school in Agassiz, has a brother who's a judge, and seems to be involved in Native political affairs; so I gave him a copy of "Target Zero" and "Orders." Again, by looking after Jennifer, I ended up in the right place at the right time to get things that I wanted to do done.

I went back to work and was safety check in that week. On October 1, I e-mailed my letter to APTN regarding the public inquiry into the killing of Dudley George and mentioned my research reports. I mailed them on Friday with my suggestions for improving the social and living conditions of Canadian aboriginals and hoped they might help me find a publisher for my life story. Later on, APTN news said there was going to be a public inquiry into the killing of Dudley George; and the news anchor, Nola Wuttunee, knew I was watching.

I originally wanted to take the third week of October off because it was Thanksgiving, but the A&W where Jennifer worked would be shutting down the next week for renovations, so I postponed my holidays again. Jennifer wanted to go to New Mexico with me in November, but I wanted some time away from looking after her. If she could have paid her own way, I would have taken her though because making her my main priority has always worked out for me.

I went back to Chilliwack again the next weekend because Jennifer was off work from Monday to Thursday. I wanted to take her to Kelowna, but her boss wanted her to be on call for work on Thursday. We couldn't come back to Squamish either because it was raining too hard and we were scared of bridges washing out and stranding us there, so on Monday I took Jennifer to Sto:lo Eagle to visit her mother. Henry Jr. was out hunting; otherwise, I wouldn't have gone there at all, but we didn't stay long because it was raining hard and could have flooded or washed out roads. Jennifer got stressed out when we got back, so we went to the bars and didn't get home until four o'clock in the morning.

On Tuesday, Jennifer was stressed out and tired, so she stressed me out again. I helped her apply for work at Sto:lo Employment

Services, an office that helps Natives find work, but nothing came of it. Then the rain stopped and sun shone, frustrating Jennifer because we didn't get to do anything. On Wednesday I took Jennifer to Sto:lo Eagle and spent the night because of the wind and rain, and she was too scared for me to leave. She went back to work the next night then went to the bars. She still drank until closing time or until she got cut off and sometime got mad and flipped out. I went back to work for a week; then on the weekend, I went back to Chilliwack even though I would have preferred to stay home. Jennifer's daughter Roberta and her boyfriend, Nicholas, from Whitehorse, also went to visit; and they were looking for work.

I went back to work and during the week tried to audition for a commercial that was being filmed in Squamish. I wanted to be the logger, but filming was being done the next week when I would be in New Mexico. I worked all week then went back to Chilliwack to drop my car off with Jennifer before flying to New Mexico; and Nicholas got noisy and obnoxious when he was drunk, and arguments started, making me wonder if he was going to cause trouble for Aaron and Jennifer. Jennifer had called me in Squamish one night, and Nicholas was drunk and noisy. She told him to keep quiet because they could get evicted, and he said, "I don't care!" I got scared he was going to get Aaron and Jennifer evicted or in trouble with the managers!

I flew to New Mexico and had another incredibly relaxing holiday. I didn't drink very much, and it felt like I was off for two weeks instead of just one. I went back to work after the weekend, and on Thursday I talked to Roberta about what I went through looking after Jennifer. I told her what happened, Jennifer's depression and injuries that just wouldn't heal until she started working on the cause of her problems instead of the symptom, and about her family's reaction toward me after everything I did for them. I could eventually understand it, treating me like an outcast, but they couldn't do enough for Alvin. If Alvin did that much for her family, it would have been a major event and no one would be able to do enough for him and do everything they could to help!

Roberta went back to Calgary, Alberta, the next day; and Nicholas went back to Whitehorse, which was a relief for Aaron and Jennifer, and I just stayed home for the weekend. It was now late November; then in early December, it finally dawned on me that if Alvin was trying to help Brenda (who needed her sleep so she could catch up on her studies) get a career, Geraldine wouldn't have said anything to her at all and would have even guarded the door to make sure no one disturbed her! She kept waking Jennifer up though and wouldn't listen when I told her to leave Jennifer alone and didn't care!

I stayed home one weekend, then the next weekend I helped Jennifer do her Christmas shopping. We got most of it done on Saturday, and on Sunday, she and Brenda went to Laughing Raven to visit Geraldine. Jennifer got depressed because it would have been her niece Amanda's birthday, but she also stressed Aaron out again. I hoped Jennifer would finally start feeling good about herself this year like I've been hoping for years now; unfortunately, it hasn't happened yet. She's still addicted to suffering and crisis.

I went back to work but started coming down with the flu. I worked as long as I could then went home and back to Chilliwack. The next day, Roberta called and said she and her husband, Timothy, were going to Chilliwack. On Wednesday, my dad ended up in the hospital with a weak heart, but he got to the doctor just in time to prevent a stroke. I came back to Squamish that night and went to work the next day, and the staff told me to just go home because I was sicker than I thought I was. I wanted to stay in Squamish until Saturday or Sunday, but my dad was in the hospital, so I came back right away. I went to visit him, but there were posters in the hospital, asking people with the flu to stay away because they don't want the patients to get sicker; so I stayed at Jennifer's place and met Roberta's husband. Roberta had been married, separated, and Nicholas came down from Whitehorse to see her.

I went on annual leave the next week, and Dad was supposed to go home on Monday but was kept in for shock treatment. He went home on Thursday, Christmas Day, though and Mother asked me to be available to help look after him for three days next week. I agreed, but Tony didn't show up at all and Marge didn't know where he was. I helped look after my dad the next day and went to the back of the reserve to check the cedar trees I planted last spring, and they all died because of the drought; and those planted earlier were damaged by horses stepping on them, which was very disappointing.

On Saturday night, Roberta talked about drinking herself to oblivion, put a bottle of Tylenol tablets in her mouth, and wanted to swallow them with whiskey in an attempt to commit suicide; but I grabbed the whiskey and threatened to dump it out if she didn't spit them out, so she spit them out in a cup. Then I washed them down the sink and knew by the way she was acting what had happened to her. Roberta would need therapy to work on the cause of her problem, not just the symptom; but unfortunately, there still seems to be very little therapy available.

I looked after my dad for three days, but he wanted to be as independent as possible. It was New Year's Eve and Aaron had been drinking every day for a while now. I stayed sober then eventually drove everyone to Laughing Raven. I thought we would all spend the night there, but Ben got mad at Nicholas and started punching him in the head; then arguments started, so I drove Nicholas and Roberta back to Chilliwack and was nervous because I had a few drinks. I didn't want them to walk back to Chilliwack, but my instincts told me I would be safe and I got back to Chilliwack okay.

Chapter 26

2004

When I got back to Chilliwack, I told Roberta a little bit about what Jennifer went through and a brief outline of what I went through looking after her and hoped that would make her realize what she went through was probably nothing compared to what Jennifer went through and still survived. I also hoped that would make her think more positively about herself, but I also told her she had to cure the cause of her problems, not just the symptom. Then I went back to Laughing Raven to pick Jennifer, Aaron, and Timothy up. They decided to go to the bars, but the heater wasn't working, so the bar closed down early; then they all went home to drink, but I didn't drink. Nothing eventful happened the next day, but I wanted to go back to Squamish because I was getting tired of Aaron's drinking and irresponsibility. I visited my dad and bought him some more chocolates because I thought he would be craving sugar since he had to quit drinking.

Jennifer got off work at six o'clock Sunday evening and had two days off, so she came back to Squamish with me. When I got back, it dawned on me that Stan Dixon, owner of *Kahtou*, an aboriginal newspaper based out of Sechelt, British Columbia, is a politician and may want a copy of my research reports. I called him, and he said he would like a copy of *Target Zero,* and Jennifer was able to stay for three days because of road conditions and weather. I stayed home and rested up for the weekend, and the next week, Bing Wong called me at lunchtime and asked me to attend the Chinese veterans' banquet and reunion in Chinatown on February 3. He also wanted me to attend the Chinese New Year parade on January 25, but we were having a surprise dinner for Isaac because he would be turning fifty. Bing also mentioned opening a museum and cultural center for aboriginals in Vancouver and wanted me to talk to Judy Maxwell, a half-Chinese, half-English lady working on a master's degree on Chinese war veterans.

On Thursday night I woke up at three thirty and couldn't sleep, drank a few beers to try and put me to sleep, but it didn't do any good; and surprisingly, I only slept lightly at lunchtime. I visited Aaron and Jennifer for the weekend; and Nicholas was drunk, loud, and noisy! He was told at least six times to keep the noise down because people had to go to work, and he said he didn't care, so I was ready to punch him out; but he left, then we called the police. The next day I was tired because of him, and Jennifer was making mistakes at work; so a few days later, Aaron told them to leave because they were too much trouble to have around.

I had applied to go on the critical-incident stress-management team and got a telephone interview when I got back to work. I was interviewed by two guys and a girl over the phone, and I mentioned a gambling-addictions counsellor sending out a request for feedback on why people with addiction problems may just give up one addiction for another. She really liked my response and offered to help me find a publisher for my life story. Then I mentioned the Chinese veterans inviting me to their banquet and reunion in Chinatown, then the lady sensed I knew much more that I was letting on; so the very next day, my application was turned down.

I went back to Chilliwack again the next weekend for the surprise dinner we were having for Isaac. Jennifer was depressed on Sunday and came back to Squamish for a rest. She went to the bars Monday night and I got a little worried about spending too much money and she got to stay an extra day because of road conditions again. At the end of January, it dawned on me that if Alex Louie's daughter, Jari Osbourne, didn't make the documentary *Unwanted Soldiers*, it's doubtful if many Canadian film companies would have made it because it exposes too much of the truth. I also decided to stop worrying about Jennifer so much because she should be responsible for her own actions; then I slept like a log at lunchtime.

On February 3 I left work an hour early to attend the Chinese veterans' banquet, but a major accident shut the highway down that day; and Percy Joe, the chief from an Indian reserve in Merritt, left a message on my answering machine, saying how happy he was that I exposed the truth about Chinese and aboriginal veterans. The next day, I called Bing Wong and told him why I didn't make it to the banquet. Bing thought I forgot about it and invited me to their meeting at the same place in Chinatown next Thursday. He wanted me to meet Judy Maxwell and said many Chinese veterans wanted to meet me. Then he said a letter I wrote was printed in the January edition of *Kahtou*.

I went to Chilliwack for the weekend and again accidentally stressed Aaron out on Saturday. Jennifer was really stressed out when she got home but calmed down eventually. I got home rather late and had a few beers to unwind, but I was beginning to hate Jennifer's family more and more because I got absolutely no recognition for what I've done to save her from suicide and get her a career! Even now, looking after her is still hard; it's gradually getting easier, but it really wore me down!

On Thursday evening I went to the Ho Ho restaurant in Chinatown for the meeting with the Chinese veterans, gave Judy Maxwell my research reports on "Target Zero," "Veteran's Affairs," and "Orders;" but she couldn't stay long because she had to fly to Hong Kong early the next morning. I hoped she would pass the information on to influential people in Hong Kong because Bing Wong said there's a strong interest in Indian culture in Hong Kong. After the meeting, we had dinner and Bing Wong paid for my meal; then Bing, Howe Lee, and I went out for coffee. They both agreed that if Jari Osbourne didn't make the documentary *Unwanted Soldiers*, it's doubtful if many Canadian film companies would have made it. Then I told Howe Lee Indians are often reluctant to open up to white people and say what happened, and before I could say anything, he said, "Because you would be called a liar!" Bing also showed me the letter I wrote that was printed in *Kahtou* and showed me the newspaper. He also gave me a letter from a professor at the University of Maryland who's writing a book on Chinese Canadian history.

This is the letter I wrote that was printed in *Kahtou*:

Re: **Researching Target Zero and Other Canadian Issues!**

When I finally found time to research "Target Zero!" I decided to go all out to do my research and ask as many people as possible for information! I even asked my father, which I rarely do, because I never seem to get a straight answer out of him! Then I finally realized questions like those probably just bring back very painful memories that he would rather just leave behind him! I'm sure many other Natives feel the same way, so they try to avoid these subjects or talking about their past! There are many other issues I thought should be exposed even though they're not government issues!

I phoned around and interviewed many people and asked if they could ask around for stories and information. I asked Harley Wylie to help me get information on sterilizing of Indian girls and selling of Indian babies in the USA from witnesses and residential-school survivors. Harley asked for an introduction letter stating who I am and what I intend to do with this information because that's what they would want to know. I made one up and it's included in this package. Unfortunately, I didn't get any responses from him yet.

I spoke to Scott Stephens, mentioned in the main letter about sterilization, and he e-mailed me a website on that subject; but it's mostly American. Canada probably wasn't any different; only it was done in more subtle manners, and the truth rarely gets exposed! Even when the truth comes out, it's usually severely distorted, or issues are minimized to the point they're barely noticeable! How Canadians usually react to the truth when aboriginals speak out is written in one of the articles I'm enclosing.

In that website there was a paper written in 1998 by Ralph P. Reed titled "Silent Genocide"! Although it's American, it sounds totally Canadian *because we were taught to be much the same way in Canada! Even when I finished high school in 1973, anything Indian was something to be looked down on, and we were taught to think of Indian spiritual beliefs as foolish superstition. For decades, Western movies probably had an influence on forming this image because we were always made out to look like simple-minded, murdering savages!*

There's a group of researchers who launched a website to get the truth on how Canada treated its aboriginal people to be taught in grade school, known as the Coalition for the Advancement of Aboriginal Studies (CAAS). I sent them a letter with my opinions, and it was printed word for word on that website. Anne Pohl, a member of the core working group, really liked what I had to say about how non-Native Canadians react to the truth when aboriginals speak out. I'm including that letter and some of Anne Pohl's research papers.

Since Anne Pohl is of Russian Jewish descent, I suggested she expose Canada's reaction to the Jewish refugees during the Holocaust! It was said in a documentary that Canada was the worst Western country for not allowing Jewish refugees in! I didn't catch the name, but one influential person was quoted as saying, "None is too many!" I thought it could have been the prime minister at that time, and only 450 Jewish refugees were allowed into Canada! I thought Anne would know how to locate and interview witnesses and survivors who are willing to expose the truth!

Then on May 21, 2003, on the History Channel, there was a documentary titled Je me souviens! *It exposed widespread anti-Semitism in Canada; and Mackenzie King, Canada's prime minister at that time, actually wanted Canada to have the worst record for allowing Jews in! It appeared Canada was just as much against the Jews as many other countries were but stopped just short of outright physically trying to exterminate them! Canada left that up to other countries!*

It's possible Native Indians weren't the only people marked for attack or extermination under Target Zero! This all appeared to be done by "silent genocide"!

I don't know what school students are taught about the Chinese coming over to build the railroad, but when I was in grade school, all we were told is they weren't allowed to bring their women with them. I always knew I was part Chinese but didn't think anything of it until Jennifer's oldest brother, Ryan, said it was because the Indian girls were the only women available to the Chinese Labourers. When I was younger, I often used to get mistaken for Chinese.

My dad said some of our relatives who were Chinese or half Chinese, half Indian went back to China. Eventually, I found out many Chinese and many half Chinese, half Indian went back to China. Tony, my oldest brother, mentioned this to me.

Denise Macdonald never heard about "Sugar and Vanilla Extract," "Target Zero," or the book Genocide Machine in Canada *even though she has a master's degree and PhD in native studies. I thought she might know why some of those who were half Chinese, half Indian went back to China. I kind of wondered if the Chinese went back because no one would hire them for work and took their sons with them. My dad said a few who went to China came back to Canada though.*

Denise said the Chinese and some of their children probably went back to China because of racism. On cafés there were signs saying "No dogs, no Chinese, and no Indians!" Lawrence, fifty-seven years old from Mount Currie, said his grandfather went to Vancouver to sell his furs. Hastings Street was the main part of town, and Indians weren't allowed there! Even in the video Unwanted Soldiers *Chinese Canadians faced much racism, and they're still alive today!*

Unwanted Soldiers *is a video about Chinese Canadians wanting to go to war for Canada in WWII but were continually turned down because the government thought they would demand the right to vote. In that documentary, Alex Louie, whose daughter made the video, dreamt of taking his family back to China because they felt there was no hope for them in Canada! Going to war appeared to help break the racial barrier! This video is available from the National Film Board of Canada. Unfortunately, nothing changed for the Indians until many years later!* Unwanted Soldiers *was broadcast on TV many times; but* Forgotten Warriors, *which about*

Canadian aboriginal soldiers, was only broadcast once that I know of, because I watch for both of them!

I asked Roney Douglas, sixty-one years old and a Cheam Indian Band member where I'm from, if his father, Grampa Charlie, ever said why many of those who were half Indian, half Chinese went back to China. Roney's father was half Chinese but never said very much about his past. Roney said it probably just brought back too many painful memories they would rather not think about!

Roney also said one of his nieces, Filomena Douglas, who is also one of my cousins, gave him a questionnaire to fill out because she's writing a book on residential-school survivors. Roney didn't want to answer it because he lived through the horrors once and didn't want to live through it again! I realized many other residential-school survivors probably felt the same way! One fellow I tried to interview is extremely hard to get a hold of. When he saw it was me on his call display, he just hung up! Some people I interviewed didn't say very much because we knew we could go on and on about what we've been through, saw happen, and heard about.

Uncle Joe said Indian girls married the Chinese and the Chinese went back to China because no one would hire them for work. He said there's a video at Coquileetza about how badly the Chinese were treated when they were brought in to build the railroad. He also said sterilizing had been going on for a long time.

Coquileetza was originally a tuberculosis sanitorium for the Indians, went on to become a preventorium, then a residential school, and now it's an education and cultural center for the Indians. It's located in Sardis, a suburb of Chilliwack. Roy Mah, in the video Unwanted Soldiers *said he fought against injustices all his life! Chinese Canadians could get a degree but weren't allowed to practice as professionals until the 1950s. John Kabong, also an unwanted soldier, said they would apply for work and get turned down. When they asked why, they were told people would feel uncomfortable working next to a Chinaman! Chinese veterans were also turned down when they applied to join the legion after the war!*

This year I finally realized that in the 1960s and '70s, when I was a child and teenager, it was extremely rare to see Indians working in stores as clerks and waitresses in cafés. I mentioned this to Roger Adolph and he didn't think of it until I mentioned it to him. Anne Acco said Saskatchewan was the worst province for not hiring Indians.

Alvin Tolley, from Quebec, said if white people (sometimes called blind pigs—see no evil! Hear no evil!) got caught selling liquor to Indians, they got a fine; and Indians weren't hired in stores or cafés unless Indians were the main customers. Eugene Harry, fifty-three years old, said he worked in grocery stores and at gas stations in Duncan, British Columbia, in the 1960s; but that appeared to be extremely rare!

In 1994 when I was doing my grocery shopping in Squamish, the clerks said they didn't mind the Indians! I responded, "You never see them working here!" They never thought of that; then I finally saw Indians working there! Before that, it was extremely rare to see Indians working in large chain grocery stores or any stores for that matter! In 1996 when I went to Whitehorse, Yukon Territory, for a holiday, it wasn't until I got well past Prince George that I started seeing Indians working in stores.

I heard about Indians applying for work and getting hired over the phone or told to go for an interview when answering ads for jobs in the newspaper. When they got to the office for the interview or the job site, Indians would be told "The job's been filled!" as soon as they saw we were Indian! Either that or we would apply for work and get turned down! Then white people would walk in behind us and they would get hired right away! From what I went through to get a career and try to find work, I can believe that!

Even in 1993 and '94, Jennifer was working for a janitorial service here in Squamish. She wasn't shown the security codes for the buildings they cleaned, but white people hired after her were shown the security codes!

Jennifer got quite a runaround when she applied to get into the residential care aide program in Chilliwack; then the instructors failed her in the practicums. They said she wasn't organized enough, but she's even better organized and more meticulous than I; only she doesn't speak out enough! Office staff where I work know I'm very well organized! Even the other students wondered why the instructors failed her.

After she went back and passed the course, she talked about not going to her graduation ceremonies! I told her she should go! "Look at the run around you got just to get into the course and what happened after you got in!" Then she said, "Look at what you went through, and you didn't go to your graduation ceremonies!"

I didn't think of that until she said it! Although I knew very little of what I know now after eight years of studying, I totally *refused to go to my graduation ceremonies when I graduated from BCIT in 1981! One reason I didn't go was because I thought I might be working and may not be able to make it! I also didn't apply because the students closed me off and wouldn't associate with me, so I thought I would be a good Canadian Indian and keep my distance! It wasn't until early February 1987 that people started calling me "too lazy to go to work"!*

Yes, I had lucky breaks most students wished they had, but I went through four years of incredibly hard times I wouldn't wish on anyone before I got those lucky breaks! I also had many things holding me back, and it really slowed me down! I couldn't go home to take a break because my mother kept telling me what to do and wouldn't listen to what I had to say no matter how much trouble she caused me! Next to Department of Indian Affairs, my family was my biggest hindrance in getting a career!

If all that wasn't bad enough, Indians I went to school with were dying and committing suicide left and right before they turned twenty-five! The Indian who cut himself up with a knife two times then committed suicide when he was twenty-two used to be my foster brother and was one year older than I!

In 1987 when applications to carry the Olympic torch came out, I threw it straight in the fireplace! I thought I would be a good Canadian Indian *and keep my distance! I totally refused to be a token Indian and make Canada look like Goody Two-shoes! Even in* Maclean's *magazine, one Indian said if we carried the Olympic torch, we would be accepted! Once that was over, we would be told to keep our distance again!*

When we get called "Too lazy to go to work!" people act like we don't even apply for work! Rose Charlie said in the 1980s one Indian had to say he was Hawaiian and another said he was Ukrainian before anyone would hire them!

I'm part Chinese and often used to get mistaken for Chinese when I was younger. I never thought of trying to speak with an Oriental accent so I would get hired when I applied for work, and couldn't even get an interview! Of all the times I applied for work with major forest companies, I only got two interviews even though I have a diploma in forestry and everything from tree planting to high-lead logging on my résumé. Most of the work I did in the 1980s was with Indian bands and tribal councils because that was the only work available, making it obvious I'm Native!

George Christopher, a black my age, lived in Ohio; moved to Regina, Saskatchewan; and now lives on the Cheam Reserve, ten miles east of Chilliwack. He said the only difference between Canada and the USA is racism isn't in words or in writing! John also remembered when Indians couldn't buy vanilla extract and could only buy small bags of sugar!

Canada could actually be even more racist than the USA; only it's just more subtle! Down there the Indians could drink in

1950 and the Japanese were let out of the internment camps before Canada let them out. In the USA, the Japanese were also given their possessions back, but that didn't happen in Canada! In the book Ten Lost Years, *it was said WWII was just an excuse to take everything away from the Japanese! This issue was minimized to just one sentence in the whole book, and I'm still trying to research it! Denise MacDonald said not mentioning anything may have been worse than minimizing it!*

American farmers from Washington used to send buses to the Indian reserves in British Columbia to get people to work their farms and orchards. Some went to Merritt, Lytton, Lillooet (to name a few places) and perhaps even went as far as Williams Lake. Not many people would do that kind of work if there was other work available because it's hard work, very low paying, and Labour intensive! Some people who were young and wild thought it was fun, but the most parents could hope for was to make enough money to buy school clothes for their children. This went on until the late 1960s when farm work was taken over by Mexican workers. In British Columbia, Indians sometimes did something else to get work during the summer because that was the only way they could get work!

Even in the American Civil War, both the North and South had Indians who were commanding officers. Ulysses S Grant's secretary of war was an Indian brigadier general.

I called Larry Whiteduck at the Assembly of First Nations in Ottawa because he works with Native veterans. He said no aboriginal soldiers were promoted to commanding officer in WWII and wives of Native soldiers who were killed in the war never got any benefits, but the wives of white soldiers who didn't come back got a pension! Indians who joined the American army got a pension though!

When I saw Colin Powell on Biography, he said 3 percent of those he grew up with did something with their life. The rest either ended up dead or in jail. When I heard that, I thought it sounded like the Indian reserves in Canada! Not many Canadian Indians in his age group did very much with their life. In British Columbia (I'm not sure about other provinces), most of them ended up as loggers, fishermen, or welfare cases, dying without doing very much with their life! That's a result of the residential schools, being placed on a useless, isolated rock pile known as an Indian reserve; being held back when we tried to do something for ourselves; or in many cases not even being hired when we applied for work.

Barbara Charlie is from North Vancouver but graduated high school in West Vancouver in 1952. She said students accepted her but some teachers were racist and Indian babies were sold to white homes because they wanted children. Barbara worked for Legal Aid and said Indians got heavy sentences for minor crimes because they weren't given proper legal representation.

Lawrence said in the late 1950s he had a cyst in his eye and came to Squamish for an operation. The operation didn't work, so he went to Coquileetza. Years later when he saw the movie One Flew Over the Cuckoo's Nest, *it reminded him of Coquileetza and seeing patients walking around drugged and in a dazed state! Whatever they were given made them act crazy!*

Lawrence said he was given many needles and one pinkish needle he was given really hurt! A former patient he talked to many years later said the same thing, so they wondered if they were being used for medical experiments. Denise MacDonald said Indians were used for medical experiments ever since colonization began but didn't know when it ended! Even when I was a child, I heard of many Indians going to tuberculosis sanitariums because it was epidemic among the Indians!

Paul Barnsley wrote an article on sterilization for Windspeaker *in June 1998, which I'm including here. Paul also told me to go out of the country to get my life story published! He said not many Canadians will want to publish it because it exposes too much of the truth!*

In the movie Marion Rose White, *one young white girl committed suicide after she was sterilized! Other girls probably did the same thing, but only one was mentioned in that movie!*

On April 23, 2003, it finally dawned on me that Indians were victims of random beatings by white people or beatings by the police because of stories I heard from victims over the years. In 1979, a friend from Merritt, British Columbia, was living in Vancouver and was beaten up by two Vancouver police constables for no reason, and they seemed to enjoy doing the beating! Alvin Tolley and Roger Adolph both said we were victims of random beatings and beatings by the police! We figured beatings by the police appeared to end in the late '70s. There was only one case I know of where the victims were the type to either provoke or justify it though!

*There's a website on witnesses and victims mentioning police in the prairies dropping Natives off outside town in freezing temperatures in the middle of the night! Of course, the police deny it happened at all, but it happened to the Indians so much they call it starlight drives! It appears to be mentioned quite regularly on CBC News (*CBC News Magazine*), and there's an ongoing investigation into this! I'm including a report from that website even though this was on CBC News again after I got the website. I haven't had much time to research this issue yet because I was busy working on this report!*

Fortunately, there's no escaping: "What goes around, comes around!" When people misbehave, they could be blamed for something they didn't do and still suffer! It appears to me that's what happened in the Fred Quilt case in the 1960s. Fred Quilt was an Indian from Williams Lake who died, and the last thing he said was "They beat me!" The police were accused of beating him and causing his death, so there was a big rally over that!

That month, Jane Byra finally made Jennifer realize she couldn't stand things being calm because at home, the only time things would be calm would be after a beating; if things were calm, she would be subconsciously expecting a beating. She drank until she blacked out because she used to black out at home because of the kind of love her dad gave her. That was probably a survival mechanism, and she was lucky she survived what she went through.

I wanted Jennifer to read a rough draft of my life story, but it was hard for her to settle down and read and said many times that when my book comes out, she's going to run away! I finally thought, *She can go right ahead, as long as she has her LPN training and tells her family not to call me!* I went to Chilliwack the third weekend of February and took Jennifer to visit her mother in Sto:lo Eagle. Henry Jr. had to escort an inmate to Fort St. John in Northern British Columbia, so he was gone for the weekend. I picked Jennifer up to go to work on Sunday but wouldn't even drink their water even though Henry Jr. wasn't home but felt bad that about feeling that way though.

I came back to Squamish, but Jennifer hurt her back at work. Judy Maxwell called me; I had a good talk with her and hoped I could talk her into reading the information I gave her and pass it on to influential people in Hong Kong. I took holidays the next week so I could look after Jennifer because of her bad back. Most of Jennifer's belongings were in storage, and Aaron and I moved them back to their apartment. I helped her unpack them, and she realized it was useless to just have everything sitting in a box, so I hoped she was finally getting over her addiction to suffering.

Brenda came down from Kelowna and Henry Jr. asked Jennifer if he could park his truck at their place while he went to a cabaret. He may have spent the night there, but I was there and offered to leave, but Jennifer wanted me to stay. She was registered to take a cashier's course the next day in Mission, so we dropped Brenda off in Laughing Raven along the way. I was allowed to sit with her in class and enjoyed the course, but I wouldn't want to do it for a living.

The next day, Aaron left around ten o'clock because his friend's wife had just passed away. Jennifer and I got lots of things organized, but she stressed Aaron out when he got home. I left later than I wanted to leave because I tried to cheer Jennifer up, but I was hating her family more and more! My acne also came back again. I only slept lightly at lunchtime when I got back to work, stayed home and rested the next weekend, and was surprised at how tired I was. I watched *Unwanted*

Soldiers again and still felt angry but felt better when I decided not to accept offers from Canadian film companies for my life story!

I went back to Chilliwack again on the weekend so I could take Jennifer to finish her cashier's course. She was stressed out over whether she would pass it or not but got 98 percent and only needed 60 percent. I wasn't allowed to join her this time, so I slept most of the day and was surprised at how tired I was. There was a dinner for Desiree the next day in Sto:lo Eagle, and Jennifer didn't want to go; but her nephew Allan, Liz's son, needed a ride over, so she went. I dropped them off but didn't stay because my dad needed someone to stay with him, and when I went to pick Jennifer up, she decided to stay in Sto:lo Eagle. I had a brief talk with Henry Jr. but still wouldn't use their bathroom or even drink their water. Psychics said he would heal in two years, but it's only been one and a half years so far; he was healing, but I still want to stay away from them. I still kept trying to help Jennifer get a job as an RCA but didn't have any luck. She got some job interviews but wasn't able to find work in that field.

On the first weekend of April, I took Jennifer to a Psychic Expo and I got a reading from a Métis psychic named Sterling. He was really good and said the years 2002 and 2003 were very difficult for me. They were hard, but not much harder than what I've already been through looking after Jennifer all these years. He said things would really pick up for me in June and I would give Jennifer my Cavalier at the end of the year, and Jennifer said 2002 and 2003 were very difficult years for her too.

I went back to Chilliwack again the next weekend because it was Easter weekend, and my mother needed a break from looking after my dad, so I spent the weekend at my parents' place. Jennifer got more job interviews, but some jobs weren't what she was looking for because she wanted to advance to LPN.

I called Jennifer and told her the federal government has a class action lawsuit against them over residential-school issues. Surprisingly, it's called the Baxter class action lawsuit. My nickname is Baxter, and I've been doing much research, gathering information and sending it out to influential people. When I told Jennifer about it, she suggested I send them my information packages.

Simon Murray, from a forest consulting company in Squamish, gave me some Douglas fir and cedar seedlings; so on Friday afternoon, I went back to Rosedale and planted some trees. That night I took

Jennifer to visit Geraldine; then Geraldine and I got into a big argument! I was going to plant some cedar trees down by the river the next day, but the area was crawling with cops; so I just visited Isaac, and his daughter Ashley said, "An Indian with a nice car like that looks suspicious!" I said, "Even in that car, people call me too lazy to go to work!" Then on Sunday, Jennifer and I went to a psychic fair because we enjoy these things.

I stayed home the next weekend and worked on the covering letter to information I wanted to send to the lawyers working on the Baxter case; then I realized how much information I found doing research during my coffee breaks. Now I was really glad staff closed me off! I had been developing another sty, and it was getting bigger until I started working on this letter. During the week, I called a lawyer's office in Toronto, Thompson Rogers, working on this case and a lawyer said they were interested in my information.

I also called Alvin during the week and told him about how Jennifer's family reacts toward me even though I had saved her from suicide and helped her and Henry Jr. get a career. I said Geraldine was proud of having been Jennifer's guardian yet she didn't want us together when we first met. Previously, Alvin told me that their family can't do enough for him. I started feeling really good in May and hoped I would be over my last hill in life this year! Previously, Phaye Sutton said I would be over my last hill in life in May, and the sty went down after sending the letter to Thompson Rogers but didn't go away completely.

Roger Adolph called me one weekend and we had a good, long talk about addiction and having to cure the cause of the problem, not just the symptom. He asked me for articles I wrote on curing the cause and got really mad when I told him the full details on how Jennifer's family treats me yet they can't do enough for Alvin. Then Roger got mad and started swearing; that was the first time I ever saw him get mad like that in the twenty-nine years that I've known him. The next day I started wondering if I should write everything in to show the *full* impact of the residential schools, incest, and child sexual abuse that carried on afterward.

Jennifer got drunk and depressed the next weekend, but I looked after her. We didn't get to bed until five o'clock or six o'clock; then at eight thirty, Ryan called and said Ben and Geraldine's house burned down and they lost their car and truck! They thought it could have been one of the daughters' boyfriend, and foul play was suspected, so I took Jennifer to Abbotsford to visit them and we spent the night at a motel with Geraldine and the kids. On Sunday, Aaron borrowed $60 off me again because he had pawned his planer and needed it to go to work; that was annoying because there were things I wanted to do with my money. Then I took Jennifer back to Abbotsford again on Sunday then came back to Squamish.

The next weekend I went to Bellingham to visit Auntie Jeanette and Mike again, and it was quite relaxing. On Sunday I had a short visit with Aaron and Jennifer and thought Jennifer would be stressed out and crabby, but she was pretty good. She was getting over the pain and anger from the past, but it must have taken incredible strength to go through what she went through and survive! I went back to Chilliwack again the next weekend, but Jennifer was stressed out again. After she went to bed, I had a few beers with Aaron and didn't realize how stressed out I was until after I drank a few beers. Jennifer was still cranky on Saturday but calmed down a bit on Sunday, then we dropped some clothing donations off at Ben and Geraldine's.

It was the end of June now, and I started feeling really good when I got back to work. Happiness had crept up on me just like a psychic said would happen in two years, and I stayed home for the long weekend to do fire patrols. Jennifer called me on Friday morning and was crying and depressed; she wanted to move away, and it felt like this was going on forever! I felt good by the afternoon though and hoped Jennifer would be over her addiction to suffering by this fall. Although I was working overtime and making good money, I still felt bored. I thought perhaps a change was coming.

Nothing eventful happened in July, but I started going through my life story and writing everything in on how Jennifer's family treated me. Previously I only wrote in how their father treated me and Geraldine being a hindrance in trying to get Jennifer a career; now I decided to write in how I don't get any recognition from her family and how Henry Jr. treats me like an outcast. It was incredibly hot that month, and Jennifer still sometimes stressed everyone out, and I stayed home on the long weekend in August so I could do fire patrols. I was enjoying my sleep on Sunday morning when Jennifer called and stressed me out; people are still affected by the misery Henry, Old Useless, caused when he was here!

I watched the Logger's Day parade, and the MLA for Squamish, Ted Nebbling, was in a car in the parade; so I waved to him, let him know I sent that information on aboriginal issues in 2001, and he realized I got the provincial government to apologize for how the Indians have been treated. Another politician, John Reynolds, was in another car. There had been a federal election earlier that year and a pamphlet was sent out asking what election issues concerned us. I made my comments, and when I got John's attention, I told him those were my suggestions; then he looked away really fast and realized I've been doing research and sending information out to influential people.

I continued working on my writings, and my sty finally went away. I went back to visit my parents the next weekend and my dad was putting in a new well, so brush had to be cleared to get the equipment in. Some of my seedlings had to be dug up, so now I had to replant some areas. Dad said he wanted to put in a well three years ago but the reserve was going to put in a water line; that didn't happen yet, so he just put in his own well.

Nothing eventful happened in August, but I feel really good off and on. I told Dave Walkem how Jennifer's family treats me in spite of everything I've done for them, and we figured it's a result of the residential schools. I worked part of Labour Day weekend in September but took two days off work to help Jennifer apply for work. I've been feeling really good off and on and hoped things will pick up for me and Jennifer would start feeling better.

I stayed home one weekend then went back to Chilliwack the next weekend, and Jennifer was sick but went to work anyway. Aaron was sick, so on Sunday I made him go to the doctor so that if he needed medication, I could help him out. He did, and it cost me $93 for the prescription. Jennifer called me the next morning and said someone broke into their car and stole Aaron's power saw and planer. His other saw was in the pawnshop, but he needed $60 to get it out but would also need help to get a new planer. Now I'm glad he pawned his saw; otherwise, he would have lost it. I was stressed out at first, but in the afternoon, I couldn't help but feel good. I also wondered if something good would come of this. I tried to buy him a new planer, but the store said I couldn't use my Visa number over the phone. I thought I might have to go back on the weekend, but by helping them out, things usually work out quite well.

I worked at getting my life story ready for editing, still adding in what I originally thought I would leave out on how Jennifer's family reacted toward me. I had already put in how Henry treated me and how Geraldine was a hindrance at getting Jennifer a career and didn't feel guilty about it at all! It was still stressful to relive what I went through though and drank a few beers even though I was getting sick.

Near the end of the week, I gave Jennifer the money she used to buy Aaron a new planer; then she asked me to go back to Chilliwack on Thursday night because she had a job interview with the Seabird Island Indian Reserve near Agassiz. I went to Chilliwack and signed Jennifer up for a first aid course the next day because I thought she would need it for her new job, took her to her job interview, which stressed her out; but eventually she calmed down. I also missed work on Monday because I was still sick and took Jennifer shopping in Abbotsford; then she got a call, and it looked like she was going to get the job.

On Friday, October 1, Bing Wong called me and invited me to the Chinese Canadian veterans' reunion and dinner in Vancouver the next day and said it could be their last reunion because they're all getting old and was glad I would try and make it. The next day, Jennifer called me two times when I was out for coffee, asking me to ask Sterling if she got the job, called me again and said she got the job and would be giving her notice; she would be leaving A&W but wanted me to call Sterling anyway.

I went to the Chinese veterans' dinner that night and aboriginal veterans were also invited, but only one showed up, Lou Schmidt; and we ended up sitting with the Korean veterans. There were pictures of the veterans when they were in uniform on display; and I was quite surprised that one veteran, Roy Mah, looked just like me when I was a teenager in army cadets, and one lady even asked if that was a picture of me. Ironically, Roy Mah fought injustices all his life, which was mentioned in the documentary *Unwanted Soldiers*; and I've been doing the same thing. Bing had some stories he wanted me to record so they wouldn't be lost but found someone else to do it. One story he told was when he would apply for work and get turned down. Then he would be told he's qualified but people wouldn't want to take orders from a Chinaman.

I went back to work during the week and wanted to go to Vancouver for karate on Tuesday, but Jennifer didn't think I should go; she somehow usually makes the right decision and it was raining hard, so I didn't go. That night, Auntie Tilley called and said they were having company from Hawaii the second week of November, so I couldn't visit them that week. Jennifer still wasn't totally sure if she got the job or not and was stressed out over whether or not she would even be able to do the job: looking after eight kids! Then she called and told me her schedule, so she got the job!

I went back to Chilliwack since it was Thanksgiving weekend, and Jennifer was stressed out over starting her new job on Monday, but I thought most of it was her addiction to suffering and not being sure of herself. She thought she would have to cook a turkey, which she's never done before, so I bought her a meat thermometer to help her out; and when she went to work, she cooked a turkey. The mother helped her, so everything worked out well. I had enough hours built up to take two days off, so I stayed in Chilliwack, drove Aaron to work, and had Jennifer's car serviced so it would be reliable for work. At the end of the month, I helped Aaron and Jennifer move into a trailer in a farmer's field near where Aaron worked. Now he was close to his job because Jennifer needed the car to go to work.

I e-mailed Lee Schmidt, Lou Schmidt's daughter, a lawyer for legal advice; and she answered right away and offered to edit my life story. I called Anne Acco, a researcher and editor for a book publishing company, and Anne said I'm bringing up Native issues at just the right time because the residential-school syndrome is now being recognized as an issue. It's coming out on people's bodies when they're sixty, but I said even as early as when people are in their forties and fifties. She also told me to write to Pemmican Publications about publishing my life story; so I told Anne the Southern Poverty Law Center in Montgomery, Alabama, used to answer my e-mails. Then after I sent them a package of information on Native Canadian issues, they *totally* stopped answering me. She said I sent them too much information, but I kept sending them information anyway but never got any response.

Joy Ward, an addictions counsellor, was one of the people I asked if I should write everything into my life story; and she thought it was a depressing, lose-lose story. But I wrote to her and told her it's a beautiful, inspirational story that will show how *something great* came of hard times I wouldn't wish on anyone! Then she said there's going to be an Addictions conference and if it's in Vancouver, perhaps I could be on the panel.

I went back to Chilliwack and took the next week off in annual leave, and my family had a Chinese dinner at home for me because it was my birthday. I helped Aaron and Jennifer get a satellite dish installed, and on Remembrance Day, I took Jennifer to visit her mother in Sto:lo Eagle. Henry Jr. was out hunting and I thought he would be gone for a few days, so I stayed there. He went back that night though and I said hi to him, but he just walked by me without saying anything. I wanted to be gone before he got back.

Jennifer and I went to the psychic fair again on the weekend and I was told to get a woman to edit my life story and things will really pick up for me next year. I thought maybe that's when I'll get the reward of sticking out a difficult situation. I had a reading from Lora Schultz again and mentioned writing to the department head of aboriginal history at the University College of the Fraser Valley. She didn't answer, and Lora said some people's jobs may be on the line if they expose too much of the truth. Time off was rather stressful because I spent too much money, but my sty went down even more. I called Stan Dixon, and he asked me to go to a forestry seminar on November 30 at the Four Seasons Hotel in downtown Vancouver.

On November 30 I went to the Four Seasons Hotel for a seminar on a Supreme Court decision that forest companies must consult Natives before they develop land in their land claims area. I met Denny Eddy there, a law student in his fifties who made a living as a musician for over thirty years. He used to play hockey with the Indians back east and didn't know there was any prejudice. Some of them were very good hockey players and played better than Phil Esposito, a star professional hockey player in the 1970s, did but weren't drafted to play professional hockey. When he asked about them years later, before he could say anything, I said, "They're dead! Either suicide or alcohol- and drug-related deaths!" I called Denny when I got back to work and sent him some articles I wrote. He offered to edit my life story; said if schools want my book, it will increase sales; and he would try and get UBC Press to publish it. He wasn't surprised at how Jennifer's family reacts toward me, said I write well, and knows much of the truth of how the Indians of Canada have been treated.

I took three days of annual leave to help Jennifer do her Christmas shopping. She was stressed out after work, so we went to the bars. She drank, but I stayed sober to drive and look after her. She wanted to leave, but another lady kept buying her another beer when her glass was almost empty, so we stayed until closing time. She was sick for the next two days, then Aaron's parents came on Saturday, so we didn't get much shopping done on Sunday. I had the horn, signal lights, and a number of small things fixed on her car, which cost $350; and it also had to be checked for a leak in the cooling system. I went back to work for a week then took the last two weeks of December off in annual leave. I helped Jennifer do her Christmas shopping and had her car checked; sure enough, there was a leak in the cooling system and would be too expensive to fix. Now I would be giving Jennifer my Cavalier this month; just like Psychic Sterling said, I would now I would buy myself a truck.

Christmas was rather uneventful, and Jennifer spent more money than I thought she should, but it's her money. I wanted her to come with me to look for a truck, but most places were closed because of holidays when she was off work. I thought we would have time to shop around the day after Boxing Day, but Ryan invited us over for a turkey dinner and I got stressed out, but we went anyway. When we got there, both Ryan and Desiree thought, *It takes an awful lot to get Baxter to come to Sto:lo Eagle!* Henry Jr. was sitting there and knew it was because of him.

We shopped around Abbotsford for a truck then came to Squamish. I had some salmon for a memorial in Bellingham in two weeks that I brought to my freezer and knew I would probably buy a truck in Squamish. We didn't have much time to shop around though because Jennifer had a work group meeting the next day. We tried to get my car loan put in Jennifer's name because she would be making the rest of the payments and it would give her a credit history, but the bank wouldn't accept it. She would need a cosigner and wouldn't accept me because the loan would still be in my name and she only had her new job for two months. My mother suggested one of her brothers cosign the loan, but I said I didn't even want the time of day from them!

Chapter 27

2005

Jennifer and I went back to Squamish to arrange buying a truck and transfer ownership of my Cavalier to her on January 3. I knew it would take a long time, and she had to go back to work at eight o'clock that night; then we had the car serviced, so we went back to Chilliwack on my truck. I took an extra day off work, and she came back to Squamish with me. The holidays had been hectic because of Jennifer's long hours at work, Christmas shopping, and looking for a new truck. The next day, Jennifer was in the bars when I got off work, so I went there to look after her but didn't start drinking until eleven thirty.

On Friday I was going to bring Auntie Jeannette some salmon for the memorial, but Jennifer suggested I stay home because of high winds and snow making driving dangerous. That night I got a call from Shihan Iyabanaka, the head karate Instructor of Canada, about grading for my black belt. He was really happy about me and Chris Gielow, a club member, taking over the karate club and keeping it going even though we were just brown belts. I just stayed home for the weekend because of high winds and snow conditions, and Jennifer borrowed some more money off me, but I didn't think she should be doing that anymore. Then I decided that when I retire, I'm just going to have fun because all my life I've been held back from having fun.

I took the next Friday off to deliver the salmon to Auntie Jeannette for the memorial and visited with them for a while then went back to Chilliwack to visit Jennifer and because my mother wanted to attend the memorial too. The memorial was held at the same time the Indian

Dancers had gathered for a powwow. It was an enjoyable occasion, and when I got back to Squamish, I felt quite relaxed compared to how stressed out I sometimes feel after Christmas. I had a good talk with Patricia Kelly about my book, and she said her friend who's an editor thought it must be quite a story and it's okay to use people's names as long as what you say is the truth.

When I got back to work, my supervisor said people were complaining about me writing letters even though I only did it during my coffee breaks; yet when I walked around, I often saw people doing things not work related on the computer and it wasn't coffee break. I thought if they knew the truth, they might not react that way, so I took many e-mails off my computer then decided I better just write my letters at home from now on and worked at learning Spanish during my coffee breaks. Near the end of January, a program titled *The Passionate Eye* broadcast a documentary titled *Indecently Exposed*, about twenty white Canadians and twenty Canadian Indians doing role play on what Indians have to live with daily. The white Canadians were quite surprised at how we actually get treated; and on the website, there were some feedback, so I wrote up a response in a covering letter to Canadian Broadcasting Corporation (CBC) in Toronto and included some letters and research reports that I had written.

In early February I wrote to Amnesty International in Ottawa, Ontario, and sent a parcel of articles I had written. I tried to register it, but the clerk at the post office said it couldn't be registered because it was a parcel; then a year later, I realized I had sent letters that size before and had them registered and the postal clerk probably didn't want to register it because of whom it was sent to. On the weekend I went to visit Aaron and Jennifer at the trailer, and a white fellow driving by called me "too lazy to go to work" but felt bad when I responded, "Would you say that if I was a white boy?"

Anne Acco offered to do an editorial commentary of my life story free of charge, so I sent her a hard copy of my manuscript and told her she's the only one allowed to read it. Patricia Kelly also suggested I divide it into two volumes because it's rather long, but I didn't like the idea of doing that. I want my story complete to show how something great can come of incredibly hard times.

I went to Vancouver to train in karate for my black belt grading and got the belt but not my certificate. The Vancouver instructor, Allan Chan, wasn't happy with my technique and wanted me to go to

Vancouver once a week for six months for more training. I finally got my black belt in karate, but it wasn't the happy occasion that I thought it would be, so my first impulse was to go home and drink then wondered if drinking was slowing me down. I thought maybe I better slow down on drinking because of karate. I kept going to Vancouver for karate but felt depressed because Allan Chan wasn't very happy with me after how hard I worked all these years, then I thought, *I feel down today. I wonder if* something good *will come tomorrow.*

When I got to work the next day, Gurdeep Pander, an author in India, had sent me an e-mail offering to help me find a publisher for my book over there. He read my letter that I sent to CAAS titled "Aboriginal Perspectives in the Classroom." Gurdeep also worked at fighting poverty, racism, and social injustice in India. I replied to Gurdeep, thanking him for his offer, and told him I would be sending him a brief outline of my life story. Then I called *Kahtou*, and the person answering the phone said my letter they published went over quite well and they got lots of comments on it. I also got sick that week and saw Roberta Smith on the news at lunchtime and where she was working. She was a journalism student when I first went to college in 1973 and wrote the article "Native Students Angry at Segregation," but unfortunately, she didn't think of saving it.

Jennifer was slowly getting better and wasn't as cranky as she usually was. When I visited her on the weekend, I also visited Patricia Kelly. She had broken up with her boyfriend and knew she could easily get me interested in her. I mentioned Gary being on the news as a survivor of the Port Alberni Indian Residential School, which was reported to have been the worst one in British Columbia. Then she said the father of her kids, Ron Hamilton, wrote a book on that school after interviewing two hundred survivors and gave me Ron's phone number so I could order a copy of the book. She said she would call him and say I'm her cousin. I didn't think she was interested in me, so I didn't get excited.

I called Ron Hamilton about the book *Indian Residential Schools: The Nuu-chah-nulth Experience* and told him I would try and have it distributed in India. Gurdeep also responded to my e-mail, liked my response, and offered to help me find a publisher over there. When I ordered the book, I included some of the articles I wrote, then wrote to Gurdeep, sent him a copy of the book and more articles that I had written.

When Easter weekend came at the end of March, Jennifer wanted me to drive her to Sto:lo Eagle for their dinner. Andrew was there and Jennifer wanted me to stay and visit, but I left right away. When I went back to pick her up, we didn't leave for an hour, so I just crashed out on a chair in the living room. I still wouldn't even drink their water or use their bathroom because I just wanted to pick her up and leave without visiting. I talked to Patricia Kelly the next day, and she was really enthusiastic about getting my book published. We knew it's going to expose much of the truth about Canada's treatment of Natives, and getting it published in India could really generate sales and expose the truth. Gurdeep was also excited and thought my book should definitely get published in India as well as Canada, which would really make waves. Previously he asked for the first one hundred pages of my manuscript to look for a publisher, but now he only asked for the first fifty pages.

In early April, I watched *Chiefs and Champions*, documentaries on successful Native athletes who also did something with their life, on APTN; but I also watch APTN news because they expose aboriginal issues and the truth. Roger Adolph was on one episode because he used to be a professional boxer, went home and became a chief, and asked me to write his life story for him. Jennifer got sick again as she sometimes does at this time of the year for some unknown reason. On APTN news there was a three-part series on sexual abuse in Native communities, and it said the person who discloses the abuse can be dejected from the family and, in some cases, from the whole community, if it's a well-respected elder. In the third and last episode one fellow said disclosure is the first most important and difficult step toward healing.

I called Isaac to see if they were going to have a dinner for our father, but he said they already had one; then he said there was going to be a psychic fair in Chilliwack next weekend, if I was interested. I tried calling Jennifer but couldn't get through, so I thought she was probably visiting her mother but *totally* refused to call her in Sto:lo Eagle unless she called me first. She called me at work the next day and she was still sick, so I went to Chilliwack to visit her. She was really sick on Saturday but went to work anyway. I helped her out at work and she called her boss to see if someone could take her place on Sunday even though she still wanted to go to work, and I tried to take her to a satellite medical clinic, but they were closed when she got off work.

Aaron and I took her to the doctor the next day and she got more medication and needed X-rays, so I decided I better take Monday off work to help look after her. Jennifer was really cranky the next day because she was sick, but I got a message from Shihan Iyabanaka. He said Allan Chan was happy with my progress, so I hoped I would get my black belt certificate soon. I went back to work; then two days later, I called Jennifer at lunchtime on April 13. She said she had double pneumonia and won't be able to go back to work until the twenty-ninth. I thought I may have to take another week off work to look after her; then I got a covering letter ready for four information packages on aboriginal issues that I sent to Gurdeep Pander in India. Jennifer was sick and cranky; then I realized it was her birthday.

I went back to Chilliwack for the weekend because I always help Isaac's kids on their birthday; and when I went to pick up Nicole, my niece, Tony was there. Helen said his liver was giving out on him because of all the drugs he's taken over the years; and Jennifer said if he passed away, my parents will go down like her dad did when Liz died. She still won't accept that Henry suffered because he wouldn't put anything down for Liz's funeral after the way he treated her and all the money he had in the bank, and I still felt angry at him, but I'm getting over it. I booked another week of annual leave to help look after Jennifer because she was really sick and needed me to help look after her and got really stressed out on Monday but calmed down the next day.

AEA sent out a message asking for letters of support to Canadian Radio-television and Telecommunications Commission (CRTC), asking to renew APTN's license for another seven years and also sent a memo stating what kind of issues we should bring up in those support letters, so I decided to send my letter by registered mail.

Jennifer also started getting severe menstrual cramps because she was near menopause and got some pills from the doctor, but they only made her feel worse. Eventually I was able to talk her into going to the hospital emergency ward, where she was given a morphine shot and some Tylenol #3's, strong painkillers that require a doctor's prescription to get. By Sunday, Jennifer was getting severe headaches and was crying off and on. She got worried about whether or not she'll be able to make it back to work and if it's affecting my job. I had to come back to Squamish to pick up some clothes, so I decided to go to work on Monday then take the rest of the week off to look after her.

I went to work Monday then went to karate in the evening and picked up the book on the Port Alberni Indian Residential School. A lady in the karate club was from Barbados and asked what a residential school was; then I realized I would have to write some things into the Introduction so the reader will know what I'm talking about. I booked the rest of the week off in annual leave to look after Jennifer and called Patricia Kelly and told her about APTN asking for letters of support to be sent by viewers to CRTC to renew their license for another seven years. Jennifer was also stressed out about my book coming out, but Patricia said it's a story that must be told. It's not only inspirational; it could also help other victims realize they're not alone in what happened so, hopefully, they'll go for help. Toward the end of the week, Jennifer started feeling restless even though she was still sick, called her boss, and said she'd be back to work on Monday. I worked on getting my letter to CRTC ready and asked Patricia to edit it and put it on computer disk because of the deadline to get the letters in. When I went to visit her, she said it was a *very good* letter that would only need a few minor changes; then she sensed that I was excited by APTN's news anchor, Nola Wuttunee.

By Saturday, Jennifer was still sick but wanted to go back to work because she felt guilty about just sitting around. On Sunday I wanted to leave early to go home and relax because I had given up ten days of annual leave to look after her by now. Toward the end of the week, Jennifer called and said she wanted to move to Agassiz because she couldn't take all the driving back and forth. I stayed home the next weekend for a well-deserved rest, called Anne Acco, and she edited the first one hundred pages of my manuscript and wanted it sent to a department of social work at a university. I sent another book on Indian residential schools to Gurdeep then called Patricia Kelly. She said she would try and get my letter to CRTC ready soon, and I hoped media exposure for Canadian Indians would bring some results.

By the second week of May, I started having a hard time going to sleep at night and woke up early; then when I started thinking about *sex*, more often, I slept heavily. I needed some more seedlings to plant on my parent's property because some were destroyed when my dad put in a new well. I wasn't going to ask Brenda Cosgrove from Chilliwack forest district then decided I should because sometimes I get things where I least expect to get them. Sure enough, she got me some cedar seedlings; at first I was slightly disappointed then thought, *Maybe it's better that I plant cedar instead of Douglas fir*.

I took the next Friday off to pick up the seedlings and planted most of them, and the next day, I went to see Patricia Kelly about the letter to CRTC. I didn't have enough time to look it over because I thought mail left at two o'clock, and wanted it sent by Xpresspost to make sure it would arrive on time. It wasn't quite ready and it took a while for her to get it ready; then I sent it off even though there was a slight bit of information that I wanted to add to it, but she had done a terrific job of editing the letter. When I went back to see Aaron and Jennifer, they were both stressed out over my book and wanted their names and place-names changed completely. The next day I took Jennifer to the flea market and worried about spending too much money. She got called back to work, and I finished planting the seedlings that Brenda gave me. Lora said May was going to be a *stormy* month for Jennifer and its half-over; hopefully, things will calm down after the storm! I mailed the book about Canadian Indian residential schools, *No End of Grief* by Dr. Agnes Grant, to Gurdeep Pander; then he phoned me from India and said he was really happy to get the books that I've been sending him because he didn't know such things were going on in Canada.

By the fourth week of May, Jennifer got depressed over her job because she wasn't getting any help looking after the kids from the parents, so I told her that at least she's probably giving them a ray of hope that they may not have if she weren't there. On Thursday she called and said she had double pneumonia. She didn't want to take time off because she was scared she could get laid off, so I told her to report it to her boss because people can die from pneumonia! The next day she went to the emergency ward and ended up in the hospital.

I worked long hours and tried to leave early and get back to Chilliwack to see Jennifer but couldn't and had to try and build up my hours so I could attend my niece Ashley's graduation. I spent most of Saturday visiting Jennifer in the hospital, and in the evening, Ryan called, so I told him where Jennifer was. I visited Jennifer again on Sunday; and Henry Jr. and his girlfriend, Cecelia, came to visit. But when they came, I just laid back in a chair and pretended to sleep until they left.

I booked another three days of annual leave to help look after her, and on Monday I went to a signing ceremony for a forest agreement between the British Columbia government and an Indian band. A film company was there filming the ceremony; and Gene MacInnes, a British Columbia Forest Service member whom I happened to be sitting beside at lunchtime, was filmed. The camera lady knew I had done something great with my life and tried not to include me in the filming, so I just sat there without looking up or showing any reaction. Kerry Crozier, the Chilliwack forest district manager, was there and wondered why I didn't work in Chilliwack; and I told him there were two incidents that I may only tell Paul Kuster and June Quipp, the former chief of my reserve, about until my life story gets published. Kerry said district managers are in a position of trust.

I casually mentioned to Gene that Gary was a non-status Indian who was trying to make us give up on our postsecondary education, then he thought, *Indians hold each other back then cry injustice.* I knew all along that Gary was a non-status Indian but didn't realize how important it was until I mentioned it to Gene. Later on I thought about everything that was going on in Gary's age group that must have made him willing to work at a job like that and follow orders, so I decided to put everything into an information package and send it to influential people.

Jennifer got mad because I wasn't at the hospital to pick her up, and Henry Jr. picked her up, but I think she was just jealous of seeing me have fun. She seemed to calm down; but in the early evening, she threw a tantrum and drove to Squamish in her car, so I followed her. She was still pretty sick the next day and wanted to go back to Chilliwack so she could look for a place to stay in Agassiz. I didn't want to go but knew that if I didn't go along with her, she would have found a way to get her own way. Ryan called us in Squamish around three o'clock in the afternoon and tried to be nice to me, but I let him know I wasn't going back to Sto:lo Eagle to visit.

On June 1 I helped Jennifer find a place in Agassiz and Aaron got really mad. I didn't answer him at first then told him she would have found a way to get her own way anyway, then Jennifer told me to leave, so I went to visit Patricia Kelly. I told her that I really liked the letter she edited then told her what I wanted her to do so I can try and find a publisher for my life story. That night, Jennifer came back to Squamish with me and told me she can't sit still because of what she went through as a child. She can't change overnight and had to change slowly like a career criminal did when he tried to live a straight life. I said it's been twenty-six years now, and I didn't think I could even bring her this far when I met her. Then she said she didn't want me calling her family anymore, but I didn't say I already considered having their numbers screened, so they can't call me.

Jennifer went back to Chilliwack the next day, but I thought she would have rested better at my place. May had been a difficult month, but hopefully, things will start picking up. I hoped that would be the final storm before a whole new beginning like Phaye Sutton predicted. I went to Chilliwack on the weekend to help Jennifer move her things to her new apartment. She was sick, but we still moved her things; and eventually, Aaron helped us. I had built up enough hours to take Monday and Tuesday off to attend Ashley's graduation; and my other niece, Deidre, was there and she said she found a letter I wrote on a computer website.

Jennifer was really cranky on Monday and Tuesday, so I took her to the doctor again. She had talked about wanting me completely out of her life for two days now, but I thought it was just the stress she was going through. She thought she would be going back to work on the thirteenth but was told not to go back until the eighteenth. I finally got to stay home for a weekend in June and worked on an information package on Indian residential schools and healing and titled the package "Assimilation" because the Canadian government said the residential schools were meant to assimilate the Indians into mainstream Canada.

I called Jennifer on Tuesday, June 14, but she was working. I didn't think she would be going back to work until Saturday. I started feeling really good; then on the weekend, I had Jennifer's car serviced and took her to Bellingham, Washington, shopping. She started feeling better, and on Sunday, I helped her straighten out her apartment then took her and Aaron out for Chinese buffet. I had enough hours built up to take Monday off and took her shopping in Bellingham again, came back, and visited again the next weekend; but she wasn't too cranky.

Near the end of June, I met Don DeHart, who grew up in North Carolina, had a bachelor's degree in intercultural studies and a master's degree in counselling, and is working with North America Indigenous Ministries (NAIM), restoring Native pride and culture to the Indians of Canada. I told Don about some information packages that I put together and sent out to influential people, then Don asked me to send them to him. Don said people who have been oppressed tend to become oppressors. Where there's money, there's jealousy. People who have been oppressed may lash out at people who try to help them because that's all they know. Now I was beginning to understand why Indians are often jealous of other Indians getting ahead of them, can sometimes be their own worst enemy, and why Jennifer often lashes out at Aaron and me.

I sent another book on Indian residential schools, *A National Crime* by John S. Milloy, to Gurdeep in India and by mid-July I got a thank-you note from him and he suggested I use his editor to edit my life story. The day after I got that message, he phoned me from India and said he liked the books and information packages that I sent him and invited me to his wedding in India. I would have liked to attend but couldn't afford to go and had already used up much of my holiday time. That night, *Forgotten Warriors*, a film documentary on Canadian aboriginal WWII veterans, was finally broadcast on TV.

On the third weekend of July, I took Jennifer to Sto:lo Eagle to visit her mother. She wanted me to spend the night there in case anything happened, but Henry Jr. and Cecelia went back. Henry Jr. didn't talk to me but seemed rather glad that I finally went to visit and felt relieved when I told him I had the strongest feeling telling me not to think about how he treated me, but still left without eating anything even though I hadn't had supper yet. Jennifer wasn't as crabby as she usually was and even gave me a key to her apartment, so I felt really good off and on while driving back to Squamish.

I sent the APTN support letter to influential people and called Patricia Kelly and told her about how Jennifer's family treat me after everything I've done for them, and she said what Jennifer's family went through is something people usually secretly take with them to their grave. I went back to Chilliwack again the next weekend because it was the long August weekend, spent part of the weekend in Sto:lo Eagle, and Ryan and Desiree were excited that I finally went back; but I didn't tell them that I wasn't going to make that a habit. When I got back to work, Derek Kingston and Jan Poulderman, contractors from Lytton, had gone to the office because they were doing work in Squamish. They were the two people I spoke to when I wrote "Grim Reality," and Derek said Billy Paul is the only one left that's still alive of his class from the residential school. Billy is only two years younger than I and said the school was like a prison.

I just stayed home the next weekend, and on Saturday I heard one of my cousins who's about eight years younger than I was depressed and threatening suicide, so I called my aunt and uncle and told them what symptoms to watch for that would indicate the decision has been made. Then I told some of my other cousins how he was feeling so they would know, called my uncle the next day, and they said he was improving. Then my aunt thanked me for showing my concern, but I told her to watch him at all times!

In the second week of August, I thought more about Gary being a non-status Indian working at trying to keep other Indians from doing something for themselves and didn't think about how important that issue was until now. In the 1990s he was mentioned on the news as being a survivor of the Port Alberni Indian Residential School, which I eventually found out was the worst one in British Columbia. He was an alcoholic because of the pain and anger of what he went through in the residential school and may have given up his Indian status because of a law that still existed right up to when I was a child. It's quite possible that many Indians he knew as a child, youth and young adult, died or committed suicide before they turned twenty-five or fell victim to alcohol addiction, because many Indians tell the same story. Then he got a well-paying job with the federal government with good benefits, a pension plan, and lucky breaks on top of that; after surviving everything he went through, he got a lucrative federal government job, so he would naturally follow orders rather than rock the boat and lose his job.

In 1973 Gary talked about going to Bermuda for a holiday; then the British Columbia Association of Non-Status Indians hired him for two weeks travelling around British Columbia, counselling students with their career goals for $60 a day plus expenses. At that time there was a café in Merritt where you could get fish plus chips for 90¢. You got toast and salad with it, and a cup of coffee was 10¢. At the bus stop at the college, there was a café that advertized toast and coffee for 40¢, so with $60 there were places he could have gone to sixty times for fish and chips or 150 times for toast and coffee.

I started sleeping more lightly at lunchtime and sometimes didn't even sleep at all. Other times, I couldn't sleep until I started thinking about sex, so I thought looking after Jennifer might be over soon. I went back to Chilliwack again on the third weekend of August and took Jennifer to Laughing Raven for a wedding. She didn't want me to go to the wedding because she said Geraldine and her son Riley were still mad at me, but when I saw them, they weren't mad at me; but I still stayed home to look after her niece's baby since she couldn't find a babysitter.

By September I had a hard time going to sleep until I accepted that *something great* is coming, then I slept heavily. I went to Chilliwack on the weekend since it was a long weekend, and at times I felt so happy it was practically impossible for me to get mad. Aaron and Jennifer weren't getting along because Aaron would disappear, not say where he was, and didn't stay home to look after her when she was sick with pneumonia. However, over the years, I often wondered how he put up with her fits of anger. Jennifer went out with another fellow named Stanley that weekend but wouldn't tell me his last name. I visited her in Agassiz and found the marked copy of her term paper "Plight of the Native Elderly" and was really happy to find it because now I had documented proof of how Canadians react to the truth that I could show to influential people. Such things happen, but proving them could be extremely difficult.

Since staff wouldn't let me sit with them during coffee breaks, I started sitting at my desk, writing letters to influential people and searching aboriginal websites. On August 24 I had exposed an incident that happened in 1995 to a staff member, so they threatened to fire me. I was told to only expose these issues when they're asked for, and I got scared and got rid of many things on my computer!

When I got back to work, I got a call from the bank saying I didn't write out my check properly for my Visa payment. That was the first time I ever did that, so I wondered if there was a reason why it happened. On the weekend I went back to Chilliwack and helped Jennifer find a place there. We found one that was rather expensive, but the managers were very nice people and they wanted a security deposit and the first month's rent. I helped her out but couldn't have done it if I didn't make the mistake on my Visa payment.

The next weekend, the third weekend of September, Jennifer's mother wound up in the hospital; so I went back to Chilliwack to visit her, and she forgot her charger for her cell phone at Aaron's trailer and asked me to go get it. When I got to the trailer, an old stray dog had shown up at Aaron's place. I went back to the hospital and read the paper to pass time. An old man, Keith, had his car stolen with his dog in it. Keith got his car back and offered a $500 reward for his dog with no questions asked, so I thought that might be his dog that showed up at Aaron's trailer.

I spent the night at the hospital and talked to Geraldine about saving Jennifer from suicide, and my mother saying she was beyond recovery when I first met her in 1980. Now she and Henry Jr. have a career and I'm trying to help Jennifer advance in her career. Jennifer had a course to go to the next day, so I helped her catch her ride then told Aaron that the stray dog might be Keith's and he was offering a $500 reward to get him back. Aaron called Keith, met him at the bank; and sure enough, it was his dog. Keith was happy to get his dog back but could only afford to give Aaron $150 since he was a pensioner. We didn't mind, and now Aaron had money to attend a family reunion, so I let him use my truck to attend. If it weren't for that dog showing up, Aaron wouldn't have had money to attend his family reunion.

The next day I helped Jennifer pack and move some of her things, and Aaron got mad because she was seeing Stanley. Jennifer said Aaron often took off on her and didn't tell her where he went, so she suspected he was doing drugs. I went back to Chilliwack again the next weekend, the first of October, and helped her move more of her things; but her mother was still in the hospital. I went back to work for a week then went back to Chilliwack again the next weekend because it was Thanksgiving and I would be taking a week of annual leave.

Nothing eventful happened that week, and I went back to work for a week and stayed home the next weekend. I called Jennifer on Sunday, and she was at the hospital because her mother wasn't doing very well; then I called her again the next day and she wouldn't answer the phone, so I knew something was wrong. She called me at 10:35 a.m. and said her mother passed away that morning. Later on she called again and got mad at me for telling Aaron and Patricia what happened. She said she would see me on Saturday, the funeral would be on Thursday or Friday, and sounded like she didn't want me to attend. She said she wouldn't need me for support because her family would all be there, and I thought her family may not make me welcome, so I may not go.

I called Jennifer on Tuesday, and she said the funeral would be on Thursday. I had enough hours built up to take Thursday and Friday off but took Wednesday off as well. I was sick but allowed to take one day off for a funeral. I helped Jennifer and Brenda buy a floral arrangement for the funeral, then they left because Jennifer wanted to be home when her mother was brought home, so I had to take the floral arrangement to Sto:lo Eagle. When I delivered it, I just dropped it off in Jennifer's car, said hi to Ben, Riley his oldest son, and Alvin. Then I said good-bye, and they were all surprised that I was leaving right away. Prayers were being held, but I wouldn't go in the house, so Geraldine went in and got Jennifer. When Jennifer went out, she asked me to attend the funeral so I could take pictures of the family. I actually wished she would have lived to see Jennifer advance to LPN, but unfortunately, that didn't happen.

My mother went with me to the funeral, but at church services we sat back, away from the family. Henry Jr. was happy I was sitting back, keeping my distance, but my mother and I left right after the burial and didn't stay for the dinner. I wanted to go for a steak dinner, but the restaurant we went to in Agassiz only served steak sandwiches. I thought that could be a sign for me not to be angry at that family because I actually wanted a T-bone steak and didn't care about the cost. Jennifer called the next day and asked why we didn't stay for the dinner, but my mother answered the phone and said it was too cold, so she just wanted to leave. I didn't want to say it was because I wanted to stay away from her family, and when I saw Jennifer later on, she said everyone asked where I was. Then everyone told her to take some food with her, so she gave it all to Stanley. I was really happy about that because I didn't want it!

I went back to work and only worked for a week then took the second week of November off in annual leave. I visited Jennifer, and we ran into Henry Jr. at the credit union. He invited her over to Sto:lo Eagle for supper, so I dropped her off then left right away. He wanted me to stay, but I left anyway. Then when I picked her up, we left right away to take her to a satellite medical clinic before they closed because she was sick again. Nothing eventful happened during my week off. but there was a psychic fair the next weekend. We saw Lora Schultz again for a psychic reading because she's very good, and we call her at home when we have a problem and want advice on what to do. Previously, Lora told me to call my book a work of fiction, but I told her I can't do that because it exposes too much of the truth and not many Canadians are willing to face the truth, let alone accept it. I would change people's names to protect their privacy, but I don't want people to think my book is fiction even though it may sound like fiction; and she said, "That's a great idea."

I was happy to get back to work because Jennifer was spending too much money, and when I got back, some staff realized I didn't get hired until I was thirty-five because no one would hire me. Then they knew it would be highly justified for me to say "Canadian film companies need not apply for my life story!"

Jennifer had been drinking quite heavily since the summer and Jane Byra, her therapist, said she's like a time bomb, and I often wondered if she could actually be very angry at her mother for not protecting her from her father. I called Jennifer during the week and told her that in some situations when children are badly abused by one parent, they hate the other parent for not protecting them; she may feel that way and not be aware of it.

I worked until the middle of December then took my usual two weeks off for holidays, and nothing eventful happened except that I got worried about Jennifer's drinking and not eating properly. I thought it was misery caused by Henry, Old Useless, so I had a letter ready to burn for him on Christmas Day because therapists said that if you've been badly hurt by someone and they die before you can confront them, writing them a letter and burning it has the same effect as confronting them. I had the letter ready for a few years now but finally decided to burn it on Christmas Day, then I registered Jennifer in Biology 12 at the college. I helped Jennifer wrap her Christmas presents even though she still lashed out at me and didn't even want me using her bathroom, so I wondered if that was happening because of how I treated Henry Jr. because she changed when I stopped feeling angry at him.

I burned the following letter on Christmas Day:

> Merry Christmas, Old Useless!   19 December 2005
>
> Merry Christmas, you *useless piece of shit*! I hope you're still miserable because everyone that was close to you when you were here, your niggers and their mates, are still miserable because of you! Everyone but Alvin!
>
> You knew *full* well I was literally going through *hell* trying to save Jennifer, your nigger, from suicide and get her a career so she can do something with her life! All you ever

did was mooch off me and make my life miserable and looking after your nigger even harder! You knew full well you were making my life miserable all those years you were mooching off me! When I ruined visits with your family, it was *payback time*!

If it were Alvin trying to save Brenda from suicide and get her a career, you and your niggers would have done everything you could to *help* him! Then no one would be able to do enough for him! You wouldn't even buy me a cup of coffee and even got mad at me for borrowing your lawn chairs when I got Andrew a job patrolling a fire! Even now your niggers can't do enough for Alvin and treat me like an *outcast!*

If you were such a hardworking man, why did your kids have to work and go hungry so you could drink? Why were you always mooching off me and making my life *miserable?* If that trip to see Isadore Tom for Jennifer's wrist wasn't just an excuse to mooch off us, why didn't you pay for it! You wouldn't even pay for your own coffee and wouldn't ever pull a stunt like that on Alvin!

If Alvin saved Brenda from suicide then got her and Henry Jr. a career, your niggers wouldn't be able to do enough for him! It was Jennifer, so it was no big deal! She's not important to anyone, especially your family! Even you acted like it was no big deal because all you ever did was mooch off me and make life miserable for me! Then you got mad when I said you sure didn't mooch off Alvin and make life miserable for him! I helped your youngest son get a career, and he treats me like an outcast and can't do enough for Alvin!

Even Geraldine was a hindrance in trying to get Jennifer a career and acts like saving Jennifer from suicide and helping her and Henry Jr. get a career was no big deal! If it were Alvin, she wouldn't be able to do enough for him, and now she's trying to tell me I can't come out with my book! She's part of your family through and through!

When the headstones were laid at Liz and Jeremy's grave site and you cried a river, I wanted to say, "Did you lose your *wallet*? Your money's far more important to you!" When she was a child, you wouldn't look after your responsibilities as a parent, yet you made your kids put your socks and shoes on for you! Then you grumbled about buying them second hand clothes and charged her for babysitting Allan when she was really down on her luck! When you stopped off where she was working, you even expected her to pay for your coffee! Look at how you treated me after everything I went through to save Jennifer from suicide! The only thing that stopped me was that I would have set both Jeremy's family and your niggers against me!

You tried to get your son to quit school because he couldn't give you any money, then you called him down for making it! Did you want him to end up a *useless piece of shit like you*! *If you thought choosing the tape* Kickboxer *would make up for the karate tournament I missed because of you, why didn't you pull the same stunt on Alvin!*

Even if you eventually bought me a cup of coffee, you probably would have said that should make up for the cup of coffee you were too cheap to buy me when we were really down on our luck! If you wanted me to forgive you, why didn't you mooch off Alvin, make life miserable for him, then tell him he's obligated to you because you did *everything* for him? You couldn't do enough for him then didn't even expect him to get up and help you when you couldn't walk! You actually expected me to walk across the room and do it!

When your granddaughter Amanda committed suicide, I tried to tell everyone to just let you stay home and save your money! They knew what I was trying to say but wouldn't give me a chance to say it!

When Emily passes away, being a pallbearer, paying for the funeral, and doing the burial are all *Alvin's* responsibilities!

If not, I don't even want to drink the water at your *house of misery*! Once Emily passes away, I'm going off on a big celebration because hopefully I'll never set foot on the Sto:lo Eagle reserve again, unless I find a woman there from another family! But I don't even want to know your family after that! Emily's funeral is your last chance to make life miserable for *Alvin*! If that's not done, I don't want to hear your family name for the rest of my life!

If being confronted is painful, that's nothing compared to the pain and misery you caused everyone around you! The only reason why I didn't wish you would *just commit suicide* is because some of your niggers might follow you! Then I thought I would rather see you live to be one hundred and suffer every minute of it! If you actually had a *happy home*, I would like to know what a *miserable home* is.

Even Alvin said if he comes back in another life and hears your family name, he'll shoot himself even though you and your niggers can't do enough for him! You called yourself *the man*! But if you were even half a man, the world would be a better place!

Your Ostracized Son-in-Law
Baxter!

Other than that, nothing eventful happened, but I felt some relief though!

Chapter 28

2006

The Christmas holidays weren't very stressful, but I spent more money than I wanted to spend as usual; normally it takes a month for me to unwind from Christmas, but not this year. I was working on an information package about the Indian residential schools and their effects on the survivors and the families of survivors, titled "Assimilation". Uncle Joe was interested in this information and was quite surprised at how Henry Jr. treated me compared to how he treated Alvin.

Since New Year's Day was on a Sunday, I had Monday off for a holiday. Jennifer seemed to be getting better, and I felt better after getting her off to work in the afternoon. She started treating me the way I treat her family but changed when I stopped feeling angry toward them. On TV there was a documentary on making the movie *Skins*, starring Graham Greene. In that documentary, Graham stated that an Indian medicine man said the poison must be exposed before a wound can be healed. Unfortunately, the painful truth of incest and child sexual abuse has to be exposed before the victims can heal the cause of their problems.

I went back to work on Tuesday and Jennifer said the college called and she didn't have the prerequisites for Biology 12, so I called the college to appeal it, but their computers were down that day. Then I tried calling Jennifer in Sto:lo Eagle two times, and Andrew answered the phone; the first time he wasn't very friendly, and I wondered if it was because I didn't stay long at their mother's funeral. Perhaps he didn't know Henry Jr. makes me *totally unwelcome* yet can't do enough for Alvin, but the second time I called, he was more friendly. I called Lora Schultz, and she reminded me that in her psychic reading, she said January would be off to a rough start.

The next week, I helped Jennifer get her books and lab coat, so she was accepted in the course. It looked like I was better off not to make my RRSP contributions again. Jennifer also came to Squamish, so I could help her study, but she was still cranky. She went to the bars one night, which stressed me out, but she still got some studying done. In the second week of January, a staff member sent out an e-mail asking for people interested in working in continuous improvement. She knew I could come up with some really good ideas but wouldn't apply because I was tired of how everyone treats me. I went back to Chilliwack on the weekend to help Jennifer with her studies. We got lots of work done on Sunday, and I took Monday off to help her some more. She was going to come back to Squamish with me, but Henry Jr. offered to help her study.

I felt really good on Tuesday morning, and Jennifer came to Squamish on Wednesday so I could help her study. She caught up with her homework and was doing good on her assignments, but it was very stressful. We both felt like giving up, hoped everything would work out but felt like she wasn't going to make it and taking the course was more trouble than it's worth. I went back to Chilliwack again on the weekend, the third weekend of January, and helped her with her studies and at work. She had her hours cut back, so she didn't have as much money as she needed, and I was getting concerned about how much it was going to cost me. On Sunday I helped her do some more studying, then we finally decided it's getting too hard on both of us emotionally and financially. On Monday I decided her going back to school right now was a mistake.

On Tuesday, Jennifer was stressed out, went to the bars, and lost her cell phone; then on Wednesday she said the course was going to cause her a breakdown, so I told her to either audit the course or drop it. Then we felt incredible relief when she decided to just drop the course. She asked me to go back to Chilliwack again on the weekend to help her get another cell phone. She was putting me deeper in debt now because she was still addicted to suffering, so I thought to myself, *Thank you, Piglet!* referring to Henry.

On Monday I called Joy Ward, and she was happy to hear from me and wanted an "Assimilation" package. On Tuesday, the end of the month, Jennifer called me at the office and said she was in a hit-and-run, so I told her to call ICBC and had trouble getting her to do it. She was also worried that $100 from work could be missing because she was too tired to think straight. January had been a rough month right up to the end. Then a week later on Thursday night, Jennifer called and said she was in another accident; someone rear-ended her, which stressed me out, but I didn't drink. Then two days later, Jennifer called me at one o'clock in the morning crying because she fell, hurt herself, and was bleeding from her nose. She was trying to visit Stanley, but he wouldn't answer his phone. I tried calling him to help her, but he wouldn't answer, so I called Jennifer back and told her to call an ambulance. Then I called her back again several times, but she wouldn't answer, but later on she called me and was at the hospital. I went back to Chilliwack again the next night to see Jennifer and give her emotional support, and on Saturday we talked to Stanley, and he thought Jennifer and I should get back together. When I went back to work on Tuesday, Jennifer asked me to call Lora and ask why she's been having so much bad luck. Lora said it's from chasing after Stanley and they should just stay friends and told me I should contact *Sharing Circle* about doing a documentary on what I went through to get a career.

I called Joy Ward the next day, and she was really excited about the information I told her I would be sending her and agreed that I should change the names of some of the people involved and where they live, to protect their privacy. I stayed home the next weekend to get a letter ready for *Sharing Circle* and the covering letter to "Assimilation" on Saturday, then on Sunday I got all the information ready to send out and mailed the packages on Monday.

I went to Chilliwack again the next weekend; and Jennifer said Henry Jr. had asked her to meet him, Cecelia, and the kids at Manning Park to go skiing, and went to the bars that night. So I visited Aaron at his trailer. Later that evening, Jennifer caught a ride to the trailer with a fellow named Peter that she met in the bars. It seemed like she still drinks and puts herself in rather risky situations.

I thought I would have a day to myself, but Jennifer wanted me to drive her to Manning Park, and when we got there, Henry Jr. looked rather serious because I was there. Andrew was in Henry Jr.'s truck and got kind of cranky because he knew I wanted as little to do with that family as possible. I wasn't going to ski to try and keep my distance from them, but Jennifer wanted me to ski, and one of Cecelia's daughters was really nice to me. After skiing, Henry Jr. told Jennifer they were having a dinner for Cecelia and she was allowed to go and sounded like he didn't want me to go. Jennifer thought the dinner was for her, but I told her it was for Cecelia. When we got back to Chilliwack, I dropped Jennifer off at a Chinese restaurant then went to her place and waited for her to call when she was ready to be picked up. When I got there, she was by herself and there was a piece of cake on the table. I asked if it was Cecelia's birthday, but she just said it was none of my business. Jennifer was either trying to get me out of her life because of Stanley or lashing out because that's what she learned from the Piglet.

We went to visit Aaron, and road conditions were wet and slippery because of snow, but Jennifer wanted to go to Abbotsford to see the movie *Walk the Line*. I wondered if she was trying to stress me out or get me to have fun because she used to always hold me back from having fun, but I followed my instincts when they told me "everything is going to work out." I wasn't going to get depressed because my family was always jealous of seeing me have fun in life. Now I'm ready to punch them in the head if they try doing that again.

In early March I knew Jennifer was drinking heavily because of anger, so I wondered if she should go to hypnotism to work on her anger to try and slow down on her drinking and break her addiction to suffering. I called Lora, and she didn't think it was a good idea. She said the psychic fair was going to Chilliwack next month, so I worked on my writing some more and didn't realize how stressful it still was. In the middle of March, I went to a coaching-skills workshop and enjoyed it. I couldn't drink coffee because it would make me shake, so I knew my stress level was going down. I also learned more about myself and why I act the way I do. I decided to use my own initiative from now on and not listen to my family because you can only call yourself a victim for so long. I also started feeling sick like a flu was coming, and my throat was getting sore.

We saw Lora Schultz at a psychic fair that month, and she really made me feel good. She told me I had to forgive *Old Useless*, Henry, for Jennifer to heal completely and also forgive myself for staying angry at him. I told Lora that I seem to sense spirits watching me when I go to the office after hours to write letters and wondered if it's my imagination. She said it's not my imagination and one spirit is crying, so I hoped it was *Old Useless* feeling *guilty* about how he treated me. Lora said I should bury some food he liked, so I thought about wild game if I got something hunting that fall; but she said that would be waiting too long, so I decided to bury some of our traditional foods, wind-dried salmon, smoked fish, rice, and a thermos of tea. I wondered if he realized how much his family lashes out at me because of how he treated them. She said Henry Jr. will invite me to his wedding, but it's going to be just as hard for him to invite me as it is for me to attend.

At the end of March, Jennifer called and was depressed because she was sick again. She got an all-expense-paid trip to Mexico from where she works and asked me for some spending money. Since it was close to her birthday, I gave it to her as a birthday present. I was still sick with a sore throat but didn't sleep at lunchtime very much, and in the first week of April, I got a letter from the Southern Poverty Law Center in Montgomery, Alabama, saying they were considering putting some of my information from "Assimilation" in their newsletter.

Easter was on the second weekend of April that year, and I buried some food on Henry's grave on Good Friday in Sto:lo Eagle. Before I buried it, I said the following words to him, "*Hello*, Piglet! You wanted your niggers to be a white Indian like you! That didn't happen because of me! I helped two of your kids get a career! I have to forgive you for Jennifer to heal *fully*! Emily was the only one in that family who wanted me to help Jennifer get a career! Unfortunately, your family pushed me to the point where I wouldn't even stay for the dinner after her funeral! Even Alvin may be miserable because he can't even hug his own daughter because of you! I have to forgive myself for being angry at you because I knew you suffered!" Then I buried the food! I thought about stopping and saying hi to Henry Jr. but changed my mind.

I kept going to work in April even though I was sick, and by the third week of April, Jennifer was really cranky over me writing my book and told me not to call her unless it was urgent. I had tried to get her to read a rough draft, but she wouldn't do it; then at the end of the month, she called me at my parents' place and wanted all her bills put in her name. I asked if she wanted me completely out of her life, and she said, "No, because I don't want to make enemies out of us." I thought she was just transferring her anger on me to avoid facing the truth even though it wasn't her fault.

In early May, the staff got a book titled *55 Years of the Vancouver Forest District/Coast Forest Region*. I wondered how many Indians were in it and the staff saw what I was doing. I was the only one, and that was for our lottery ticket winnings, not for work. I kept going to work even though I wasn't feeling well, and at the end of the week, two ladies at work told me to go to the doctor because I was coughing so much. I've been sick for at least a month now and finally went to the doctor at a satellite medical clinic. I met Cindy Lewis there, a lady I went to college with in 1973, and we talked about things that were going on in our lifetime; and people who heard us were probably surprised that these things had actually gone on in our lifetime.

The next week I took four days off work then went back to work on Friday even though I wasn't feeling very well. I went back to Chilliwack for the weekend, and Jennifer still drank and put herself in dangerous situations. She said Geraldine and Brenda were also mad at me over my book coming out, and Aaron suggested I go to my parents' place that night. On Saturday, Jennifer worked until four o'clock in the afternoon; then I took her shopping in Bellingham. I was sick and didn't want to go, but at least I kept her out of the bars and hoped it would make her feel better. Jennifer was scared that something could have happened to her when she was drinking, but I told her my instincts tell me nothing happened. She wouldn't listen, so she called Lora, and Lora also said nothing happened.

I went back to work even though I was sick and to do late check-in, because I needed the money but was coughing so much it disturbed the lady in the cubicle next to me, so I went home. I went back to Chilliwack again for the long weekend in May even though I was sick, and Jennifer was rather cranky and told me I should have gone to the doctor. I visited Patricia Kelly that weekend, and she said Jennifer was really lucky to have me help her out the way I do. I went to a doctor at a satellite clinic again, and he said I had a virus that could last two weeks more.

Since Monday was a holiday and I had asked for the forms to fill out at work because I would be off work for more than five days and had to go back to Squamish for X-rays, I stayed in Chilliwack for two days because Jennifer had her car brought to an auto-body shop for repairs but was given a courtesy car. I went home Wednesday, and at one o'clock in the morning, Jennifer called and said she bumped something in the courtesy car while she was on her way to visit Aaron. I got scared and tried to tell her to stay home and not drive anywhere, but she wouldn't listen; so I wondered if part of this was happening because I still had a hard time forgiving Piglet, Henry.

I went for X-rays and to the doctor the next day, and Jennifer called me from Aaron's place, upset over what happened. She didn't remember where she hit something that put a dent in the car, and I told her she should listen to people who try to help her. I went back to Chilliwack, picked them up, and we looked around for the hubcap she lost and where the accident could have happened. Then we went back to the auto-body shop, and the manager was calm about everything and said he would get an estimate of what it would cost to fix the car. I had been so stressed out that I forgot my medical card at the hospital and my forms in Squamish, then I thought, *Maybe something good may come tomorrow.*

The next day, Jennifer said she can't keep running and has to face reality; she tried to escape reality by drinking then realized that's not the answer. The results of drinking were worse than the results of not drinking. There were canoe races and an Indian festival at Seabird Island, so I dropped Jennifer off there on Saturday. I wanted to go, but I wasn't feeling well. I picked her up in Agassiz the next day, and she was still cranky toward me and didn't even want me talking to her family and said she didn't want me to make her a martyr.

I didn't go back to work that week because I was still sick, and on Monday I picked Jennifer up after work, then we went to visit Aaron. She flipped out and took a taxi to town; then I realized that I have to completely let go of my anger toward Henry or she may just carry on that way. Jennifer said she was stressed out over me coming out with my book, so I started hoping something positive actually came of Henry's time on earth, then I felt relief right away and hoped Jennifer would start feeling better. Jennifer came back in the morning and I drove her to work. She was still stressed out though, and damage to the courtesy car would cost $1,226, but I still felt she got off lightly though and didn't get caught drinking and driving. Then when Aaron got home from work, he got stressed out and told me to leave, so I wondered if it was because I'm writing my book and they don't want me to do it.

On Wednesday I visited Jennifer at work and she was nice to me, didn't lash out at me, and asked me to phone her later on; and I felt really good when I tuned my mind in to see what was coming. On Thursday, June 1, I was thinking of making my RRSP contributions when Ed Kelly, my cousin, called my parents' place for me. At first he thought he was talking to my dad then offered me a seven-millimeter

Remington Magnum rifle with a Leupold scope for $900. Isaac and his black friend Chris both said it was a great buy, so I bought it because I hoped to do lots of hunting when I found the time.

On Saturday I drove Jennifer to work then went to the canoe races at Cultus Lake, talked to Ryan, Desiree, and Andrew a bit and thought Henry Jr. might invite me to his wedding. I didn't want to attend but would have gone if he invited me, but I definitely would have missed the dinner. Jennifer went to the bars in the evening, and I finally accepted that Henry suffered for what he did wrong because I clearly saw the things I was doing to him happening back to me. I still ignored it though because I wanted him to suffer as much as possible; however, I listened to signals telling me not to be angry at Henry Jr. Jennifer was nice to me the next day, didn't lash out at me, and even gave me her work schedule. Even Isaac gave me a spring salmon, so I thought the anger that I held toward Henry was coming back to me in all directions. Normally, Isaac is cranky toward me, so I don't say very much to him.

I came back to Squamish and tried to go back to work on Monday but was too sick, so after two hours, staff told me to just go home. I missed work for the rest of the week then went back to work the next week even though I was still sick. On Tuesday I got another letter from the Southern Poverty Law Center in Montgomery, Alabama, rejecting my submissions and sent back the information package titled "Assimilation". They said they only publish their newsletter two times a year and they get so many submissions they have to screen them. I didn't mind though because at least I got a response from them in writing.

I had fieldwork for the next three days, which wasn't too bad because it was mostly just driving around, but I was still sick; and on Friday I wanted to stay home, but Jennifer wanted me to go back to Chilliwack, so I went. She had asked for this weekend off to go to the canoe races in Lummi but had to work, then we argued slightly then went to bed at Aaron's trailer. She was stressed out over having to work this weekend when she had asked for time off, so she started drinking as soon as she woke up on Saturday morning. She said she can't stop drinking and laid some of the blame on me; so I drove them to town, went back to my parents' place, then came back to pick them up. Jennifer thought she lost her bank card, which also stressed her out, but she went back to work from eight o'clock to ten o'clock the next morning. She still talked about wanting to go to the Lummi canoe races, but I told her she didn't have time because she had to go back to work at four o'clock; so we drove around to garage sales, and she realized people often ruined my fun and her father did it deliberately. I told her I had enough hours built up to take Monday off; then she realized she had been compensated for her lost fun.

Nothing eventful happened for the rest of June, but the end of the month was a long weekend, so I went back to Chilliwack to visit Jennifer; and Henry Jr. got married on July 1. She was cranky the day before the wedding then called me at five forty-five in the morning to go to Sto:lo Eagle and help her get ready for the wedding. She said I could visit Ryan and Desiree because she knew I didn't want to go to her brother's place.

Rhonda was down from Kamloops for the wedding and stayed at Ryan's place. She told me how the Piglet drove her around and did everything for her, so I told her how he knew I was literally going through *hell* trying to save Jennifer from suicide and get her a career yet all he did was mooch off me and make life miserable for me. Then he turned around and said he did everything for us and we were obligated to him, but I still managed to get Jennifer and Henry Jr. a career and get absolutely no recognition for it and wasn't even invited to the wedding!

Jennifer went to the bars on Sunday then called me and asked me to pick her up and drive her to Aaron's trailer, so I picked her up; but when we got to the trailer, she really lashed out at me and told me to leave. She called me again at six thirty the next morning and asked me to drive her to her place to get changed then drive her to work. She didn't remember lashing out at me, but she got a letter from the Residential School Settlement regarding compensation for going there and the letter asked if it was a fair settlement. I asked if I could bring it back to Squamish with me so I could write to them and say Canada got off extremely lightly for how the Indians have been treated, tell them what it's like to have parents who survived those schools, and we're still suffering incredibly because of what they went through. Jennifer still lashed out at me, and it took an awful lot to let me have the package for two weeks just so I could voice my opinion.

I went back to work, and on Thursday night I couldn't sleep, so I worked on the letter to the Residential School Settlement at three thirty in the morning. Then at 6:35 a.m., I *finally* realized the seriousness of not being invited to Henry Jr.'s wedding after everything I went through to save his sister from suicide and get both of them a career! I stayed home the next weekend and worked on a letter regarding the Residential School Settlement because the deadline to voice opinions was August 25. I thought what they were offering was an insult and Canada was getting off without even a slap on the wrist for all the suffering the Indians went through because of the residential schools then being held back by the government when we tried to do something for ourselves! Jennifer called on Sunday and lost her cell phone again. I often worried about how much she's been drinking but don't know what to do about it, but in the morning, I started feeling really good.

I went back to Chilliwack again the next weekend, the second weekend of July. Jennifer went to a wedding and I worried about her drinking but felt really good like I don't have to worry. I picked her up the next morning, drove her to work, then went to my parents' place. My mother took me out for breakfast and I told her how staff at work treat me and about Wesley Pierre committing suicide. She got depressed because she didn't know he committed suicide; then I told her he also cut himself up with a knife two times and lost his front teeth in a car accident, then realized the waitresses and customers were listening to me. I took Jennifer shopping after work, and she tried to accept that what happened to her wasn't her fault and she seemed to be getting better.

I stayed home the next weekend and worked on my letter and information package to the Residential School Settlement. I rushed to get it in well before the August 25 deadline and had it ready by Monday and included the letters that I wrote to *Sharing Circle* and other information. I went to the post office to register it, and the clerk who wouldn't register an information package to Amnesty International looked at it and thought she wouldn't register it; but I was served by another clerk, so in the next information package I sent out, I reported how she wouldn't register some of my letters.

I visited Jennifer again the next weekend then went back to work even though I was feeling sick again. I also had late check-in that week and needed the money. On Friday, Jennifer called me at 8:10 a.m., depressed and drinking because Stanley found another girlfriend, and she wanted to move to Nanaimo. Gurdeep called and was now living in Squamish and wanted to put some of my articles in his magazine, so I said he could as long as he changed her name.

I also got a letter from the Residential School Settlement saying my information would be forwarded to the appropriate court. It was the first weekend of August and a long weekend, so Jennifer asked me to go to Chilliwack because she had two days off; and on my way, I also decided to send a copy of "Assimilation" to the Residential School Settlement.

On Sunday night Jennifer went to Aaron's trailer and lashed out at me, then on Monday she slept most of the day and I was still coughing, heavily at times. Then on Monday she worked from four o'clock in the afternoon to midnight then at eight o'clock the next morning because they were short of workers. I did some brushing of my trees then felt really sick and coughed so heavily that coughing hurt my head. I was only going to take one day off, but Jennifer wanted me to take a whole week off. I called in sick on Tuesday morning and checked into getting Jennifer's transcripts so she could apply for licensed practical nurse (LPN), training at Sprott-Shaw Community College. It's a private college, but their training is recognized by the association of LPNs. Jennifer was drinking quite heavily, got really cranky, and lashed out at Aaron and me; then we went for an interview and she had all the required courses except for Biology 12.

Although I was off work for another week, by Sunday I was still coughing heavily and spitting up yellow goo, then I tried to accept that Henry admitted that he was suffering for everything he had done wrong in his life when he was in the hospital in 1990. I knew he suffered, but I still couldn't swing back at him hard enough for how he treated me. I went back to work even though I was still sick, and did some fieldwork but couldn't work as hard as I normally do; and on Friday I was coughing so much it disturbed other staff, so I was told to go to the doctor again. Jennifer called and asked me to go back to Chilliwack. I had enough hours to take Monday off as well, so I stayed and helped her straighten out her apartment. Spending the day with her was stressful, but I felt good at times. I went to the bank, and on my way back, I saw a black male driving a freight truck for a major grocery-store chain and told him that if he was an Indian, he would be lucky if he even got an interview.

I went back to work even though I was still sick, and Jennifer wanted me to go back on the weekend. I wanted a weekend of rest, but on Saturday night, she called and asked me to go get her. She said she had been drinking and lost her wallet with $300 in it, so I rushed to

Chilliwack to see her, but she was gone. I called her home and she was there but didn't turn her phone off after the call so I couldn't call her again, but my instincts told me everything was all right, so I went over to Aaron's. Jennifer called the next day and said she had her wallet but she was really sick. She was sick all day then came back to Squamish with me. I was still sick and was starting to feel better, but Jennifer was sick all day Monday; in the evening she started lashing out at me, so I knew she was getting better.

On August 30 I was getting annoyed at Jennifer's irresponsible spending habits, but my instincts told me everything was going to work out, and Gurdeep called and asked me to meet him the next day. The next day I realized that by looking after Jennifer instead of advancing to RPF, I'll probably make far more money through my life story than if I had become an RPF and worked as a professional forester. I gave Gurdeep an information package that I was going to use to find a publisher and some videos that I got from the National Film Board of Canada. I followed the proverb, "If you put people ahead of things, everything will find its place," and things seemed to be working out quite well.

The next weekend, the first weekend of September, was a long weekend; so I went back to Chilliwack. I saw Patricia Kelly when I dropped some information packages off at Uncle Joe's, and we rather mutually agreed that she may not edit my life story. She's a very nice-looking girl but didn't seem interested in me. On Monday I brought Aaron some tobacco and groceries and he was cranky, so I wondered if he was on drugs and if I should stop visiting him, but he called and apologized the next day. I had enough hours built up to take three days off and could have booked in sick because I wasn't feeling well; then on Friday and Saturday, I went to BCIT for a seminar to prepare for the registered forest technologist (RFT) exam.

I worked for a week; then the next week, I did the late check-in, so I kept working even though I was sick. Then I decided to give the group of Canadians I told the *full* details of how Jennifer's family treated me after everything I did for them written permission to expose it to try and justify changes as long as they used the fictional names that I had chosen for them. I finally realized that when I was at BCIT, there was an East Indian student would have been accepted but he chose to be alone and there was also a small Filipino student who was accepted, but the Indians were closed off.

I tried calling Alvin that week, but Brenda answered and sharply said he doesn't even want to talk to me anymore. I thought she would just hang up, but she said, "Good-bye!" then hung up. That felt so good I wanted to celebrate but thought I better wait until the weekend because I was sick and doing late check-in. On Friday I went out for Chinese food then went home so full I couldn't drink. I called Aaron that night and told him that if Alvin ever did as much as I did for that family, they wouldn't be able to do enough for him; the only way they're ever going to stop me from coming out with my life story is if Alvin ever did that much for them and got the exact same treatment that I got, then I would burn everything!

I stayed home for the weekend and studied for my registered forest technologist's exam, put on by the Association of BC Forest Professionals (ABCFP) for forest technicians to write an exam after a minimum of two years' forestry experience to become an RFT. If a forest technician had enough work experience, they only had to write the first half of the exam; but on the application, there was an optional question, "Are you aboriginal?" so I said yes, thinking nothing of it. Then I was told I had to write the *full* exam, and I appealed it but had to be careful of what I said because they threatened to fire me for exposing the truth. I told them what they saw on my BCIT transcripts was only the second half of what I went through to get a career and had many things holding me back and slowing me down. You may not believe what I went through in the first half and what was going on all the time I was getting my career, but they wouldn't budge.

I had been calling Joy Ward about my life story, and she was one of the chosen few who heard the full details of how Jennifer's family treated me. She was getting more excited the more I spoke to her because I still kept her in suspense of what went on. She also mentioned Lorna O'Toole might be able to help me find a publisher and had connections with film companies who might be interested in my life story.

I stayed home again the next weekend to study for the exam, but on Wednesday night, Jennifer called and lashed out at me. She said Geraldine and Brenda were both mad at me for coming out with my book. I wondered if Geraldine sensed that I exposed how she reacted toward me when I first met Jennifer and kept putting her back in school yet she didn't even want us together. Then Jennifer called the next day and didn't remember lashing out at me, and I said, "Psychics said you survived to tell the story"; but she snapped, "I'll tell the story when I'm good and ready!"

I was still feeling sick even though I had been resting up. I was allowed to take two days off to study for the RFT exam but only took a half day off before the exam. We had to leave early to get to Vancouver to write the exam, and the staff were surprised that I was the only one out of ten people who had to write the *full* exam even though I got my diploma years before some of them. I mentioned that to the fellow monitoring the exam, Rob Wood; and he was told my application was sent in late, so they made me write the full exam. I said they were all sent in the same package and I was probably the first one to have my application ready, and he said, "Hey! I only work here."

Since it was Thanksgiving weekend, I took the next week off in annual leave and went to Chilliwack, and Jennifer's job was still stressing her out. Previously, Lora said she was transferring her anger from what was really bothering her to her job and saying her job was stressing her out, but I still helped her look around for another job and another apartment. On Friday she went to visit Aaron and admitted she has to love herself before anyone can love her, and I was starting to forgive people who had done injustices to me in the past. She also found a new apartment, and it looked like the landlords were going to give it to her.

On Sunday, October 15, a program on Global TV titled *Listen Up* stated the churches were told, "Kill the Indian in the child!" by the Canadian government. I sometimes wondered about that because Indians from across Canada told the same story about how they were treated in the Indian residential schools no matter which Christian faction operated the school.

In the fourth week of October, the staff were sent to a course in Abbotsford titled *Investment in Excellence*, training about overcoming obstacles that prevent people from achieving their goals. It made me feel really good even though I applied similar things that I learned from books that I already read. Previously I thought I'd come as far as I was going to go in my career then realized I could go even further. I was finally able to get Lorna O'Toole's phone number and called her. She talked about movies, documentaries, getting my life story published, legal implications, knew a good copyright lawyer, and sounded anxious for me to copyright my life story.

I went to Chilliwack for the weekend, and two people from my reserve died in a house fire and there were suspicions that they were murdered. The funeral was the next Friday, so I went back to Chilliwack Thursday night. Jennifer was going to go to a rock concert Friday night, but it was postponed because the lead singer got sick. She went to the bars Thursday night, stressed me out, and wanted me to spend time with her the next day; but I wanted to go to the funerals. She went to the bars again the next night then called me to take her home, but someone played the juke box, so she got up and danced. Then she went to the cabaret and the place was cited for serving her when she had too much to drink, so she was told to leave by the police, who were in plainclothes. When we got to the truck, she really flipped out and lashed out at me; kicked the dashboard of my truck, breaking the dials on the radio; then took her clothes off and said I lowered her self-esteem, dignity, and self-respect, exactly what Piglet did to her! She broke the zipper on my coat, ripped some buttons off my shirt, tried to run off naked; but I dragged her back, and eventually she calmed down. Then I drove her to Aaron's trailer, and she didn't have her shoes, so I had to go back and get them.

The next day I called Lora for a psychic reading over the phone; it was very good. Then I told Jennifer I would put the writing on disks in my safety-deposit box at the bank, so she felt better but wanted the key to my box. I agreed and that took a huge load off her mind and she stated feeling better right away. She also agreed to read my manuscript before she would make a decision on what to do with it. It appeared to me that she mainly wanted to control what's going on; then she started talking about writing her own life story.

I turned fifty-one that week and Jennifer took me out to the Keg, a chain restaurant that specializes in steaks, for my birthday; and in the afternoon, I called Lorna O'Toole about my manuscript for her to read, and she mentioned a confidentiality contract. I was also asked to participate in a karate demonstration at a mall in Richmond where most of the stores are owned by Orientals. I felt good that Allan Chan, the head instructor in Vancouver, wanted me to participate; so I attended.

I went back to work, but before I went back, I helped Jennifer apply for work where a new home for the elderly was being built in Sardis. That's closer to where she lives and the kind of work she was trained for and wanted to get into. She was called and told to take a two-day course in medical administrative-assistance living first. They would hire her after she took the course, so she started feeling better. I was supposed to go to the hospital in North Vancouver for breathing tests, but the highway was shut down because of trees blowing over, so I went back to the office. I still felt sick, but I was getting better; and on the weekend, Gurdeep brought my manuscript back because he was going to India for a month. He suggested I self-publish my book in India, and he could help me do it and agreed that it's a very beautiful story.

I worked all week even though I was still sick and went back to Chilliwack for the weekend. Jennifer was going to move to her new apartment and was moving this weekend. It was also the only time help was available because everyone was working. We helped the former tenants move their things out first because it was heavy and they couldn't move it themselves; then Jennifer went to the rock concert Saturday night with Henry Jr. and his wife. I was happy about it because it snowed and he drove them to Vancouver and she spent the night in Sto:lo Eagle. Jennifer called me the next morning as she was on her way back to Chilliwack, and it was near white-out conditions, snowing and blowing so hard you couldn't see where you're going.

We got the big things moved into Jennifer's apartment, but it was stressful. We had help, but Aaron had hurt his hip, so I didn't call him; but he was still mad about it. It snowed heavily and highways were shut down, so I stayed at Jennifer's place, and on Monday I decided to stay in Chilliwack because I had enough hours built up to take three days off. I helped Jennifer finish packing and moving her things; then Aaron called. He had run out of diesel for his heater, was freezing in his trailer, and scared to go to sleep because if the electricity went off, he could freeze to death! I picked him up, bought him something to eat, then helped him pack some clothes and move to Jennifer's place. He mainly just drove to help move things then spent the night at Jennifer's place. I went back to my parents' place to spend the night and pick up my things.

On Tuesday I helped Jennifer move the rest of her things; then Aaron and I helped her unpack and get settled. Then I decided to stay one more day because it was cold out and the roads were still icy. On

Wednesday morning I called the office to say I would be taking the rest of the week off because roads were bad and more snow was expected in the afternoon. We went to the bars that night for a few hours; then at two thirty in the morning, Jennifer told Aaron and me to leave, so I drove him to my parents' place. It was still snowing, so there was no traffic; but we were still nervous though because we had been drinking, but we made it to my parents' place. On Thursday I drove Aaron to Abbotsford to pick up his WCB check, which had been lost in the mail. Jennifer called and apologized for what she did, but Aaron was still mad at her. Jennifer's been really lashing out at us lately, but I still stayed until Sunday to help her unpack and get settled. She wanted me to stay longer and I didn't look forward to going back, not because staff close me off, but because I usually have nothing to do most of the time.

When I got back on Monday, I got my marks for the RFT exam and it said I barely passed the exam. We needed 60 percent to pass, and they said I got 60 percent in part A and 63 percent in part B. I felt *totally* disgusted and wondered, what happened? The letter said the following:

> November 27, 2006
>
> Annis Gregory Aleck, RFT
> Ministry of Forests & Range
> 42000 Loggers Lane
> Squamish, BC V0N 3G0
>
> Dear Mr. Aleck,
>
> We are pleased to inform you that you passed the 2006 RFT Registration Exam held on October 6, 2006. Congratulations!
>
> Your marks are as follows:
>
> | | |
> |---|---|
> | **Part A** | **60%** |
> | **Part B** | **63%** |
>
> Council approved your official status as Registered Forest Technologist (RFT) on November 27, 2006.

We would also like to take this opportunity to invite you to attend an Inductees' Luncheon at our Annual General Meeting (AGM). The ABCFP will cover the cost of your luncheon as congratulations for passing your exam.

This year we had an extra-ordinary number of people writing the exam (over 900 in total) due to the closing of the transition period for RFT memberships. Due to space constraints at the venues is impossible for us to honor all of the successful exam writers at the same Inductees' Luncheon. You are therefore invited to choose to attend the luncheon at ExpoFor 2007 in Harrison Hot Springs or at ExpoFor 2008 in Penticton. You may want to attend the Inductees' Luncheon in Penticton if you or your family live in the Okanagan or if you want to be part of the ABCFP's 60th anniversary celebrations. If you live close to Harrison Hot Springs, you may want to attend the 2007 Inductee's Luncheon. The option is yours. Whichever choice you make, you must register for the luncheon to ensure a seat is reserved for you. Of course, as our guest you will not be charged for your attendance.

The Harrison Hot Springs' Inductees' Luncheon will be held on February 22, 2007. Attire for the luncheon is semi-formal-business attire is expected. Please do not wear blue jeans. Information on the Penticton luncheon will be available at this time next year.

You may invite guests to the luncheon. Please make sure that they register and purchase the required meal ticket. The ExpoFor 2007 registration form is enclosed with your November/December issue of **BC Forest Professional.** Online registration will also be available on our website by late November.

The ABCFP is committed to ensuring that all inductees will be given the opportunity to attend an Inductees'

Luncheon and be introduced to their family and peers as full members of the profession. We thank you in advance for your patience as we try to ensure all inductees get their chance to attend and be recognized for the hard work and dedication required to become a fully registered member of the forestry profession.

Personally, and on behalf of the Board of Examiners and Council, I extend sincere congratulations and best wishes, once again, on your successful completion of all requirements for registration.

If you have any questions or concerns regarding this letter, please feel free to contact the Registration Department at 604.687.8026 or at *admissions@abcfp.ca*.

Yours truly

Jerome Marburg, LL.B
General Counsel & Registrar

Then on Monday, December 4, 2006, 3:16 p.m., I got this e-mail from Amanda Molson from the ABCFP:

Hello Annis,

Please be advised that the exam results that were mailed to you contained a processing error where the data from our database merged incorrectly into our form letter. Whether or not you passed the exam was not affected. Your correct marks are as follows

Part A	**60%**
Part B	**63%**

We apologize for any confusion that this may have caused. If you have any questions, please feel free to contact the registration department at 604-687-3264, or at *admissions@abcfp.ca*.

Thank You

Amanda Molson
Registration Coordinator
Association of BC Forest Professionals
Tel: (604) 331-2327
Fax: (604) 687-3264
Email: amolson@abcfp.ca

Website: www.abcfp.ca

Later on I got the e-mail from ABCFP saying my marks were reviewed and didn't change. I wondered if they did that because I fought unfair treatment right up to when I wrote the exam. One staff member who wrote the exam was told his marks went up; then I decided not to make any more suggestions unless it was for safety.

The next weekend, Jennifer asked me for some money for her fine for driving without insurance, so I put the money in her account; but the judge wouldn't accept her guilty plea because it wasn't her fault her pay wasn't deposited on time. She and Aaron drank that night and she flipped out again and the police went to her apartment. I wished there was something I could do for her because I know she's just transferring her anger from Henry to those who try to help her.

A staff member who was retiring at the end of January held the staff Christmas party at his place. Jennifer wanted me to go to Chilliwack that night, but I didn't go because I thought she was just trying to keep me from having fun again.

I took the last two weeks of December off in annual leave like I do every year, and on Monday, Aaron's parents dropped by and gave him a Ford Ranger 4×4. Now that he's not tied to living in his trailer, I hoped he would start being more responsible. Jennifer got called to work with the elders because all the other workers had booked in sick, but she jumped at the opportunity because she wanted to transfer to working with the elders. I wanted to start shopping early the next morning, but she was tired. She was supposed to have the next two days off as well but got called to work. That cut into her shopping time, but she was told they would try and transfer her to working with the elders. One elder patient Jennifer looked after had a bed they didn't want, so I offered to deliver it to Ryan Jr. in Hope. I called Ryan and arranged for him to help deliver it, and he told me he told all his siblings that if it weren't for me, Jennifer would have been an invalid; but I didn't tell him she would have committed suicide if it weren't for me.

I finally realized what Lora meant when she said I had to forgive myself for staying angry at Henry for Jennifer to heal. When I forgave myself for staying angry at him, I felt a big load come off my chest. Aaron had time off work and went for physiotherapy after hurting his hip then ended up staying at Jennifer's place because it was closer to his physiotherapy.

Christmas was uneventful, and after Christmas, I wanted to go back to work because I felt like I had been off for three weeks. Jennifer spends too much money when I'm around and was getting really cranky and telling me to leave in spite of how much I tried to help her out. Then on December 30, Geraldine called and said her husband's twin brother, Gerald, collapsed and died the day before. Jennifer and I went to Laughing Raven, and the next day I took her to see a psychic named Renel, who was originally from South Africa. Renel said the ABCFP couldn't fail me completely on my RFT exam, so they slashed my marks and that my marks should have been in the high 80s, in the top 5 percent of those who wrote the exam. I got really disgusted and told myself I would expose all this to influential people when I got more copies of the book *55 Years of the Vancouver Forest District/Coast Forest Region*!

Chapter 29

2007

On New Year's Day, Jennifer was cranky in the morning then told Aaron and me to leave even though we try to look after her. Aaron went partying with some friends then asked me to go back to his trailer to party with three men and four women, but the women all looked like addicts, so I didn't go. Then I went back to visit Jennifer and helped her get to work, and she asked me to stay at her place one more night. She said Aaron could stay too but no visitors, so I picked him up and took him to Jennifer's place. Aaron couldn't make it to his physiotherapy the next day because he was sick. I still had a sore throat and felt like I've been off work for a month and wanted to go back to get away from Jennifer. I went back to work for two days then took Friday off to attend Gerald's funeral and was surprised to see Henry Jr. there but didn't say very much to him. Two weeks later, Jennifer called me early in the morning, angry and stressed out because her car got towed. She had been drinking, flipped out, got mad at Aaron, then went to sleep in her car. Then the police went and had her car towed away, so she called me the next day for some money to help her get her car back. It bothered me, but my instincts told me not to worry about it.

I kept going to work even though I was still feeling sick, and in the third week of January, I finally made the suggestion that all Forest Service vehicles should have fluorescent triangles in them in the event of an accident, vehicle breakdown, or coming upon the scene of an accident. That's been on my mind ever since I started this job, but I finally spoke up. I sent it to the district manager as a suggestion for our next staff meeting, but he sent it directly to the clerical supervisor to carry it out. In early February I started feeling sick again. My throat was still sore, but at least I wasn't coughing like I was before; and by the middle of the month, I was still feeling sick.

I finally managed to contact Lorna O'Toole again and agreed to meet her at a karate instructor's meeting in Surrey and gave her a rough draft of my manuscript. She was really enthusiastic about helping me out with getting my book published and liked my information packages on Canada's treatment of aboriginals and other minorities and thought the information packages were to be kept confidential like my manuscript, but I told her that information was meant to be exposed.

In the third week of February, I went to my Inauguration for passing the RFT exam but only went because it was in Harrison Hot Springs. There were many people there, and people who knew me got angry when they heard that I had to write the *full* exam. Jennifer was supposed to have the day off but got called in because other workers had booked in sick. She needed time off to go to a course and was getting burnt out. Then she got stressed out because she had to go back to work, so she went to the bars after work and stayed out late. I went to get her; but that got her angry, so she didn't go home until three forty-five in the morning and just told me to leave. I slept in her car then went to wake her at five o'clock; but she couldn't get up, so I pretended to leave but slept at her place until six fifteen then went to see Aaron and asked him to take Jennifer to Rosedale to pick up her car when she wanted it back.

I went back to the inauguration, which was going on for two more days, and arranged for Jennifer to take the medical administration course at a later date. People congratulated me for passing the exam, which made me feel good, and restored some of my faith in Canada. I was tired at the end of the day and worried about Jennifer's drinking and was surprised that my instincts told me that everything was going *great*! On the third day of the inauguration, I ran into old friends and made new acquaintances who were also surprised that I had to write the full exam. I sometimes wondered if I was the first aboriginal to graduate in the forestry program at BCIT, and a fellow who used to instruct there told me I was. Then I was given some Douglas fir seedlings, which I planted on my reserve, and felt good about my inauguration.

On Saturday, Jennifer worked with the elders during the day; then at the group home at night, she wanted to work full-time with the elders and worked with them again on Sunday. I drove her to Sto:lo Eagle after work and visited with Ryan and Desiree but wouldn't go into Henry Jr.'s house. I wanted to leave early but left late but wasn't as angry at the Association of BC Forest Professionals as I used to be. Then I told a Native client who does salvage sales, Don Baker, how staff at work treat me and he said he would complain right up to Victoria where the head offices are!

I called Denny Eddy on the first weekend of March, and he was happy to hear from me and said he was going to try and get UBC Press to contact me about writing my life story. I also called Lorna O'Toole and she suggested I get my book published first then see about getting it made into a movie, which was my original intention. Lorna also said Japan, China, and Germany, especially Germany are all interested in aboriginal issues; then I told her psychics said some people may try to hurt me for exposing the truth. She responded, "Just call me! I'll have a string of lawyers on their trail so fast!" Then she suggested I attend the Surrey International Writers' Convention in September or October.

On the third weekend of March, I visited my parents, and my mother warned me to be careful of what I expose; and we talked about dysfunction caused by the Indian residential schools and what survivors are being offered is an insult. Then she told me Tony had been in a car accident. I went to town to visit Jennifer, and on my way, I stopped off to say hi to Helen; and Tony's girlfriend, Marge, was there. But as soon as I pulled in the driveway, she went in the house, so I knew something was wrong! I asked Helen about Tony's accident, but she wouldn't say anything. When I went back to work, on the news I saw Mission had a black mayor and I wondered, if he was Indian, would he have even been elected to council?

Near the end of March, Jennifer called and said she had to be out of her apartment by the weekend because the building was being renovated, so I took Friday afternoon off to help her move her things into storage and spent the night at my parents' place. I went to the Popkum Market just down the road for a case of beer and saw Tom, sitting in a truck between two other fellows, pretending it wasn't him. The next day I found out Tony wasn't in a car accident. He was kidnapped at the Popkum Market, driven up Chilliwack Lake Road, knifed near a major artery in his leg, and left for dead! He walked about fifty feet, called for help, and collapsed; and luckily, some people heard him and called an ambulance! Tony had been in the hospital for three weeks now over a drug debt to Tom, who arranged for people to do it to him!

By the first weekend of April, Jennifer was transferred to working full-time with the elders, got a $4-an-hour raise, but worked less hours. She was really happy about that though because it was less stressful than working in the group home. She didn't have a home right now, often slept in her car even though there were places she could go, and was drinking quite heavily.

On the first weekend of May, I sent out an information package titled *Working for the British Columbia Forest Service* to influential people; and the clerk in the post office knew it was serious because of how thick it was, how many copies were being sent; and a copy was sent to the Southern Poverty Law Center in Montgomery, Alabama. On the second weekend of May, I visited Jennifer and we drove around and got things done. Stanley saw us together and got jealous even though he knew I saved Jennifer from suicide and got her a career. I thought maybe if I found a girlfriend, he might accept me being friends with Jennifer, but there didn't seem to be anyone interested in me. I started to slow down on drinking, felt really good, and thought maybe I should start looking for a girlfriend again. It's been thirty-one years since I stopped looking for one.

I went back to Chilliwack again the next weekend because it was a long weekend; and on Sunday I got Steven Point, an aboriginal judge, to sign my passport application. Then I told him about the information packages that I've been putting together and he and his wife, Gwen, were both surprised at the issues that I researched and exposed; then Gwen said it was PhD material. I gave them the information packages that I had with me. They said they were interested in all my other information packages and asked if I would be interested in speaking in front of a class and insisted that I have breakfast with them.

Jennifer slept most of the day then went with me to my parents' place. Monday was a holiday and we didn't have to work, but Jennifer still said she didn't sleep very well. She said she dreamt someone told her to learn to be happier then asked me to take two days off work, so I called the office and booked in two days of annual leave. Jennifer still didn't have a place to stay but had an appointment to view an apartment; then a week later, she called and said she got the apartment, so I started making arrangements to help her move in.

The first day of June was a Friday and I had enough hours built up to take the day off, so I took it to help Jennifer move her things out of storage; and Albert Murphy showed up again to help us move. I borrowed my dad's truck to help her move; then we helped an old lady named Kathleen Harry move her things. Her son got her evicted and no one was available to help her, so we helped her move. When I told my dad, he was happy we did that because he went to school with her and didn't even know if she was still alive. After Kathleen told a story of how she was treated by the nuns in the residential school, I was surprised she even survived, let alone went on to become a nurse; and she said she had her story recorded so it wouldn't be lost. I told her about many Indians I went to school with died or committed suicide before they turned twenty-five, and she said, "Because they were molested!"

Aaron and Jennifer went to the bars after moving her things and I went to my parents' place; then at five o'clock the next morning, Aaron called and asked me to drive him home because his hip was sore and he had a hard time walking. After I dropped Aaron off, I went to Tim Horton's for coffee and Jennifer called and asked me to help look for her purse; so I went to her place and it was there. Some of our friends were there and they all started drinking when they woke up, but I didn't drink because I had to drive back to Squamish. Everyone was having a good time; then I felt Jennifer getting incredibly stressed out. They went to the bars and drank until they were cut off; then I drove them to the Cultus Lake canoe races. I enjoyed it and was glad Henry Jr. wasn't there because I didn't want to see him. I drank two beers before I drove home though because I was stressed out to the point my chest was hurting; then the next day, I bought a case of beer after work and drank it because I didn't realize how stressed out I was.

Two weeks later, my family had a dinner for my dad because it was Father's Day, but I couldn't make it; then my mother called and said Uncle Howard Dolan passed away that day. Two days later, I called my mother, and she said the funeral would be on Thursday and I might be asked to be a pallbearer. I had enough hours built up to take Thursday and Friday off, so I went to the funeral then visited with Aaron and Jennifer. On Saturday, Jennifer wanted to go to the canoe races at Lummi Island, but I didn't think I would be allowed across the border because I sent my birth certificate in to apply for a passport. I was glad of that because I didn't want to see Henry Jr. and told myself that each time I don't see him for a year, I'm going to treat myself to a steak dinner, so Jennifer went with two of her clients that she looked after at work.

I went back to my parents' place because there was a salmon barbecue at the band hall and met a black fellow from Mississippi there, Joseph Haney, who was working as an addictions counsellor. I thought he was younger than I because he didn't have any gray hair, but he was two years older than I. I told Joseph about things I saw happen in my lifetime, the issues I researched and put into information packages, and he was totally blown away by what went on! Then I gave him copies of the information packages and said he could expose it wherever he wanted.

Near the end of June, Jennifer asked me about registering her in Biology 11 because she wanted to advance in her career because she's no quitter. I also noticed that I was developing a sore throat but didn't think it was anything serious. In the middle of July, I started reading the book *The Secret* because it was given to us at work, applied what it said, and realized I have to forgive people who did me an injustice in the past, especially Henry. Patricia Kelly called and sounded like she might actually be interested in me, so I went back to Chilliwack at the end of July; and Jennifer started jogging to slow down on drinking. She wanted to buy some mouthwash but didn't want the brand Henry Jr. used because she was mad at him, so on my way back to Squamish, I wondered if she's finally facing reality on how he treats us.

I was sick. so I took a few days off then went back to work; and on the long August weekend, I went back to Chilliwack. Aaron wanted to go to his family reunion in Parksville on Vancouver Island; so he, Jennifer, and I went over on Jennifer's car. I was rather reluctant to go because I thought ferry traffic would be heavy because of the long weekend, but it wasn't too bad. Jennifer got stressed out on the way back; then she and Aaron started drinking. I didn't drink though because I wanted to slow down on drinking. I stayed home the next weekend and worked on my manuscript and enjoyed it. Jennifer called me on Sunday and said she hurt her back and had to take a few days off work. Then I finally decided that I can't do anything for Isaac anymore because he never does anything for me yet often gives lavishly to other people.

When I got back to work, I went to the doctor because my throat was still sore, often making me slow and tired. I did my employee-performance development plan (EPDP) with my supervisor, Dave Southam, and it didn't go over very well and thought it could be from drinking. I don't know why things like this keep happening to me because it makes me feel like a born loser; then when I went over my manuscript again, I realized I still have much anger in me and it's probably coming out on my body.

I went to Chilliwack on the weekend. Jennifer was visiting Aaron Friday night, and Aaron's neighbours were over visiting. She told them she wouldn't be here if I didn't help her out and then I helped her get a career. She's finally acknowledging that I saved her life then got her a career, because last year she blamed me for everything that her father did to her.

Jennifer got sick, so on Sunday I took her to the doctor and Aaron helped look after her all week; then on Friday, Jennifer called and said our friend Jim's son died, but didn't know how he died. I called my mother on Sunday, and she said Jim's son committed suicide and he was the last person anyone ever expected to do that. The residential schools weren't only hard on those who survived and their families; they were also hard on the second generation because many of them still fall victim to addiction and commit suicide! Jennifer attended the funeral and asked me to help her out with her rent because she missed a week of work when she hurt her back. Although I wrote my life story out six times and was now touching it up, it was still stressful to relive what I went through in 1986 and '87.

On Friday I went out to the woods to do a survey and got disoriented. I knew I could get lost if I tried to find my way back, so I just found another trail and followed it. I knew it was taking me farther away from the truck, but it would take me to a road by the railroad tracks where I could radio the office and arrange a ride back to my truck; but luckily, when I got to the railroad tracks, a heavy-equipment operator was just finishing work and gave me a ride back to my truck. I didn't realize I got disoriented because of how my throat was affecting me.

I continued working on my manuscript, and when I reached "1990," I started feeling bad about how I treated Henry; now I hoped I had *finally* let out all my anger toward him! It was early September now, and Jennifer decided to drop her biology class because it was too hard for her to work and study at the same time; and I knew it wasn't the right time because she still has too much anger in her to be able to concentrate on her studies. My throat was still acting up, but my acne appeared to be going away.

In August I filled out an aboriginal-employee-retention survey, which was supposed to only take five to ten minutes to complete, but it took me over an hour because I brought up many issues. I started at eleven o'clock and worked past noon. The staff saw me working on it, so they knew it was important and didn't think I would be back from lunch until 1:10 p.m.; but I went back right at one o'clock. Luckily, it said everything would be kept confidential because I exposed some very important issues.

I entered the writer's contest using an outline of my life story and paid my fees to attend the International Writers' Convention in Surrey. The convention would be on for three days and writers could attend all three days. I decided I would only go on Sunday because Jennifer had her medical administration course on Friday and Saturday in Vancouver and wanted me to drive her there.

Toward the end of September, Shihan (a sixth-dan karate black belt) Allan Chan, the head karate instructor of Vancouver, came to Squamish to instruct the class. Chris Gielow and I were getting discouraged with karate training because we only do one night of training a week, get very little practice and instruction; so our techniques were sloppy. Shihan Allan still came down on us because of our poor technique even though it wasn't our fault, so now I wanted to transfer to a town where I could get better karate training. On October 1, CTV News mentioned the Chinese Canadians fighting for Canada in WWII and how they were treated, exactly five years to the day when I sent information on Chinese Canadian and aboriginal soldiers to two different news stations in Vancouver by registered letter and they didn't even respond.

I took the next week off in annual leave; and on Thursday, Patricia Kelly asked me to go for a beer with her, so we went to a pub in Agassiz. She had two beers, I drank pop, and we played pool and talked about what we've been through. I told her Chichel Siyam (the Creator, Christians would say God) put a wall around me and wouldn't let anyone near me because I had to look after Jennifer. Other ladies seemed to sense that wall or that they shouldn't get involved with me, and she said she could sense that wall too. She was slightly interested in me, didn't want me to go home with her, then later on changed her mind about me, which I knew she would do.

I told Jennifer to get her pictures taken on Saturday for her passport application because it takes a long time to get a passport, and for some reason, that flipped her out; so she went to the bars then drove over to Aaron's even though I told her I would pick her up at the bars. Then Aaron called me on the cell phone, so I told him to go outside and make sure she didn't drive because I'd be right there; but when Aaron got outside, the police were there because Jennifer hit someone, didn't know it, and kept driving. Then the police took her to jail and had her car towed away. Fortunately, a cop there said the person she hit wasn't hurt very badly; but it stressed Aaron and me out, so I bought a fifteen-pack of beer.

Jennifer called me at six o'clock the next morning when she was let out of jail. Now she was worried about losing her job, driver's license, and going to jail; so she asked me to call a psychic. The psychic phone numbers weren't in the newspapers, so we called a psychic named Sanatra; but she wasn't home. She also got her car back that day, but it cost her $116.26. The mirror on the passenger side was broken, and we all realized she was lucky because the person she hit could have been killed! I was surprised she got her car back that fast and hoped she would slow down on her drinking, but she still blamed me for what happened; then Sanatra eventually called at ten forty-five that night. I went back to work and still felt tired and had been feeling tired for quite some time now. I called Uncle Sal in New Mexico and told him an emergency came up, so I couldn't make it to visit; and he said they were going to Arizona anyway.

I had enough hours built up to take Friday off, so I went back to Chilliwack to take Jennifer to her medical administration course in Vancouver. It was a two-day course, Friday and Saturday; so we thought we would just come to Squamish Friday night. We stopped at Park Royal Mall in West Vancouver to shop around a bit and got a flat tire. I was worried about getting it fixed because we had to go back the next day, and I didn't want to drive without a spare tire. They also decided to start the class at seven thirty instead of eight thirty the next morning. I changed the tire and knew the nearest tire shop was just across the street and hoped we could get there before they closed. Fortunately, the tire shop was supposed to close at five o'clock; but a tire delivery was late, so they were still open. The tire was worn out, so I had to buy a new tire and knew she would have to replace the other three tires the next day. After her course was over the next day, we went back to the tire shop and had her other three tires replaced; it was a good thing their delivery was late because they ended up selling a new set of tires.

I went to the writers' conference in Surrey the next day and enjoyed it! I didn't know what to expect or where to go for different types of stories that were being sold, but everything worked out quite well. I met many other interesting people and other writers as well. At the end of the month, I got into trouble again for not doing my job properly, so I told Jennifer and she wasn't very supportive as usual. She just told me not to focus so much on her anymore, so I worked for a week then took the second week of November off in annual leave again.

I had arranged to meet Lorna O'Toole in Aldergrove, just past Abbotsford going toward Vancouver, the next day to discuss my manuscript, getting it published, and trying to get a film contract for it. I took Patricia Kelly along to meet her so we could discuss how my book was doing and they could give me their opinions. Lorna said I was lucky to survive what I went through and Patricia agreed; then they both said it's a story that must be told. I told Patricia she was lucky she didn't start working on it earlier because of changes I made and incidents that I almost didn't write in then helped her apply for a job in Abbotsford on our way back.

During the summer, my right shoulder started getting sore and kept getting worse. It reached the point where I couldn't even lift it up to touch my left shoulder, so I couldn't go hunting again that fall.

I had quit drinking before my holidays because I thought that could be what was making me tired and forgetful, but it didn't do any good; I still felt the same way. I went back to work and went to the doctor who sent me to the lab for blood tests. Jennifer called me when I got back and told me to go for counselling, so I applied through the British Columbia employee family-assistance program at work. On Saturday I finished touching up my life story on computer disks and my back started getting sore and my ribs were also incredibly sore for some reason; then I realized what a fool I was years earlier to do surveys when I had a bad back then told Jennifer to take time off work when she was sick. I stayed home and rested all weekend and still felt tired.

I went to the counsellor, Mary Leslie, and she made me realize how much negative energy was draining me and suggested a good method of letting it go. She said for every person that I'm angry at, just before I go to sleep at night and when I wake up, "Wish them all well!"

When I started doing that, I felt like I could forgive Henry soon. I went back to Chilliwack, and by Saturday I tried again to accept that Henry probably suffered even after he passed away because his wooden grave marker turned *black* in less than a year even though it was treated with preservatives. When I accepted that he suffered for what he did wrong, I felt a whole lot better; and my mother finally told me to start doing things for my own enjoyment, but previously, whenever I tried to do that, she or someone else would deliberately ruin my fun.

When I accepted that Henry suffered for *everything* that he did wrong, it felt like I could see him in front of me; and he wasn't the least bit angry. Now I hoped I would get better and wouldn't lose my job and tried to drop my manuscript off with Patricia Kelly, but Jennifer slowed me down. Then I realized that Jennifer's family may have gotten stronger because they survived what he put them through. I had another appointment with Mary Leslie when I got back to work, and she told me to leave the past behind me and to look forward and really liked it when my nephew said to me, "When are you going to live happily ever after?" I realized that I should start looking forward with enthusiasm because the past is what made me stronger and that's why I'm where I am today! I went to the doctor the next day for my lab-test results and he said I have hypothyroid; that was what was making me slow and tired all the time. He told me to take pills for three months, go for lab tests again, then see him.

I stayed home the next weekend, and in the first week of December, I wrote the following letter to Henry:

Henry—I have to Forgive You! December 5, 2007
(c)copyright Annis Aleck 2007

I have to forgive you for how you treated me because holding on to the anger is like a dragging a ball and chain behind me! I know you suffered for what you did wrong because when I lashed out at you, I saw it happening back to me! I didn't care though because I was blinded by anger and was willing to accept it as long as I could make you miserable!

You knew full well wanting you to eat the grease out of the pan while everyone else had ham and turkey was justified, yet you were angry at me about it until you died! There's absolutely no excuse for not putting anything down for Elizabeth and Jeremy's funeral, especially after the way you treated her, and you suffered for it! Jennifer's life wasn't worth the time of day to you because you knew full well *I was literally going through* hell *trying to save her from suicide and get her a career so she could do something with her life, yet all you did was mooch off me and make life miserable for me! Then you couldn't do enough for Alvin!* You were absolutely nothing but a burden to everyone but Alvin! You never did amount to anything!

I was too blinded by anger to see you suffering while you were here and after you passed away! Even after you passed away, I'm sure you suffered, because your wooden grave marker turned black *even though it was treated with preservatives! You just pushed me to the point where I didn't care if I suffered as long as I could do something to make you miserable! Now your family has practically* ostracized *me! If I get rich and successful, I'll be giving them* exactly *as much as you gave me for saving your daughter from suicide and getting both her and Henry Jr. a career!*

I know you're a victim of what you went through, but all you had to do was treat Alvin the way you treated me if he ever did that much for your so-called happy *family! You choose to do* absolutely nothing *but mooch off me and make life miserable for me when you knew I was trying to save Jennifer from suicide and get her a career! Then you choose to treat Alvin like* royalty!

Your niggers learned from you to ostracize me and treat Alvin like royalty*! Now he wants* absolutely nothing *to do with me, but if I get successful, I'm going to have Alvin and Henry Jr.'s numbers screened so they can't call me! Now you've suffered for what you did wrong because you made the choice to treat everyone the way you treated them! You even suffered after death, but it was your family's choice to react and take the path they choose in life! I have to accept that you suffered for what you did wrong, and if your family suffers for how they* *treated me, there's nothing I can do about it because I don't even want to know them!*

From
Baxter, Your Ostracized Son-in Law!

I had enough hours to take Friday off and wanted to burn it that day, but Aaron asked me to help him out with things he had to do in town. We picked Jennifer up in the bars and she just lashed out at us, so I drove her home and spent the night at Aaron's. Jennifer called the next day because I still had her cell phone, and I offered to take her Christmas shopping; but she went shopping on her own and told me not to worry about her. I went to my parents' place and burned the letter to Henry, and he seemed to be there looking at me, smiling and admitting that he was a burden that never amounted to anything; so I felt a whole lot better after that but still felt tired.

I had another appointment with Mary Leslie when I got back to work and she made me realize that Henry was blinded by his own pain and anger, so he couldn't see that he was driving Jennifer to suicide and didn't care that he was making my life miserable. I was a threat to him by making him lose control of Jennifer. He didn't want his kids to grow independent of him because he would lose control of them, so he tried to keep them from growing up. He was *totally* insecure, so he felt he had to control *everything* around him.

I went on annual leave the next week because I always take two weeks off at Christmas. On Monday I took Jennifer Christmas shopping in Abbotsford, and at the end of the evening, she seemed happy and that really made me glad I was able to save her from suicide. I went to the doctor in Agassiz the next day and he told me to go back on Friday and get a cortisone shot. On Friday the doctor said I have frozen shoulder; my shoulder has frozen up on the inside. I started getting bored but was also concerned about losing my job, but things seem to work out well for me as long as I don't get lazy or drink too much.

Nothing eventful happened at Christmas, but two days after Christmas, Jennifer called and woke me up at seven fifteen and I couldn't go back to sleep. I turned the TV on and watched *Bury My Heart at Wounded Knee* and was surprised that one Indian warrior who fought at the Battle of the Little Bighorn went on to become a doctor, changed his name to Charles Eastman, and that he had a white woman for a wife. Now I was glad Jennifer woke me up because that made me wonder when the first Canadian aboriginal became a licensed physician in Canada.

At the end of December, I got Patricia Kelly to sign a contract for editing my life story and decided not to go chasing after her because she's not interested in me. She's a very nice-looking girl, but if women aren't interested in me, I give up right away. My shoulder still hurt and the cortisone shot seemed to be doing more harm than good. That night, Jennifer called and said Stanley was jealous of me and not to call her; she'd call me.

Chapter 30

2008

I still had a bad shoulder when I got back to work; and the physiotherapist said I had frozen shoulder, it froze up on the inside, and to see a doctor because it may just have to run its course. Then Jennifer's grandmother passed away on the weekend. I had an appointment with Mary Leslie, and she's been helping me let go of my anger from the past and said I was frozen with anger and it was coming out on my body. I decided to go to the funeral. Church services were held at Laughing Raven, and while driving over, I accepted more that Henry suffered for everything he did wrong and there was nothing anyone could have done to prevent it from happening back to him. When Alvin arrived, he seemed happy to see me; but Henry Jr. and I avoided each other until the evening when he seemed to accept me, so I wondered if it was because I was still trying to forgive his father.

Jennifer missed two days of work after the funeral because of arrangements that still had to be made and because she was worried about her court case. I tried telling her to think positively, but she wouldn't listen as usual. Mary Leslie helped me let go of more of my anger, showed me how much it was affecting me, and then asked me to write something positive, leave the past behind me because it's over and made me the person that I am today. This month has been pivotal for me, like a fortune cookie said.

On *Exhibit A: Secrets of Forensic Science*, a series on police science investigations narrated by Graham Greene, the actor, there was a documentary about a hairdresser killing aboriginal women by pouring alcohol down their throats in the 1980s on Vancouver's downtown east side where the impoverished drug addicts live. He killed six Aboriginal women then killed a white girl, which sparked a police investigation, and he was charged for killing the white girl; but no charges were laid for killing the aboriginal women. Graham said this was going to be made into a movie documentary, and when I found out it was titled *Unnatural & Accidental*, I ordered it from Amazon but accidentally ordered two copies.

Near the end of January, I accidentally did some damage to a BCFS truck without realizing it; and when I filled out an accident report, I got scared for my job. But my instincts told me not to worry because I didn't deliberately do anything wrong. Then I thought, *Things went bad today. Perhaps something good will come tomorrow.* Sure enough, APTN news said the truth commission will be doing a major investigation into when the RCMP were ordered to kill the Inuit sled dogs in the 1950s and '60s. This was a forced relocation of the Inuit to the communities and would expose the history of the Arctic. The RCMP denies it happened at all, but people can expect it to say that; so I wondered if I helped initiate this investigation because as soon as I heard about it, I reported it to influential people.

The next week, APTN news did a three-part series on the RCMP killing of the Inuit sled dog, and some people who were alive when it happened told how devastating it was to the Inuit people. *Canadian Geographic* also did a documentary on Inuit sled dogs, how important they were to the people, and the role they played in surviving in the Arctic. Dogs were everything to the Inuit people. They weren't only used for transportation; they also protected them from predators, helped with hunting seals and polar bears, kept them warm at night, were used for trading, and their fur made the best clothing. Dogs were probably used as food once they were no longer useful for work, and once the Inuit were moved into the communities, they couldn't go back to the land because they didn't have any well-trained dogs. Some people went to the hospitals in the south after contracting diseases. Some didn't come back, and I thought some of the women may have been sterilized because the Canadian government secretly ordered Inuit girls sterilized and they were almost automatically sterilized when they went south to the hospital.

Previously I ordered *Freedom's Land: Canada and the Underground Railroad* from CBC but didn't know how much of it was true, if the story was distorted or not, and if any incidents had been deliberately left out. I mailed that and the unopened copy of *Unnatural & Accidental* to the Southern Poverty Law Center in Montgomery, Alabama, with a covering letter stating how Canadian film companies often distort the truth and leave out important issues.

In February I went to the doctor and was told I'll be on pills for the rest of my life because of my thyroid, but I still felt tired and forgetful most of the time, so I wondered if the medication wasn't strong enough. In the first week of March, on Monday, Ashley, Isaac's daughter, called and said my dad was rushed to the hospital and was in intensive care and his heart stopped twice on the way to the hospital! I got really depressed; and Ashley called again and said my dad's pacemaker wasn't working, they'd put another one on him, and another doctor will see him before anyone can visit him. I went to work the next day then called Sarah, David's youngest daughter; and she said my dad had a 20 percent chance of living, so I called Jennifer and told her what happened. She told me to call Auntie Jeanette, so I called her then called Auntie Deedee in Ohio. I got really upset and called Isaac an hour later and he said Dad was starting to come around, so I decided to take the rest of the week off because I knew I couldn't concentrate!

I went to Chilliwack the next day, and when I got to the hospital, my cousin Cheryl Trainer was at the door. She walked me up to my dad's room, and I was glad she was there because I was falling apart; but other people smiled like she was my girlfriend. David showed up for a little while then left, and my dad passed away at 6:10 a.m. Naturally that hit us all hard because he was a *great man*, so I was glad I didn't go back to work! The next day, Isaac, my mother, and I went to the funeral home to choose a casket and make funeral arrangements; and on Wednesday, Randy, Isaac's friend from childhood, came over from Nelson, British Columbia because he was like part of the family. On Thursday, Isaac and Randy went to town to make more funereal arrangements, but I didn't go with them because I thought Isaac would feel better if I wasn't there.

On Sunday, arrangements were made for a burning to be done by Sparky, an Indian from Sto:lo Eagle; and when he came to the house, I asked him about burning a cup of bacon grease for Henry, and Isaac said, "*Baxter!*" I got annoyed because he was deliberately being obnoxious and should stay completely out of things that involve Henry! I felt like punching him in the head and told it to Sue and

Sarah that night after having a few drinks but forgot Ashley was in the living room. Then I told them about standing up to someone three times my size for a knife fight and didn't care if I won or lost! That was the first time I ever told my family about it and cried slightly even though I tried not to!

The funeral was on Tuesday, and I drove my mother in her car to pick up Tony and Marge. Mother told them what time we would pick them up and Marge was ready on time, but Tony acted like it didn't matter at all. Mother went in the house to get him and we still had to wait, so I said, "We have to wait for His Majesty!" and Marge said, "Shut up, Baxter, or I'll slap you!" It's annoying the way Tony just doesn't care about anything.

Jennifer took the day off work to attend the funeral, and Ryan and Desiree were also there.

On Thursday, APTN news said that Amnesty International said Canada had been losing it's good image starting two years ago, so I wondered if I was part of it because that's when I started reporting some of the truth to them. Before I left Rosedale, I started writing a letter; and Nicole, Isaac's youngest daughter, saw me writing. Although she's only eleven years old, she knew that I write research reports exposing the truth about how Canada has treated the Indians.

I went back to work even though I was still tired, forgetful, and unable to think clearly; and Dave Southam told me to bring a union shop steward to my next performance review because I haven't been able to work properly for quite some time now. I contacted Chris Braun, the shop steward, did the performance review in April; and it went very badly, so I was told to get a medical report from the doctor. Unfortunately my regular doctor is very busy and I usually have to book an appointment two weeks ahead of time when I want to see him. The doctor told me it's better to stay with one doctor so they'll know what's happening, but on April 14 anyway, I went to another doctor who gave me a stronger dosage of thyroid pills and put me on antidepressants; then I took the next two weeks off in sick leave.

I went back to work for a week then booked in sick again; and at the end of April, Stan Dixon, owner of *Kahtou*, an aboriginal newspaper based out of Sechelt, British Columbia, called and asked for some of the articles I wrote on residential schools to put in his paper. He said to only make them about two and a half pages long because some of the reports I wrote were ten pages long. He wanted a picture of me and said I could be asked to speak at conferences and get paid for it.

I worked for a week then went on sick leave for three months from May 3 to July 25. I tried to go back to work after three weeks, but Dave Southam told me to go home until the doctor said I could go back to work. On the third weekend in May, I went to the canoe races and soccer tournament at Seabird Island for the first time in years and saw Henry Jr. there but avoided him. When we walked by each other later on, we both just looked the other way; but his wife said hi to me, and I didn't see them there the next day.

Stan Dixon published the article I wrote on the Residential School Settlement, which mentioned two other articles that I wrote, "Grim Reality" and "Sugar and Vanilla Extract"; so I called Stan, and he agreed that those and other articles I wrote should also be put in his newspaper. I also put two information packages together, (1) *Aboriginal Issues* and (2) the *Immigrant Journey*, for British Columbia's 150th anniversary and sent them to the Royal British Columbia Museum in Victoria. The information was reviewed and I was told to shorten it and put it in story form, not a letter, but they couldn't expose the Immigrant Journey without permission from the Chinese Veterans' Association because they could get sued. On June 11, on TV, the prime minister and leaders of other political parties issued an apology to the Indians because of the residential schools. It was a long time coming, but it was good to see them stand up and tell the truth without holding back. However, I thought it should have been broadcast on other stations, not just APTN and one other station.

In June while visiting my mother, I started cutting the grass with a push lawn mower and fell rather hard and hurt my ribs. I thought I was just bruised and would get better, but it didn't; so Jennifer told me to go to the doctor. The doctor sent me for X-rays, which indicated that I had dislocated my ribs, so he sent me to a chiropractor; then Jennifer told me to take another month off work. The chiropractor said the central nervous system, spinal cord, controls everything; and when the back is out of alignment, it impairs body functions connected to that part of the nervous system. My spine was misaligned where concentration, sinuses, and digestion were controlled; that's why I've been having health problems for the last three years.

In the third week of June, I met with Dave Southam, the district manager and Chris Braun about my medical report, and the district manager changed the cutoff date of my sick leave because the doctor's medical report hadn't gone in yet. It went in the next day, and I gave a copy to Chris Braun and to the district manager in an envelope marked Confidential. Then I applied to Mental Health for counselling as was suggested by Dr. Fabian, a psychiatrist, and wait for the doctor's recommendations. On Wednesday, July 23, I had a meeting with management and Chris Braun and was told to go back to work on Monday. I was also told to see Dr. L. at the Vancouver General Hospital on August 6 at four o'clock and if I missed the appointment, it would cost $750, which I would have to pay for myself. No one knew what kind of doctor he was, but I was told I could use a company vehicle and get a hotel room for the night.

I called Geraldine on the weekend and she said Jennifer took the RCA course to follow her footsteps because of all the money she was making, and to me it appeared she wanted to be credited for Jennifer taking the course and doing something with her life. Geraldine also felt proud of having been Jennifer's guardian, but I said I made Jennifer take the course at a recognized institution so she could work off Indian reserves. She also took the course because there weren't many other opportunities for her to get a career, but she enjoyed the work.

I was supposed to meet with management on Wednesday that week, but a major rock slide shut the highway down between Squamish and Vancouver, so it was rescheduled for the next day; but I forgot about it even though I had it written down in my journal. Even though I had three months off, I was still tired, forgetful, and unable to think clearly; so I decided to quit drinking to see if that would help. I made it to see the Dr. L. at the Vancouver General Hospital because the rock slide was cleared up on time. The doctor was a psychiatrist and complete jerk who thought I was being friendly and personal when I asked him his age and nationality; but it was because immigrants from a country affected by European colonialism often have a chip on their shoulder, an expression for being very angry about something, and treat the Indians like we were part of it. He said that if we didn't attend the residential schools, we weren't affected by them and the obstacles and setbacks that I went through while getting my career were my fault. I was in the first generation after the residential schools, so my home life was difficult; and the second generation also has a high rate of suicide and addiction. Racism is very hard to prove, and even if it could be proven, it's quite likely nothing would be done about it.

Psychiatrist's Report: He said I'm of average intelligence and have a narcissistic and passive-aggressive personality.

Narcissistic Personality: People routinely overestimate their abilities and inflate their accomplishments and are often preoccupied with fantasies that confirm and support their grandiosity of their sense of being superior, special, or unique. Such fantasies often involve admiration and special privileges they think should be forthcoming. Persons with narcissistic personality disorder often feel envious of others, begrudging them their successes or possessions and are particularly prone to feel that they deserve the achievements, admiration, and privileges of others. He said I revealed a number of narcissistic personality traits during the interview and voiced exaggerated and persistent complaints of personal misfortune. He also said I have a tendency to fantasize and imagine things; my thought pattern was characterized by some "magical thinking" with elements of superstition most likely related to my First Nations cultural background. He probably didn't know what happens when people think "evil thoughts" and acknowledge feelings and hunches when they come. I had to remain calm; otherwise, I would have just put myself in a worse situation than I was already in.

Passive-aggressive Personality: People often feel cheated, unappreciated, victimized, and luckless; they grumble, whine, and tend to blame their misfortunes on others. They also express envy and resentment toward those they believe are more fortunate or powerful than they. Patients often undermine their own progress by undoing their accomplishments, role of martyr, the aggrieved, the misunderstood, and the contrite. They may also take on the sick role, the aggrieved, the misunderstood, and the contrite. They may also take on the sick role, complaining to others of various body ailments.

I told the psychiatrist saving Jennifer from suicide was an ordeal I wouldn't wish on anyone and he said I shouldn't have done it, so I responded, "Would you say that if it was your daughter or your sister?" He said he would send them for professional help, wouldn't write that in his report, and said I repeatedly asked him personal questions during the appointment. He said he was a qualified medical doctor as well as psychiatrist. I thought being a doctor and psychiatrist were fields to save people from physical, mental, and emotional problems, not push them away and ignore them if they're extremely depressed and contemplating suicide! I was quite stressed our after seeing him but didn't drink.

The psychiatrist totally ignored the fact that life was hard on the families of residential-school survivors in spite of a pamphlet from the *British Columbia Medical Journal* recognizing the residential-school syndrome as a medical issue by Dr. Brasfield, a psychiatrist in private practice and clinical associate professor in the department of psychiatry at University of British Columbia (UBC), and research report by UBC psychologist Michael Chandler that I showed him. In a CBC Radio interview on November 19, 2001, Michael Chandler was told the suicide rate among First Nations youth is the highest of any cultural group in the world and some Indian bands have a high rate of suicide yet some where suicides almost never happen. It was the Canadian government that forced the Indians to attend residential schools then held us back when we tried to do something for ourselves.

I continued working and going for counselling at Mental Health but just couldn't function properly at work. Stan Dixon called and asked for some more submissions, so I sent him some; and Jennifer was supposed to go to court in the first week of September, which was stressing her out, but it was postponed again. In the second week of September, I noticed I could breathe better and wondered if that had been affecting my work. I called Isaac again and he had deliberately pushed his ignorance too far again; and I felt like beating the shit right out of him, so I had to buy a case of beer to calm down! I probably would have, but I already saw him have bad luck from deliberately doing things wrong; but he refuses to acknowledge that "what goes around comes around"!

I didn't think I would have anything to write for *Kahtou* for October, but on September 15, Stan Dixon asked me to write an article on the election campaigns for the coming federal election. He said people campaigning for prime minister never mention the aboriginals, and he suggested I call it "Are We the Forgotten People?" so I wrote the article and titled it "Federal Elections 2008: Are Aboriginals the Forgotten People!"

On September 24, I did my performance management review with Dave Southam, and it was dismal! I told Dave how I've been feeling but wasn't able to get a medical report from the doctor, got sick again, and took the first two weeks of October off in sick leave; but on October 2, I got a letter saying that I have until November 17 to improve my job performance. Otherwise, I'll be terminated. On Monday, October 6, I had another meeting with Dave Southam, management, and Chris Braun; and my job performance was dismal again to say the least and I needed a report from the doctor. I had a medical report from the chiropractor, but it wasn't acceptable because they're not registered in the College of Physicians and the doctor couldn't sign it even if he agreed with the report because it hasn't been scientifically proven what chiropractors say they can cure.

The next day I took Jennifer to Surrey to apply for her passport right at the office so she would get it on time for her trip to Mexico. We visited Ben and Geraldine on our way back. She called them Mom and Dad and said I was like a father to her because I looked after her and pushed her to get a career. Then she said I saved her life; she knows that, but she rarely mentions it and still lashes out at me.

I had to go back to Squamish for a doctor and chiropractor appointment, and the doctor said the symptoms I described to him were depression; so he doubled my dosage of antidepressants and made another appointment for me in two weeks. Then Jennifer called and said her cousin Jim would do a spiritual healing for me on Sunday at one o'clock; so the next day, I called Keith Cameron, the aboriginal liaison worker for the BCGEU, and said he's going to try and get me to see an aboriginal psychologist.

I went back to Rosedale since it was Thanksgiving weekend; and on Sunday, Jennifer took me to see Jim, who worked on me spiritually and said I have to follow my life's calling or I'll be six feet under (i.e., dead). I knew that my life's calling was looking after Jennifer; then later on, a psychic said it's also exposing the truth of how aboriginals in Canada have been treated. Then Jim told me to stay off coffee, tea, salt, and sugar for the next week to ten days; so I started right away. The next week, I still felt slow and tired most of the time and met with Chris Braun and Katie Riecken, the BCGEU staff representative. They both said they didn't think very much of the psychiatrist, and Katie told me to get a doctor's referral to see a psychiatrist at UBC before I see the one who has worked with residential-school survivors.

In the last week of October, I still wasn't feeling any different even though I had quit drinking for over two weeks. I had to travel to Campbell River on Vancouver Island for a course, and on the third day, Jennifer called me at one thirty in the morning. She was depressed and crying and said she had to see a lawyer about the residential school and talk about her past. I didn't get a chance to tell her that it's the first, most difficult, and most important step toward healing; so I called her when I got home, and she said she was going to meet with the lawyer on Tuesday and wanted me there. I told her I couldn't make it but could be available over the phone though.

I went back to work and had enough hours built up to take Friday and Monday off, which gave me a five-day weekend because Tuesday was Remembrance Day. I went back to work, and the next weekend, I called Joy Ward about writing an article for *Kahtou* on the residential-school syndrome, and she gave me some advice and told me to include something positive. I felt a whole lot better after talking to her and realized that could be why I'm still having trouble with depression. I was probably still angry at Jennifer's family and didn't realize it.

I went back to the office on Monday and got fired because I couldn't get a medical report saying that I had something affecting me. The district manager offered to get me a ride home, but I went on my own and picked up a bottle of whiskey on my way. Then I called my mother, told her what happened, and she said it's my anger; so I told her everyone always tries to keep me from having fun!

The next day, Jennifer called and said she would be meeting with the lawyer on Thursday at five o'clock and wanted me to either be there or available on the phone, so I decided to be there. I went to Chilliwack on Thursday and the lawyer, Christian Voth, went to talk to her about her residential-school experience. I was glad I was there because I told him of all the times she went to the psychiatric ward for depression and how many times she tried to commit suicide since I met her. Christian asked if she was able to hold a steady job and about staying in school, so I told him I put Jennifer back in school until she got a career.

I helped Jennifer at work the next day, but she got a letter regarding her court case, which got her depressed; so she went to the bars after work, and eventually I joined her. She got depressed but felt better in the morning; then on Saturday, the building manager spoke to her about tenants complaining about strange people with keys coming into the building. Aaron argued a bit but should have kept quiet, and the manager said she knew she could trust me though. Aaron had been going in her apartment to feed the fish while she was on holiday, but tenants still complained; so Jennifer should have told the manager.

On December 2, I got a letter from work stating that I was now officially laid off, and Jennifer called and said she started reading the book *Women Who Love Too Much* and wanted to go to Al-Anon meetings like the book suggested. She still puts herself in dangerous situations and wants to stop because she's getting tired of it. I still felt tired most of the time and didn't do very much, and Jennifer found Lora Schultz's phone number. I called Lora; and she said lucky breaks will come in the last week of January and, in February, as a result of losing my job.

Nothing eventful happened until Christmas Eve when Ryan called and said their uncle Dennis, in Seattle, Washington, went to the hospital with a collapsed lung and was put to sleep. Jennifer got quite depressed about it, and I thought he may pass away! Christmas was on Thursday, and I drove Jennifer to Sto:lo Eagle to have Christmas dinner with Henry Jr. and his family. I didn't say very much, but I used the bathroom and had a cup of tea, which is more than I usually do at that house. I went back to Rosedale and thought Jennifer would spend the night there, but she called me later on to take her back home. Henry Jr. was at work when I got there, so I talked a little bit with Cecelia.

On Sunday, Jennifer wanted me to take her to Seattle to visit her uncle Dennis, and I didn't want to go; but Derral said that if Dennis passed away and she hadn't visited him, she would get really depressed and it would prolong her drinking. I also knew Jennifer would go with or without me, so I got my nephew Ric to look up on his computer where the hospital was and how to get there. When we got to the hospital, Henry Jr. and Cecelia were already there, and my going stressed him out. I couldn't stand looking at Dennis the way he was sleeping with breathing tubes attached to his face because that's how my dad looked when he passed away, so I sat in a chair and pretended to doze off. Then Henry Jr. told me to just go wait in the waiting room and sounded like he couldn't stand me! Then he realized that I didn't stay for the dinner at his mother's funeral because of the way he treats me! I went to the waiting room; then Henry and Cecelia left and I took Jennifer back home.

Chapter 31

2009

There was heavy snowfall; and I still felt slow, tired, and unable to think clearly. I wanted to come back to Squamish, but it was snowing too hard and the neighbour had to clear the snow off the driveway, but there wasn't much room to park without getting stuck in the snow. My nephew Ric left early in the morning when it was still dark and backed into my truck because he couldn't see it and because of the way it was parked. I felt bad about it because his insurance would go up, so I paid him $300 that he would have to pay to get his car fixed even though I didn't have very much money and was on employment insurance (EI). Jennifer was taking driving lessons in Abbotsford on Saturdays to learn to drive a standard transmission vehicle, so I drove her to Abbotsford; and after her driving lesson, she wanted to shop around in the thrift shops. I didn't want to, but I found the book *How a People Die* by Alan Fry. Vivian Ignace recommended I read it many years ago, but I didn't buy it because it's fiction. When I decided to read it, I couldn't find it; now I finally found it.

When I got back to Squamish, Bing Wong called and invited me to the Chinese Veterans' Association banquet and he would pay for my ticket. Previously I forgot to ask if any Chinese Canadians were made commanding officers in WWII. Bing said there was only one commanding officer serving in combat, Lieutenant Wilfred Seto, who served in Italy but got sent back because soldiers didn't like taking orders from a Chinaman. Most of the Japanese were well behaved but still lost everything even though very few did anything wrong, so I told him about the book *Redress: Inside the Japanese Canadian Call for*

Justice by Roy Miki. It exposed how WWII was just an excuse to take everything away from the Japanese.

When I read the book *How a People Die*, it accurately described the living conditions of Indians living on reserves in the 1960s, the high rate of alcoholism, and problems it caused. Although it was classified fiction, it could easily have been a true story; Alan Fry may have had to call it a work of fiction to avoid lawsuits and to get the book published. Canadian publishers aren't known for publishing the truth exactly the way things happened; even when they say the book or movie is nonfiction, the stories are usually so distorted that there's very little, if any, truth to what they're saying. Aboriginals who were adults in the 1960s could easily be called "the lost generation" because much of their life was wasted by excessive drinking.

Near the end of January, Bing Wong called and asked me to go to the Chinese New Year parade and try and get into exporting beetle-killed wood from aboriginals to China. Pine beetles have been devastating pine forests and killing the trees because winters haven't been cold enough to kill them off. Once the trees are dead, they have to be harvested within a few years or they become worthless for lumber.

Then when I started writing "2008," I realized that anger was the cause of my health problems. I went to Vancouver on February 1 for the Chinese New Year parade and was asked to march in the parade with the aboriginal and Chinese veterans; then we went to the Ho Ho restaurant in Chinatown and met people who wanted to organize log exports to China through aboriginals. Steven Point, British Columbia's first aboriginal lieutenant governor, was there and he wanted the truth of aboriginal and Chinese Canadian history taught in grade schools and knew I was already working on it. Then Bing Wong, Brian Chromko, and I went out for coffee; and Bing told me how some businesses succeed and some don't, and he wanted to help aboriginals get successful businesses operating.

The Chinese Veterans' banquet was held at the same restaurant on Tuesday, and Brian Chromko told me whom to contact about exporting logs to China. Bing Wong wanted it to go through the Chinese Veterans' to avoid corruption, and if it succeeded and made a profit, then we would share in the profits. I met Woodrow Wilson, a former lawyer and now a Haida storyteller and writer and now works with movies. He said he knows someone who might be interested in making what I went through to get a career into a documentary, so I e-mailed him the career stories that I sent to *Kahtou* but never heard from him again. All this was happening because Jennifer wanted to see the band Aerosmith in concert and asked me to find out when they were coming to Vancouver.

I went back to Chilliwack on the weekend to visit Jennifer because she was stressed out over her court case coming on February 18 involving the car accident; then I came back to Squamish on Tuesday for a doctor's appointment and felt incredibly tired on my way back. I felt like I was almost going to fall asleep while driving, but I made it back okay. I still felt incredibly tired the next day and had to go to the dentist for an emergency appointment. I needed a root canal done, but it had to be approved by DIA first. I felt incredibly tired all week, and on Friday, my teeth were incredibly sore; so I had to go to the dentist right away, not wait two weeks. The dentist squeezed me in and now I needed two root canals and my jaw hurt so bad I had to drink until I passed out. I knew it was caused by extreme anger, but it was hard not to be angry all the time.

I went back to Chilliwack on Tuesday because of Jennifer's court case on Wednesday. It cost her $1,200 for the lawyer, and I paid half of it. She didn't listen when Aaron and I told her to think positively, so she was extremely scared and nervous; then when her case came up, the judge dismissed it because the witnesses hadn't been subpoenaed by the female cop who arrested her and the judge wasn't going to adjourn the case again. That was a big relief because it could have been much worse even though we were prepared with a good lawyer.

Near the end of February, Stan Dixon called and asked me to write an article on living under the Indian Act, how it suppresses us and keeps us in poverty for his newspaper. I told him that was perfect timing because I could combine it with a book review on *How a People Die* because it accurately describes life on the Indian reserves in the 1960s. I called him a week later, and he and Dave Lakes, his office worker, really appreciated the articles that I've been writing. Dave said they get lots of feedback from people who like the issues that I've been exposing.

In the second week of March, Jennifer got sick, so I went to Chilliwack to look after her. I got there Tuesday but had to leave on Thursday for a doctor's appointment even though she was still sick. The doctor gave me a full physical checkup, and when I told him about my job, he said I was bored with it so my body shut down; sitting in the office drove me crazy because I prefer active outdoors work. I felt a whole lot better now that I knew for sure what happened, but I kind of wondered if that was the problem all along. I was limited in how far I could advance in my career because I was just a forest technician, not a professional forester, so there was no challenge or stimulation to my work. The government held me back in more ways than I realized. In 1981 a psychic said my career was going to be full of deceit, which got me upset because I didn't want to believe him; but looking back over the years, I see that he was right.

In March we met with log brokers and discussed farming sea cucumbers and met interesting people from the Nass River valley in Northern British Columbia. If the business got operating and made a profit, then we would be paid; but Brian Chromko said the government put restrictions on log exports, so our prices would be too high to compete with Russian log exports. If things changed in the future, I made contacts where I could get a supply of logs.

In the fourth week of March, *APTN Contact* discussed aboriginal postsecondary education funding and why it shouldn't be cut off, so I wrote an article on that for *Kahtou*. Education is an equalizer, and aboriginals were held back from getting educated, well-paying jobs through the residential-school system and their spin-off effects. It should be kept available and increased until the aboriginals' lifestyle and living conditions are the same as those of the majority of Canadians. At the end of March when I filed my EI claim, I was told that I was now off medical benefits and they would review my claim, which could take up to three weeks. The lady asked if I could go back to my old job, and at first I reluctantly said yes then reluctantly said no. She asked why, and I reluctantly said, "Because of depression"; and she said, "That's okay." I got a letter the next week, early April, saying I wasn't going to get any more EI benefits; and I got depressed but seemed to get signals saying not to worry.

I was optimistic about what was happening, and by the third week of April, I was starting to feel better and getting my energy back. Then Service Canada said I got my final EI payment, which got me down, so I phoned in to appeal it; and they said they were going to call me back. Service Canada was supposed to call back the next week on Monday but didn't, so I called them at four o'clock and they said a decision had been made, so I would get EI again. It was time to call in my report, so now I would get paid for two pay periods; and the next day, I got a call from a BC Government Employees' Union (BCGEU), who said they have a strong case for my job because of my medical history.

In the first week of May, Isaac called and was angry at me because of when I was ready to beat our mother to a pulp right in front of our dad. He threatened to shoot me, told me not to go around, and said all I had to do was stay away! He was always taking advantage of me, never showed any appreciation for all the times I got him work, didn't ask for anything for room and board, and was always there for him and his family! Then he deliberately pushed his ignorance too far just to be obnoxious, so we got into a big argument and he just hung up. I only went back when I couldn't find work and had no choice, so the next time I saw him, I told him he didn't know how close I came to beating the shit right out of him! If he ever threatened to shoot me again, I would put him in the hospital! Then he started easing up and wasn't as jealous of me as he used to be, but he was still very close to getting the shit beat out of him!

Two days later I called Longhouse Publishing in Mission, British Columbia, and talked to Anne Mohs; and she was excited to see the book review I did on *Amongst God's Own*, a book on the Mission Indian residential school by Terry Glavin. Then I told her my parents and many of my relatives attended St. Mary's Indian residential school in Mission, I'm writing an autobiography, and she recommended I contact a professional editor, Lisa Kenney. I did a covering letter for the book review and included a letter I sent to the Southern Poverty Law Center to show how Canada likes to distort the truth. The next day, the dentist called and said DIA wasn't going to pay for my root canals and to ask if my Indian band would help me; otherwise, I'll have to pay for it myself. I called Lisa Kenney that, day but she wasn't home, so I just left a message. She called back and we briefly discussed my manuscript and what it's like to be aboriginal; but we couldn't meet until the first week of June, a month away.

In the first week of June, Shihan (a high-black belt karate instructor) Einar Gunderson called and said he had my black belt certificate. Both he and Shihan Yabanaka, the head karate instructor of Canada, appreciated the work Chris Gielow and I did to keep the Squamish karate club operating and us training without an instructor, so our technique wasn't at black belt level. The next day, Bing Wong called and asked me to attend a luncheon for him in Vancouver on Sunday, then we could meet with log brokers.

On Friday, Jeff Fisher, RPF, gave me two boxes of cedar seedlings that I could plant rather than throw them away; so I picked them up then met with Lisa Kenney in Abbotsford. We had a good discussion and I gave her a rough draft of my life story. I planted some trees on Saturday then went to Vancouver for a luncheon with Bing Wong. It was a very good meal and met with Tom Duong and Dan, and we talked about exporting pine logs to Mexico and hemlock logs to China. Then I went back to Rosedale and finished planting the seedlings the next day.

I went back to Squamish for a dentist appointment then Simon Murray of. JCH Forestry said he had a box of cedar and Douglas fir seedlings that had to be planted right away. He said the forest nursery had many boxes of seedlings that were going to be destroyed and asked if I wanted any. I said I would take as many as I could fit in the back of my truck, and he said I could fit ten boxes in there. I said I could pick them up on Friday and got excited because I could now plant areas that I wanted to plant and hoped it would rain soon. I planted all the trees on the Indian reserve, but it took time because it's hard work and I'm not a young man used to doing physical work.

In the third week of July, the BCGEU told me Tom Yachnin would be my lawyer representing my case; and the dentist called and said I would have to pay for my root canals, $1,405.80, because DIA wouldn't help me. Then a record heat spell began with temperatures breaking records; it lasted three weeks, and when I checked the trees I planted, most of them died. Many survived on my mother's property but I knew they may not survive if it didn't rain soon. I went to Rosedale the second weekend of August, and it finally rained for two days. I wanted to leave early for karate, but Jennifer wanted me to stay longer, so I stayed. I canned some salmon and did lots of running around for Jennifer, Isaac, and his daughter Nicole; then Isaac finally showed some appreciation. I ran into Uncle Joe and Auntie Irene, and they both had stories to tell of when laws were still discriminating against the Indians and how we were treated by the police, so I had them published in *Kahtou*.

In the third week of August, I brought a résumé and registered with Sitsma Employment Services on the Squamish Nation Indian reserve for work. I never thought of applying to be a security guard but put my name in for training; there weren't very many jobs to apply for, and places where I applied never called back. Then I got an annual survey form from the Federal Liberal Party of Canada and very few people got the survey; and as I was writing a response, I wanted to check issues under the Assembly of First Nations website, and they wanted personal stories to help fight aboriginal poverty. I wrote a paper titled "Making Aboriginal Poverty History" and had it published in *Kahtou*; then I included that, the two-part series on what I went through to get a career, and an article on laws that were clearly discriminating against the Indians sent with the survey and sent it by registered letter. Then Jennifer bought me a coffee mug with Mickey Mouse saying with open arms "I ♥ Dad."

I went back to Rosedale for the second and third week of September to brush out my seedlings, and on September 14, I had to take my niece Sarah to the hospital for antibiotics because she was expecting a baby. I ran into Ryan there because his uncle Bruce was in the hospital, but I didn't want to visit him because I might run into Henry Jr. I spent the night at Jennifer's place and called Patricia Kelly just for something to do, and she asked me to drive her to Seabird Island to apply for a job. I said I could do it on Wednesday because I was still doing my brushing.

When I took Patricia to Seabird Island, the chief, Clem Seymour, said the Union of British Columbia Indian Chiefs (UBCIC) was having a three-day assembly at Harrison Hot Springs; so we went there. I took her there again the next day, and when people had a chance to say something about them, I mentioned the college students being segregated in 1973. When UBCIC found out, much trouble was created but Gary was the only one to get fired, and he was only following orders. On Friday her kids missed the school bus, so I drove her daughter Siyam to school, and she was in grade 8. Siyam said schools still say, "Everyone gets equal treatment in Canada and Indians came over from Asia on a land bridge," and we both thought we would look more Oriental, if that was true.

In the fourth week of September, Tom Yashnin called and asked if I wanted to try and get my job back or try for a settlement. I asked for a settlement because I didn't think there were many other job openings in other forest districts or government departments. Then I went to the Squamish Nation band office to sign up for basic security training, which started the next week. The security training started on Monday, and on Wednesday I got a job interview with a company hiring security guards for the Olympics. What the security company was offering sounded too good to be true, so I automatically thought there was a catch, and people at the course heard stories about that security company; so I didn't sign on with them, and eventually they were mentioned on the news.

In the second week of October, I went to the police station to get my fingerprints because I would need them to get my security license and told the cop taking my fingerprints that laws were clearly discriminating against the Indians when I was a child. In the 1970s when I was getting my career, I thought about being a cop; and a friend who was also trying to join the police force suggested I apply to the Vancouver Police because they don't have any aboriginal constables. Then the cop realized that no one would hire the Indians in the 1970s.

Tom Yashnin called that day and said I might get a small settlement and if I could deposit it directly into my RRSP, I may not have to pay any taxes on it, and he would get back to me. Tom called the next day and said they don't want to give me a settlement or even retrain me and he would call next week. Tom called a week later and said I won't get a settlement and may not even get money for retraining, so I said I didn't want my job back because of too much unjustified harassment. I went to my grievance hearing the next week at the Coast Plaza Hotel in Vancouver near Stanley Park, and Tom said the best he could get for me was a $2,000 training allowance and I couldn't work for the British Columbia government again, but I didn't want to anyway.

That weekend, Tom Harry, owner of Sko-mish Valley Security Services, asked me if I could start working for him. I was happy to work because my EI would run out soon and the money I made working would be tax free because Tom's office is on Indian reserve. Security started at a new London Drugs store that was still under construction, and at first, the work was inside the building. On one shift I spent six hours sitting in my truck and thought time would drag by, but when I thought about love and lust, time flew by. After the job at London Drugs was over, we did security at a gaming center and gas station that were under construction. I found working in security rather enjoyable because I read many books that I never got around to reading before and borrowed books from the library. I also worked on my life story and articles that I wrote for *Kahtou* while at work. Work was rather slow in November and my EI claim ran out. Then in December, a staff member quit; so I got more shifts but had to work Christmas Day, Boxing Day, and New Year's Eve.

Chapter 32

2010

I continued working in Security at the Gaming centre and Gas station construction sites and used the time to work on my life story. I had repeated myself a number of times to get my feelings of anger out so now I was reviewing my work and deleting incidents that I repeated or thought weren't important. It was still stressful to re-live what I went through so I took a few chapters to work in a binder, looked it over, decided what changes should be made then made the changes on my computer at home.

Then at the beginning of February we did 2 weeks of security for Natives from across Canada attending a youth conference. Natives were given much recognition at these Olympics, Indian Dancers did their dances at the opening and closing ceremonies and an Aboriginal museum and cultural centre was built in Whistler where many events were held. I thought that was great because I don't know if we were mentioned at all during the 1976 Olympics in Montreal, Quebec and possibly only mentioned as carrying the Olympic Torch in the 1988 Olympics in Calgary. Then with the 1988 Olympics in a magazine an Indian fellow said we would be accepted while carrying the torch then told to keep our distance again once it was over.

We worked long hours for the 2 weeks when the Olympics were going on then when it was over we only got part time work. That was disappointing because I wanted to put more money on my bills but couldn't. The Gaming Centre was built in time to open the Olympics but we still did security at the Gas Bar which was still under construction. Security was only part time work now so I used my time to work on my life story and had it finished to date by the end of March. I thought I wasn't doing too badly on my bills then Aaron called and said the top plate of his dentures cracked and asked to borrow $320 to get it fixed. Since people can't eat very well without teeth I helped him even though it brought my bills up again. He was on welfare and couldn't afford to get them fixed but at least he wasn't drinking or on drugs anymore.

Security at the Gas Bar ended on April 9 and Tom Harry thought he was going to get some more contracts so I didn't apply for Employment Insurance. I felt bored one day so I went to Employment Resources, an office that helps people find work, put resumes and job application letters together, has job listings and computers for people to look for work. Since I was bored I looked up my name on the internet and was surprised to find that an American named Annis Aleck wrote an article on the "Jewish Holocaust and it sounded like it was written by me so I went home, looked it up on my computer then sent it to a few people. Then I wrote a response and sent it to the American named Annis Aleck. Here's what it was:

Jewish Holocaust

By an American named Annis Aleck, 2006-11-23

I agree, it is really odd that they'd wait all these years to make this story public but nonetheless how is it possible to forge or recreate so many documents? It would take a vast conspiracy and hundreds if not thousands of people many years to forge these documents. Making sure everything was accurate while fabricating hundreds of thousands of accounts would be virtually impossible. It seems rather probable that the holocaust did happen but I also believe that the Israeli people use it a little too often to make people feel sorry for them and then take advantage of them. I hate how we have the holocaust shoved down our throats as Americans. Every day it seems like a new movie, book, or television show comes out regarding the holocaust. I believe that it's ignorant for people to believe that Jews are the only people that have ever had to go through hard times or have been the only victims of genocide. I believe that more people were killed by the Nazis than the amount of Jews that were killed. Also, people hardly ever mention the slaughter imposed by Stalin most likely because a lot of the territory we gave to the Soviet Union after WW II was were Stalin imposed his harshest policies and slaughtered the most people. Americans don't want to face the fact that we basically turned these people and their countries over to Stalin to have them slaughtered. So, people never mention the genocide we took part in. We basically vanquished the entire race of Native Americans within the United States. This was genocide people and we were the ones that did it.

If "6 million" actually died, why wait so long to open up these "archives"—unless a lot of the content is BOGUS . . . .

Also, very convenient to wait until ALL the purported "eyewitnesses" have died, don't you think.

So, 10,000 died or perhaps 25,000—but the allegation has been "6 million"—quite a different number—and how come so many "eyewitnesses" lived to tell about it—why were they spared by the big bad Nazis—perhaps to tell us all about this infamous "Holocaust" when the war ended—yeah sure—and Hitler was a Jew.

It has always been a fishy story, told to support the Zionist petition to the UN, through the USA, for the creation of Israel.

Response to Jewish Holocaust

Canada was just as much against the Jews during the Holocaust as most other countries were but appeared to leave exterminating them to other countries. I asked a lady of Russian-Jewish descent to research and expose Canada's reaction towards the Jews during the Holocaust of WW II then the Prime Minister at that time got put into the Hall of Shame in March 2005. In the series "Canada: a People's History", episode 14 at a Jewish Death camp there was a warehouse full of food that could have kept them from starving but they were cut off from it so they called the warehouse Canada. Fortunately some Jews survived the death camps to tell the story because they were rescued by the allies. Canada tries to keep the truth of how they treated minorities hidden but I've been researching and exposing it to influential people and publishing it in a newspaper.

Canada also tried to exterminate the Indians like the USA but used subtle methods like diseases, the Residential Schools, oppression and sterilization of women rather than war fare. It's said genocide was successful in Prince Edward Island, PEI, one of that Atlantic Provinces but it may have only been the Beothuk who were exterminated though. In the 1995 Canadian statistics of incomes of Native elders compared to non-Native elders there's no information on PEI. On the internet in PEI "census returns after 1901 are deemed confidential by Stats Canada and are unavailable" but doesn't say why. After the Residential Schools Indians who tried to do something for themselves were held back by Department of Indian Affairs, DIA, a branch of the Federal Govt. This didn't only happen to those who went for Post Secondary education but even those who applied to take a trade were often put in a course different than what they wanted or applied for. I don't know when this ended but it was still going on in the 1970's when I was getting my career.

In the 1950's and 60's the Royal Canadian Mounted Police, RCMP, were ordered to kill the Inuit, formerly called Eskimos, sled dogs and people can't live off the land in the Arctic without dogs. It would have been more merciful to shoot the people but that was illegal yet it wasn't illegal to starve them to death. Dogs were everything to the Inuit people and as soon as I heard about this I reported it to influential people, including Amnesty International. Now a major investigation is being done and naturally the RCMP deny it happened at all but some Inuit who survived are telling the story.

I was born in 1955 and laws were still discriminating against us right up to 1964 but we still face discrimination in the 21st century. Many Indians I went to school with didn't live to be 25, they either committed suicide or died of an alcohol related death. Many other Canadian Indians tell the same story only in my case the one that cut himself up with a knife 2 times, lost is front teeth in a car accident then committed suicide when he was 22 used to be my foster brother. In 2000 I wrote a paper on the high rate of suicide and alcohol and drug related deaths among the Indians titled "Grim Reality". Also in 2000, Harinder Mahil, British Columbia, BC, Commissioner of Human Rights said Aboriginals have 10 times the national average suicide rate. It's illegal to outright kill people but not illegal to drive them to suicide and kill themselves. Many Aboriginals aren't physically dead, just physically existing as alcoholics, drug addicts and welfare cases.

The truth of Canada's treatment of Aboriginals doesn't usually get exposed exactly the way things happened unless the story is told by the Aboriginals themselves. Usually when Canadians say they're saying what happened the stories are so distorted there's very little, if any truth to what they're saying. The truth can often be very slow to come out, even how the Americans tried to exterminate the Indians didn't come out for decades, possibly when *Bury My Heart at Wounded Knee* first got published. I've spoken out to the media and not only did they not say one word about what happened they didn't even leave a message on my answering machine saying they got the information. That was no surprise but a major disappointment because of all the time and effort it took to find the truth. My friend's daughter is 14 and in grade 8 said schools still tell the students, "Everyone gets Equal Treatment in Canada."

It's said there's 2 ways to exterminate people, genocide and put them all on welfare. In 1970 Alan Fry wrote a book titled "How a People Die". Although it's labelled fiction it accurately describes living conditions on Indian Reserves in BC in the 1960's. Alan may have had to call it fiction just to get the book published and avoid law suits. Indians often drank because of the pain and anger of what they went through in the Residential Schools then fell victim to alcoholism and the problems it causes. Genocide was attempted in many countries in the 20th century as was illustrated in "Worse that War" by Daniel Jonah Goldhagen, son of a Jewish Holocaust survivor but I'm mainly interested in exposing the truth about Canada.

It seems rather ironic that we have the exact same name, have very similar views and opinions and your paper is well written and sounds like it could have been written by me. Since Annis isn't a very common name people sometimes think I'm a woman but I'm a man. I've been writing for Kahtou, an Aboriginal monthly newspaper since June 2008, exposing much of the truth about Canada's treatment of Aboriginals and a little bit about Chinese Canadians. People willing to face and accept the truth say the Indians of Canada are some of the world's most oppressed people. Right up to the late 1960's in southern BC they went to the USA just to get a low paying job working on the farms and orchards.

In the third week of April Jennifer had a court hearing for her Residential School experience which was held at a hotel in Chilliwack. She had asked that me and Ryan be allowed to attend and a lady there who worked on Residential School cases suggested she go to a treatment centre on Vancouver Island. Treatment centres aren't only for people with drug and alcohol addiction problems but also emotional stress. Then I visited my mother and Aunty Tilley and cousin Robin were there and we went to Isaac and Helen's for supper. As I was leaving I told Isaac that if he ever threatened to shoot me again I would put him in the hospital! He was lucky I haven't beaten the shit right out of him already!

By May I wasn't called back to work so I applied for Employment Insurance, EI, again and was eligible for benefits but my claim wasn't back dated to when I got laid off so I lost $1,200. That was disappointing because I could have used the money to pay for my truck insurance, now I had to put it on my credit card and go deeper in debt. At the end of May I realised that I may have done something wrong that I knew I shouldn't have done, I didn't do it again when asked because I knew it was wrong and could suffer for it.

That month there was an ad in Kahtou for an Indigenous Independent Film making course at Capilano University in North Vancouver from July 5 to 9. I applied to take the course to expand my job skills, perhaps get into another line of work and maybe even find someone who would want to put what I went through to get a career into a documentary. I asked other people earlier but they weren't interested or didn't have the money.

On June 1, I felt stressed out and thought about buying a case of beer but flipped a coin and it told me to buy a bottle of whiskey instead. When I went to buy some pop to mix with it I run into John Howe, an RPF who owns a Forest consulting company and asked if he had any spare tree seedlings so he told me to call Tom Cole at Richmond Plywood, a forest company. I called Tom and he told me to ask Chris Nunn at N&R, another Forest consulting company. I called Chris Nunn but he couldn't give me any seedlings right away because he was trying to sell them. I had also applied for the job as a silviculture surveyor that they advertized but he said my chances of getting it were extremely remote because they had so many applicants. I was happy about that though because I was trying to find other work.

Then in the second week of June Jeff Fisher gave me some more cedar seedlings and Chris Nunn said he could give me some more douglas fir seedlings. It was getting late in the season for tree planting but I thought it was still worth the risk of trying to get a crop of trees established on my Reserve. I planted as many trees as I could for 2 weeks, which is hard, back breaking work and I'm not a young man then took a 2 week break. I also needed a week off so I could take the Digital Film making course.

When I started the Digital Film making course I showed the lab assistant Tobi Caplett the outline of what I went through to get a career that I had published in Kahtou and she agreed that it could be made into a documentary. We were divided into groups of 4 people and told to do a three minute edit of an Aboriginal film that we saw as children that gave us an impression of what it was like to be Native. I was grouped with 3 other women and we choose the movie *Unnatural & Accidental.* I told them the story the movie was based on and the movie distorted the story so much that it came out as a completely different story.

One lady in my group, Kerry Sugiyama, worked for APTN got really mad when she heard the truth and some viewer's reaction. Then Kerry looked up the serial killer and found the names of 10 Aboriginal women that he killed and one lady in my group, Melanie, not her real name, thought he may have killed her mother. Melanie said her mother was found dead in a hotel room from alcohol consumption. I really enjoyed the course but didn't want to go back to college or university for 2 years to make a career of it. I already spent enough time in college and didn't think anyone would hire me at my age.

I went back to Rosedale to plant more trees and brush out seedlings that I planted last year. When I finished the planting and brushing I was going to take Patricia Kelly out for lunch to discuss editing but she wasn't home so I went to the Mandarin restaurant which serves a Chinese buffet. I run into Jennifer's uncle Sunny Boy and cousin Larry so I had lunch with them. Sunny Boy said Henry Jr. was building a giant house, the biggest in Stolo Eagle then called him and Andrew assholes. Then he said he's surrounded by assholes because both of them live in a house on either side of him.

In the third week of July I developed a rash on the right side of my chest and thought it would go away but I flipped a coin and it told me to go to the doctor. The rash got worse before I was able to see him and he said it was shingles caused by stress so I wondered if it was from wanting to beat the shit right out of Isaac? That day Rey Francis from Xlibis Publishing in Bloomington, Indiana called me and we talked about getting my book published. Previously I had gone on the computer to look for a Literary Agent for first time authors to find a publisher and now I got a response. I told Rey I would send him some of the articles that I wrote for Kahtou and a brief outline of my life story to give him a sample of my writing.

In the third week of August Rey Francis called again and said he liked my articles and agreed that *Jewish Holocaust* sounded like it was written by me. Xlibis has a number of self publishing packages offered, depending on what the author wants and can afford and offered me the Platinum Package, the best package at half price if I agreed to buy it before the end of the month. It sounded good but I was reluctant to buy it because I owed too much money on my credit cards already. The next day I looked at what the Platinum Package offered and decided that was too much material for me and I wouldn't be able to sell that many books on my own. Then I looked at the Executive Service Package, the second best, and decided that would suit my needs much better and was cheaper so I asked if I could get it at half price. Then my TV broke down so I said I wouldn't be able to afford it unless it's at half price so Rey had to ask permission to reduce the cost.

That week I got a petition in my email for a "Walk for Justice" by Gladys Radek to pressure the Federal Govt. for a Public Inquiry into the almost six hundred missing and murdered Aboriginal women across Canada. There was a column beside the signatures for comments so I signed the petition and my comment was, "If these were White women that went missing and murdered would there be a need for a Walk for Justice? Aboriginal women are people too!"

Since I didn't have a TV I spent more time working on my book and enjoyed it. I went over it completely, changing the names of the people, the names of the Indian Reserves and making adjustments. It was still stressful but was getting easier all the time.

Near the end of August Jennifer called and said she was invited to a dinner at Stolo Eagle and when I asked her what it was for she said Henry Jr. was having a house built and it was a house warming. I knew he wouldn't want me there and I heard Brenda was coming down from Kelowna. The next day I asked Jennifer if Alvin was there and she said he was but closed her ears when I said, "Did Henry Jr. lay out the red carpet for him?"

There had been a record dry spell that year and I knew many of the seedlings I planted may not survive. Some people on the Reserve had built a sweat lodge by the Health Building and I wanted to go for a sweat to see what it was like. If my Dad was still alive he may have tried to keep me away from them because they're not scientifically proven and he tried to keep me away from our old traditions. The sweat was scheduled for a certain day then got delayed so I was going to go back to Squamish but Sue was staying with my mother and suggested I stay for the sweat. This was organized by Mike, the Alcohol & Drug councillor working for the Reserve.

The fellow conducting the sweat was Arthur (Art) Clifford Shofley, an Aboriginal elder who had worked at conducting traditional ceremonies and as an Aboriginal Spiritual Care Specialist. Sue originally planned on attending but didn't make it and I was surprised Aaron and three other people were there. The sweat was incredibly hot with the steam from water poured over the hot rocks and Art sang Aboriginal songs and drummed. Art had been doing sweats for 50 years and said that was one of the most intense sweats he's ever done even though there was only 5 people there. I knew there was an incredible amount of anger from the people there and I had much anger in me that I just didn't know how to deal with. The sweat seemed to just lift it off and take it away so I felt a whole lot better when it was over and thought I should go at least 3 more times. Art said I'm over my last hill and anger, now things are all downhill and will be easier for me!

I went back to Squamish then on Sunday Tony called and said Aunty Jeannette passed away the other day and he's going down for prayers tomorrow. I called mother and she said she's going down for prayers too so I said I would go with them then went to Chilliwack the next day and we were all going to go down with Isaac. We left early because we knew we would be delayed at the border because of Tony's criminal drug record but when we got to the border we were turned back then delayed on the Canadian side. Isaac got arrested, handcuffed and taken to jail in Chilliwack by an RCMP constable. Isaac owed a fine and was making payments on it but a clerk thought he should have been making larger payments because he had 3 part time jobs. Work was very sporadic for him so he paid what he could and when he went to court the next day the judge said that should never have happened.

I went to the Health Building 2 days later for an appointment with Mike for counselling on my anger. Mike said people who are gifted get tested, sometimes severely if they're exceptionally gifted. Saving Jennifer from suicide and getting her a career was an ordeal I wouldn't wish on anyone then I wondered if she was gifted too? She was lucky she survived what she sent through before I met her then breaking her depression and getting her a career was also an extreme test of my patience. Then I showed Mike the letter I wrote to Dr Clare Brant and told him about standing up to someone 3 times my size for a knife fight.

In the last week of September I called Kahtou and found out they're an international paper that gets distributed to many countries in the world. Then I decided I should put a brief outline of my life story in the paper to show the effects the Residential Schools had on the families of those who survived. Then on October 1, Rey Francis called and offered me the Executive Service publishing package at 80% off but I had to decide right away so I accepted it, saving me $5,400.

The next week I went to Adrienne Boots for a psychic reading and she said I still have much anger festering inside me that I have to work on releasing through sweats, hunting, etc. That night my mother called because she was concerned about my anger and almost told me to stop visiting if I wanted to stay that angry. She said I always blame my anger on someone else and didn't want me to drink at her house anymore! She was one of the main causes of my anger and no matter how much trouble she caused me she still kept telling me what to do! Not only that, everyone was jealous of seeing me have fun in life and tried to hold me back, even my Dad accused me of being religious when I was happy and now she's saying my anger is all my fault!

Black Tusk Fire & Security also called me to their office in Whistler for a job interview as a security guard. I went for the interview and got some work in Whistler doing security. When I went to work one day the security guard getting off work, Mark, had to wait for his ride. Mark said he was from Washington, DC and knew about Aboriginal women being sterilized 2 years ago from when he worked in security at a college in Langley.

Thanksgiving weekend was coming up and my mother said we may not have a Thanksgiving dinner this year because my cousin Barney's wife was sick and doesn't have very long to live so everyone was going down to see her. I called Stan Dixon about putting a brief outline of my life story in Kahtou and he wanted an article on what Christmas meant for Aboriginals, even if it's just a short story.

In the middle of October Jennifer called when she was drinking and told our friends that I saved her life. She sometimes gives me recognition for what I've done, Ryan sometimes gives me a little bit of recognition but other than that her family acts like it was nothing. If it was Alvin who did that much for Brenda everyone would have done everything they could to help then they wouldn't be able to do enough for him!

In the third week of October I had an appointment with Lois Hansen, a councillor who works with people affected by the Residential Schools. It went well and she wanted to see the articles that I wrote for Kahtou. In the afternoon I went for another sweat, it went well, wasn't as intense as the first and I let go of more anger. On the weekend I realised that I'm almost 55, never had a chance to raise a family or buy a home and wondered what was going to become of my life. My whole life was spent looking after Jennifer.

In early November I started feeling better and felt like I was getting my sense of humour back again, I felt like I lost it before I left the BC Forest Service. Then Xlibis called about a contract for my book so I signed it and sent it to them. On my birthday I didn't drink and woke up happy! I was 55 now and eligible to start drawing my pension. My cousin Sharon Shackelly in Merritt called and was happy for my suggestion of physical fitness as a safety factor for fire fighters. When it escalated to unit crews who were employed full time for up to 8 months of the year it helped many Natives in remote communities and her son had worked at it for 14 years now.

Then I interviewed a few Aboriginals about what Christmas was like for them when they were growing up and it wasn't long and I had 4 pages of hand written information. This would work out to 2 ½ pages when typed, the maximum length for Kahtou. Many Aboriginal families were poor and alcoholic when they were growing up so there were many stories to tell. I almost didn't interview James because his step father worked but he had quite a story to tell. I called Dave Lakes at Kahtou that week and he said Kahtou is distributed worldwide, even to Germany and they haven't gotten any negative feedback on the issues I exposed yet. I heard there's a strong interest in Native culture and languages in Germany and they're also interested in how Natives have been treated in Canada and the USA.

In the third week of November I got Jennifer to attend a sweat and she got Aaron to come too. She was probably scared to go and seemed to drag her feet getting ready but felt better when it was over. Sue was also there and said I looked a lot more relaxed after attending the sweats. I had another appointment with Lois Hansen the next day and she liked the articles and the outline of my life story.

On the weekend I got a job working in Security at Chances Gaming Centre, the gambling operation where I did security while the building was under construction. I was happy about that because now I could put higher payments on my bills without dipping into my savings. I wasn't scheduled for very many hours at first then a security guard who wasn't very happy working there walked off the job so I got more hours of work.

In the TV series "Nazi Hunters" Josef Mengele was hunted down for performing medical experiments on Jewish children and sterilizing women in inferior races to create a master race. Canada secretly ordered Indian and Inuit girls sterilized right up to the early 1970's and Indians were used for medical experiments but my cousin with a PhD in Native studies doesn't know when it ended but it's possible it went on right up to the 1960's.

When Christmas came we had our dinner the day before Christmas because the turkey pan wouldn't fit in the oven at my mother's place so Isaac always cooked it. He had to work Christmas day so our dinner was a day early. Then my mother finally realised how much trouble she caused me when she made life so boring for me that I barely made it through grade 11 then had a hard time getting going again. Isaac's Black friend Noel, who's 6 years younger than me came over for dinner and I told him how staff treated me when I worked for the BC Forest Service. The men closed me off and the women didn't only close me off they did things that got me in trouble, made me look bad and interfered with my work even though I tried to be nice to them. I also told him I was the first Native to graduate in the Forestry program at BCIT and Helen and Nicole were sitting there listening to what I was telling him.

I had to go back to work on Boxing Day, the day after Christmas at the Gaming Centre and got extra work in Security with Black Tusk. Now that I no longer work for the BC Forest Service and Security is only part time work I can draw my pension and become a writer. I started looking for Roger Adolph, a former professional boxer who asked me to write his life story for him so I could start working on it. Canada and Canadians couldn't turn me into a White Indian, ie. Welfare bum no matter how hard they tried! Here's the article I wrote for Kahtou on Christmas for Aboriginals:

Christmas for Aboriginals

Stan Dixon asked me to write about what Christmas meant for Aboriginals after surviving the horrors of the Residential Schools, trying to find work and the kinds of jobs they were able to get. Some had a normal Christmas celebration but for some families sometimes there was no Christmas because they were poor because Canada tried to keep us living in extreme poverty. Stories can still be told, even while they were in the Residential School.

My Dad mentioned that when he was in the Residential School Santa Claus was just another person because they weren't allowed to go home at Christmas. My mother said he got a book on his first Christmas but he didn't know how to read yet.

A close relative said they didn't have a Christmas as a child because they had no money, only $15 a month in Relief for the family, if they got extra money it would have went to her step father. The first time there was even a hint of Christmas she was about 8 years old, perhaps younger when her sister bought a cake. She started St Mary's Residential School in Mission, BC at 7 and wasn't allowed to go home during the year then in grade 6 she was allowed to go home at Christmas. There were approximately 300 students at St Mary's and a cannery near the school that contributed some food because some students did some work for them but there was no such thing as Christmas. Eventually she got a black doll that was very small and stationary for a while then it was upgraded to a bigger doll. The boys got a truck and everyone got the same thing. For her life was better in school than at home because her step father was very abusive towards her mother but she was only one of two people I've met that said life was better in school than at home.

Uncle Percy Roberts said when he was very young there was no Christmas then he got gifts from school but the kids at home didn't have any so small gifts started. Then there was some oranges and a turkey when Indians started getting welfare in the late 1950's.

Paul Johnny, born in 1947 said Christmas was just another day because they couldn't go home from the Residential School for Christmas or Easter. He left the school to play hockey though which was a relief for him. Christmas was just a religious holiday, no special event for him. Paul was against all religions but started celebrating Christmas for his kids.

Greg, not his real name, from Lytton, BC was physically handicapped, a heavy drinker and separated from his wife but kept the kids. He said he couldn't afford a turkey so he just cooked a salmon which was readily available so Christmas must have been just another day for his kids. Greg attempted suicide several times, woke up in the hospital after one attempt then jumped out a window and was finally successful.

Mike, an Alcohol and Drug Councillor in my age group said as he was growing up there was lots of drinking at Christmas, the drinking came before the presents. He lived with a foster family and was treated as 2nd class even though they were related. He got new clothes at the beginning of the school year and at Christmas so it wasn't toys like most children got.

Jamie, 2 years older than me didn't have a Christmas celebration except with his grandmother, then had a dinner and presents. His step father was a chronic alcoholic, always violent, threw the tree out after the first day when drunk and kicked the kids out in a drunken rage. When the step father was sober they had a turkey dinner with his step grandmother combined with traditional foods but Jamie still hated his guts through and through and didn't think there were any kids on that Reserve that weren't molested.

My cousin, Sharon Shackelly is one year younger than me and has 3 brothers older than me said sometimes there was no presents or hardly anything but had a turkey dinner. The parents were poor and away a lot but were there for Christmas so it was nice to have everyone together. Frozen huckle berries were a treat and they sometimes got toys from an Anglican Priest. Some of her cousins had bannock for lunch and were ashamed of it but she sometimes got cake with icing. Since the parents were away a lot Sharon took her younger siblings and hid in the mountains so they wouldn't get taken away.

Maria, not her real name, born in 1961 and the lady that mentioned racism in Duncan, BC in *Aboriginals and Immigrants, Part 4* said as a child they celebrated Christmas with a turkey dinner and presents. Then when her parents separated she lived with her mother and had 2 different step fathers. One step father was jealous of her mother spending money on her because he wanted it spent on his kids. Then when she was 15 she moved back to her father's Reserve and cooked a dinner. Her father and his friends came home drunk, knocked the tree over and dishes were broken so she just joined the party. After that Christmas was just a party.

The girl I called Jennifer was born in 1962 and her father went to school with my father in the Residential School. Presents couldn't be opened until her father got up and sometimes he wouldn't get up until 2:00 in the afternoon. Sometimes his friends would come over and party, the kids would have to run for them, a big mess would be made and the kids would have to clean it up. One year they didn't even have a turkey dinner but luckily the grandparents invited them over. Another year all her older sisters got for Christmas was a potato peeler so they just kind of looked at it but I don't know what Jennifer got.

Since the Residential Schools didn't prepare the Indians to get an educated, professional job they had to settle for labourer's jobs. On the coast there were jobs in logging and fishing but these jobs kept them away from their families for extended periods of time. There was also work in fish canneries but this was all seasonal work. This wasn't available in the interior of BC or the prairie provinces, a fellow who used to live in Alberta said they either worked the farms or in arts and crafts. In BC Indians sometimes started forest fires then applied for a job fighting fires or in the southern part of BC worked the farms and orchards in the USA. Since Indians had to either do something illegal or leave the country just to get a low paying job it's quite possible Christmas was just another day for many Aboriginal families. In Merritt I sometimes saw Indians come to town on horseback or horse and wagon with parents and children on the wagon, a family friend said he saw a wagon with 10 kids on it. I don't think any family would choose to live that poor when the majority of Canadians were working and providing a comfortable living for their family.

Before I got a permanent job with the BC Forest Service I had to travel to wherever work was available. In 1978 I worked in Lower Post, BC's most northern town and the rate of unemployment and alcoholism was phenomenal! I also worked near other isolated Reserves where there was just nothing there for work and very little for entertainment. Extreme poverty and boredom often causes social problems like alcoholism, addiction, sniffing glue and other insolvents and in many cases suicide or attempted suicide. On October 30, 2010 Aboriginal People's Television Network News broadcast an Aboriginal community of 1200 people near Fort Hope, Ontario where 50% of the population is addicted to prescription pills but this probably isn't the only one. A Police Constable there said some people commit crimes so they can go to jail so they can get away from the community. In communities like that Christmas is probably just another day to them. Sharon Shackelly said they may have wanted to go to jail for the winter for a warm place to stay with 3 meals a day.

Last August I received a petition for a "Walk for Justice for the Missing and Murdered Women of Canada" to pressure the Govt for a Public Inquiry by Gladys Radek, there's been almost 600 missing and murdered Aboriginal women in Canada over the last 4 decades. On the petition there's a column for signatures and for comments. I signed the petition and my comment was, "If these were White women who went missing and murdered would there be a need for a Walk for Justice? Aboriginal women are people too!" No matter what life style they lived they still had family who loved them, they were either someone's daughter, sister, mother, aunt or loved one. Christmas can be painful not knowing what happened to their missing or murdered loved one, no closure and that the killer or killers may still be free, seeking more victims.

Epilogue: Things I saw happen and stories I heard.

I grew up in the middle of town and my parents said very little about what they went through so I didn't feel different than anyone else. As I was growing up I remember often seeing Indians drunk on the streets and people could tell the Indian Reserves by the extreme poverty, the rundown houses and most of them had wells, outhouses, wood stoves and many didn't have electricity or running water. I was too young to think anything of it though.

When I was about eleven years old my mother sent me to the grocery store to buy something and as I was standing in line at the cash register the customer in front of me asked the clerk where there was a bar. The clerk said, "Right across the street.

The customer said, "I don't know if I'm allowed in there. That's where all the Indians hang out."

Then the clerk said, "You should have seen them before when they hung out at the Coldwater Hotel! Oh . . . ."

Although I was young I was mature for my age and just shrugged it off but the clerk just snubbed me.

When I was a child our neighbour and his wife were Chinese and their son and David became friends because they were the same age.

My dad said when he was in school the other kids bullied him, they used to corner him and push his face in the snow even though he was a nice guy and was always nice to us.

On my first job in 1971 I went haying, stacking bales of hay on a ranch and the boss's wife cooked for the crew. She mentioned a Japanese fellow who was very bitter about how he was treated by the Canadians and took it out on the prisoners of war and became known as one of the worst sadists. My dad said he was bitter about how everything was taken away from the Japanese during WW II and twenty years later a documentary was made about him, calling him "The Kamloops Kid".

I tried to be athletic in high school and in 1972 I went to a track meet in Williams Lake and on both sides of the street on that one city block there was nothing but drunk Indians, some of them past out and some staggering along the sidewalk with a gallon of wine loosely held in a brown paper grocery bag in each hand. Since I was only 16 at the time I was too young to realize why they were like that and how much it makes other Canadians think of us as being nothing but a bunch of lazy, useless drunks. When I started working for the BC Forest Service in 1991 when I ran into Indians my age and older I would ask them if they travelled around BC in the 1960's to mid 70's and they always knew what I was talking about and that I was referring to Williams Lake.

I went to college right after finishing high school in 1973 and was only 17 so I couldn't go to the bars until a year later and the Indians used to drink in a bar that was called the Nelson Place, at the corner of Nelson and Granville Streets in Vancouver. One time in 1974 I was in the bar I went to the washroom and a white fellow, about 40 years old tried talking to an Indian fellow and the Indian said with extreme bitterness, "I don't like whites!"

"You don't like whites," he said then he looked at me and said, "What are you doing here?"

"Just relieving myself," I replied.

"That's a good way to put it," he said.

Another time when I went down there and went to the washroom there was 2 Indian fellows who were friends when another Indian came in and started talking about god. The taller Indian got mad right now and yelled, "Just lay off with that god business!" and made a swift kick for his groin but stopped within a fraction of an inch then said, "Do you want me to send you where god is?"

In the summer of 1975 when I was tree planting a forestry student working there asked me why there are very few Indian students in university and I didn't know why. When tree planting was over I got a job with the CN Railroad and was having a beer in a bar in Terrace with one of the caboose men, they still had cabooses back then. He complained about Indians with a chip on their shoulder over of past injustices that happened over 100 years ago that he had nothing to do with.

Like most people I didn't know why the Indians were like that then eventually learned that they were very bitter about how they were treated in the Indian Residential Schools. Many Indians said they were very badly treated and beaten just for speaking their own language even if they didn't know a word of English. Dad said when he was there it was ½ a day of class and ½ a day of work, the schools did nothing to prepare them for the outside world and the clergy staff were more interested in teaching the Indians religion than in educating them. He wanted to be an engineer but couldn't get his grade 12 in school, he could only go as far as grade 8. When I worked in Cache Creek in 1985 one fellow there said he worked harder at the Residential School than at any other time in his life, a couple kids froze to death when they ran away from there and he was younger than my parents.

St. Mary's Indian Residential School in Mission where my parents attended was first opened in 1860 and the Indians couldn't get their grade 12 there until 1952 because Uncle Joe was one of the first Indians to get his grade 12 there. Up to 1947 it was ½ a day of classes and ½ a day of work and Indians were forced to attend these schools by legislation. As a child I remember seeing a commercial on TV showing young Black students in school and the ad saying, "A mind is a precious thing to waste. Please give to the United Negro College fund." I didn't know that many Indians in Canada never had a chance to do something with their life because of what they went through in the Residential Schools. Most people believe we get equal treatment because the schools keep drilling that into our heads.

There's many things Canadians don't know about how the Indians have been treated because nothing is said about it in school and when books and the media say they're exposing what happened the stories are usually so distorted that there's very little, if any truth to what they're saying. Some examples of blatant racism legislated by the Govt. that didn't change for years are:

- Indians didn't have the right to vote in Provincial elections until 1949 but some people say it was 1952. Perhaps it varied with different provinces.
- Indians didn't have the right to vote in Federal elections until 1960.
- It was illegal for Indians to practise their religious beliefs or hold festivals until 1951. If we got caught we served 2 to 6 months in jail.
- Indians weren't allowed to "pre-empt" (take-up land) in BC between 1866 and 1951.
- Indians weren't allowed to hire lawyers or pursue land claims between 1927 and 1951.
- It was illegal for Indians to have liquor of any kind, not even homemade wine in our own house on the Indian Reserves. Then in 1960 we were allowed to drink in the bars but not at home then in 1964 we were allowed to drink like everyone else but those who drank too much were **Blacklisted** and not allowed to buy liquor anymore.
- It was illegal to practise Indian Art until 1955, the year I was born.

I never really thought about when it was illegal for Indians to have liquor until many years later, even though we weren't even allowed homemade wine in our own house on the Indian Reserve. Then my mother said sugar sales were restricted to try to keep us from making homemade wine so I did some research and wrote a paper on it titled "Sugar and Vanilla Extract". Although I held back information and only went back to when I was a child it was 7 pages long, hand written, which was about 4 ½ pages typed then I had to shorten it to 2 ½ pages to get it published in Kahtou. Here it is:

Sugar and Vanilla Extract!

Laws were clearly discriminating to the Indians right up to the early 1960's! I wasn't going to bring up the issue that it was still illegal for Indians to have liquor of any kind, not even home made wine in our own house on the Indian Reserves to influential people until I was told about sugar sale restrictions to try and keep us from making home made wine!

In the process of researching that issue I found out about vanilla extract then wrote the following report! This article has been slightly modified from its original version!

Most of the issues I brought up so far to influential people dealt with obstacles Indians had to face while getting a career or even just getting a job. There was one law that was clearly discriminating against the Indians that most people don't believe ever existed in Canada yet it still existed when I was a child, I was born in 1955. Since it didn't involve work or career goals I wasn't going to mention it but last year just before Christmas I found out there was more to it than most people, even Indians, realised. I also thought you should see how clearly discriminating laws were as late as the early sixties.

When I was a child it was still illegal to sell liquor to the Indians. We weren't even allowed home made wine on the Indian Reserves and the penalties were quite severe! Therefore Indians drank vanilla extract and called it Black Magic. I sometimes saw or heard of Indians drinking vanilla extract as a child and on my first job in 1971 part of the crew talked about drinking Black Magic. Like any other drink some people developed a taste for it so that became their preferred drink. I also heard Indians drank shaving lotion, Listerine and after shave as well because that was all they could get.

As I said in a previous article Indians drank because of the pain and anger of what they went through in the Indian Residential Schools and often fell victim to alcohol addiction. Many Indians gave up their Indian status so they could drink without getting a heavy fine or do time in jail. Giving up their Indian status was known as enfranchising. Some of my friends in grade school were non status Indians because their parents enfranchised so they could drink. This was rather common knowledge to the Indians right down to my age group but no one was totally clear as to when this law was modified then completely removed.

Retired RCMP constables who joined the force in the late 1950's sometimes put workshops on in Squamish. They said in 1960 Indians were allowed to drink in the bars but not at home. Then in 1964 they could drink like everyone else. Two or 3 years ago I called Dept of Justice and asked what the fines were for underage drinking on the third offence in 1960? The lady who answered got really defensive and snapped, ***"Why don't you check the library?"***

Last year just before Christmas my mother said at one time it was illegal to sell sugar to the Indians to keep us from making home made wine. I checked into it because I thought probably sugar sales were just restricted so we couldn't make wine. If she had told me earlier it would have been easier to research this issue because most of those people who would have remembered have past away or are too old to remember it clearly. Their kids may not know very much about it either because they could have been in the Residential Schools for 10 months of the year.

Alvin Tolley said back east sugar sales were restricted until 1960 so the Indians couldn't make moonshine. If the Indians drank moonshine it was hard to tell if they were drinking because you couldn't smell it on their breath. Indians couldn't buy sugar in large quantities and this was enforced by the Indian Agent. In northern communities Hudson's Bay Company had a set amount of sugar they could sell and when that ran out the Priests sold sugar and tripled their prices. In 1985 liquor sales were introduced on Indian Reserves because of a change in the Indian Act.

When I checked into sugar restrictions in BC one of my cousins in Merritt, BC, Dewey Shackelly, suggested I call Don Moses, an Indian from Merritt who's older than me and has a degree in Political Science and Economics. Don said he worked in a grocery store in the late fifties and said they couldn't sell vanilla or lemon extract to the Indians because they might drink it. If they knew the Indians weren't going to drink it they sold them small bottles but the Indians could have been charged if they got caught with it. One of my Dad's friends in Merritt, Jimmy Fountain, said at one time vanilla extract was boot legged on the Indian Reserves.

I thought it was kind of late to find out what the penalties were for having vanilla extract because most of the people who would have known are too old to remember or have passed away. Their kids may not know either because they were probably taken away and put in the Residential Schools. However, on May 1, I called Jimmy Fountain and he said it was illegal to sell vanilla extract to the Indians and the penalties were the equivalent of having liquor. When Indians were first allowed to drink in the bar there was also an "Induction List". If Indians drank too much they were put on the "Induction List" and could be hauled off to jail without charges. That could explain one of the incidents I saw as a child.

The next day I called Roger Adolph in Lillooet and Dewey Shackelly again and they knew when it was illegal to sell vanilla extract to the Indians and about the "Induction List"! On the weekend I called Alvin Tolley and surprisingly he didn't know about Indians drinking vanilla extract. But, he said telephone operators on party lines would spy on the

Indians, report when they were partying and the RCMP would break the doors down and arrest the Indians. Naturally this would scare the wife and kids!

All the issues I brought up should make you realise Canada definitely isn't what we're taught to believe it is! Usually when Indians speak out or protest people automatically think we want special treatment or a hand out. Hopefully things will change and Natives will be better represented at the professional level in all fields of employment and our standard of living will equal that of the majority of Canadians. Issues I brought up should help justify policy changes for Equity and Diversity when this is brought up and Indian's complaints might be well justified in most cases! But, in some cases they're not justified.

It's quite possible Gary gave up his Indian Status so he could drink without getting a heavy fine and serving time in jail and was very bitter about it. Then I decided to write another article on this subject for Kahtou because there was many more stories to expose. I wrote another research paper titled "Absolutely No Alcohol for Indians in Canada" and didn't hold anything back. Here it is:

Absolutely No Alcohol for Indians in Canada!

(c) copyright Annis Aleck 2009-08-16

History books say the law passed making it illegal for Indians to have alcohol was put in place to protect the Indians but if Aboriginal reporters were there history would have been written differently. These history books were probably written either by an Englishman or White Canadian because there's individuals in every society who fall victim to addiction and lose everything. Since the English wrote their own history books whenever they colonized a country they only told what they wanted to be heard, maximizing the good things they do and saying very little, if anything about what they actually did. The French traded rum with the Indians but after the English defeated them they didn't want to trade alcohol with the Indians so this law was probably first implemented during the fur trade.

When I wrote ***Sugar and Vanilla Extract*** *I held back information and only went back to when I was a child. Now I'm going back to the earliest stories that I heard and not holding anything back! My Dad* *was born in 1928 and as a child lived in a shack made of cedar shakes with a dirt floor in an isolated area. He didn't remember what year it happened but 2 squads of Police cars came searching for homemade wine, did a thorough search checking the pig pen, chicken coop and root cellar and didn't find anything. His younger brother Don, not his real name, said it was a common occurrence for Police to check Indian homes for homemade wine.*

Roy Lewis, a Black originally from the Dominican Republic fought for Canada in WW II had to carry a letter with him stating he wasn't an Indian so he could drink. Lawrence said one of his uncles fought in the war and was on the front line all the way through. When he got back to Canada he got as far as Calgary, Alberta and they wouldn't serve him in the bars even though he was still in uniform. His White buddies tried arguing for him but it didn't do any good so they went out and drank in an alley. Don's wife, Doreen, not her real name, said 2 of her cousins fought in WW II, one was in a tank that destroyed 8 German tanks and the other won numerous medals. When they got back to Canada they weren't even allowed to take a case of beer home with them. Indians were allowed to fight in the war but weren't allowed to drink when they got back and were very bitter about it! When I was working in Enderby, BC in 1984 a Korean War veteran said he served 2 months in jail for drinking when he got back.

In 1957 my Dad and Uncle Albert were at a wedding when they and other Indians got caught with beer so they spent the night in jail and my Dad got a $15 fine. Professional tree falling for logging, known as fallers, even in the interior of BC when it was still done with power saws is a high paying job because of the danger involved and the skill required to do it safely. Around that time my Dad mentioned hiring a crew of fallers and paying them $14 a day so $15 was lots of money back then. In 1960 Roger Adolph got a $50 fine for underage drinking on his third offense under the Indian Act. When I was a child everything cost 10 cents, regular sized chocolate bars, ice cream cones, potato chips, candied popcorn and we were happy when we could buy a 10 cent bag of candy! The Police were searching my grandparent's house and my cousin Eddie Dale, who's 2 years younger than me led the Policeman by the hand and showed him where the wine was brewing behind the stove. Then he said, "And there's another one in the closet and it's been there for days and days!" so my grandfather got a $25 fine for having homemade wine in his own house on the Indian Reserve and Eddie Dale was nicknamed Days and days.

Some Status Indians were able to go to the bars and liquor stores if they could pass for another race though. One lady from Sumas Reserve said her father was extra dark and could pass for an East Indian so he was able to drink. One WW II veteran from Cheam Reserve could pass for a Chinaman so he dressed like a Chinaman so he could drink. One of his brothers could pass for a Mexican so he was sometimes able to drink. White people and other immigrants were allowed to drink in Canada but not Indians unless they enfranchised and gave up their Indian Status. In Merritt, BC my Dad said there was an Art Alex who enfranchised so he was able to drink because they had the same name and didn't know it wasn't him.

When I worked for the BC Forest Service retired Police Constables sometimes instructed courses for us. They said in 1960 Indians were allowed to drink in the bars but not at home then in 1964 they were allowed to drink like everyone else but previously they served 2 months in jail for drinking on their third offense. They didn't mention that if Indians drank too much they could still be put on the Induction List and put in jail without any charges being laid. Naturally all hell broke loose when Indians were finally allowed to drink because of all the tension that had built up and it took some time for things to settle down. One day when I was 6 or 7 years old I went to a Chinese Cafe to buy some candy and my Dad's friend, Harold, was sitting there by himself quietly drinking a bottle of pop. Harold had been drinking but other than that all he was doing was drinking his pop when a Cop hauled him off to jail, but the Cop was polite. To a young child it seemed like a joke and he only went to jail for 2 hours. Many years later I realised he wasn't doing anything wrong!

If driving the Indians to drinking through the Residential Schools and giving them heavy fines or time in jail for drinking wasn't bad enough Cops sometimes beat up the Indians after arresting them! My Dad mentioned one Indian was arrested then the Cop beat him up after he was hand cuffed. When the Indian was let go he asked the Cop to try it again but the Cop backed down. Another Indian who used to wrestle professionally was put in jail. Then 2 big Cops went in the cell to beat him up but backed down after he threw them both on the floor.

One of my brothers said in Vancouver Indians were beaten up in the elevator at the Police station or under the Cambie Street Bridge. In some towns Indians were taken outside of town and dropped off and there's no way of telling how many of them died that way! That was the first time I heard of Indians being dropped off other than in the prairies and Paul Johnny said it was common knowledge so he didn't mention it to me. Both Paul and my brother mentioned a Police Constable in Williams Lake, BC who was really bad for beating the Indians up so the Indians laid a trap for him! When he went to arrest some drunk Indians a bunch of them were hiding and waiting for him, gave him a severe beating then threw him into a rail box car. The Cop was eventually found in Edmonton. In 1971 Fred Quilt, an Aboriginal from a Reserve near Williams Lake died and the last thing he said was, "They Beat Me!" People blamed the Police for beating him and causing his death but the Judge refused to do an inquiry into the incident so Native and non-Natives held rallies and protested against the Judge's decision. There's a website titled Fred Quilt of Williams Lake with information on this incident and the first web title is 'Help Kill Indians, Join the RCMP'—CBC Archives. It tells some of what happened when the investigation was done but it wasn't set up to do justice for the Indians and in 1970 a number of Indians lay in waiting for that one Cop and gave him a severe beating.

Uncle Don said it was nothing unusual for the Police to take Indians outside of town, beat them up and let them find their own way back. Two of his uncles were taken away by the Police and never heard from again! One fellow, Earl, was taken outside of town several times, beaten up and sometimes didn't know which way it was back to town. Paul Johnny said Indians were taken outside of town in freezing temperatures in the middle of the night and didn't know which way it was back to town and this is still going on! I first heard of it happening to Neil Stonechild in the book Starlight Tour when he died in 1990. I heard of it happening again in 2000 when the Indian got his coat and shoes taken away when he was dropped off outside of town in freezing temperatures! Of course the Police deny these things never happened at all but it happened so often the Indians called it Starlight Tours!

In 1982 when I was managing tree planting contracts in Lytton, BC the other supervisor, Buck Thomas was as tall as me but stocky, I'm 5ft 8 inches tall. Buck said when it was illegal to sell Liquor to the Indians this great big Cop beat him up then threw him in jail. The next day he said, "You got me when I was drunk, why don't you come in and try it again!" The cop went in and got a good beating and when another cop about as big as me said, "Do you need some help?" Buck said, "This is between him and me so stay out of it or you'll get yours!" After beating the Cop up they became good friends. The Govt and Police went to ***GREAT*** *lengths when they tried to keep us from drinking!*

In 1976 while riding a transit bus in Vancouver there was 4 or 5 off duty transit drivers sitting in the back and one of them said, "As far as I'm concerned the only good Indian is a dead one!" and they all laughed along with him. I wasn't going to write it in but it's the truth but that could be an isolated incident because most of them were quite civil. In 1990 at a physiotherapist's office on the front cover of a magazine there was people protesting against the Smoke house, where the coastal Indians practice their religious beliefs. I never heard of people doing that against other religions unless it wasn't published or I missed it.

I heard vague stories that the Indian language was used for radio communication during WW II but this was rarely mentioned. I also heard, 2 times, once in high school and once in my first year of college that Eskimos, now called Inuit, made the best airplane mechanics. Dad also said Indians made excellent snipers because they were crack shots and good in the woods but that's the only time I heard it mentioned but an ex-soldier said they were also good in reconnaissance. Unfortunately the Indians didn't get the same benefits that white soldiers got and if a white soldier was killed or missing in action his wife got a pension but the wives of aboriginal soldiers didn't get any benefits. My dad met a fellow, Ross, who said for how he was treated when he got back he would have been better off if he didn't come back. My cousin Richard Band said they had to lose their Indian status before they got the same benefits the other veterans got but one veteran who served in the American army said he got the same benefits as the other veterans.

Information from the National Aboriginal Veterans Association:

Some Native WW II veterans never got any benefits or didn't get anything for 50 years and it wasn't upgraded, for some it was only retroactive for 3, 5 or 8 years. The nurses eventually got benefits and it was retroactive but wasn't upgraded for many years. Some Indians were tricked into giving up their Indian status before they went overseas because they had to be Canadian citizens to go to war and others were tricked into giving it up when they got back. Indians who lost their status were no longer Canadian citizens and it's possible those who didn't come back either the church, DIA or the Indian agent got their benefits.

Only a few Indians were allowed in the Air Force and none in the Navy so most had to join the army. When Indians got back they couldn't get very good jobs because of the quality of education they got in the Residential Schools, couldn't own property or even move back to the Reserves and it was illegal to get lawyers to represent them in court. Natives who worked for the railroads or in the Post Office lost their Indian status and on the ferries from Victoria, BC to Seattle, Washington and from Vancouver to Nanaimo Indians weren't allowed on the upper deck.

Charles George, one of Isaac's friends, said his father died of war wounds so his mother couldn't look after the children so they were put in foster homes. They were kept in one place until the work run out then they were shipped to another home so he lived in five different foster homes. When the Indian children turned sixteen they were kicked out of school by the Children's Aid Society and weren't told about post secondary education available to Native students. It's quite possible many other Indian families experienced the same thing.

During the Hungry Thirties when my parents were children it's said a single white male got $10 a month in relief but it wasn't reported that Indians with a family only got $5 or even less a month. A family friend who's older than my parents said some Indians didn't even get that, all they were given was a sack of rice and a sack of beans. Ironically I also heard stories of white people asking the Indians for work in exchange for food. It's possible many Indians in the 1930's couldn't speak English very well or may not have known how to read and write very well so were easy victims of unscrupulous Indian agents, this was mentioned in a book that I read. In January 2000 I read on the computer that in 1969 there was only 800 Aboriginal people with post secondary education in Canada.

When I was 14 I heard a rumor that in some towns Indians would start a forest fire then apply for a job fighting fires and I thought it was a big joke. Then I heard it again when I was applying for a job in Lillooet I heard it again and still thought it was a big joke. Then after what I went through to get a career and find work and stories other Indian told me about applying for work, how hard it was to get hired and how they were treated after they got hired I realized they probably did that because it could have been the only way they could get work. I don't speak out until things are confirmed by people who witnessed what was going on or were involved in what happened. I asked Aunty

Beatrice in Merritt and she said that was why they did it and why Indians often went down to the Washington or other states to work the farms and orchards.

I told a friend, Keith about it and he acted like it was common knowledge and said the major forest fire in the Kootenays in 1985 was started by an unemployed Indian who needed work. I said they had to pull a stunt like that just to get a low paying job and he said, "Well at least they got a job. I was going to keep that incident confidential until I got my life story published then after the way the Association of BC Forest Professionals treated me when I wrote the Registered Forest Technologists exam in 2006 I decided to expose it so Canadians will realize that racism and social injustice can bite you in the ass like a rattle snake.

In 1995 Percy Joe, the Chief of an Indian Reserve in Merritt had a meeting with forest companies. He said the Indians might as well burn the forests down because at least they'll get some benefits out of them because none of you have hired any Indians, and all their mouths dropped. I exposed this incident to a staff member when I worked for the BC Forest Service then I was told not to expose these issues unless they're asked for otherwise I'll be suspended then terminated.

One of my dad's friends, Andrew, was a journeyman carpenter and told me about going to a construction site, applying for work and getting turned down then a white fellow walked in behind him and was told he could start work the next day. When Andrew got a job later on a white fellow was promoted then asked Andrew how to do some work and Andrew said, "Like a darn stupid fool I showed him what to do."

One of Ron Gabriel's sons, Steve who's younger than me took a course to be an electronic technician. Steve applied for work then hid behind the door after applying and heard them say, "Another fucking Indian looking for work!"

Many other stories like that can be told and some stories can be told of Indians making suggestions and white people taking credit for their suggestions. I originally wanted to work for a large forest company because of the benefits and opportunities for promotions but of all the times I applied for work I only got 2 interviews inspite of my qualifications and that I also made some very good suggestions in places I worked over the years. Then when I finally got a permanent job with the BC Forest service I was mistreated to the point I decided to stop making suggestions unless it was for safety even though they always gave me recognition for my suggestions.

Bing Wong told me that one year a group of anti-Asians wanted to destroy a Chinese community in Vancouver's Coal Harbor and there was too many of them to fight off so they asked the Indians for help. This fight was mentioned in the Vancouver Sun newspaper on September 1, 2007 under "Asian History Milestones in BC" but didn't mention the Indians helping them out. Bing Wong said wherever there was a China town there was an Indian village because we were pushed to the edge of town and society and expected to stay there. Next to Vancouver's China town there used to be an Indian village but it would be very hard to prove now, except for the high number of impoverished alcoholics and drug addicts who live there.

In elementary school when I used to deliver newspapers I read about a group of anti-Asians who wanted to destroy a Japanese community on Powell Street in Vancouver but the Japanese were ready for them, fought them off and won. This riot happened in September 1907 and was also reported in the Vancouver Sun on September 1, 2007. Powell Street isn't very far from China town and it's possible the Chinese and Japanese may not have gotten along very well and the communities may have been separated by an Indian village. I wondered if the Japanese also asked the Indians to help them out in that fight but I haven't been able to find out.

Many Canadians seem to envy the Indians or are jealous of us because the Govt. made it look like we have everything given to us on a silver platter but it's more like we had everything taken away from us and we were held back when we tried to do something for ourselves. Children learn what they live and if they were beaten and abused as children they often beat and abused their own children or went to the other extreme and were too lenient which can also be devastating. The Residential Schools, being held back or put in a career different than what we wanted or applied for created many dysfunctional families which we'll probably feel the effects of for some time to come. People are usually happiest when working with their natural talents and "Happy Work = Happy Home". If people aren't happy at work it could affect their productivity, their family life and eventually their health which could have been the object of DIA treating Indians that way. In 2010, I think it was on "APTN Contact" it mentioned that only 4% of the Canadian population is aboriginal but 60% of the children in the child welfare system is aboriginal. There's also a highly disproportionate number of aboriginals in jail but the statistics appear to vary, depending on who's speaking out.

Some Natives just want to leave the past behind them and live their life today because it just brings back bitter memories that there's nothing they can do about. Unfortunately bringing up the past can also drive some people to suicide or the pain and anger can come out on their body and cause health problems like strokes, diabetes, heart attacks and in some cases early death if it's not dealt with. For other people like me it's a catharsis and important to expose past injustices we're still feeling the effects of and how Indians who wanted to do something with their life weren't only held back by the Govt. but also by how Canadians treated us when we were hired. I heard some Indians mention that they couldn't make it to management positions because they're Indian and I wondered if that was exaggerated but now I know it's true. Then when we cry racism and social injustice Canadians tend to believe it's not racism as long as nothing's in words or in writing.

I was probably better off than many Indians whose parents went to the Residential school in my age group because my dad worked hard, provided for the family and made sure we grew up in the middle of town and all finished high school. Life was still hard on me though because I was a scapegoat and didn't get the same treatment that my brothers got then when I tried to get a career I had to go through setbacks and obstacles that I wouldn't wish on anyone. Fortunately some people also get stronger when they go through hard times. The hard times I went through gave me the knowledge, the strength and determination to break Jennifer's depression so she wouldn't commit suicide, giving her the gift of life. Then I got her a career so she could do something with her life. She was "Almost a Born Loser!"

Edwards Brothers Malloy
Oxnard, CA USA
November 24, 2014